EATING GRASS

EATING GRASS

The Making of the Pakistani Bomb

FEROZ HASSAN KHAN

STANFORD SECURITY STUDIES

An Imprint of Stanford University Press

Stanford, California

Stanford University Press
Stanford, California

Library of Congress Cataloging-in-Publication Data

Khan, Feroz Hassan, author.
   Eating grass : the making of the Pakistani bomb / Feroz Hassan Khan.
      pages cm
   Includes bibliographical references and index.
   ISBN 978-0-8047-7600-4 (cloth : alk. paper) —
   ISBN 978-0-8047-7601-1 (pbk. : alk. paper)
   1. Nuclear weapons—Pakistan—History. 2. Pakistan—Military policy.
I. Title.
U264.5.P18K43 2012
623.4'5119095491—dc23

                                   2012015835

Printed and bound by CPI Group (UK) Ltd, Croydon, CR0 4YY

Typeset at Stanford University Press in 10/14 Minion.

Contents

Map, Tables, and Figures

MAP

TABLES

FIGURES

Preface

This book took six years to compile. What began as a simple quest to compress a holistic account of the Pakistani nuclear program turned into a Rubik's cube. As a first-time writer setting out to pull together a balanced and objective account on a subject considered taboo for decades, I ran into the proverbial Clauswitzian "fog of war," where a maze of claims and counterclaims made the research difficult.

Like many aspects of Pakistan's politics and history, its nuclear story is awash with controversies and competing narratives. Yet, the most intriguing aspect during the course of this research was facing the challenge of the relentless disinformation campaign unleashed on the Pakistani nuclear program. Gore Vidal's famous quotation emphasizing that a "[d]isinformation campaign has metastasized to a level where myth threatens to overthrow history" aptly applies to the case study of Pakistan. This was one reason that galvanized my efforts in telling the story of the Pakistani nuclear program and my interest in writing this book.

In the case of new nuclear states—such as India, Israel, and Pakistan—the necessity to keep the nuclear weapons program covert in order to resist international proliferation pressures has added another layer of opacity. The habits that come with decades of secrecy do not disappear overnight just because the country has conducted a declared nuclear test. Furthermore, as with many developing countries, the Pakistan government does not open its national archives to outside scrutiny, especially on matters of national security. Even nonofficial accounts, such as newspaper and journal articles, are difficult to access with collections often incomplete.

On top of these challenges, reconstructing the Pakistani case is vexing because its nuclear history is still contested by those who took part in the program. As this study will show, the establishment of two rival organizations—the

Pakistan Atomic Energy Commission (PAEC) and Khan Research Laboratories (KRL)—created an intense bureaucratic rivalry, in which members of both organizations have sought to highlight their own successes and minimize the accomplishments of the other.

While the rivalry has waxed and waned, it frequently led to poisonous interpersonal relationships. That bitterness has frequently affected the accounts of those who took part in the interlaboratory issues. Further, the deliberate attempt to compartmentalize the program has meant that very few individuals (perhaps none) have had a complete view of the effort. As with all accounts of Pakistani history, nuclear developments are also part of a broader pattern of civil-military relations, in which control over nuclear decisions has frequently been an indicator of political strength. Given the success of the nuclear program, military and civilian leaders have considerable interest in highlighting their role.

My experience as former director in Pakistan's Strategic Plans Division (SPD)—the secretariat of Pakistan's National Command Authority (NCA)—provides insight in terms of information and analysis. The last decade of my thirty-two years in the military were dedicated to the Pakistani nuclear program. It all began with a little-known event in Pakistan's nuclear history when President Ghulam Ishaq Khan and Prime Minister Nawaz Sharif resigned from their respective offices in July 1993, and handed over responsibility for the nuclear program to Chief of the Army Staff General Abdul Waheed. This charge eventually fell to Major General Ziauddin—Director General Combat Development Directorate—under whom I was posted from the end of 1993 until the SPD was formed.

In 2003, I joined the faculty at the Naval Postgraduate School (NPS) along with my close friend and colleague Dr. Peter R. Lavoy, who was at the time director of the Center on Contemporary Conflict (CCC) in the Department of National Security Affairs (NSA). Under his leadership, I was involved in several research projects on South Asia that included two major military crises—"The Kargil Conflict" and the "2001–2 India-Pakistan Military Standoff." Since that time, I have continued to work on a litany of research projects relating to South Asian security and strategic stability, including the completion of this book.

Dr. Lavoy was enthusiastic when I proposed researching this book. We began the research as coauthors. Our first task was to request from the Pakistan government and authorities in Islamabad cooperation and guidance in facilitating the research, including interviews, access to public documents, and archives.

The proposal was accepted after careful coordination and processing in Islamabad, where Pakistani authorities laid strict rules for our interviews, which we respected. We were not allowed to interview serving scientists, or active-duty officials. Retired officials and scientists were cleared for interviews only if they were willing to talk voluntarily. On our part, we ensured that SPD carefully scrutinized our questionnaires for any sensitive matter or inadvertent overstepping. When necessary, authorities facilitated the research with "background briefings" by concerned government departments.[1]

This book, then, relies on several types of source material in an attempt to overcome these challenges, while always being cognizant of their limitations. By far the most important contribution comes from interviews with key civilian leaders, military officers, and nuclear scientists. With the extraordinary approval of the Pakistani government, I was granted permission to interview for the first time many officials about their role in Pakistan's remarkable nuclear history. These interviews were compared with a variety of other sources. U.S. declassified documents provided considerable information about U.S. perceptions of the covert Pakistani effort, and showed the U.S. understanding of Pakistan's motivations and technical milestones at various periods of history.

There are wide arrays of Pakistani accounts discussing nuclear developments. Many of these accounts come from participants in the feud between Pakistan's two rival laboratories, with friendly journalists producing slanted accounts. A similar distortion is evident in many contemporary Pakistani articles. Reports in the U.S. press, while better, frequently lean toward sensationalism or showcase leaks that were provided with a clear policy agenda in mind. To navigate this hazardous terrain, the author has relied on his own personal knowledge of Pakistan's nuclear and military history to help ascertain what is true and what is merely propaganda. To the extent possible, this text will highlight these controversies and describe the evidence that led to conclusions when evidence is contradictory. In some cases, the evidence is too ambiguous to draw any conclusions.

Even with the assistance of interviews, there remains resistance to scrutiny. Several key officials did not yet believe it was time to write the history of Pakistan's nuclear weapons program. The Abdul Qadeer (A. Q.) Khan proliferation network scandal that became public in 2004 formed a backdrop for the interviews. Khan's role in Pakistan's nuclear developments, already divisive given the interlaboratory rivalry, became a national controversy in Pakistan. Many individuals approached for this study were wary of inserting themselves into an arena of such contentious politics, fearing that whatever they said would be misunderstood or distorted. Such fears were accentuated by Western accounts that many Pakistanis felt demonized by the accomplishments of the nuclear program. When someone knocked on their door asking for an interview, they were understandably suspicious. Even so, a surprising number of individuals were willing to talk on the record. Some officials asked that portions or all of their interviews occur without direct attribution, and their wishes to remain anonymous have been honored in this text.

Despite these limitations, the book that follows provides the first comprehensive account of the Pakistan nuclear weapons program. While incomplete, as all histories are, this account substantially improves upon existing prior accounts. In part, it does so by assiduously following scholarly convention, which is too frequently discarded in works published in Pakistan. Throughout the text, on-the-record and anonymous interviews are cited directly. When information was provided on background, I have attempted to verify the information in a citable format. When clear written or interview evidence is not present, I have attempted to signal uncertainty or lack of clarity in the text. The hope is that this work is the first of many nuanced, scholarly, and clear-headed accounts on this topic. It does not seek to glorify or demonize those who took part in these decisions, but rather chronicle, as best it can, the role that numerous individuals from many organizations contributed to Pakistan's present nuclear capability.

Additionally, it is important to highlight that interviews conducted for this research would not have been possible without the approval of former president Pervez Musharraf, and with the consistent support of Lieutenant General Khalid Kidwai, director-general of Pakistan's SPD; both of whom were gracious enough to provide their own inputs at various times. No words can sufficiently thank them and the staff at SPD for their positive outlook and for providing all necessary assistance and guidance.

In 2007, Dr. Lavoy left his post at NPS, after which I carried the baton for completing this book. As a consequence, this work is devoid of the wisdom, quality, and style that Peter Lavoy would have provided as coauthor. He was dearly missed as I struggled to write, but his words of encouragement throughout these years strengthened my resolve to finish this book.

I owe a word of gratitude to all the others who made a great impact on this book over the past five years. First are the three editors who contributed to the completion of this book in no small order. Anya Erokhina, a graduate of the

Monterey Institute of International Studies (MIIS) and aspiring scholar, helped me with both the research and writing of the initial draft. Mansoor Ahmed, now a lecturer at the Quaid-e-Azam University, Islamabad, did extensive research for all of these years; his contribution is exceptionally appreciated. Lisa Donohoe Luscombe helped compile and develop the final manuscript. The research team at the CCC helped me keep pace with narratives, events, and records of the interviews. Those who made an immense contribution include Christopher Clary, Adam Radin, Puja Verma, Kali Shelor, Rebekah Dietz, and Nick Masellis.

In addition, thanks go to a series of close friends and enthusiasts from the Monterey Bay area, Dr. Lois Lagier, Roderick and Suzanne Dewar, whose consistent support and lens as interested, well-read laymen on the subject brought important perspectives that helped refine the subject matter. Also to several of my professional colleagues, scholars, and South Asian experts in and out of government, for their invaluable encouragement, support, and friendship: Dr. James Wirtz, Dr. Zachary Davis, Dr. Michael Krepon, Dr. George Perkovich, Dr. William Potter, Mr. Robert Swartz, Mr. Toby Dalton, Ms. Kathryn Schultz, Dr. Scott Sagan, Dr. Siegfried Hecker, and Dr. Michael Elleman. I am especially indebted to Dr. Michael Wheeler and Mr. David Hamon for their consistent support in the completion of this work. My Pakistani colleagues also deserve sincere recognition for their consistent encouragement: Dr. Maleeha Lodhi, Dr. Rifaat Hussain, Dr. Zafar Jaspal, and Dr. Salma Malik. I owe a special thanks to the Directorate of Arms Control and Disarmament, SPD, for their consistent support. Brigadier (ret.) Naeem Salik and Air Commodore Khalid Banuri, two directors that succeeded me, deserve special gratitude for their consistent help.

Finally, thanks go to my family—from California to Islamabad—Mahreen, Mahvish, Sarem, and Haider, to whom belongs the future. They bore the burden of my distractions and moods as I burned the midnight oil.

Pakistan: Key Characters

Governors-General

Mohammad Ali Jinnah 1947–48
Khwaja Nazimuddin 1948–51
Ghulam Mohammad 1951–55
Iskander Mirza 1955–56

Presidents

Iskander Mirza 1956–58
General Mohammad Ayub Khan 1958–69
General Agha Mohammad Yahya Khan 1969–71
Zulfiqar Ali Bhutto 1971–73
Fazal Elahi Chaudhry 1973–78
General Mohammad Zia-ul-Haq 1978–88
Ghulam Ishaq Khan 1988–93
Farooq Khan Leghari 1993–97
Rafiq Tarar 1997–2001
General Pervez Musharraf 2001–8
Asif Ali Zardari 2008–present

Prime Ministers

Liaquat Ali Khan 1947–51
Khwaja Nazimuddin 1951–53
Mohammad Ali Bogra 1953–55
Chaudhry Mohammad Ali 1955–56
Husain Shaheed Suharwardy 1956–57

Iftikhar I Chundrigar 1957 (Interim)
Feroz Khan Noon 1957–58
Zulfiqar Ali Bhutto 1973–77
Mohammad Khan Junejo 1985–88
Benazir Bhutto 1988–90
Ghulam Mustafa Jatoi 1990 (Interim)
Mian Mohammad Nawaz Sharif 1990–93
Balak Sher Mazari 1993 (Interim)
Moeenuddin Qureshi 1993 (Interim)
Benazir Bhutto 1993–96
Malik Meraj Khalid 1996–97 (Interim)
Mian Mohammad Nawaz Sharif 1997–99
Zafarullah Jamali 2002–4
Chaudhry Shujaat Hussain 2004 (Interim)
Shaukat Aziz 2004–7
Mian Mohamad Soomro (Interim)
Yusuf Raza Gilani 2008–2012
Raja Pervez Ashraf 2012–present

Army Chiefs

General Sir Frank Messervy 1947–48
General Sir Douglas Gracy 1948–51
General (Field Marshal) Mohammad Ayub Khan 1951–58
General Mohammad Musa Khan 1958–66
General Agha Mohammad Yahya Khan 1966–71
Lt. General Gul Hassan Khan 1971–72
General Tikka Khan 1972–76
General Mohammad Zia-ul-Haq 1976–88
General Mirza Aslam Beg 1988–91
General Asif Nawaz Janjua 1991–93
General Abdul Waheed 1993–96
General Jehangir Karamat 1996–98
General Pervez Musharraf 1998–2007
General Ashfaq Pervez Kayani 2007–present

Director Generals

Lt. Gen. Ziauddin, Combat Development Directorate 1993–96
Lt. Gen. Zulfiqar Khan, Combat Development Directorate 1996–98
Lt. Gen. Khalid Kidwai Strategic Plans Division 1999–present

Heads of Scientific Organizations

Dr. Abdus Salam, Nobel Laureate
Chief Scientific Advisor to president of Pakistan, 1961–74
Chairman Pakistan Space and Upper Atmosphere Committee (SUPARCO), 1961–64
Founder International Center for Theoretical Physics, Trieste, Italy, 1964–93

Pakistan Atomic Energy Commission (PAEC)

Dr. Nazir Ahmad, April 1956–March 1960
Dr. Ishrat Husain Usmani, March 1960–March1972
Mr. Munir Ahmad Khan March, 1972–April 1991
Dr. Ishfaq Ahmad, April 1991–April 2001
Mr. Pervez Butt, April 2001–April 2006
Mr. Anwar Ali, 2006–9
Dr. Ansar Pervez, 2009–present

Khan Research Laboratory (KRL)

Dr. Abdul Qadeer Khan, July 1976–April 2001
Dr. Javed Mirza, April 2001–March 2006
Mr. Karim Ahmad, April 2006–present

National Engineering and Scientific Commission (NESCOM)

Dr. Samar Mubarkmand, January 2001–November 2007
Dr. Muhammad Irfan Burney, November 2007–present

Abbreviations

ABMs	antiballistic missiles
ACDA	Arms Control and Disarmament Agency (United States)
ACDA	Arms Control and Disarmament Affairs (Directorate) Pakistan
ACR	annual confidential report
ADW	Airport Development Workshop
AEC	Atomic Energy Council
AEMC	Atomic Energy Minerals Center
AFSC	Air Force Strategic Command
AHQ	Air Headquarters
ALCM	air-launched cruise missile
ARGONAUT	Argonne Nuclear Assembly for University Training
ARS	Army Reserve South
ASFC	Army Strategic Force Command
ATGM	antitank guided missile
ATS	Air Transport Support
AWC	Air Weapons Complex
BCCI	Bank of Credit and Commerce International
BJP	Bhartiya Janata Party
BMD	ballistic missile defense
BNFL	British Nuclear Fuel, Ltd.
C3I	command, control, communication, and intelligence
CAA	Civil Aviation Authority
CANDU	Canada Deuterium-Uranium
CAP	combat air patrol
CBMs	confidence-building measures
CCC	Center on Contemporary Conflict

CCS	Cabinet Committee on Security
CD Directorate	Combat Development Directorate
CENTO	Central Treaty Organization
CEP	circular error probability
CFL	ceasefire line
CGE	Canadian General Electric Company
CGS	Chief of General Staff
CHASHNUPP-1	Chashma Nuclear Power Plant
CIA	Central Intelligence Agency
CIRUS	Canada India Research Utility Service
CJCSC	Chairman Joint Chief of Staff Committee
CJSC	Joint Chiefs of Staff Committee
CNC	Computer Numerical Control
CNS	Center for Nuclear Studies
COAS	Chief of the Army Staff
COCOM	Coordinating Committee for Multilateral Export Control
CPC	Chemical Plants Complex
CTBT	Comprehensive Test Ban Treaty
CTBTO	Comprehensive Test Ban Treaty Organization
CTC	Counterterrorism Center
CWO	Civil Works Organization
D_2O	deuterium oxide
DCC	Defense Committee of the Cabinet
DCC	Development Control Committee
DESTEM	Decision Support System
DESTO	Defense and Science and Technology Organization
DGCD	Director General Combat Development Directorate
DGISI	Director General Inter-Services Intelligence
DGMI	Director General of Military Intelligence
DGMO	Director General of Military Operations
DGSPD	Director General Strategic Plans Division
DIB	Director of the Intelligence Bureau
DIL	Directorate of Industrial Liaison
DMO	Director of Military Operations
DNP	Division of Nuclear Power
DPRK	Democratic People's Republic of Korea
DRDO	Defence Research and Development Organisation

DTD	Directorate of Technical Development
E&R	Evaluation and Research Directorate
ECC	Employment Control Committee
EME	Electrical and Mechanical Engineering
EMIS	electromagnetic isotope separation
ERL	Engineering Research Laboratories
FATA	Federally Administered Tribal Area
FBR	fast breeder reactor
FCAs	foreign currency accounts
FCNA	Force Command Northern Areas
FDO	Fysisch Dynamisch Onderzoek
FMCT	Fissile Material Cut-off Treaty
FSF	Federal Security Force
FWO	Frontier Works Organization
GHQ	General Headquarters
GIK	Ghulam Ishaq Khan
GOC	General Officer Commanding
GPS	global positioning systems
GS	General Staff
HE	high explosive
HEU	highly enriched uranium
HFF	Heavy Foundry and Forge
HMC	Heavy Mechanical Complex
HMX	Her Majesty's Explosive
HRP	Human Reliability Program
IAEA	International Atomic Energy Agency
IAF	Indian Air Force
IBGs	integrated battle groups
ICS	integrated circuitry
IGMDP	Integrated Guided Missile Development Program
IISS	International Institute for Strategic Studies
IJI	*Islami Jamhoori Ittehad*
IMF	International Monetary Fund
ISI	Inter-Services Intelligence
ISNSE	International School of Nuclear Science and Engineering
JAERI	Japan Atomic Energy Research Institute
JI	Jamaat Islami

JSHQ	Joint Services Headquarters
JSSC	Joint Services Staff College
JVC	joint verification commission
KANUPP	Karachi Nuclear Power Plant
KCP-II	Kundian Chemical Plant-II
KfK	Karlsruhe Nuclear Research Centre
kg	kilograms
KNFC	Kundian Nuclear Fuel Complex
KNPTC	Karachi Nuclear Power Training Centre
KRL	Khan Research Laboratories
kt	kilotons
LET	Lashkar-e-Tayyaba
LEU	low-enriched uranium
LIS	laser isotope separation
LOC	Line of Control
LSG	London Suppliers Group
LTTE	Liberation Tigers of Tamil Eelam
MFN	Most Favored Nation
MMRCA	Medium Multi-Role Combat Aircraft
MNSR	Miniature Neutron Source Reactor
MO	Military Operations Directorate
MOU	Memorandum of Understanding
MRD	Movement on Restoration of Democracy
Mt	megatons
MTCR	Missile Technology Control Regime
MTO	Maritime Technology Organization
MWd/t	Megawatt day per ton
MWe	Megawatt [electrical]
NAM	Non-Aligned Movement
NAP	National Awami Party
NASA	National Aeronautics and Space Administration
NCA	National Command Authority
NCNDT	National Centre for Non-Destructive Testing
NDC	National Development Complex
NEFA	North East Frontier Agency
NESCOM	National Engineering and Scientific Commission
NGO	nongovernmental organization

NLC	National Logistics Cell
NLI	Northern Light Infantry
NMCC	National Military Command Centre
NNWS	non–nuclear weapons states
NPS	Naval Postgraduate School
NPT	Treaty on the Non-Proliferation of Nuclear Weapons; Nuclear Non-Proliferation Treaty
NRRC	Nuclear Risk Reduction Centre
NSA	National Security Affairs
NSC	National Security Council
NSFC	Naval Strategic Force Command
NSG	Nuclear Suppliers Group
NTG	Nukleartechnik GmbH
NTI	Nuclear Threat Initiative
NWFP	North West Frontier Province
OIC	Organization of Islamic Conferences
ORSORT	Oak Ridge School of Reactor Technology
OSTs	Officers on Special Training
PAEC	Pakistan Atomic Energy Commission
PAF	Pakistan Air Force
PAKNUR	Pakistan Nuclear Reactor
PAROS	Prevention of Arms Race in Outer Space
PARR	Pakistan Atomic Research Reactor
PCB	Printer Circuit Board
PCSIR	Pakistan Council for Scientific and Industrial Research
PEL	Pakistan Electron Limited
PIA	Pakistan International Airlines
PIDC	Pakistan Industrial Development Corporation
PIEAS	Pakistan Institute of Engineering and Applied Sciences
PINSTECH	Pakistan Institute of Nuclear Science and Technology
PLA	People's Liberation Army
PML	Pakistan Muslim League
PMO	Project Management Organization
POF	Pakistan Ordnance Factories
PPP	Pakistan People's Party
PRC	People's Republic of China
PRP	Personnel Reliability Program

PTBT	Partial Test Ban Treaty
PTV	Pakistan Television
Pu	plutonium
PUREX	plutonium uranium extraction
R&D	research and development
RAPIDS	Reinforced Army Plain Infantry Divisions
RCD	Regional Cooperation for Development
RIAD	Radioisotope and Applications Division
RV	re-entry vehicle
SAARC	South Asian Association for Regional Cooperation
SAMs	surface-to-air missiles
SCOPE	Scomi Precision Engineering
SDW	Special Development Works
SEATO	South East Asian Treaty Organization
SES	Scientific and Engineering Services Directorate
SFC	Strategic Force Command
SGN	Saint-Gobain Technique Nouvelle
SLBMs	submarine launched ballistic missiles
SLCMs	submarine-launched cruise missiles
SMG	Strategic Missile Group
SNEPP	Study [of] Nuclear Explosion for Peaceful Purposes
SPD	Strategic Plans Division
SRBM	short-range ballistic missile
SRR	Strategic Restraint Regime
SSG	Special Services Group
SUPARCO	Space and Upper Atmosphere Research Commission
SWD	Strategic Weapons Development
SWO	Special Works Organization
SWU	separative work unit
TELs	transporter-erector launchers
TLAMs	*Tomahawk* missiles
TNW	Tactical Nuclear Weapons
TOT	transfer of technology
TROC	Tritium Removal by Organic Compounds
UAV	Unmanned Aerial Vehicle
UCN	Ultra-Centrifuge Nederland
UF6	uranium hexafluoride

UKAEA	United Kingdom Atomic Energy Authority's
ULFA	United Liberation Front for Assam
UML	Uranium Metal Laboratory
UNMOGIP	UN Military Observer Group in India and Pakistan
UNSC	UN Security Council
UO2	uranium dioxide
USAID	United States Agency for International Development
USEXIM	U.S. Export-Import Bank
UTN	*Ummah Tameer-e-Nau*
VCOAS	Vice Chief of the Army Staff
VDT	Van Doorne Transmissie
VMF	Vernidge Machine Fabrieken
W&E	Weapons and Equipment Directorate
WAPDA	Water and Power Development Authority

Pakistan. Reproduced from Dan Caldwell, *Vortex of Conflict: U.S. Policy Toward Afghanistan, Pakistan, and Iraq* (Stanford University Press: Stanford, CA 2011); based on map at the CIA web site, https://www.cia.gov/library/publications/the-world-factbook/geos/af.html.

EATING GRASS

1   Introduction

On May 28, 1998, Pakistan announced the test of five nuclear explosive devices
in the Chagai Hills in the western province of Baluchistan. A mere seventeen
days after neighboring India had shocked the world with its first nuclear tests
since 1974, Pakistan's response came as a surprise to many observers. Some had
doubted that Pakistan possessed the capability to construct a nuclear explosive.
But even those who thought that Pakistan could test a weapon were aston-
ished by the speed of the Pakistani reaction. Many observers wondered how
a poor country recovering from catastrophic wars and national dismemberment—and struggling with national identity crises—could devote its limited
state resources to acquiring such potentially destructive technology.[1]

This book examines how and why Pakistan managed to overcome the wide
array of obstacles that stood between it and nuclear weapons. It unravels the
interplay of personalities and organizations involved in developing the bomb
against a backdrop of political, security, and economic constraints, as well as
opportunities. It contributes to the established tradition of academic work that
examines the causes behind nuclear proliferation by telling the Pakistani nuclear story. While excellent academic accounts describe the origins of the other
key nuclear weapons programs (for example, those of the United States, the
Soviet Union, China, Israel, and India),[2] existing accounts of Pakistan's pursuit
of the bomb either have been journalistic, have focused almost exclusively on
the A. Q. Khan nuclear proliferation network, or have included Pakistan only
in a broader discussion of nuclear weapons in South Asia.[3]

Pakistan's nuclear program evolved under immensely complex and challenging security circumstances. Structural generalizations do not explain the
complexities of its historical existence and evolution unless a holistic account is
understood. This book examines that historical experience—a blend of cultural
nuances, idiosyncrasies of personalities, and the multitudinous pulls of domes-

tic politics, regional crises, and geographical compulsions, as well as technical challenges, global politics, and international barriers to nuclear materials and know-how. Nuclear technology is now nearing seven decades of development, but nuclear politics and technological determinism remain the quintessential factors in international relations, especially for developing states. Fascination in mastering the mystery of the atom is as much alive today as it was in the early fifties, when many of the developing world states broke free from the yoke of colonialism. Despite the many decades of the nuclear age exposing the dangers and blessings of nuclear energy, atomic weapons are considered a life-line for states like Pakistan and Israel, "orphan states" in the international system, outside the U.S. nuclear umbrella.[4] In this sense, the story of nuclear Pakistan is sui generis among nuclear weapon–capable states in contemporary times. Although many of its compulsions and rationales are comparable to those of other nuclear powers that earlier decided to take the same path, what would cause Pakistan to fulfill almost literally its vow to "eat grass or go hungry" in its quest for the nuclear weapon? Why and how did Pakistan stand in defiance of the world to acquire a capability described by Bernard Brodie as the "absolute weapon"?[5]

To understand the heart of the Pakistani quest, this study examines these and several related questions: What conditions sparked the shift from a peaceful quest to acquire nuclear energy into a full-fledged weapons program? How was the nuclear program organized? What role did outside powers play in Pakistan's nuclear decisions? How did Pakistan overcome the many technical hurdles encountered in the process of developing nuclear weapons?

Like the history of the Pakistan state, the story of Pakistan's nuclear program is one of unwavering resolve and dedication. Pakistani senior officials tapped into the genius of young scientists and engineers and molded them into a motivated cadre of weaponeers. Building on this reservoir of talent, the program outlasted perennial political crises and persisted despite poor civil-military relations. The young nation's leaders and scientists were united by their fascination with the new nuclear science and consciously interwove nuclear developments into the broader narrative of Pakistani nationalism. They were unwilling to allow India's strategic developments to go unanswered, and the more assiduously the program was opposed by India and the West, the more precious it became. It evolved into the most significant symbol of national determination and a central element of Pakistan's identity.

Pakistan's enduring rivalry and strategic competition with India turned bitter over subsequent decades after a series of wars and crises. The last major war in 1971 resulted in humiliating military defeat and dismemberment of Pakistan, which simply reinforced its belief that its adversaries were determined to destroy the very existence of the new state. This perception united the nation-state into a "never again" mind-set that found succor in the acquisition of a nuclear capability. However, as this book will show, there were twin causes for its national dismemberment in 1971—external aggression and internal instability. The development of a nuclear capability and robust command system might partially address one-half of the equation—that is, deterrence against external threat from India. But Pakistan has so far failed to address the other more dangerous half that threatens national survivability—domestic dissension and internal conflict. It was Pakistan's inability to develop a viable political system that failed to bring harmony and nationalism to a religiously homogeneous but ethnically and linguistically diverse people. Although the quest to acquire a nuclear weapons capability was fundamentally drawn from outside threats, East Pakistan's geographical separation, with a hostile India situated between the two wings of the country, was a vulnerability waiting to be exploited.

Theory and Approach

Why do states pursue nuclear weapons, and how do they do so? What, if anything, is unique about the Pakistani case? The realists (neorealists) would suggest that states are concerned primarily with maximizing security.[6] When faced with external threats and an unfavorable distribution of political, economic, and military capabilities with its adversaries, government officials have two fundamental options. They can either *bandwagon*, by accepting the dominance of the stronger state and relying on it for continued safety, or seek to "balance" against the power asymmetry and security challenge posed by the adversary. The option to bandwagon frequently requires the weaker state to compromise its national sovereignty.[7] The second option can be achieved through the pursuit of alliances (external balancing) or through the development of military capabilities (internal balancing).[8]

According to Kenneth Waltz and Stephen Walt, states usually choose to balance against the most serious foreign threats to their security; rarely do they bandwagon—that is, accommodate or appease the powers making these threats.[9] Further, defense planners generally prefer internal balancing because it leaves less to chance and less to the will of others; however, this strategy requires levels of national determination and resources that are beyond the reach of most countries, including Pakistan. While allies were crucial in the prenuclear era to help states fend off foreign aggression, realists recognize that nuclear weaponry has made internal balancing both more feasible and more urgent, especially to states such as Pakistan that face security threats from nuclear-armed neighbors.

All nuclear weapons development programs constitute a response to insecurity and a form of balancing against foreign political or military threats. States will choose to build nuclear bombs if the pursuit of other time-honored policies—such as strengthening their conventional military capabilities, acquiring different weapons of mass destruction, or aligning with foreign powers—are either not available or insufficient to provide the security for the state.[10]

An alternative explanation by Jacques Hymans surmises that ideas produced by national, cultural, or individual attributes and idealist approaches can explain much about worldviews, motives, and decision-making styles of specific state leaders who engage in nuclear proliferation.[11]

To understand why some countries pursue nuclear deterrence—and certainly to understand how they operationalize that deterrent—one must understand the strategic culture of the country in question. The passion and fervor with which Pakistan acquired nuclear weapons are only partially explained by realism. What is necessary is to supplement realism with more fine grained predictions derived from Pakistan's unique *strategic culture*— "a collectivity of the beliefs, norms, values, and historical experiences of the dominant elite in a polity that influences their understanding and interpretation of security issues and environment, and shapes their responses to these."[12] This book does not make the case that strategic culture can replace the explanatory power of realism. Rather, it argues that strategic culture is important to understand how Pakistan reacted to changes in the regional balance of power. Strategic culture stands as an important intervening variable between changes in the material bases of power and state behavior.[13]

"Strategic culture" is a slippery term, which presents challenges to any study employing it. The definition used in this account, proposed by respected Pakistani scholar Hasan Askari-Rizvi, argues that historical experiences have important explanatory value in the development of beliefs and in assessing how a given state responds to a given threat to national security.[14] Strategic culture is the mediating lens through which national leaders view reality, which, while not permanent, is slow to change. National elites are socialized into a strategic culture, and in the process come to share these beliefs, norms, and values. Frequently, strategic culture will be a source of constancy in the midst of a changing international environment. This study pays particular attention to assessing episodes when national leaders took decisions that would make sense only in the context of certain strategic beliefs, norms, and historical experiences.

Peter R. Lavoy has chronicled a similar narrative in his history of Indian nuclear development, where he argues that Jawaharlal Nehru and Homi Bhabha played the role of "nuclear mythmakers."[15] Lavoy defined "nuclear mythmaking" as an approach adopted by national elites (mythmakers) who want government to adopt a national security strategy of acquiring nuclear weapons by emphasizing the country's insecurity and poor international standing; portraying this strategy as the best corrective measure; articulating political, economic, and technical feasibility; successfully associating these beliefs with existing cultural norms and political priorities; and finally convincing national decision-makers to act on these views.[16]

This account describes these factors as "beliefs" that grew out of existential threats in a historical narrative that was internalized through generations and that forms the inherent cognitive disposition of the people. Lavoy provides an analytical pathway as to how myths turn into strategic beliefs. He examines primary and auxiliary assertions that drive leaders to convince decision-makers and ultimately create a popular national goal.

The primary beliefs are based on two levels of relationship. The first level is the relationship between nuclear weapons acquisition and the military dimension of security, which lays the foundation on which the second level develops in terms of a state's political status and its influence in international affairs. These levels are supplemented by four auxiliary requirements, which relate to articulating political, economic, strategic, and technological feasibilities. The state must have the developed capacity to manage political problems associated with developing nuclear weapons and their impact on relations with important states; the wherewithal to meet financial costs associated with acquisition or development of nuclear technology, including the possibility for other spin-offs such as industry, agriculture, and medicine; the capability to develop operational nuclear weapons and to devise options for their effective use in military operations; and the infrastructure and capacity to overcome the numerous technical difficulties associated with developing nuclear weapons with the possibility for industrial spin-offs. When leaders acquire the capability to articulate the six interrelated factors with panache and convincing aplomb, it is a matter of time for them to become embedded in the strategic culture of the nation-state.[17]

The person who spearheaded the idea of nuclear Pakistan was Zulfiqar Ali Bhutto. In Pakistan's early history there was no consensus about the desirability or utility of nuclear weapons. Only a few individuals, most notably Bhutto, believed that acquiring them was critical for Pakistan. However, following the devastating loss of East Pakistan in 1971 and the Indian nuclear test in 1974, opinions favoring nuclear weapons, held only by a minority, became national consensus—the necessity of nuclear weapons became a mainstream belief. This belief eventually determined the discourse of Pakistani nuclear thinking that evolved gradually—first into developing a nuclear weapon capability that took some twenty-five years, and later operationalizing it after being forced to demonstrate that capability.

In the Indian case, the shock of losing the 1962 war with China combined with the Chinese nuclear test at Lop Nor in 1964 eventually led to the Indian test in 1974.[18] Prime Minister Jawaharlal Nehru's and Indian Chief Scientist Homi Bhabha's arguments became dominant, even though neither survived to see the ascendency of those beliefs. In the Pakistani case, Zulfiqar Ali Bhutto played a similar role and nurtured the nuclear program throughout the important decade of the 1970s.

Today, there are three important strategic beliefs regarding nuclear weapons that were largely absent when Bhutto took power in 1971 but have since become dominant in Pakistani strategic thought. First, nuclear weapons are the only guarantee of Pakistan's national survival in the face of both an inveterately hostile India that cannot be deterred conventionally and unreliable external allies that fail to deliver in extremis. Second, Pakistan's nuclear program is unfairly singled out for international opposition because of its Muslim population. This feeling of victimization is accentuated by a belief that India consistently "gets away with" violating global nonproliferation norms. Third is the belief that India, Israel, or the United States might use military force to stop Pakistan's nuclear program. Today, these three beliefs—nuclear necessity for survival, international discrimination against Pakistan, and danger of disarming attacks—form the center of Pakistani strategic thinking about nuclear weapons. Collectively, these convictions have served to reinforce the determination of Pakistan's military, bureaucratic, and scientific establishment to pay any political, economic, or technical cost to reach their objective of a nuclear-armed Pakistan.

Zulfiqar Ali Bhutto was able to capture this all-encompassing narrative even before there was any national consensus on the nuclear matter. As far back as 1965, he famously told the *Manchester Guardian*: "If India makes an atom bomb, then even if we have to feed on grass and leaves—or even if we have to starve—we shall also produce an atom bomb as we would be left with no other alternative. The answer to an atom bomb can only be an atom bomb."[19] He continued to push for nuclear developments as foreign minister in the 1960s and played a critical role during his period as national leader in the 1970s. By the time he was removed from power in 1977, his thinking on nuclear matters had been institutionalized throughout the establishment. Ample patrons in the military, bureaucracy, and scientific communities would ensure the nuclear program's success in the 1980s and 1990s. Today the national narrative around the need for nuclear weapons is intertwined with Pakistani nationalism to a level that it is almost treasonous to think otherwise.

Nuclear Themes

While it is too strong a statement to say that every nuclear state has the same historical experience, it is useful to highlight the similarities. Underneath the unique strategic beliefs of Pakistan are several themes that are similar to those found in the histories of other nuclear aspirants. Three threads interweave through the fabrics of many nuclear weapons acquisition stories: national humiliation, international isolation, and national identity. When Pakistanis look back on their history, these themes are recurrent and provide a conceptual foundation from which specific strategic beliefs emerge.

National Humiliation

At the core of the nuclear weapons acquisition narrative rests national humiliation—the phrase "never again" is repeated over and over in nuclear histories. For many nations, fears produced by past humiliations are frequently reinforced by concerns about nuclear blackmail. The Soviet Union, after experiencing the ravages of invading Nazi armies, refused to accept the danger that came from an American nuclear monopoly.[20] China's nuclear ambitions were fueled by a century of foreign interference, a brutal Japanese occupation, and U.S. nuclear threats in the 1950s.[21] India's national humiliation stemmed from colonial subjugation, an embarrassing defeat in its border war with China in 1962, and strategic disparity following the Chinese nuclear test at Lop Nor in 1964.[22] Israel is a state created to ensure that "never again" would the Jewish people face risk of national extermination, and nuclear weapons became perceived increasingly as central to that requirement in the context of enduring Arab-Israeli enmity.[23]

For Pakistan, the memories—both firsthand and passed down—of the fall of Dhaka, the loss of East Pakistan, and the capture of ninety thousand prisoners of war by India are seared into the collective memory. The tragedies of 1971 left Pakistan reeling, and were followed by the subsequent blow of the 1974 Indian nuclear test. Together, these events allowed nuclear enthusiasts to take charge and led to the ascendance of Zulfiqar Ali Bhutto and his belief in the necessity of nuclear arms. Nuclear weapon efforts were redoubled after India's underground explosion at Pokhran three years later. The asymmetry in strategic capability between India and Pakistan reinforced the feeling of insecurity that had lingered after Dhaka's fall. The Pakistani nuclear weapons program was the only way to prevent such humiliation in the future and to preserve Pakistan. "Never again" would Pakistan be subject to disgrace at the hands of others.

International Isolation

Some nuclear weapons states find themselves on the receiving end of international demonization, which serves only to buttress national resolve to develop advanced technology. While the Russian experience was somewhat different—it is difficult to call a nascent superpower isolated—the USSR was the target of Western castigation for its socialist way of life. Nuclear weapons were not only a security imperative but also proof to the West of Soviet scientific advancement. China found itself ideologically disconnected not just from Western foes but also, and increasingly, from its former Soviet patrons. Israel faced opprobrium from much of the postcolonial world, and criticisms grew as Soviet-backed pan-Arabism emerged as an important political force in the 1950s.

Many nuclear aspirants are also harshly reminded that to the extent they have international support, such support is insufficient or, more often, ephemeral during periods of profound political crisis. Israel's early history showed that the United States would subordinate Israel's interests during periods of tension in an attempt to maintain stability between the superpowers. Israel's battlefield successes in 1947–48 and 1967 occurred with little foreign support. Soviet backing did little to ease Chinese hardships in Korea or to face U.S. threats in other crises regarding Taiwan in 1955. Tensions between Soviet Premier Nikita Khrushchev and Chinese communist leader Mao Zedong grew in the mid-1950s, ultimately leading to the cessation of Soviet assistance to the Chinese nuclear program in 1959. India found itself isolated: it initially received neither U.S. nor Soviet assistance in its 1962 war with China. Delhi's calculations had gone woefully wrong when its forward policy on the disputed territory provoked a border war with China. But, unfortunately for India, it occurred simultaneously with the Cuban Missile Crisis between the two Cold War superpowers. Following China's nuclear test in 1964, India's hawks began to dominate the debate. The mood of the nation was summed up in a famous speech of renowned Indian scientist Homi Bhabha: "[A]tomic weapons give a State possessing them in adequate numbers a deterrent power against attack from a much stronger State."[24] Eventually the bomb lobby in India would prevail, while India continued to believe it was on its own. In 1965, India was disgusted that the United States had cut off aid to both India and Pakistan, despite Delhi's belief that Pakistan was the aggressor in the five-week-long Second Kashmir War.

For Pakistanis, history showed that outsiders would not assist them in confronting security threats, particularly during the periods of most pressing need. Pakistan's alliance with the United States provided no benefit in the 1965 war and proved traumatically insufficient to stop military defeat in East Pakistan in 1971. While Pakistan entered into an alliance with the United States primarily to answer the Indian threat, the United States viewed the alliance solely through the prism of superpower competition and had little interest in Pakistan's fears about India. Similarly, Pakistan's all-weather friendship with China translated into little material support for Pakistan when it counted most, in either the 1965 or 1971 wars. After Pakistan embarked seriously on the nuclear path, it increasingly was the focus of Western proliferation concerns. Conspiracy theories that Pakistan was being targeted for its "Muslimness" grew, along with resentment. This perception of international isolation only served to reinforce the Pakistani state's devotion to achieving nuclear self-sufficiency.

National Identity

Most nuclear programs are not initiated with national identity as a driving factor, but often they eventually become integral to national self-perception and are thus perpetuated by their symbolic place in national identity. Sacrifices associated with the nuclear program made in the face of international opposition, combined with the belief that nuclear weapons are the only answer to prevent future humiliation, confer symbolic meaning upon the nation's sense of self. By 1971, all five permanent members of the UN Security Council were recognized as nuclear weapons states by the Treaty on the Non-Proliferation of Nuclear Weapons (NPT), and nuclear weapons were perceived as the currency of international power. "Mythmakers," be they Chinese, Indian, or Pakistani, often argued that nuclear weapons were necessary not simply to check aggression but also to wield greater influence on the global scene. This perception is well captured by Mao's statement to senior Chinese officials in 1958 that, without nuclear weapons, "others don't think what we say carries weight."[25]

Moreover, the scientific, technical, and logistical challenge of nuclear development elicits pride in societies that are able to harness their national potential to join what is arguably the most elite club in the world. Especially for countries that might have quite a mixed bag of indicators of modernity and progress, nuclear weapons are a potent symbol of the national scientific establishment's strength. This achievement is then typically employed by national elites in their effort to gain political legitimacy and influence at home. In Pakistan, the contrast between its status as a semi-industrialized developing country and its technological expertise was particularly striking, especially for those involved in the nuclear weapons development efforts. N. M. Butt, a retired Pakistani nuclear physicist, took pride in the fact that Pakistan's nuclear developments occurred in "an ocean of ignorance" in a country that possessed "lame high technology."[26] A. Q. Khan boasted of Pakistan's success in uranium enrichment: "A country which could not make sewing needles, good bicycles or even ordinary durable metalled roads was embarking on one of the latest and most difficult technologies."[27]

Pakistan's sense of national identity has a complex relationship with its Islamic identity. The perception that Pakistan is a victim of discrimination—that the world is opposed uniquely to an "Islamic bomb"—became a source of pride. Of the Muslim polities, only Pakistan has managed to cross the nuclear threshold. This nuclear accomplishment gave Pakistan certain preeminence in the Islamic world. It is perhaps no surprise, then, that Zulfiqar Ali Bhutto, the force behind the nuclear program, pivoted Pakistani foreign policy to enhance ties to other Muslim countries. Moreover, Bhutto adroitly leveraged these relationships to garner financial support for Pakistan's nuclear program. Such global prominence, in Pakistani thought, harkened back to past civilizational glory, to the time when the Mughal Empire shared the global stage with the Safavids and the Ottomans. Additionally, for Pakistan, a country conflicted over whether it is a secular or theological Muslim state, nuclear weapons were a symbol of cohesion—they became one of the few issues about which there was national consensus.

Chapter Summary and Roadmap

This book divides Pakistan's nuclear history into five phases. Part I recounts Pakistan's early days, when its fragile domestic political state was devoid of leadership in the face of emerging rivalry with India. Pakistan was barely surviving when the United States found a strategic ally by virtue of its geographical location and U.S. compulsion to "contain" the communist threat. Under these circumstances, Pakistan found new life as a member of U.S.-led military alliances. President Eisenhower's Atoms for Peace program through the 1950s fascinated the young nation and influenced the creation of the Pakistan Atomic Energy Commission (PAEC). Pakistani youth, under the vision of the father of the nation, Muhammad Ali Jinnah, were determined to acquire knowledge, and the new science was the greatest source of excitement. This part delves into the initial reluctance of Pakistani leaders to pursue a nuclear weapons program. President Ayub Khan kept the program focused on peaceful civilian purposes in the 1960s, much to the consternation of his young, hawkish foreign minister, Zulfiqar Ali Bhutto. The most prosperous period of Pakistan's history began to crash with decisions that led to war with India, diminished the alliance with the United States, and gave birth to the bomb lobby around the time the world was debating the most famous treaty of the nuclear age—the NPT. This part ends with Chapter 4, which recounts the disastrous 1971 war with India, the ascent of Bhutto to national leadership, and Bhutto's call to Pakistani nuclear scientists to begin a weapons development program in a meeting in Multan in January 1972.

Part II examines the subsequent steps taken by Pakistani leaders and scientists to develop a full-fledged nuclear research and development program. Pakistan's early, multipronged, and somewhat disjointed efforts to obtain fissile material were given greater urgency following the Indian nuclear explosive test in 1974. More important, the PAEC's attempts to secure a plutonium-based fuel cycle were stymied by the international nonproliferation regime. In fact, following the Indian nuclear test, the regime was focused not on India but on stopping Pakistan from following suit as a means to stall the cascading effect on nonproliferation. The more India's nuclear activities were tolerated, the more the Pakistani sense of discrimination grew, captured in Chapter 6, "Punishing Pakistan."

Under these circumstances Pakistan developed the front end of the fuel cycle and established the road to nuclear ambition. The program was developing at a slow pace, but institutions and infrastructures grew steadily. Zulfiqar Ali Bhutto then recruited A. Q. Khan to develop a uranium enrichment capability, whose mastery by a developing country was a revolution of sorts in the nuclear world. Despite global export controls, two related but distinct procurement networks emerged to meet the needs of the PAEC's plutonium route and the uranium route of the Khan Research Laboratories (KRL). The procurement was possible in the grey areas of nuclear trade and evolved into one of the most troubling tales in the history of nuclear weapons: that of the A. Q. Khan nuclear proliferation network. The penultimate chapter of Part II describes the scientific, technical, and experimental work necessary to develop a nuclear weapon design. Chapter 10 describes the slow reemergence of the plutonium fuel cycle, which was initially blocked in the 1970s but became increasingly important to Pakistan's nuclear developments in the late 1990s and 2000s.

Part III of the book narrates the steps taken in the 1980s and 1990s to weaponize Pakistan's nuclear devices and develop delivery means, culminating in the May 1998 tests in the Chagai Hills. This part also covers a complex historical phase of the country under the military regime of General Zia-ul-Haq. In this period, Pakistan's ideological character was redefined in more theological terms—a shift away from the founder Jinnah's vision of Pakistan. The interplay between the domestic dimension and regional and international shifts made Pakistan a central player in the Cold War battlefront in Afghanistan in the 1980s. Religious zealots were armed in the name of faith to defeat the infidel Soviet forces in Afghanistan by waging *jihad* through asymmetric guerrilla war. The Soviets were eventually defeated, and the Cold War ended. In this period three nuclear-tinged military crises and near-wars occurred with India, while the nascent nuclear weapons program continued apace.

Production of fissile material was achieved, and the program's focus shifted to acquiring delivery systems. Chapter 12 examines the multiple routes Pakistan explored to acquire an ensured capability—including fighter aircraft and liquid- and solid-fuel missiles—to deliver nuclear weapons to enemy targets. When the aircraft route became stalled as a result of nuclear sanctions, the effort shifted to ballistic missiles. Pakistan struggled to sustain its covert nuclear program in the face of sanctions and the emergence of post–Cold War norms and arms control. Pakistan's nuclear capability had not been demonstrated, but Islamabad was under intense diplomatic pressure to cap and roll back the program to mitigate crippling sanctions. Pakistan faced the choice of "eating grass or giving up the bomb." Part III ends with India's mid-May 1998 surprise test and the Pakistani government's decision to respond in kind, and the national euphoria following the success of the late-May Pakistani tests.

Part IV describes the steps taken after 1998 to turn Pakistan's nascent nuclear weapons program into an operational deterrent. Once again Pakistan transitioned from a decade of democracy to a military government under General Pervez Musharraf. Chapter 15 explores why nearly three decades of U.S.-led nonproliferation policies failed to prevent Pakistan from going nuclear, and concludes by examining the burst of U.S. diplomatic activity at the end of the Clinton administration aimed at restraining post-test nuclear deployments in South Asia.

This new nuclear environment evolves in the context of two serious crises with India and major steps taken by Pakistan in 1998 and 1999 to institutionalize command and control over its nuclear arsenal. Chapter 18 examines a 2001–2 military standoff and explores what role nuclear weapons played in the resolution of these crises. By the end of the Musharraf era, Pakistan's thinking on nuclear doctrine and force posture had developed substantially, and this planning is described as Part IV closes.

Part V identifies the challenges facing Pakistan today. Chapter 19 returns to the A. Q. Khan network and explains how Khan converted the import network he had overseen into an export enterprise that culminated in an international scandal as the network unraveled. The chapter reveals a view from inside Pakistan as to how the network activities came to light under the command and control system, what led to Khan's removal from KRL, and how the nuclear trafficking activity moved away from Pakistan into the world—vulnerable and waiting to be unraveled. The impact of the network on Pakistan and the consequences for nonproliferation continued to haunt Pakistan, especially after the United States offered a lucrative nuclear deal to India and continued to isolate Pakistan.

The book concludes with Chapter 20 by examining Pakistan's role in the new nuclear order. It provides an overview of how Pakistan is managing its nuclear arsenal following a return to civilian rule in Islamabad, while it faces unparalleled terrorist and insurgent threats. Pakistan's nuclear future will be determined within the overall context of strategic stability in South Asia. As India and Pakistan both pursue conventional and strategic force modernization, there is a potential arms race in the making. Which nuclear future will prevail is unknown. This book tells the story of Pakistan's pursuit of the bomb in the light of the wisdom of an old African proverb: "If you wish to know where you are going to go in the future, you must first know where you have come from."

Part I:
The Reluctant Phase

2   Atoms for Peace at the Crossroads of History

In 1953, in the aftermath of the armistice on the Korean Peninsula and the So-viet leader Joseph Stalin's death, the new U.S. administration under President Dwight Eisenhower reconsidered the policy of "containment" regarding the So-viet Union. Worried about an escalating arms race with a rising nuclear power, Eisenhower attempted rapprochement with the new Soviet administration. In his famous "Chance for Peace" speech he offered an olive branch, but his efforts proved futile; the Cold War between the USSR and the United States deepened.[1] The Eisenhower administration then adopted a more aggressive policy of "con-taining" the communists' potential global expansion. Washington was eyeing the periphery of Eurasia for strategic alliances, and Pakistan's strategic location atop the Indian Ocean caught its attention.

Pakistan, a six-year-old sovereign state, was yet to evolve as a nation. Nev-ertheless, when the newly appointed U.S. Secretary of State John Foster Dulles planned a visit to Asia, the *New York Times* favorably described Pakistan as "de-veloping an Eastern area of substantial strength, which can be vital to the whole of the free world."[2] The Dominion of Pakistan, however, was still reeling from the violent partition of India during its independence from the British Empire in 1947. The country was in tatters—communal riots, political instability, ethnic rivalries, mass migrations of Muslims and Hindus, and a lack of basic needs had hindered nation-building and civilian rule. At the same time that the glowing *Times* editorial appeared on January 23, 1953, Pakistani Foreign Minister Zafrul-lah Khan was at the U.S. State Department pleading for emergency food aid.[3]

At this crossroads, between a new nation heading toward its demise and U.S. Cold War exigencies demanding military alliances and "containment," arrived Atoms for Peace, promising atomic energy technology for all nations willing to forgo the development of nuclear weapons. On December 8, 1953, President Eisenhower stood before the UN General Assembly and outlined his Atoms for

Peace proposal. He sought to address the global challenges posed by nuclear science and technology in a bipolar thermonuclear age.[4] The new technology was seen as a panacea by the struggling Pakistan, a way toward economic development, legitimacy, and nationhood.

A Moth-Eaten and Truncated Muslim State

In the spring of 1953 the wounds of partition were still visible in the young Pakistani state.[5] The dream of a Muslim homeland in South Asia appeared in doubt. Leaders in India saw Pakistan as temporary, nonviable, and likely to collapse. Even Lord Mountbatten, the last viceroy, who oversaw the partition of British India, had predicted that the new nation of Pakistan would more closely resemble a tent, or *nissen* hut, than a permanent building. By that time, the six-year-old country was an orphan. Governor-General Mohammad Ali Jinnah—the *Quaid-e-Azam* ("Great Leader")—and his chosen prime minister, Liaquat Ali Khan—the *Quaid-e-Millat* ("Leader of the Nation")—had passed from the scene. The founding father of Pakistan, Jinnah succumbed to illness in September 1948, having governed Pakistan for just over a year of its independent existence. A Pashtun gunman assassinated Liaquat Ali in 1951. Their departure left a void in Pakistan's leadership that, to some extent, was never filled.[6] In this period of political turmoil, Pakistan was still struggling to formulate a written constitution and to unite its various factions.

Partition from India and independence ought to have brought an end to communal violence between Muslims, Hindus, and Sikhs, but Britain's hasty and "shameful flight" from the subcontinent created new and more intractable problems.[7] Lord Mountbatten had rushed the process of independence along at an absurd pace. The viceroy's worst blunder was the impetuous drawing of new borderlines through the middle of Punjab and Bengal. The trauma of partition had left Pakistan structurally and geophysically vulnerable to India. Three issues were at the root of Pakistan's animosity toward its neighbor. First, the new border, as drawn, was perceived as neither fair nor just, and the partition's manner of execution led to horrible consequences that continued to affect future generations. For example, Jinnah lamented that the border demarcation had left a "truncated and moth-eaten" Pakistan, with vulnerable and arbitrary boundaries.[8] Further still, no one expected that the partition would be accompanied by such bloodshed and widespread migration, as more than 10 million refugees from minority communities on both sides of the new border sought to relocate to the other, hundreds of thousands dying in the process.[9] Second, the division of civil and military assets had been inequitable. Pakistan had been expected to get one-fourth of the cash balance of rupees, but India held back and delayed, making excuses. The military division was even more acute. Pakistan received no more than 3 percent of its share of ordnance stores, and neither tanks nor ammunition was ever delivered. Pakistan's perception that India was foot-dragging on completing the division of assets reinforced the Pakistani belief that India was not reconciled to partition and was betting on failure for the infant state. In Pakistan's view, the third and most glaring example of injustice was the accession of the Muslim-majority state of Jammu and Kashmir to India by its Hindu ruler, which led to the First Kashmir War in 1948 and would become a casus belli for decades to come.

Domestically, Pakistan was bursting from within, facing immense challenges to national consolidation and its identity. A hostile India separated the two wings, East and West Pakistan, by a distance of a thousand miles. East Pakistanis, predominantly Muslim Bengalis, were agitated with the West Pakistanis over a host of issues, but most importantly over nonacceptance of their native language, Bengali, as a national language.[10] Following Liaquat's death in 1951, a Bengali politician, Khawaja Nazimuddin, had taken over as prime minister. Governor-General Ghulam Mohammad then sacked Prime Minister Nazimuddin in April 1953, believing him to be too weak to shepherd Pakistan's government during that critical period, and replaced him with another Bengali, Mohammad Ali Bogra. Despite having two consecutive Bengali prime ministers following Liaquat's assassination, East Bengal nevertheless felt disrespected by the ruling elites in Karachi and Lahore. After all, Bengalis noted, Dhaka, the capital of East Pakistan, was the 1906 birthplace of the All India Muslim League and, in 1911, the first city to raise a voice for the preservation of Muslim rights when the British rulers revoked the 1905 partition of Bengal under Hindu pressure, redividing the province along linguistic lines. In 1953, the Bengalis took to the streets to call for, among other demands, Bengali as the second national language in addition to Urdu.[11] Language riots the previous year had left many dead on the streets of Dhaka and Chittagong, East Pakistan's largest port city.

In West Pakistan, there was unrest on the streets of Lahore, the cultural and commercial capital of Punjab. Pakistan's most resource-rich and fertile province, Punjab braced itself for violence once again, barely six years after Mountbatten's vivisection of the province. Angry Muslim clerics began to target the Ahmadi community, a religious sect that venerated a nineteenth-century prophet named Mirza Ghulam Ahmad, who was castigated by orthodox Muslims.[12] The religious schism flared to national prominence. Free from the Hindus and Sikhs, who had fled western Punjab, Muslims now wanted the removal of Jinnah's handpicked foreign minister, Sir Zafarullah Khan, an Ahmadi, by declaring the Ahmadi sect as non-Muslim and Khan hence unfit for office.[13] Pakistani Punjab prepared itself for another bloodbath, barely six years after witnessing the bloodiest migration in human history. Pakistan's military was called in and martial law declared in Punjab, foreshadowing the limits of civilian authority and more declarations of martial law in the decades to come.[14]

Other separatist forces threatened Pakistan. Baluchistan, a tribal preserve on the brink of armed resistance against the state, simmered with rebellion. The Baluchis had reluctantly accepted the new federal order; however, they failed to understand its implications and were unable to give up their antiquated tribal system (*Sardari*). For example, the country's biggest natural gas field had been discovered in Sui, Baluchistan, the previous year. From the Baluchis' perspective, the Punjabi-dominated central government was milking and exploiting their resources.[15] Rather than becoming a source of strength and prosperity, therefore, the gas field became a source of grievance, lending strength to many insurgencies to follow.

The Sindh province also became a hotbed of ethnic and socioeconomic unrest. Sindhis had hoped for a better future in modern Pakistan as its feudal lords (*waderas*) maximized their gains after the departure of the Hindus. But Muslim immigrants from India (*muhajir*) chose to settle predominantly in Sindh. These "New Sindhis" settled mainly in urban areas, especially in Hyderabad and the port city of Karachi. Karachi, the national capital, was made a federal district, which was perceived as robbing the best of Sindh from Sindhis.[16] Migration southward of Punjabis and Pashtuns into Sindh added salt to the wounds, creating further alienation among the Sindhis.

In Peshawar, the capital of North West Frontier Province (NWFP), disenchanted Pashtuns demanded the return of Khan Abdul Jabbar Khan's provincial government. Popularly known as Dr. Khan Sahib, he was the brother of Ghaffar Khan, leader of the populist Red Shirt (*Khudai-Khidmat*) movement. Ghaffar Khan, the "Frontier Gandhi," had led a Pashtun nationalist movement in opposition to the creation of Pakistan, with support and sympathy from Afghanistan and India's Congress Party.[17] Pashtuns demanded their province be named Pashtunistan after their ethnic identity, rather than after a cardinal direction.

Also in 1953, across the wild borderlands of western Pakistan, King Zahir Shah of Afghanistan appointed his cousin, Mohammad Daoud Khan, as prime minister. Daoud, who vowed to unite the Pashtuns under a single Pashtunistan banner, questioned the contours of the border between Pakistan and Afghanistan. Kabul had always refused to accept Pakistan as a successor state to the British, had voted against its membership in the United Nations in 1947, and in 1949 had unilaterally revoked the 1893 border agreement it had made with the British Empire. Pakistan's newly inherited mountainous western border was now disputed, porous, tribal, and lawless. Although Afghanistan remained a buffer against Cold War communist expansion—just as it had shielded British India from the southerly expansion of the czars in the nineteenth century—the last thing Pakistan desired was an unsettled western neighbor as it prepared to face its principal rival, India.[18]

Meanwhile, in the same year, the U.S. Central Intelligence Agency (CIA) successfully toppled the Mossadeq government in Iran in a coup, returning the pro-Western Reza Shah Pahlavi to the throne in Tehran. For the next two decades, the Pahlavi dynasty would ensure the smooth flow of oil to the West and act as a Western bridgehead in the strategic Persian Gulf. The ripple effects of developments in Iran would be felt in Pakistan far into the future. While Iranian Shia clerics, alienated from the Western-influenced elites in Tehran, gained sympathy among Pakistani Shia, under the shah the relationship between Iran, Pakistan, and Turkey would grow into an organization called the Regional Cooperation for Development (RCD). This partnership would also form the centerpiece of a U.S.-backed military alliance (the Central Treaty Organization, or CENTO) against communist expansion.

Pakistan and the Early Cold War

Oblivious to the chaotic situation within and around Pakistan, the Eisenhower administration was eager to explore Pakistan's strength and abilities. When Secretary Dulles made his visit to South Asia in May 1953, he found an anxious Pakistani leadership willing not only to cooperate but also to enthusiastically make available its "potential both in manpower and bases." The Americans were impressed with the "martial and religious qualities of the Pakistanis, especially its military leader General Muhammad Ayub Khan," even though they noted that the political situation was disordered.[19] Dulles was convinced of finding in Pakistan "one country with a moral courage to do its part in resisting communism." Army Chief Ayub Khan took it upon himself to commence the foundations of a military alliance. His visit to the United States in September 1953 would be the "turning point" in laying the foundation for probably the most critical and enigmatic military relationship during the Cold War and one that has continued through the post-9/11 world order.[20]

Vice President Richard Nixon's trip to Karachi followed a visit to New Delhi, where Nixon found Indian Prime Minister Jawaharlal Nehru "the least friendly leader he had met in Asia."[21] With Pakistan, however, Nixon was impressed. "Pakistan is a country I would do anything for. The people have less complexes than the Indians."[22] At another occasion he remarked, "The Pakistanis are completely frank even when it hurts."[23]

In the year following Nixon's visit, the United States began assisting Pakistan's armed forces with training and equipment for new infantry battalions, an armored division, and modern aircraft. In 1954 and 1955 Pakistan became a formal member of two U.S.-led alliances, the South East Asian Treaty Organization (SEATO) and the Baghdad Pact—later, CENTO.[24] SEATO was formed in Manila in September, in the midst of the Taiwan Straits crises. During the preparation for the pact, Pakistan wanted the SEATO shield to cover aggression from all quarters (namely India), not just from communist states. Dulles refused and even added an explicit clarification to the treaty that it would deal only with communist aggression and that the United States had no interest in embroiling the alliance in India-Pakistan disputes. Inside Pakistan, the military was skeptical of any benefit from the final treaty, given its failure to address India.[25] Throughout 1954, the modalities of the U.S.-Pakistan military alliance were under discussion as the United States agreed to strengthen the Pakistan Army. General Ayub Khan assured the U.S. leadership that Pakistan did not want dominance over India; it wanted only to protect itself. During Ayub Khan's interaction with U.S. military leadership, he explained that Pakistan was vulnerable to communist and Indian pressure, as well as suffering from internal difficulties. The alliance should therefore have a proportionate distribution of sacrifice. Further, Pakistan had a crushing financial burden, especially in relation to its defense expenditure.[26] It was clear to the two countries by now that while an alliance was mutually beneficial, they had divergent objectives.

Those same years saw U.S. debate regarding the bolstered Pakistani military's impact on India's security. To placate India, Eisenhower issued a policy statement pledging that any aid to Pakistan misused for aggression would result in "appropriate action" by the United States and the United Nations. Pakistani

Prime Minister Muhammad Ali Bogra recognized this limitation and responded in turn that Pakistan would not provide bases or any other military facilities to the United States. However the military, led by Ayub Khan, knew the tremendous boost that American-led military outposts would provide to Pakistan's security. The risk of housing the bases, of course, was reaction from communist countries, as well as neutral countries such as Egypt.[27]

Indeed, the Soviets reacted sharply to the U.S.-Pakistan alliance and courted India and Afghanistan by supporting their resentments toward Pakistan. Meanwhile, Afghanistan's request for military aid from Washington was rebuffed. Kabul then reached out to Moscow, which obliged. Pakistan now was sandwiched between two officially nonaligned countries but de facto allies of the Soviet Union. In November 1955, Soviet leaders Nikolai Bulganin and Nikita Khrushchev visited Srinagar, the capital of Indian-administered Kashmir, and declared that Kashmir belonged to India, adding fuel to the regional rivalry. Thus India had secured a Soviet veto in the United Nations against any resolution on Kashmir.[28]

A significant development took place in 1955. In April an Afro-Asian Summit was held at Bandung, Indonesia, that provided Pakistan with an opportunity to initiate high-level contacts with the countries vying for leadership in the nonaligned world. Here, Pakistan and China recognized their importance to each other. Sensing an emerging nexus between Moscow, Kabul, and Delhi, Pakistan could not afford to alienate China. At the same time, Chinese Prime Minister Chou En-lai was quick to realize the significance of Pakistan in China's national security.[29] Pakistan's alliance with the United States was China's ticket to improved national security, given Pakistan's shared border with China's volatile Muslim-majority Xinchiang province and their shared competition with India. Pakistani Prime Minister Bogra requested a meeting with Chou En-lai to explain that Pakistan's membership in SEATO was not directed at China. Chou En-lai immediately understood and responded that he would call upon Bogra that afternoon.[30] This meeting marked the beginning of what would become an "all weather friendship" between China and Pakistan.

Compelled by geographical location, regional threats, and domestic politics, a weak and fragile Pakistan had chosen to play power politics. It was, however, caught in a catch-22: Pakistan's survivability now depended on alliance with the United States, yet keeping all of its eggs in the American basket would risk alienating China. Pakistan's dilemma at this juncture was analogous to Israel's, where the centrality of the United States was deemed essential for national survival, yet the "necessity of locating an alternative partner" was also felt. France had provided that partner in the early 1950s.[31] In its search for security and survival, Pakistan ensured its national security by making use of a two-pronged approach: engaging in *external balancing* through its alliances with the United States and China, as well as its dependence on international institutions such as the United Nations; and engaging in *internal balancing* through the formation of professional armed forces that would meet both external and internal military threats. As time passed, however, Pakistan found international institutions capricious and alliances unreliable. Bolstered by such realizations, Pakistan determined that only by matching India's threats could its security be ensured. This acute sense of insecurity and isolation became a central tenet of its security policy. Subsequent events in the region reinforced Pakistani vulnerabilities.[32] Facing a constellation of outside foes and domestic threats, Pakistan was confronted early on with the challenge of balancing between the dictates of national security and the demands for economic development—a dilemma the country has continually struggled with throughout its independent history.

Atoms for Peace

President Eisenhower was conscious of the danger of nuclear proliferation. "Atomic realities of today comprehend two facts of great significance," he said in his 1953 Atoms for Peace speech. "First, the knowledge now possessed by several nations will eventually be shared by others—possibly all others. Second even a vast superiority of weapons and a consequent capability of devastating retaliation, is no preventive, of itself . . . . "[L]et no one think that vast sums for weapons and systems of defense can guarantee absolute safety."[33] Going on, he categorically stated, "[T]he United States pledges before you—and therefore before the whole world—its determination to help solve the fearful atomic dilemma—to devote its entire heart and mind to find a way by which the miraculous inventiveness of man shall not be dedicated to his death, but consecrated to his life." He added, "[If] the fearful trend of atomic military buildup can be reversed, this greatest of destructive forces can be developed . . . to serve the peaceful pursuits of mankind."[34]

Consequently, in August 1954 the United States modified the U.S. Atomic Energy Act to allow for nuclear assistance and technology transfer just when the U.S.-Pakistan relationship was being forged. This was a radical departure from the previous American policy of nuclear secrecy. At the time, the United

States led the world in nuclear science and technology, and while the idea of sharing was noble, it would become the engine for transfer of essential know-how for future proliferant states. Under Atoms for Peace, the United States supplied research reactors to forty countries and the highly enriched uranium needed to fuel them.[35]

The plan, which allowed the United States to transfer nuclear technology and materials to countries that pledged not to use this assistance for nuclear weapons manufacturing, simultaneously would "strengthen American world leadership and disprove the Communists' propaganda charges that the United States is concerned solely with the destructive uses of the atom."[36] In the following year, the United States called for an International Conference on the Peaceful Uses of Atomic Energy in Geneva, under the auspices of the United Nations. Some twenty-five thousand participants attended this meeting, which was the largest scientific conference at the time. Two prominent scientists from South Asia played leading roles in the event. The conference was presided over by an Indian physicist and founder of the Indian nuclear program, Homi Bhabha, while a Pakistani scientist, Abdus Salam, who would be Nobel laureate, served as the scientific secretary.[37]

The Pakistani press welcomed the proposed assistance for peaceful uses of atomic energy. Pakistani Foreign Minister Zafarullah Khan, who a year earlier had knocked at the door of the State Department seeking emergency food aid, lobbied for the new technology by reassuring the West that Pakistan was not interested in developing an atomic bomb.[38] A U.S. Atoms for Peace exhibit team visited Pakistan in 1954, which greatly helped spread awareness in the young country about the benefits of nuclear technology for socioeconomic development.[39] The U.S. Agency for International Development also displayed a large exhibit at the New Delhi Trade Fair that included a thirty-foot-high reactor diagram, "hot" laboratories, and many working models of nuclear power reactors.[40] The developing world was impressed with this new science and its availability. But as Pakistan was poor, underdeveloped, and unstable, thoughts of its going nuclear were far away. Nevertheless, the "new science" excited young Pakistani students more than did the other more established fields.[41]

Partition did not evenly divide the subcontinent's scientific capital, just as other elements of national power had been unjustly distributed. As early as 1942, in part because of the urging from Indian Prime Minister Nehru and the Indian National Congress, the British government supported the establishment of the Indian Council for Scientific and Industrial Research, which oversaw several national laboratories throughout India.[42] After the partition, however, the Council and the laboratories were all located on the Indian side of the dividing line.[43] During Pakistan's early years, issues of national survival, not scientific progress, occupied Pakistan's leaders. So it was not until October 1954 that Pakistan's minister for industries announced a plan for the establishment of a national atomic research unit as part of a new body for scientific and industrial research in Pakistan, whose name was copied from its Indian progenitor: the Pakistan Council for Scientific and Industrial Research (PCSIR).[44] Although important, this body was not initially a major contributor to the emerging nuclear infrastructure.[45]

Instead, the history of the first decade of Pakistan's nuclear endeavors is the story of a trio of Cambridge-educated physicists, who would build institutions and, equally important, identify and train the next generation of Pakistani scientists. In 1954, Dr. Rafi Mohammad Chaudhry oversaw the formation of the "High Tension Laboratory" in the Physics Department of Government College, Lahore, in order to carry out nuclear research. Chaudhry, both as an institution-builder and teacher, proved to be one of the most influential figures in creating the scientific foundation for Pakistan's subsequent nuclear efforts.[46] He had trained under Ernest Rutherford, the leading British nuclear physicist of his era, at the renowned Cavendish Laboratory of Cambridge University, completing his dissertation in 1932.[47] Chaudhry had returned to India, becoming head of the Physics Department at Aligarh University, the preeminent Muslim higher education institution in what is now the Indian state of Uttar Pradesh. At the time of partition, Mark Oliphant—a leading Australian physicist who worked with Rutherford and Rafi Chaudhry in Cambridge—corresponded with Pakistan's founder, Mohammad Ali Jinnah, and suggested to him that he hire Chaudhry. Apparently in response to Oliphant's advice, Jinnah worked to secure Chaudhry a position at Government College, Lahore, in 1948, when Chaudhry migrated from India to Pakistan.[48]

As early as 1952, Prof. Rafi Chaudhry constructed a particle accelerator at the university, a larger version of a model designed by British physicists John D. Cockcroft and Ernest Walton at Cavendish Laboratory in the mid-1930s. Upon its completion, the 1.2-megavolt accelerator was perhaps the most advanced nuclear accelerator in Asia.[49] He also founded the High Tension Laboratory in 1954 and remained its head until 1965. During his tenure at Government College, Lahore, he would oversee the training of many of Pakistan's best physicists, earning him the title of *ustadon-ka-ustad* ("teacher of teachers") in the scientific community.[50] Throughout his career and well into his retirement, he earned a variety of awards for that work. When one of his students, Munir Ahmed Khan, subsequently introduced him to President Zia-ul-Haq in 1986, the military dictator raised his hand and saluted Chaudhry for his contributions to Pakistan's nuclear development.

For a few years in the early 1950s, Chaudhry was a colleague of another brilliant, Cambridge-educated Pakistani physicist, Abdus Salam. Salam, who would become the first Muslim and first Pakistani to receive the Nobel Prize in physics, in 1979, for his work on the interaction between particles, studied at Cambridge several years after Chaudhry.[51] Upon finishing his graduate studies in Great Britain, he returned to Pakistan in 1951. As a rising star, he received faculty appointments at both Government College, Lahore, and Punjab University. Salam considered himself a devout Muslim, though he belonged to the Ahmadi sect. He was disheartened to see, upon his arrival, his birth province in the throes of anti-Ahmadi riots. Salam was also appalled at the grim state of affairs in Pakistan, particularly in the field of science. He had returned to Pakistan hoping to establish a world-class scientific institute but quickly concluded that Pakistan was not yet ready for such a venture. In a retrospective essay, he wrote, "Of indigenous science and technology, or indeed of any technological manpower development, there was neither need, nor appreciation, nor role . . . . In that extreme isolation in Lahore, where no physics literature ever penetrated, with no international contacts whatsoever, and with no other physicists around in the whole country, I was a total misfit. In no uncertain terms, it was made plain to me that my dream of founding a school of research in physics was to remain a dream." By 1953, he had decided that institution building was best done outside of Pakistan. Nevertheless, throughout his life he would continue to advise the Pakistan government on nuclear matters, serve on Pakistani scientific and research bodies, and regularly scout for talented Pakistani students that could advance physics in Pakistan.

If Chaudhry at root was an educator, and Salam a scientist, the third member of the Cambridge trio can be summarized as an administrator, albeit a controversial one. Nazir Ahmad, like Chaudhry and Salam, also undertook his graduate education in the United Kingdom at the Cavendish Laboratory under Rutherford's guidance. A few years older than Chaudhry (Nazir Ahmad and Rafi Chaudhry were decades older than Salam), Nazir Ahmad finished his Ph.D. at Cambridge in 1925, after which he returned to India.[52] The job prospects for even accomplished physics graduates in British India were limited, and Nazir Ahmad's initial appointments were at the laboratory associated with the Central Cotton Committee of India. He moved to a series of economic appointments in the mid-1940s, and, after partition, he served in Pakistan's planning and economic development bureaucracy. His physics background did not go unnoticed by the new state, however, and he continued to advise on nuclear matters. In 1955, he led Pakistan's delegation to the International Conference on the Peaceful Uses of Atomic Energy in Geneva. Upon his return, and in response to the U.S. Atoms for Peace initiative, Pakistan decided to upgrade its ad hoc nuclear activities by creating a more formal Pakistan Atomic Energy Commission (PAEC) with Nazir Ahmed as its first chairman.[53] Under Ahmed's leadership, the new institution's charter outlined its primary objectives: planning and development of peaceful uses of atomic energy, the establishment of the Atomic Energy and Nuclear Research Institute, installation of research and power reactors, negotiation with international atomic energy bodies, personnel selection and training, and the application of radioisotopes to agriculture, health, and industry.[54]

Early on, Pakistani scientific leaders identified the lack of trained physicists and engineers as a crucial deficiency that its nuclear program would have to rectify. In that context, in 1957 the PAEC established a small laboratory with limited facilities in a shed at West Wharf, Karachi, to provide basic training to scientists and engineers to prepare them for further studies. Specially selected individuals would be sent for short training courses of under a year that were available in Europe or the United States. Then, having completed their studies, they would return to Pakistan and conduct their own elementary research and development, instructing the next generation of students.

Just as Pakistan decided that it needed more scientific talent, the availability of nuclear education expanded dramatically. Pursuant to the Atoms for Peace initiative, the United States decided to train nuclear scientists and engineers from foreign countries beginning in 1955. At the Argonne National Laboratory, administered by the University of Chicago, the United States established a school to accomplish that task. Similar international outreach programs existed at North Carolina State University and Pennsylvania State University, among others. On March 14, 1955, at the opening session of the Argonne international program, President Eisenhower personally addressed some forty students from twenty countries, saying: "You represent a positive accomplishment in the Free World's efforts to mobilize its atomic resources for peaceful uses and the benefit of mankind."[55]

Two years later, in 1957, a research reactor, the Argonne Nuclear Assembly for University Training (ARGONAUT), was set up at Argonne, deepening the education available for foreign students. Students were trained in reactor theory, nuclear physics, and engineering laboratory experiments. Following their studies, nuclear engineering graduates received an opportunity to work and intern in various U.S. national nuclear laboratories; many of them, if they did not return to their home countries, went on to join the International Atomic Energy Agency (IAEA) upon graduation. By 1959, Argonne's international school had 420 alumni in nuclear science and engineering from forty-one countries.[56] Pakistanis participated actively in the training available in the United States and elsewhere, and by the end of the 1950s PAEC had signed several bilateral agreements with U.S. national nuclear laboratories including Oak Ridge, Brookhaven, and Argonne.[57]

On August 11, 1957, Pakistan and the United States signed an agreement in Washington for cooperation in civilian and peaceful uses of atomic energy. Under the agreement the United States would supply a research reactor to Pakistan and help with the design, construction, and operation of power reactors, so long as total assistance did not exceed $350,000.[58] This small dollar amount meant that Pakistan could afford only a swimming pool–type reactor, a design suitable for research and training but not power generation.[59]

The PAEC was dissatisfied. They wanted a heavy water reactor that could be used for power generation in addition to more advanced scientific research. Among other benefits, heavy water allows for naturally occurring uranium—as opposed to enriched uranium—to be used in reactor cores; however, separating heavy water from regular water requires large-scale facilities. Heavy water molecules consist of one oxygen atom and two deuterium atoms, an isotope of hydrogen having an extra neutron in the nucleus; while naturally occurring, they are quite rare, accounting for about only one in three thousand water molecules. Nazir Ahmad implored the ministries of Finance and Foreign Affairs to allocate $1 million, or arrange a loan from the U.S. Export-Import Bank (USEXIM), in order to procure a heavy water reactor like the "CP-5" reactor in operation at the Argonne National Laboratory.[60] But the domestic institutions had different national infrastructure priorities, such as the Warsak Dam in the NWFP.[61]

In March 1958, PAEC chairman Nazir Ahmad wrote a letter to the chairman of the Pakistan Industrial Development Corporation (PIDC), Ghulam Farooq, requesting procurement of a heavy water plant that could produce 50 kilograms (kg) of heavy water per day. This plant, proposed to be installed in Multan, a city in the Punjab province, would use by-products from a nearby fertilizer plant. But the PIDC showed no interest in this plan. The PAEC was deeply disillusioned with the response of PIDC, as well as that of the Ministry of Finance.[62]

Aside from fund allocation, the PAEC push for a CP-5 reactor met another obstacle. The United States was reluctant to sell Pakistan a CP-5 reactor because by-products of a heavy water reactor could have military applications, though proliferation concerns at the time were not as acute as they would later become. Instead, the United States was willing to assist only with comparatively proliferation-safe light water reactor technology.[63] The issue remained unresolved for three years. Not until 1959 did the Pakistani government approve the construction of the modest swimming pool–type research reactor.[64] The PAEC was still unhappy. The PAEC was demanding a quality power reactor, especially knowing that India had received one. The minutes of the meeting recorded the dismay of the board: "The installation of the swimming pool type reactor might adversely affect the progress of peaceful uses of atomic energy which we would like to achieve in the country, and in view of our expanding national requirements, it might be necessary to consider the installation of a power reactor, with a large number of facilities."[65] Still grappling for options, Pakistan looked to Canada, which had offered a Canada Deuterium-Uranium (CANDU-type) heavy water reactor to India in 1955; Pakistan sought a similar reactor, but the Canadian price of $7 million greatly exceeded Pakistan's budget.

The difficult path toward the acquisition of a reactor defined Nazir Ahmad's tenure as PAEC chair, which ended in 1959 with few concrete results. As early as June 2, 1958, Ahmad was complaining that the procurement of nuclear reactors had been unnecessarily delayed for "nontechnical" (that is, financial and administrative) reasons. He demanded financial and administrative autonomy for the PAEC so that it could carry out its objectives. In the memories of the PAEC scientists, Nazir Ahmad's tenure as the PAEC chair is judged harshly for his failure to secure a reactor. Former scientists are likely to understate Ahmad's challenges in educating a young bureaucracy about the promise of nuclear science, and they certainly understate the accomplishments of the young PAEC in identifying and training the personnel that would be crucial to the program's later success.

The Decade Draws to a Close

As Ahmad struggled with the bureaucracy, Pakistan continued to face serious political instability. Clashes in East Pakistan, sudden power shifts, and failed government appointments led to frequent changes in the central government. Even Indian Prime Minister Nehru was prompted to comment, "The government in Pakistan changes before I change *dhoti* [pants]."[66] Young military officers of the time found the behavior of the political leadership very disturbing, especially when it provoked negative comments from the comparatively more stable India.

Defense Secretary Iskandar Mirza and Army Chief General Ayub Khan emerged as powerful players during this tumultuous period. The two men had similar worldviews. They viewed strong armed forces as essential. They believed that Pakistan must have a secular outlook, as envisioned by Jinnah, and rejected any role in politics for clerics, who were threatening that Pakistan would become a theocratic polity. Finally, their experiences with politicians had left them with little faith in the parliamentary system, and a belief in the necessity of a presidential system with strong central government.

On March 23, 1956, Pakistan was renamed as a republic. This day was the sixteenth anniversary of the Lahore Resolution, when the All India Muslim League laid the foundation for an independent nation-state. A new constitution, which had been debated and drafted since 1947, was promulgated, establishing a parliamentary system. Iskandar Mirza became president of Pakistan for the next two and a half years, during which period the prime minister's office changed hands four times, an indication that the state of Pakistan was in disarray and that the system's breakdown appeared imminent.

3   Ayub's Non-Decision and the Nuclear Bomb Option

Under the new constitution of the Republic of Pakistan in 1956, a highly centralized system of governance emerged, marred by continuous struggle between the president and Parliament, with the balance of power clearly lying in favor of the former. Rather than encouraging democratic principles and ensuring public participation in the political process, President Mirza began to consolidate his position.[1] The four provinces in West Pakistan were merged into a single entity, to be treated as one federal entity at par with East Pakistan. As a result, authority was concentrated in the hands of Punjabi and Muhajir elites who held civil bureaucratic positions, resulting in much resentment from other ethnic groups—the Bengalis in the east, and the Pashtuns, Sindhis, and Baluchis in the west wing of the country. Meanwhile, religious groups jockeyed for influence and dominance, hoping to seize the opportunity to turn Jinnah's Muslim Pakistan into a theocratic Islamic Pakistan entity.[2]

In the following decade, despite all internal discords and political experiments, the new republic of Pakistan made remarkable progress. By the mid-1960s the country saw economic growth averaging about 6 percent annually, prompting the Harvard Development Advisory Group to declare Pakistan a model developing country.[3] The Pakistani armed forces were modernizing as new industries, agriculture reforms, and energy production were slowly improving socioeconomic conditions. Young Pakistani scientists, engineers, physicists, and chemists were receiving scholarships to study abroad at top universities of the world in nuclear science and advanced technologies. The Pakistan Atomic Energy Commission (PAEC) was creating a "soft technology" base by developing a cadre of highly qualified experts. However, Pakistan was far behind in acquiring "hard technologies." Hardware was expensive, and unlike India's, Pakistan's basic technical infrastructure was poor and nearly nonexistent. Pakistan was enormously underdeveloped, and its limited resources, despite emerging economic promise, compelled the nation to prioritize more important developmental goals over available nuclear energy opportunities.

Amid these challenges, the rise and fall of four personalities over the decade of the 1960s determined the course of nuclear history in Pakistan. Ayub Khan, who would become the unquestionable ruler of the decade, and his brilliant young minister Zulfiqar Ali Bhutto were the two leaders whose close alliance and subsequent rivalry would determine the country's destiny. Their national-level decisions on domestic political dispensation and national security policy created new strategic alliances, military crises, and wars—and laid the foundation of nuclear discourse in Pakistan. Two scientists, Dr. Abdus Salam and Dr. Ishrat Hussain Usmani, would chart the course of science and technology advancement for peaceful and military applications. The curious intersection of these four personalities determined the nuclear policies at a time when the international community was debating how to address the proliferation of nuclear technology for military purposes. The atmospherics of the somewhat promiscuous nuclear trade environment prevalent at the time were about to change with the completion of the Treaty on the Non-Proliferation of Nuclear Weapons (NPT) negotiations.

The historic rise of two distinctly opposite personalities—General Muhammad Ayub Khan and his protege Zulfiqar Ali Bhutto—is a story of how personal idiosyncrasies and political decisions amid cross-cutting domestic politics, regional security dynamics, and global geopolitical tensions affected the nuclear discourse. Two opposing camps would emerge, one pragmatically advocating caution and slow gradual process, the other enthusiastically pushing for nuclear acquisition and development. All the while Pakistan was also losing its sense of political direction and coherence as the decade neared an end.

Answer from Heaven

Two years after the 1956 constitution went into effect, the governmental system neared collapse. By then President Mirza and Army Chief General Muhammad Ayub Khan had emerged as the two most powerful figures in the country. General Ayub Khan had approached retirement in 1955, but he was given a four-year extension, causing some resentment among the army's many hopefuls waiting in the wings for the vacancy.[4] By the fall of 1958, Ayub Khan would be the unquestioned ruler of Pakistan.

Born in the humble home of a noncommissioned officer in 1907 in the village Rehana in the North West Frontier Province (NWFP), Ayub Khan rose to become the first commander-in-chief of the Pakistan Army at the age of forty-four. After his father sent him to the prestigious Muslim University in Aligarh, the tall, handsome Pashtun was selected to go to the prominent Sandhurst Military Academy in Great Britain. Following Sandhurst, his quality education was matched by considerable experience on the ground, first on the Burma front against the Japanese threat to India in World War II, then as commanding general officer of the 14th Division in Dhaka (East Pakistan) from 1948 to 1950. There he witnessed Bengali dissatisfaction with Pakistan's policies. In January 1951, the same month Ayub Khan was made army chief, a conspiracy to overthrow the civil government was discovered. The newly appointed army chief's acumen in acting against the "Rawalpindi Conspiracy" established his credentials and loyalty.[5] Despite the breakup of the conspiracy, a Pashtun gunman assassinated Prime Minister Liaquat Ali Khan on October 16, 1951, for reasons that remain unclear.

President Mirza trusted his close friend and associate Ayub, whose forceful personality stood out in the political tumult. Ayub focused on modernizing the army to facilitate its task of defending the national frontiers and maintaining domestic order. He was concerned with changes in the U.S. administration's attitude toward Pakistan and, at the same time, India's increasingly antagonistic stance. In April 1958, Ayub Khan visited the United States amid a tense political climate and a deteriorating economic situation in his country. Ayub was worried that Washington would support India at a time when Delhi was moving closer to the Soviet Union and, having secured a veto in the United Nations, was hardening its position on Kashmir. India was also threatening to cut off the waters of the Ravi and Sutlej rivers, the lifeline to the Pakistani agricultural heartland and national breadbasket.

On May 1, 1958, General Ayub cabled President Mirza from Washington after his meetings with the Dulles brothers—Secretary of State John Foster Dulles and CIA director Allen Dulles—and informed him that India had "cleverly convinced top-ranking Americans that their [India's] military build-up was checkmating China ... but somehow Americans believe it to be true .... I am amazed at their ignorance and gullibility, when the best part of the Indian Army is either concentrated along the Pakistan border or is within 10 day's call of the border."[6] Ayub's primary mission was to get U.S. military aid to Pakistan, and the Washington meeting brought him one step closer to that goal.[7] By mid-summer 1958, General Ayub Khan was seen as the architect of the U.S.-Pakistan alliance. On June 9, Prime Minister Feroz Khan Noon extended Ayub's service by another two years, saying, "You are still very young, being 51 years of age . . . . Pakistan at this juncture cannot afford to lose your services."[8] By this time, Ayub was convinced that his power and popularity within the country and internationally made him indispensable to the armed forces and the nation.

Within the two years of his term, President Mirza had rotated through a series of three prime ministers and had faced a separatist leader in Baluchistan. Ayub convinced Mirza that democracy was not a luxury Pakistan could presently afford. Mirza, who thrived on political intrigue and maneuvers, agreed and on October 7, 1958, declared martial law.[9] The move was applauded by a public frustrated with the prolonged uncertainty and continued ineptitude of national governance.

After martial law was declared, Mirza's rule lasted only twenty days. Ayub Khan felt that Mirza's scheming might eventually threaten the discipline of the army and decided it was time to show Mirza the door and demonstrate where the ultimate power rested. Ayub's rise to power, which came to be called the October Revolution, ushered in a period of stability and growth in Pakistan for the next decade. The mood of the nation at the time was aptly covered on October 10, 1958, in an editorial in *Dawn,* the most prestigious English language daily: "The way things were going, so much more damage would have been done . . . it might have been too late to save it from collapse . . . . Now that a break has been made with the past system and [a] new one has been ushered in . . . the peaceful revolution [might have been] the *answer from heaven* [emphasis added]."[10] A decade later, in 1968, Samuel Huntington would effusively describe Ayub's rule: "More than any other political leader in a modernizing country after World War II, Ayub Khan came close to filling the role of a Solon or Lycurgus or 'Great Legislator' on the Platonic or Rousseauian model."[11]

By nature Ayub was a cautious man—prudent and disciplined. He loathed brusque and adventurous ideas and proceeded only after careful analysis. Altaf Gauhar, his close associate and biographer, described him as a man who knew "the art of moving on slowly."[12] Ayub's critics would accuse him of being weak and indecisive in his military leadership, but he believed in "patience" and "consulting the best brains" before arriving at major decisions.[13]

Ayub's secular outlook and moderate religious beliefs could be attributed to a number of experiences: his early schooling under Sikh teachers, whose "rituals and Punjabi songs he found absorbing";[14] his stay in the Aligarh Muslim College, where he refined his Urdu and matured intellectually; and his Sandhurst military education, where he was trained to respect civilian rule and developed a personal habit of reading and writing with an "insatiable desire for more."[15] Ayub Khan was enigmatic, with many of his actions and decisions apparently contrary to his primary traits and values. While he seemed to be "a man in a hurry to leave his mark on Pakistan," on some issues, including his decisions on the direction of the nuclear program, his instincts were just the opposite.[16]

He had seized political power in a military coup, abrogated the constitution, and enforced national discipline. Within three months of the October Revolution, Ayub Khan withdrew the military to the barracks and reinstated civil life, though with the military directing public administration from the top. He appointed cabinet ministers primarily from his military colleagues and from bureaucrats who avoided discredited politicians, some of whom he attacked as "disruptionists, political opportunists, smugglers, black-marketeers and other such social vermin, sharks and leeches" in his first speech as martial law administrator.[17] Ayub's personnel choices included two prominent persons—Manzur Qadir, an eminent lawyer whom he made the foreign minister, and the brilliant Zulfiqar Ali Bhutto (originally chosen by President Mirza), who quickly was entrusted with half a dozen government portfolios, including fuel, power, and natural resources, as well as control over the atomic energy effort. Bhutto's impressive commission was remarkable given his youth and relative inexperience.

Zulfi, as Bhutto was fondly called, had risen to prominence rapidly. After completing studies at the University of California at Berkeley and Oxford University, he left for Karachi in 1954 to practice law. During the final years of the protracted constitutional debate, Bhutto, hailing from the Sindh province, achieved some notice for his vociferous opposition to the one-unit scheme that had merged four provinces into West Pakistan. Success in his law practice plus the land inherited from his family and that of his wife provided material backing to his already formidable intellect and charisma. Bhutto would generously invite senior generals and bureaucrats to his home and farmlands for wining, dining, and hunting.[18]

President General Ayub Khan learned to rely on both the experienced Qadir and the young Bhutto as eloquent, vocal supporters of the rewriting of a new social contract for Pakistan by way of referendum, local democracy, and executive order, as well as a centralized system of governance.[19] During this transformation of the Pakistani regime, Ayub viewed indiscipline, political dissent, and media criticism as impediments to national progress. So important was national discipline and order, that despite his liberal, educated demeanor, he looked around the country and saw only citizens "behaving like a wild horse that had been captured but not yet tamed."[20]

Though Ayub Khan was central in building Pakistan's relationship with the United States, it was the decade of his rule that also saw a gradual downward trend in the U.S.-Pakistan relations. U.S. officials thought Pakistan was too demanding and obsessed with India. Washington reiterated to Karachi (then capital of Pakistan) that U.S. military aid was not intended for use against India. Pakistan insisted that U.S. officials were either naive or simply insensitive to the nascent country's security concerns. In the decade that Ayub Khan continued to hold power, he emphasized to his American interlocutors that not only was India the real threat to Pakistan, but it was also a proxy of the Soviet camp. However, the United States remained unconvinced, a fundamental mismatch of perception in the U.S.-Pakistan security relationship that has persisted to this day.

Nevertheless, even as early as 1958, the army gained several infantry divisions and armored brigades as a result of Ayub's untiring courtship of the United States. As its numbers grew close to 200,000, the army took the opportunity to reorganize and modernize. Pakistan received M-1 rifles, jeep-mounted recoilless rifles, antitank weapons, M-48 Patton tanks, F-86 Sabre jets, B-57 bombers, and, most notably, modern F-104 Starfighter aircraft.[21] In return, it leased to Washington for ten years the Badaber Air Base in Peshawar, Pakistan, where the United States housed the "6937th Communication Group" and supported U-2 Spy plane launches. Unfortunately, two years later, on May 7, 1960, Francis Gary Powers (call sign Puppy 68) was shot down, prompting Nikita Khrushchev to warn the Pakistani ambassador in Moscow that he had circled Peshawar in red on the Soviet map.[22] Khrushchev threatened, "If any American plane is allowed to use Peshawar as a base of operations against the Soviet Union, we will retaliate immediately."[23] Ayub realized that U.S. support for Pakistan had costs as well as benefits.

Recognizing waning U.S. interest in Pakistan's security problems, the Ayub regime reached out for rapprochement with both China and India. Pakistani Foreign Minister Manzur Qadir proposed a border agreement with China in November 1959 that would eventually demarcate the several-hundred-mile Sino-Pakistani border in northern Kashmir.[24] At the same time, Ayub Khan had reached out to Indian Prime Minister Nehru to negotiate the Kashmir issue. While results of these talks were minimal, the World Bank was able to settle India-Pakistan disagreements on water rights and water distribution between the two countries, leading to the Indus Waters Treaty, signed on September 19, 1960. The Eisenhower administration left office in January 1961 convinced that it had achieved good relations with both India and Pakistan.

By that time, Zulfiqar Ali Bhutto was a key cabinet minister and close political advisor to President Ayub Khan. It was Bhutto who suggested in 1959 that the president's rank should be elevated from general (four-star) to that of field marshal (five-star). The president was delighted at the "brilliant idea."[25] Bhutto was also responsible for administering Ayub's "Basic Democracies" scheme and establishing the foundation for the new constitution that came into effect in 1962, along with identifying and implementing ideas to strengthen the "revolution."[26] Bhutto's real ambitions, however, lay elsewhere. What he truly wanted was to emerge as the architect of national security and external affairs policy.

In September 1959, while addressing overseas Pakistanis in Dorchester, England, Bhutto described energy and power as the two keys to Pakistan's industrial future. Bhutto, despite not holding the foreign affairs portfolio, would act as if he did, to the chagrin of the senior and more sober Manzur Qadir, who held the portfolio. President Ayub encouraged the exuberance and energy in the personality of the youthful minister.[27]

Meanwhile, China was constructing a road through Aksai Chin that would link Tibet to Xinjiang. Aksai Chin was a portion of territory from the disputed princely state of Jammu and Kashmir that Pakistan eventually would cede to China in 1963. China's actions created tension between India and China, primarily because India claimed Aksai Chin along with the entirety of Jammu and Kashmir. Bhutto had the foresight to recognize the significance of the development and apprised Ayub about the relevance for Pakistan's Kashmir position. At first, Ayub dismissed Bhutto's concern by stating that the dispute was India's problem. But Bhutto persisted, arguing that by not taking a specific position, Pakistan was essentially recognizing India's authority over that portion of Kashmir. He wrote a letter to President Ayub as well as to Foreign Minister Qadir, saying, "We shall have to examine the whole question in depth and not let the India-China situation regarding Kashmir drift and develop to our detriment."[28] Ayub Khan, although deeply engrossed in the Indus Waters Treaty negotiations with India, ultimately noticed Bhutto's shrewd political thinking and, in April 1960, appointed him minister for Kashmir affairs.[29] Bhutto's youth, energy, and charm thrust him into the limelight, bringing him closer to the president, often overshadowing other senior ministers such as Manzur Qadir and Mohammad Shoaib, Ayub's finance minister.

Bhutto led a delegation to the United Nations in 1960, where he abstained from voting on Peking's membership in the United Nations, which drew U.S. displeasure. Fearing political discord, Foreign Minister Qadir retracted Bhutto's voting power in the United Nations. Bhutto forcefully argued with the president about the importance of maintaining a position of neutrality in order to strengthen Pakistan's position among the Third World countries and in the Sino-Pakistani friendship as a counter to Indian hegemony in South Asia. The Pakistan Foreign Ministry, in the meantime, was committed to the U.S.-led alliance and considered Bhutto's suggestion of "neutrality" a contradiction, which also appeared to follow Nehru's nonaligned policy.[30] By now Bhutto was openly crossing swords with Foreign Minister Qadir, a challenge that President Ayub Khan ignored so as to encourage the younger politician, who had the advantage of both eloquence and conviction.

Bhutto's global vision and experience in the United Nations had convinced him that "in a world dominated by great powers and filled with the fear of a nuclear holocaust, the umbrella of world organizations was the best protection for small non-nuclear states."[31] Bhutto kept Kashmir on top of the UN agenda, describing India's aggressive occupation of Kashmir as a "grave threat" to international peace. Stanley Wolpert observes, "[N]either Ayub [nor] Qadir had ever used such strong language in public pronouncements on Kashmir."[32] The two statesmen believed in subtle, calibrated foreign policy without making waves, while Bhutto enjoyed stirring the waters.

Indo-China War

In May 1962 Pakistan and China formally announced their intention to begin border negotiations in October, provoking reactions not only from Delhi but also from Washington. Ayub clearly indicated to his Western allies that as a sovereign state, Pakistan had the right to demarcate the border with its neighbor.

Meanwhile, border talks between India and China had stalled, and bogged down even more when India took a hard-line negotiating position and executed aggressive troop movements toward a disputed border with China known as the McMahon Line. In September and October 1962, India established posts in another disputed territory, the North East Frontier Agency (NEFA). By October, just when the Cuban Missile Crisis between the United States and the Soviet Union was at its peak, war broke out between India and China. The United

States rushed to provide India with arms as Nehru pleaded for U.S. assistance. Ayub Khan was concerned over the arming of India, but the Kennedy administration urged the Pakistani leader to make "a positive gesture of sympathy and restraint" toward India.[33] Although Ayub Khan assured Washington that Pakistan would not take action against India, he rebuffed the notion that India, having initiated the conflict by its aggressive policies and provocation of China, deserved any sympathy.

Even while making these assurances, Ayub Khan was under domestic pressure to exploit India's weakened position by launching an attack on Kashmir.[34] Lieutenant-General Abdul Malik Majeed was an instructor at the Pakistan Army's Command College in Quetta at the time. Now retired, he recalls that there was a strong belief throughout the army that Pakistan should take advantage of India's vulnerability in its war with China. The general opinion, he recollects, was "unanimous to take advantage of the situation. Ayub Khan, however, did not succumb to pressure."[35]

As U.S. aid poured into India, the United States urged Pakistan to put its border talks with China on hold. At the same time, the U.S. demanded that Ayub Khan make public assurances that Pakistan would not attack India. While U.S. pressure was not appreciated, Ayub was especially offended that Kennedy did not consult him before sending military aid to India, a discussion that he believed had been promised the previous year during a visit to the United States. Pakistan was now more preoccupied with ensuring that the U.S. military aid to India would not be used against Pakistan. Ayub insisted that the best way forward was to quickly resolve the Kashmir issue in order to eliminate the India threat once and for all.

The impact of the Sino-Indian conflict was a defining moment for the U.S.-Pakistan alliance. From Ayub's standpoint, his agreement not to intervene in Kashmir should have been rewarded with a serious negotiation leading to the settlement of the issue. Many in the U.S. government also thought the environment was propitious to settle the Kashmir dispute, but could not have foreseen events to come.[36] President Kennedy decided to send a high-level team headed by Assistant Secretary of State for Far Eastern Affairs Averell Harriman to South Asia to aid in conflict resolution. Meanwhile, Britain paralleled this effort by dispatching Secretary of State for Commonwealth Relations Duncan Sandys.[37] Throughout the following year of 1963, both teams would face deep frustration in their efforts to find a solution to Kashmir. Then, on Friday, November 22, 1963, President Kennedy was assassinated, marking the end of serious American mediation between India and Pakistan on the Kashmir issue. All future U.S. intervention would be for either conflict prevention or crisis management.

Immediately after the Sino-Indian War, Ayub replaced Foreign Minister Mohammad Ali Bogra—who was seriously ill—with Zulfiqar Ali Bhutto. This decision had a major impact on Pakistan's security policy in the 1960s. During that time, Pakistan was negotiating on three tracks: one with the United States and United Kingdom on regional issues, another with India on Kashmir at the Foreign Minister level, and a third with China on border demarcation. Bhutto's major achievement as foreign minister was the conclusion of the boundary agreement with China on March 2, 1963. Coming on the heels of the India-China war and failed talks on Kashmir, this agreement was a classic Machiavellian move on the part of Bhutto.

Delhi was furious, charging before the UN Security Council that Pakistan had unlawfully ceded two thousand square miles of "Indian territory" to China. This accusation gave Bhutto the opportunity to retaliate. He resurrected the issue of India's occupation of Kashmir and nonadherence to UN resolutions, declared it "outrageous" for India to claim sovereignty, and called for an impartial plebiscite in Kashmir. Bhutto insisted that Pakistan had not ceded any territory to China, but rather, China had given Pakistan its rightful 750 square miles and asserted that, "by agreeing to delimit and demarcate its boundary with China, Pakistan helped to improve the region's prospects for peace."[38] He pushed further, asking India to come to an agreement with Pakistan "here and now," so that both Indian and Pakistani forces could be withdrawn from Kashmir in a synchronized manner under the auspices of the United Nations.[39]

Throughout 1963 Zulfiqar Ali Bhutto's popularity in Pakistan grew. He was traveling worldwide, rhetorically echoing Third World popular sentiments, ridiculing India's negotiating positions on Kashmir, all while praising China. He urged President Ayub to review Pakistan's membership in the South East Asian Treaty Organization (SEATO) to placate the Chinese. Bhutto even rejected a "no war pact" with India, calling it "sinister."[40] He believed this idea was designed "to lull [Pakistanis] into a false sense of security . . . [only] to become victims of Indian aggression." Referring to China, Bhutto assured a domestic audience in the national assembly, "We have friends . . . [and] assurances from other countries that if India commits aggression against us they will regard it as aggression against them."[41]

In an incident in December 1963 at Hazratbal Shrine in Kashmir, a sacred relic was stolen that was said to hold the Holy Prophet Muhammad's hair. This incident triggered anti-Indian unrest throughout Kashmir, which eventually forced India to release the popular Kashmiri leader Sheikh Mohammad Abdullah, who had been detained for eleven years. Fearing the movement might evolve into secessionism, Delhi sent in the Indian Army. But this move only helped to fuel more violence and widespread chaos. Foreign Minister Bhutto gathered the support of China, Indonesia, and many other countries for the Kashmiri cause. Then, on May 27, 1964, Indian Prime Minister Nehru passed away. At his funeral, Bhutto met several leaders of India, whom he urged to resolve the Kashmir dispute. However, they clearly were not serious about settling the issue, and by mid-1964 Bhutto was convinced that the only remaining solution was a military one.[42]

At the time of Nehru's death, the popular Kashmir leader Sheikh Abdullah was visiting Pakistan and had met Ayub Khan, who was greatly impressed with him. In Nehru's death, Ayub saw an opportunity to bring an end to the "bitterness and recrimination" between the two countries.[43] While a noble goal, his focus was quickly diverted to the domestic arena for the 1964 elections that, although he emerged victorious, proved challenging.

Staying Ahead of the U-2

Winning the election freed Ayub Khan to the international stage. Bhutto had long championed "neutrality," and by this time had convinced Ayub not to put the proverbial eggs in the American basket and to open up establishing relations with both the Soviet Union and China. President Ayub Khan made back-to-back visits to Beijing in March 1965 and Moscow in April. These two visits clearly indicated that foreign policy had shifted to encompass more than just the U.S.-Pakistan alliance. China apparently welcomed Ayub Khan, as he was accorded the most enthusiastic welcome given any visitor in the history of modern China up to that point. During the visit, Premier Chou En-Lai and Ayub Khan signed a boundary protocol on the basis of a ground survey of the border.[44] Upon his return, Ayub was sworn in for a five-year term on March 23, 1965.

The visit to the Soviet Union was significant, being the first by a Pakistani head of state. Historically, relations between Pakistan and the Soviet Union had been strained, and the Gary Powers U-2 incident in 1960 had not improved ties. Unlike in China, there was no rousing welcome, and the weather was cold. At first Ayub's meeting with Prime Minister Kosygin and Foreign Minister Andrei Gromyko was like an encounter with strangers. But it soon became a frank exchange among the three. Ayub explained the complex relationship between India and Pakistan and complained that the Soviet Security Council veto against a Kashmiri plebiscite only served to block a resolution to the dispute in Kashmir. He argued that settlement of the Kashmir issue would be an act of friendship and mercy to the people of India, as it would allow that country to focus on more pressing issues such as poverty and other socioeconomic concerns.

Kosygin and Gromyko insisted that Kashmir be resolved bilaterally between India and Pakistan and complained of Pakistan's membership in SEATO and the Central Treaty Organization (CENTO), as well as American U-2 flights launched from Pakistani soil. Ayub assured the Soviet leadership that "there was no military life left in the pacts, and Pakistan would never serve as an instrument of U.S. policy."[45] Ayub went on to apologize for the U-2 incident of 1960 and assured the Soviet statesmen that no American offensive weapons would be allowed at Badaber communications base at Peshawar. At the end of the meeting, Ayub invited Kosygin and Gromyko to visit Pakistan, noting that Gromyko "had been to the east and west but never to Pakistan." Gromyko replied in a light vein, "I always keep ahead of the U-2."[46]

The result of the visit was an official apology to the Soviet Union about the U-2 incident by way of Ayub's repeated assurance that the military alliances seemingly pitted against the Soviet Union were obsolete. The Soviet leadership acknowledged the historic nature of the meeting with Ayub. Kosygin summarized the visit's importance: "In one day we have achieved more than what others take years and sometimes fail to achieve."[47] In the minds of both Ayub Khan and Zulfiqar Ali Bhutto, this triumphant moment was a turning point in removing Pakistani policy from its reliance on the United States.

Meanwhile, back home a new crisis was brewing between India and Pakistan that would eventually erupt into an armed conflict. After Nehru's death in May 1964, Lal Bahadur Shastri was sworn in as prime minister. Shastri was not as charismatic as Nehru, but he was shrewd in humility.

The India-Pakistan War of 1965

President Ayub Khan returned from the Soviet Union on April 10, 1965, only to be hurriedly called to army headquarters and briefed on a situation across the border of Sindh province, in a place called the Rann of Kutch.

Between Sindh, Pakistan, and Rajasthan, India, lay some twenty-three thousand square kilometers of desolate, dry salt beds and marshes, once part of the Arabian Sea.[48] The boundary of the area had never been demarcated and thus was patrolled by both sides. In February 1965 India decided to evict Pakistani border troops from an old fort called Kanjarkot. Pakistan countered by deploying its forces. On March 6, 1965, the Pakistan Army's 8th Division issued a crisp order to its 51st Brigade: maintain de facto control of Kanjarkot and do not allow violation of the territory.[49]

While Ayub was in the Soviet Union, Indian Prime Minister Shastri warned before India's Parliament that Pakistani intrusions in the area must end. Zulfiqar Ali Bhutto issued a stern rebuke to India on April 15, calling the event "the latest example of Indian chauvinism."[50] Earlier, Pakistan had captured Sardar Post in the area in a small skirmish. This move led to a small-scale operation involving the Pakistan Army's 6th Brigade, the "Battle of the Bets" (*bet* being a local word for raised mound). In the third week of April the battle escalated slightly, and the Pakistani division contemplated an offensive maneuver to destroy a causeway, which would have cut off Indian forces. Ayub Khan disallowed this tactic in order to avoid further exacerbation of the clashes and instead ordered consolidation of Pakistani forces.[51] Pakistan managed to defend the territory, hold its ground, and, even at a tactical level, display better military leadership than its opponent.

Unable to push the Pakistani troops out of the disputed region, the Indians declared the skirmish to be "the wrong war with the right enemy at the wrong place."[52] On April 28, 1965, the international community became involved as UN Secretary General U Thant pressed for cessation of hostilities. However, Pakistan deemed itself victorious at Rann of Kutch. Coupled with the successful visits to China and Russia, Pakistani leaders began to feel a sense of superiority over India. These emotions certainly provided them with increased confidence, contributing to their decision that the time was ripe to launch a war over Kashmir.

Under Foreign Secretary Aziz Ahmed, the Pakistani Foreign Office had established a department entirely devoted to the region of Kashmir. It comprised high-ranking officials, such as the secretary of defense, the Director of the Intelligence Bureau (DIB), the Chief of General Staff (CGS), and the Director of Military Operations (DMO) of the Pakistan Army. Foreign Secretary Aziz Ahmed was to coordinate a series of activities, named Operation Gibraltar, to "defreeze" the stalemate on Kashmir and stir the waters in preparation for an offensive.[53] These efforts would include Pakistani infiltration into Indian-held

Kashmir and formation of an uprising by exploiting India's heavy-handed response to the Hazratbal shrine incident and its subsequent re-arrest of Sheikh Abdullah in May 1965. Three fundamental assumptions lay behind these plans: (1) the action would remain confined to the disputed territory of Kashmir, (2) the subsequent uprising in Kashmir would be significant enough to tie down Indian forces, and (3) Pakistan's international alliances would preclude an Indian attack across the international border.

If Operation Gibraltar was a success, a second plan—code-named Grand Slam—was created to follow closely on its heels. The Pakistan Army would cross the cease-fire line in Kashmir and take control of a choke point called Akhnur, thus cutting off Indian forces in Kashmir from overland contact with Delhi. While it was risky, Foreign Minister Bhutto assured Ayub that India was not in a position to "risk a general war of unlimited duration."[54] Bhutto surmised that Pakistan enjoyed relative superiority and consequently had two alternatives: either to act preemptively and courageously in self-defense, or wait until India took the initiative to choose the place and time to attack and ultimately defeat Pakistan.[55] Eager to see Operation Gibraltar unfold, Bhutto convinced Ayub of the plan's merits.

The infiltration in Indian-administered Kashmir began on July 24, 1965, and continued throughout August. But the plan remained shrouded in secrecy from the very people who were to enact it, causing its execution to be deeply flawed. First, the strategy was based on the lingering euphoria of the Rann of Kutch "victory," heavily supported by an alliance of Foreign Ministry officials and enthusiastic generals, whom Army Chief General Mohammad Musa Khan disparaged as "brainwashed" and "Bhutto converts."[56] In addition, achievement relied on a successful information warfare campaign, but forced secrecy prevented effective coordination between the Pakistani and Kashmiri leadership. Finally, the most dangerous aspect was the mandatory exclusion of both the air force and navy chiefs from joint planning, as they were not considered "sufficiently security minded."[57] Even the army was not fully informed, as the operation was de facto, solely compartmentalized to the 12th Division—in Murree, a hilly station located forty miles north of Islamabad—whose commander, Major General Akhtar Malik, was the central figure for planning and execution of the operation.

By the time Operation Grand Slam began on September 2, the fundamental assumption that India's hold on Kashmir was weak had already changed. Within two days of the offensive, it was clear that the infiltration had failed and the objective of capturing the strategic choke point of Akhnur in a swift offensive maneuver was meeting resistance. The commander of the operation, General Malik, was abruptly replaced with a new commander, General Yahya Khan, who converted the offense to a defense. On September 6, India attacked, crossing the international border and threatening Pakistan's second-largest city and its cultural heart, Lahore, located barely fifty miles from the border.

By noon that day, President Ayub Khan was preparing to address the nation when the U.S. ambassador to Pakistan told him, "Mr. President, the Indians have got you by the throat."[58] Ayub assured him, as he did the nation in his speech, "Any hands on Pakistan's throat will be cut off." For two subsequent weeks, war spread in West Pakistan, and the entire nation united behind Ayub as never before. A thousand miles away, however, East Pakistan lay defenseless. The 1965 war ended with Pakistan's having successfully defended Lahore and countered a major Indian offensive north of the region in the Sialkot sector north of Lahore. But in many other areas across the international border, in Sindh as well as in Kashmir, Indian forces made significant gains. Eventually, the two countries arrived at a military stalemate.[59] Though this outcome gave Pakistan an "illusion of victory," in reality the Pakistani objective of liberating Kashmir by use of proxy followed by a military invasion had failed.[60] Moreover, the aftermath of this war set Pakistan on a downward slope after the remarkable growth and prosperity achieved in the early part of the 1960s.

Lieutenant-General Majeed later summed up those days by drawing a comparison with a subsequent flawed Pakistani incursion near the town of Kargil in 1999, attributing the failures to the "ambitiousness of the planners, misconceptions about the Kashmiri uprising, miscalculations about India's reaction, and immaturity in military thinking."[61] Majeed speculated that, at an operational level, Pakistan could have succeeded had there been solid execution, proper organization, adequate training, and suitable weapons. Even with the reality of rudimentary training and poor force organization, Majeed felt that the objective could have been achieved, at least in Kashmir, had a change of command not taken place in the midst of a military offensive. The prime reason for the change in command, in Majeed's assessment, was that Major General Akhtar Malik was a defiant general. Though people subsequently would point to Malik's Ahmadi sectarian denomination, that factor was not significant at the time. Regardless of the level of Pakistan's operational success, according to Majeed, India would still have attacked across the international border toward Lahore, and Pakistan had not planned for this occurrence.

During the war, Pakistan reached out to the United States and China. Its appeal to the United States did not fall on sympathetic ears and was referred to the United Nations instead. As if such a rebuff was not sufficient, on September 8, the Johnson administration decided to suspend military and economic aid to both India and Pakistan. An argument ensued between Ambassador McConoughy and Bhutto, as the latter accused Washington of poor treatment toward its ally by rewarding Indian aggression. McConoughy responded by questioning whether Pakistan had considered the consequences when it planned, organized, and supported guerilla operations in Kashmir.[62] The next day, when the U.S. Congress passed the resolution to stop aid, Bhutto was bitter, concluding this "would mean that Pak-U.S. relations could not be the same again."[63] The U.S. decision was made simply to underscore its position that it would not become entangled in an India-Pakistan conflict.

China was more understanding, but not as helpful as Pakistan had expected or hoped. On September 7, China condemned India's "criminal aggression," and, referring to other incursions on the Tibetan border, warned that it should "end its frenzied provocation activities or bear the responsibility for all consequences."[64] Five days later, China issued India an ultimatum: "Dismantle all military works on the Chinese side of the border within three days."[65] India, believing China's actions to have been at Pakistan's behest, reached out to the United States, Britain, and the Soviet Union for backing. India received assurance of support from all three countries in the event of a Chinese attack. On September 18 India reported Chinese activities in the Ladakh area of the India-China disputed border, in the north-eastern portion of Kashmir, where India and China had fought three years before.

The very next night Ayub Khan, along with Bhutto, secretly flew to China to complain of the Western powers' support of India. The Chinese advocated a "people's war" and advised Pakistan to "keep fighting even if you have to withdraw to the hills."[66] A "people's war," however, was not a feasible strategy in the India-Pakistan environment. Pakistan's mainland was under attack, leaving Pakistan with virtually no strategic depth: should it fail to defend itself right at the border, the advancing Indian armed forces would slice through the country. It was clear by the end of the meeting that China would not provide a "quick fix" for Pakistan's problems—Pakistan had expected China to agree to open a second front with India in order to force a break in India's military momentum toward Lahore. As Pakistani Information Minister Altaf Gauhar summarized, "The whole Foreign Office strategy was designed as a quick-fix to force the Indians to the negotiating table. Ayub had never foreseen the possibility of the

Indians surviving a couple of hard blows, and Bhutto had never envisaged a long drawn out people's war. Above all, the Army and the Air Force were totally against any further prolongation of the conflict."[67] Ayub was left with no choice; Pakistan accepted a UN-sponsored cease-fire on September 22, but against the advice of Foreign Minister Bhutto.[68]

The 1965 war cost the country politically, economically, and militarily. It was the last attempt to snatch Kashmir by military force, and Pakistan's international position—especially with the United States—began to deteriorate from this point onward, while its reliance on China began to increase. In retrospect, Lieutenant-General Majeed noted that Premier Chou En-lai had advised the Pakistani government in the classic style of Sun Tzu: to go slow, not to push India hard, and avoid a fight over Kashmir "for at least 20–30 years, until you have developed your economy and consolidated your national power." Chou advised that Pakistan's greatest assets were its natural and human resources, and that by fighting a war it would lose its collective strength and allow Indian domination. Although Majeed believed India certainly held some responsibility for pushing Pakistan into a war, he admitted that "sane and analytical political thinking" was missing in Pakistan. He branded Bhutto as an impatient, "clever and feudal-minded politician." A broad-stroke analysis would reveal that the Pakistani political leaders after Jinnah and Liaquat had not "gone through the political mill," and thus led with an underdeveloped political philosophy.[69]

This war also confirmed to both India and Pakistan that U.S. interest in South Asia was minimal. In the aftermath, the United States intentionally allowed the Soviet Union to broker peace and detente. Secretary of State Dean Rusk summed up the U.S. position: if the Soviets succeeded, there would be peace in the subcontinent, which is good for the United States. If they failed, they could get a taste for the frustration of dealing with India and Pakistan.[70] In January 1966 at Tashkent, the Soviet Union finally brokered an agreement that essentially returned the situation to the status quo. Hours after signing this agreement Indian Prime Minister Shastri died of a heart attack. Ayub Khan never recovered domestically from the political trouble that followed and only accumulated more enemies, including his own protege Bhutto in West Pakistan, who resigned and transformed himself from Ayub's loyal lieutenant into his "most acerbic critic,"[71] and an increasingly popular Bengali politician Sheikh Mujibur Rahman in East Pakistan.

The war also had a significant impact on Pakistan's military aid. Until then, the United States had been the principal supplier of Pakistan's military equipment. But Islamabad was hit much harder by the U.S. arms embargo than was India, since the latter had more military ties with the Soviet Union. The United States shut the door to export of tanks, aircraft, and artillery to Pakistan—though it agreed to sell spare parts for previously supplied arms. Pakistan began to replace American equipment with arms from China and later even from the Soviet Union.[72] It would not be until the arrival of an old friend to the White House, Richard Nixon, that Pakistan would return to prominence in U.S. policy in Asia. By that time, however, Ayub Khan had already left the scene.

PAEC Focus and Accomplishment

The prerequisite for any state embarking on a nuclear weapons program is a complex base of material and people with a diverse set of skills and experience. A 1968 UN study estimates that a full-fledged nuclear weapons program requires some five hundred scientists and thirteen hundred engineers—physicists, chemists, and metallurgists; civil, military, mechanical, and electrical engineers; machine-tool operators with precision engineering experience; and instrument-makers and fabricators. The history of the nuclear age has shown that secrecy surrounds all nuclear weapons endeavors. Skilled workers of this nature are not publicly acknowledged, and their employment is often disguised. Further, the state needs to have a certain industrial base within its territory or access to one, and considerable experience in engineering, mining, and explosives. In addition, for a program to remain clandestine, sufficient foreign exchange and covert business deals with foreign partners willing to do business must generally be held as a state secret.[73]

The notion of starting a nuclear weapons program—given the political, economic, and security struggles of Pakistan in the late 1950s—was a daunting, almost inconceivable objective. What was achievable at the time was to harness the national talent and build what would become the backbone for a nuclear *energy* program. Nazir Ahmed, the first head of the PAEC, had taken the early steps toward creating the human capital necessary for a true nuclear energy infrastructure. By 1960, one of Bhutto's many ministerial assignments was Fuel, Power and Natural Resources, which included the PAEC. Bhutto was not content with the modest steps Nazir Ahmed had taken in the 1950s. Remembering his own role in the Pakistani nuclear program, Zulfi Bhutto wrote from his jail cell in 1978, "When I took charge of Pakistan's Atomic Energy Commission, it was no more than a sign board of an office. It was only a name. Assiduously and with granite determination I put my entire vitality behind the task of acquiring nuclear capability for my country."[74]

While Zulfiqar Ali Bhutto was foreign minister, Dr. Ishrat Hussain Usmani was serving as the chief controller of imports and exports in the Pakistani government when he caught Bhutto's eye. Professor Abdus Salam, who was chief scientific advisor to the president of Pakistan, also found that Usmani's qualifications and talent were being wasted on bureaucratic assignments and thought that a role for him in the PAEC would be right for the country.[75] Ultimately, President Ayub Khan appointed Usmani as chair of the PAEC in 1960 and changed the future of the organization. Bhutto and Usmani were two strong personalities; both were aristocratic and brilliant, but they hardly saw eye to eye. One of Bhutto's first moves after becoming the president of the country in 1972 was to remove Usmani and appoint a new head of the PAEC.

A graduate from Aligarh Muslim University with a master's degree from the University of Bombay, Usmani belonged to a cultured family in Delhi. In 1939, at the age of twenty-two, he completed his Ph.D. in electron diffraction from Imperial College, University of London, under Nobel Laureate P. M. S. Blackett and Sir G. P. Thomson. Upon returning to India in 1942 he joined the Indian civil service. At partition, he opted to leave India and join the new Pakistani government.[76]

Dr. Ishfaq Ahmad, who later would become chairman of the PAEC (1991–2001), described his first meeting with Usmani in the early 1960s. Science was not performing well in Pakistan at the time, but, Usmani told Ishfaq, nuclear science was something different. He went on, "We have Salam's backing, and the army has assured us of the funds." Usmani would send people abroad for training on "all aspects of nuclear technology." He realized that without a trained workforce, Pakistan could not move ahead. Later, after China became the fifth nuclear weapons power in 1964, Usmani hinted at India's and Pakistan's nuclear future when he said in a number of speeches, "If there will be a sixth nuclear weapon state, then there will be a seventh one."[77]

During the 1960s Pakistan's main thrust was not only to train a labor force from abroad but also to build an indigenous power plant capability. PAEC chairman Usmani laid down three objectives: to construct nuclear power plants and so alleviate the shortage of conventional energy sources; to apply nuclear knowledge (radioisotopes) to agriculture, medicine, and industry; and to conduct research and development on problems of national importance.[78] It was from this third task that Pakistan's nuclear weapons program would eventually grow. In an interview with the author, Ishfaq Ahmad characterized Usmani as sharp, with an understanding of the cascading effect of nuclear proliferation. But he was a visionary, not a maverick; he simply wanted Pakistan to be well prepared for the future.

The Nucleus

All of Usmani's objectives were contingent on the availability of trained labor. His aim was to give the PAEC solid footing and produce a "nucleus" of adequately trained scientists—Pakistan needed some five hundred before it could embark upon a nuclear program.[79] Usmani prioritized recruitment and training of scientists, setting a pattern of enlisting the most promising students in physics, chemistry, and engineering from all of Pakistan's universities and then sending the best abroad for higher education. Usmani gained a reputation for honesty and had the backing of Bhutto and Salam for his recruitment initiative. He would select fifty students each year, based purely on merit.[80] Selected young scientists—many were proteges of Professor Chaudhry in Lahore—were enrolled as Officers on Special Training (OSTs) and given a nuclear orientation course at the Atomic Energy Centre in Lahore. These young scientists and engineers were then sent abroad to Western universities and research establishments to obtain Ph.D.s in nuclear sciences and find postdoctoral research opportunities.

Usmani created a professional atmosphere of research and intellectual growth. His dynamic and autocratic personality had a communication style that was always seen as challenging his subordinates to rise to the heights. His animated style of communicating was described by one of his close associates: "His eloquent King's English seemed to fill the spacious room and beyond to hold the entranced gathering in a state of ecstasy and awe."[81]

One endeavor was to establish a quarterly journal, which he entitled *The Nucleus*, reflecting his penchant for training the young and talented into a technical force.[82] He approached the director of the Atomic Energy Center, Lahore, with the task: "Durrani, I don't suppose you could launch a journal of the Pakistan Atomic Energy Commission?" When Mr. Durrani said, "I am happy to grasp that nettle," Usmani replied, "Good luck, then, you can count on me for support." The first edition of *The Nucleus,* in January 1964, contained messages from Zulfiqar Ali Bhutto, then Pakistan's foreign minister, and Professor Abdus Salam.[83] Usmani then mandated a subscription for officers of the PAEC, with cost to be deducted from their annual salaries. *The Nucleus* also received international acclaim.

In an April 1964 article published in *Trade and Industry* magazine, as well as in several public speeches, Usmani projected a forty-year plan for East and West Pakistan's electricity demands, proving that the national energy needs could not be met with conventional sources. He was frustrated by the lack of support for and understanding of the future of nuclear energy in the government bureaucracy. At the First International Conference on Nuclear Physics in 1967 in Dhaka, he famously stated, "There are fossils in Pakistan Government who would prefer fossil fuel."[84]

Usmani created a work culture that kept the entire PAEC motivated and on their toes, rewarding performers with generous salaries and perks such as travel abroad. He would not hesitate to subject average performers to "embarrassing public dressing-downs."[85] He sent his best and brightest only to the highest-quality institutions around the world, such as North Carolina State University, which in 1953, was the first to establish a nuclear engineering program. The University of Michigan, Pennsylvania State University, and Massachusetts Institute of Technology also had several new programs that welcomed trainees from abroad. The U.S. government encouraged enrolling students from abroad by providing financial stipends as an element of the Atoms for Peace initiative. The PAEC also utilized well-established Ph.D. programs in nuclear physics, nuclear chemistry, materials science, geology, agriculture, nuclear medicine, and other nuclear sciences offered by universities in Canada, the United Kingdom, Australia, France, and other countries.[86] Pakistani scientists were trained at British atomic energy establishments at Harwell and Winfrith, in the Chalk River Nuclear Laboratory in Canada, and at the universities of Birmingham, Manchester, Sydney, Toronto, Stanford, and Rochester.[87]

During several world tours Usmani established personal contacts at U.S. national laboratories, which by then had begun to open up their facilities under the auspices of Atoms for Peace, and through U.S. promotional efforts to encourage worldwide development of nuclear power plants for energy production. He also had access to earlier U.S. research and development work that had been declassified to foster the diffusion of nuclear science. However, physical separation of the classified and open facilities remained a problem within the United States. It was under such circumstances that Usmani began to seek opportunities available at Oak Ridge National Laboratory in Tennessee and Argonne National Laboratory near Chicago.[88]

Funding for the PAEC "trainees" generally came from the U.S. International Cooperation Administration, which later became the United States Agency for

International Development (USAID).[89] Argonne National Laboratory near Chicago had been the first to establish an International School of Nuclear Science and Engineering (ISNSE) in 1954 to provide a one-year training course in reactor engineering. The first semester of ISNSE was conducted at North Carolina State University and Penn State University.[90] Oak Ridge National Laboratory conducted a somewhat higher level course at its Oak Ridge School of Reactor Technology (ORSORT). It offered two options for specialization: reactor operations and reactor hazards evaluation.[91] Upon their return home, the young trainees applied their skills and expertise in the PAEC's evolving projects, as new ones proceeded abroad. However, because of better job prospects overseas, not all scientists returned after their training, hampering progress in the nuclear program.[92]

Ayub Khan's government, between 1960 and 1968, spent roughly 724 million rupees for the development of nuclear technology, Rs. 400 million of which was exclusively spent on the Karachi Nuclear Power Plant (KANUPP). The majority of this spending occurred after 1965; the second national five-year plan (1960–65) contained only Rs. 46.5 million for nuclear spending.[93] The plan specified how the funds were to be divided between training of nuclear scientists and engineers, exploration of radioactive materials, and establishment of a nuclear research institute (Institute of Nuclear Research and Technology).[94] In addition, the Ayub government planned to establish a 300-megawatt (MW) nuclear power plant in West Pakistan and a 400-MW plant in East Pakistan.[95] However, given the already emerging financial constraints, these plans could not completely materialize.

Quest for Power Plants

Usmani began his tenure at the PAEC by commissioning a series of feasibility studies on the introduction of nuclear power in Pakistan. Two American firms, Gibbs & Hill and Internuclear Company, were tasked to conduct a joint study. In May 1961 a report entitled "Study of the Economic Feasibility of Nuclear Power in Pakistan," known as the Gibbs & Hill Report, became the standard reference on nuclear policy for the PAEC.[96] Usmani also urged the International Atomic Energy Agency (IAEA) to undertake an authoritative analysis of the energy picture in Pakistan. The 1962 IAEA report, "Prospects of Nuclear Power in Pakistan," concluded that the growing electricity requirements of Karachi could be well met by nuclear power instead of natural gas. Usmani, supported by Bhutto and Salam, began building up a case for the inevitability of nuclear power as an economic alternative energy source. Usmani argued, "[It] would be clean, pollution-free and perfectly safe, and the beneficial spin-off in developing the industrial infrastructure and scientific base could be revolutionary."[97] Usmani picked up the efforts where his predecessor had left off. Whereas Nazir Ahmed had failed to secure a reactor, Usmani successfully concluded an agreement with Canada for a Canadian Deuterium (CANDU)–type 137-megawatt electrical (MW[e]) reactor to be built in Karachi.

Pakistan signed the turnkey contract on May 24, 1965, with the Canadian General Electric Company (CGE), in addition to a memorandum of understanding on safety policy and procedure. The memorandum required the establishment of an independent nuclear safety committee that would oversee safety appraisals, site evaluations, and other regulatory requirements. By late 1965 a special ordinance had been enacted by the president of Pakistan that was the first Pakistani legal document pertaining to nuclear safety and radiation.[98]

The formal approval to establish the KANUPP had been granted on January 5, 1964, by the Executive Committee of the National Economic Council. The understanding was that the project would be paid for through loans from the Canadian government, but under condition that the plant would be subject to IAEA inspections.[99] Pakistan's Foreign Office initially objected to the safeguards conditions, arguing that the Canadians had attached no such condition when they sold Canada India Research Utility Service (CIRUS) to India in 1954. Even the United States, in providing heavy water for moderation of the research reactor, did not insist on any conditions, though it was known at the time that heavy water–modulated reactors had proliferation risks. (Conversely, the United States was reluctant to provide a CP-5 reactor to Pakistan in 1959, fearing the proliferation consequences.) The Canadians responded quickly, pointing out that India had paid for its reactor in full, and should Pakistan want to avoid IAEA safeguards and inspections, it too could pay in full.[100] This financial barrier pitted Bhutto's Foreign Office and Shoaib's Finance Ministry against each other, as two distinct groups emerged. Those in the Finance Ministry viewed nuclear developments as laudable, but they were skeptical that Pakistan's scarce resources were best used on such an expensive and perhaps unattainable endeavor. On the opposing side, nuclear scientists and some bureaucrats in the Foreign Ministry were convinced that only by keeping pace with India could Pakistan ensure its security, and they apprehensively watched as the window of opportunity to purchase nuclear capabilities narrowed with the coming nuclear nonproliferation debate.

Agha Shahi, at that time serving in the Foreign Ministry, recalls this period in an interview with the author: "When the Indians got this CIRUS reactor, 40 MW with no restrictions, then we became concerned. I tried to get the same terms for our CANDU reactor, but the Canadians insisted on stringent measures. I was arguing that we couldn't accept discriminatory terms. But in those days, our economic and finance ministers were so strong, and they were always looking for foreign aid . . . other people higher up in the ministries overruled me . . . so we signed on the dotted line, but under very stringent safeguards."[101] In 1965 Pakistan's ambassador to Canada, Sultan Mohammad Khan, wrote to President Ayub Khan urging him to accept the periodic inspections, "since the power plant was for civilian use and practically free. However, should a situation develop where we could not allow inspections, then we would have to face the problem of finding a non-Canadian source of fuel, and it would be up to our nuclear scientists to develop ways and means to keep the nuclear plant operational."[102] Ayub's long-term policy focus was on economic development, and he saw nuclear energy in that light. It is not clear if Ayub's decision to accept the KANUPP deal was influenced by his scientific advisors Dr. Abdus Salam and Usmani, but what seems probable was that all of them were keen to acquire as many facilities as possible, without jeopardizing other military and economic interests.[103]

While the Foreign Office and Finance Ministry bickered, Ayub's attention was elsewhere. He was euphoric after having won elections in 1965, completed successful back-to-back visits to China and the Soviet Union, and emerged victorious at Rann of Kutch. Further, he was enthusiastic about his plans to "defreeze Kashmir" and prepare for Operation Gibraltar. With so much going on, Ayub was not focused on nuclear developments.

Nevertheless, nearly two years later construction of KANUPP began. It was finally completed in early 1971, went "critical" on August 1, 1971, and was inaugurated on November 28, 1972 by Zulfiqar Ali Bhutto.[104] Ishrat Usmani's persistence and energy had led to the construction and successful operation of what was heralded as the first nuclear power plant in the Islamic world. Rather sadly, Usmani was not invited at the inaugural. Over the years, for inexplicable reasons, Bhutto had begun to dislike Usmani. Dr. Ishfaq and several other former PAEC officials told me that both were strong personalities and had different visions about Pakistan's nuclear future.

Application for Agriculture and Medicine

Usmani's second tier of nuclear planning was to absorb the newly returned trainees into agriculture, medicine, and other industrial applications. Radioisotopes can be used as tracers to study movement of fluids in humans, animals, and plants. Nuclear radiation can also be employed for treatment of cancer, development of new varieties of crops, and several other applications. Under Usmani's stewardship, two atomic research centers were formed in 1961 and 1962, at Lahore and Dhaka, respectively. These centers' nuclear science facilities were unmatched anywhere in Pakistan.

The Lahore center boasted a 14-mega (million) electron-volt (MeV) neutron generator and a subcritical assembly of magnox-clad natural uranium rods, while the Dhaka center housed Pakistan's first computer, an IBM 1620. Under Professor Rafi Choudhury, the Lahore Government College Physics Department had trained many scientists able to operate nuclear accelerators and other complex equipment. The two centers aided in the creation of a wide repertoire of nuclear-related applications for both peaceful and weapons programs.

The initial enthusiasm and success of the first two centers encouraged an explosion of nuclear-related research and development (R&D) institutions. In West Pakistan, three nuclear energy agricultural research centers were established—at Tando Jam in Sindh, Faisalabad in Punjab, and Peshawar in NWFP. Furthermore, nuclear medical centers were initially launched in public hospitals in Lahore, Islamabad, Peshawar, Multan, and Quetta, and then expanded nationally to include remote places such as Gilgit in the northern areas. For the industrial application of nuclear energy, several plants were established in Lahore and elsewhere. The establishment of the Centre for Space and Upper Atmosphere Research (SUPARCO) was set up at Karachi in 1964, indicating the spillover effects of the scientific interest and zeal unleashed by the nuclear program.[105] Given the numerous centers sprouting up all over Pakistani territory, Usmani created a Directorate of Industrial Liaison (DIL) to interface between local industries and nuclear power centers.[106]

The Taj Mahal of Nuclear Pakistan

Usmani's third objective, to create a premier research establishment, became the cradle of Pakistani nuclear achievement. The Pakistan Institute of Nuclear Science and Technology (PINSTECH), located in Nilore, near Islamabad, was an architectural masterpiece, designed by the world famous Edward Durell Stone with a Mughal garden structure. Lieutenant-General Syed Refaqat, former chief of staff to President Zia ul-Haq, described PINSTECH as the Pakistani equivalent of Agra's Taj Mahal.[107] Usmani carefully monitored the construction and furnishing of the facility. He conceived an edifice that inspired and motivated not only scientists but all of Pakistan, as he gave the nation a building that embodied the pride, grandeur, and progress that it desired and espoused. In the PINSTECH visitor's book, Edward Stone inscribed these words: "This . . . has been my greatest work. I am proud that it looks like it belongs in this country with such a rich architectural heritage. I am grateful for the inspired guidance of Dr. Usmani."[108]

The PAEC selected a 5-MW swimming pool–type reactor, called the Pakistan Atomic Research Reactor (PARR-1), to be housed in the new PINSTECH building.[109] This reactor was designed to use highly enriched uranium fuel supplied by the United States through the IAEA, installed in a dome-shaped building constructed by the U.S. company AMF Atomics.[110] PINSTECH was constructed in two stages—in the first stage, the reactor building and ancillary facilities were completed; the second stage would not come for almost a decade.

On December 21, 1965, a week after Ayub Khan returned from what was called a "pathetic and sad" visit to Washington, where he received "no warmth, and mere formality," there was suddenly reason for celebration as the reactor at PINSTECH reached criticality: a self-sustaining fission chain reaction was initiated inside the reactor.[111] This event formally heralded Pakistan's entry into the atomic age. Six months later, on June 22, 1966, the PINSTECH reactor attained full power of 5 MW.[112]

PINSTECH had two strategic goals: research and development, and the production of skilled labor for the greater national project. By the mid-1960s PINSTECH was training about 350 nuclear scientists. One report estimated that by about 1967, three thousand Pakistani nuclear science students were studying in various universities at home and abroad. PINSTECH alone had the capacity of training one hundred plant engineers annually. A reactor school was established in 1967. By the end of the decade, Pakistan had a reasonably large skilled workforce and rudimentary infrastructure in the KANUPP and PARR-1 facilities.

These early institutions would come to form the core of a broader set of nuclear science and educational institutions in Pakistan. The PINSTECH reactor school was later upgraded into a full-fledged Center for Nuclear Studies (CNS) in 1976 and became affiliated with Quaid-I-Azam University in Islamabad. It produced a trained cadre for the nuclear program, especially after the 1974 Indian nuclear weapon tests, when Western universities had begun gradually closing the doors to Pakistani students in nuclear science and technology. Eventually CNS became a university in 1997 and is currently known as the Pakistan Institute of Engineering and Applied Sciences (PIEAS).[113] Subsequently other institutions, such as Ghulam Ishaq Khan (GIK) Institute of Science and Technology in Tarbela in NWFP would also broaden the base of scientific education.

The second stage of PINSTECH development would be launched in the early 1970s, when the PAEC pushed it to become a leading research and development institute in addition to an educational institution. Starting with only four divisions in 1966, it would be expanded to nine by 1992.[114] That year the PAEC claimed to employ more than two thousand scientists, engineers, and technicians at PINSTECH.[115] PAEC chair Munir Ahmad Khan recalled his achievement just before his death in 1999: "Within a few years PINSTECH became, and is still, the leading nuclear center in the entire Muslim world."[116]

As PINSTECH expanded its research activities and undertook more classified work of national importance, the great architectural masterpiece became increasingly shrouded from public view. Explaining his anguish over this loss, Lieutenant-General Syed Refaqat said to the author, "Nilore is not just a matter of pride that we had a reactor, but a matter of pain; in the whole of Pakistan there is no better piece of architecture created in the last sixty years . . . . [N]ow what we have done with this is—we have camouflaged it, we have painted it, colored it, put bars around it, we have machine guns spread all over the place. You can't reach it, you can't see it, you can't identify it."[117]

Now or Never

A watershed event for the South Asian security landscape was the Chinese nuclear test on October 16, 1964. Nehru had died in May of that year, and his successor, Prime Minister Lal Bahadur Shastri, presided over a weak Indian government. He called the Chinese test a "shock and danger to world peace."[118] U.S. intelligence immediately estimated India's likely reaction and concluded that India could produce and test a device within one to three years of a decision to do so.[119] In India, open debate surrounded the weapon's preparation, timeline, and cost projections. Homi Bhabha, chair of the India Atomic Energy Program and the architect of India's nuclear program, led the financial debate, citing U.S. sources claiming "a 10-kiloton explosion would cost $350,000 . . .

while a 2-megaton explosion [equivalent to 2 million tons of TNT] would cost $600,000." This discussion was especially significant because that same year the country was in the midst of a major food shortage.[120]

The Indian press continued to question whether or not India should "rush into a mad race for nuclear arms," urging caution "that India could not afford to get into a program of manufacturing and stockpiling atom bombs without serious repercussions on its economy."[121] As George Perkovich summarized, "The food crisis and related political turmoil, not the Chinese nuclear test, preoccupied the Indian polity. Indian consumers confronted scarce supplies of basic food stuff[s] . . . . The growing crisis stemmed from complex factors; defense spending certainly contributed to it. The defense budget for 1964, the equivalent of 1.8 billion, amounted to 28 percent of government spending."[122] These challenges notwithstanding, Indian Prime Minister Shastri approved a study of peaceful nuclear explosions, dubbed the "Study [of] Nuclear Explosion for Peaceful Purposes (SNEPP)."[123]

Meanwhile, that same year, neighboring Pakistan's economy was booming, averaging a 6 percent growth rate, prompting the "model developing country" designation by the Harvard Development Advisory Group.[124] With President Ayub focused chiefly on elections, the Rann of Kutch, and the 1965 war, the nuclear debate in India was hardly noticed by anyone other than Bhutto, the Foreign Ministry, and the PAEC—then engaged in negotiations for a CANDU-type reactor for Karachi.

However, the failure of the 1965 Kashmir War deeply changed the nuclear perception in Pakistan. The Kashmir issue, instead of being resolved, remained a major irritant in India-Pakistan relations and apparently would not be resolved through military means. India's military was far stronger than Pakistan had imagined, and Pakistan's alliance with the United States had limited utility.[125] These insights, combined with the upcoming negotiations on the NPT and India's nuclear activities, shifted Pakistan's security perceptions and inspired the nuclear weapons enthusiasts to create a true bomb lobby. It was under these circumstances in 1965 when Zulfiqar Ali Bhutto made the famous euphemism of "eating grass" in his interview with the *Manchester Guardian*.[126]

Two Camps

Having faced multiple domestic and regional problems, crises, and wars, the Ayub regime split into two camps regarding the development of the atomic bomb. Ayub's advisors such as Foreign Minister Manzur Qadir, Information Minister Altaf Gauhar, Finance Minister Shoaib, Deputy Chairman of the Planning Commission Saeed Hassan, and Army Chief General Musa Khan would belong to a camp urging caution. The other, more ambitious, camp was led by Zulfiqar Ali Bhutto, Aziz Ahmed, and Agha Shahi and was housed largely in Pakistan's Foreign Ministry. Munir Ahmed Khan, a Pakistani nuclear scientist then working at the IAEA who would head the PAEC in later years, befriended Zulfiqar Ali Bhutto and came to support Bhutto's ambitions. Bhutto's group, including some generals close to the foreign minister, would support an aggressive security policy and would eventually form the core of a bomb lobby. The two top scientific advisors at the time, Dr. Abdus Salam and PAEC chairman Ishrat Usmani, were torn between the two camps. They felt that prudence required caution, but at the same time the availability of nuclear technology would not last for long.

The dialectic between these two camps drove Pakistan's policy choices. While both lobbies had powerful opposing arguments, there was often commonality between their views. For example, there was no disagreement that bolstering nuclear energy and acquiring nuclear technology was in the long-term interest of the nation. Both sides eventually agreed that Pakistan should diversify its external relationships and no longer rely solely on the United States. Interestingly, the two influential camps were at one point divided over development of friendly relations with China. While the Bhutto pro-bomb camp pressed for closer relations with China, the Shoaib anti-bomb camp was skeptical of relations. Ayub Khan was himself cautious but willing to expand relations with China. The border agreement of March 1963 with China was Ayub's decision when he became convinced of the need for Chinese assistance.[127] Both camps would, however, disagree over the timing and urgency of nuclear weapons acquisition.

Nuclear Enthusiasts

Zulfiqar Ali Bhutto and his close associates in the Foreign Ministry believed the window of opportunity to compete with India was beginning to close, and the costs of a U.S. alliance were starting to outweigh the benefits. At the same time, they detected new opportunities to exploit the growing tension between India and China and to reach out to the Soviet Union. Meanwhile, the international community, beginning with a draft resolution at the United Nations by Ireland in 1958, was moving toward a nonproliferation treaty that sought to prohibit the spread of nuclear weapons. Bhutto and his Foreign Ministry associates realized that the growing debate on the nonproliferation norms would make acquisition of nuclear technology much more difficult.[128] They perceived the situation as "now or never." Agha Shahi, who would later rise to become foreign minister and architect of Pakistan's external policies, describes his thinking at the time: "We are now moving into a nuclear age. India is going to develop nuclear weapons. . . . Pakistan should make progress in nuclear technology . . . . This is the last chance for us . . . because the nonproliferation treaty [is] in discussion . . . and after that we don't know—the situation will be unpredictable."[129]

The nuclear enthusiast camp built its case around five arguments. First, the Chinese nuclear bomb test had changed the security paradigm of South Asia. With nuclear facilities outside of IAEA monitors and safeguards, India was surely pursuing a weapons capability. Second, because of the disappointing outcome of the U.S.-Pakistan alliance, big powers could no longer be relied upon for national security. Third, the NPT debate had already commenced, and sooner or later severe restrictions on nuclear trade would be enforced. Fourth, the asymmetry in conventional weaponry between India and Pakistan was already widening, and, with India's nuclear ambitions, the gap would be unreachable. Fifth, a nuclear weapons program would necessitate an expansion of Pakistan's scientific infrastructure and human capital, becoming a pillar of support for Pakistan's high-technology goals.

In 1965 Zulfiqar Ali Bhutto requested Rs. 300 million for the purchase of a nuclear reprocessing plant from France in an effort to match a similar plant installed in India in 1964. Agha Shahi recalls the view from the Foreign Ministry: "It was at that time we became suspicious that India—while talking of nuclear disarmament and fighting for nuclear guarantees to non-nuclear states against the threat of attack—was heading towards development of the bomb."[130] However, the reprocessing plant purchase was turned down for financial reasons.[131] The bomb lobby would continue to push for the plant even after Zulfiqar Ali Bhutto was forced out of office in June 1966.

Munir Ahmed Khan, later chairman of the PAEC, recalled that in October 1965 he had met Zulfiqar Ali Bhutto in Vienna. Munir explained to him that he had been to India's CIRUS facility at Trombay in 1964 and saw for himself that India was well on its way to making the bomb. Bhutto asked Munir to meet Ayub Khan in December during Ayub's upcoming visits to the United Kingdom and the United States and try to convince the president of the urgency of a weapons program. On December 11, Munir Ahmed Khan did meet the Pakistani president at the Rochester Hotel in New York. The president had a lot on his mind: the 1965 war fiasco and defeat, a weapons embargo from the West, and the economic consequences in the aftermath of the 1965 war. Moreover, he did not have a very pleasant visit to the United States. In his encounter with President Lyndon Johnson, Ayub was "disappointed," and Johnson found his guest "subdued, pathetic and sad. He had gone [on] an adventure and been licked."[132] President Ayub might have been well aware that the meeting with Munir Ahmad Khan was set up by Bhutto, whom he held responsible for influencing his decision to go to war with India. President Ayub was obviously in no mood to entertain any more of Bhutto's adventures.

In the meeting, Munir informed President Ayub that there were no restrictions on nuclear technology; it was freely available. India was soaking it up, and so was Israel. Even when Munir explained that the cost was estimated to be no more than $150 million, Ayub was unmoved. Munir recalls, "Ayub Khan listened to me very patiently, but at the end he said that Pakistan is too poor to spend that much money. Moreover, if we ever need the bomb, we will buy it off the shelf."[133] Meanwhile, Mr. Bhutto was pacing up and down the hotel lobby. When Munir came out of the meeting, Bhutto asked him what had happened. He told Bhutto, "The President did not agree." Bhutto replied, "Don't worry, our turn will come!"[134]

Years later, at the inauguration of KANUPP, Munir Ahmad Khan addressed then-president Zulfiqar Ali Bhutto and said:

> I remember the day in October 1965 when I had the opportunity of discussing with you the tremendous potential which atomic energy had and the role it could play in the development of our country. You not only listened but insisted that I present my view to higher-ups. I went. But my pleadings made no impact and I was dubbed as another mad man who thought like Zulfiqar Ali Bhutto. But the times have changed and so has the destiny of our country.[135]

Four years after the 1965 war, when Bhutto was campaigning against Ayub Khan, he summed up his thinking on the role of nuclear deterrence in his book *The Myth of Independence*:

> All wars of our age have become total wars . . . and it will have to be assumed that a war waged against Pakistan is capable of becoming a total war. It would be dangerous to plan for less and our plans should, therefore, include the nuclear deterrent .
> . . . India is unlikely to concede nuclear monopoly to others . . . . It appears that she

is determined to proceed with her plans to detonate a nuclear bomb. If Pakistan restricts or suspends her nuclear program, it would not only enable India to blackmail Pakistan with her nuclear advantage, but would impose a crippling limitation on the development of Pakistan's science and the technology . . . . Our problem, in its essence, is how to obtain such a weapon in time before the crisis begins.

In hindsight, it is clear that Bhutto anticipated eventually gaining political control of the country, allowing him to end the military's dominance over national security policies.

Nuclear Cautionists

Those individuals urging greater caution and more limited nuclear ambitions are usually perceived in Pakistan as antinuclear, which is not entirely correct. The group was not monolithic, but all saw national interest through the lens of their own organizational interests. Most notable in their caution were the country's finance and economic managers, while the military and scientific communities were more pragmatic than cautious. Overall, this camp took a holistic view, with six major reasons for not pushing enthusiastically for nuclear weapons. First, they considered Pakistan's already weak alliance with the United States to be in further danger as a result of aggressive security policies, especially in regard to Kashmir. Second, Pakistan's economy was financially sound, but dependent on outside help; staying in the good graces of the World Bank and International Monetary Fund (IMF) was a priority. Third, they believed that the conventional military balance with India, as well as military modernization, would erode if military supplies and aid were interrupted. Fourth, the Atoms for Peace program was helping to create a base of both soft technology ("the nucleus" of trained personnel) and hard technology transfers, albeit under IAEA safeguards. Fifth, the camp was dismissive and doubtful of India's ability to acquire nuclear technology. Finally, in their assessment, the nuclear weapons arms race and strategic competition were luxuries of the big powers with lots of resources. For small developing countries like Pakistan, nuclear energy technology was associated with poverty alleviation and development, rather than military improvement.

In the period after the 1965 war, Ayub Khan became even more cautious than before. The impact of the war, Pakistan's unsteady relations with external powers, and Ayub's waning domestic popularity led him to be almost too guarded against firm decisions. Ayub doubted his judgment when listening to the hawkish camp. He believed, as his subsequent diaries and biographies reveal, that he had previously erred in listening to the advice of the Foreign Ministry. Ayub agreed with the rationale for reaching out to China and the Soviet Union, which he did with all sincerity, but he wanted to do it without damaging relations with the United States. By the mid-1960s, Ayub was walking a triangular tightrope and gradually weaning away from alliance politics and toward nonalignment. His thinking is summed up in his autobiography *Friends Not Masters* in the following words:

> The big power rivalries, the diffusion of the focus of world power by the emergence of China, and the end of the U.S.-U.S.S.R. tussle for world supremacy, all are hard realities, but they need not be a source of weakness for small nations acting in concert. With a little farsightedness, it should be possible to create such as constellation of power, interlinked with one other . . . ever since the Soviet Union and the United States have come closer to accepting the gospel of coexistence, the need for their wooing of smaller countries for support has receded.[136]

In his autobiography, which covers the period from his youth until 1966, he makes no mention of nuclear weapons. Those urging against hasty, bold decisions seemed vindicated. Ayub intuitively entered a mindset not to repeat the mistake of 1965, becoming extracautious and reluctant to make any rash decisions on security policies, even if a compelling rationale were presented to him. Ayub Khan was always hesitant in nuclear-related decisions. As Agha Shahi explains, "We got concerned when India got the reactors from Canada without safeguards. We wanted it on the same terms for our KANUPP but were overruled. Then after the Chinese test, we pointed out India's nuclear preparations to the leaders but to no effect."[137]

At this time in Pakistan there was animated debate inside government circles about the possibility of acquiring a fuel fabrication facility, heavy water plant, and reprocessing plant from France (as discussed in the following chapter), but President Ayub did not prioritize the issue.[138] Agha Shahi explained in an interview with the author that "both Usmani and Salam were saying that this is the opportunity to get it [the reprocessing plant] when we could conclude an agreement for merely $25 million and that too without stringent safeguards." However, Ayub would not budge. On another occasion, Shahi explained how he had tried to convince President Ayub once again of the opportunities presented by the reprocessing plant, before his departure for a meeting with French President de Gaulle in 1967. Shahi was friendly with Defense Secretary Nasir Rana, who regularly played golf with the president, and so Shahi asked him to convey a message to Ayub: "We are moving into the nuclear age. India is going to develop nuclear weapons, and it is happening. We should close the deal with France and get the reprocessing plant." Shahi received Ayub's reaction through Nasir: "Why is the Foreign Office so jittery? What will India do with nuclear weapons? How will they deliver the nuclear system?" Agha Shahi exclaimed, "I was shocked beyond words. How was the bomb dropped on Hiroshima? Was it not from a transport aircraft?"[139]

Ayub's Final Decision

In the end, Ayub never explicitly rejected the bomb option. He simply decided not to decide. From his dairies we can extrapolate his thought process. It is worth quoting from them at some length, because they detail the president's thinking on nuclear matters. On January 28, 1967, Ayub notes:

> It is heartening news that the USSR and UK have signed a treaty not to use the celestial bodies for military purposes and in any case not to use them as a base for nuclear weapons. It is a big step forward and I hope that [a] non-proliferation treaty would come soon. But meanwhile the beginning of another ruinous nuclear armament race is in sight between America and Russia. . . . This would be a terrible waste as this expenditure or a portion of it spent in the needy world could change the history of mankind. . . . Wasteful and purposeless. Nuclear power has put a terrible power of destruction in the hands of mankind. Its military use might well cause utter ruination of human civilization. These weapons are today in the hands of a few countries. Efforts, which I do not think will succeed, are being made to prevent their spread. Time will come when their production might well become simpler and cheaper and even the small countries might have them. In that case the world will be a very, very dangerous place to live in . . . because nuclear weapons and territorial nationalism are incompatible and deadly danger to the survival of the human race.[140]

Ayub elaborated further, making mental connections between nuclear weapons, poverty, and scientific progress:

> It is a common belief amongst the Muslims that doomsday will come in the fourteenth century—that is, of the Hijra. Well, does not the development of nuclear weapons make this a distinct possibility? Another somber thought that faces the world . . . is the shortage of food and the population explosion. No amount of application of science to land is going to fill the food gap because of so many limitations and insurmountable difficulties, especially human ignorance.[141]

Ayub's thoughts on nuclear proliferation and fears regarding nuclear use were quite clear. Ayub's belief is written on the masthead of the Atomic Energy Center in Dhaka, words he reportedly spoke in a 1962 speech at the center's inauguration: "We are too poor not to afford nuclear technology." Ayub Khan's motto for the center can be seen as his desire to connect nuclear technology with the struggle against poverty. In his imagination perhaps, less-developed East Pakistan was more associated with poverty than West Pakistan. Ayub clearly had an image of nuclear technology as a key for progress, but also a source of danger.[142]

By mid-June, Ayub Khan had had enough of Bhutto. He asked him politely to take "a long leave abroad for health reasons," and as quid pro quo for an honorable departure, asked him not to make political speeches. On the night of June 20, 1966, Bhutto left Islamabad by train for Lahore, as news of his sacking spread throughout the country. At Lahore thousands of students and well-wishers flocked around him shouting, "Bhutto *zindabad* (Long live Bhutto!)" and "United States *murdabad* (Down with the United States!)." Bhutto did not make a speech but tearfully waved at the crowd who garlanded him, kissed his hands, and carried him on their shoulders.

Bhutto went to Europe and on August 13, 1966, he spoke to a large gathering of Pakistani students:

> I am not supposed to be in good health, but I can assure you no matter how poor my health, it is sufficient for India. . . . Pakistan is the voice of a hundred million people articulated on the purity of an ideal . . . . [T]hough India is threatening us with the atom bomb . . . science and technology are everyone's right . . . . Progress and scientific technology cannot be restricted. If India has the bomb, that does not mean that we are going to be subjected to nuclear blackmail.

Bhutto declared,

> Pakistan without Kashmir was a body without a head, and it's a very beautiful head . . . . We are the proletariat of the world . . . therefore, we have to cooperate, collaborate, get together, assist one another . . . and finally the right cause and justice must prevail . . . . Our people deserve it. For centuries they have lived in misery, squalor, filth, and poverty.[143]

By 1966, the divergence of Ayub's and Bhutto's visions had become very clear, and soon competition between the two seeped into the scientific organizations, the bureaucracy, the military, and the political leadership. For his part, Bhutto made his rationale very clear: if India was making the bomb, Pakistan should make it. Time and time again, the leader's rhetoric emphasized the importance of nuclear technology. It was about competition and balancing.

The rift between the two statesmen determined the trajectory of nuclear Pakistan, because when Bhutto came to power in 1971, he brought with him not only a particular political philosophy but also a deep faith in nuclear deterrence.

4   Never Again

In 1968, Ayub's health was deteriorating. While his administration celebrated the tenth year of the "October revolution," dubbed the "Decade of Development," his erstwhile protege Zulfiqar Ali Bhutto was campaigning against his mentor to launch a new political movement that he called the "people's revolution." Concurrently, yet another revolution was brewing for Bengali independence in East Pakistan, with India's active involvement and encouragement.

Throughout the late 1960s, Bhutto had paraded his campaign against Ayub under two major banners. Bhutto's first line of attack was against the capitalist-based economic policy, which benefited twenty-two elite families, leaving the rest of the population by the wayside. Utilizing familiar Marxist rhetoric, he played upon the romantic appeal of socialism prevalent among the youth at the time. His second line of rhetoric was Ayub's failures on national security issues. In his speeches, Bhutto raised the suspicion that Ayub had bartered away Pakistani national interests in the 1966 Tashkent peace accord brokered by the Soviet Union. He accused Ayub of being spineless against India's hostile intentions and increasing nuclear ambitions, and promised to reveal the alarming secret about Ayub and respond to these issues when his time came.

After Bhutto was sacked as foreign minister in 1966, he visited Paris and London. In Paris he discussed the prospects of forming a political party with his friend J. A. Rahim; this discussion would eventually lead to the birth of the Pakistan People's Party (PPP) by the end of the following year.[1] In his visit to Europe Bhutto continued his anti-India rhetoric, focusing on Delhi's nuclear program and making dry remarks in his speeches. He convinced the youth in particular that he was the voice of the Pakistani people and that everyone's focus and concern should be India, which was "threatening us with the atom bomb."[2] By framing the conflict in terms of self-preservation, Bhutto could raise the battle cry as the man "standing by the people of Kashmir and upholding the right of self-determination." As Wolpert writes, after hearing his fiery rhetoric, Ayub and his colleagues began to view Bhutto as "dangerous, a Maoist as well as a madman."[3]

Also around this period, negotiations on the Nuclear Non-Proliferation Treaty (NPT) in the United Nations had begun. At the UN debate in 1966, Pakistan's new foreign minister, Sharifuddin Pirzada, supported the call for a world conference against proliferation of nuclear weapons.[4] Bhutto, who was celebrating his thirty-ninth birthday in his hometown of Larkana, Sindh, promptly reacted to his successor's statement in the United Nations on January 4, 1967:

> Pakistan will always find it difficult to quantitatively keep pace with India, but qualitatively we have maintained a balance in the past, and will have to continue to maintain it in the future for our survival. It is for this reason that as Foreign Minister and Minister-in-Charge of Atomic Energy, I warned the nation sometime back that *if India acquires nuclear status, Pakistan will have to follow suit even if it* entails *eating grass* . . . . My criticism of the [UN] resolution is not opposed to national interest and security. Quite the opposite; it has been made in the interest of the nation and should be welcomed. It is dangerous to take aim with a gun loaded with blank cartridges.[5]

Eventually, Bhutto's "people's revolution" would lead to the fall of the Ayub regime and his military rule in 1969, only to be replaced with martial law again under General Yahya Khan. The new military regime would decide to dismantle the "one-unit scheme" that had previously unified the four provinces in West Pakistan and hold fresh national elections on the basis of one person, one vote. To date, the 1970 elections are reputed to have been the most free and fair elections in the nation's history. However, rather than bringing national harmony and encouraging public participation, they resulted in a power struggle between the majority parties of East Pakistan (the Awami League) and West Pakistan (the PPP). The military regime would be unable to handle the power transfer, and tensions in East Pakistan would mount.

A Pakistani military crackdown on March 25, 1971, would prove to be the proverbial last straw. The strike on Bengali dissidents morphed into a civil war, and refugees poured into India. For the second time in a quarter-century the subcontinent was about to witness a bloody partition. After nine months of violence, massive internal displacement, and transborder migration into India, Delhi finally intervened militarily, resulting in a major war in November and December 1971 and Pakistan's subsequent surrender in Dhaka. The defeat would be the tipping point, turning what could have been a short conflict into an "enduring rivalry." Ultimately, Pakistan's humiliation would lay the foundation for a shift in the once-peaceful nature of the nuclear program.

Psychology of Defeat and Strategic Culture

No other event in the history of Pakistan left as indelible a mark as the humiliating defeat of 1971, a key theme of Pakistani strategic culture today. States and societies that have suffered catastrophic military defeats and experienced threats to their identity and existence develop an angry determination never to allow a repeat of such humiliation. States that continue to face significant security threats eventually gravitate toward nuclear weapons as the ultimate security guarantee.[6] In a nuclear-armed world, those states without firm security guarantees from allies and facing threats from large neighbors not reconciled to the state's existence are essentially "orphan states."[7] The memory of the holocaust among the Jewish people and the enduring rivalry with the Arabs over their right to exist remain the motivations behind Israel's nuclear objectives. Stephen Cohen described Israel and Pakistan as being in an identical dilemma over the security and survivability of their respective states. He ultimately concludes that for these states, conventional military forces and strategic alliances with great powers are not sufficient to ensure national survivability, and hence they put faith in the invincibility of atomic weapons as their ultimate savior.[8] Though China and India are not as structurally weak or as vulnerable as Israel and Pakistan, their underlying motive to develop nuclear weapons was somewhat the same. The Chinese, after suffering threats and humiliation in the 1950s, vowed "Never Again" as an "angry determination to make a difference to the strengthening of the New China."[9] To date, India's humiliating defeat in the 1962 border war with China remains at the core of Indian nationalism and its security narrative; the sense of disgrace is the driving force behind its rivalry with China, as well as modernizations of India's military and nuclear forces.[10]

Indeed, Zulfi Bhutto would galvanize the nation by evoking a deep sense of nationalism to "never again" suffer defeat and dismemberment. Like the Chinese, the Pakistanis vowed to strengthen and build a "new Pakistan" that would become the term du jour in the early 1970s. The "never again" resolve was so central in Pakistani thinking that technical barriers, political sanctions, and security threats did not construct an antinuclear sentiment, but instead did just the opposite. In the 1950s, China had vowed to produce the bomb on self-reliance after the Soviet Union unilaterally abandoned its nuclear assistance. Likewise, Pakistan vowed to find all possible means to obtain the technology to develop a nuclear capability, especially after Western partners would abandon them in the 1970s. Eventually, possessing the bomb would be perceived as the ultimate guarantee of national self-reliance.[11]

In the five years after Ayub Khan signed the Tashkent accord with India and faded away from the scene, two firebrand political leaders, Bhutto and Mujib, and the controversial military leader General Agha Muhammad Yahya Khan, would determine the fate of the country. Together they would run Pakistan into the ground and oversee its eventual dismemberment. India found an opportunity not only to physically undo its archenemy—the state of Pakistan—but also to declare Jinnah's two-nation theory a failure. And all this occurred under the shadow of the highly complex dynamics of the Cold War at the system level.

The Bengali Nationalist Movement and the PPP

Sheikh Mujibur Rahman, who in 1966 was head of the Awami League Party in East Pakistan, released a six-point platform that, in short, demanded virtual autonomy for his constituency—East Pakistan. He called East Pakistan *Bangladesh*, "Land of Bengal," and appealed for a separate military force. In an attempt to quell the movement, Ayub labeled Mujibur Rahman a secessionist, and in subsequent months hundreds of Bengalis were arrested or killed while participating in riots.

In December 1967 Pakistan's Inter-Services Intelligence (ISI) uncovered what became known as the Agartala Conspiracy, a plot against the government involving Mujibur Rahman and his contacts with Indian intelligence.[12] Also that month, President Ayub toured East Pakistan and was "almost kidnapped, [and] nearly assassinated."[13] Zulfiqar Ali Bhutto, upon learning of the Agartala Conspiracy, wrote to the Foreign Ministry accusing India of fueling the unrest and warning that this hostile neighbor was "determined to dismember Pakistan."[14]

In the same month, Mujibur Rahman was arrested, and the PPP was formed at the residence of socialist scholar Dr. Mubashir Hasan in Gulberg, Lahore. A year earlier, with his friend J. A. Rahim, Bhutto had written a manifesto for a new socialist-based political party, boasting that very same name. The manifesto began with a fourfold motto: "Islam is our faith, democracy is our polity, socialism is our economy, all power to the people." In addition, the party's rhetoric was not short on relentless criticism of Ayub Khan, lashing out at the president's system as "half-democratic, half-dictatorial, half a war with India, half a friendship with China, and resisting America by half." He went on, "Where is the security? . . . We were supposed to be a second Japan. I do not see where this second Japan is."[15]

Bhutto's disparagement of India was popular within military circles. His rhetorical attacks—complete with references to guns and blank cartridges— were applauded. However, this narrow security mindset had its consequences, as Lieutenant-General (ret.) Majeed Malik recalled in an interview with the author: "The Pakistani military strategy was essentially India-centric, and due to the proximity of major communication centers like Lahore and the railroad communication generally close to the border, the entire military planning was focused on fighting a war in the plains of West Pakistan." The vulnerability of East Pakistan did not figure prominently in Pakistani security thinking.

Bhutto's opposition movement was an influential recipe for a culture of defiance in Pakistan, where a domestic political hero defines himself with anti-Western rhetoric and cloaks himself in the ethos of socialism. His clever blend of socialism, Islamism, and security threats attracted the populace and the military, and would allow him to feed his nuclear ambitions into the mix, resonating with the nuclear enthusiasts into the late 1960s and beyond. Defiance of the West would become synonymous with the quest for nuclear weapons capability. Gradually the socialist streak would be replaced in the late 1970s by Islamist trends. Thus anti-Westernism, social-Islamism, and nuclear enthusiasm would become entwined in Pakistani domestic political culture.

Pakistan on a Tightrope

In March 1969 hundreds of thousands of students and PPP supporters virtually brought West Pakistan to a halt.[16] Many leaders were arrested and imprisoned in both East and West Pakistan. Both Ayub and Mujib called for new elections in the country, which Ayub Khan agreed to hold but to not participate in. To placate the masses, Ayub released Bhutto from his latest stint in prison and also released Mujibur Rahman. Once free, the two returned to their native provinces, where crowds numbering in the thousands welcomed them. In a last ditch-effort to maintain control, Ayub Khan called a roundtable conference from March 10 to 12 for all political parties. Bhutto boycotted the meeting and fueled public pressure on Ayub to step down. Ayub finally yielded. On March 25, 1969, amid a spiraling crisis within the country, Ayub handed over power to Army Chief General Agha Mohammad Yahya Khan, who then declared martial law but also pledged to hold free and fair elections.

Earlier, in January 1969, Pakistan's old friend Richard Nixon had entered the Oval Office. Nixon was determined to reverse the quagmire in Vietnam. South Asia, however, did not figure prominently in U.S. foreign policy. As Kissinger wrote in his memoirs, "The U.S. policy on the subcontinent was, quite simply, to avoid adding another complication to our agenda."[17] The Soviet Union, however, had strategic interests in the region. In May of that year, in the wake of a series of clashes between the USSR and China along the Sino-Soviet border, Prime Minister Alexei Kosygin paid a visit to Pakistan in order to evaluate the nature of political change in the country. In his second visit in a year, the Soviet premier sought to open a trade route through Afghanistan and Pakistan to reach India. General Yahya was initially amenable; however, the Pakistani military and civil bureaucracy dissuaded him from accepting the proposal, arguing that it held too many costs. First, both Beijing and Washington might see that Pakistan was moving closer to the Soviet camp. Second, by opening a trade route for India—halted since 1965—Pakistan would lose its geographical leverage and relevancy. Yahya, though not politically savvy, did not want to rebuff the Soviet overtures. Within a month of this offer, he visited Moscow and extended Pakistan's friendship while also seeking Soviet military assistance. With Sino-Soviet relations deteriorating, Prime Minister Kosygin told him bluntly that if Islamabad desired help, it would need to distance itself from China. This reaction echoed President Lyndon Johnson's response to Ayub's request for military aid several years before: "[If] Islamabad wanted more arms aid [from the United States], it would have to distance itself from Beijing."[18]

Clearly Islamabad was being pushed into a corner, as both the United States and the Soviet Union were asking it to choose between them and China. Since Islamabad was not willing to do that, Moscow moved decisively closer to Delhi. Two years later, the Soviet Union and India signed a Treaty of Friendship, whose manifestation proved disastrous for Pakistan.

In August 1969, President Nixon visited Pakistan after visiting New Delhi and received a warm welcome in Lahore reminiscent of his first visit in December 1953. But Nixon had a hidden agenda: unbeknownst to the world at the time, he secretly requested Yahya to help open a discreet diplomatic channel between Washington and Beijing. Islamabad found this situation ironic.

Only a few years before, the Johnson administration had rapped Pakistan on the knuckles for its growing relationship with China, but the new Nixon administration was now exploiting that same closeness for its own geopolitical objectives. Pakistan's triangular tightrope walking had made it a pawn between the three great powers. However, Yahya complied, and two years later, in July 1971, he helped arrange a secret visit for Henry Kissinger to Beijing, a geopolitical somersault of global power politics that would change the landscape of the Cold War. With this external focus, Pakistan had made no progress in alleviating its own security concerns—the imbalance with India was growing, and domestically the country was in political turmoil.

Elections in 1970

Yahya reversed some of Ayub's political reforms by restoring West Pakistan to its original four provinces and abolishing the electoral college system of the 1962 Constitution, which allowed the election of the president through elected representatives. He restored popular demand by declaring that elections would be decided on the basis of adult franchise—that is, "one person, one vote."

Yahya Khan had confidently gone ahead with the elections, expecting that diffusion of electoral votes and infighting among the political parties would result in a hung parliament, forcing him to remain in power as arbiter of the country. Yahya was shocked with the election results: Mujibur's Awami League swept 160 out of 162 seats in East Pakistan, and Bhutto's PPP won 81 seats in West Pakistan, giving him a clear majority. Such political dominance from only two parties resulted in a power struggle as they vied to form a government. President Yahya Khan knew that Mujibur Rahman had won the majority and logically he was to be the future prime minister, but several fundamental questions arose: How could a satisfactory governing arrangement be achieved that would balance two popular victorious parties in two wings of one nation? Would Mujibur Rahman's rise to power reduce his insistence upon Bengali autonomy? Would Zulfiqar Ali Bhutto be willing to take the opposition seat? Yahya juggled to resolve this seemingly irreconcilable puzzle, but in vain. After several abortive and inconclusive rounds of talks, there was a serious political breakdown.

By March 1971 all party negotiations had failed to bring about an end to the political stalemate. Angry Bengalis were assembling in protests in Dhaka, and the armed forces of Pakistan were coming under immense pressure to ensure the integrity of the country. Meanwhile, West Pakistanis were being harassed, kidnapped, and killed inside East Pakistan. Among the brewing conflicts and growing polarization of Pakistan's two ends, Indian intelligence operatives intensified their subversive activities by exploiting Pakistani miseries and openly abetting the Bengali rebels. As tens of thousands of East Pakistani refugees fled to India, many of them volunteered to be trained for the insurgency. India established hundreds of training camps and prepared a rebellion force that would famously be known as the Mukti Bahini ("Freedom Fighters").[19]

As the crisis intensified, Lieutenant-General Sahabzada Yaqub-Khan—who would later become Pakistan's foreign minister in the 1980s—resigned from the Eastern Command in 1971, on the grounds that there was no military solution to the political problem in East Pakistan. In an earlier meeting with President Yahya Khan and his chief of staff, Yaqub-Khan had insisted, "The situation in East Pakistan has been transformed after the elections to such an extent that for an 'open sword' martial law action, we would not be able to enlist political support from any party or group, however small."[20] His advice was ignored.

War with India in 1971

On March 25, 1971, the Pakistan Army began to disarm the East Pakistan Rifles (a paramilitary organization that had joined the Bengali rebels), launched a crackdown on the violent protest in Dhaka, and arrested Mujibur Rahman on charges of treason and secessionism. These actions marked the beginning of the end of a united Pakistan, as East Pakistan plunged into civil war.

While the army had some forty-five thousand soldiers in the region at that time, [21] they were ill equipped: they lacked heavy armaments and tanks and had only one aircraft squadron, at Dhaka, to provide air support. Several units of Bengal-origin soldiers had deserted, killing their West Pakistani officers and escaping to India.[22] Three regiments—namely, the 1st, 3rd, and 8th East Bengal Regiments—were regrouped in India as part of the Mukti Bahini. The revolutionaries, now exiled, established a headquarters at a location nicknamed Mujibnagar—named after Mujib—inside the Indian city of Calcutta. Throughout the summer of 1971 the U.S. embassy in India tried to mediate between New Delhi, Islamabad, and Mujibnagar, but to no avail.[23]

From March until November 1971, all military forces in East Pakistan were engaged in fighting in the tropical hilly jungles, rivers, and swampy marshlands typical of the delta region. By July, as monsoons set in and the Pakistan Army crackdown continued, a reported 6.9 million refugees poured into neighboring India, spread throughout a thousand camps. Between March and October, the army reasserted its control over East Pakistan, and also managed to create new paramilitary forces, some of which were composed of students recruited from *madrasas*. The active involvement of India and the rampant insurgency made political options difficult for Yahya's regime.

Four possible solutions were contemplated to break out of the quagmire: the first was to a call the national assembly into session as was originally planned after the elections; second, to grant amnesty to those who had gone to India and hand over power to Mujibur Rahman; third, to start over with a new election; and fourth, to grant only selective amnesty and charge a committee to draft a new constitution. Yahya opted for the last solution, rejecting new elections, and continued the ban on the Awami League.[24] The military regime now found itself pulled in three different directions: between a very deep domestic crisis, escalating tensions with India, and deep anger with the Soviet Union for signing a twenty-year Treaty of Friendship with India over Pakistan's mediatory role in Sino-U.S. rapprochement.[25]

From November 21 to December 3, Indian forces marched from multiple directions into three strategic areas of East Pakistan with armor and air support as well as thousands of Mukti Bahini forces. The Pakistani garrison was simultaneously fighting a civil war and a conventional war to defend the territorial integrity of East Pakistan. Any ground lost to the combined Indian and Mukti Bahini forces would provide the geographical space to declare a "Free Bangladesh." Spread thinly on the borders and also fighting a deep insurgency, the army had little hope of both defending the territory and reversing the civil war. Nevertheless, in an attempted strategy based on the idea that "defense of the East lies in the defense of the West," on December 3 the Pakistan Army launched an attack from West Pakistan in the hope of reversing the Indian advances. It did not succeed.

The war now was reaching a peak and spreading in both wings of Pakistan. The Indian Navy successfully conducted a blockade of all ports of East Pakistan and in the west, effectively attacking the Pakistani coastline and destroying key targets around Karachi and other Pakistani lifelines. Within three days the Indian Air Force was able to establish air superiority, and both wings of Pakistan's territory were strategically dissected and isolated. The only choice left to Pakistan was to launch a riposte with the last reserves of its strike corps in West Pakistan.[26]

By the second week of December Mukti Bahini units were able to establish operational bases on three sides of the capital of Dhaka. India then launched the final assault on the capital of East Pakistan on December 15. The next day the Pakistani military commander in East Pakistan, Lieutenant-General A. A. K. Niazi, outmaneuvered and outnumbered, formally surrendered. International intervention to stop the Indian invasion, as well as Pakistan's subsequent humiliation, did not materialize.[27]

Pakistan lost the 1971 war for several reasons, including strategic blunders, poor leadership, and weak military strategies. A commission headed by former Chief Justice Hamoodur Rehman studied the debacle, but because of the sensitivity of the information, the report was not released until twenty-five years later. The Pakistani military also launched its own investigation, presented to its forces on January 31, 1972, but it was never published.[28]

The war left an indelible mark on the Pakistani psyche. More specifically, it was India's direct role and the Pakistani government's perception of their hostile neighbor's intentions that lent the most weight in the national narrative. Did India merely want to support a Bangladeshi insurgency and help create an independent state, or did it have other, larger objectives in mind?

Before Pakistan's military began its crackdown on Dhaka in April, India openly exploited the situation in East Pakistan, as was widely recorded in Indian parliamentary debates and statements of officials and scholars. Immediately after the crackdown, Indian defense analyst K. Subramanyam remarked that the situation "presented India with an opportunity the likes of which will never come again."[29] Moreover, with the Soviet Union–India Treaty of Friendship, India gained a proactive superpower behind its policies. At the same time, Pakistan was secretly brokering the U.S. rapprochement with China and had high, but mistaken, hopes of U.S. support against any external aggression inspired by the Soviet Union or its ally. Another factor contributing to this exaggerated sense of reliance on the United States was the fact that President Nixon openly despised the Indian leadership and even directed his administration to "tilt" in favor of Pakistan. Clearly, the United States was equally aware of India's plan for a lightning blitzkrieg, as reflected in Henry Kissinger's memoirs, but did nothing to discourage it.[30]

India's leadership had larger goals than merely humiliating and dismembering Pakistan. Mrs. Gandhi had a strong desire for India to be recognized as a major Asian power; therefore the defeat of its neighbor would demonstrate her country's dominance.[31] In addition, the "Bangladesh factor" had to be neutralized in such a manner that a refugee surge from East Pakistan would not destabilize India's northeastern states. A final factor was Indian 1971 war planning vis-à-vis the Kashmir sector and its impact on Indo-Pakistani relations for decades to come.

In a December 4 meeting, Indian defense ministers pushed for a decision to annex the Pakistani portion of Kashmir. After considerable discussion, Mrs. Gandhi concluded that India was to remain in a war of defense on the western front. However, Indian forces were to seize tactical high-regions during the battle in Kashmir, which would not be returned to Pakistan after the war was over. Additionally, in Western Pakistan, India also undertook a limited offensive in the Sindh province, threatening main Pakistani communication lines between Lahore and Karachi. As planned, after the war India withdrew from all areas in Punjab and Sindh but not from Kashmir. Once the peace treaty was negotiated at Simla in July 1972, the ceasefire line (CFL) was rechristened the Line of Control (LOC). Even here there were portions left undemarcated because of terrain and inaccessibility. This mistake would later become a source of major military crises—for example, when India decided to occupy the Siachin Glacier (1984) and Pakistan occupied the heights in Kargil (1999).

The timeline of events as they unfolded in 1971 would explain the Pakistani leadership's anxieties of a full-fledged Indian invasion. Throughout that year, Pakistani intelligence observed India training, financing, and directing Mukti Bahini operations from training and refugee camps surrounding East Pakistan. In November Mrs. Gandhi took an extensive world tour, essentially marketing to the globe India's position. Her main argument for military intervention lay on humanitarian grounds. Meanwhile, war preparations commenced as India strike formations began to concentrate around East Pakistan. By the third week of November, Indian forces had begun cross-border attacks on East Pakistan.

At that point, President Yahya Khan approached Nixon for help. The latter then appealed to both India and Russia's Kosygin in an effort to stop the war, but Delhi refused. On December 2, Pakistan formally asked for U.S. assistance under the 1959 bilateral agreement between the two states, but the U.S. State Department overruled the request. Desperate, on December 4, a day after Pakistan opened the front on West Pakistan, the matter was taken up in the UN Security Council. While eleven out of the fifteen members voted in favor of a ceasefire and withdrawal, the expected Soviet veto killed it. Three days later, on December 7, the UN General Assembly overwhelmingly voted for a ceasefire, but to no effect—Indian forces continued to advance. The only support that

Pakistan received was from China and some military equipment imports. But to Islamabad's surprise, India seemed untroubled by the possibility of Chinese intervention in the war, or the emerging U.S.-China rapprochement.

On December 8 Henry Kissinger briefed President Nixon in the Oval Office, having received a CIA assessment about Indian objectives. Kissinger reported that according to the CIA, Mrs. Gandhi spelled out three objectives for Indian forces: liberation of Bangladesh, incorporation of southern Pakistan–administered Kashmir into India, and lastly, destruction of Pakistani ground and air forces to completely eliminate the threat.[32] By December 10, by which time the writing on the wall was clear, Nixon intervened, spoke directly to Brezhnev in Moscow, and ordered a task force comprising eight ships, including the aircraft carrier *USS Enterprise,* to enter the Bay of Bengal.[33] But these efforts proved futile as, over the next five days, East Pakistan began to fall. On December 16, Indian Prime Minister Indira Gandhi stood before the Indian parliament and, amid a thunderous standing ovation, stated that India had "avenged several centuries of Hindu humiliation at the hands of Muslim emperors and sultans."[34]

Zulfiqar Ali Bhutto had been meeting Nixon and Kissinger at Key Biscayne, Florida. When he arrived back home to Karachi, he was heralded by a mass meeting of the PPP yelling such slogans as "death to Yahya Khan, and long life to Bhutto." The defeat in East Pakistan had riled up new sentiments of anger and frustration within both the public and the armed forces.[35] Within the army, an address by Lieutenant-General Hamid Khan at the National Defense College was interrupted by shouts of "bastards," "drunkards," and "disgraceful" from his officers.[36] Faced with an enraged populace, the Yahya regime could do nothing else but hand over power to Bhutto upon his arrival. On December 20, 1971, President Yahya and several other generals stepped down and Bhutto became Pakistan's first civilian chief martial law administrator. Bhutto appointed his old friend Lieutenant-General Gul Hassan Khan as army chief. Within a month of taking power Bhutto called a meeting of Pakistan Atomic Energy Commission (PAEC) scientists at Multan. The bomb lobby was now in power.

A Perfect Storm for Military Support of Nuclear Weapons

Although Bhutto, along with some foreign ministry bureaucrats and scientists in the PAEC, had been lobbying to shift the nuclear program toward weapons capability as a counterforce to India, the army had not always been fully on board with the idea. In the spring of 1967, PAEC chairman Usmani was invited to the General Headquarters (GHQ) of the Pakistan Army, which had a tradition of inviting guests each week to speak on a wide variety of security-related subjects. Usmani's talk was entitled "The Mysteries of the Atom." For the first time ever, military officers were introduced to the role of a power reactor and the entire nuclear fuel cycle in the development of nuclear weapons. Usmani went on to describe the two separate paths to fissile (bomb-grade) material—the uranium path and the plutonium path. He explained to the officers—who, according to one of the attendees, Lieutenant-General (ret.) Syed Refaqat, were by then bored—how reprocessing spent nuclear fuel can create more reactor fuel. Recalling this experience, Refaqat said, "Nobody understood the earlier part of his presentation—that had lots of charts, graphs, tubes, atoms and fuel flowing this way and that way—but he then paused and said, 'Gentleman, once you have achieved this you can also make a bomb.' Suddenly, the entire audience woke up. Usmani explained to the officers how fissile material is produced and how a thin line existed between civilian use and military. When Usmani finished his speech, the officers gave him a standing ovation."[37]

According to Lieutenant-General Refaqat, who at the time was of the rank of major, Usmani's presentation marked the beginning of the military's passionate support for the bomb. "At least I saw it for the first time in 1967," he said, "and it has not died down." When asked if the military was concerned about nuclear developments in India, which had by that time already set up a reprocessing plant at Trombay, Refaqat replied, "We [the military] were not monitoring the Indian nuclear program. It was his [Usmani's] job and the job of the political leadership. We were concerned with our little professional matters of the day. The reaction of our so-called intellectual military did not come about until India tested in 1974."[38] Lieutenant-General Majeed Malik, who was Director of Military Operations (DMO) at Army GHQ in 1969 and 1970, agrees with Refaqat's assessment that nuclear weapons did not figure in Pakistani military thinking until Usmani's technical explanations. Within military circles, a much greater concern was the effect of the U.S. weapons embargo, put in place after the 1965 war.[39] However, when coupled with Bhutto's political rhetoric and Usmani's sophisticated lecturing, the combined effect began to change the strategic culture in Pakistan. The military, in the 1960s hitherto resistant to the idea of nuclear weapons, began to view the role of these weapons as an equalizer to conventional force imbalance, accentuated as a result of the U.S. embargo.

By the late 1960s, deteriorating military supplies had reduced the combat potential of Pakistan considerably. The army, once accustomed to using sophisticated American military equipment, was now receiving "a few cannons and primitive aircraft from China."[40] The U.S. arms embargo forced the Pakistanis to look for weapons, equipment, and transports from the Soviet Union and China. Such a motley mix of arms and equipment in the inventory posed new challenges to the armed forces, in making them compatible and cohesive. For example, an infantry company in an exercise with an armored unit would typically carry Chinese small arms, communicate on American wireless sets, and be transported by Russian-made vehicles into the field to carry out joint maneuvers with American tanks.

Along with Chinese military equipment and aid, however, came a new technique that Pakistan had never experimented with before: reverse engineering. "The Chinese had perfected the art of reverse engineering, because they were under worse embargoes, worse sanctions, and worse barricades than anybody else, except of course Cuba."[41] At the time it was realized that there was no possibility of direct transfer of emerging technologies, and therefore "reverse engineering [was] an act of salvation."[42] The Chinese benefited from this relationship as well. Pakistan possessed Western arms and equipment, and despite embargoes still had access to more advanced equipment through its connections to the Western world. The arms embargo from both Cold War superpowers pushed Pakistan and China into a technological quid pro quo—new techniques in exchange for access. Over time, as nuclear establishments emerged, this collaboration of evolving technical fixes and troubleshooting would become crucial.

By the late 1960s the conventional force gap with India was widening, the arms embargo was beginning to hurt, and with the NPT concluded, the era of Atoms for Peace was coming to an end. Furthermore, the Pakistan domestic political scene was in a state of unrest. The combination of all these factors created a "perfect storm" in Pakistan for a change of course toward the pursuit of nuclear weapons.

Usmani, Mahmood, and the Young Scientists

Among the hundreds of scientists and engineers that PAEC sent to Europe and the United States for training in various fields of nuclear science and technology was Sultan Bashiruddin Mahmood, who returned to the PAEC in the late 1960s. Sultan and another scientist, Abdul Majeed, would become famous for their meeting with Osama bin Laden in the summer of 2001.

After completing his Ph.D. in science and nuclear engineering at the University of Manchester in the United Kingdom, Bashiruddin Mahmood worked in the UK's Atomic Energy Authority on nuclear reactors, then at Risley Design Centre, a small facility thirty miles outside of Manchester. His job at this facility exposed him to design work for nuclear power plants, reprocessing plants, and enrichment facilities. In an exclusive interview with the author in December 2006, Mahmood said that he was popular and well respected for his innovative approach to finding technical solutions pertaining to reactor stabilization. Asked how he came up with the solutions, Mahmood replied, "I got the idea from Allah." Mahmood explained how he gained experience from the South Africans, who were then working on uranium enrichment at Risely. In the late 1960s the British ran the South African program, and these scientists would discuss their experiments and techniques over dinner. Mahmood claimed that he gained expertise and knowledge from mere discussion in the cafeteria.[43]

In 1967 he returned to Pakistan and was posted to the Atomic Energy Center in Lahore under the supervision of nuclear physicist Naeem Ahmed Khan. These two men, along with another young scientist, Samar Mubarakmand, who would later play a critical role in the development of the nuclear weapons program, formed a study group on enrichment, extensively reviewing literature for about eight to nine months. In late 1969 and early 1970, Mahmood began working under Mr. Yusuf, an East Pakistani senior member of the PAEC, but they did not develop a harmonious relationship. Aside from Mahmood's personal disagreements with his supervisor, the uprising in East Pakistan underscored the political polarization within the ranks of the PAEC, which included many Bengalis on its staff. These conditions made it very difficult for young scientists and engineers to work productively.

Mahmood had a rebellious streak. To the chagrin of his superiors, at PAEC he presented his viewpoints with force and passion. In a departmental meeting presided over by his boss, Yusuf, Mahmood stood up in front of everyone and said, "This program is no program at all. We should be doing things like designing reactors, reprocessing and enrichment, and fabricating fuel." Yusuf reacted by threatening Mahmood: "You are doing politics, and I'm getting reports about you." Mahmood retorted, "We are not doing any politics. We are asking for work from you. Check our records. No one else has as good a record as us." As he later recalled, "We had joined PAEC with an inspiration to work on the nuclear weapons side."[44]

The object of Mahmood's rebellion went beyond his immediate boss. He wanted to challenge the highest authority in PAEC—the aristocrat and PAEC chairman Dr. I. H. Usmani. Now a reputed hero for his defiance, Mahmood was able to convince two more young engineers, Chaudhry Abdul Majeed and Haji Ibrahim, to join him. Together, the three wrote a handwritten report to Usmani demanding to commence a nuclear weapons program. The letter listed the facilities required to jumpstart such a program and expressed confidence that the expertise and know-how to develop nuclear weapons was available in the PAEC.[45] The manner in which the letter was delivered was explained in his words:

> "I. H. Usmani used to stay in the guesthouse of PINSTECH," recalled Mahmood. "I took the report and gave it to the guard at the guesthouse. I. H. Usmani had an imposing and fearful personality, like an old British style bureaucrat, and he would instantly launch a verbal assault on a person. He came out in a rage and said, "Who is he to tell me what to do and what not to do? Get out! We ran out after handing the report. Majeed and I ran towards the outside."[46]

Such young engineers were seen as indulging in politics, which was not allowed for any public servant, and was therefore considered a serious breach of discipline.

Then came the Indo-Pakistani war of 1971 and the subsequent fall of Dhaka on December 16 of that year.[47] Young scientists and engineers in the PAEC were shocked, as was the entire nation. The day after East Pakistan fell, Sultan Bashiruddin Mahmood and other young, rebellious men decided to launch a protest against General Yahya Khan, an activity that was banned under Section-144 of the law, whereby no public gathering of more than three persons at one place was allowed.[48] As Sultan recalled,

> On the day of the protest, we reached a point Faizabad, in Rawalpindi, and held placards. The police asked the demonstrators to keep a distance of five feet between each person and walk two at a time so as to abide by the law. The group had planned to walk from Faizabad to Chandni Chowk, and from there proceed to the Liaquat Garden where they would hold a rally. But the demonstration increased to about 200–250 people, and soon Pakistani citizens began to line the streets and the rooftops to witness the event. But the police stopped us at Chandni Chowk, so we made the speeches there.[49]

Mahmood claims that diverse media circuits covered these protests, including the BBC. There was a common thread in all the speeches that day. Bashiruddin Mahmood recounts the contents of his speech:

> It was not the failure of the Army, but it was a failure of technologists and if we had built the bomb, today India would not have dared to do this. It was not a military but a technological defeat. That was the slogan for the birth of the bomb. At least it gave a realization of what we must do. The people who first came to PAEC were from the middle class. They were not interested in this type of research. Here [to PAEC], very good people came, mostly belonging to the lower or middle class, but very capable people. And there was no element of corruption in them. They had a lot of sincerity. They had a great passion and love for Pakistan.[50]

The day after the protest, the scientists and engineers who participated were served citations by their supervisors in PINSTECH for indiscipline and indulging in political activities. In his usual rebellious tone, Mahmood defiantly explained to his boss, "You can take my explanation. I admit I have done it. I wanted you to come along with us, but since you did not and were left behind, it was not in your destiny to be part of it." Mahmood later claimed to the author that his leadership gave courage to PAEC employees, and they continued to hold many demonstrations. The young group then formed a body called the "Association of Nuclear Engineers for a Nuclear Pakistan" in PINSTECH. Sultan Mahmood was its general secretary. PAEC chairman Usmani was appalled at this kind of indiscipline within the PAEC, an organization he had nurtured for over a decade with care, proficiency, and style.

This was the beginning of new era that Bhutto fondly called the *Awami Daur* (The era of people's rule). Bhutto encouraged a culture of public indiscipline; the rhetoric of his speeches resonated the bourgeoisie ethos as the means of his popularity, which was dubbed as democracy and freedom of expression.

Bhutto's Early Days in Power and the Scientific Conference at Multan

In his first speech to the nation as president, Bhutto spoke in English, apologizing for not speaking in Urdu, because "the world [is] listening." Bhutto pleaded to the nation, "We have to pick up the pieces to make a new Pakistan, a prosperous and progressive Pakistan, as envisaged by Quaid-i-Azam [Jinnah]."[51] He only asked time of his people, time to remove martial law, restore

Pakistan's pride, and pave the road for an equal society where "the poor man in the street can tell me to go to hell."[52] A month later, speaking to a journalist from the *Baltimore Sun*, Bhutto smacked of confidence. "If you Americans think Franklin Roosevelt had an amazing first 100 days, watch us."[53]

Upon assuming power, the new leader would sleep only three or four hours a night and spend much of his time traveling all over the country and abroad.[54] One important stop would be China, to meet Mao Zedong and Chou En-lai. Accompanied by Army Chief Lieutenant-General Gul Hassan and Air Marshall Rahim Khan, Bhutto received a large welcome in China despite the January snowfall, and left with Beijing's support.

Within a month of taking the presidential seat, Zulfiqar Ali Bhutto announced that a scientists' conference would be held in Quetta, although he didn't quite know himself what the agenda might be. In response, Sultan Bashiruddin Mahmood's Association of Nuclear Engineers for a Nuclear Pakistan sent the new president a private message. Mahmood recalls, "We were the bomb lobby. So I sent a telegram to Bhutto, saying that I represent the engineers of the Atomic Energy Commission at PINSTECH, and we should be given a chance to speak."[55]

Bhutto acknowledged the telegram, and informed PAEC chairman Usmani. The next day PINSTECH director S. A. Hasnain called Mahmood and asked, "Have you sent a telegram to the President? The chairman is very angry with you." Mahmood replied, "Yes, he has been angry for a long time now."[56] Hasnain made it very clear to Mahmood that his so-called bomb lobby would not receive PAEC financial support for the conference. Unaffected, Mahmood and his two colleagues, Chaudhry Abdul Majeed and Mahmood Ahmad Shad, traveled to the conference at their own expense.[57]

The scientist's conference was moved to Multan, scheduled for January 20, 1972. By that time Bhutto had two clear-cut goals for the meeting. The first was to provide support for the nuclear program and its Pakistani scientists and engineers. But the second and probably more important goal was to announce publicly the new PAEC chair, removing Usmani from office for reasons that will be discussed later. Many scientists attended, some of whom would later play a major role in the Pakistani nuclear program, such as Dr. Ishfaq Ahmad, Dr. Inam-ur-Rahman, Dr. Noor Muhammad Butt, Dr. Zafarullah, and Dr. Sakhi Muhammad Bhutta.[58]

After arriving in the host city, Mahmood and his colleagues learned that the highly respected Prof. Abdus Salam had also come to attend the scientist's conference and was staying at a local hotel. Upon their meeting, Prof. Salam cautioned young Mahmood against indulging in inappropriate activities that could cost the young scientist his career—such engineering talent should not be thrown away. In this vein, he advised Mahmood and the others to observe the proceedings without participating.[59] But having already challenged his immediate boss, still-acting PAEC chair Usmani, Mahmood was even more eager to address the president and express his views. Dr. Salam told him, "OK, write down your views and bring them to me."[60] Mahmood and Majeed wrote a two-page, handwritten speech and gave it to Salam, who kept it on his person.

The next day the conference was held at the home of Nawab Sadiq Hussain Qureshi, then chief minister of the Punjab province. His house in Multan was known as "the White House," and attendees met under a *shamiana*, or tent, that was erected on the huge lawn. Contrary to some misconceptions, this gathering of scientists was not a closed-door or secret meeting. Dr. Ishfaq Ahmed recalls: "Anybody could come in, and I spotted many foreigners sitting there, including journalists. There were at least 400 people under the *shamiana*." When Sultan Bashiruddin Mahmood and Abdul Majeed reached the venue, they were miffed to find that their allotted seats had already been taken and they had to settle for space in the press area, located somewhere in the rear.[61]

Three people were on stage: Bhutto, Usmani, and Salam, available to listen to remarks and answer questions. While scientists and university professors made up many of the attendees, Ishfaq remembers that anyone who raised his hand was allowed to speak. He recalls one man in particular who raised his hand and said, "I am the only Pakistani who has ever seen a nuclear bomb."

Interested, Bhutto asked, "Where have you seen this?"

"In a museum in the United States," the man replied, smiling mischievously. Bhutto smiled in return.

Questions and speeches continued, including remarks by Ishfaq and Usmani, and all the while Bhutto listened patiently. As Sultan Bashiruddin Mahmood remembers, Usmani called the speakers by name from a prepared list. After some time, Mahmood realized that he would not be called onto the stage, so he raised his hand like a schoolboy. This act caught Bhutto's eye, and after two to three more speakers, Bhutto stopped Usmani and said, "No, that young man!"[62]

Sultan Mahmood climbed on stage and he addressed Bhutto:

> So far the people who have come, they have said that you are a very great man. But nobody has talked about what we should do. Perhaps the conductor of the bus who takes us to PINSTECH knows better than them! When the bus stops there, the bus

conductor shouts, "Nilore bomb factory, Nilore bomb factory." This is the public impression of what is happening in that building, but we know that there is no program like that, and what Pakistan needs today is to make a bomb.[63]

Two more speakers followed Mahmood, after which Bhutto announced, "That is all," and stood to speak. According to Mahmood, the president explicitly mentioned the bomb, saying, "We are fighting a thousand year war with India, and we will make an atomic bomb even if we have to eat grass. So in how many years can you do it?"[64] At this, Mahmood recalls, "There was excitement; with some saying five years, some seven, some said ten. People were raising their hands. Someone was jumping. There was shouting, like in a fish market. Bhutto said, 'OK, OK, five years.' Then someone shouted three years."[65] Encouraged by the audience's eagerness, the president candidly communicated the gravity of the decision, but also promised the assembled scientists and engineers his full support. "I shall provide you the resources and the facilities, so can you do it?"[66]

Asked about Bhutto's reaction to this, Dr. Ishfaq Ahmad, says:

Bhutto just smiled at the enthusiasm of the participants. He knew they were just novices. The original intent of the meeting was to have a small group to review our capability and where we stood, and to announce a change in leadership. But then things got out of hand and it became a *tumasha* [public drama].[67]

Contrary to Mahmood's account, Ishfaq stated that Bhutto never used the word "bomb" during the Multan meeting. While he did read elsewhere of Bhutto's stating, "We will eat grass but make the bomb," Ishfaq categorically denies that the president said it at that particular conference. In Ishfaq's account, Bhutto only indirectly referred to a nuclear weapon by hinting that he expected the scientists to meet the challenge "if something happens." By this, everyone attending understood him to mean, "If India explodes a nuclear device." In such an eventuality, Bhutto went on to say, "I expect you to deliver. You'd better deliver."

After that portion of his speech, Bhutto still had the task he originally set out to accomplish—to announce the new PAEC chair. Finally, Bhutto remarked, "I am very proud of what you people have done in the PAEC, but there is always a time to come and a time to go." Turning to Usmani, he said, "You have been chairman now for twelve years. I think it's time that we make a change. I hereby appoint Munir Ahmad Khan as the new chairman of the Atomic Energy Commission."

The suddenness of his announcement shocked Usmani as well as all the attendees, but Bhutto made it as though it were business as usual. His brutal act made it clear to all who was in charge. Bhutto always believed nuclear affairs were his brainchild; the atomic energy portfolio moved with him wherever he went. He wanted singular glory for his singular vision.

Bhutto and the newly appointed PAEC chair, Munir Ahmad Khan, had developed a friendship since their first meeting in 1965. In his frequent visits to Europe he often stayed with Munir Ahmad Khan, where he was serving in the IAEA. Munir described the alliance between him and Bhutto as the real "bomb-lobby" and one akin to the "Nehru-Bhabha" alliance in India.[68]

By the time Bhutto announced that Munir was the chair of PAEC, Munir had gained significant experience working in different capacities within the IAEA,[69] mostly related to nuclear power reactors.[70] After lauding Munir's youth and "splendid career" at the IAEA in his speech, he announced that he was appointing I. H. Usmani as secretary of Science and Technology,[71] the ministry to which PAEC reported. Bhutto, however, told Munir later that evening that PAEC would no longer be reporting to any ministry and that Usmani would "not be allowed to interfere in PAEC affairs." He told Munir to report directly to him.[72] The PAEC has remained under direct presidential or prime ministerial control ever since.

Following his appointment as PAEC chair, Munir flew to IAEA headquarters in Vienna and started packing for his return to Pakistan. In interviews with the author, his family said that Munir had left a lucrative position for a job with a meager salary of Rs. 3,325 per month.[73] Boasting about the perks and privileges left behind and the sacrifice made in order to serve one's country was a common theme in the Pakistani scientific culture. Most scientists who were sent to study abroad a decade earlier had settled into jobs, married in the West, and were raising families. They worked in technically sophisticated environments and a Western scientific work culture. Pakistan's technical environment was backward, its work ethos was underdeveloped, and it offered few resources or perks to those returning home. With no incentive except for the patriotic call to serve their country, Pakistani scientists regarded the development of the nuclear bomb as the highest national duty, and acquisition of nuclear capability the ultimate national cause.

Usmani's Removal: Under a Cloud of Suspicion

Munir Ahmad Khan officially took over Dr. I. H. Usmani's seat as PAEC chairman on March 15, 1972.[74] Usmani's conciliatory appointment as secretary of Science and Technology was short lived; he also was fired from that position. Subsequently, he would make a career at the United Nations, specializing in energy and environmental issues. The causes for Usmani's removal from the PAEC and the Ministry of Science and Technology were shrouded in mystery. Almost all scientists interviewed by this author unanimously acknowledged the great contributions Usmani made to the foundations of the Pakistani nuclear program. But at the same time, Usmani had many detractors who often expressed pessimism over the PAEC's state of affairs. The loudest and most powerful of these critics was Bhutto.

There are three probable reasons why Bhutto sacked Usmani. First, his aristocratic style would have clashed with Bhutto's more socialist approach. Second, the president held many grudges against Usmani for the former chair's public criticism of his policies. For example, as the PAEC was searching for a reliable contractor in the United States for its first research reactor, Bhutto was pushing for a local civilian contractor.[75] Usmani refused because Bhutto's choice of contractor was inexperienced and would not be able to do the job well, but Bhutto considered this a harsh rebuff and held a grudge. Many years later, Usmani publicly criticized Bhutto's decision for appointing an engineer as finance minister, stating that the man was unfit to do the job. As Ishfaq recalls, "Bhutto was not one who would forgive such things." Finally, a more justifiable reason for Usmani's removal was his caution, a trait Bhutto believed would hinder the PAEC's bold steps toward nuclear weapons. Munir Ahmad Khan seemed more pliable and able to keep sensitive information secret. The president was searching for an active way to permanently fire Usmani from public office, and a suspected espionage plot between the United States and Pakistan gave him that needed excuse.

In an interview with the author, Agha Shahi said that Usmani left under a cloud because many suspected him of being a CIA informant and helping the agency gather Chinese nuclear test data. After all, during that time, Pakistan was perhaps among the few countries with direct flights to China. One such flight flew from Dhaka to Shanghai. Allegedly in 1971, an espionage operation had Pakistan International Airlines (PIA) planes sprayed with special paint that attracted particles containing nuclear isotopes, which would then stick to the aircraft's surface. These planes would purportedly collect data during flights over Chinese territory.[76] Agha Shahi recalls that he was present in March 1973 or 1974 when Chinese Prime Minister Chou En-lai raised the sensitive subject with Bhutto. He expressed concern that despite the great trust between the two nations, Pakistani planes were being used against China. Bhutto's response to Chou En-lai was that he had already remedied the situation by removing Usmani.

Ishfaq Ahmad, however, provides an entirely different explanation for the espionage allegation, dismissing any notion that PIA planes or the PAEC was involved in clandestine operations. Ishfaq Ahmad explains that in 1971, the head of Dhaka Atomic Energy Center, Mr. Anwar Hussein, complained that the Chinese above-ground nuclear tests released radioactivity that had traveled into the atmosphere over East Pakistan. Hussein then had ordinary adhesive tape placed on PIA planes operating out of Dhaka, but upon discovering this, China immediately suspected CIA involvement. Even when the issue was resolved, the Chinese felt offended that, being a trusted friend, they had not simply been asked for their assistance. Given Beijing's reaction, the PAEC issued a directive to the Dhaka Center to stop this practice, and the matter was closed.

But Bhutto suspected that this act was indeed espionage, conducted by Usmani at the behest of the Americans. This incident was Bhutto's excuse to remove Usmani for good. In an attempt to sully Usmani's name, he put Usmani and Anwar Hussein on trial for espionage. But after the latter apologized for having acted without permission, a judge concluded that the matter was trivial, and neither of the men could be charged. Rumors are hard to quell, however, and thus Bhutto still managed to remove Usmani from his PAEC office.

S. N. Burney, who served three consecutive PAEC chairs, recalled Dr. Usmani's departure from the PAEC:

> [Usmani's] ouster was heralded with jubilation by some and seen as unfortunate by others. With a broken heart, he left PAEC to head the newly formed Ministry of Science and Technology, an institution which he always described as a "paper tiger," to be tried later for prying into the affairs of a friendly country and be compulsorily retired.[77]

Indeed, Dr. Usmani did not receive the respect and credit due to him after years of contribution and dedication to the nuclear program. But it was time for a new era, and the Multan meeting served as its symbol with the appointment of Munir Ahmad Khan. The country's scientific capabilities, as well as morale, had declined after East Pakistan's fall, since Dhaka Atomic Energy Center was located in the lost region, with all its computers, facilities, and most important, nearly 50 percent of the PAEC's trained personnel. Scientists and engineers needed new, energetic leadership and vision to boost their enthusiasm and confidence, which some would say came in the form of a nuclear bomb.

In some respects, the Multan Conference seemed to point in no other direction than to a "bomb decision" as the future of the nuclear program. But at that stage, Pakistan was still a nascent nuclear state. The country had the appropriate labor force, a mining capability (to some extent), and one power reactor at KANUPP. Beyond that there was little infrastructure or money to launch a full-fledged nuclear program. As Ishfaq Ahmad put it, "We required the three M's: Manpower, Material and Money." Describing the capacity around this time, Dr. Usmani is quoted by the Western press as saying, "Bhutto had asked me to take our nuclear program to its logical conclusion. But I refused. Pakistan just didn't have the infrastructure for that kind of nuclear program. I'm not talking about the ability to get ten kilograms of plutonium. I'm talking about the real infrastructure."[78] If this quotation were true, Bhutto would have seen it as a refusal to follow orders.[79]

Although it was commonly believed that Usmani was reluctant to take responsibility for a weapons program, he was actually gradually building up a "standby nuclear capability"—which was much more discreet than a full-blown program that would have drawn unwanted international attention.[80] Studies have shown that lack of adequate technical capability does not dissuade highly motivated states from going nuclear. In a strategy known as "nuclear hedging,"[81] they first try to develop latent capacities before proceeding to a functional nuclear program, and usually a catastrophic event or shock triggers the shift from a simple "capability decision" to a "proliferation decision."[82]

Was Usmani really not interested in Pakistan's developing at least a "just in case" contingency? According to Dr. Ishfaq Ahmad, Usmani "always thought that if India did something, Pakistan would have to respond. No chairman of the PAEC would hold a different viewpoint."[83] Usmani also feared the cascading effect of nuclear proliferation and knew that Pakistan would have been prevented from embarking on the pathway only if India had refrained. Ishfaq stated that Usmani "hoped that India would not cross the barrier."[84] Recalling a conversation between Salam and Usmani, Ishfaq paraphrased Usmani's contention regarding India's choices:

What the Indians should have done [in response to China's test in 1964] was to have placed before the international community all components of their device and declared that India has the capability of conducting a nuclear explosion any time it wants, but that as disciples of Gandhi and Nehru [they] would not breach the proliferation barrier. India would then hold the high moral ground to ask the other five [nuclear weapon] countries to disarm rather than adding a sixth one.[85]

Ishfaq had served two PAEC chairs before becoming chairman for a ten-year tenure. He witnessed a harmony of infrastructure buildup, facility construction, and human resources training as a prelude to launching a nuclear weapons program. India's subsequent 1974 test turned Pakistan's policy option into an imperative.[86]

Part II: The Secret Nuclear R&D Program

5   The Route to Nuclear Ambition

Zulfiqar Ali Bhutto had finally taken the helm of the new Pakistan, leaving the trauma of East Pakistan (now Bangladesh) behind. The country was geographically coherent but still politically divided. Bhutto was simultaneously the president and the chief martial law administrator of the country.[1] He was determined to chart Pakistan firmly on a course toward a nuclear weapons program, but the journey would be fraught with obstacles and domestic challenges.[2] Bhutto was well aware of the limits of Pakistan's capacity—the country had only one IAEA safeguarded power reactor, which had yet to be commissioned into active service. President Bhutto brought the PAEC directly under his control, but because of multiple political, military, and economic crises, he would not have the luxury of overseeing the weapons program.

On Bhutto's directive, the PAEC began pulling out all the stops to open up a broad base of nuclear options—it recalled scientific talents from abroad, tapped into open resources, and utilized every available avenue—all to acquire the necessary technological abilities. Bhutto's nuclear policy was clear—he would pursue everything that the reluctant Ayub had shelved or rejected.

His revolutionary zeal was analogous to China's in the mid-fifties. After the Korean War, the Indo-China clash, and the Taiwan Strait crises, the Chinese leadership concluded that a technologically backward country would continue to suffer humiliation; since the nuclear weapon symbolized modernity, it feverishly began to pursue strategic weapons.[3] Pakistan suffered a similar sense of degradation. Determined not to repeat that experience, the country was spurred to pursue a weapons capability as well. Bhutto thus directed the PAEC to launch three parallel secret programs simultaneously—producing plutonium through reprocessing, enriching uranium, and developing nuclear weapon designs (for details, see subsequent chapters).

Meeting Bhutto's directive proved an arduous assignment. The Nuclear

Non-Proliferation Treaty (NPT) went into force in 1970, bringing about a number of informal restrictions in the flow of technology and expertise. U.S. supplies under the Atoms for Peace program, such as highly enriched uranium (HEU) for the Pakistan Atomic Research Reactor (PARR-1), were gradually withdrawn, and even Canada began to slow the provision of supplies before cutting them off completely in 1976. As an outlier in the nonproliferation regime, Pakistan and its nuclear activities came under more scrutiny, causing the scientists to become more resourceful and innovative in developing indigenous capabilities. India's nuclear test in May 1974 was a death knell for Pakistan. The United States stopped all levels of cooperation and forced Canada, Germany, and France to back away from contracts and agreements. The first formal nuclear sanctions were put in place on April 1979 by the Carter administration.

In the meantime, the political environment both regionally and domestically occupied Bhutto's attention. While the PAEC worked to overcome the technical challenges of developing a complete indigenous fuel cycle, Bhutto attended to relations with India and Afghanistan, alliances with the Middle East, China, Russia, and North Korea, and his domestic political agenda. While raising funds for the nascent nuclear weapons program, he would introduce a "new Pakistan" to the Muslim world before having to face the impact of the Indian nuclear test on the Pakistani program.

Bhutto's New Pakistan

Between 1972 and 1974 four major issues would consume Zulfiqar Ali Bhutto's energies. The first item on his agenda was rapprochement with India, needed in order to settle postwar issues concerning prisoners of war and withdrawal of troops from captured territories. Second was to write a new constitution for Pakistan and create a new domestic political order. Third, Bhutto had to reorient the national economy along socialist lines, to keep in line with the Pakistan People's Party (PPP) manifesto. Lastly, he would reorient Pakistan's foreign policy, retaining critical partnerships with the United States and China while looking for support in the Middle East. Faced with all of these tasks, Bhutto was still determined to pursue his nuclear ambition, but first he needed to find funding and hardware for the nascent program.

In the end, Bhutto succeeded remarkably well on all four fronts. Mrs. Indira Gandhi and he signed an accord at Simla in July 1972 that included the return of ninety-three thousand prisoners of war and 5,131 square miles of territory that India had seized during the war.[4] The agreement also marked a new relationship between India and Pakistan by recognizing the former's regional primacy. All major issues with India, including Kashmir, would take a back seat for the foreseeable future.[5]

On the Afghanistan front, however, a new complication arose. In July 1973 Bhutto was touring Europe when Sardar Mohammad Daoud Khan overthrew his cousin and brother-in-law King Zahir Shah. Daoud declared Afghanistan a republic and at the same time resurrected the call for a "Pashtunistan," an issue that had been dormant since the 1960s. The claim for Pashtunistan included a significant portion of Pakistan's North West Frontier Province (NWFP) and Baluchistan—essentially all land west of the Indus River. Daoud's cordial relations with Moscow and New Delhi also caused security concerns inside Pakistan. This dramatic shift created a strategic quagmire for Bhutto. With King Zahir Shah gone, Pakistan could no longer focus its military resources on one front—India. Rather, its leadership was divided, protecting both the Afghanistan and India borders.

Despite these regional developments, Bhutto was able remain attentive to domestic issues. For example, he cooperated with all political parties in order to compose the new constitution, presented on April 12, 1973, after which he named himself prime minister. This achievement was remarkable in building political consensus and defining Pakistan's civil-military relationship, which had bedeviled the country since the 1950s.[6] In addition, Bhutto instituted a new, more socialist economy by nationalizing major industries. His finance minister, Dr. Mubashir Hassan, was a known socialist, and his close associates included J. A. Rahim and the health minister, Khurshid Hasan Meer.[7]

Bhutto's socialist ideals influenced his foreign policy orientation, which would look toward the Middle East, where Muslim brethren, oil, and money were in abundance. Pakistan's democratically elected "people's government" would not allow the poor "to eat grass or go hungry," and Bhutto vowed to fulfill the election slogan of *Roti Kapara aur Makan* (Bread, Clothes, and Housing). Bhutto reached out to natural, socialist allies such as China, Russia, and North Korea. The president's socialist bent even realized itself in fashion: party workers would wear Awami dress (*Shalwar Kameez*) and for all formal occasions, a new standard dress, Maoist-style tunic and trousers, leaving behind the traditional *Sherwani* and cap that Jinnah had adopted.[8]

Reestablishing new ties with the Muslim Middle East, Bhutto visited eight countries in January 1972 and championed the cause of the Islamic world in the wake of the 1973 oil crises and Arab-Israeli War. In February 1974 he hosted a summit for thirty-eight Islamic countries on behalf of the Organization of Islamic Conference (OIC). Bhutto had molded himself into a Third World nonaligned leader.[9]

Bhutto reaffirmed close ties with China, established new relations with North Vietnam and North Korea, and tried his best to normalize relations with Moscow. In addition, to appease these countries, he announced Pakistan's withdrawal from the South East Asian Treaty Organization (SEATO). Despite this and his anti-American rhetoric during his tenure as foreign minister, Bhutto as president maintained good relations with the United States.[10] With Nixon in office, Pakistan had a friend in the White House, and Bhutto even offered to construct a new port at Gwadar, on the Arabian Sea, for the United States. After examining the pros and cons, however, Washington politely declined.[11]

Even with all the aforementioned accomplishments, Bhutto's presidency was plagued with challenges. In the summer of 1972, riots erupted in his own province of Sindh after the government attempted to replace Sindhi with Urdu as the official language. Simultaneously, an insurgency in Baluchistan morphed into a near civil war, coupled with much unrest in the NWFP. The Pakistan Army, still reeling from the military defeat in East Pakistan, was once again thrust into an internal battle. And in 1975 the assassination of Bhutto's close associate in Peshawar, Hayat Sherpao, forced the president to remove the provincial government of the National Awami Party (NAP).

In his first year in power, Bhutto had a political showdown with his own newly appointed army chief, Lieutenant-General Gul Hassan Khan. The general felt that Bhutto and his advisors were not only interfering in the army's internal affairs but also illegally aiding civilian power.[12]

Gul Hassan and other military leaders, such as Air Force Chief Rahim Khan, were reluctant to place the military in conflict with civilians, especially after the disastrous loss of East Pakistan.

These challenges to his leadership led Bhutto to create the controversial Federal Security Force (FSF), which could control internal security without relying on the army.[13] The civil-military tension that this move caused eventually resulted in the unceremonious dismissals of both Gul Hassan and Rahim Khan at gunpoint.[14] Bhutto replaced Gul Hassan with Lieutenant-General Tikka Khan, a highly controversial appointment after the general's actions in East Pakistan earned him the name "Butcher of Bengal."[15] Ironically, Tikka Khan was once again asked to quash an insurgency, this time in Baluchistan, and would receive the unenviable distinction of being the "Butcher of Baluchistan" as well.[16]

As Islamic fundamentalists gradually gained influence in the country, Bhutto attempted to appease them. Simultaneously he came into conflict with socialist political colleagues, some of whom were his close confidants. Bhutto displayed arrogance of power by simply dismissing founding members of the PPP, such as J. A. Rahim, Finance Minister Mubashir Hasan, and Health Minister Khurshid Hasan Meer. J. A. Rahim's removal was especially harsh, as members of the FSF pushed their way into Rahim's house, beat him with fists and rifle butts, and dragged him into custody. By then, the FSF was fourteen thousand strong and growing, making the army and others within the country increasingly uncomfortable.[17] With socialist stalwarts pushed aside, Bhutto began to look more to right-wing colleagues in his cabinet and party. His appeasement of the mullahs would later be seen as his start down a slippery slope of concessions.

Anti-Ahmadi religious riots, absent since 1954, began to reoccur. At the center of the tensions was a riot that began at Rabwah, the mecca of the Ahmadiyya community in Pakistan. Unlike in the 1950s when the government stood up to the clergy and diffused the challenge by invoking the court, this time Bhutto pandered to the religious parties, possibly because of the financial influence of Wahhabis in Saudi Arabia, leading him eventually to declare Ahmadis as non-Muslims. This step had a profound impact on the nuclear program, as Pakistan's chief intellectual in the nuclear field, the future Nobel laureate Dr. Abdus Salam, was an Ahmadi. The scientists and technicians who were either Ahmadis themselves or close prodigies of Abdus Salam would be seen as suspect and face discrimination. As will be shown later, this move had a negative effect on nuclear progress, as these minorities were kept away from the secret program.[18]

Given all of these national challenges, Zulfiqar Ali Bhutto did not stay deeply involved in the nuclear program, to the disappointment of many scientists.[19] If Bhutto did find a moment to attend to nuclear matters, discussions were probably held in strict secrecy between him and PAEC chairman Munir Ahmad Khan. However, no evidence or record of such meetings exists. Munir Ahmad Khan was known for his secrecy, and throughout his PAEC career the right hand did not know what the left hand was doing.[20]

Mastering the Nuclear Fuel Cycle

While Bhutto struggled to get the nation back on its feet, the scientists confronted technical and economic obstacles in their quest to fulfill Bhutto's dream. The PAEC had a large challenge ahead, as it had to meet two requirements simultaneously: security (nuclear weapons) and development (nuclear energy). The PAEC was now running into new difficulties, as the NPT was now in force, placing restrictions on the flow of nuclear technologies and expertise.

As an outgrowth of Article 3 of the NPT, a Nuclear Exporters Committee, comprising major Western countries, was formed. Commonly referred as the Zangger Committee—named after its chairman, Claude Zangger—its mandate was to draft a "trigger list" of sensitive nuclear material and equipment whose trade would be restricted or denied to non–nuclear weapons states (NNWS) that were members of the NPT. Those outside the NPT, such as India, Israel, and Pakistan, would be subjected to IAEA safeguards. The committee created guidelines and a common understanding among the exclusive members regarding supplies and exchange of information. In three years' time, the Zangger Committee created a list that restricted supply of sensitive material and equipment, or applied conditions to their supply. Most of the technologies used in nuclear trade also had other uses and applications in conventional industries. It would take many years to identify such "dual-use" items, whose ostensible purpose would be benign but could also be secretly used for nuclear application.[21]

After India conducted its first nuclear test in 1974, it became obvious that the material used to build the bomb came from the installations and technology that were offered under the spirit of Atoms for Peace. The violation caused supplier conditions to become stricter and to be subsumed under the London Suppliers Group (LSG). Many developing countries considered such export control regimes to be the design of a supplier cartel of Western nations intended to deprive NNWS of technology. Pakistan felt it was an unusual victim of these emerging norms under the regime, especially because India's abuse of Atoms for Peace resulted in the nonproliferation regime's focus on Pakistan. A common sentiment within Pakistan is that Pakistan was punished for India's sins. This sense of discrimination in Pakistan would help to propel the nation down the nuclear weapons path.

Worried that the window to develop the weapons option would be short-lived, the PAEC created an ambitious plan to work simultaneously on the front end and the back end of the nuclear fuel cycle—the stages that uranium undergoes in order to power a nuclear reactor and become available for a nuclear weapons development program.[22]

The front end of the cycle begins with the mining of uranium. Uranium is a slightly radioactive metal that is found in the earth's crust and is composed of three isotopes—uranium-238, uranium-235, and uranium-234—with proportions of 99.284 percent, 0.711 percent, and 0.0055 percent, respectively. The main ingredient for producing both nuclear energy and a nuclear explosion is fissile material—that is, elements with nuclei that can break apart in a chain reaction called fission. Some of the more common fissile materials are uranium-235 (U-235), uranium-233 (U-233), and plutonium-239 (Pu-239).[23] Only U-235 is naturally occurring and is fed into the nuclear fuel cycle; the other two are by-products of the nuclear fuel cycle in a nuclear reactor. When the U-235 nucleus absorbs a neutron, it readily splits apart releasing energy and one or more neutrons. The presence of U-235 in natural uranium is rare, however, so to achieve a critical mass of this material to power a nuclear reactor, the uranium feed needs to undergo enrichment. Once the percentage of U-235 reaches a critical mass through enrichment, enough atoms can split to release energy as well other neutrons, continuing the cycle and creating a "chain reaction" inside the nuclear reactor—or a nuclear bomb.

It is this chain reaction that enables fissile materials to be harnessed for peaceful nuclear energy or diverted from the fuel cycle for military purposes. The key difference is that in a nuclear reactor, enrichment of approximately 5 percent U-235 is necessary, and moderator materials, such as heavy water, control the chain reaction. However, a chain reaction in a nuclear weapon requires some 90 percent of U-235 and remains uncontrolled, taking place in a very short time—a tenth of a microsecond.[24]

While nuclear reactors use different types and quantities of fissile materials depending on their design, nuclear weapons require a minimum amount of a particular fissile material in their center, officially dubbed a "significant quantity" by the IAEA. For example, a significant quantity of 25 kilograms (kg) of highly enriched uranium (HEU; 90 percent or more of U-235) and 8 kg of Pu-239 is the minimum required to create a nuclear explosive device.[25] While most countries seeking a nuclear weapons capability choose one fissile material over the other, some may choose both.

In order for the fissile material to be utilized for either civil or military means, the original uranium source must go through a series of industrial processes that are encompassed in the nuclear fuel cycle. The process by which uranium is prepared for nuclear reactor use is called the "front end" of the fuel cycle and includes mining, milling, conversion, enrichment, and fuel fabrication. The "back end" of the fuel cycle consists of the steps taken with the spent fuel—uranium that has already been used in a nuclear reactor. These stages include storage, reprocessing, recycling, and disposal.

The front end of the fuel cycle begins with the exploration process, which is the search for natural uranium ore deposits that, once found, are mined and prospected. Next, milling extracts the uranium from the ore, refines it, and then purifies it. Eventually, this uranium ore concentrate is converted into a solid form called uranium oxide (U_3O_8), often referred to as "yellow cake."

At this point a country has two choices. It can convert the yellow cake into a gas called uranium hexafluoride (UF_6) for the purpose of uranium enrichment, which is the process that separates U-238 from U-235 in order to increase the proportion of the latter isotope. Or, that same solid can be used to make natural uranium fuel rods that are then fed into a reactor. The type of reactor determines which fuel is the appropriate choice.

If a country chooses the first option, the UF_6 is then enriched to varying degrees. It is important to note that gas must be highly purified for it to undergo the process. Low-enriched uranium (LEU) has 3–19 percent of U-235 and typically is used for peaceful nuclear energy purposes. HEU has 20 percent or more of U-235; an enrichment level of 20 percent or less is common for research reactors. Uranium enriched above 90 percent is weapons grade.[26]

Although there are numerous technologies used for enrichment, all are highly involved and complex. Gaseous diffusion, gas centrifuge, aerodynamic separation, electromagnetic isotope separation (EMIS), and laser isotope separation (LIS) are all feasible options. If a country wants large quantities of enriched uranium, the first three are the most commonly used methods. Of these, gas centrifuge enrichment is the most cost- and energy-efficient, but also one of the more complex because it requires specialized equipment, metallurgy, precision-engineering, and a highly sterile and stable environment. While the other enrichment methods have been tried, they have proven to be either too expensive or too inefficient.

Thus, if a country decides that it needs HEU, it must choose one of these enrichment methods—but even so, the beginning stages are the most difficult. The most energy, time, and money are spent in the first stage—increasing the U-235 from 0.07 percent in uranium's natural state to 3–4 percent. After that initial hurdle, the next stage, from 4–19 percent (LEU), becomes relatively easy.

Reaching 20 percent enrichment or beyond is then a matter of time and intention. Therefore, any country that can produce LEU is usually considered to be on the threshold of producing weapons-grade uranium in a matter of days or weeks, depending on the technology used.

As with natural uranium, the enriched UF6 is converted into uranium dioxide (UO2) powder. This powder can either be made into pellets for nuclear reactor fuel rods or be formed into the core of a nuclear weapon. To fabricate the fuel rods, the pellets are inserted into thin tubes, usually made of alloys, ceramics, zirconium alloy (zircalloy), stainless steel, and aluminum cladding. The rods are then sealed and assembled in clusters to be used in a nuclear reactor, such as a heavy or light water power reactor.[27] After fueling the reactor for several months to three years, depending on the type of reactor and fuel, the rods are removed and replaced with fresh fuel. The removed fuel, called "spent fuel," is then placed into a water pond to cool.

In the back end, the cooled spent fuel undergoes a chemical process, known as "reprocessing," to collect the by-products of the fuel cycle: Pu-239 created from decayed uranium isotopes, as well as any remaining uranium. First the fuel rods are dismantled and chopped up, and then the plutonium and uranium are separated from other impurities and products via a solvent, most often tributyl phosphate. Pu-239 is the most usable fissile material for a nuclear weapon, but the amount of Pu-239 needed to ensure its proper fission (at least 93 percent) is difficult to attain, given that there is only 1 percent of plutonium in any given batch of spent fuel.[28] Finally, the extracted Pu-239 is converted into a solid to be used for more fuel rods or diverted to a military program for use in a nuclear weapon. This illustrates the fine line between the uses of fissile material for peaceful and military purposes.

Needless to say, mastering the nuclear fuel cycle is no small feat—and these are only some of the challenges that Pakistani scientists in the 1970s would face in the decades to come. It was one thing to make predictions rhetorically for nuclear weapons production, but it was another to overcome not only the numerous technical challenges but also the political and economic difficulties ahead.

Foundations of a Nuclear Program

The PAEC's primary task was to assess Pakistan's capacity for the ambitious program. At the time, Pakistan had a basic nuclear infrastructure comprising the Pakistan Institute of Nuclear Science and Technology (PINSTECH), the 137-MW Karachi Nuclear Power Plant, and the Atomic Energy Mineral Centre in Lahore. This infrastructure allowed Pakistan to mine uranium ore, mill it, and convert it into yellow cake—only the beginning stages of the fuel cycle.

Two months after the scientific conference at Multan, Munir Ahmad Khan presented a plan to President Bhutto for approval.[29] As Munir Khan recalled, the plan "envisaged complete control of the nuclear fuel cycle, and building numerous plants and facilities for the generation and application of nuclear know-how."[30] As Munir Khan recalled in a speech, "Once the decision had been taken to build the bomb, we started looking at both routes," meaning plutonium and highly enriched uranium.[31] The PAEC's plan included building the facilities and expertise that would make possible progress in both directions— nuclear weapons and nuclear energy.[32]

Faced with the challenge of developing both ends of the fuel cycle simultaneously, Pakistan had no choice but to seek assistance from abroad. In 1970 the NPT was enforced, and a nascent international nonproliferation regime—comprising the NPT, IAEA safeguards, and export control agreements—had begun taking shape. The international community was greatly concerned about the misuse of nuclear technologies and thus, any country seeking them would need to sign the NPT and abide by stringent IAEA safeguards. By 1975, the industrialized countries, led by the United States, had set up the LSG (later known as the Nuclear Suppliers Group), which prevented the transfer and export of all nuclear materials, technology, and facilities to those countries that had not signed on to the new nonproliferation standards.[33]

Given this strict international environment, Bhutto approved the PAEC's plan within two hours of receiving it, but with two major directives. Bhutto turned to Finance Minister Mubashir Hasan, and said, "I hereby abolish all the several committees dealing with Atomic Energy in various Ministries. You give [Munir] the money as he puts in a request."[34] Munir tasked Dr. Muhammad Yunus Khan, head of the PAEC's Directorate of Nuclear Fuels and Materials, with the planning and launching of nuclear fuel cycle projects. The directives addressed foreign suppliers. First, no foreign contract on the construction of a nuclear power plant could include any clause inhibiting Pakistan's own scientists from constructing or reproducing a similar plant indigenously.[35] Also, the country could not allow external financing to become hostage to the international nonproliferation regime, a certainty if Pakistan initiated a program without safeguards.[36]

Pakistan was steering a risky course. As a non-NPT member, the country was aiming to acquire nuclear weapons with foreign technological and financial assistance while refusing to become an NPT signatory. Moreover, the Pakistani leadership wanted the rights to copy technological designs for its indigenous program without incurring penalties and while remaining on the "good side" of the international system.

Yunis Khan and Munir decided on a two-pronged strategy: acquire the necessary plants, facilities, and equipment from foreign supplier countries while developing parallel indigenous facilities outside safeguards. Dr. Ishfaq Ahmad and many PAEC scientists told the author that the PAEC did not see this approach as abusing foreign contracts. Pakistan's policy was to abide by legal contracts with its foreign suppliers and remain in good standing with the IAEA and international partners. In Ishfaq's view, it was the nation's right to use its experience and knowledge gained abroad as it saw fit for its national interests.[37] There existed no plan to misuse the spent fuel from any foreign-supplied reactors or to divert it from a safeguarded reactor to a military program; rather, the aim was to obtain experience and use the "know-how gained from this cooperation to indigenously produce parallel capabilities that could yield a bomb."[38] This strategy was identical to the one adopted by India during its participation in the U.S. Atoms for Peace program.[39] Conceptually, it remains the foundation of Pakistan's policy and a principal reason for the country's refusal to join the NPT.[40]

Pakistan entered into several agreements with supplier countries for the acquisition of fuel cycle facilities, such as a nuclear fuel fabrication plant, a heavy water reactor, and a nuclear fuel reprocessing plant, all under IAEA safeguards.[41] In 1973, Pakistan negotiated the purchase of a nuclear fuel fabrication plant for the Karachi Nuclear Power Plant (KANUPP) from Canada, but Canada stopped the transfer at the last minute, even though it was already in port, ready to be shipped.[42]

Pakistan then entered into an agreement with West Germany for the supply of a heavy water production plant for KANUPP, but this agreement was also canceled after the formation of the LSG.[43] Ishfaq recalls of the West Germans, "They also promised, but never delivered."[44] It was clear to the Pakistanis that Western countries were reneging on their contracts under pressure from the United States as well as the tightening nonproliferation regime.

In its quest for a reprocessing plant from the French, to be discussed later, Pakistan had to justify its desire for a nuclear energy program. Thus the

PAEC initiated a joint study with the IAEA to determine Pakistan's nuclear power requirements, and the resulting report made a strong case for nuclear energy.[45] A twenty-five year plan for the construction of twenty-four nuclear power reactors in an integrated nuclear complex that would yield a capacity of 5,000–6,000 MW of electricity was born out of this study.[46] The PAEC had immediate plans to build eight nuclear power plants in the coming years in order to provide the technical and economic rationale for the reprocessing plant.[47] As part of the larger scheme, in the first twelve years, four large projects were to be launched.

However, the grand plans for Pakistan's nuclear energy program gradually became deeply affected by the emerging international nonproliferation regime, specifically the LSG, as well as the tense international atmosphere after the Indian test. With Jimmy Carter's arrival in the White House, the United States began to rethink Atoms for Peace, and all civilian nuclear cooperation with Third World countries, especially Pakistan, was viewed with suspicion. European supplier states followed suit, leading to what effectively amounted to an international embargo on nuclear power cooperation. But even with all of these nuclear sanctions and nonproliferation barriers, the PAEC was able to establish major institutions and installations that would help complete the front end of the fuel cycle within five years of the scientists' meeting at Multan.

The Commissioning of KANUPP

As groundwork projects continued, the PAEC commenced the second stage of PINSTECH's development by adding new laboratories and divisions.[48] These included the Radioisotope and Applications Division in 1972, the Nuclear Materials Division in 1973, and later the Nuclear Chemistry Division, the Nuclear Engineering Division, the Solid State Nuclear Track Detectors Lab, and the Computer Division.[49] By the mid-1970s, the scientific community was determined to achieve self-reliance in all areas of nuclear science and technology, and PINSTECH became the main research and design center for the PAEC's nuclear fuel cycle.[50]

Anticipating that Pakistan could not indefinitely depend on foreign supplies of nuclear fuel for KANUPP, PINSTECH initiated an indigenous program for the production of uranium oxide fuel in 1973.[51] Not until two years after the Canadians cut off fuel supplies was the first fuel bundle for KANUPP produced.[52] The Canadian's supply cut-off shocked the PAEC at the time, but the scientists accepted the challenge to produce indigenously. Consequently, as several PAEC scientists told the author, this setback became a blessing in the long run.[53]

To accommodate the expanding projects, both classified and unclassified, the PAEC reorganized itself and created a new division called the Directorate of Technical Development (DTD). The DTD procured diagnostic equipment and precision machines that would later build explosive lenses (see Chapter 9).

The commissioning (start-up) of KANUPP had been particularly difficult for PAEC after East Pakistan separated from West Pakistan. The organization lost nearly half of its trained labor force from the region and was left with fewer than three hundred personnel.[54] Several East Pakistani scientists and technicians were then serving on various projects in West Pakistan; many wanted to stay in their jobs in new Pakistan. Sultan Bashiruddin Mahmood recalls that in the aftermath of the 1971 war, Bengali scientists in general were distrusted, but especially at KANUPP, where they were often pushed aside. "The environment was such that even if some had wanted to stay, they were left with little choice but to leave," he said.[55] Even the Canadians working on KANUPP's final stages were forced to leave after the Indian naval boat attacks on Karachi during the war, and many of them never returned.[56] Indeed, the PAEC had a large void to fill. And as mentioned above, a few years later the newly declared minorities—the Ahmadis—were pulled away from the classified program. These self-inflicted wounds only compounded the technical challenges ahead.

Thus KANUPP became a symbol for the PAEC's successes and failures. More was at stake as the electricity supply to Pakistan's largest metropolis, Karachi, was dependent on KANUPP's successful commissioning. Recalling the anguish of the time, Sultan Bashiruddin Mahmood said, "KANUPP was in a crisis situation, and if the leadership had not responded to the situation appropriately, it could have been a failed power station. Munir Khan through his contacts in the IAEA and diplomatic skills brought back some Canadians to the KANUPP plant, but not for long."[57]

To alleviate KANUPP's acute shortage, the PAEC initiated a new training program at the Karachi Nuclear Power Training Centre (KNPTC). This center became the main training ground for current and future generations of nuclear power plant engineers and technicians.[58]

Inaugurating KANUPP

The PAEC's efforts bore fruit as President Zulfiqar Ali Bhutto finally inaugurated KANUPP on November 28, 1972, announced his nuclear policy, and reaf-

firmed his commitment to nuclear development. He remarked, "The inauguration of KANUPP is a historic occasion for Pakistan. It symbolizes our people's
determination to keep pace with modern technology. We want to be part of this
nuclear age and in harmony with the march of time. We believe that in order to
accelerate the economic and social development of Pakistan, to overcome the
poverty of our people, we must use the latest technology and techniques available to the modern epoch. Nuclear energy fits into this pattern. I will remember
the struggle we had to go through to get KANUPP sanctioned and to launch
other atomic energy activities in the country. The powerful vested interests opposed it. If they had their way, we would not be inaugurating this nuclear plant
today."[59]

President Bhutto then addressed the significance of nuclear technology and,
turning to Munir Ahmad Khan, stated, "[S]oon after assuming this office, I not
only placed the Atomic Energy Commission under my direct control but also
asked you [Munir Khan] to return to the country and serve the nation." Encouraging PAEC workers, he continued, "I want this program implemented in
the speediest manner. I believe that Pakistan's survival lies in using nuclear research, nuclear technology, and nuclear power for the betterment of its people.
The government will give the fullest support to the PAEC, and this country will
make the necessary resources available to bring the promise of atomic energy to
the people of Pakistan at the earliest possible time. I want first class science in
Pakistan because nothing less is acceptable. And I wish Pakistan to be increasingly self-reliant in all aspects of technology."[60]

Bhutto was aware that his audience was not solely domestic. He announced,
"Pakistan believes in using atomic energy for peaceful purposes and as an instrument for development and progress. We have placed our nuclear facilities
under international safeguards of the IAEA. We would like to see other countries in our region do the same." Next he echoed a phrase from Eisenhower's
famous Atoms for Peace speech at the United Nations by declaring, "[T]he most
menacing problem in the sub-continent is that of poverty and misery of its
peoples. Atomic energy should become a symbol of *hope* rather than *fear*. For
this reason, we should welcome if this entire sub-continent by the agreement of
the countries concerned could be declared to be a Nuclear Weapon Free Zone
and the introduction of nuclear weapons be banned the same way as the Latin
American countries have done."[61]

Soon after the commissioning, KANUPP faced another major technical
challenge when heavy water leaks were reported. KANUPP is a CANDU-type

reactor that uses heavy water as both a moderator and coolant. Canada was also supplying heavy water for it, but at the high prices. Pakistan could not afford persistent heavy water leakages. With no available foreign assistance, KANUPP'S principal engineer, Sultan Bashiruddin Mahmood, designed a device that could detect heavy water leaks in CANDU-type reactors. He later patented it as the "SBM-Probe," proudly using his own initials for its name.[62]

For Pakistani scientists, overcoming KANUPP's initial problems on their own was considered a major accomplishment. As Dr. Ishfaq Ahmad recalls, the "buzzword within the PAEC then was a Punjabi word, *joogaardh*, meaning to innovate or improvise . . . . [We] could pick up pieces of junk and put them together and make it work." He explained that because of technological limitations, "Pakistan did not look for fancy things. If we needed a belt for the starter, and didn't have one, we substituted with a bicycle chain." Ishfaq went on, "This did not mean that we encouraged people to be unsafe, but emphasized that ultimately the scientists must deliver." In Ishfaq's words, PAEC culture taught, "Don't demand we need this or that—but find a *joogaardh* and improvise if you can."[63]

Given the difficulties, it was natural to approach China for assistance, though Chinese scientists had never been exposed to a Western power reactor. With Beijing under Coordinating Committee for Multilateral Export Control (COCOM) restrictions throughout the Cold War, the Chinese welcomed exposure to the Canadian power reactor at Karachi. The Chinese scientists and technicians justified working on KANUPP outside of the export control restrictions by reasoning that any know-how gained on nuclear safety from the IAEA safeguarded facility was within the realm of legality. The interaction with the Chinese helped Pakistani nuclear scientists learn reverse engineering techniques, just as Pakistani-Chinese cooperation in military equipment had been of assistance earlier.[64] There are no records available on the technical details or the type of help the Chinese provided that led to the proper functioning of KANUPP. However, new engineering techniques, coupled with *joogaardh*, reverse engineering, and technical boosts from the Chinese together provided a way out of Western sanctions.

Throughout 1973, the team of nuclear engineers working at KANUPP conducted detailed studies on the feasibility of building an indigenous, safeguards-free nuclear reactor, based on another Canadian design, the NRX-type reactor. But acute shortages of trained technical expertise in the PAEC forced the project to be shelved. The project would restart in the mid-1980s in the form of the Khushab heavy water reactor project (see Chapter 10).[65]

While work to commission KANUPP went on, Munir Ahmad Khan informed Sultan Bashiruddin Mahmood that there would be a secret team, headed by Dr. Sardar Ali Khan, to work on replicating India's CIRUS reactor at Trombay. The team included Sultan Bashiruddin Mahmood, Dr. Pervez Butt (who would later become PAEC chairman from 2001 to 2005), and seven other junior engineers. Mahmood claims that after only eight months of hard work, preliminary designs were presented to Munir.[66] Later in 1984, Pervez Butt recalled in an interview with the author, "[O]ur team worked tirelessly, I did the mechanical part, Samar Mubarakmand did the electronic part, and Shabbir did the chemical portions. When we merged our work and presented, Munir Khan could not believe it."[67]

It is important to note that KANUPP and India's CIRUS reactor were fundamentally different.[68] As Sultan Bashiruddin explained to the author, KANUPP uses uranium oxide fuel, whereas CIRUS uses uranium metal fuel. In the case of the former, spent oxide fuel has so many impurities that quality plutonium cannot be extracted from it through normal reprocessing. Thus, metal fuel is the preferred option for a nuclear weapons program. Sultan Bashiruddin Mahmood explained, "It is a myth to believe that KANUPP's spent fuel could have been diverted to extract plutonium, even if IAEA safeguards were bypassed. Munir Khan's secret instructions to his scientists were to 'work on a design identical to the Indian CIRUS reactor.'"[69] Munir was not directly violating any international contracts by copying the design and building a similar reactor under a classified program. Reflective of a growing culture of defiance and anger at the West, one PAEC scientist told the author, "[S]eeking knowledge and technological advancement was not the exclusive domain of the West. They [the West] believe it is a matter of entitlement, privilege and exclusive domain. The developing world must be kept deprived from seeking knowledge and technological advancement. After centuries of exploitation, suppression and colonizing, they feel offended if we get the knowledge and utilize that experience for our motherland. This has nothing to do with the spread of nuclear technology but is a racist and apartheid attitude."[70]

Financing the Program

Prime Minister Bhutto's primary challenge was to raise the necessary finances to fund the nuclear program, which could only be accomplished with the help of friendly countries. To this end, soon after the Multan Conference of January 1972, Bhutto embarked on a tour of Muslim states in the Arab World and the Middle East. These countries included Iran, Saudi Arabia, the United Arab Emirates, Turkey, Syria, Morocco, Egypt, Algeria, Tunisia, and Libya. The trip was aimed at rehabilitating the country's status and image in the Muslim world and introducing a "new Pakistan." During this time, Bhutto also visited the People's Republic of China, where he met Chairman Mao Zedong.[71] In his visits, Bhutto criticized Western hypocrisy and lamented the West's betrayal of Pakistan, despite the country's loyal membership in the Western military alliances, the Central Treaty Organization (CENTO) and the South East Asian Treaty Organization (SEATO).[72]

Bhutto's most significant visit was to Libya, where he struck up a personal friendship with Colonel Muammar Gaddafi and possibly discussed nuclear cooperation.[73] Libyan and Pakistani officials then met in Paris as early as 1973 to discuss the terms and conditions of nuclear cooperation and financial aid to Pakistan, all under the direction of the two countries' leaders.[74] Ongoing negotiations for a reprocessing plant contract between Pakistan and France made a meeting between Libyans and Pakistanis more feasible.[75]

Estimates of Libya's financial assistance to Pakistan's nuclear program vary from $100 to $500 million. According to one estimate, Libyan loans and investments totaled $133 million in 1979 alone.[76] Libya's assistance apparently involved the diversion of up to 450 tons of yellow cake, acquired from Niger, to Pakistan between 1976 and 1982. Also, Libya controlled significant uranium deposits in the Ouzo Strip in Chad in 1973, which may have also added to its contributions.

In a quid pro quo arrangement, Libya had hoped to gain full access to Pakistan's nuclear program in return for its uranium and financial assistance but was not successful. Pakistan did, however, agree to train Libyan nuclear scientists at PINSTECH, in return for approximately $100 million. One Western publication alleges that Pakistan International Airlines (PIA) planes were involved in bringing cash from Libya, as much as $100 million per flight, so that these financial transactions would not show up in Pakistan's official books.[77] Bhutto even renamed the new Lahore cricket stadium Gaddafi Stadium in honor of the Libyan leader.[78]

Generally, during the Bhutto years Pakistan's relations with Libya remained close, although they began to wane during the presidency of his successor, Zia ul-Haq.[79]

In February 1974, leaders of thirty-seven Islamic nations gathered for an Islamic Summit Conference in Lahore that was chaired by the host, Z. A. Bhutto.

At this conference, Bhutto called for a new spirit of Islamic unity: "Israel had gorged and fattened on the West's sympathies, nurtured itself on violence and expanded through aggression. But now with the oil weapon and a new military strength, the balance was shifting. This may well be a watershed in history. We are emerging today out of nearly half a millennium of decline. It is time that we translate the sentiments of Islamic unity into concrete measures of cooperation and mutual benefit."[80]

Z. A. Bhutto's diplomatic skill in harnessing the support of other Muslim states brought in "Moslem oil money."[81] In a December 1974 interview, he revealed that Iran and the Arab countries had given Pakistan some $450 million in loans, which he described as "just the beginning."[82] Soon after that, on February 15, 1975, Bhutto approved that same amount in loans for fuel cycle facilities, including a centrifuge plant for the enrichment of uranium, a uranium mine at Baghalchor in Dera Ghazi Khan (BC-1), and the Chemical Production Complex (CPC) in DG Khan. Some funding was also sent to the Wah Group, where a theoretical physics team was working on nuclear weapons design.[83] However, pan-Islamic support for the nuclear program would end in 1979 with the overthrow of the shah in Iran and the downfall of Bhutto through a coup d'etat by Zia ul-Haq, resulting in Bhutto's execution.

Uranium Prospecting and Exploration

Jumpstarting the front end of an indigenous nuclear fuel cycle would prove to be problematic, not only because of the restrictions imposed by the nonproliferation regime but also because of the simultaneous back-end objectives. Even so, the PAEC would boast of three major achievements in the initial years that would free them from foreign supplies: locating and processing indigenous uranium, fabricating nuclear fuel, and producing uranium hexafluoride gas.

The PAEC's first task was to find uranium ore deposits and convert them into pure oxide gas and metal.[84] At the time, the Lahore Atomic Energy Minerals Center (AEMC) had little experience in mining on an industrial scale. Skilled labor was scarce, and the drillers and miners trained were "among an illiterate labor force" available in the region.[85]

In 1959, the PAEC discovered radioactivity in the Swalik Mountain Range in Dera Ghazi Khan (DG Khan) in South Punjab, and geological surveys confirmed accessible deposits of uranium.[86] Drilling commenced in a one-hundred-kilometer belt in the areas of Rakhi, Baghalchur, and Rajanpur throughout 1963.[87] In 1970, headed by Ishfaq Ahmad, scientists and engineers of AEMC designed and built a pilot plant with a capacity of ten thousand pounds per day for the concentration of mined uranium ore. The pilot plant was designed and fabricated by Muhammad Shabbir.[88] However, formal announcement of the uranium discovery and the pilot plant was made much later, on December 27, 1973.[89]

Uranium exploration efforts continued after Bhutto and into Zia ul-Haq's era, well into the 1980s. As geological mapping, radiometric measurements, drilling, and subsurface excavations improved, more deposits of uranium ore were revealed at Thatti Nasratti and Isa Khel. These areas were said to possess three zones of uranium ore below the surface.[90] A further uranium survey of sixty thousand km discovered significant reserves of uranium ore in the Tharparkar desert in the Sindh province, in NWFP between Mansehra and Thakot, and in the Sonmiani range indicating the presence of four megatons (Mt) of heavy minerals, most importantly uranium. Regions bearing this valuable radioactive element were also discovered in the Eastern Potohar region, on both sides of the Indus River.[91] As illustrated by the extensive milling projects, Pakistan appeared blessed with many natural deposits.

In the late 1980s, the Zia ul-Haq government allocated a sum of $1.5 million for a nuclear mineral survey and another $4.5 million for an ongoing uranium exploration project in Dera Ghazi Khan. Another milestone in uranium exploration was achieved in 1987 when the Solid State Nuclear Track Detection Laboratory of PINSTECH fabricated Chromium kF39, which is a valuable substance used in uranium exploration. The following year, PINSTECH developed an innovative technique called "in-situ leaching," which allows for the extraction of metals from uranium ore without the need for conventional mining.[92]

Uranium Mining, Milling, and Refining

But the shine of the initial discoveries soon tarnished. The uranium deposits found in Baghalchor, near Dera Ghazi Khan in southern Punjab, were of low quality. The ores consisted of only a few kilograms of uranium per ton—compared with the much higher concentration of uranium Pakistan was receiving from Canada. One can imagine the disappointment. In addition, Western countries denied Pakistan the equipment needed to mill and refine the uranium. Eager to overcome this challenge, Pakistan found two alternative sources in Africa—Niger and Libya. In the late 1970s Pakistan acquired 110 to 150 tons of yellow cake from Niger, which was shipped in parts through Libya, Benin, and France. Pakistani scientists assert that this was not a clandestine sale, but was made under the supervision and knowledge of the IAEA and the French Atomic Energy Commission. Pakistan had also pledged to place that shipment of uranium, intended for KANUPP fuel, under IAEA safeguards.[93]

In addition, between 1978 and 1980, Libya purchased about 1,000 tons of yellow cake from Niger, which was not under any IAEA supervision, and then transferred up to 450 tons of that purchase to Pakistan.[94] The yellow cake received from Nigeria and Libya was eventually used as feedstock for the production of UF6.[95]

In addition to the newly found African assistance, the PAEC wanted to bolster its own domestic capabilities and began to create an indigenous design for a uranium extraction plant. In a little over a year, AEMC, Lahore, assisted by other industries within the country, completed the plant. Pakistan was no longer dependent on external supplies for that stage of the fuel cycle.[96] Muhammad Shabbir, who would be in charge of the CPC, said, "PAEC started refining uranium where the Canadians and Australians stopped."[97]

Pakistan then established the Baghalchor (BC-1) facility, which consisted of an ore storage mill, a ball-grinding mill, a sulfuric acid plant, a solvent extraction plant, and a tunnel drier. Except for the ball grinding mills that were imported from the United States, all the other units of the uranium refining plant were manufactured in Pakistan.[98] Sultan Bashiruddin Mahmood was assigned the task of expanding BC-1's capacity, which he claims to have expanded to four times its original capacity.[99] A decade later, in November 1986, PAEC held an exhibition, "Atoms for Development Exhibition—1986," which highlighted its achievements in discovering uranium and refining it at the uranium mill at DG Khan—entirely through indigenous efforts.[100]

Nuclear Fuel Fabrication

After India's nuclear test, Canada abruptly shifted its nuclear cooperation policies and insisted that all customer states must sign the NPT and open all their facilities to safeguards. On December 23, 1976, the supply of nuclear fuel, heavy water, spare parts, and technical support to KANUPP was cut off. Therefore, Pakistan had to develop an indigenous nuclear fuel capability and achieve self-reliance in this critical aspect of the nuclear fuel cycle.[101] Having intensified uranium exploration and extraction and yellow cake production, the PAEC set up a uranium refining plant to obtain pure UF6 that could then be manufactured into fuel for KANUPP.[102]

On the banks of the mighty River Indus, at Kundian, near Chashma, Pakistani scientists planned to construct a nuclear fuel fabrication facility. As in the case of mining and exploration, they possessed little knowledge about the exact measurements, critical materials, and machinery. The personnel at PINSTECH boasted only a very basic familiarity with the entire process; so it was no surprise that left without foreign support, Pakistan faced many more challenges.

One of the first steps was to find a critical material, zircalloy, required to manufacture the tubes in which uranium oxide pellets would be placed in order to fuel a reactor. Exploration discovered sand on the beaches of Baluchistan to contain heavy amounts of zirconium. PINSTECH scientists then established a pilot plant, the Kundian Nuclear Fuel Complex (KNFC), to separate other elements in the sand to obtain pure zirconium.

The commissioning of KNFC, with an annual processing capacity of twenty-four Mt of natural uranium oxide into fuel, provided the PAEC with more boasting rights in the face of Western technological denials. Built indigenously, there was no obligation to place it under IAEA safeguards. Currently, KNFC manufactures fifteen hundred fuel bundles for KANUPP and includes a small zirconium oxide and zircaloy-4 production plant.[103] Yet another achievement—the completion of a nuclear fuel manufacturing plant at Chashma—was announced on August 31, 1980. The indigenous fuel from KNFC and Chashma saved Pakistan $40 million every year. In the ten years that KANUPP was loaded with Pakistani fuel bundles, not a single fuel pellet failed.[104] Many years later a proud PAEC chairman claimed, "Pakistan produced the first ton of purified uranium oxide and metal before it produced the first ton of copper or any other mineral using local ore and indigenously developed technologies."[105]

Uranium Conversion: The Chemical Production Complex

As mentioned earlier, a critical element of the "front end" is the production of UF6. UF6 is enriched through ultrahigh revolutions of thousands of gas-centrifuge machines arranged together in what is known as *cascades*—many centrifuges hooked together. One PAEC scientist characterized the production of UF6 gas as a long, intricate process that uses hazardous, toxic, and radioactive materials.[106]

For Pakistan, acquiring a foreign supply of uranium hexafluoride was next to impossible, and even if it were available, attempts to acquire it would reveal the secret centrifuge project pursued in the late 1970s. As with the other facilities, Islamabad had no other choice but to build its own UF6 production center, and scientists were again faced with mastering a complex and unfamiliar technology in a relatively short period of time.[107]

In 1975–76, PAEC began work on the CPC, colocated with the aforementioned Baghalchur-I uranium mining and milling facility, in the Southern Punjab province. Apart from security considerations, this area was selected because of the abundance of natural uranium ore. "At least half the steps leading to the development of a nuclear device were completed and mastered in the two PAEC facilities located at BC-1 and the CPC."[108] The CPC produced two products: uranium dioxide for KANUPP and uranium hexafluoride for the centrifuge program in Kahuta.[109] Reportedly, the current estimated annual production capacity of CPC is two hundred tons of UF6.[110]

The PAEC team at CPC consisted primarily of four people: Dr. Muhammad Yunus (supervisor), Dr. Muhammad Shabbir (also director of Fuels and Materials, PAEC), Dr. Aminuddin Ahmed, and Dr. N. A. Javed. The CPC was considered a huge leap in nuclear development. In the words of Munir Khan, it is "small by international standards, but unique in the world, because it receives ore and sand and rocks, and ships out pure finished products of uranium, zirconium and other materials I don't want to name at this point. Like PINSTECH, it is also the pride of Pakistan . . . . The CPC perhaps remained one of the best kept secrets of Pakistan's nuclear program, not only from the prying eyes of the satellites but also intelligence agencies on the ground, the international media and miraculously from the people of DG Khan itself."[111] The CPC was indeed kept under a closed door, as it had its own landing strip and not even the Punjab province government knew of its existence.[112]

By 1980, the Kundian Nuclear Fuel Complex, the Baghalchur-I facility, and the Chemical Production Complex were ready and producing sufficient amounts of high-purity yellow cake, uranium hexafluoride gas, uranium metal, uranium oxide, and nuclear fuel for KANUPP.[113] In the meantime, as Chapter 7 will explain, Pakistan was proceeding apace to master the enrichment process through gas centrifuge methods at Kahuta.

The technical barriers and sanctions imposed by the nonproliferation regime in the 1970s did not stop Pakistan from pursuing its nuclear ambitions. Diplomatically there was little hope that the world would understand Pakistan's point of view or accept its actions as a necessary response after India conducted a nuclear test in 1974. Each of the PAEC's small achievements bred a larger culture of defiance, as scientists overcame political and technical obstacles in pursuit of their goals. Although the entire program was kept a secret, professionals recognized and idolized the great minds in their field. N. M. Butt, former director general of PINSTECH, sums up the impact:

> The embargo alerted the nuclear scientists and engineers of Pakistan and they adopted the strategy of using their own expertise and skills to make things indigenously, which were previously purchased from the Western suppliers. The embargo by the West was therefore beneficial for developing in-house R&D in all high technology branches of nuclear technology. The fuel fabrication technology gave the scientists and engineers a confidence to acquire further expertise in the area of nuclear technology. So the embargo policy of the West in fact made Pakistan more nuclear capable rather than hindering its capability.[114]

India's "Peaceful Nuclear Explosion"

At 8:05 a.m. on the morning of May 18, 1974, India carried out its first test of a nuclear device at the Pokhran test site, in the Rajasthan desert, approximately fifty miles from the Pakistani border. Soon after the test, the chairman of the India Atomic Energy Commission, Homi Sethna, called Prime Minister Indira Gandhi's office and told her principal secretary, P. N. Dhar, "The Buddha is smiling."[115] Soon afterward, the All-India Radio interrupted its regular transmission and aired a special announcement, "At 8:05 a.m. this morning, India successfully conducted an underground nuclear explosion for peaceful purposes at a carefully chosen site in western India."[116] India had gone nuclear by exploding a device with a yield of about ten kilotons (kt).[117]

On the day of the test, Chairman Munir Ahmad Khan and Ishfaq Ahmad were attending a meeting at the University of Peshawar. During the seminar, Vice-Chancellor Ali Khan handed a small note to Munir. After reading the note, Munir whispered to Ishfaq, *Mai pai gaye hai* ["The old lady (Indira Gandhi) has shown her prowess"]. The same note asked Munir to immediately call the prime minister. Bhutto exploded in anger. "Why are you sitting in Peshawar?" Bhutto went on, "You didn't inform me that the Indians had exploded a device. We heard it over the BBC." Munir canceled a scheduled press conference with the remark that "you cannot expect me to be talking about onions and tomatoes when India has just exploded a nuclear device close to Pakistan's border."[118] Munir and Ishfaq rushed back to Islamabad. The next day Munir met the prime minister, and later told Ishfaq, "Bhutto was very upset, very annoyed." He questioned Munir about why he didn't know that India was testing a bomb. Munir had little explanation.

The Pakistani seismic stations at the time were not adequate to detect such tests promptly. Consequently, Bhutto directed the PAEC to build its own monitoring system to detect nuclear explosions, which was later placed in the Seismology Department. Within months of India's test, Ishfaq was made a member of the PAEC, entrusted to oversee the classified nuclear program and begin searching for an appropriate Pakistani test site. In September 1974, Ishfaq selected the Chagai site for Pakistan's future nuclear testing. Two years later, Brigadier Sarfaraz, then serving as chief of staff in the Quetta corps, received orders from General Headquarters (GHQ) to provide helicopters and other services to Dr. Ishfaq Ahmad and Dr. Ahsan Mubarak for a secret reconnaissance mission of a nuclear site. In 1976 an organization called Special Development Works (SDW) was created that would work directly under the Chief of the Army Staff (COAS). Brigadier Muhammad Sarfaraz headed this organization; for the next six years, he would work closely with Ishfaq Ahmed and his team to secretly prepare the test site in Baluchistan.

Even though Pakistan had no nuclear device, or even any fissile material at that time, preparations for a nuclear test were already underway. The rush may have been one of Munir's efforts to placate Prime Minister Bhutto's growing restlessness, or perhaps it truly was Bhutto's deadline for Munir to conduct a test.

The Mughals Next Door: Bhutto's Immediate Reactions

The day after the Indian test on May 19, 1974, Bhutto called a press conference at the Governor's House, Lahore, to announce Pakistan's response to what was perceived as a qualitative new threat. He stated, "There is no need to be alarmed over India's nuclear demonstration. It would indicate that we have already succumbed to the threat. This would be disastrous for our national determination and to maintain the fullness of our independence. Let me make it clear that we are determined not to be intimidated by this threat. I give a solemn pledge to all our countrymen that we will never let Pakistan be a victim of nuclear blackmail. This means not only that we will never surrender our rights or claims because of India's nuclear status, but also that we will not be deflected from our policies by this fateful development. In concrete terms, we will not compromise the right of self-determination of the people of Jammu and Kashmir. Nor will we accept Indian hegemony or domination over the Sub-continent."[119]

Three days later, on May 22, 1974, Indira Gandhi wrote a letter to Bhutto: "We remain fully committed of our traditional policy of developing nuclear energy entirely for peaceful purposes. The recent underground nuclear experiment conducted by our scientists in no way alters this policy. There are no political or foreign policy implications of this test. We remain committed to settle all our differences with Pakistan peacefully through bilateral negotiations in accordance with the Simla Agreement."[120]

Bhutto responded in turn on June 6, 1974: "It is well established that the testing of a nuclear device is no different from the detonation of a nuclear weapon. Given this indisputable fact, how is it possible for our fears to be assuaged by mere assurances, which may in any case be ignored in subsequent years? Governments change, as do national attitudes. But the acquisition of a capability, which has direct and immediate military consequences, becomes a permanent factor to be reckoned with. I need hardly recall that no non-nuclear weapon state, including India, considered mere declarations of intent as sufficient to ensure their security in the nuclear age."[121]

A few days following the letter, Munir Ahmad Khan said, "India's test had opened the floodgates for nuclear weapons and unless decisive action is taken, the membership of the nuclear club will not stop at six."[122] That same summer the U.S. ambassador to India, Patrick Moynihan, met Mrs. Gandhi. In a meeting with this author in March 2002, he recalled his conversation with the Indian prime minister. As they walked along the green lawns of the prime minister's house, Ambassador Moynihan asked Mrs. Gandhi what led her to decide to conduct the test. Receiving an unsatisfactory answer, Mr. Moynihan replied, "Madame Prime Minister, the Mughals next door are not going to sit idle. Sooner or later, you will be condemned to [be] sandwiched between two nuclear neighbors, China and Pakistan."[123]

Reaction within the Military

The Indian nuclear test was a defining moment for the Pakistani military. Until then, it had been seemingly oblivious to the implications of the nuclear ambitions in the neighborhood and ignorant of the development in India. Still reeling from the shock and defeat of the last war, the military had its hands full. It was in the process of restructuring its ranks, modifying its strategic orientation, reintegrating prisoners of war, and requesting release of soldiers left behind in Indian jails. The military had struggled with severe deficiencies and equipment losses since the war, and was grappling with the opening of the new strategic front after the Daoud-led coup in Afghanistan. After the Indian nuclear tests, Lieutenant-General Syed Refaqat summed up the sentiments within GHQ:

> The worst was to come two years after the separation of East Pakistan, when India conducted the nuclear test. Our memories echoed that when Pakistani forces had surrendered to Lt. Gen. Arora Singh in East Pakistan at Dhaka, Indian Prime Minister Indira Gandhi declared in the parliament, "Today I have wiped away the ignominy of 1,000 years from the good face of India." Now while she was in power, you have this nuclear test. We were stunned. We were baffled. We did not know what to do. I can tell you how unprepared we were for this when India conducted the test. I was a Brigadier in Kharian, about 80 miles from Islamabad. The next day I was visiting GHQ where Chief of General Staff Lt. Gen. Abbassi, considered the best intellectual mind in the army at that time, called me over. He asked me to begin the strategic and tactical implications of the Indian nuclear test. At that time the military thinking was purely in military-operational terms. We all thought in terms of primitive military ideas such as what would become of the Pakistani bridgehead were we to launch a tactical riposte against India. The army was so extremely simplistic, almost innocent, about the implications of a nuclear bomb. This showed we had no doctrine—we had not studied this subject in all seriousness, even though the army had an idea that a nuclear program was on its way. It would take some time for the army to become aware of the use of nuclear technology—you don't fire a nuclear weapon so close to your own troops or your own civilians.[124]

In October 1974, U.S. Secretary of State Henry Kissinger visited India, and with reference to the country's nuclear capability remarked, "India and the USA now shared another common tradition."[125] Kissinger reaffirmed that the United States would continue to supply nuclear fuel to India's two General Electric Tarapur reactors, despite the now-established fact that India had used the U.S.-supplied heavy water in the CIRUS reactor to produce the fuel for the nuclear bomb. The Pakistanis saw this decision as more than a double standard, as Kissinger would continue to offer carrots (and sticks) to dissuade Pakistan from doing the same.[126]

In the wake of these grave developments, Prime Minister Bhutto launched a diplomatic offensive. Writing to world leaders, he made it clear that "Pakistan was exposed to a kind of nuclear threat and blackmail unparalleled elsewhere . . . . If the world community failed to provide political insurance to Pakistan and other countries against nuclear blackmail, these countries would be constrained to launch nuclear programs of their own . . . . [A]ssurances provided by the UN Security Council were not enough."[127]

Pakistan also urged other non-nuclear states to call upon the nuclear powers and the five permanent members of the UN Security Council to extend a nuclear umbrella to those states that were under the threat of nuclear blackmail. Bhutto announced his intention to elicit strong Chinese support via a letter to Peking for bilateral nuclear cooperation. Such an agreement did in fact take place two years later, in 1976.[128]

As part of the diplomatic offensive, Pakistan formally presented a proposal in the United Nations for the establishment of a nuclear free zone in South Asia. While this proposal did receive the support of the majority of UN member states, the nuclear weapon states abstained. Therefore, it was clear to Pakistan that the world powers had accepted the new reality of a nuclear India and that "Pakistan would have to face a de facto India alone."[129] Prime Minister Bhutto realized that "Pakistan had no choice but to acquire essential nuclear technology under safeguards, if possible, without it, if necessary, in order to neutralize India's nuclear edge."[130]

Unrelenting, Pakistan brought its concerns to the IAEA Board of Governors on June 8, 1974, and stated that it did not consider the so-called peaceful Indian nuclear explosive to be any different from a nuclear weapon. At the end of the debate, one IAEA senior official told Munir Ahmad Khan, "Even though it was India which had carried out the nuclear explosion, it would be Pakistan which would be punished for that."[131] This remark would become prophecy in the years to come.

While most of the world powers expressed concern over India's nuclear test, they stopped short of condemning India. The most notable reaction came from Canada, makers of the CIRUS reactor from which India had extracted the plutonium for the device. Canada cut off all nuclear cooperation not only with India but also with Pakistan, despite the latter's having accepted IAEA safeguards in all of its bilateral agreements.[132]

Canada's actions illustrated a greater concern within the international community regarding the vulnerability of the global nonproliferation regime, and Pakistan paid the price. The aforementioned London Suppliers Group was formed at this time, in anticipation of future actions from other developing countries. This coalition effectively prevented nuclear cooperation with those countries that had not accepted full-scope safeguards and not signed the NPT.[133]

The Defense Committee of the Cabinet

Prime Minister Z. A. Bhutto called a meeting of the Defense Committee of the Cabinet (DCC) on June 15, 1974. Bhutto remarked, "The explosion has intro-

TABLE 5.1

Pakistan Nuclear Infrastructure

Function	Facility/Project	Organization	Capacity
FRONT END OF NUCLEAR FUEL CYCLE			
Uranium Processing(Mining and Refining) U308	Baghalchur-1; Nuclear Materials Complex, D. G. Khan; Issa Khel and Qabul Khel	PAEC	40 tons/yr[a]
Uranium Conversion (UO2/ UF4/UF6 Production)	Chemical Plants Complex, D. G. Khan	PAEC	200 tons/yr UF6[b]
Uranium Enrichment	Kahuta/Khan Research Laboratories	KRL	100–150 kg U-235/ 15–30,000 SWU[c]
	Chak Jhumra, Faisalabad (Under Construction)	PAEC	150–600,000 SWU[d]
Nuclear Fuel Fabrication	Kundian Nuclear Fuel Complex KNC-I	PAEC	24 MT/yr
	Pakistan Nuclear Fuel Complex (Under Construction)	PAEC	
BACK END OF NUCLEAR FUEL CYCLE			
Heavy Water Production	KCP-I, Khushab Nuclear Complex	PAEC	13 MT/yr
50 MWt Plutonium /Tritium Production Reactors	KCP-II, Khushab-1 Reactors/ Khushab Nuclear Complex	PAEC	9–12 kg Pu-239
Tritium Production Plant	Khushab Nuclear Complex	PAEC	5–10 grams/ day
Fuel Reprocessing	New Labs, PINSTECH KNC-2 Chashma Reprocessing Plant	PAEC	20–40 tHM/ yr 100 tHM/yr
NUCLEAR WEAPONS COMPLEX			
Trigger Mechanism	R-Labs, DTD	PAEC	
Neutron Source	Fast Neutron Physics Group, DTD	PAEC	
High Explosives	Wah Group, DTD	PAEC	
Precision Engineering/ Quality Control/High Speed Electronics	Wah Group, DTD	PAEC	
Weapon Design	Theoretical Physics Group	PAEC	
Nuclear Testing	Diagnostic Group Chaghi/Kharan/Kirana Hills	PAEC/SDW KRL[e]	
Uranium Metallurgy/ Machining of U-235 Weapon Core	Uranium Metal Lab, PINSTECH/KRL	PAEC KRL[f]	
Plutonium Metallurgy- Machining of Pu-239 Weapon Core	New Labs, PINSTECH	PAEC	
Nuclear Weapons/ Delivery Systems	National Development Complex (1990–2001)[g] NESCOM (2001 to date) nuclear power reactors	PAEC/ NESCOM	
KANUPP	Karachi	PAEC	137 MWe
CHASNUPP-1	Chashma	PAEC	325 MWe

CHASNUPP-2	Chashma	PAEC	325 MWe
CHASNUPP-3 and 4 (under construction)	Chashma	PAEC	340 MWe each
	RESEARCH REACTORS[h]		
PARR-1	PINSTECH, Nilore	PAEC	10 MWe
PARR-2	PINSTECH, Nilore	PAEC	27 Kw

[a]Uranium mining capacity is being expanded to meet the growing feedstock requirements of the plutonium as well as advancement of HEU programs.

[b]CPC is also expanding its capacities according to the Institute of Science and International Security. See http://isis-online.org/uploads/isis-reports/documents/PakistanExpandingCPC_19May2009.pdf.

[c]Some reports indicate P-3 and P-4 are already operating. With the introduction of P-3 and P-4 centrifuges, the plant capacity would likely increase to 75,000 SWU or more. The HEU annual production capacity could then be between 200–250 kg.

[d]This non-classified project, which will be under IAEA safeguards, was approved by the Pakistan's Central Development Working Party of the Pakistan's Planning Commission in July 2007. As of yet it is unclear whether or not work has commenced on the project.

[e]In March 1983 PAEC conducted first Cold tests in Kirana Hills, near Sargodha. In 1984 KRL also conducted cold tests on weapons designs. Since 1987 nuclear weapon designing and testing were the sole responsibility of PAEC, which included the 1998 tests at Chagai and Kharan.

[f]KRL is responsible for machining the U-235 Core. PAEC is responsible for machining the Pu-239 Core. Other forms of uranium metallurgy are undertaken at Uranium Metal Labs.

[g]The National Engineering and Science Commission (NESCOM) now has four organizations under its jurisdiction: National Development Complex (NDC), Air Weapons Complex (AWC), Project Management Organization (PMO), and Maritime Technology Organization.

[h]All imported power reactors are under IAEA safeguards.

duced a qualitative change in the situation between the two countries. Pakistan will not succumb to nuclear blackmail." The meeting was attended by Foreign Minister Aziz Ahmad, Foreign Secretary Mr. Agha Shahi, Finance Secretary Mr. AGN Kazi, Secretary of Defense Major-General (Ret.) Fazal-e-Muqeem Khan, the three chiefs of staff of the armed forces, Pakistan People's Party Secretary General J. A. Rahim, and Information Minister Kausar Niazi.[134] This gathering was the first formal institutional meeting to conclude that the only viable option for Pakistan was to develop a nuclear deterrent capability. From that point onward, the nuclear program had officially shifted from merely acquiring a nuclear capability to decisively pursuing weapons.[135]

During this DCC meeting Munir Khan was traveling abroad, so Member (Technical) Riazuddin attended. Bhutto sought a complete progress report on the status of the nuclear program. The meeting deliberated the difficulties and challenges of producing fissile material and creating a bomb design. Since Bhutto was pressed for time, the DCC decided that the work to obtain fissile material and to design a nuclear device would occur simultaneously.[136]

6   Punishing Pakistan

By the mid-1970s, Prime Minister Bhutto was at the peak of his power, but he was quickly losing political allies as well as the patience of his colleagues. His fascination with socialist ideals was gone; the founding members of Pakistan's People's Party (PPP) were equally disillusioned. Bhutto thought that by appeasing Islamist opponents, he could bring pragmatism to his politics and stall his plummeting popularity. Instead, this strategy led Bhutto down a slippery slope of concessions from which he never recovered.

In the spring of 1976 Bhutto handpicked a new army chief, Zia-ul-Haq, whose appointment superseded the rank of many senior generals. It is not known whom the retiring Army Chief Tikka Khan recommended as his successor, but apparently Prime Minister Zulfi Bhutto was smitten with Lieutenant-General Zia-ul-Haq's sycophancy. In particular, the impressive reception that Zia had arranged when Bhutto visited the Multan garrison in 1975 certainly must have earned him partiality. Breaking military tradition, Zia-ul-Haq, corps commander in Multan, had ordered officers and families to line up on the streets and give a rousing welcome to the beloved leader.

Bhutto's decision to appoint Zia-ul-Haq changed the fate of the country and raises several questions: Had Bhutto examined the military dossiers of all senior generals before making his final selection?[1] If so, how could Bhutto have ignored some concerning traits of Zia-ul-Haq's military career, all of which were recorded in his dossier? Did Bhutto deliberately select a military leader believing him to be a sycophant that would keep the military subservient and under his control?

General Zia-ul-Haq's Islamic bent and his adventurous character were evident in his reputation, and even his military record foreshadowed his impact on the course of history.[2] In 1970, then-brigadier Zia-ul-Haq was posted to Jordan as King Hussein's military advisor and subsequently played a controversial role in military operations against the Palestinian uprising, famously known as "Black September." Zia allegedly exceeded his advisory capacity by actively directing military operations. The uprising was crushed, but Zia's conduct came under scrutiny, especially by the Pakistani embassy. Brigadier Zia-ul-Haq did not enjoy amicable relations with the Pakistani ambassador to Jordan, and the two had often clashed over mundane administrative issues. Eventually, Zia-ul-Haq's reporting officer in Jordon, Major General Nawazish, gave him an "adverse report," which should have ended his military career.[3] But Zia challenged the report. His plea was accepted, and shortly thereafter, he was promoted to the rank of major general and assigned to the prestigious command of the I Armored Division in Multan.

Friction soon developed between Zia-ul-Haq and his immediate superior—Corps Commander Lieutenant-General Muhammad Sharif. Writing the annual confidential report (ACR) of Major General Zia-ul-Haq, the corps commander observed Zia's tendency to bypass the chain of command. This comment was very similar to what the Pakistani embassy in Amman had reported earlier. Army Chief Tikka Khan supported the corps commander's assessment and wrote in his remarks that "the general officer must adhere to the advice of his corps commander."[4] Once again, however, Zia's career advancement was not adversely affected, as he was later promoted to the rank of three-star general, replacing Sharif as corps commander in Multan. Zia-ul-Haq's professional military record was impressive, and his conservative nature and religious convictions were never obstacles; rather, they were assets to Yahya Khan's military regime, which had a reputation for drunkenness and debauchery that was blamed in part for the 1971 disaster. In all probability his conservative background and straightforward professional record overshadowed some of his less desirable traits.

Thus, Prime Minister Bhutto was likely oblivious to Zia's negative traits when he made him the army chief. He promoted both Muhammad Sharif and Zia-ul-Haq to the rank of four-star general and appointed the two rivals to the positions of Chairman Joint Chiefs of Staff Committee (CJSC) and Chief of Army Staff (COAS), respectively. It is the author's view that there is only one plausible explanation for Zia's promotion—to exploit the cleavage between the two senior commanders. Bhutto made a Machiavellian move to keep the two men focused on each other and thus keep the military away from the domain of civilian power. And as usual, the sycophant Zia continued to publicly praise the prime minister in a manner and with an eloquence that boosted Bhutto's ego.[5]

Bhutto was acutely conscious of the need to modernize the armed forces.

In February 1975, he successfully negotiated with President Gerald Ford to lift the decade-old U.S. arms embargo, and Pakistan became the recipient of U.S. equipment and helicopters once again. While the military was fully supported for force modernization, the nuclear question was still a point of contention and debate.

Bhutto's Focus on the Nuclear Program

After India's nuclear test, Bhutto set the nuclear weapons program into high gear, and from 1974 onward it was the highest national security priority. However, the program needed oversight in order to efficiently handle diplomacy, procurement, finances, and many other issues for which Bhutto had little time. He nevertheless continued to be the ultimate decision-maker for the program. Although little is on public record, it is believed that Munir Khan reported to Bhutto on the program's progress in one-to-one meetings. In addition, Bhutto's military secretary, Major General Imtiaz Ali, was specifically directed to keep the prime minister regularly informed on the nuclear program. Eventually he established an interministerial coordinating committee to undertake the tasks listed above, as well as to generally smooth over any bumps in the nuclear program.

In the remaining three years of Bhutto's tenure, Pakistan pursued all options to bring the nuclear fuel cycle to its logical conclusion, which would open up the prospects for both a military weapons program and a civilian program for nuclear energy. Bhutto realized that after the India nuclear test, the international community would act quickly to close the window of opportunity for the procurement of technical capability. In spite of the interministerial coordinating committee, the nuclear program continued to face difficulties in diplomacy, financing, and technical capacity. Ultimately, Bhutto did not see the nuclear fuel cycle's completion during his time in office, and he blamed the United States for his lack of progress.

The prime minister correctly anticipated that time was at a premium and Pakistani efforts would meet many obstacles. The United States also correctly read Bhutto's intentions, especially after the Indian nuclear test. Islamabad, however, expected the United States to understand Pakistan's strategic anxiety after the test and was disappointed when, instead of penalizing India, the United States was eyeing Pakistan's procurement activities, while also dissuading Western allies from nuclear cooperation with Pakistan. Pakistan's strategy was to keep its procurement activities within the limits of commercial law of the country and, if necessary, operate within the legal grey areas (explained further in Chapter 8). When individuals were caught, Pakistan would at times officially deny U.S. allegations and disassociate itself from any illegal activities. At other times it would privately explain to the United States that it had to do what was in its national interest. Pakistan would then use diplomacy to mitigate the damage, especially during critical periods of the Cold War when Pakistan's role was strategically significant to U.S. security objectives. This cat-and-mouse game of sorts would last for three decades.[6]

As revealed in the previous chapter, Canada and Germany had followed America's lead by refusing to supply a nuclear fuel fabrication plant and a heavy water production plant, respectively. The United States then mounted pressure on France to abrogate its agreement to supply a commercial fuel reprocessing plant. Given this trend, Pakistan thought that to avoid conflict, it had to stay ahead of the game.

To gain France's trust, Pakistan agreed to all conditions posed by the foreign supplier: the PAEC was ready and willing to accept all conditions for imported plants and equipment, to place facilities under IAEA safeguards, and to meet any other legal obligations demanded by the exporting country. Pakistan's policy at the time was to acquire nuclear capabilities without violating international law, hurting its diplomatic posture, or jeopardizing the PAEC's good standing with the IAEA. Further, the country could not afford to imperil its political and economic support from international organizations, as Bhutto's economic policies had all but crippled the economy.

Pakistani officials would later point out that, unlike India, Pakistan did not violate any international safeguards agreements and always abided by foreign contracts. However, their concerns and pleas fell on deaf years. From the Western perspective, India's test was a fait accompli, and the real concern was the cascading effects of horizontal proliferation. Pakistan was an obvious state of focus. A nonmember of the NPT and known to be in strategic rivalry with India, Pakistan would certainly react in some way to India's provocation; thus, even peaceful acquisition of nuclear technologies would have military intentions. Rather tragically for Pakistan, the more it advertised its anguish and security predicaments to the world, the more supporters it lost. Pakistan was on its own to fend off its troubles with India.

In December 1976, Canada abruptly cut off all supplies, including nuclear fuel, heavy water, spare parts, and technical support for KANUPP. PAEC scientists told the author that the sudden withdrawal of personnel had endangered the safety of the power plant. Former PAEC chairman Ishfaq Ahmad commented, "Our pleas to the Canadians about nuclear safety were of no avail."[7] The Pakistani diplomatic and scientific communities were now incensed that Canada, although it had reasons to be upset with India's actions, was projecting its anger onto Pakistan. As former PAEC chairman Pervez Butt told the author, "They [Western countries] were not simply denying us technology, their aim was to cripple the existing nascent nuclear infrastructure."[8] Ishfaq Ahmad added, "The frustration and anger at Western countries eventually turned into national resolve, which was a blessing in the long run; it actually put Pakistan on the path of nuclear self-reliance."[9] The sense of betrayal was analogous to China's situation in the mid-1950s, when the Soviet Union withdrew its support. China was left to face technical and resource challenges on its own, which aroused national resolve for self-reliance. Under the dynamic leadership of Nie Rongzhen, director of the Defense Science and Technology Commission, the Chinese nuclear program flourished.[10] Clearly, when Pakistan turned to China for help on the safety of KANUPP, China was not only sympathetic; it had other incentives—especially an opportunity to examine a Western-made power reactor.

However, for Pakistan, the political and technical challenges in the mid-1970s were much greater than those for China in the late 1950s. Under the populist leadership of Zulfiqar Ali Bhutto, public support for the nuclear program had developed quickly. Government rhetoric about injustice, discrimination, and unfair treatment of Pakistan gained popular appeal and bolstered the "never again" theme. With each passing year, Western-imposed obstacles were deemed challenges that Pakistan would gladly undertake. However, the government line also sparked widespread belief that the West was determined to prevent a Muslim country from acquiring a nuclear capability. This perception, coupled with Pakistani security predicaments, exacerbated the national sense of isolation. By the mid-1970s, Bhutto had lost faith in his alliance with the West and directed his foreign policy to the Non-Aligned Movement (NAM) and the Organization of Islamic Conference (OIC). Bhutto openly championed the causes of the Third World, the north-south divide, and Islam.

In addition, the prime minister's socialist leanings led him to search for stronger friendships in the East. His overtures to China and North Korea to acquire conventional defenses brought the defense and strategic organizations of the three countries into business with each other.[11] Pakistani scientists quickly adopted reverse engineering techniques and new methods of technical substitution. Bhutto was confident that his Western-trained Ph.D.s in science and technology would be capable of mastering these arts, thus allowing them to copy and customize new technologies.[12]

Munir Ahmad Khan followed Zulfiqar Ali Bhutto's lead and instructed his employees to copy Western technologies while building nuclear facilities. The nature of the Pakistani nuclear program would continue to follow this pattern. However, this strategy often was not easy to realize. As former Pakistani Foreign Minister Abdul Sattar told the author in an interview, certain contracts, such as that for France's reprocessing plant, included clauses that banned copying or reproducing designs.

In addition to restrictions in private contracts, the newly formed London Supplier Group (LSG) and U.S. legislation were presenting more hurdles for Pakistan to overcome in its search for foreign nuclear technologies. One such piece of legislation, the Symington Amendment passed by the U.S. Congress in 1976, was attached to then-existing U.S. exports controls. It stipulated the halt of all military and economic assistance to any non–nuclear weapons state (NNWS) that built a uranium enrichment or reprocessing plant and did not accept full-scope NPT safeguards on its entire nuclear program. India's test preceded the law, but Pakistan fell subject to it in April 1979, during its pursuit of the French reprocessing plant. In August 1977, the Glenn Amendment was passed by the U.S. Congress, stipulating the cancellation of all security assistance to any NNWS that exploded a nuclear device. Again this amendment exempted India because of timing, but Pakistan remained vulnerable.[13]

On April 4, 1979, Zulfiqar Ali Bhutto, the political father of the Pakistani bomb, was hanged. Just two days later, on April 6, the Carter administration applied the Symington Law to Pakistan and suspended aid.[14] Although there was no direct causal relationship between the U.S. sanctions and Bhutto's death, some theorize that Zia-ul-Haq's disregard for President Carter's appeal for clemency may have triggered Washington's anger.[15] If the Symington law was intended to punish Pakistan, it only bolstered Pakistan's determination to pursue its nuclear program.

Pursuit of the French Reprocessing Plant

Munir Khan had spent thirteen years in the IAEA in the Nuclear Power and Reactor Division and had many friends and contacts in Europe. He had a keen understanding of power reactor and reprocessing technologies and was well aware of France's pioneering role in reprocessing and plutonium extraction. After his appointment as PAEC chair, Munir returned to Vienna to officially end his employment with the IAEA. There he met a French delegate to discuss the possible sale of a reprocessing plant to Pakistan.[16]

France was eager to make profits from nuclear commerce with developing countries.[17] Pakistan was just as enthusiastic to tap into the French source, as it would contribute to reprocessing know-how and help train Pakistani scientists in the back end of the fuel cycle. Other Western countries, such as West Germany and Italy, were also willing to share reprocessing technologies, as they had with Brazil.[18] However, since France was not a signatory to the NPT at the time, the PAEC concluded that the country might not feel overly obligated to insist on stringent conditions or safeguards.[19]

French firm Saint-Gobain Technique Nouvelle (SGN) specialized in spent fuel reprocessing and plutonium extraction through the solvent extraction method.[20] Former PAEC scientist Muhammad Afzal, a chemical engineer who had also studied nuclear engineering in Australia, was involved in the negotiations with France at the time. The scientist was very experienced, and gained further expertise while working for the Australian Atomic Energy Commission on a pebble bed reactor.[21]

Afzal claims that although no serious efforts were made, the idea to acquire a reprocessing plant had existed in Pakistan since the early 1960s, after the PAEC learned of India's reprocessing plant at Trombay. Ishfaq Ahmad Khan supports this claim, stating that purchase plans for a reprocessing plant were "on the drawing board" in the late 1960s, and even then, SGN was a willing partner.[22] Indeed, a Planning Commission report cites the approval of the Executive Committee of the National Economic Council (ECNEC) for the purchase of reprocessing plants, a fuel fabrication facility for KANUPP, a thirteen-ton per annum heavy water plant for Multan, and a plutonium extraction plant.[23]

In Pakistan's initial talks with SGN after 1972, Afzal explains, the reprocessing plant under consideration was modest, boasting only a thirty-ton capacity. During negotiations, however, SGN suggested a plant with a capacity of one hundred tons of reactor fuel, as it was cost-effective at only a marginal difference in price. Since Pakistan's long-term plans would require a larger plant, Pakistan agreed, and the two parties began to discuss whether the transfer should be on a turnkey basis or whether SGN should design the plant and Pakistanis construct it. Finally, they settled on the second option.[24]

Two separate agreements were signed by the PAEC and SGN to build an industrial-scale reprocessing plant at Chashma, in the Punjab province. The first contract, signed in March 1973, was for the "basic design" of the plant; the second, signed on October 18, 1974, called for a "detailed design" and the plant's construction. In the latter contract, SGN promised to provide blueprints, designs, and specifications; procure equipment from suppliers; and put the plant into operation. In exchange, SGN would earn $10 million, and other French contractors would earn upward of $45 million. France was also trying to secure more orders—at least three to four 600-MW power reactors, Mirage fighter-bombers, and other hardware for Pakistan and other Arab states.[25]

French experts raised questions about the economic and industrial justification for a reprocessing plant with a capacity of one hundred tons per year in Pakistan. In response, the PAEC presented France with the October 1973 IAEA report justifying the construction of twenty-four nuclear power reactors in Pakistan by the end of the century. However, the IAEA plan came under criticism, especially after the Indian nuclear test, because of doubts regarding Pakistan's true intentions.[26] It remains uncertain whether the plan to build twenty-four power reactors was a ruse to justify the ongoing purchase of a one hundred–ton reprocessing plant, or vice versa.[27] PAEC's excessive energies devoted to the purchase of the reprocessing plant were raising doubts about its use for peaceful purposes. Nevertheless, from a technical standpoint, the reprocessing plant would have yielded enough fuel to reduce Pakistan's dependence on scarce uranium reserves and increase the country's self-sufficiency.[28]

After India's 1974 nuclear test, France insisted that the reprocessing plant be placed under IAEA safeguards.[29] Although displeased, Pakistan decided not to cause a confrontation and agreed to the new demand, referring the French request to the IAEA Board of Governors. Finally the sale was approved in February 1976, and in the following month Pakistan and the IAEA reached an agreement. The Chashma reprocessing facility would now be under full IAEA inspection and safeguards, and Pakistan pledged not to divert the materials for nuclear weapons manufacturing or any other military purpose.[30]

As both negotiations for IAEA safeguards and SGN designs were in progress, the French began to shift their position, expressing concern that once Pakistan had obtained the detailed design, there would be little need for outside help to construct it indigenously.[31] The French began to offer a variety of options intended to let the purchase pass, while ensuring the facility's peaceful use. A new design for the plant was offered to Pakistan, whose end product would be mixed-oxide fuel rather than plutonium. Munir Khan tried to reason with his French counterparts that Pakistan had no intention of acquiring or building breeder reactors; hence mixed-oxide fuel would be of no utility. Foreign Secretary Agha Shahi formally rejected the modified French proposal, insisting that Pakistan had met all of its obligations and agreed to IAEA safeguards, and thus would not accept any modifications to the original agreement.[32]

Given this setback, Pakistan's leadership assessed that the SGN deal would never go through. Soon Islamabad began to believe that Western powers had accepted India's de facto entrance into the nuclear club, but were determined to block Pakistan by every possible means. It was obvious that France was acting under immense pressure from the United States, and by that time, Kissinger was directly pressuring Bhutto, with carrots and sticks, to stop his pursuit of a nuclear program.

Even with these doubts, the Pakistanis decided to continue negotiating with the French. Some PAEC critics claim that Chairman Munir Khan was obsessed with the plutonium route, so he could not give up the possibility of acquiring a reprocessing plant.[33] Others explained to the author that the continuation of the French deal was part of a larger plot to distract international attention from the secret work being done on highly enriched uranium.[34]

PAEC scientists told the author that once they determined France would not deliver, discussions were protracted to extract the maximum amount of knowledge about the reprocessing technology, plant designs, and construction details. According to Weissman and Krosney, by August 1978, "SGN had transferred 95% of all the detailed engineering designs and drawings for building the reprocessing plant to PAEC, including the plans for the chopping machine."[35]

If Bhutto had planned to continue to press France on the deal as a strategy to protect the secret highly enriched uranium (HEU), Pakistani diplomats abroad were seemingly not in sync with this national strategy. As Islamabad was placing pressure on France to honor the deal and individual scientists prolonged negotiations to acquire knowledge, Pakistani diplomats made undisciplined remarks. Frustrated with Western double standards, for example, in 1977 Pakistani ambassador to the United Nations Iqbal Akhund remarked, "We can do it ourselves if we don't get the reprocessing plant."[36] These words caused diplomatic embarrassment for the Pakistani ambassador in Washington, Sahabzada Yaqub-Khan, who was burning the midnight oil convincing the Carter administration not to impose nonproliferation sanctions on Pakistan. Yaqub-Khan told the author that Iqbal Akhund's remark inspired the United States to consider invoking nuclear sanctions against Pakistan. This incident exemplifies the significance of nuclear-related rhetorical statements within Pakistani nuclear policy, a feature of Pakistan's subsequent nuclear history that would be demonstrated time and time again.[37]

Indeed, the Chashma reprocessing plant provoked much controversy, both in Pakistan and abroad. Critics at home questioned the utility of this reprocessing facility for the nuclear weapons program, as it was under full-scope IAEA safeguards, while others outside Pakistan expressed doubts about the efficacy of those very same safeguards. Another contentious issue was the fact that the 137-MW KANUPP, also under IAEA safeguards, was the only source of irradiated or spent nuclear fuel for Chashma reprocessing. This point raised the question of whether, should the reprocessing plant be acquired, the PAEC would then violate international safeguards on KANUPP and divert the spent fuel for reprocessing at Chashma.

Theoretically, this scenario was possible. KANUPP's spent fuel, if and when reprocessed, could yield enough plutonium for a few weapons. According to a 1978 CIA analysis, KANUPP could produce between 132 and 264 pounds of reactor-grade or weapons-grade plutonium, depending on how the reactor was optimized for operation.[38] But the IAEA safeguards were far too stringent, making diversion extremely difficult.

As mentioned in the previous chapter, Sultan Bashiruddin Mahmood described a technical obstacle to extracting quality plutonium from the uranium oxide fuel used at KANUPP. In his assessment, normal reprocessing would not have yielded weapons-grade plutonium.[39] Further, the chemical process required to extract plutonium would have entailed greater penalties and fewer dividends. According to Bashiruddin, had Pakistan decided to cheat on its international obligations and divert the spent fuel from KANUPP, it would have taken many years, been "highly impractical," and at best would have provided enough material for "barely a weapon or two." In all interviews conducted by the author, PAEC officials denied the existence of any plan to divert spent fuel secretly from either KANUPP or any other safeguarded facility, including the 5-MW PARR-1. They unanimously asserted that to date, there is neither evidence nor even a hint of Pakistani intentions to violate the safeguards. These scientists insist that it would have been highly foolish on the part of Pakistan to think along such dangerous lines, especially considering the IAEA's vigilance after India's nuclear test.[40]

Ultimately, Pakistan's plans to acquire plutonium took another path. PAEC planned to indigenously build a 50- to 70-MW NRX-type reactor, which would be outside the scope of any safeguards. Following the inauguration of KANUPP in November 1972, a team of nuclear engineers, including Sultan Bashiruddin Mahmood and Pervez Butt, was formed to prepare a blueprint. The team spent a year preparing the design, but the project was shelved, primarily because of a shortage of labor and finances, to be discussed in further detail in Chapter 10.[41]

New Labs: Indigenous Plutonium Extraction

As negotiations with France continued for the commercial reprocessing plant, the PAEC secretly commenced work on a pilot-scale reprocessing facility. This plant was one-tenth the size of the Chashma plant, and once completed, would produce enough weapons-grade plutonium for one to three bombs per year.[42] Located near PINSTECH, this small plant was known as "New Labs."[43]

In late 1969 the UK Atomic Energy Commission was working on reprocessing technology via the company British Nuclear Fuel, Ltd. (BNFL). The original nuclear chemistry lab, dubbed "hot cells," had been designed by BNFL in 1971, but it could produce only 360 grams of plutonium per year. Pakistan contemplated buying the British design, but it had no capacity for expansion and most likely required IAEA safeguards. Pakistan then looked to Belgian firm Belgonucleaire, whose design allowed for expansion and did not demand safeguards.[44]

In March 1973, a three-member PAEC team comprising Abdul-Majid Chaudhry, Khalil Qureshi, and Zafarullah Khan went to Belgium to negotiate and eventually train with Belgonucleaire. This company owned Eurochemic, a plant in Mol, Belgium, with a known record of separating 678 kilograms of plutonium from two hundred tons of fission material between 1966 and 1974.[45] The Pakistani team received training in the design of the pilot-scale reprocessing facility, as well as in reprocessing of spent fuel.[46] Mr. Abdul Majeed Chaudhry would later take over as the head of the New Labs reprocessing project and remain in that role until 1991.[47]

The primary objective of New Labs was to train PAEC scientists and engineers in the sensitive field of reprocessing. The same trained personnel could then be hired to work on the larger commercial reprocessing plant being built at Chashma. Upon completion, New Labs had the capacity to reprocess 10–20 kg of spent reactor fuel annually, and the plutonium obtained was sufficient for at least two to four atomic bombs each year.

Nuclear Waltzing: Bhutto and Kissinger

Within three months of India's nuclear tests, President Richard Nixon re-signed. Pakistan had truly lost a friend; as Nixon himself said in 1970, "No one has occupied the White House who is friendlier to Pakistan than me."[48] With the change of command, Secretary of State Henry Kissinger became more influential in U.S. foreign policy matters and began a tour of the Asian subcontinent in October 1974. Visits to Pakistan and India were on his agenda, but even before arriving he made his preferences clearly known with references to India as a "preeminent power in the region," and public assurances of a continued supply of nuclear fuel for India's Tarapur reactor.[49] To Pakistanis, Kissinger was giving obvious signals that India's nuclear test was accepted as fait accompli, and that the U.S. visit was merely to stall a Pakistani response.

At this time, the Pakistani economy was in dire straits following a poor wheat crop. Bhutto was requesting food aid while simultaneously expanding the nuclear program—seemingly unconscious that he was delivering on his promise of eating grass. National morale, already low, was further diminished by India's nuclear test, which highlighted the deficiencies and weaknesses in Pakistan's national defense forces—shortcomings that were further exacerbated by a decade under the U.S. military embargo. It was under such circumstances that Bhutto and Kissinger entered into a verbal banter over Pakistan's nuclear program.

Given Pakistan's difficult position, Bhutto approached the Ford administration for only two things—economic assistance, particularly food aid, and an end to the arms embargo. He made various indications to the United States that if Pakistan's conventional forces were bolstered, nuclear weapons might not be necessary. In an interview with the *New York Times*, Bhutto stated, "If security interests are satisfied, if people feel secure, and if they feel they will not be subject to aggression, they [will] not want to squander away limited resources in [the nuclear] direction." In another interview, he said, "It was not that Pakistan wanted toys . . . . Pakistan sought sufficient arms to permit it to defend itself."[50] Seemingly convinced, Washington provided Bhutto with four hundred tons of wheat and about $78 million in development loans.[51]

In February 1975, Bhutto made another visit to the United States, this time to the nation's capital, just at the time when concerns were rising over Pakistani nuclear capabilities, particularly the purchase of reprocessing fuel. Nevertheless, the prime minister was successful again, and on February 24, Washington officially removed the arms embargo that had been imposed on Pakistan for the past ten years. This gesture was not unconditional, however. Military purchases were restricted to cash sales only, such that assisted grants or concessional sales were prohibited in order to "dampen possible Congressional criticism and the Indian reaction."[52]

U.S. officials were no less concerned about Pakistan's purchase plans for the French reprocessing plant, which, in their assessment, was far too large for the fuel requirements of KANUPP. They quickly concluded that the plant's ultimate purpose was none other than to supply the fuel for a plutonium weapons program. In preparation for Bhutto's visit, the State Department sent Kissinger a note saying, "The [government of Pakistan] is trying to develop an independent nuclear fuel cycle and the technical skills that would make the nuclear explosion option feasible."[53] Nevertheless, the Ford administration avoided introducing this issue at the top level; instead, the Pakistan embassy's charge d'affairs, Iqbal Riza, received American complaints. The demarche sent to the embassy said, "[L]ifting the arms embargo would encourage Pakistan not to pursue the politically risky and costly development of nuclear explosives."[54] This course of action, coupled with the arms embargo lift, reflected a U.S. policy at the time—conventional military aid would stall nuclear weapons development.

By the beginning of 1976, the nonproliferation regime had begun to tighten its export controls because Pakistan, as well as several other countries including Argentina, Brazil, South Korea, and Taiwan, were all engaged in troubling nuclear activities. Leading the way, the United States embarked on "muscular diplomacy" to derail suspect programs.[55] In February 1976 Kissinger met Bhutto in New York and suggested that Pakistan forgo its French reprocessing plant purchase. In return, Pakistan's needs would be addressed through alternative means, such as the creation of an international fuel reprocessing facility in Iran. Needless to say, no headway was made during that meeting.

In another attempt to dissuade Pakistan from its nuclear path, Kissinger visited Pakistan in August 1976. At the same time, U.S. elections were sparking debates, and Democrat Jimmy Carter's agenda specifically targeted Kissinger and his relaxed response to India's nuclear test. As Dennis Kux writes, "Kissinger and Ford were under pressure to demonstrate that they were doing everything possible to prevent Pakistan from continuing its effort to match India's nuclear capability."[56]

Thus Kissinger's second trip to Pakistan was an attempt to remedy his mistakes. He arrived with an offer of 110 A-7 attack bombers for the Pakistani Air force in exchange for canceling the reprocessing plant purchase, indicating that Congress would most likely approve such a deal. And as a stick, he brandished a possible Democratic victory, hinting that when in power, Carter would certainly make an example of Pakistan.[57] Since that meeting, the popular myth in Pakistan has been that Kissinger threatened Bhutto with "a horrible example," meant as an ultimatum.

At an official dinner in the city of Lahore, Kissinger and Bhutto engaged in nuclear banter in the midst of toasts. Raising his glass, Bhutto declared, "[Lahore] is our reprocessing center and we cannot in any way curb the reprocessing center of Pakistan." When Kissinger's turn for the toast came, he replied, "All government must constantly 'reprocess' themselves and decide what is worth reprocessing."[58] As these statesmen were tipping their glasses, back in the United States, senators John Glenn and Stuart Symington "adopted amendments to sections 669 and 670 of the foreign assistance bill to bar assistance to non-NPT signatories that imported uranium enrichment or nuclear fuel reprocessing technology."[59]

In the meantime, Pakistan's military and civilian leaders, including the Air Force chief, Zulfiqar Ali Khan, advised the prime minister not to accept the aircraft in exchange for nuclear capability. Both the United States and Pakistan were surprised at each other's position. Pakistanis were surprised at the intensity with which the U.S. was pursuing the nuclear question, and the Americans were surprised that Pakistan declined a substantial military package.

Later that year, Jimmy Carter won the U.S. presidential election, just as Bhutto announced a Pakistani election to be held in March 1977. Upon assuming the presidency, Carter quickly turned down the Pentagon's recommendation to sell the A-7 attack bombers to Pakistan. In response, Bhutto threatened to quit CENTO, claiming that it discriminated against Pakistan. Pakistan did indeed leave the treaty in 1979 and joined the NAM.

But the Pakistani prime minister had to focus on his domestic situation, as large protests against him began to spread that accused him of rigging the elections. The domestic situation in Pakistan continued to deteriorate, and Bhutto was forced to seek help from Saudi Arabia. He flew there on June 17, 1977, all the while blaming both Moscow and the United States for his troubles.[60] He truly suspected that the U.S. had funneled money to his Islamic opponents, who then spurred the protests. Restless, the Pakistani military led by Zia-al-Haq overthrew Bhutto on July 5, 1977. From that day onward U.S.-Pakistani relations rapidly deteriorated.[61]

Pakistan was not the only country in the region with political upheavals. In India, Mrs. Gandhi's government lost the Indian election, and for the first time in the country's history, a new political party, the Janata Party, came to power. In Iran, trouble was also brewing against the shah, who would eventually be overthrown in 1979. And in Afghanistan, the Daoud regime would face domestic tensions that eventually led to the end of his reign in 1978.

Three months after Zia took power in Pakistan, in September 1977, State Department nuclear specialist Joseph Nye, Jr., visited Islamabad and threatened to cut off economic assistance if the French reprocessing plant purchase succeeded. At that time, Pakistan was receiving only $50 million in aid annually, so the new leader had no incentive to agree and clearly informed Nye that he intended to proceed with the project. In response, U.S. nuclear sanctions were applied and only food aid continued. This point was the lowest in U.S.-Pakistani history.[62]

Around this time, unbeknownst to the United States as well as the Pakistani public, Pakistan's nuclear elite embarked on the highly enriched uranium route to nuclear weapons.

7   Mastery of Uranium Enrichment

The popular narrative surrounding Pakistan's uranium enrichment is one of nonproliferation and export control failure. There is little focus on the domestic environment and the intense demands Pakistani experts had to meet. Such was the pressure and determination: the more hurdles the scientists had to overcome, the more their resolve increased. In an organizational culture where the end justified the means, and left with so few alternatives, the Pakistani leadership turned to self-reliance and creativity to overcome the nonproliferation barriers erected. Eventually it was the leadership of A. Q. Khan, a leading Pakistani scientist, and competition within the Pakistani scientific community that led to the project's success.

The little-known domestic story is one of professional jealousies, claims and counterclaims, and innovation surrounding Pakistan's centrifuge enrichment project. Among other sources, this account is based primarily on two interviews, with Sultan Bashiruddin Mahmood and Javed Arshad Mirza.[1] The former was a predecessor to A. Q. Khan's reign at Engineering Research Laboratories (later KRL) and the latter, the successor to A. Q. Khan in 2001.

A Man Called A. Q. Khan

In the state of Bhopal, India, the headmaster of a local school, Abdul Ghafoor, chose to retire in 1935. The following year, in April, he and wife, Zulekha, had their youngest son—they named him Abdul Qadeer Khan, famously known as A. Q. Khan.[2] A decade later, during the traumatic years that surrounded India's partition, Bhopal was the scene of intense Hindu-Muslim riots. Abdul Ghafoor's Muslim family was profoundly affected by the prejudices of the Hindus and decided to immigrate to Pakistan in August 1952, eventually settling in Karachi.[3] In 1953, seventeen-year-old Abdul Qadeer Khan received admission to D. J. Sindh Govt. Science College in Karachi. His friends characterized him as a decent man who prayed regularly, but avoided indulging in religious discussions. After earning a B.S. from Karachi University, he stayed in the city for three years to serve as an inspector of weights and measures, and then left for West Berlin. A. Q. Khan traveled across Europe, earning degrees along the way—an M.S. from the Technological University of Delft, Holland, and a Ph.D. in copper metallurgy from Catholic University of Leuven, Belgium, under the supervision of Professor Martin Brabers.[4]

As A. Q. Khan pursued a higher education, Pakistan underwent the tragic events of 1971 and its humiliating defeat at the hands of India. This historical episode not only changed the map of the region but also influenced A. Q. Khan in particular, who recalled personal humiliation and forced migration to Pakistan. When India conducted its first nuclear test in 1974, he was well settled in Holland with his wife, Hendrina (Henny) Khan, and two daughters—Ayesha and Dina. The Indian nuclear test transformed both the security landscape in the region and the "man from Pakistan."[5]

A. Q. Khan's dissertation on exotic metals and their ability to withstand high rates of deformation made him a prime candidate for metallurgy-related jobs, especially on centrifuge-based designs.[6] He accepted a job offer at Fysisch Dynamisch Onderzoek (FDO), a subsidiary of Vernidge Machine Fabrieken (VMF), which worked closely with Ultra-Centrifuge Nederland (UCN), a member of the Uranium Enrichment Consortium (URENCO). As an employee at the URENCO plant in Almelo, Netherlands, he gained crucial knowledge of centrifuge-based enrichment operations. Fluent in German, French, and English, he was often asked by his managers to translate German reports on centrifuge technologies, including those related to the German-1 (G1) and German-2 (G2) models.[7] Khan was focused on his work and family in the Netherlands when destiny knocked on his door, bringing with it fame and notoriety.

Following India's nuclear test, in August 1974, he wrote a letter to Prime Minister Bhutto, volunteering his expertise in gas centrifuge technologies to the country. The letter went seemingly unnoticed and probably was treated as another "nut case."[8] A. Q. Khan persisted, however, and sent another letter on September 17, 1974, this time through the Pakistani ambassador in Holland, explaining the significance of highly enriched uranium (HEU) as an alternative to the plutonium path to the bomb. Finally, the letter caught the attention of the prime minister, who remarked that the "man makes sense."[9] Within Pakistani circles, Khan's letter to Bhutto is considered analogous to Albert Einstein's famous first letter to President Franklin Roosevelt dated August 2, 1939. Both letters changed the course of history.[10]

Frustrated with the lack of progress on the plutonium front, Bhutto was intrigued by Khan's proposal and asked Military Secretary Major General Imtiaz Ali to investigate both A. Q. Khan's background and centrifuge enrichment as a whole. A. Q. Khan was soon invited to meet Zulfiqar Ali Bhutto and Major General Imtiaz Ali in December 1974. Bhutto was impressed with A. Q. Khan's credentials and instructed him to speak with PAEC chairman Munir Ahmad Khan. Before returning to Holland, A. Q. Khan met Bhutto again, this time in the presence of two senior civil servants—Secretary General of Defense Ghulam Ishaq Khan and Foreign Secretary Agha Shahi.[11] A. Q. Khan was instructed "to stay longer in the Netherlands to learn more."[12]

Initial Attempts

The origins of uranium enrichment in Pakistan date back to 1967, when I. H. Usmani asked Ishfaq Ahmad, then the director of the Atomic Energy Mineral Center, to research enrichment technologies.[13] A small group of famous young scientists and engineers, including Samar Mubarakmand, Sultan Bashiruddin Mahmood, and Muhammad Hafeez Qureshi, did so, but with few results.[14] A. Q. Khan's letter must have been a catalyst for a change in direction. In several interviews with the author, Pakistani scientists recalled that the sudden rise of interest in highly enriched uranium coincided with A. Q. Khan's letter and his winter visit.

According to Sultan Bashiruddin Mahmood, in October 1974, Munir Ahmad Khan gave him only a week to prepare a technical feasibility report on centrifuge technologies, emphasizing the "strict secrecy of this assignment." As Bashiruddin Mahmood explained, "Munir Khan was in a great hurry—he wanted a detailed report on centrifuges the next day—Bhutto's military secretary Major General Imtiaz Ali was enquiring about it."[15] Bashiruddin Mahmood then prepared a fifteen-page handwritten report examining the relative advantages and disadvantages of different enrichment techniques.[16] Based on the report, the PAEC concluded that the gas centrifuge method was the most feasible. Along with cost, efficiency was the most attractive feature, considering Pakistan's limited industrial and technical capacity.[17]

A summary of gas centrifuge mechanics and technical requirements will paint a more accurate picture of the challenges associated with this enrichment process. As mentioned in Chapter 5, uranium enrichment is the process that separates U-235 from U-238 in order to increase the proportion of the former isotope. Separation is measured by the kilogram separative work unit (SWU), representing the amount of uranium processed and the degree to which it is enriched.[18] The gas centrifuge exploits the mass difference between these two isotopes (three neutrons) by spinning uranium hexafluoride gas (UF6) at extraordinarily high speeds (twice the speed of sound), forcing the lighter U-235 to the center, where it can be "scooped off" at the top. These centrifuges must be arranged in cascades, or groups of centrifuges, as each cascade enriches the material only slightly before feeding it into the next. Although this process may sound fairly simple, the specialized materials and precision engineering necessary are very difficult to achieve.

The necessary ingredient for the enrichment process, UF6 , must be free of any impurities, as impurities may condense and trigger blockages in the valves and piping of the cascades, causing the centrifuges to crash. Once this gas is produced with the highest degree of purity, it is then ready to be fed into the centrifuge, a machine made of many complex parts. The main components are (1) rotor and end caps; (2) bearing and suspension systems; (3) electric motor and power supplies; (4) center post, scoops, and baffles; (5) the vacuum system; and (6) the casing.[19] The first challenge is to acquire the specialized materials for these parts. High-strength, corrosion-resistant materials, such as maraging steel, aluminum alloys, titanium, glass-fiber resins, or carbon fiber, are essential for most of the aforementioned components.[20] Maraging steel specifically provides not only protection but also the capacity for faster rotor speed.[21]

The second challenge is to construct a perfectly balanced centrifuge rotor (an almost impossible task) that can rotate at supercritical speeds (about 100,000 rpm). In addition to the complex engineering necessary for the construction of the other centrifuge parts, a method must be devised to control the temperature and convection in the vacuum. Now imagine replicating this precision engineering in cascades of about three thousand centrifuges.[22]

Given Pakistan's lack of resources and technical know-how, building a gas centrifuge enrichment plant from scratch was a major feat. Undeterred and seemingly naive of the challenges, in October 1974 the PAEC formally launched a secret uranium enrichment plan code-named Project 706.[23] Sultan Bashiruddin, the project manager, recalled with confidence, "[We] had the complete design and know-how of the Zippe-type centrifuge machine, and it was enough for an intelligent team to build [upon] it. It had a rotor of aluminum, and was good enough for enrichment. It was the basis of gas-centrifuge technology and the URENCO machines were also improved versions of the Zippe design."[24] PAEC scientists believed that once the mechanics of one machine were mastered, then that technology could be replicated several times.[25] But this was not the case.

As Javed Mirza pointed out, Sultan Bashiruddin's version of the story is too simplistic. He insisted that none of the project's employees "knew anything about centrifuges, except A. Q. Khan." The scientists and technicians gained expertise only through trial and error and on-the-job learning. Agha Shahi agreed with Javed Mirza—the program was going nowhere until A. Q. Khan arrived.[26]

Phases of Project 706

As mentioned in Chapter 5, on February 15, 1975, Prime Minister Bhutto approved $350 million for several PAEC initiatives, which included the uranium enrichment plant.[27] The plan was to complete Project 706 in three phases: Phase I would establish an experimental test bed of a few centrifuges in Chaklala; Phase II would include a working test bed for prototype centrifuges in Sihala; and Phase III would install production-scale cascades at the main plant in Kahuta. The swiftness with which Prime Bhutto approved the budget approval was probably the result of the A. Q. Khan December 1974 meeting with the prime minister and complemented by frustrations surrounding the slow progress in plutonium production.

Project 706 was concealed by yet another name, Airport Development Workshop (ADW), by virtue of its location. The Islamabad International Airport shares space with the Pakistan Air Force's military garrison, Chaklala, which had existed since the nineteenth century.[28] Several dilapidated military barracks stood near the airport, and PAEC chairman Munir Khan approached Defense Secretary Fazal-e-Muqeem to allocate them for the secret project. A boundary wall was quickly constructed to cordon off the project, and barracks were converted into necessary facilities. One barrack held the centrifuge bed (Phase I), and another became a hostel where PAEC technicians resided in a literal state of quarantine.[29] As Javed Mirza described it, they were "very old barracks" with "hot tin roofs," with "ceiling fans that blew more hot air," and "lots of snakes" that resided in the building basement.[30]

Within this walled compound PAEC scientists, engineers, and technicians were trained in basic metallurgy, high-strength magnets, high-frequency inverters, and the like, yet none of those employees were aware of the training's purpose.[31] The more famous scientists who trained at these facilities were Ghulam Dastagir Alam (G. D. Alam), Anwar Ali, Javed Arshad Mirza, Ashraf Chaudhry, Dr. Fakhar Hashmi, and Ijaz Khokhar. These men later formed the core of Pakistan's centrifuge program, with Alam as the head of design and development.[32]

Sihala was chosen for Phase II of Project 706, some thirty miles east of Islamabad. Just like Chaklala, an army barracks was designated for the project. Under the PAEC plan, the pilot project would enrich uranium to a maximum of 10 to 12 percent before launching a system for higher grades of enrichment at the main plant.[33]

Sultan Bashiruddin Mahmood claimed that in December 1974, he and the director of general civil works, Mr. B. A. Shakir, were tasked to find a suitable site for Phase III of the project, the main uranium enrichment centrifuge plant. Sultan Bashiruddin and Army Engineer-in-Chief (E-C) Major General Shafqat Syed carried out reconnaissance for several days and eventually chose Kahuta in the second week of January 1975.[34] This account is at odds with A. Q. Khan's claim that actually, it was he who selected the site.[35]

The site, known as Sumbal-gah, was chosen for a variety of reasons. In addition to being close to the capital, it had a nearby water stream and mountains covering three sides, which provided protection.[36] Apparently the selection of the site did not receive formal military approval, as security personnel would later complain about its proximity to the Indian border and Indian air force bases. But the most important factor was its proximity to the central government, military headquarters, and the scientists living in Islamabad whose recruitment was a priority at the time.

The Pakistan Army created two separate organizations to assist the nuclear project: the Civil Works Organization (CWO) and the Special Works Organization (SWO). The CWO supplied all the construction and technical support and employed officers and soldiers from smaller organizations. These included the Corps of Engineers, the Corps of Electrical and Mechanical Engineering (EME), and the Corps of Signals, which provided the communication and electronic expertise. The SWO, tasked under Brigadier Muhammad Sarfaraz, constructed the nuclear tests sites in Baluchistan. The many departments and working teams assigned to Project 706 functioned under code names, thereby ensuring secrecy and security.

The army designated Brigadier (later Lieutenant-General) Zahid Ali Khan

Akbar and Colonel (later Major General) Anis Syed, both from the Engineers Corps, to acquire land under government rules for construction of a military garrison in Sumbal-gah and for equipment procurement for Project 706.[37] As the initial experiments proceeded, assistance from the aforementioned organizations began to increase. Some of the prominent names from EME included: Brigadier (later Major General) Abdus Salam, Colonel Majeed, Colonel Bashiruddin, Brigadier Sajawal Khan Malik, and Colonel Kazi Abdur Rasheed.[38]

The years 1975–76 were focused on developing the enrichment program's basic infrastructure. While procurement efforts were being conducted outside Pakistan (to be explored in Chapter 8), the stringent export controls on dual-use items made importing difficult. Forced to find an indigenous solution, the PAEC created the Directorate of Industrial Liaison (DIL), which carried out a comprehensive survey of more than three hundred local businesses that could potentially produce basic gas centrifuge components, and gave them subcontracts to do just that.[39]

Information Transfers

While jumpstarting Project 706, the PAEC realized that it would "need more know-how ... on how hexafluoride gas is put in and removed, how the cascades and adjacent facilities are designed." As Sultan Bashiruddin explained, "[A]ll this information was absolutely non-available."[40] In order to help with this laundry list of essentials, Munir Ahmad Khan decided to tap into his own resources.

Italian scientist Maurizio Zifferero was Munir Khan's former colleague at the IAEA, when both served as deputy directors general. Munir Khan sent Sultan Bashiruddin Mahmood to meet Zifferero at the Italian Casaccia Nuclear Research Centre outside Rome. After a detailed visit and lunch with Italian scientists, Bashiruddin claims to have obtained complete engineering drawings of both the plant and its centrifuges.[41]

Bashiruddin brought the drawings back to his hotel *and copied them*. Although he could not make out some of the symbols because they were in Italian, a later visit by two Italian scientists provided further translation.[42]

All this foundational work was occurring as A. Q. Khan was still in the Netherlands gaining valuable information from his work at the URENCO plant in Almelo. By 1975 he was already assisting Project 706 by passing copied URENCO designs to the PAEC.[43] At the time, Shafique Ahmad Butt (S. A. Butt) was the PAEC's chief procurement officer posted in the Pakistani embassy in Brussels. An engineer by profession, S. A. Butt's role in procuring critical technologies for Pakistan was significant. In the summer of 1975, S. A. Butt invited A. Q. Khan and Sultan Bashiruddin to his home. The three scientists spent two days in Butt's attic discussing A. Q. Khan's access to the centrifuge technologies, particularly his access to some failed centrifuge parts from Almelo that had been sent to FDO for analysis, as well as the documents that he was given to translate.[44]

After this meeting, the three men traveled to A. Q. Khan's home in Holland to develop an arrangement for information transfers. Abdul Quddus Khan, A. Q. Khan's older brother, was working for Holland's KLM Royal Dutch Airlines at the time. He was chosen to be the middleman, as he would not be an obvious suspect. A photocopy machine was installed in Quddus's house, and copies of the designs would then be passed along to S. A. Butt, who would then dispatch them via diplomatic pouch to Islamabad, where they would eventually end up at the home of Munir Ahmad Khan. In addition, S. A. Butt was authorized to furnish A. Q. Khan with money to recruit others for the job. Specifically, certain photographers were willing to be bribed for information, including one by the name of Fritz Veerman, who would later become the famous whistle-blower on A. Q. Khan's activities.

As related by Bashiruddin, "We asked A. Q. Khan to visit Pakistan in the Easter Holidays of 1975. He stayed in my home . . . [a]nd brought some documents with him also. That meeting with A. Q. Khan was also useful for us."[45] A. Q. Khan's knowledge of copper metallurgy was apparently required to supplement the nascent experiments at Chaklala.

Bashiruddin continued, "A. Q. Khan told us about the components that he brought with him, and from where the component had been retrieved. He also brought some broken pieces of components. He stayed for 5–7 days and we had a good discussion with him."[46] At the time, A. Q. Khan had advanced information about the G-1 and G-2 centrifuge models that were under development in Germany. A. Q. Khan spent sixteen straight days in what was dubbed the "brain box" at URENCO, translating twelve volumes of these centrifuge designs.

These accounts support the perception that the centrifuge components and designs were stolen from the West; however, Javed Arshad Mirza insists that there is more to the story. "You can say some designs, photocopies of drawings and notes that A. Q. Khan brought were with the group, but as far as mechanical machine and experience how to run the plant and how to do the process control, we had to learn all that ourselves." For example, "It would be impossible to work on the drawings and make a centrifuge run; balancing a running centrifuge at such high speeds is not an easy job. And we had to have a perfect balance."[47]

Toward the end of 1975, A. Q. Khan was transferred to a less sensitive section in FDO, and it may have been possible that he was fearful of his illicit activities being discovered. Simultaneously, the prime minister's office was encouraging him to return to Pakistan permanently.[48] Certain PAEC employees, including Sultan Bashiruddin, claim that A. Q. Khan insisted on returning; however, that cannot be verified. Western publications and sources allege that A. Q. Khan was less than discreet, and his rash style was bound to attract suspicion. For example, a flurry of official visits resulted in diplomatic cars parked outside his home until late hours of the night. More important, Khan indiscreetly inquired about sensitive and classified technological details, which was bound to place him and others under suspicion.

Thus, in December 1975, A. Q. Khan left Europe and arrived in Pakistan, formally joining the enrichment project in April 1976. He was given the title of director of research and development under Sultan Bashiruddin Mahmood's ADW project. But A. Q. Khan was miffed—his qualifications and experience should have merited better status.

Clash of the Khans

Working conditions in Europe were starkly different from those in Pakistan during that time, and the transition was difficult for A. Q. Khan. In order to serve his country, he left a lucrative job and a comfortable life with his European wife and children. But he was not repaid for this sacrifice—instead the pay was meager and initially less than that of his colleagues.

In addition, the work ethos itself was not pleasant in Chaklala's decaying buildings, as PAEC management did not create a healthful working environment, but rather one that was competitive and "hostile."[49] For example, there was no air conditioner in any of the buildings, making work during the hot summer months unbearable. When employees requested one, Chairman Munir Khan turned it down, on the pretext that a group of junior officers were not entitled to such luxuries.[50]

Sultan Bashiruddin was one of the causes of the poor working environment in Project 706. Though personally skilled and knowledgeable, his poor managerial skills caused precious hours to be wasted on conferences and petty administrative tasks, leaving little time for substantial work.[51] In addition, Sultan Bashiruddin's hiring practices came under scrutiny. For example, he insisted on interviewing and selecting new employees on his own and did not include any of his subordinates in the hiring process. Many employees viewed this as nepotism, making the working environment even less pleasant.

Eventually A. Q. Khan began voicing his complaints, leading to a direct competition between the two Khans—one that would last throughout Pakistan's nuclear history. For example, he was in favor of wholesale procurements and openly derided the progressive indigenization instituted by Munir Ahmad Khan and Bashiruddin Mahmood. A. Q. Khan would later say, "If Pakistan had tried to develop indigenous capability for each and every part and component, it would have proven very costly and time consuming, and who knows the project might have been aborted at the very initial stage because of this."[52] However, the project's leaders insisted that indigenous development was absolutely critical for the long-term sustainability of the enrichment program.[53]

It was obvious that A. Q. Khan was not particularly happy with his new employment, and there are a wide variety of stories circulating regarding A. Q. Khan's behavior during this transition. While Bashiruddin Mahmood alleged that he distracted employees by engaging them in gossip and grumbling, Javed Mirza sympathized with A. Q. Khan's sacrifice and family troubles, insisting that he "never complained" and always focused on work.

But the competition and hostility between Sultan Bashiruddin and A. Q. Khan worsened as controversies arose within Project 706. During the summer of 1976, A. Q. Khan accused Bashiruddin Mahmood of buying substandard maraging steel that had been purchased from West Germany. Major General Imtiaz Ali brought this issue to Prime Minister Bhutto's attention, who ordered a high-level investigation.[54] Certain PAEC officials believe that the inquiry was done purposely to discredit management, but this motive is difficult to confirm.

Another political storm began within the nuclear program when Sultan Bashiruddin Mahmood, Munir Ahmad Khan, and Dr. Riazuddin were accused of belonging to the Ahmadi sect, which had been declared non-Muslim by the National Assembly in 1974. Since the latter two held close relationships with Dr. Abdus Salam, an Ahmadi, this intended slander was the easiest way to discredit their credentials. Not only was being Ahmadi viewed as unpatriotic, but also, under the norms, a minority could not serve within a classified government program. Coupled with the maraging steel controversy, the association with the Ahmadi sect gave the impression that the PAEC leadership was disloyal and determined to sabotage the program. Eventually, an investigation led by Inter-Services Intelligence (ISI) determined in January 1977 that none of the accused was Ahmadi.

It is unclear whether A. Q. Khan sparked these accusations, but some PAEC officials alleged that it had been because of growing jealousies. According to Sultan Bashiruddin, "A. Q. Khan was very ambitious, extremely ambitious, and he wanted to take over, he had certain ideas in his mind."[55] Javed Mirza and several officials told the author that A. Q. Khan drew attention to the mediocrity of others, perhaps because within the PAEC culture he was discriminated against for being a Mohajir (an Urdu-speaking immigrant) from India in a world dominated by the Punjabis, some of who referred him as "that Bhopali" (a reference to the place of his birth).[56] There was seemingly no end to the ethnosectarian schism in Pakistan, a scourge that had destroyed the unity of the country. The scientific community had already been depleted by the loss of East Pakistanis (Bengalis) in 1971 and was damaging itself through petty jealousies and self-destructive bigotry.

Although Sultan Bashiruddin was eventually exonerated of both accusations, he was removed from Project 706 and transferred. Some in the PAEC say that A. Q. Khan was unrelenting and allegedly wrote to Prime Minister Bhutto denouncing Munir Ahmad Khan's leadership of the nuclear program and threatening to leave unless he was put in charge of the entire enrichment project.

As provocative as the story about A. Q. Khan's takeover may be, there are competing and presumably more accurate accounts. According to Javed Mirza, Dr. A. Q. Khan inherited the enrichment project under the directive of none other than Prime Minister Bhutto. He did indeed voice many of his complaints to Bhutto, but instead of demanding a higher position, simply asked to be relieved of his duties.[57] Furious, Bhutto asked Foreign Secretary Agha Shahi to intervene and remove Sultan Bashiruddin.

Agha Shahi told the author that Bhutto had also lost faith in Munir Ahmad Khan and wanted to remove him from the PAEC chairmanship. But Shahi counseled Bhutto away from this decision and instead suggested that the centrifuge program be simply pulled away from his leadership. Recalling the day, Agha Shahi said, "I told Bhutto, '[L]eave things as they are, don't remove the present leadership, because disgruntled people will say all kinds of things.'"

Shahi suggested, "You give independent charge to this man, A. Q. Khan. Let us see if he can produce results."[58]

On July 17, 1976, Foreign Secretary Agha Shahi accompanied Munir Ahmad Khan and A. Q. Khan to Bashiruddin Mahmood's office. Shahi asked him to hand over the keys to the office, the workshops, the storage, as well as all the essential documents, drawings, and all other records to A. Q. Khan.[59]

Was the change in leadership warranted? Debates continue as to the progress of the enrichment program by that time. Bashiruddin claims that A. Q. Khan inherited large amounts of technological progress, while Javed Mirza insists that there were no real developments at all. When asked, "What was the progress of the centrifuge program when A. Q. Khan took over from Sultan Bashiruddin?" he replied, "Nothing. We were too busy on meetings."[60] Regardless of the claim, the enrichment project simply continued in fits and starts.

In this context, a Project Coordination Board was established to supervise Project 706, with A. Q. Khan, as project head and secretary of the board, reporting directly to the prime minister's office.[61] Its membership consisted of Mr. A. G. N. Kazi, deputy chairman of the Planning Commission; Mr. Agha Shahi, foreign secretary; Mr. Ghulam Ishaq Khan, secretary general-in-chief; and Mr. Munir Ahmad Khan, PAEC chair.[62] The enrichment project now had a new director and a new name—Engineering Research Labs (ERL). The official division between ERL (later renamed Khan Research Laboratory) and the PAEC occurred only after Pakistan's nuclear test. Until that time, it was still an undocumented project under the PAEC.[63]

Eventually, the ERL team would succeed in 1978, when Pakistan's first enrichment would be completed.[64] But the road to this achievement was long and tedious.

Enrichment Trials, Tribulations, and Successes

After forcibly taking power from Prime Minister Bhutto, General Zia-ul-Haq injected his political preferences and paranoia into the PAEC and Project 706. The new president had a particular dislike for Munir Khan, because of the Ahmadi investigation and his close relationship with Bhutto. General Zia's conservative Islamic mindset and suspicions of Ahmadis led him to believe that these minority groups infiltrated the PAEC. Intelligence sleuths would investigate anyone associated with Nobel laureate Abdus Salam, purge all confirmed Ahmadis, and sideline the suspected ones.

Zia was equally concerned with Western moles and spies within the nuclear program, and this paranoia was reflected in his managerial style. While it is hard to assess the effects of Zia's oversight, it is safe to say that an intense security culture permeated the PAEC.

In light of his deep suspicions, General Zia made a variety of administrative changes, including the separation of ERL and PAEC. The virtual divorce between ERL and the PAEC caused intense competition between the two entities. On the one hand, this rivalry spurred more innovation within Project 706. On the other, miscommunications and jealousies led to controversies that slowed progress.

Specifically, Zia-ul-Haq induced brisk competition between the two in order to gain information on both while maintaining what he felt to be a healthy, yet aggressive, environment.[65] Within the limited circles that were aware of this tension, the competition was referred to as the clash of the Khans: Centrifuge Khan vs. Reactor Khan. However, this same rivalry caused one entity to undermine the other. For example, out of spite Munir Ahmed Khan stopped sending new employees to ERL, forcing A. Q. Khan to recruit and hire on his own. Munir was seemingly skeptical of the project's success and viewed it as a waste of resources. Javed Mirza recalls Munir saying, "No one in the world has used the centrifuge method to produce weapon grade material . . . . [T]his is not going to work, he [A. Q. Khan] is simply wasting time."[66] A. Q. Khan interpreted these doubts as threats to his centrifuge program.[67]

To make matters worse, another controversy grew within the government circles, alleging that Munir Khan may have had a conflict of interest. According to Agha Shahi, Munir's loyalty was divided between Pakistan's bomb effort and his own desire to become IAEA chair.[68] This accusation remains unsubstantiated, although it is possible that after constant attacks, Munir may have naturally felt that a return to the IAEA would earn him more respect.

The competition between the PAEC and ERL also led to several miscommunications, further mistrust, and the eventual breakdown of any dialogue between the two organizations. For example, as centrifuge experiments were taking place, the Chemical Plants Complex (CPC) was tasked to produce the UF6 that was to be fed into the completed cascades. However, the CPC did not know the level of purity that ERL needed for its machines, and ERL did not trust them to produce gas of good quality. As mentioned earlier, the level of UF6 purity is extremely important to enrichment success, yet even with their common goal at risk, the rivals could put their own interests aside, and the two refused to initiate communications.

The technological complexity of producing the gas worsened the situation, leaving ERL unsure if the CPC could indeed complete the task. A special team of PAEC scientists and engineers were recruited and foreign experts consulted to solve the frequent glitches related to UF6 production. The CPC was under pressure because, reportedly, General Zia had given Munir Ahmad Khan a six-month deadline; after "a few more weeks, and if PAEC failed, [General Zia] could hang the scientists." This threat was a grim reference to Bhutto's hanging only a few months before. It also reflected Zia-ul-Haq's poor opinion of PAEC performance and leadership. Nevertheless, Munir Ahmad Khan met the deadline in 1980 and requested that Dr. Ishfaq Ahmad personally go to Islamabad and inform General Zia of their success.[69]

But this success was belated, as A. Q. Khan had approached China two years earlier and received fifteen tons of UF6.[70] This move was not meant to undermine Pakistan's ability to produce indigenously, but rather to ensure that Project 706 continued on schedule. And indeed it did, as China's gas was most likely used in Pakistan's first round of enrichment while the PAEC was still struggling with UF6 production. When the CPC finally sent its first consignment to ERL, A. Q. Khan was wary of its quality and refused the shipment. This step sparked further debate, and another high-level investigation ensued that eventually demonstrated that CPC's UF6 was indeed of the right purity.[71]

PAEC officials at CPC agreed "1979–80 was the most difficult period for our project since doubts were being expressed about our ability to operate the plant and produce UF6. When we started producing UF6 and sent it to [ERL] they were taken by surprise as Dr. A. Q. Khan somehow had become convinced that PAEC would never be able to produce UF6 in required quantities."[72]

The intense competition between the PAEC and ERL permeated almost all facets of the nuclear project. Although the controversy over the UF6 was resolved, certain PAEC officials remain bitter to date. Even after thirty years, Sultan Bashiruddin Mahmood held exceptionally strong feelings about those times, demonstrated by his lasting opinion of A. Q. Khan. "A. Q. Khan was mentally sick. His mental sickness was such that he wanted everything in his possession, in his control, and he wanted that 'I should be known that I am the super-genius, I am every body.'"[73]

Even with these delays and controversies, the project did manage to enrich uranium successfully, but not without years of trial and error. It was A. Q. Khan's managerial skills and perseverance that drove progress. Javed Mirza told the author, "A. Q. Khan was a loner. He used to say, 'I have no lobby. I am alone and too much pressure is being put on me. Everyone thinks I am wasting their time.' . . . He concentrated and made sure we got the money, tools, equipment, and materials . . . . He said, '[Y]ou recruit the people, put in your best and the job has to be done.' He worked and made us work seven days a week, from morning till midnight. Everybody."

The R&D on indigenous centrifuge production began as early as the first months of 1976, and the first experimental centrifuges began to be tested and rotated by June 1976.[74] This effort continued unabated following A. Q. Khan's appointment as head of the project.

Learning to Rotate

Javed Mirza had been posted to PINSTECH to begin work on the electronics of a foot-long centrifuge. He recollected a day when he and his colleagues first tested the rotation speed of their prototype motor. While they had begun to congratulate each other on the machine's successful rotation, the centrifuge exploded with such force that a splinter flew off, broke through its glass casing, and cut clean through the neck of a glass bottle lying on a shelf. The splinter ended up embedded in the ceiling and has been left there as a memento.[75] Mirza recalls, "It was then that we realized we all had a narrow escape. We then had a clever idea. We turned the machine around towards the wall . . . , so next time if it crashed it would hit the wall. These were our learning steps."[76]

To analyze the speed and rotation of the centrifuge, the team installed a glass window with a strobe light in the centrifuge case to determine "if the speed of rotation was equal to the speed of strobe lights or double or triple." As Mirza explained, "A crude magnetic device was built using a bent rod with coils around it and then we magnetized it and then by using some coil outside we were able to get the signals. . . . From that crude beginning we have now refined it, but the concept remains the same—as if placing a 'simple coil' over the telephone and you can pick up a conversation."[77]

More pilot-scale centrifuges were made, each with its individual problems. Some exploded, others did not rotate, while others failed to separate uranium isotopes.[78] Balancing the centrifuges while they spun at high speed was a critical engineering problem. The ERL team faced two major challenges in this regard—the frequency of earthquakes in Pakistan and a flaw in the original Dutch design. As will be explained later in this chapter, after a traumatic experience the first challenge was resolved. A ten-foot concrete foundation was laid in the main Kahuta centrifuge hall that would absorb the tremors before they could reach the cascades. The second challenge was more complex.

At the base of the centrifuge casing was a bottom bearing that took the weight of the rotor as it spun. The rotor itself hinged on a thin needle, and adjacent to that was a tiny cup of lubricant to reduce friction. This tiny system was located in a groove, but had to be etched inside, completely erect and without the slightest tilt. Any minute irregularity in the design would result in a crash. And indeed, Project 706 was experiencing crashes at all stages of the program. The Dutch design had an unwanted tilt, and only when A. Q. Khan applied his knowledge of the German G-2 design was the problem solved.

The next step was to develop integrated circuitry (ICS) technology, of which there was no precedent in Pakistan. The team was able to build, ab initio, a Printer Circuit Board (PCB) by 1976 using only a pen and marker on a copper board. The vacuum and rotors were built next, with the help of Dr. Fakhar Hashmi and imports of small inverters. Eventually the team built four aluminum rotors, and by late 1977, Project 706 boasted the development of Pakistan-1 (P-1) rotors.

From Rotating to Cascading

Experiments on cascades and isotope separation were divided between the Sihala and Kahuta sites. A pilot-scale plant of 52 centrifuge machines was built in Sihala that eventually grew to accommodate 164 machines. The goal was to conduct trials at Sihala in order to solve all the technological problems before moving the plant to the Kahuta site, which was still under construction at the time. As Javed Mirza phrased it, "We did not wait for all buildings to complete. We assembled one big cascade and partitioned it. As one part [of the cascade] was ready we put machines in Kahuta while the other was being built and assembled."[79]

The delicate process of trial and error began once again. Although 164 machines were not many, the team was confident enough that this number would suffice for the initial stages. However, there were times when the entire complex would crash because of flaws in the cascade logic. As the project progressed, Project 706 would have to build and rebuild many more machines to meet its needs.

By the end of 1977, the team had passed over the initial humps and was confident that the machines would operate effectively. Javed Mirza explained that these experts did not simply learn how to turn the machines, but also to ensure that there were "counter currents inside the machine that could help enrich the uranium." Mechanical and temperature differences allowed the UF6 to flow from top to bottom, and it was here that lots of research and development was done. Under the dynamic leadership and administration of A. Q. Khan, there were three outstanding contributors—G. D. Alam, Fakhar Hashmi, and Anwar Ali—all who helped achieve the first enrichment.[80]

Cascading to Enriching

At the Sihala plant, on June 4, 1978, at 2 a.m., a centrifuge machine succeeded in separating U-235 from U-238, thus accomplishing centrifuge enrichment. Dr. G. D. Alam instantly declared to his fellow scientists and engineers, "Gentlemen, today we have achieved enrichment in Pakistan."[81] Dr. Javed Mirza ran to retrieve a piece of paper, dated it, and all present, including Anwar Ali and Ijaz Khokar, signed their names to it.[82] In an interview with Pakistani television *Aaj*, however, A. Q. Khan provided an earlier date of April 6, 1978.[83] Munir Ahmad Khan described this team of scientists and engineers as "the best brains of PAEC."[84]

Dr. A. Q. Khan reported this milestone to the Project Board: "We in the project would like to inform the Board that a machine has been developed and tested which has resulted in predicted performance. We have succeeded in producing laboratory samples in which natural uranium hexafluoride has been enriched. The technological problems of running the machine at high speed and physical problems of moving the gas within the rotator in appropriate direction have now been overcome. For the first time, on June 4, 1978, natural uranium hexafluoride was enriched into U-235 in any developing country of the world. Today we are now probably the 5th country in the world which has succeeded in enriching uranium."[85]

The news soon spread. Munir Ahmad Khan informed an imprisoned Zulfiqar Ali Bhutto of this success under the pretext of bringing him vitamins and fruits.[86] Not particularly adhering to the strict secrecy within the PAEC, on February 2, 1979, A. Q. Khan wrote to his friend in Canada, Abdul Aziz Khan, of the great success at ERL. "June 4 is a historical day for us. On that day we put 'air' in the machine and the first time we got the right product and its efficiency was the same as the theoretical . . . . As you have seen, my team consists of crazy people. They do not care if it is day or night. They go after it with all their might. The bellows have arrived and like this we can increase the speed of our work."[87]

The next enrichment success came after many years of procurement efforts that will be explored in Chapter 8. In A. Q. Khan's letter to Abdul Aziz Khan, he wrote of the first attempts being made to link up groups of centrifuges in cascades. He said in reference to the work in Sihala, "Everybody is working like mad. The first eight are working fine, after that we started the four together . . . . [T]hey worked all right, then we distributed the sweets."[88] He also revealed that "work on the big plant was also speeding up, with the main laboratory buildings, centrifuge hall B-1 and administration block almost finished."[89] He added, "We hope by April, many groups of centrifuges would be transferred there [Kahuta],"[90] and expressed his desire to have more staff, as the work was increasing. "Unless this work is completed," he said, "I am not going to budge from here."[91]

By this time, the London Suppliers Group had placed a stranglehold on all shipments and exports of nuclear-related materials and equipment, directly affecting Pakistan's enrichment project. In yet another letter, A. Q. Khan shared his disappointment: "All our material has been stopped; everywhere they are making us delayed. The materials, which we were buying from British and Americans, have been stopped. Now we will have to do some work ourselves."[92]

Nevertheless, construction work on the Kahuta plant continued unabated, and by February 1979 the pilot centrifuge plant at Sihala was successfully running a test-cascade of fifty-four machines. The outer ring of the Kahuta plant was completed by 1981, and the centrifuge halls were being prepared for the installment of hundreds of centrifuge machines.[93] President General Zia-ul-Haq visited the Kahuta plant on May 1, 1981. Expecting a rudimentary workshop, he could not believe the state-of-the-art operational cascades in the facility, the likes of which he had never seen. Delighted, he changed the name of ERL to KRL, or Khan Research Laboratories, after its director, Dr. A. Q. Khan. In A. Q. Khan's words, this was "a distinction that was unmatched in the scientific world since no living scientist had been bestowed the honor of the naming of an organization after him."[94]

The joy had lasted a few months when President Zia braced for a new shock. In September 1981, a powerful earthquake measuring 6.1 on the Richter scale shook Islamabad and the surrounding area. Pakistani scientists at Kahuta were on a lunch break when the earth shook, forcing them to run to work stations only to hear the sounds of explosions. Some four thousand centrifuges operating in the Khan Research Laboratory had crashed. The earthquake had unbalanced the rotors, operating in a vacuum at some 65,000 revolutions per minute (RPMs); they hit their casings and turned into powder, making sounds like hand grenades exploding. Within minutes President Zia-ul-Haq was informed. According to A. Q. Khan, he told the president, "We [have] a clean slate and would have to start from the beginning." A. Q. Khan nevertheless assured the worried president that "unexpected disasters do happen ... but we have all the required facilities, materials and know-how." Within two years, claims A. Q. Khan, "we had installed five thousand machines and were producing weapons-grade enriched uranium."[95] As mentioned above, KRL scientists and Pakistan Army engineers then redesigned the centrifuge beds so as to make them resistant to shocks.[96]

President Zia-ul-Haq was not having a particularly good year in 1981—except for the support from President Reagan, who had taken office that January. Pakistan's western borders were in a state of war threatened by the Soviet Union, but also were the base from which guerrilla war was waged for the entire decade. In that summer Israeli planes destroyed an Iraqi nuclear plant at Osirak. This created new ideas in Delhi to emulate the Israeli feat, and ripples of fear spread in Islamabad. The September earthquake and resulting "clean slate" apparently panicked Zia, and that explains why he reached out to China. Zia-ul-Haq sent his emissary Lieutenant-General Naqvi to China; Naqvi received some fifty kilograms of HEU on loan and even a crude bomb design purported to be a copy of China's fourth nuclear test of 1966, which will be explained more in later chapters.

Undoubtedly the project's success was the result of years of hard work and the dedication of hundreds of Pakistani scientists and engineers, but, more important, the result of A. Q. Khan's leadership and resolve. In 1990, A. Q. Khan recounted the various milestones of the project. He said, "A country which could not make sewing needles ... was embarking on one of the latest and most difficult technologies. Only 7 countries in the world (USA, UK, France, USSR, China, Germany and Holland) possessed this technology. Of the whole nuclear fuel cycle, enrichment is considered to be the most difficult and most sophisticated technology. It was a real challenge to my colleagues and me. The problem was very clear to us. We were not going to find out new laws of nature but were dealing with a very difficult and sophisticated engineering technology. It was not possible for us to make each and every piece of equipment or component within the country. Attempts to do so would have killed the project in the initial stage. We devised a strategy by which we would go all out to buy everything that we needed in the open market to lay the foundation of a good infrastructure and would then switch over to indigenous production as and when we had to."[95]

The skill of the scientists and engineers—those men who managed to understand the complex enrichment technologies and were able to re-create them in Pakistan—was also applauded internationally. "At the same time, we received many letters and telexes from abroad and people chased us with figures and details of equipment they had sold to Almelo, Capenhurst, etc. They literally begged us to buy their equipment. We bought what we considered suitable for our plant and very often asked them to make changes and modifications according to our requirements. One should realize that all this equipment was, what we call, conventional technology. It was normal chemical process and vacuum technology equipment, which had 1,001 uses in other disciplines. Notwithstanding the fact that we were handicapped by not being able to hold open discussions with foreign experts or organizations, we attacked all the problems successfully. Our scientists and engineers not only designed and ran good centrifuges but designed the cascades, worked out the header piping system, calculated the pressures, developed the control philosophy and developed software and hardware for it. It was a hundred percent Pakistani effort and success story."[96]

In this regard, he further said, "An enrichment plant needs a lot of precautions or fail-safe systems. We designed them all. We welded thousands of feet of aluminum pipes of the header, and of the feed and collection systems. Once the western propaganda reached its climax and all efforts were made to stop or block even the most harmless items, we said enough was enough and started indigenous production of all the sophisticated electronic, electrical and vacuum equipment."[97]

He went on to add, "Kahuta is an all Pakistani effort and is a symbol of Pakistan's determination to refuse to submit to blackmail and bullying. It is not only a great source of personal satisfaction to me, but is also a symbol of pride for my colleagues. While preliminary work was being undertaken at Rawalpindi and procurement was being done for the most essential and sophisticated equipment and materials, we were manufacturing the first prototypes of centrifuges; we were setting up a pilot plant at Sihala and were preparing blueprints for and starting the construction of the main facility at Kahuta. It was a revolutionary and bold step and it virtually ensured our success in a record time."[98]

TABLE 7.1

Development of Enriched Uranium Route

Process/Step	Facility	Launched	Completed	Product	Organization
Uranium Exploration	Dera Ghazi Khan; Exploration commenced at Qabul Khel (1992), Siwalik Hills etc during 1970s	1961	1977	Decommissioned in 2000. Replaced by Nuclear Materials Complex-1	PAEC
Uranium Processing (Uranium Mine and Mill)	Baghalchur-1 (BC-1), DG Khan	1975	1977	Yellow Cake/ Uranium Concentrate U3O8	PAEC
Uranium Conversion	Chemical Plants Complex, DG Khan	1975	1978–80	Uranium Oxide UO_2; Uranium Tetra fluoride UF_4; Natural Uranium Hexafluoride Gas, UF_6	PAEC
Uranium Enrichment	Chaklala, Sihala, Kahuta	1974	1980	Enriched Uranium Gas U-235	PAEC/ADW 1974–76 ERL 1976–81 KRL 1981 to date
Uranium	Uranium Metal Laboratory	1976	1978	Enriched Uranium U-235 Metal	PAEC 1978 to date
Metallurgy/ Machining of HEU core	KRL	1987			KRL 1987 to date

On June 23, 1983, a secret memorandum from the U.S. Department of State titled "The Pakistani Nuclear Program" (now declassified) assessed that Pakistan was "facing difficulties in making the centrifuges machine work and that the Pakistanis have not yet produced any significant quantities of highly enriched uranium." The memo indicated that the United States believed the Pakistanis were seeking cooperation from China to overcome the difficulties. It predicted that once operational difficulties were over, within two to three years, Pakistan could produce sufficient fissile material for a single device and, with sustained operations, up to several devices per year.[99]

However, it would take KRL another two years to produce enough weapons-grade uranium for one nuclear device. Although the number of operational centrifuges of the P-1 model continued to increase, at least two more earthquakes—apart from the one in 1981, described above, and another in 1983—destroyed hundreds of centrifuges before Pakistani engineers learned how to design shock-resistant beds.[100] Nevertheless, essential materials continued to be procured from abroad, while at the same time Pakistan began producing centrifuge components and maraging steel indigenously.[101]

It was in January 1984 that A. Q. Khan first publicly announced that Pakistan was able to enrich uranium. He told the Urdu magazine *Qaumi Digest* that he considered it his greatest achievement to have done in seven years what had taken the West twenty years to accomplish—the enrichment of uranium to weapons grade. These claims were repeated in two more Urdu daily papers, *Nawa-i-Waqt* and *Jang,* in February 1984.[102] An International Institute of Strategic Studies dossier of May 2007 aptly noted, "During the 1980s and 1990s, the mastery of uranium enrichment became the quintessential symbol of national pride, scientific and technical modernity, and independence from foreign powers."[103]

The Changed Political and Security Landscape

While the internal struggle for uranium enrichment was continuing, external struggles were also taking place. As if the technological challenges were not enough, changes in Pakistan's leadership and foreign relations, as well as in sanctions, all had an impact on the centrifuge project.

On July 5, 1977, after four months of violent protests against the rigged March election that returned Bhutto to the presidency, the Pakistan military seized power. Zia-ul-Haq would rule Pakistan for the next eleven years, during which time the region would undergo tremendous upheaval and violence, the impact of which still resonates today.

Also in 1977, Jimmy Carter assumed the presidential office with a strong nonproliferation agenda. Indeed, his policies affected the global nuclear industry, as new export controls were enacted, new export cartels emerged, and a campaign to create robust norms against proliferation was created. Not surprisingly, this policy led to much friction between the United States and Pakistan. The military coup against Bhutto triggered another layer of sanctions on top of the already existing nuclear sanctions. The Carter administration even considered using force to destroy Pakistan's nascent nuclear capability if sanctions did not work.

Well aware of the American attitude toward the Pakistani program, Zia tightened security and command over Project 706. After all, the country was in a dangerous position, faced with poor economic performance, political upheaval, and international sanctions. The people of Pakistan were truly "eating grass" as the nation came close to bankruptcy between 1978 and 1979.

In this environment, three major changes took place in Pakistan's neighborhood. The first was the Indian National Congress defeat by the Janata party. Second, Afghan President Daoud Khan was overthrown by a bloody coup led by communist leader Nuruddin Tarakki, leading to Islamic tribal leaders revolting against the regime and, eventually, the Soviet invasion of Afghanistan in 1979. The invasion posed a direct threat to Pakistan and completely changed the political geography of the region. Finally, Pakistan lost a close ally that same year when the shah of Iran was removed by the triumphant return of Ayatollah Khomeini. The Islamic Revolution of Iran brought about yet another ideological split within the Muslim community.

These dramatic regional shifts—and Pakistan's new role as a central player between the two global superpowers in the South Asia region—provided a window through which Pakistan could push through its nuclear program. The inter-lab rivalry, tense domestic political situation, rapid change in the regional security landscape, and global politics bolstered the path to successful enrichment. However, technical challenges remained, and open market supplies were cut off by the growing nonproliferation regime. Deeply determined, Pakistan learned to negotiate foreign procurement networks in markets ranging from white to grey to black. Any means were justified in pursuit of a nuclear deterrent.

8   Procurement Network
in the Grey Market

Western accounts of Pakistan's procurement strategy focus exclusively on A. Q. Khan, whose role is cast either as spy or kingpin of an elaborate network that ran like a nuclear Wal-Mart.[1] For A. Q. Khan and others who were involved in procurement activities, however, acquiring the necessary knowledge and components for the nuclear program was a call to the highest level of national service at a time when Pakistan's security and survivability were at stake. Dedicated people who were determined to overcome all technical and political hurdles placed before the Pakistani nuclear program were prepared not just to "eat grass" but also to take extraordinary risks—at times with their lives—in the underworld of nuclear procurement, all in the name of technology and national capacity.

Three significant factors handicapped Pakistan and created the necessity for a procurement network. First, no other country with similar nuclear ambitions faced such stringent nonproliferation barriers. Contemporary proliferators such as Brazil, Argentina, South Africa, India, and Israel had crossed the critical thresholds well before the nonproliferation regime tightened its screws. From Pakistan's perspective, however, its exclusion was not just a matter of timing—Pakistan believed it was targeted because it was the only Muslim country acquiring such weapons at the time. Many other states in the Islamic world were gradually convinced of this belief as well. Saudi Arabia, Libya, the UAE, and, to an extent, Iran (under the shah) were determined not to let the Pakistani nuclear ship sink.

Second, Pakistan was extremely vulnerable and did not have any leverage of its own. Beset with huge economic burdens, domestic political unrest, and regional security concerns, it was largely dependent on international institutions and aid. Although Pakistan was aware that Western countries were not sympathetic to its security anxieties, it knew that its alliance with the West was critical and largely unavoidable. Islamabad could afford neither confronting nor abandoning the West.

Instead, Pakistan sought more reliable strategic relationships via alliances with China and North Korea. A three-pronged strategic policy surfaced: (1) retain an alliance with the West and seek technological assistance, (2) seek financial support from oil-rich Islamic countries to sustain the economy, and (3) seek strategic substitutes with assured allies when Western technology was not available.

The third and most serious handicap was the rapid deterioration of the regional security situation, summarized at the end of Chapter 7. The dramatic alteration of the geopolitical landscape—especially after the Islamic Revolution in Iran and the Soviet Union's invasion of Afghanistan—created a new strategic environment for which Pakistan had no preparation. Pakistani armed forces faced potential aggressors on two fronts. Although the country enjoyed the benefits of being a frontline state as long as the Soviets lasted in Afghanistan, the socioeconomic and security costs were substantial and the resulting anarchy in the region still threatens Islamabad today.

It was under such circumstances that the lack of Western nonproliferation concerns opened up a new window of opportunity for Pakistan's nuclear deterrent. The technical hurdles forced scientists and officials to tap into any and every source that would help Pakistan complete its fuel cycle. Where rules were lax, critical supplies were procured from the West, and when nonproliferation barriers increased, those supplies were found by other, less explicit means. It is important to remember that while uranium enrichment became a top priority, plutonium production still continued, but at a slower pace. Thus Pakistani officials searched for materials that met the needs of both ends of the nuclear fuel cycle.

Tom and Jerry in the Open Market

As mentioned in the previous chapter, S. A. Butt played a key role in procuring critical technologies for Pakistan. Essentially, he simultaneously wore the hats of secretary, consultant, recruiter, and distributor. He kept an eye on legally available technologies and shipped them through fastest means.

When pressure mounted on France and other European countries to scuttle the Pakistani nuclear program, Butt's sole procurement strategy was to purchase all possible critical items before they were tagged by the nuclear supplier club's list.[2] A cat and mouse game ensued between the European suppliers and

Pakistani demands, as Pakistani buyers raced to acquire goods, dodging obstacles and slipping away. This became possible because the Western bureaucracies were slow to act. A. Q. Khan and his suppliers stayed one step ahead of their pursuers for almost three decades.

Initially, Pakistan participated in purchases of key components from the open market. As rules tightened, however, willing suppliers shifted to the grey market. Most published Western accounts blame either U.S. policy-makers or intelligence agencies for turning a Nelson's eye on Pakistani procurements. Perhaps the United States might have barred critical supplies to Pakistan early on, but the exigencies of global security trumped nonproliferation concerns.

S. A. Butt's dedication, coupled with Khan's connections and ability to bargain, allowed Pakistan to buy things that would have otherwise been impossible to acquire. As A. Q. Khan's professor, Martin Brabers, explained, "[In] buying equipment, [A. Q. Khan] knew all the companies, he knew so many people abroad in many countries. . . . Why, he knew so many languages, and he is so charming [that] he managed to buy many things that other Pakistanis would not manage to buy."[3] And in A. Q. Khan's own words when asked how he developed the supply chain: "Since I had been living in Europe for 15 years, I knew about their industry and suppliers very well. I knew who made what. People accuse me of stealing lists of European suppliers, but that is rubbish. I had a doctorate in engineering. I had a valuable job in Holland; I would travel from one corner of Europe to the other. I also knew the addresses of all the suppliers. When I came to Pakistan, I started purchasing equipment from them until they proscribed the selling of equipments to us. Then we started purchasing the same equipment through other countries, for example, Kuwait, Bahrain, UAE, Abu Dhabi and Singapore. They could not outmaneuver us, as we remained a step ahead."[4]

The Pakistani approach was innovative. Although initially pursuing entire machines and technologies, Pakistan eventually began to acquire components of enrichment technology and equipment from small, high-technology Western firms. Once the individual components—from yellow cake, to gasification/solidification units, to centrifuge parts—found their way to Pakistan, PAEC scientists and engineers would assemble them to achieve mastery over the enrichment cycle.

As a counterpart to A. Q. Khan's efforts, another significant cross-section of Pakistan's network was at play: Europe's business community, which found ingenious ways of keeping the Pakistan procurement pipeline flowing. At first, all activities were conducted within legal bounds, but when laws changed and rules tightened, the supply patterns adjusted accordingly and grey areas of legal interpretation emerged. Butt was always careful; when he assessed that procuring a particular item was clearly illegal in one country, he tapped into another European country where laws and export restrictions acted in his favor. Butt and his team would eventually create a supplier network that worked with "fantastic cleverness."[5]

But Pakistan did not purposefully design a network. Rather, it was a product of intense domestic demand and of Western business interests. Willing suppliers were looking for profits—some unwittingly contributing to the establishment of a network, others with full knowledge of their product's end use. Indeed, many business people had no regrets about helping Pakistan acquire a nuclear deterrent.[6] For them, India had cheated the world by testing a nuclear device and dubbing it a "peaceful nuclear test" (PNE), posing a direct threat to Pakistan.[7]

Sultan Bashir Mahmood believes that 1975 was the most important year for PAEC procurements. He insists that significant acquisitions from abroad were made under his supervision before A. Q. Khan took over in July 1976. Other sources reveal that more advanced technologies and critical components could have come only after A. Q. Khan was made the head of Project 706. After Engineering Research Labs (ERL) was separated from the PAEC, S. A. Butt continued to deal with PAEC-related work, even though ERL had hired its own agent in Bonn, Mr. Ikram-ul-Haq Khan.[8]

Regardless of individual contribution, the series of procurement events documented in this chapter illustrate the dynamic nature of Pakistan's efforts. From maraging steel to cascade pipes to inverters and everything in between, Pakistan actively sought out opportunities, instilled business competition, and worked ahead to stay ahead of the nonproliferation regime.

In 1975, S. A. Butt sensed an opportunity rising, as German unhappiness over the numerous legal strains placed on nuclear commerce surfaced. Under U.S. pressure the Germans put on hold the sale of eight power reactors, a uranium enrichment facility, and a plutonium reprocessing plant to Brazil (then a nonsignatory to NPT). If completed, that deal would have yielded multibillion-dollar profits. The German industry was frustrated that nonproliferation and moral arguments selectively hurt European business, while U.S. nuclear industries such as Westinghouse and General Electric thrived.[9] It is therefore no surprise that Germany was the main supplier of components to Pakistan.[10]

For example, in 1975 there was a major purchase of three "roller, high compression machines" from Dusseldorf Germany, which boasted a dual-use application to make stainless steel utensils and casings for artillery shells.[11] This machine was subsequently used to build the aluminum rotor for centrifuges.[12] Some European suppliers were very generous, and offered to sell items not on the Pakistani wish list. In this particular case, the same Dusseldorf supplier volunteered to sell a device that machined metal into an extremely thin, highly uniform file sheet. The businessman told Pakistani purchasers, "Some far eastern country had placed this order which never picked it up." Sultan Bashiruddin said, "We jumped at the offer, making prompt payment and shipping it to Pakistan Ordnance Factories [POF]. It arrived within 45 days."[13]

Two other important procurements were also made that year: an electronic beam welding machine and a ring magnet charging machine.[14] These purchases were part of the initial PAEC strategy to undertake large-scale procurements in an effort to avoid future shortages.[15]

G. D. Alam also participated in Pakistan's procurement project, specifically within the enrichment program. In 1976, he was A. Q. Khan's right-hand man and accompanied him, along with S. A. Butt, to Europe on a secret assignment to acquire critical components for uranium hexafluoride (UF6) handling.

Another very important purchase from Germany was a uranium conversion facility designed to convert UF4 to UF6. The West German firm Leybold-Heraeus, based in Hanau, was famous for its vacuum technology products. G. D. Alam told the Germans that the Pakistanis were looking for a "box-like plant" to handle UF6 gas. The Leybold executives discussed several designs with Alam, who suggested modifications that would meet Pakistan's requirements. Alam's hosts were eager to secure the deal and replied, "We know exactly what you want."[16]

Within a fortnight of their visit, the Swiss and German hosts sent detailed designs to the PAEC, which immediately placed orders worth some 6 million deutschemarks. The orders were completed a few months after Alam's visit to Europe. The conversion plant was sent via a firm in Austria, routed through Dubai and, like other critical equipment, arrived in disassembled form in Pakistan.[17] Leybold Heraeus also supplied S. A. Butt and G. D. Alam with a machine that made centrifuge rotor-tubes.[18] Building closer ties, an employee at the Leybold Heraeus, Gotthard Lerch, traveled to Pakistan and eventually became part of A. Q. Khan's suppliers network.

German companies were chosen as the primary suppliers because A. Q.

Khan and his colleague Fakhar Hashmi recognized that German expertise in machine tools and precision engineering was second to none and contributed greatly to the enrichment industry as a whole. In addition, since Germany was not a nuclear power, it employed more lenient export controls.

Competition for Pakistan's business among European firms continued, even in the more restricted advanced technology market. Thus U.S. public nonproliferation reprimands produced modest results, as demonstrated by Germany's meager response to nearly one hundred demarches. But the Pakistanis detected this international pressure and quickly made use of extensive contacts. The German magazine *Stern* reported that about seventy German firms conducted nuclear-related business with Pakistani-associated enterprises throughout the 1980s.[19]

At the time, Switzerland's Chur Valley was famous for its centrifuge equipment production, and so earned the name "Vacuum Valley." Among the many firms located there, CORA Engineering was known for its custom-made gas and solidification units.[20] These units convert solid UF6 into a gaseous form for feeding the centrifuge and then after enrichment turn the gas back into solid form.[21] But luckily for the procurement agents, it was not placed on the "trigger" list of banned nuclear-sensitive items. CORA instantly obtained a supply order from the Pakistanis, and by the summer of 1978 the company was able to complete the customized plant. This unit was quite large and required three specially chartered C-130 planes to transport it to Pakistan.[22]

In the same famous Swiss valley lay another firm, Vakuum Apparat Technik (VAT), well known for its high-vacuum valves. Vacuum tubes and valves were dual-use items, suitable for both gas centrifuges and nonmilitary items, and not included in the export controls lists at the time. Defending the sale to Pakistan, a VAT official later said, "The parts for Pakistan were not crucial components. They were not parts of the isotope-separation equipment."[23] In addition to equipment, Pakistan also gained the support of Fredrich Tinner, a Swiss engineer and export manager of VAT. Eventually he established his own firm and continued to provide valves to ERL and other world customers.[24]

In another procurement effort, G. D. Alam and Javed Arshad Mirza traveled to the Fysisch Dynamisch Onderzoek (FDO) with a letter to A. Q. Khan's former colleague and friend Fritz Veerman.[25] Included was a request for very detailed technical specifications.[26] A. Q. Khan wrote:

> Very confidently I request you to help us. I urgently need the following information for our research program. Etches for pivots: a) Tension- How many volts?;

b) Electricity- How many amperes?; c) How long is etching to be done?; d) Solution (electrolytic) HCl or something other is added as a solution. If it is possible, I would be grateful for 3–4 etched pivots. I would be very grateful if you could send me a few negatives for the pattern. You would be having negatives of these. Lower shock absorber. Can you provide a complete absorber for CNOR? Please give my greetings to Frencken, and try to get a piece for me. . . . Fritz, these are very urgently required, without which the research would come to a standstill. I am sure you can provide me with these. These things are very small, and I hope you will not disappoint me.[27]

However, this attempt to obtain information was not successful. After reading the letter, Veerman turned to the two Pakistani scientists and in a state of agitation said, "Dr. Khan calls me, 'my dear friend,' and has asked me for information that is secret and I cannot provide him. This is the end of our business with Pakistan."[28] Alam and Mirza barely escaped arrest before Veerman reported the letter to his superior, who then forwarded it to the Dutch intelligence service.[29] Consequently, the Dutch government used this and other letters to institute a case against A. Q. Khan.[30]

Despite this setback, further attempts to procure more materials proved to be successful. Another Dutch firm, Van Doorne Transmissie (VDT), agreed to provide Pakistan with sixty-five hundred hardened steel tubes through a procurement network that became known as the "Pakistani pipeline." The first batch of three hundred tubes was sent to Pakistan on November 2, 1976, and the remaining order was completed in September 1979.[31] Although the Dutch government tried to prevent the sale, the absence of legal provisions and the assistance of middleman Henk Slebos allowed the bulk of the order to be completed.[32] S. A. Butt placed another order worth 40 million deutschmarks for rolled rods and ten thousand small parts with Aluminium Walzwerke of Singen in West Germany.[33] Butt had also placed an order for ten thousand bellows with a French firm, but only a part of the order could be shipped via Belgium since the French government intervened. However, enough technology was transferred "to enable the Pakistanis to make the rest themselves."[34]

By far the most significant event in the enrichment project was the procurement of high-frequency inverters from the British firm Emerson Electric. These components were especially important as they ensured uniformity in power supply to the centrifuges. Typically, inverters are used in textiles, and since Pakistan was well known for its textile fabric exports, this industry was an ideal front for importing the inverters.

S. A. Butt had begun making inquiries in Europe, and after a bit of searching, a West German firm called Team Industries, owned by Ernst Piffl, agreed to
supply the inverters. An initial order of thirty-six to forty inverters was placed
for about £30,000 to £40,000 each, and Ernst Piffl approached Emerson Electric for the product.[35]

The first batch was sent in December 1977, and the entire order was completed by August 1978.[36] But the Pakistani engineers found flaws in the inverter
models sent by Emerson. Some speculate that either the company deliberately
sold faulty models to undermine Pakistan, or simply assumed that Pakistani
scientists would not detect the flaws and thus they could get rid of a bad product. Unexpectedly, ERL scientists sent back a list of complex modifications for
subsequent inverter shipments. Needless to say, Emerson engineers were surprised. One employee remarked that from that moment on, another "Anglo-
Saxon" prejudice about Pakistani incompetence went down the drain.[37]

Even with the initial purchase made from Ernst Piffl, the centrifuge program
required at least 150 more inverters.[38] Shifting away from Emerson, A. Q. Khan
placed an order for additional inverters with the British firm Weargate, which
was owned by his old friends Peter Griffin and Abdus Salam (not to be confused with Pakistani Dr. Abdus Salam or Major General Salam, EME corps).[39]
Griffin claims that the supplier change occurred because Piffl was charging an
exorbitant price.[40] Others such as G. D. Alam simply believe that A. Q. Khan
wanted the moneymaking contract to go to his friend, with whom he could
share the profits.[41]

But these purchases did not go undetected. Piffl disclosed the entire inverter
affair to a British Labour MP, Mr. Frank Allaun, who was widely known for his
nonproliferation views. He of course sounded the alarm within Parliament, accusing Pakistan of procuring inverters for an ultracentrifuge project.[42]

Why the leak? One possibility is that after receiving the list of desired modifications, Emerson may have suspected the converters' actual end use. Another
is that Piffl was upset that the new Pakistani order was given to a rival firm.
Regardless of the reasons, Britain placed inverters on its export control list,
making it impossible for Griffin to secure more shipments for Pakistan.

The exposure of Pakistani imports from Britain alerted various intelligence
agencies around the world. The Israeli Mossad, in particular, viewed Pakistani
procurement as making possible an "Islamic bomb." Mossad was well known
for kidnapping and secretly assassinating scientists and suppliers who were assisting Egyptian and other Arab nuclear aspirants. Israelis were contemplating

similar ends for European procurement agents who were helping Pakistan.[43] Peter Griffin experienced firsthand the power of Mossad when he was caught in the crosshairs of its agents. In their book *Deception: Pakistan, the United States, and the Secret Trade in Nuclear Weapons,* Levy and Scott-Clark relay an incident in which Griffin was sitting at a bar in Bonn when a stranger sat down next to him. "'You're Peter Griffin,' he said. 'We don't like what you are doing, so stop it.' Griffin took this as a serious threat, recorded all business dealings, placed them in bank vault, and advised his wife that if anything untoward should happen to him she should give everything to their son Paul."[44] It is unclear whether A. Q. Khan or his other business colleagues knew of this threat and if so, what steps they took to prevent disclosure of the network or become more discreet in their dealings.

Now exasperated over the inability to purchase needed high-frequency inverters, A. Q. Khan wrote to his friend Abdul Aziz Khan in Canada on October 8, 1978: "Work is progressing but the frustration is increasing. It is just like a man who has waited 30 years but cannot wait for a few hours after the marriage ceremony."[45] While ERL engineers began to reverse engineer the imported inverters,[46] Abdul Aziz Khan helped to arrange a new avenue of procurement. In July 1980, Pakistani officials Anwar Ali and Imtiaz Ahmad Bhatti reached Montreal, Canada, to receive capacitors and resistors (individual inverter components) from the U.S. firm General Electric, Ltd. Eleven shipments worth $170,000 successfully reached Pakistan via a Dubai-based company before Canadian authorities stopped the last shipment.[47]

In another letter to Abdul Aziz Khan, A. Q. Khan hinted that inverter procurements were also made from the former Soviet Union: "The dam is ready and a week ago we put the flow of water in it and now it is filled. It has become quite scenic. Presently we are trying to obtain some information about where we can get the fish and put them in it so that our angler friends could have a good time. Hopefully in winter there will be ducks from Russia."[48]

Pakistan's supply of luck was large, but it was not limitless. As A. Q. Khan's audacious attempts to acquire sensitive technologies caught the attention of business and governments around the world, international pressure mounted on countries to control nuclear trade, and they slowly roused themselves to the task. Bilaterally and through multilateral organizations, states slowly harmonized export controls to prevent Pakistan and others from seeking and exploiting weak national regulations. Simultaneously, state regulators sought control further down the production chain.

But even with the rising barriers, one main strategy sustained the procurement network—as soon as Pakistani officials found one firm that was either unwilling to deal with them or was suspicious of their intent, they always found a willing substitute. These companies were in competition with each other, and Pakistan offered a high price. Reflecting back, Khan noted the eagerness of European firms to do business with Pakistan. "They literally begged us to buy their equipment. We bought what we considered suitable for our plant and very often asked them to make changes and modifications according to our requirements."[49]

Extra Hands

In addition to establishing European connections for equipment and parts, Pakistan continued strategic cooperation with China on a wide range of weapons purchases, some of which included nuclear components. One of the most closely guarded secrets in Pakistan is the specific nature of its nuclear agreements with China. None of the individuals interviewed by the author was forthcoming on this topic. Thus, the story of Sino-Pakistani cooperation is based solely on the author's limited personal knowledge, some credible Western public sources, and conjecture drawn from available records.

Reportedly, Z. A. Bhutto signed a strategic agreement with China in May 1976 that included military, nuclear, and other civil agreements. This cooperation became increasingly important in the mid-1980s when nonproliferation barriers deeply affected Pakistan's nuclear weapons program. One critical factor the two nations had in common was denial of certain Western technologies. Thus, their relationship was mutually beneficial—every piece of technology that Pakistan managed to acquire would be available to the Chinese for reverse engineering, providing Pakistan an opportunity to develop its engineering expertise. For example, it is possible that the inverters Pakistan began to produce indigenously were originally reverse engineered by Chinese specialists.

In addition to providing the benefits of expertise, China furnished Pakistan with UF6 and some highly enriched uranium (HEU) before Pakistan enriched as explained in the previous chapter. Further cooperation was marked by the import of forty tons of heavy water and a 1994–95 import of five thousand ring magnets to Khan Research Laboratories (KRL).[50] Beijing is also reported to have supplied a weapon design to KRL in the early 1980s—the same design it had tested in 1966. (See Chapter 9 for more details regarding cooperation in the weapons and ballistic missile fields.)

All of these purchases and agreements for cooperation required money. The Pakistani economy was in shambles throughout the time that the procurement network was forming, yet officials were still able to pay premium prices for expensive technologies. It was generous countries such as Libya and Saudi Arabia that financed the Pakistani economy as a whole, and mitigated the impact of Western sanctions. Nevertheless, despite economic and military aid, Pakistani officials had to devise a way to sustain the nuclear program. The answer came from the Bank of Credit and Commerce International (BCCI) and its Pakistani owner, Hassan Abidi. Islamabad's finance minister invited Abidi to establish a BCCI branch in Pakistan, tax free, so that every operation would be tax exempt. In exchange for such favorable conditions, BCCI would pay funds and fees directly back to the government—much less expensive than taxes. For example, one bank payment came in the form of a BCCI $10 million grant to G. I. Khan Institute at Tarbela, which is a private science and technology institute that also happened to be directed by A. Q. Khan.[51] Thus the BCCI paid for Pakistan's nuclear program via front companies and institutions, until its collapse in 1991.

Procurement Strategies

Pakistani officials utilized numerous strategies to consolidate the multiple channels, connections, and techniques during their procurement efforts.[52] These included:

- Diplomatic channels. Almost all the Pakistan embassies around the world helped procurement efforts by using their diplomatic dispatches;
- Staying ahead of the curve. Pakistani imports adjusted and shifted as different export controls were applied. Purchases shifted from buying entire units to acquiring smaller, independent components to unfinished products;
- Needle in the haystack. Pakistan would buy many benign and unsuspected technologies and hide a critical component within the lengthy purchase;
- Willingness to pay high prices. Pakistan would offer to pay twice the original price;
- Reverse engineering. Pakistan would purchase samples and then reproduce them domestically;

- Multiple attempts and connections. At least three or four different agents would buy from different companies. Once a set of choices was established, the agents would evaluate the ease of exportation and transportation;
- End-user justification. Pakistan would provide the supplier with numerous front companies and legitimate reasons for procurement, which could then be later verified;
- Diverse intermediaries and shipping routes (trans-shipment). Very few direct transportation routes to Pakistan existed; most items would go through intermediaries and numerous countries before reaching their final destination;
- Help from sympathetic countries. China, North Korea, and friendly Islamic countries would be willing conduits of shipments or sources of money;
- The Pakistani diaspora. Professionals scattered around the globe would contribute extensively to the nation's cause;
- Connections with a variety of entities. Pakistan had made friends with numerous individuals, companies, and businesses around the globe;
- Front companies. Pakistan created so many that they overwhelmed the system.

All of these strategies and partnerships allowed Pakistan to stay ahead of the global export control regime from the mid-1970s to the mid-1980s. A complex network of middlemen, financiers, importers, and front companies would work together to supply the Pakistani nuclear enterprise. Unfortunately, once Pakistan's own requirements were complete, this network would then acquire a life of its own, as other interested countries would be attracted to its benefits.

9   Building the Bomb

Pakistan began to review and evaluate atomic bomb designs within a year after the Multan meeting in 1972. Bhutto and the PAEC were expected to slowly hedge toward a weapons capability. However, Bhutto's approach was quite the opposite—it seemed as though he were trying to make up for lost time, and his impatient nature spurred him to keep a quick pace. He was caught between two schools of thought: one that advocated uranium enrichment and an HEU-fueled gun-type device, and another that backed the plutonium (Pu) program and a Pu-fueled implosion-type bomb design. Eventually, it was decided that the implosion method was the best choice for a nuclear bomb design.

Both Khan Research Laboratories (KRL) and the PAEC competed intensely under Bhutto, and eventually under Zia-ul-Haq. Zia realized that the highly classified activity should be under centralized control and a single command. Both for security as well as technical efficiency reasons, the president would make two decisions. First, he would decide to maintain the development of the metallic uranium core at KRL rather than transport it to the PAEC. Second, Zia would end the bomb design competition between the two organizations.

For a decade the PAEC worked discreetly on the bomb design. In the early 1980s, however, Zia-ul-Haq deliberately sparked a competition on bomb design between the two organizations, hoping to turn interlaboratory rivalry and the egos of the two Khans into a positive dividend for the country. The competition for the bomb design lasted about six years, after which the president reversed his decision, returning the bomb design project to the PAEC. Besides the technical reasoning (explained later), apparently the president concluded that A. Q. Khan was too indiscreet and pompous to be trusted with such a high-level national secret.[1] Also, his earlier distrust of Munir Khan had waned in the last years of Zia-ul-Haq's life.[2]

A commonly held belief in the West is that Pakistani nuclear weapon designs were simply a result of China's passing on its design in the early 1980s. However, China's help was a supplemental contribution to an ongoing effort. The experiments on nuclear devices and the development of weapon designs and means of delivery took nearly twenty-five years after the theoretical study commenced in 1972. The air force and Pakistani scientists worked for more than a decade before they could confidently claim the capability to deliver weapons from the wings of a fighter aircraft. The weapons tested in 1998 had undergone decades of experiments, cold testing, and computer simulations. As disclosed to the author in several interviews and background briefings, most notably with Riazuddin and Samar Mubarakmand, several organizations within the PAEC experimented on many aspects of bomb design from early 1970s to the 1998 nuclear tests.[3]

Although a plutonium implosion device is more technically challenging than an HEU bomb, the Pakistani leadership's decision to build an implosion device was motivated by political factors: India's nuclear test and its consequences on the regime, U.S.-led efforts to stifle Pakistani response to India's challenges, and the open business environment in Europe coupled with vulnerabilities in the nascent nonproliferation regime.

Bomb construction was also enabled by outside forces that ranged from the India missile program in the 1980s to the Soviet invasion of Afghanistan. Indeed, as in the case of the HEU program, Pakistan's bomb building experiments were tucked into the window of opportunity provided by the political timelines of regional security posturing and the superpower rivalries.

Nuclear Weapons Technology

There are two types of nuclear weapons design: gun-type and implosion. The former is a simpler design and typically uses HEU, while the latter is considerably more complex and uses Pu, although HEU is also possible.

A gun-type design earns its name because it is detonated much like a bullet from a gun. One subcritical mass of uranium is fired through a "gun tube" into another mass to form one supercritical mass, causing an explosion. The implosion method is also very aptly named, as it involves a subcritical core of plutonium that is compressed by a symmetrical implosion of conventional explosives into the core, creating a supercritical mass and causing a much larger nuclear explosion. Since Pakistan was originally pursuing plutonium, pilot bomb designs employed the implosion method, and when there was little progress on the back-end of the fuel cycle, HEU became the substitute material for the same bomb design.

Aside from converting the fissile material into a suitable form for a bomb, Pakistani scientists had to undertake a series of important stages. First, they needed to choose between a solid core design and a levitated core design, the latter involving the support of the fission material (plutonium or HEU) in an airspace inside the tamper cavity—a more technically complex design but one that can double the explosive yield of the device. Once that was chosen, a series of computer programs and mathematical equations had to be developed to calculate criticality and yield, and to design the triggers.[4] Next, the explosives and propellant systems required the production of explosive material, lenses, detonators, and the main high explosive (HE) charge. Non-nuclear testing took place on neutron initiators, firing set performance, and metal shell dynamics.

Explosive lenses are a primary component of the implosion design and very difficult to develop, especially in a nascent technical program. They have to be homogenous—shaped with high precision and free of impurities—for precise control of the detonation speed. Simultaneously with producing the lenses, weapon designers must begin to fabricate the fissile core, which involves casting and machining the plutonium or HEU pit, constructing the neutron initiator and nonmetallic components, and installing all of these into the weapon's structural casing. Then the HE charge, propellant, and lens systems are placed alongside the warhead electrical system. The neutron initiator is especially important, since it initiates the fission chain reaction. Timing is key, because if the chain reaction begins too soon, the result will be a fizzle yield (much less than desired), and if the chain reaction occurs too late, there will be no yield at all.

Once the core is assembled, the high explosives are amassed to generate symmetrically convergent shockwaves into the core, compressing the fissile material so that it reaches supercriticality, causing an explosion. Supercriticality requires that all shockwaves converge uniformly and simultaneously, which is possible only through the use of explosive lenses.

A pure fission weapon involves this combination of a fission core and conventional high explosives. Boosted fission or thermonuclear systems, however, incorporate either deuterium-tritium or deuterium-deuterium mixtures. These isotopes of hydrogen are components of heavy water that can be extracted through a process of separation and purification.[5] When included in a bomb design, these isotopes exponentially increase the yield of the nuclear weapons system.

Typically a nuclear weapons design project involves four to five select groups that work separately, but simultaneously, as each step progresses. Once a weapon is tested and the warhead is prepared for a delivery system—either a missile or aircraft—an arming system is developed. This system includes a mechanical safing device and multiple firewalls and codes to prevent unauthorized access, tampering, or misuse.[6]

As mentioned previously, Pakistan experimented with an HEU implosion design, with an eye toward its long-term plutonium production capability. In the words of Riazuddin, "Pakistan scientists had a double challenge. The path to producing HEU as fissile material is more challenging than extracting plutonium; designing an implosion device is far more difficult than the gun assembly. So we took the hard pathways on both counts."[7]

The Directorate of Technical Development (DTD)

In March 1974, the PAEC established a department dubbed the Directorate of Technical Development (DTD), which was perhaps the best kept secret of Pakistan's nuclear program. The DTD coordinated the work of all the specialized working groups involved in the bomb effort, thus allowing for centralized control and synergy.

DTD controlled and handled all aspects of the design, fabrication, manufacturing, and testing of the atomic bomb. Under the silent and discreet directives of PAEC chairman Munir Ahmad Khan, all work on the bomb design was to be kept in the highest level of secrecy, above all other aspects of the nuclear program.[8] Working under the ambit of DTD were: the Wah Group, the Theoretical Group, the Fast Neutron Physics Group, the Diagnostics Group, the High Explosive or HMX Group, the High-Speed Electronics Group, and the High-Precision Mechanical Group. The name of DTD was unknown to the public until after the 1998 tests, when the organization issued a statement saying that "it had fulfilled the mission for which it was established more than 20 years back."[9]

Theoretical Physics Group

Soon after the Multan Conference in 1972, Dr. Abdus Salam and Munir Ahmad Khan traveled to Pakistan to meet with President Bhutto. What transpired in that meeting will never be known, for all three interlocutors are no longer alive. However, the significance of the meeting came to light a few months later, in October 1972, when Salam, who was the head of the International Centre for

Theoretical Physics in Italy at the time, summoned two Pakistani theoretical physicists working at the center—Dr. Riazuddin and Dr. Masud Ahmad. Salam informed them of Pakistan's decision to pursue a nuclear weapons program, and asked them to return to their country and report to the PAEC for a bomb design project, what was to be the Pakistan equivalent of the Manhattan Project.[10]

The two recruited scientists held impressive credentials. Riazuddin was a theoretical physicist who received his Ph.D. from Cambridge University; he was later made Member (Technical) of the PAEC in December 1973. In 1966 he joined the University of Islamabad (later renamed Quaid-e Azam University), where he established the Institute of Physics. Riazuddin was secretly working as project director of the bomb design and the triggering mechanism.

Masud Ahmad was Riazuddin's Ph.D. student as well as a research fellow in Trieste, Italy. He went on to work at PINSTECH and also taught at the University of Islamabad. Another young mathematician, Dr. Tufail Naseem, joined the small team. This group of experts formed the beginning of what became known as the Theoretical Physics Group.[11]

Riazuddin and others traveled worldwide to study the open literature on bomb designs and their necessary systems. But Riazuddin explained that bureaucratic restrictions limited their research. "The financial crunch was so severe that the PAEC could only provide $1000 for literature purchases from abroad for the project. We had to spend from our own pockets."[12]

Before setting out on their research, the team held private brainstorming sessions and developed two main objectives. The first was to calculate the size of the critical mass—the amount of fissile material necessary for an explosion. Their main goal was to create a design that required the minimum amount of fissile material necessary for a significant explosive yield. The second was to study the high-explosive dynamics needed for a triggering mechanism. Until that time, no work of the kind had been done in Pakistan.[13]

Dr. Riazuddin recalls, "We were the designers of the bomb, like the tailor who tells you how much material is required to stitch a suit. We had to identify the fissile material, whether to use plutonium or the enriched uranium, which method of detonation, which explosive, what type of tampers and lenses to use, how the material will be compressed, how shock waves will be created, what would be the yield."[14]

Once the Theoretical Physics Group had traveled abroad and gathered information, the next five years were dedicated to developing mathematical methods for calculating critical mass size and reflector and tamper designs toward the goal of reducing the size of the needed fissionable material.[15] The group completed its conceptual design in 1978 when the HEU program was quickly advancing.[16] By that time the PAEC had expanded into twenty directorates, each boasting seven hundred to a thousand scientists, engineers, and technicians.[17] As Munir Ahmad Khan later recalled, "We were simultaneously running 20 labs and projects under the administrative control of PAEC, every one the size of KRL."[18]

The Wah Group

It soon became obvious that making the explosive lenses required a dedicated team of developers.[19] In March 1974, Munir Ahmad Khan summoned a meeting to jumpstart this project. Mr. Muhammad Hafeez Qureshi was joined by Dr. Zaman Shiekh (the only high-explosive expert in Pakistan at the time), Ghulam Nabi, and Tariq Suleja.[20] These men were the first members of what came to be known as the "Wah Group," derived from the location of their project.[21]

At the head of this group was Qureshi, who was also the head of the Radioisotope and Applications Division (RIAD) in PINSTECH at the time. He had obtained a degree in mechanical and nuclear engineering from the University of Michigan and a degree in physics from Karachi University, and had become one of the first PAEC members in the mid-1950s.[22] In the mid-1960s, he was part of the team that commissioned Pakistan's first nuclear research reactor, PINSTECH.[23]

The Pakistan Ordnance Factories (POF) group in Wah was the obvious location for a project that involved high explosives. It was situated about thirty miles from Islamabad and consisted of several facilities that produced weapons for the Pakistan Army.[24] The Wah Group was located there and focused its initial efforts on the explosive lenses, or as Dr. Salam referred to them, "explosive breasts"—a term that made Sheikh blush.[25]

Dr. Samar Mubarakmand contended, "The explosive used in a nuclear bomb is a very special type of explosive. It is not to be purchased from anywhere in the world, nobody would sell it to you. So we had to put up our own plant for this and we had to have chemical engineers that would operate this plant and make the explosives."[26]

At first Hafeez Qureshi and his Wah Group began work only with very basic equipment and facilities. When he expressed concern that there was no Computer Numerical Control (CNC), Munir Ahmad Khan replied, "If the Americans could do without CNC machines in the 1940s, why can't we do the same now?"[27] Eventually, however, these machines were acquired, along with other state-of-the art facilities for precision manufacturing and quality control.[28] The POF in Wah manufactured atomic bombs of various shapes, sizes, dimensions, and configurations.

The Fast Neutron Physics Group

The Fast Neutron Physics Group was created as a part of the larger Wah Group. With Dr. Samar Mubarakmand as head, this group was key to the development of the weapon's trigger mechanism. A full-fledged laboratory for the production of a neutron initiator and reflector was later set up in the PAEC.[29]

Munir Ahmad Khan selected Dr. Samar Mubarakmand for his academic and technical background. He had earned his M.Sc. in physics from Government College, and in 1966 he obtained a Ph.D. in experimental physics from the University of Oxford under the supervision of Professor Dr. D. H. Wilkinson, a renowned experimental nuclear physicist. Mubarakmand returned to Pakistan and joined the Atomic Energy Centre in Lahore to work in fast neutron spectrometry, but moved his research to PINSTECH in 1972.[30]

Samar Mubarakmand's group was tasked to develop a reflector and/or tamper to surround the fissile material and prolong the time the material holds together under the extreme pressure of the explosion. In other words, it allows more time for more chain reactions to occur before the core goes critical and explodes—increasing the efficiency of the weapon.[31]

Developing the Trigger Mechanism

Scientists and engineers worked at a specialized laboratory in the PAEC, known as the R-Labs, to develop the trigger mechanism for the Pakistani nuclear device. It was here that the detonation procedures were established and equipment made. The main challenge was to allow for the simultaneous detonation of the explosive lenses in a minute fraction of time—fifty nanoseconds.[32] To meet this challenge, R-Lab technicians developed special high-speed electronic switches, or krytons, that triggered the thirty-two or more high-explosive lenses in the bomb.[33]

An ultrahigh precision manufacturing facility was built at the POF in Wah in order to combine the various components of the nuclear device from different facilities. As Dr. Samar explained in a speech to the Khwarzimic Science

Society, November 30, 1998, "[T]he bomb has got explosives, it has metallic uranium which comes from Dr. Khalil Qureshi, our top metallurgist, and he converts the gas from Kahuta into metal and then he does the coating and machining.[34] . . . The device has to be rugged so that if you want to have deliverable weapons, you do not have problems. You can put them on aircraft or missile. All the facilities for explosives and chemical manufacture, explosive machining and electronics transfer their products to the manufacturing facility, and Dr. Mansoor Beg was the Director of that facility."[35]

Production of Uranium Metal

The Uranium Metal Laboratory (UML) was established in 1976. Later in the 1980s when KRL was able to enrich weapons-grade material, this facility was used to convert UF6 into the nuclear bomb core.[36] A 1985 CIA report on Pakistan's nuclear program stated, "UML fabricates and machines parts for a nuclear device implosion system. UML is located at the New Labs complex at PINSTECH, and although it is organizationally part of the Directorate of Nuclear Fuels and Materials, personnel associated with UML respond to the directions of officers within the Directorate of Technical Development and use DTD funds and channels to procure materials."[37] Dr. Khalil Qureshi, head of UML, led technical experts from PINSTECH in utilizing chemical and metallurgical techniques and reduction furnaces to produce uranium metal from the enriched UF6, which had to be physically moved from KRL to UML. This transfer of sensitive material raised numerous security concerns. A. Q. Khan made a case to President Zia-ul-Haq, who agreed that the task of producing uranium metal and the bomb core should be done at a single location, thus avoiding the risks of transportation. And so KRL began to both enrich and metalize uranium. This was necessary both for secrecy and the security of the bomb program.

The Diagnostics Directorate

The Diagnostics Directorate was established in 1980 and first headed by the experimental physicist Dr. Samar Mubarakmand. This directorate was charged with administering the hot and cold tests that measure the expected yield, trigger mechanisms, explosive lenses, and so forth of various bomb designs. State-of-the-art CNC machines and high-speed computers ran the necessary diagnostic techniques.[38]

Dr. Samar explained the genesis and mandate of the Diagnostics Directorate. "There can be two approaches [to testing the bomb]: either to detonate a bomb and sit back and clap or to treat it as a scientific experiment—try to get the maximum scientific data from the nuclear detonation. We chose to do the latter and for that we had established another Directorate—the Diagnostics Directorate."[39]

The PAEC had developed the expertise to measure the yield and efficiency of the their device. A team of three to four hundred people had performed many cold tests and practiced remote control detonations over several years.[40] Samar Mubarakmand told the author that during a test in 1983, he had been in a van too close to the site and was thrown under the debris when the cold test explosion occurred.[41] Eventually, however, the team developed a very sophisticated process of performing remote experiments at Chagai. They increased the distance from which they detonated the devices from fifteen km for the first five to a distance of forty-five km in the end.[42] As Dr. Samar explained, "One must remember that the phenomenon is a single shot phenomenon. It is a very fast process . . . less than a nanosecond. So in this time, one must do all the measurements and if you miss the data, it is the end of it, it is finished and would not repeat. So it is a single shot event." The diagnostics team developed the ability to measure the yield not only of the devices that they themselves had detonated but also eventually devices exploded across Pakistan's border.[43]

Selecting the Nuclear Test Sites

In the summer of 1974, Z. A. Bhutto directed the PAEC to commence a search for an appropriate site for a nuclear test. In the words of Ishfaq Ahmad, the government told the PAEC, "[W]henever you would be ready, you would detonate the bomb, [and so that year] we began preparing nuclear test sites."[44]

Over the span of ten days, a team led by Ishfaq Ahmed and Ahsan Mubarak explored the area between Turbat, Awaran, and Khusdar to the south, Naukundi to the east, and Kharan to the west.[45] Their objective was to find a suitable location for an underground nuclear test since Pakistan had signed the Partial Test Ban Treaty (PTBT) in 1963, and thus an atmospheric test was not an option.[46]

After a hectic and careful search, the team found an ideal site for a hot test in a 185-meter mountain in the Ras Koh Hills in the Chagai Division of Baluchistan. These hills matched all of the PAEC's requirements based on a study done by the Geological Survey of Pakistan under Mr. Muhammad Hussain Chughtai. The mountain was bone dry and capable of withstanding a twenty to forty kiloton nuclear explosion from the inside.[47] The test site at Ras Koh is generally referred as Chagai.

In the same year, Brigadier Muhammad Sarfaraz was summoned by President Zia-ul-Haq to create and head the Inspectorate General of Special Development Works (SDW), a subsidiary of the PAEC.[48] This division prepared Pakistan's nuclear test sites and assisted the PAEC with cold and laboratory tests.[49] In addition, SDW built twenty-four additional sites for cold tests at Kirana Hills, forty-six short tunnels, thirty-five underground accommodations for troops, and other associated facilities.[50]

SDW designed and constructed two to three horizontal and vertical shaft tunnels for twenty-kiloton nuclear devices, along with the related facilities and infrastructure such as the Telemetric Seismic Recording Station. The sites had to be completed by December 31, 1979, and in such a way that allowed them to be utilized on short notice (less than a week).[51] Although the exact deadline was not met, the nuclear test sites were ready in 1980, well before Pakistan had developed a nuclear weapon.[52]

Directly within Ras Koh lay the 3,325-foot-long horizontal shaft that was shaped like a fishhook to be self-sealing, as the tunnel would collapse with the impact of the explosion.[53] A second site—a 300- by 200-foot L-shaped vertical shaft—was prepared in the Kharan Desert, approximately 150 km west of the Ras Koh test site. Both test sites had an array of extensive cables, sensors, and monitoring stations.

Much R&D and many feasibility studies went into the designing of the tunnels for the tests. "The designing of the tunnels was also a very intricate thing. It was not just blasting a hole into a mountain. Again there is a lot of science. If you have a straight tunnel and you put the bomb at the end of the tunnel, you plug the tunnel with concrete and explode the bomb, the concrete is really going to blow out and so all the radioactivity is going to leak out through the mouth of the tunnel. We did not want this to happen. The tunnel is not designed safe but is designed in the form of a double-S shape and when we detonate the bomb, the pressures are very great. They move the mountain outward and you use the force of the bomb to seal the tunnel. When the rock expands under the explosion, the rock moves in the direction so that it seals the tunnel. So the tunnel collapses inward by the force of the tunnel. This is how you seal the tunnel through the force of the bomb. Dr. Mansoor Beg is an expert in this. Apart from the manufacturing things, he is the one who does all the calculations and gives it to the geologists who do this work."[54]

Actual work on the construction of the Chagai site began in earnest in early 1978. By the end of the year, Mr. Mahmood Chughtai along with fifty of his men had encamped at the site. Brigadier Sarfaraz and his SDW took over all construction work of the site. Chughtai proved to be very helpful in procurement and supply of vital equipment needed in excavation and digging. Adequate measures were taken to camouflage the construction activity—even some livestock and goats were brought in to create the look of a local village encampment. Apart from a select few, most believed or were led to believe that copper mining was carried out there. No one knew the true purpose of the activities at the Ras Koh Hills.

After completion, the Chagai site was left unused until Pakistan's May 1998 hot test. Zia-ul-Haq ordered the delay, allowing only cold tests per a deal he had brokered with the Reagan administration in 1981.[55]

Cold Test Program

A cold test essentially is the actual detonation of a complete nuclear bomb, with natural uranium in the core instead of HEU or Pu. Therefore once detonated, no fission reaction takes place.[56]

Prior to the test, the DTD and its associated groups had begun preparing the site at the Kirana Hills near Sargodha, in the Punjab province. First an advance team was sent to clear the test tunnel of any wild animals and other obstructing objects. Afterward, the Diagnostics Directorate equipped the site with diagnostic tools and computers. Finally, the Wah Group brought the nuclear device in a partially assembled form, along with high-speed electronics and her majesty explosives (HMX).[57] By the end, nearly twenty cables linked oscillators to vehicles carrying diagnostic equipment in order to monitor performance and its related factors.[58] The primary objective was to see if the neutron initiator had generated a high-neutron flux, which provides confidence that the bomb will work. The test also validated the performance of the explosive lenses, trigger mechanism, and design parameters.[59]

The element of secrecy forced the scientists and engineers to transport materials and equipment themselves instead of hiring professionals. They had to acquire specialized licenses and to drive the heavy trucks and trailers for hundreds of kilometers.[60]

The first cold test was detonated by a push-button method under the direction of Dr. Ishfaq Ahmad in March 1983. "When the detonation took place, most of the wires were severed that were supposed to transfer the data to the oscillators. At first, the test team had blank faces when they first looked at the computers, giving the thumbs down signal, indicating that nothing had happened. However, a closer examination of the oscillators indicated that in fact two of them had worked which showed that the neutrons had been generated and the chain reaction taken place." This realization instantly transformed the mood from disappointment to immense happiness, as tears of joy rolled down the team members' cheeks. Munir Ahmad Khan later recalled, "On March 11, 1983, we successfully conducted our first cold test of a working nuclear device. That evening, I went to General Zia with the news that Pakistan was now ready to make a nuclear device."[61] This test became a milestone in Pakistan's nuclear history.

Dr. Samar Mubarakmand recollected the apprehension and triumph of the first cold test under a mantle of secrecy. "If you have a cold test and you detect neutrons, you can be more than 100% sure that if you put enriched uranium in the same bomb, it is bound to give you fission."[62] He continued, "We realized that 'today we have become a nuclear power,' but we could not express it because we were told to keep it secret. Pakistan's nuclear capability was confirmed the day in 1983 when the PAEC carried out cold nuclear tests. . . . The tests, however, were not publicly announced because of the international environment of stiff sanctions against countries that sought to acquire nuclear capability."[63]

After a second successful cold test was carried out, the PAEC had two options. One was to conduct a hot test as soon as the fissile material was available. The second was to develop a smaller, more rugged and deliverable bomb. Should the PAEC conduct a hot test without improving the bomb's design? President Zia declined on the grounds that the time was not appropriate.[64] Therefore, the PAEC went on to the task of miniaturizing the bomb design without the benefit of hot tests.

PAEC Deliverable Design and the PAF

From 1983 to 1995, the PAEC carried out twenty-four cold tests in the Kirana Hills in a series of two dozen 100- to 150-foot-long tunnels—all of which tested different bomb designs. New designs periodically developed by the Theoretical Physics Group were cold tested at regular intervals. The success rate of these cold tests was claimed to be almost 100 percent, which raised suspicions that the results were distorted by the diagnostic team to demonstrate positive outcomes.[65]

The PAEC began to develop the design for a deliverable bomb in 1988. The

National Development Complex (NDC) and the Air Weapons Complex (AWC) were simultaneously created in order to spearhead this project. The NDC was to prepare a nuclear warhead for the Pakistan Air Force (PAF), and the AWC was to assist NDC in aerodynamics. As Samar Mubarakmand explained to the author, "A bomb has to be tested for its ruggedness, radar systems, vibrations, environment, acceleration, to make it into a weapon system."[66] PAEC was able to obtain advanced explosive lens designs through a combination of a decade of research work carried out by the Theoretical Physics Group and a procurement network. This capability allowed PAEC scientists to reduce the Chinese CHIC-4 bomb's original size by more than half and the weight to around 500 kg in the first stages of modifications; later, "with further experiments and design modifications under the leadership of Dr. Masud Ahmad, the R block scientists and technicians brought it down to 220 kg, which was perfect for Pakistan's delivery systems."[67]

According to Hafeez Qureshi, one of the leading scientists on the bomb project, in preparation for the cold tests, the bomb was always brought from the R block into the Sargodha base during the dead of night in a covered vehicle. The lights of the air base would be off as two F-16s waited on the tarmac—one for carrying the device, and the other for photographing its drop. The PAEC team was instructed to carry out these exercises such that they would not be detected by surveillance satellites or by possible spies on the ground.[68]

Between 1988 and 1995, PAF (Air Weapon Complex) and PAEC (NDC) conducted several cold test simulations in which PAF would drop the bomb to explode at 500 meters above ground, and NDC would pick up the neutron release through the telemetry.[69] In May 1995, PAEC finally succeeded in getting the desired results after several years of aerial drop cold tests. The success of the air deliverable test was reported to the Chief of the Army Staff, General Abdul Waheed. He was so pleased that he directed Samar Mubarakmand to begin R&D on an indigenous solid fuel missile system (missile development will be covered in Chapter 12).[70]

By the summer of 1995, Pakistan had a nuclear device deliverable by fighter aircraft. Hafeez Qureshi, head of the DTD at the time, stated proudly, "The device . . . had the entire characteristics and safeguards of a weapon produced by any of the five nuclear weapon states."[71] Samar Mubarakmand explained to the author, "The device would activate only in the enemy territory when the pilot has entered the code, and once he has safely left Pakistani territory. If for any reason there is an accidental drop on Pakistani territory, the device would drop like dead weight."[72]

TABLE 9.1

Bomb Design

Theoretical Design	Theoretical Physics Group	Dec. 1972	Theoretical Design of the atomic bomb	Organization
Neutronics	Fast Neutron Physics Group	1978	Neutron Source	PAEC
High Speed Electronics	Wah Group	1974	Krytrons	PAEC
Chemical High-Explosives	Wah Group	1974	RDX-HMX Explosive Lenses	PAEC
Machining and Manufacturing	Wah Group and UML	1974 1978	Ultra-High Precision Machining, Mating and Manufacturing of Nuclear and Non-Nuclear Components of the bomb	PAEC
Neutron Reflector/ Tamper	Beryllium Metal Plant	1977 –78		PAEC
Nuclear Testing	Diagnostics Group	1980	Cold and Hot Nuclear Test Procedures, Equipment, Facilities and Sites.	PAEC

After the first successful aircraft delivery test, the joint exercises continued, but expanded to developing and perfecting various bombing techniques. Maneuvers included "conventional free-fall," "loft bombing," "toss bombing," and "low-level" attack techniques. In the years following these exercises, the PAF's F-16 and Mirage-V aircraft were adequately prepared to deliver a nuclear weapon into enemy territory. It took over two decades for Pakistani physicists and technicians to design a nuclear device, develop a triggering mechanism, and prepare warheads for delivery.

Who Made the Bomb

PAEC was aware that KRL also worked on the nuclear bomb design. Apparently on May 1, 1981, the same day Zia-ul-Haq visited ERL and renamed it KRL, he instructed A. Q. Khan to pursue a nuclear bomb design for a cold test and granted extra funding for the project.[73] Above and beyond a general desire to ensure the security and efficiency of the bomb design program, President Zia was also especially mistrustful of the possibility of Ahmadi experts working within the PAEC, even though several inquires to that effect had proven otherwise. During Zia's tenure, the patriotism and loyalty of the Ahmadis was suspect, and so the members of these sects were removed from all sensitive government departments, especially from military and scientific programs.[74] In addition, Zia's initial skepticism of Munir Khan (since he was a Bhutto loyalist) provided A. Q. Khan with yet another opportunity to exploit the president's mistrust and Islamist leanings.[75] These circumstances allowed A. Q. Khan the permission and protection to develop a separate bomb design.[76]

As mentioned in previous chapters, Western sources claim that China had provided Pakistan with fissile material in exchange for centrifuge technology assistance.[77] Zia-ul-Haq hoped to exploit the close relationship with the Chinese further in order to protect Pakistan from potential preventive attacks.[78] As explained in Chapter 7, the impact of Israeli attack on Osirak and the crash of the centrifuges in 1981 forced Zia-ul- Haq to realize that the nuclear program was vulnerable not just to preventive strikes but also to natural calamities. Zia-ul- Haq then dispatched Lieutenant-General Syed Zamin Naqvi and A. Q. Khan to request bomb-grade fissile material and bomb designs. Their visit bore fruit as Pakistan then received the Chinese CHIC-4 weapon design along with fifty kilograms of HEU in 1981, material sufficient for two bombs.[79] A. Q. Khan confirmed in a purported 2004 letter to his wife, "The Chinese gave us drawings of the nuclear weapon, gave us 50 kg of enriched uranium, gave us 10 tons of UF6 (natural) and 5 tons of UF_6 (3%)."[80]

According to A. Q. Khan's accounts, the Chinese nuclear material was kept in storage until 1985. When Pakistan acquired its own uranium enrichment capability and wanted to return the fissile material, China responded that "the HEU loaned earlier was now to be considered as a gift . . . in gratitude" for Pakistan's help with Chinese centrifuges. It was then that KRL "promptly fabricated hemispheres for two weapons and added them to Pakistan's arsenal."[81]

The bomb design controversy is shrouded in claims and counterclaims, with KRL and PAEC claiming credit. In a controversial move in 1982–83, Zia-ul-Haq ordered the PAEC to deliver bomb designs (which included the Chinese CHIC-4 design), including those created by the Wah Group, to Lieutenant-General Naqvi. As explained elsewhere, President Zia at this time did not fully trust Munir Ahmad Khan, so he attempted to shift under supervision of the trusted A. Q. Khan. Although initially reluctant to transfer the designs, the PAEC was told that the president simply wanted to keep them in safe custody in GHQ. The Wah Group leaders—Hafeez Qureshi and Zaman Shiekh—were displeased as they handed over the crown jewels of their work, including the explosive lens designs.

While the PAEC was aware of KRL's duplicate efforts on the bomb design, they knew that A. Q. Khan's team lacked the necessary expertise to create a deliverable weapon.[82] But only a fortnight after Hafiz Qureshi delivered the PAEC designs to General Naqvi, he received a call from the explosive factory informing him that an official from KRL had appeared with the same explosive lens specifications that had been developed by the Trigger Group. That the PAEC and KRL had developed the same design was not coincidence. According to Qureshi, "[T]he designs collected from PAEC had been passed on to KRL."[83] If Qureshi's claim is indeed true, it would explain how eventually KRL had been able to reduce the original, heavy CHIC-4 design to less than half its original weight. Without the theoretical physics work and sophisticated lenses expertise of the PAEC, KRL would not have been able to reduce the size of the lenses and produce a smaller bomb. However, KRL attempted to do so without adequate expertise and were probably working on a design half the size of the original design. A bomb design discovered in Libya in 2004, purportedly acquired through the A. Q. Khan network, detailed a weapon of less than 1 meter in diameter and 453 kg,[84] leading to speculation that it was the same design KRL might have been working on. In reality, the bomb design exposed in Libya was not the one Pakistani scientists worked on and eventually tested.[85] Some quarter-century later, to the horror of Pakistan, another Pakistani weapons design—different from the Chinese design—was purportedly found on a computer in Switzerland that was supposed to be part of the infamous A. Q. Khan network. It is unclear whether this was a Pakistani design or not; many U.S. experts claim this was the case.

In March 1984, exactly one year after the PAEC announced its first successful cold test, KRL conducted its first cold test in the Kirana Hills near Sargodha. By December, President Zia-ul-Haq was informed that successful colds tests had been completed, and KRL was ready for further presidential orders to begin the hot tests.[86] The product, however, was still a large bomb that could be delivered only by a C-130 cargo aircraft with no assurance of delivery accuracy.

In early 1987 President Zia ordered that KRL leave the bomb design project and transferred the work to the PAEC leadership. There were three main reasons for Zia-ul-Haq's change of mind: (1) technical considerations, (2) A. Q. Khan's indiscretion, and (3) competition. First of all, the PAEC was far ahead of KRL in terms of R&D and technical capacity (advanced lens, design, and theoretical groups, for example).[87] Second, A. Q. Khan demonstrated his indiscretion in January 1987 when he agreed to be interviewed by Indian journalist Kuldeep Nayyar during the peak of the Brasstacks military crisis (see Chapter 11). The publication of the interview on March 1, 1987, embarrassed Zia-ul-Haq and created an internal controversy, resulting in the dressing down of A. Q. Khan by authorities and the immediate transfer of the R&D back to the PAEC.[88] Finally, competition between Munir Khan and A. Q. Khan had increased to a level that Zia realized was no longer effective or efficient.

However, it is possible that A. Q. Khan defied Zia-ul-Haq's orders and continued to work secretly on specific designs in KRL based on knowledge and material gained from the Chinese. Even with the competing claims and surrounding controversy, it is clear that both the PAEC and KRL were designing a nuclear device. This fact leads to two conclusions. The first is that, unbeknownst to India, Pakistan had an active deterrent that it could have delivered with a C-130, if pushed against the wall. The second, though latent, conclusion is that the end product that A. Q. Khan's clandestine nuclear supply network was peddling was not the Pakistani blueprint, but rather one that his team had secretly created. Consequently, the Pakistani bomb tested in 1998 was made from designs perfected at the National Defense Complex, later subsumed into the National Engineering and Science Commission (NESCOM).

10   Mastery of Plutonium Production

Plutonium (Pu) has been the preferred fissile material for nearly all nuclear weapon states for its technical and strategic advantages. It is relatively easy to extract from spent reactor fuel and is most suitable for lighter, smaller weapons. New designs in technically advanced countries now require as little as 4 kg of Pu to make a small nuclear bomb. From a scientific standpoint, mastering Pu production automatically encompasses mastery over the front and back end of the nuclear fuel cycle, which also yields tritium—ideal for boosted fission warheads and thermonuclear bombs.

The technical issues discussed in Chapter 5 noted one key aspect of nuclear proliferation—that it is practically impossible to acquire Pu technologies in a clandestine manner. It is comparatively easier to hide gas centrifuge imports because they arrive in small bits and parts, but the components required for nuclear reactors and reprocessing plants are not concealable. For this reason, Pakistan made little attempt to hide its quest to acquire plutonium-based technologies. In an interview with a local magazine, Munir Ahmad Khan stated clearly that "the acquisition and development of nuclear technology is our basic and inalienable right and no power on earth can take this right away from us."[1]

Pakistan began courting the French for a reprocessing plant and pursued the acquisition with more urgency after the Indian 1974 nuclear test. However, international concern prompted France to extract concessions from Pakistan, drag its feet, and ultimately back out of the deal altogether. Paris had a series of unprecedented demands: prior agreement to IAEA safeguards, extra payment to Saint-Gobain Technique Nouvelle (SGN) to restart work, and use of an older power plant design at Chashma. Pakistan reluctantly submitted to these requirements, only to see France stall because of intense U.S. pressure via both warnings and offers to share nuclear technology.[2] Pakistani negotiators sensed that the French were not going to follow through with the deal, but continued to play along in order to extract all information possible on reprocessing technologies.

Meanwhile, in 1973, the PAEC planned to replicate India's CIRUS, which was an NRX-type natural uranium fueled, heavy-water moderated plutonium production reactor. The project was given the acronym PAKNUR (Pakistan Nuclear Reactor), which would later be resurrected as the Khushab project.[3] After only a year, PAKNUR was shelved because of a lack of resources, and Pakistan began to bide its time and move the Pu project to the backburner. Indeed, it was the international focus on Pakistan's plutonium route in the 1970s that allowed Islamabad to secretly pursue its HEU program. However, in the 1980s and 1990s, the tables turned as international attention took aim at A. Q. Khan and the HEU program, which allowed Pakistan to quietly renew the pursuit of plutonium production capabilities.

As emphasized earlier, the last two decades of the twentieth century were met with shifting global changes, which affected the regional landscape as well as domestic political challenges in Pakistan. These events essentially proved to be ideal distractions for Pakistan to continue progress on the plutonium route. By the end of the first decade of the twenty-first century, Pakistan's potential for producing Pu had far exceeded expectations.

Sources of Plutonium in Pakistan

Theoretically, Pakistan has more than one reactor source for plutonium: PARR-1, the Karachi Nuclear Power Plant (KANUPP), Chashma, and Khushab all produce varying qualities of plutonium. However, only the Khushab production reactors are dedicated to producing weapons-grade plutonium. Dr. Ishfaq Ahmad explained that as a "matter of state policy, nuclear installations acquired from external sources were kept under IAEA safeguards; only indigenously produced nuclear facilities would be dedicated for military purposes."[4] As the national requirement for civilian use expanded, power reactors remained transparent and under IAEA safeguards, allowing PAEC scientists to proudly tout their impeccable IAEA record. As a non-NPT (Nuclear Non-Proliferation Treaty) state, Pakistan was not obliged to keep indigenous plants under full scope safeguards as required for the non-nuclear NPT signatory states. For all externally acquired facilities, however, the supplier countries required safeguard requirements of supplier countries.

Many questions surround Pakistan's plutonium sources, regarding which one actually supplied the plutonium for the country's nuclear weapons. Western analysts surmise that Pakistan could have diverted the fuel from KANUPP or other sources, yet Pakistani sources deny having any such plans. Instead, they say, the leadership planned to build reactors dedicated to the military program indigenously.

PARR-1

The 5-MWt (thermal) Pakistan Atomic Research Reactor (PARR-1), a swimming pool–type reactor obtained under the U.S. Atoms for Peace Program, was never designed to produce plutonium in significant quantities. It remains a research reactor, primarily to carry out experiments for radioisotope production and other peaceful applications. PARR-1 can produce only 100 grams of Pu annually and has always been under safeguards. In 1991 its power output was doubled to 10 MWt (thermal), which is at least three times less than 10 MWe (electric). This change increased the burn-up rate and explains why the quantity of plutonium produced eventually decreased.[5] The low plutonium yield and the safeguards did not make it a feasible source of fissile material for nuclear weapons.

KANUPP

The KANUPP is a Canada Deuterium-Uranium (CANDU)–type heavy water reactor that uses natural uranium as fuel. It has been under IAEA safeguards since its commissioning in 1972. When Canada cut off supplies of heavy water, spare parts, and nuclear fuel in December 1976, the KANUPP reactor faced a possible shutdown unless Pakistan could produce its own nuclear fuel and heavy water.[6] Under these circumstances Bhutto struck a deal with Beijing: in return for technically supporting KANUPP, China would have access to KANUPP's Western technology. Until that time, China had not been exposed to a Western facility and was happy for the opportunity to learn from it. Such cooperation created a framework of trust and reciprocity between Pakistan and China that eventually led to broad-based nuclear cooperation. Pakistani scientists and engineers learned the art of substitution and reverse engineering, which would be applied when Western technologies were denied or when the Pakistanis were abandoned by Canada, Germany, and France.

Technically, KANUPP is a ready source of plutonium. It is a 137-MWe reactor that can yield between 60 and 120 kg of weapons-grade plutonium if operated at low burn-up. According to an April 1978 CIA assessment of Pakistan's nuclear program, KANUPP had by then accumulated approximately 200 kg of reactor-grade Pu, which was enough material for thirty to 40 bombs.[7] Like other CANDU-type reactors, if KANUPP burns slowly it can produce plutonium that is 80 percent rich in Pu-239 content, close to weapons grade.[8] Ironically it was Canada's backing away that further constrained KANUPP from operating at full capacity—it slow burned by default, not by design.

There have been speculations that Munir Ahmad Khan planned to divert the spent fuel from KANUPP.[9] However, almost every PAEC scientist stated clearly that there was never a premeditated plan to divert spent fuel clandestinely. If there had been a national emergency and supreme national interest had demanded it, Pakistan might have withdrawn from safeguards with full notice to the IAEA, but "there never was any plan to trick or violate IAEA safeguards."[10] On the contrary, Munir insisted on demonstrating unflinching commitment to upholding international safeguards agreements, and because of this conviction, some officials suspected him of being more loyal to the IAEA than to the national nuclear program.[11] Munir Khan followed Bhutto's directive, which he recalled years later: "The initial plan was not to divert or misuse foreign supplied reactors and a reprocessing plant to produce nuclear weapon fuel, but rather to use the know-how gained from this cooperation to indigenously produce parallel capabilities that could yield a bomb."[12]

In 1980 and 1981 the PAEC indigenously developed the capability to produce fuel bundles for KANUPP's core. The reactor is designed to refuel without shutting down, a process called on-line refueling. From a safeguards standpoint, such a process makes it difficult for outside inspectors to know exactly how much fuel is being consumed, and consequently how much may have been diverted to military use.[13] It follows, then, that the IAEA became concerned in 1981 when the PAEC produced its own fuel rods and began to refuel the reactor.

The PAEC contended that, legally, the safeguards were no longer applicable, since Canada had unilaterally reneged on its contractual obligations. Despite internal objections within the PAEC, as the indigenous fuel was loaded into KANUPP, the PAEC never withdrew from the safeguards.[14] Instead Pakistan agreed to enhance its obligations by placing the Pakistani fuel under IAEA safeguards.

The removal of safeguards from KANUPP would have created unwarranted controversy. First, by implication KANUPP would have then become a military power reactor, thus making it a target for a preventive attack. Its location made it vulnerable to an outside attack, and after the 1981 Israeli attack on Osirak in Iraq, Pakistan was unwilling to take the risk. In addition, alienating the IAEA and the international community would have been unproductive, especially given that the Cold War powers were already providing Pakistan's nuclear program with an effective cover by focusing their attention on Afghanistan. Even Munir Khan realized that nonadherence to international safeguards agreements would have isolated Pakistan from any possible nuclear cooperation at a critical time when both the PAEC and KRL were striving to expand the nuclear power program.[15] The PAEC wanted to ensure that its good standing with the IAEA was not compromised. Indeed, IAEA director Hans Blix certified there was no diversion of spent fuel from KANUPP.[16]

Chashma Power Plant

In 1976 the PAEC planned to build a 600-MW nuclear power reactor at Chashma. A year after the military coup, however, Zia-ul-Haq's priority was elsewhere. The economic downturn and the nuclear sanctions imposed upon the country had turned the hope for the purchase of a French power reactor into a pipe dream.[17]

By the mid-1980s, the economic situation had improved and the secret nuclear program had passed through a critical period, especially when bomb cold tests were successfully conducted.[18] Zia-ul-Haq's government now had the time and resources to pursue a nuclear power reactor once again. To this end, the PAEC floated several tenders for reactors, but by that time the international community was deeply averse to supplying such sensitive technologies, particularly to Pakistan. And so Pakistan turned to its trusted friend China.

On September 15, 1986, the two countries entered into a new nuclear cooperation agreement that promoted peaceful uses of atomic energy.[19] China would supply two 325-MW nuclear power reactors to Pakistan, both of which would be under IAEA safeguards. In 1989 China supplied the first reactor at Chashma, which is now commissioned and operating as the Chashma Nuclear Power Plant (CHASHNUPP-1). The second reactor (CHASNUPP-II) is under construction at the time this book is being written. Unlike KANUPP, the CHASHNUPPs are light water power reactors that run on high burn-up, produce electricity, and are not good sources of weapons-grade plutonium.[20] To date, CHASNUPP is in good standing with the IAEA.

Islamabad always had plans to construct an indigenous reactor and reprocessing facility in order to produce plutonium for strictly military purposes and intended that all externally supplied facilities for civilian use would be under IAEA safeguards.[21]

Khushab-1 Production Reactor

By 1983, HEU production, enrichment facilities, and fuel cycle facilities had been established and were well under way, allowing the Zia government to restart the plutonium production project that had been put on hold for so many years. The PAEC encouraged President Zia-ul-Haq to resume this project, insisting that the back end of the nuclear fuel cycle would remain incomplete without a dedicated plutonium production reactor and a heavy water plant.[22] Zia was now convinced that pursuing the Pu route would guard against unforeseen setbacks to the HEU program. His decision was clearly affected by fears of a counterproliferation strike like the one Israel conducted successfully at Osirak, and the massive destruction of the centrifuges at Kahuta due to earthquake, back to back events in 1981.[23]

In anticipation of this new project, 1984 marked key organizational changes within the PAEC. The Directorate of Industrial Liaison (DIL), which was originally conceived to help the secret centrifuge program at Chaklala, was merged into the new Scientific and Engineering Services (SES Directorate). The SES Directorate was then placed under Sultan Bashiruddin Mahmood, who became the head of the Division of Nuclear Power (DNP). DNP was responsible for the development of both civil and classified nuclear reactor projects.

In 1985, the erstwhile PAKNUR project was restarted as the Khushab production reactor project, later renamed Khushab Chemical Plant-II (KCP-II). In a 1986 meeting, Munir Khan formally announced the decision to all top directors. Most subordinates thought Munir was overambitious and were reluctant to accept the responsibility. Finally, Bashiruddin Mahmood agreed to become the head of this project.

In 1987 work began on the 40–50 MWt Khushab reactor for the sole purpose of plutonium production. Since there were no expectations of foreign help, the project depended heavily on Pakistan's local industries. A consortium of twenty Pakistani companies was established that contributed to the development of the Khushab reactor project. These companies included the Heavy Mechanical Complex (HMC), the Heavy Foundry and Forge (HFF), the Ittefaq Foundry, Star Mughal Engineering, Pakistan Electron Limited (PEL), DESCON Engineering, and KSB Pumps.[24] Dispelling reports of foreign assistance, Munir Ahmad Khan insisted that it was a completely indigenous project.[25] However, despite increased reliance on domestic resources, the PAEC continued to procure critical items from foreign sources. For example, special aluminum tubes and boron were procured from West Germany, allowing the uranium metal fuel plant at Kundian to operate.

Defense considerations informed site selection for the Khushab reactor, leading to the choice of an isolated desertlike location deep inside the Punjab province. There was no major population center nearby, but it was in proximity to the PAF base in Sargodha. Although the site may have been secure, its location and arid terrain made delivering fresh water difficult, causing delays in the program.[26]

Sultan Bashiruddin, assisted by Afzal Haq Rajput, headed the reactor design project. The team modified the basic CIRUS design, resulting in a heavy water cooled, heavy water moderated reactor. Sultan Bashiruddin informed the author, "It was also designed to use natural uranium metal fuel instead of natural uranium oxide fuel, because metal fuel is better suited for obtaining weapons-grade plutonium."[27] A separate uranium metal manufacturing plant was constructed at the Kundian Nuclear Fuel Complex.

While construction of the Khushab reactor progressed, the international community questioned Pakistan's capability to produce a nuclear reactor indigenously. A 1992 study conducted by the U.S. Department of Defense claimed that Pakistan had limited capability and lacked the necessary infrastructure to manufacture and test critical nuclear components. The report also indicated that Pakistan was not self-sufficient in the production of "most important nuclear materials, including beryllium, boron carbide, hafnium, zirconium, lithium, graphite and high-purity bismuth."[28]

However, this report seemed unaware of the PAEC's 1986 success in the indigenous mining of uranium and zirconium and preparation of zirconium alloys, or of its already existing fully fledged National Centre for Non-Destructive Testing (NCNDT).[29] In contrast, a 1988 *Nuclear Fuel* report suggested, "PAEC is 'very proud' of its present capabilities in enrichment, reactor technology, and fuel fabrication, and there was no doubt that PAEC had the means to build the [Khushab] plant."[30]

Another experienced nuclear engineer, Pervez Butt, was appointed head of SES and tasked with the production of a specialized HMC—dubbed HMC-III—exclusively for Khushab and future indigenous reactors and other fuel cycle projects.[31] HMC-III developed into a high-technology manufacturing initiative that created an industrial infrastructure base for the indigenous nuclear program.

The reactor project also provided a diverse and all-encompassing training platform for Pakistani scientists, engineers, and technicians. Throughout the duration of the program, Pakistani experts were trained in a wide array of fields: reactor designs and construction, reactor safety, nuclear and reactor materials, metal fuel fabrication, heavy water and tritium production, aluminum alloy production, and more. This opportunity was ideal for the Pakistani scientific community to learn and master critical portions of the nuclear fuel cycle.[32]

New Laboratories (New Labs)

The New Labs were formally launched in 1973, at around the same time that the PAEC entered into an agreement with France's SGN for the procurement of a reprocessing facility in Chashma. Throughout the drawn-out ordeal with SGN, Pakistan and the New Labs reaped the benefits from continued communication with these specialized European firms. For example, just when the contract was signed, SGN offered the PAEC a "universal machining unit" that was reportedly meant for the New Labs reprocessing facility. This machine was later used to remove the cladding that held the KANUPP irradiated fuel rods, marking the first reprocessing stage in Pakistan.[33]

While SGN delayed the termination of its contract with Pakistan until August 1978, the PAEC continued to procure equipment and materials. By the time the SGN consultants had left in 1979, an estimated 95 percent of the reprocessing facility's blueprints had been transferred to the PAEC.

In April 1978, a CIA study on Pakistan's nuclear program predicted that in the absence of a large-scale French reprocessing plant, Pakistan would certainly opt for a smaller solution: "The acquisition of facilities which would enable Islamabad to quickly respond to an Indian weapons program with one of its own has become an inescapable corollary of any nuclear explosive plan. For this reason, Islamabad could conceivably opt to build a small scale reprocessing facility on its own. There have been descriptions in the open literature of such 'quick and dirty' installations. Most if not all the needed materials are available in the open market."[34]

Indeed, the PAEC was considering a small-scale option and found Hans Waelischmiller Company, a West German firm that specialized in the sale of "highly specialized lead shielding for protection against radiation, and special remote control equipment to move and manipulate radioactive substances, all essential equipment for hot cells and reprocessing plants."[35]

In addition to the German and French (SGN) firms, Pakistan had also forged a relationship with the Belgian firm Belgonucleaire, which facilitated the building of New Labs. A 1981 Belgonucleaire employee's visit to Pakistan is believed to have been in connection with the shipment of equipment that dealt with low-active liquid waste, an essential part of the "hot cell" system at the New Labs.[36]

The French firm SGN was responsible for "engineering the reprocessing facility itself and would later back away from the contract, but Belgonucleaire designed the overall building." The Belgonucleaire's managing director at the time, Jean van Dievoet, reportedly said, "[T]he Pakistanis themselves did the construction," and his firm's job was "to prepare the design and help the Pakistanis buy the needed equipment. This involved drawing up lists of specifications for various pieces of equipment and advising on the evaluation of offers from would-be suppliers. Belgonucleaire was also given the added task of designing the basic services for the building, including ventilation, water, heating, and the like." More important, Belgonucleaire was also given the job of "designing the fuel re-fabrication laboratory in New Labs, which handles the plutonium from which atom bombs can be made."[37]

The previously mentioned CIA assessment report of 1985 calculated that New Labs contained a pilot-scale fuel reprocessing plant, a fuel handling and refabrication facility, a plutonium metallurgy lab, and a waste treatment lab.[38] Although plutonium metallurgy was done at this facility, the Uranium Metal Lab (UML) also had the capacity to conduct machining and surface protection. Samar Mubarakmand credited Khalil Qureshi for his effort to establish UML work, and attributed the successes of the New Labs to three scientists: Chaudhry Abdul Majid, Dr. Zafarullah, and Dr. Javed Hanif.[39]

Progress continued, and by 1983 scientists at New Labs believed that they were ready to begin reprocessing, possibly using the PUREX method,[40] although there were concerns of inadvertent radioactive releases.[41] New Labs was an unsafeguarded facility. This project was launched in 1973, some three years before Pakistan had agreed to accept IAEA safeguards on the French reprocessing project. In 1979, when a query was made by the IAEA about the New Labs reprocessing facility, Pakistan's official response was that "there was no reprocessing facility in Pakistan about which they were obliged to tell the IAEA anything at all."[42] This was a clear indication that PAEC had drawn a line with the IAEA: a subtle reminder that Pakistan was not an NPT member, and would deal with IAEA only on the bilaterally agreed mandate.

As early as 1982, cold test experiments were carried out in New Labs, and some five years later fuel reprocessing hot tests were conducted.[43] Hot test experiments at a reprocessing facility are a prelude to full operation, as soon as spent fuel is available. Thus, Pakistan was fully prepared to handle any spent fuel for reprocessing that could have been made available to PAEC by 1987.[44] By 1998, New Labs had expanded its capacity and could handle all the spent fuel available from the Khushab reactor and extract about 8–15 kg of plutonium annually—enough for two to three nuclear explosive devices per year, assuming that each weapon requires 4–8 kg of weapons-grade plutonium.[45]

PAEC Training

The training of PAEC scientists and engineers was critical for acquiring mastery over the back end of the fuel cycle and reprocessing technology. European training centers were the best options, especially since Munir Ahmad Khan had many helpful contacts in Europe. One such center was Karlsruhe Nuclear Research Centre (KfK), which signed an "Agreement on Cooperation in the Area of Peaceful Uses of Atomic Energy" with the PAEC in 1974.[46] For two decades KfK and PAEC constantly exchanged experts and held joint seminars.

Through this agreement, the PAEC learned a great deal in the fields of jet nozzle uranium enrichment, fuel reprocessing, hot cells, fuel production, and waste treatment.[47] Two of New Labs' directors, Mr. Abdul Majeed Chaudhry and Dr. N. A. Javed, gained much of their technical expertise on hot cells at KfK.[48] Cornelius Keller, director of the Nuclear Technology School at KfK, visited PINSTECH in 1983 and is said to have been aware that Pakistan was able to produce plutonium.[49]

New Labs was not only a pilot-scale facility but also a full-fledged training center since its inception in 1973. Technical experts trained at New Labs stayed on to expand the facility or to work on the much larger Chashma reprocessing plant.

Heavy Water Production

Heavy water is an essential element in the production of plutonium because it is often used as a moderator for reactors that use natural uranium fuel. The importance of heavy water causes it and all of its components to be on the export control list of the Nuclear Suppliers Group.[50] Deuterium oxide (D_2O) is another name for heavy water, because it has two deuterium atoms in place of the two hydrogen atoms present in ordinary water. Heavy water is produced by NPT states such as the five nuclear weapons states, Canada, Argentina, and Norway, while India, Pakistan, and Israel are the only non-NPT states that are producers.

West Germany had pledged to supply a heavy water plant to Pakistan under IAEA safeguards but, like France and Canada, had backed out after the 1974 Indian nuclear test and canceled the contract.[51] Belgonucleaire, however, was a more willing partner and helped Pakistan construct a 13-MT heavy water facility in Multan by 1980.[52] But this single facility could not meet the needs of the Khushab reactor; therefore, the construction of another heavy water production facility, known as the Khushab Chemical Plant-1 (KCP-1), began in 1987.[53] Dr. N. A. Javed led this project, for which he was later decorated with a high civil award (Sitara-i-Imtiaz) in 1996.[54]

The PAEC obtained the necessary components for this new heavy water plant from various European companies that maintained close relationships with S. A. Butt. The facility, based on hydrogen sulphide exchange technology, required towers that were manufactured by only a handful of companies. Since these towers were on the restricted list for exports of the European supplier states, the PAEC approached an Arab businessman who operated several oil and gas fields in the Middle East. This businessman agreed to import the facility, but listed it as a petrochemical or gas-purification plant in order to bypass the nonproliferation barriers. The plant was customized according to N. A. Javed's specifications and was shipped from Holland to the Middle East (probably Dubai) and then to Karachi. Just like the hexafluoride plant, this shipment was huge and required a special Pakistan Naval Shipping Corporation ship. Once in Karachi, the plant was then transported by road to Khushab, where it was further modified.[55] Currently, this heavy water production plant also supplies the KANUPP reactor, in addition to a newly built 15-MT heavy water gradation plant.[56]

Tritium Production

As mentioned in Chapter 9, tritium is a radioactive isotope of hydrogen, which along with deuterium boosts the fission chain reaction in a weapon in order to increase the yield two or three times.[57] Only pure tritium that is free of any contaminants would be nuclear weapons usable. Tritium is either produced by irradiating metallic lithium-6 targets in a reactor or is extracted as a by-product of nuclear fission in heavy water reactors like Khushab. For the latter option, a tritium recovery or tritium enrichment facility is required—two very expensive components.[58]

In 1982, the PAEC approached West Germany for the acquisition of a tritium recovery/production facility, and by 1985 the two finalized an agreement with the firm Linde AG.[59] Meanwhile, the United States caught wind of these negotiations and warned Bonn about the impending deal. As reported by Mark Hibbs in March 1989, "Linde AG, one of a handful of firms in the world with expertise in the field of cryogenic distillation of hydrogen isotopes, could have supplied a heavy water detritiator with capability to purify the tritium gas product."[60] Apparently the German firm ignored the warnings and maintained that the facility provided to Pakistan would not produce a pure form of tritium.[61]

In addition, another West German firm, Nukleartechnik GmbH (NTG), received a license in 1985 to export a tritium plant to Pakistan. Because West German export regulations prohibited the sale of tritium plants, NTG listed its export as a "heavy water purifier" and shipped it to Pakistan, where it was installed at the Khushab nuclear complex in 1987. Speculators assume that the PAEC obtained tritium by irradiating lithium-6 targets in an unsafeguarded heavy water research reactor—that is, Khushab. Soon after the installation of the tritium facility, however, one NTG official and physicist, Peter Finke, carried out tests with PAEC officials. Finke later maintained that NTG had sold only a "training plant" to PAEC for the purification of contaminated heavy water being used in KANUPP, and had no connection with nuclear weapons.[62]

Only four to five grams of tritium are needed to boost a fission warhead, and capacity estimates for the tritium facility were in that range per day.[63] The tritium purification and enrichment system that was procured by the PAEC was based on a process called Tritium Removal by Organic Compounds, or TROC. NTG's chief, Rudolf Maxmilian Ortmayer, helped PAEC acquire the TROC system from a tritium laboratory in the Max Planck Institute of Plasma Physics, West Germany. S. A. Butt and Dr. Hasibullah, PAEC's main procurement officials posted in Europe, reportedly played key roles in arranging these technology transfers through cultivated relationships with German companies.[64]

It is important to note that, as of 2011, Pakistan's capacity to produce tri-

TABLE 10.1
Development of Plutonium Route

Process/Step	Location/Facility	Launched	Completed	Product	Organi-zation
Uranium Exploration	Dera Ghazi Khan; Exploration commenced at Qabul Khel (1992), Siwalik Hills etc during 1970s	1961	Decommissioned in 2000. Replaced by Nuclear Materials Complex-1	Uranium	PAEC
Uranium Processing (Uranium Mine and Mill)	Baghalchur-1 (BC-1), DG Khan	1975	1977	Yellow Cake/ Uranium Concentrate U3O8	PAEC
Uranium Conversion	Chemical Plants Complex, DG Khan	1975	1978	Uranium Oxide Uo2; Uranium Tetra-fluoride UF4	PAEC
Nuclear Fuel Fabrication	Kundian Nuclear Fuel Complex KNC-I;	1975	1978	Nuclear Fuel Elements for Nuclear Reactors	PAEC
	Uranium Metal Fuel Plant for Khushab Plutonium Reactors	1987	1992		
Plutonium Production Reactors (KCP-II)	Khushab-I (40–50 MWt)	1985	1997	Weapons-Grade Plutonium-239	PAEC
	Khushab-II (50-MWt)	2002	2010		PAEC
	Khushab-III (50-MWt)	2006	2011		PAEC
	Khushab-IV (50–100 MWt)	2011	2014 expected		PAEC
Heavy Water Production	KCP-I Khushab Nuclear Complex	1986	1996	Heavy water for Khushab Reactor Complex	PAEC
Tritium Production	Tritium Production Plant, Khushab Nuclear Complex	1987	1998	Tritium gas	PAEC
Plutonium Metallurgy and Machining of Pu-Core	New Labs/ UML, PINSTECH	1973 1976 2000	1981	Separating plutonium from spent nuclear fuel and producing Pu-239 metal	PAEC
Fuel Reprocessing	Chashma Reprocessing Plant KNC-2	1976	1978 1979 halted. Now being retrofitted and nearing completion[a]		PAEC

[a]Chashma Reprocessing Plant (KNC-2) is not yet commissioned. There are presumptions it may be put into operation soon as Khushab-2 and Khushab-3 has enough spent fuel ready for reprocessing.

tium was very limited. With a half-life of twelve years, any previous stock held in inventory, say in 1998, would no longer be available. Two production reactors at Khushab reportedly under construction would enable Pakistan to produce tritium, should it decide to resume production. However, such a project is worthwhile only if plans to conduct thermonuclear tests are in Pakistan's future. Samar Mubarakmand told the author that, to his knowledge, the current administration has no apparent ambition or desire to conduct fusion tests, which would entail colossal experiments, a dedicated program, and large capital inputs. Unless a series of hot tests are conducted, a thermonuclear experiment is useless.

The Completion of the Back End

In 1989 *Der Spiegel* reported, "There is no doubt that Munir Ahmed Khan . . . has secretly developed his country into a nuclear power; the bomb puzzle is complete. He had many individual parts—ranging from transformer sheets to uranium conversion—supplied by small West German firms, using a network of agents to this end."[65]

It took a decade for Pakistan to build the Khushab reactor, the nascent reprocessing facility at New Labs (which was completed by 1981), the heavy water plant, and the metal fuel production plant. At the same time that Pakistan tested its first HEU weapon in 1998, Khushab was commissioned. As the new century approached, Pakistan was on the threshold of achieving both routes to nuclear weapons—HEU and Pu.

The mastery of the plutonium route added the last piece to Islamabad's technological puzzle—in spite of international doubt, Pakistan had mastered the entire fuel cycle. This achievement allowed Pakistan the option to produce smaller and more compact Pu-based weapons in addition to HEU-based weapons. The availability of Pu also enabled Pakistan to combine the two fissile materials in new warhead designs and made available a wide array of options with which to build its nuclear forces.

Part III: Covert Arsenal and Delivery Means

11   Military Crises
and Nuclear Signaling

From the 1960s to the 1970s, Pakistan transitioned from initial reluctance to go down the nuclear path to a firm resolve to acquire nuclear weapons technology at all costs. However, no other period of Pakistani history better reinforced the strategic belief that a nuclear weapon was the only salvation for the nation than the events of the 1980s and crises with India. Three major military crises with India occurred in the 1980s. Although they were ultimately diffused, they validated Zulfiqar Ali Bhutto's decision to acquire a nuclear weapons capability. Subsequent military crises and near wars in the 1990s and 2000s reinforced a belief in the invincibility of nuclear weapons—that nuclear capability ensures defense against physical external aggression and coercion from adversaries, and deters infringement of national sovereignty. The decade of the 1980s created a context through which the Pakistani leadership would formulate the strategic beliefs that would lay the foundation for acquiring these weapons: (1) nuclear weapons were the only guarantee for national survival, (2) India will aggressively exploit Pakistan's vulnerabilities, and (3) India and Israel, with U.S. support, were willing to lead preventive attacks against Pakistan.

Under the leadership of Zia-ul-Haq, Pakistan had begun to stray from Jinnah's vision of a secular, moderate state for the Muslims of India toward an Islamic state that bred political Islam. Such a shift in national culture occurred both because of the Zia regime's Islamic leanings and the ideologically based asymmetric war against the Soviets in Afghanistan, which was overwhelmingly supported by the Western sources. The impact of these policies on the socioeconomic fabric of the Pakistani state and society can still be seen today. Domestic insurgencies, violent extremism, and terrorist activities span across the region.[1]

At the regional level, aside from the Iranian Islamic Revolution and the Soviet invasion of Afghanistan, two other events greatly influenced the entire region in the 1980s: the entente between the United States and China, which resulted in U.S. recognition of the People's Republic of China (PRC), and the return to power in India of Mrs. Indira Gandhi's Congress Party. These dramatic shifts shaped the region's history and influenced both Pakistan's security policy and its nuclear program.

Beginning in 1971, the United States moved closer to Pakistan's most trusted neighbor, China, in an effort to solve certain regional concerns. Within Beijing, the tightening of Sino-American relations was welcomed, as China sought to throw off the legacy of isolation and trade restrictions and find acceptance as a global player.[2] Islamabad's facilitating role in U.S.-China relations in the 1970s had made Pakistan a pivotal state, and Sino-American cooperation to defeat the Soviet Union in Afghanistan relied on Pakistan as a conduit for arming the *mujahideen* (freedom fighters) against the Soviet forces.[3] China saw it as logical that Pakistan's security needed bolstering as Pakistan became trapped between China's two nemeses—the Soviet Union and India.

On Pakistan's opposite border, India demonstrated its solidarity with the Soviet Union and encouraged the Soviets to inch closer at the Khyber Pass, a strategic link on the border of Afghanistan and Pakistan, forcing Pakistan into "the jaws of a nutcracker," as expressed by a former official.[4] Mrs. Gandhi approved a speech delivered by Indian UN ambassador Brajesh Mishra to the United Nations that declared Soviet armed intervention in Afghanistan as legitimate and appropriate in response to the "meddlesome activities in the region of some outside powers."[5] The Soviets immediately rewarded Mrs. Gandhi with an arms deal worth $1.6 billion—the largest in Indian history.[6] India's condoning of the Soviet aggression in the South West region also hurt the improving relationship between the United States and India, as the Carter administration was in the midst of wooing dominant states—referred to as "regional influentials"—in the important regions of world.[7]

Meanwhile, President General Zia-ul-Haq faced not only threats on both borders, but also U.S. sanctions on two counts: nuclear proliferation and the military coup that derailed democracy in Pakistan. In September 1979, the United States formally withdrew the A-7 aircraft deal that was earlier offered to Bhutto. On a visit to Islamabad, Joseph Nye, Jr., assistant secretary for the State Department, issued an unambiguous warning that economic assistance would be cut off under the Foreign Assistance Act should Pakistan continue with its nuclear program.[8] Zia-ul-Haq, however, had no incentive to oblige. At the time U.S. aid to Pakistan was a meager $50 million, and domestically the nuclear issue was a hot topic and a symbol of national pride. After the Soviet invasion of Afghanistan, Carter offered $400 million in aid to help build Afghanistan resistance. Zia decided to bide his time. He declined the $400 million, dubbing it as "peanuts" while he waited for a more sympathetic U.S. president to be elected.[9] Robert Wirsing accurately sums up the Pakistani anxiety at the time: "The ranks of its allies were diminishing at that very moment when ranks of its enemies were swelling. Never before had Pakistan been quite so isolated and quite so threatened at the same time."[10] As surmised in the first chapter of this book, when states face significant national threats and an acute sense of isolation, the fervor to acquire the absolute weapon increases exponentially.

Into the Valley of Death

Before addressing any of the regional issues surrounding Pakistan's borders, President General Zia had to settle a single outstanding domestic issue. Dismissing all international appeals for clemency, Zia allowed that Zulfiqar Ali Bhutto be hanged on April 4, 1979, in Rawalpindi, following the Supreme Court's decision that had indicted him for conspiring in the murder of a political opponent—a decision that is widely held as controversial and one that has had disastrous impact on civil-military relations as well as those between executive and judiciary. Two days later, Washington suspended aid to Pakistan pursuant to the Symington Amendment to the Foreign Assistance Act. Apparently, this suspension was not a response to Bhutto's execution, but rather Zia-ul-Haq's failure to compromise with the United States on the nuclear issue. In March of that year, Deputy Secretary of State Warren Christopher had visited Islamabad and sought reliable assurances on the nuclear program. Zia assured him that the program would remain peaceful in nature but did not accept safeguards and declined to abstain from "peaceful nuclear tests."[11]

The application of nuclear sanctions on Pakistan cracked the amiable twenty-five-year relationship, originally forged by President Eisenhower and John Foster Dulles. But even under this strain, other emerging factors forced Washington to rethink the strategic significance of Pakistan.

Defense planners in the Pentagon and the intelligence community in Langley were concerned by the developments in Afghanistan and Iran. Numerous listening posts in Iran had been lost after the Islamic Revolution, leading the United States to seek improved intelligence and defense cooperation with Pakistan.[12] Zia realized that the United States had lost strategic space in the region. On the one hand, he foresaw the ensuing advantages—legitimization of his military rule, economic growth, and the redress of conventional force imbalances—all to the chagrin of India.[13] On the other hand, intelligence cooperation with the United States required increased information and surveillance activities inside Pakistan that could compromise Pakistani national secrets, especially covert acquisition of sensitive nuclear technologies.

Zia-ul-Haq had little choice but to gamble. The nuclear issue could be mitigated with diplomacy, and the risks associated with U.S. intelligence gathering could be addressed with improved counterintelligence.[14] Meanwhile, Washington policy-makers debated between cooperating with Pakistan to defeat the Soviet Union by asymmetric means or punishing Pakistan to prevent nuclear proliferation in a Muslim country.[15] Strategic imperatives and rational calculations brought Washington to the conclusion that the Pakistani nuclear program could be slowed but not derailed—thus defeating the Soviet Union in Afghanistan took precedence. Meanwhile covert operations to spy on or possibly slow the Pakistani nuclear program continued.

Fears of Preventive War

In 1977, before his government was overthrown, Zulfi Bhutto in his public speeches had rhetorically hinted at Western conspiracies against his regime for his staunch belief in the nuclear program, and subsequently he maintained that he was thrown out because of it. Such allegations were never proven, however. Bhutto nevertheless till his death believed that Zia-ul-Haq would either be incapable of pursuing the nuclear program or might trade off for conventional weapons or financial aid.[16] The nuclear program, however, not only accelerated but reached fruition during the reign of Bhutto's successor.

Western intelligence activities did increase, especially after the French withdrew from the reprocessing plant deal in 1978 when, as explained in the previous chapters, Pakistani nuclear facilities were beginning to expand. During this period a mysterious rock was discovered in the vicinity of the newly constructed centrifuge facility in Kahuta. A shepherd grazing his cattle in the area suddenly found his dog barking at the rock. The shepherd suspected something amiss and reported to the police, who discovered a hidden electronic device inside it. Additionally, the now-alerted Pakistani intelligence found that Western embassy officials and their visitors seemed to find the Kahuta valley attractive for picnics and sightseeing.

In the summer of 1979, Kahuta, a place that seemed to be shrouded in mystery, piqued the curiosity of officials at U.S. missions in Islamabad. Robert Galluci, director of the Bureau of Near Eastern and South Asian Affairs at the State Department, was one of several officials who wanted to visit Kahuta personally. The U.S. embassy promptly arranged a "picnic" for him as well as for political officer Marc Grossman (who in February 2011 would be appointed as special representative for Afghanistan and Pakistan) and another intelligence officer. At the time, the Engineering Research Laboratories (ERL) uranium enrichment facility at Kahuta was heavily guarded and fenced off with barbed wire but, with access to the surrounding hills, was easy to photograph.[17]

Recently quoted in a publication about U.S. intelligence assets around Kahuta, Galluci recalled the details of how the United States had penetrated the Kahuta facility: "We had human intel, electronic intel, intel of every conceivable nature . . . wiretaps, satellite overheads, and highly sensitive on-the-ground intel, both human and technological . . . augmented by U.S. data-collecting operations made possible by the infiltration of [a] high-tech surveillance device into the arid area surrounding the heavily guarded Kahuta hills, a place no U.S. or European spies could get near."[18] The Pakistani security agencies throughout the 1980s stepped up counterintelligence and were conducting major sweeps in the area to sift rocks from devices.[19]

Since the late 1970s, officials in Washington, DC, have been exploring more direct means to disrupt the Pakistani nuclear program. Secretary of State Cyrus Vance asked Joseph Nye, Jr., to research the pros and cons of covert action or an air strike against Kahuta. Gerard Smith, an arms control expert leading an interagency group, also presented a paper exploring similar options. However, the purported plan was leaked to the *New York Times,* and Islamabad was left fuming with anger, prompting the United States to deny any plans for a preventive strike.[20]

Refutation aside, it was apparent that the United States was concerned about the progress of the Pakistani nuclear program. Officials were convinced that Pakistan would soon be ready to test a nuclear device. On September 14, 1979, in testimony before the General Advisory Committee on Arms Control and Disarmament, the assistant director of the Arms Control and Disarmament Agency (ACDA), Mr. Charles Van Doran, expressed his suspicion that Pakistan would test a device around the upcoming U.S. presidential elections, since "it would be politically handy for them to have some great show of strength at that time."[21]

Such fears lent themselves to a discussion in the ACDA of options for a preemptive attack. It was revealed that the Israelis were also interested in taking proactive steps against the Pakistani nuclear program, presenting an "Entebbe Two" option. This designation was a reference to the 1976 Israeli commando raid at Uganda's Entebbe Airport to rescue hostages of a hijacked plane. However, before this plan could be explored further, Mr. Burke of the *New York Times* wrote a piece identifying an Entebbe-type attack as an option to disrupt Pakistan's program. Mr. Van Doran explained that this public announcement made the option unusable: "Well, we were a little bit hindered. . . . [It] makes it harder to consider that [Entebbe Two] was an option when Mr. Burke thought it up publicly and exposed it and had it categorically denied."[22]

In October of the same year, President Zia-ul-Haq sent Foreign Minister Agha Shahi to the U.S. capital. In a meeting with Secretary of State Cyrus Vance, he found Mr. Gerard Smith also present. Recalling the discussion, Mr. Shahi said that Gerald Smith began his conversation by stating, "Don't you know you are entering the Valley of Death? Do you think you are enhancing your security by what you are doing? The Indians are far ahead of you. They can utterly destroy you."[23] Shahi continued, "I paused for a moment and said, 'Mr. Gerard Smith, I am at a great disadvantage talking to you. You are perhaps the foremost expert on all things nuclear. I am a layman . . . but one doesn't have to become [a] weapons expert to understand the strategic, psychological and political implications of possessing nuclear capability . . . . [If] I remember at the time of [the] Cuban missile crisis . . . it never occurred to President Kennedy to give [an] ultimatum to Khrushchev . . . . [He] then agreed to pull out Jupiter missiles from Turkey and committed not to invade Cuba and then Khrushchev agreed to pull back the missiles from Cuba. From this we understand [that] the value of nuclear capability is in its possession as deterrent, not in its use, because it is a doomsday weapon.' There was total silence."[24]

Meanwhile Islamabad was buzzing with conspiracy theories and rumors of preventive attacks on Pakistani nuclear sites. The combination of reports about Western embassies spying on restricted areas and intelligence intercepts confirmed that Pakistani nuclear facilities were in danger. This threat led to increased security and vigilance. Counterintelligence surveillance around sensitive sites grew, and the movements of Western embassy officials were tracked.

On June 7, 1981, Pakistan's fears took on new proportions when Israeli jets attacked and destroyed the Iraqi Osirak nuclear power reactor with U.S.-supplied planes, munitions, and spy satellites. In the summer of 1981, Israeli intelligence agents threatened European suppliers such as CORA Engineering, Heinz Mebus, and Peter Griffin with mysterious bomb explosions and threats, all in an effort to discourage business with Pakistan.[25] In addition, Pakistani intelligence picked up leads of Israeli and Indian intelligence collaboration and discovered that the Indian air force had begun planning a strike on Pakistan's nuclear facilities.[26] India conducted a feasibility study on an Osirak-type attack against Pakistan at its Combat College, and the Indian Air Force conducted a series of exercises related to this study, some of which used top-of-the-line Jaguar aircraft.[27] Meanwhile, Israel offered a new proposal that would accomplish New Delhi's goals. Under this new plan, Israeli planes would take off from an Indian Air Force base in Jamnagar, refuel at a satellite airfield somewhere in northern India, and in the final stage, the planes would track the Himalayas to avoid early radar detection before penetrating Pakistani airspace. Mrs. Gandhi approved the plan, but U.S. warnings forced both India and Israel to abandon it.[28]

To Pakistani officials, however, the signs were clear—their nuclear facilities were under the threat of a preventive strike. Both the Karachi Nuclear Power Plant (KANUPP) and Kahuta were vulnerable, so President Zia tasked Chief of General Staff Mirza Aslam Beg to improve their defenses. PAF planes scrambled and began combat air patrol (CAP missions), which soon became a part of the normal operational routine. Since then, the skies above Kahuta have been no-fly zones.

Dr. Javed Mirza, who was working in Kahuta at the time, described the change in security to the author: "[W]hen we first shifted to Kahuta, there was no security. It was all open except for the barbed wire. One fine morning we went to work and found guns everywhere. The army was everywhere and that was the time when they got the threats from somewhere that Indian commandoes were coming."[29]

Islamabad could no longer remain complacent about the threats against its nuclear installations. The Pakistani threat perception from the outset of the program was the fear of an "insider" spy or saboteur within the program who would carry out espionage at the behest of an "outsider." The discoveries of "mysterious rocks," the frequency of picnics by Western embassy officials, and now Israel's attack on Osirak and India's contemplating doing the same only exacerbated these concerns. Protecting the nuclear program from outside intelligence became the primary concern for the regime, and after that period formed the basis of Pakistan's future threat perceptions. This perspective, in turn, contributed to the nature of oversight and the evolution of a nuclear security culture, as will be explained in the chapters ahead.[30]

Reagan and Zia: New Terms of Contract

In 1981, President Reagan took office with two clear objectives: roll back the Soviets from Afghanistan and slow down Pakistan's nuclear program. President Zia was offered $3.2 billion in U.S. aid for six years (1982–87), and in response Zia sent a strong team to negotiate the new terms of engagement with the United States.[31] After frank exchanges, an arrangement was agreed upon, built on four pillars:[32] (1) U.S. security assurances, (2) Pakistani sovereignty, (3) covert intelligence cooperation, and (4) Pakistan's assurances of the peaceful use of nuclear technology.

The first pillar, U.S. security assurances to Pakistan, was addressed by simply reviving the countries' 1959 bilateral agreement. The second was a response to Zia's concern over U.S. interference in Pakistan's domestic affairs. The Reagan administration agreed not only to remove the military sanctions but also to refrain from pressuring Islamabad on democracy and human rights issues. The third pillar attended to the modalities of supporting a covert war against the Soviet Union. It was agreed that Pakistan's Inter-Services Intelligence (ISI) would lead the covert operations, while the CIA would provide the resources and refrain from direct contact with the *mujahideen*.[33] Finally, Pakistan agreed to keep its nuclear program low key and peaceful and pledged not to conduct hot tests. The Pakistanis were satisfied to note that the "U.S. could live with Pakistan's program as long as Islamabad did not explode the bomb."[34]

Armed with this new agreement, President Zia-ul-Haq was ready to craft a more appropriate nuclear policy. Along with assurances to President Reagan that Pakistan would not conduct a nuclear test, Zia also directed the Pakistan Atomic Energy Commission (PAEC) to strengthen IAEA safeguards on KANUPP rather than removing them, as the latter would create unnecessary controversy. President Zia-ul-Haq issued four secret directives to the nuclear establishment that were believed to be the result of his pledge to President Reagan that he would "never embarrass his friend."[35] The four directives included: (1) not to further produce highly enriched uranium (HEU); (2) not to machine the already produced HEU, if any, into a weapon core; (3) not to conduct hot tests; and (4) not to transfer any hard technological or soft knowledge to any other country or entity.

Meanwhile, Zia had the enrichment project sped up and increased security on the nuclear installations. He turned his attention to the rising tensions with India. Mrs. Indira Gandhi had returned to power in New Delhi just when the Soviets were establishing themselves in Kabul. Pakistan was very vulnerable to its two nemeses, and the United States was its only recourse.

Indo-Pak Military Crises and the Nuclear Dimension

Relations between India and Pakistan were relatively calm through the early 1980s. Nearly a decade had passed since the last war between the two, and in the new Pakistan, old rivalries with India were fading to mere cultural and sports activities. With the return of Mrs. Gandhi to power, however, not only did political tensions begin to increase but, in addition, subtle shifts in strategic thinking began to reshape India's posture toward its neighbors. State-sponsored think tanks in Delhi propounded the dominant position of India: the defense and military establishments contemplated aggressive postures, new military doctrines, organizational changes, and strategic modernizations, all of which had a direct impact on regional relations. From the mid-1980s onward, India had major military crises with nearly all its neighbors: Pakistan in 1984, 1986–87, and 1990; China in 1986–87; Sri Lanka in 1987–88; Maldives in 1988; and Nepal in 1989.[36] However, the relationship most adversely affected, and that seemingly never recovered, was with Pakistan. The India-Pakistan military crises had a profound effect on Pakistan's nuclear development in the region.

Strategic thinking in India after the 1971 war gradually evolved throughout the early 1980s. K. Subramanyam, known as the "doyen of the India security community,"[37] is widely believed in Pakistan to be the most influential voice of India's security policies in the Indian establishment.[38] Subramanyam's writings in the 1980s, which set the security debate in the region, revolved around three major themes. First, India's large defense posture and powerful military is not hegemonistic or menacing to its neighbors; rather, this image of India is largely a projection made by India's enemies. Second, Pakistan is the root cause of the problem in the region primarily because of the nature of the state (authoritarian and ideological) and is challenged by the rise of a secular, institutionally stronger, and democratic India. Structurally, India dominates and is ordained to rise. India's neighbors, especially Pakistan, must accept this inevitability. Finally, an Indo-centric system is the ultimate destiny of South Asia, once extra-regional powers (implying the United States and possibly China) set the region free from interference and foreign influences.[39] From the Pakistani standpoint, accepting this logic would imply bandwagoning onto the rise of India, which would make Pakistan an irrelevant entity and undercut the very raison d'etre of its creation as a separate state.

The Pakistani narrative rejects Subramanyam's philosophy on all three counts. From Pakistan's perspective, India continues an aggressive policy both within the country as well as toward all its neighbors, powerful and weak alike. India has not settled any issues peacefully with any of its neighbors; with the passage of time, a policy of intransigence and dominance compounded what were initially reasonably resolvable issues. Second, Pakistan accepts its structural weaknesses, which necessitate military interventions, but it always returns to democracy as the natural disposition of its people. Indian hawks, from the outset, have had issues with the "nature of Pakistan" and are opposed to the ideological basis of its separation from India, while Pakistan maintains that Muslims in India live under constant threat of fundamentalist Hindu forces. Finally, from Pakistan's perspective, India's geophysical domination does not imply that smaller nation-states must capitulate their sovereignty to Indian hegemony. The right to independent foreign policy, seeking balances and alliances, is endemic to the nation-state pathway to survivability. Pakistan reserves the right to seek friendships with outside powers based on its geographical advantages, ideological affiliations, and political and economic potential. It thus refuses to accept India's bullying and insists on independently maintaining close ties with the United States, China, and Islamic countries. Pakistan does not see India taking its neighbors along in a benign manner; on the contrary, India is rather Machiavellian in its security policies.[40]

These competing security dialectics between India and Pakistan coincided with major military modernizations around both countries. India continued to receive military armaments from the Soviet Union, and Pakistan gradually began to receive U.S. military equipment after a long hiatus, primarily as a result of its role in the Afghan war.[41] The qualitative and quantitative edge, however, was always with India, and it continued growing. By the middle of the 1980s the Indian military lead over Pakistan in personnel was 2:1, in tanks 2:1, in surface warships 4:1, and in combat aircraft 3:1.

The advent of nuclear weapons under such a competing strategic environment, both at the conceptual and military levels, compounded the security situation. From a strategic point of view, a nuclear capability within Pakistan would alter the influence and coercive power of the predominant India, as a nuclear Pakistan would neutralize Indian geopolitical maneuvering aimed at isolating it. Conversely, with nuclear capabilities, both sides would feel secure and comfortable in accepting amicable conflict resolution, which in turn would make the rise of India beneficial for the entire region.[42]

Yet the early 1980s was a period of intense vulnerability for Pakistan and its nascent nuclear program. With plentiful geophysical exposure, strategic anxieties were natural, even absent the fear of preventive strike. In Pakistan's case, more than one party was interested in destroying its nuclear capability, and this threat exacerbated the sense of urgency to speed up the program and close down the window of vulnerability through astute policy-making and diplomacy.

Thus, in the summer of 1983, Pakistani Army strike formations (two corps) conducted a military exercise in southern Punjab with the objective of testing the combat efficiency of Pakistani counteroffensive capabilities. Important to the exercise was the perception of threat, the ingredients of which were found in the exercise narrative: India foments insurgencies in interior Sindh (East Pakistan style), builds up offensive forces close to the Pakistani border, and prepares to assail as soon as opportunity avails; Pakistani forces countermobilize. The war game starts with the Indian Air Force (IAF) conducting a partially successful attack (Osirak-style) on a Pakistani nuclear installation at Kahuta, as the Indian Navy blockades a Karachi port and the insurgency in Sindh province picks up momentum. This strategic threat perception existed well before India actually contemplated identical plans, which unfolded partially in 1984 and again in 1986–87 (see below).[43] Indeed, Pakistani strategic planning, rooted in perceptions of the times, later became the genesis of the four thresholds or nuclear redlines, which were made public in the midst of military crisis in 2002 (see Chapter 18).

As Indian and Pakistani relations emerged from the relative calm of the early 1980s, the two countries began accusing each other of interfering in internal ethnic disputes.[44] The Pakistani establishment charged India with meddling in the Sindh province under a Pakistani coalition known as the Movement on Restoration of Democracy (MRD). The campaign turned into a major uprising in 1983, prompting the Pakistani Army to deploy two infantry divisions and gunship helicopters. By the same token, India accused Pakistan of providing sanctuary and support to the Sikh insurgency that was raging in Punjab.

This volatile environment resulted in three major military crises that came perilously close to war. During that period, Pakistan had crossed a critical threshold and had acquired a nuclear capability. In each of the military crises there existed a nuclear dimension, subtle nuclear signaling, and varying degrees of outside intervention. The regional landscape had changed beyond recognition by the end of the century.

The Siachin Glacier and Golden Temple Crises

Operation Meghdoot

On April 13, 1984, Pakistan's Force Command Northern Areas (FCNA), deployed in the northernmost fringes of the Line of Control (LOC) in Kashmir, observed Indian helicopters dropping forces on the heights of the Soltoro Range in the Siachin Glacier region. The Siachin Glacier is wedged between the Chinese border and the LOC that was left undemarcated after a point (map coordinate NJ 9842) in the 1948 ceasefire line (CFL) because the area was considered inhospitable and inaccessible to either party. Pakistan rushed in troops to stall the Indian advance, which had already captured two unoccupied glacial passes, but Islamabad's ill-prepared forces failed to dislodge the entrenched Indian troops. This clash, euphemistically called "the war on the roof of the world," was the fiercest armed conflict between India and Pakistan since the 1971 war. Small-scale tactical operations along the LOC in Kashmir continued throughout the mid-1980s, mostly at heights above 15,000 feet.[45]

All disputes in South Asia come with competing narratives. From India's standpoint, the military operation, code-named Meghdoot (Cloud Messenger), was a preemptive occupation because India believed Pakistan had contemplated occupying the same territory a year earlier.[46] Pakistan rejected this narrative and claimed that Indian intrusion on these heights had begun in the 1970s on a small scale and was continuing.[47] Pakistan, however, had procrastinated in its decision to conduct a military operation to dislodge the Indian incursions in March 1984, which had allowed India to seize the initiative the following month in April and mount a major operation to occupy nearly two-thirds of the glacier before Pakistani forces reacted to stall further occupation.[48]

The 1984 Indian military action on the Siachin Glacier was considered by Pakistan to be a blatant violation of the 1972 Simla Accord, which forbade the use of military force to occupy territory, even if it was unoccupied and contested.[49] This event triggered a "series of moves and countermoves at [a] tactical level along the Line of Control in the inaccessible snowbound Northern Areas."[50] Operation Meghdoot and its consequences laid the foundation for the many later crises that occurred in Kashmir.

Pakistan was convinced that the Simla 1971 peace treaty and detente (1977–79) were no assurance of national security and that India would go on the offensive at the first opportunity. The threat perception of preventive attacks and conspiracies was reinforced as one crisis followed another. The foundation of Pakistan's later security and nuclear policies would strongly reflect the doctrines and security frameworks of successive Indian governments.

Operation Blue Star

Around the same time that Operation Meghdoot was planned, India was facing a massive Sikh uprising in Punjab, just across the Pakistani border.[51] The Indian government for over a decade had largely ignored the Sikh community's call for equal rights and protection, and unrest had gradually evolved into militancy. When Mrs. Gandhi returned to power, she had refused to make political compromises to resolve the issue. A heavy-handed crackdown on the Sikhs resulted in an open revolt, which led to an armed insurgency and gradually transformed into a secessionist movement lasting nearly two decades. The Punjab crisis was one of the most brutal and violent ethnonationalist secessionist movements that India faced in its independent history. It came to a head in the 1980s, resulting in the deaths of approximately twenty-five thousand people in Punjab.[52] The Indian government blamed Pakistan, alleging that its neighbor had only abetted the conflict.[53]

In 1984 Sikh insurgents sought refuge in Harminder Sahib, famously known as the Golden Temple, one of the holiest of Sikh shrines. A violent struggle broke out in the temple when the Sikhs, led by Garnail Singh Bhinderwala and his supporters, refused to surrender and prepared to lay down their lives. In June of that year, the Indian Army had laid siege to the Golden Temple and later assaulted it with tanks and guns, destroying the temple and eventually killing the insurgents in a bloody resistance. Operation Blue Star succeeded militarily, but it became a symbol of Sikh separatism; in its aftermath mayhem spread all over India for years, including Sikh revolts within the military.

Missing Jaguars

As described earlier, ever since the Israeli preventive strike at Osirak in Iraq in 1981, India had contemplated mimicking the Israeli feat. In 1982, a plan for a preventive strike on Kahuta was presented to Mrs. Gandhi but in the final analysis was shelved. By October of 1984, however, Indian military leaders again urged Mrs. Gandhi to order a strike on Pakistan's Kahuta centrifuge facility.[54]

U.S. intelligence satellites had detected two Jaguar squadrons missing from the Indian Ambala airbase (three hundred miles from Kahuta).[55] When U.S. intelligence discovered India's plans, the U.S. ambassador in Islamabad, Deane Hinton, issued a subtle public warning that apparently put an end to the discussion.[56] The United States also assured Pakistani officials that "[if] the United States sees any signs of an imminent Indian attack, Pakistan would be notified."[57] Pakistan's Vice Chief of Army Staff, General K. M. Arif, acknowledged, "Our friends let us know what the Israelis and Indians intended to do and so we let them know how we would respond."[58]

It is unclear if India backed down because of the U.S. warning, or whether Prime Minister Gandhi declined to oblige the Indian military. Politically, India might have rationally concluded that attacking a vital ally of the United States at the time—when the Soviets were trapped in a debilitating asymmetric war—would have been counterproductive. From a military perspective, India might have abandoned the plans because its element of surprise had been lost. Pakistan made open preparations to meet both an air threat and a possible assault from the ground.[59] K. Subramanyam, chair of India's Joint Intelligence Committee, acknowledged the loss of the surprise factor. Subramanyam determined that reports of an increase in Pakistani air defenses around Kahuta were "proof, if any more were needed, that our covert intentions to hit Kahuta were not secret anymore."[60]

The crisis was a burden not only for Pakistan: India feared a Pakistani pre-emptive strike. A senior Indian IAF officer reportedly said, "If they think you're going to attack Kahuta, they may pre-empt you."[61] The ensuing tension made the risk of strategic miscalculation extremely high.[62] Unbeknownst to Indian security hawks at the time was Pakistan's secretly acquired nuclear weapons capability. As related in Chapter 9, at Pakistan's request China had provided at least fifty kilograms of HEU (sufficient for two bombs), as well as the Chinese CHIC-4 weapon design.

Had India attacked Pakistani nuclear installations in 1984, it undoubtedly would have initiated a full-scale war. Pakistan would have retaliated in kind against an Indian nuclear installation. The region was simply lucky; it escaped a fourth war.

On October 31, 1984, Mrs. Gandhi was assassinated by two of her Sikh bodyguards in response to Operation Blue Star. What followed for several years was a Hindu backlash—a killing rampage of Sikhs across all of Punjab and other regions of India. It took nearly a decade for India—with cooperation from Pakistan—to bring Punjab under control. The assassination of Mrs. Gandhi did put an end to the 1984 escalations; however, it did not help to relieve the tensions between India and Pakistan, nor did the Indian Army abandon the idea of carrying out a preventive strike against Kahuta. Indian military planners would wait for new leadership and a propitious moment; even if the moment did not come about, they were capable of creating one.[63]

The Brasstacks Crisis

General Krishnaswami Sunderrajan (Sunderji) became the Indian Army Chief in February 1986. Sunderji was reputedly a soldier with an intellectual bent, especially famous for his flamboyant leadership style and hasty decisions.[64] Immediately after assuming command, he was eager to reform the Indian Army. General Sunderji's rise to the top coincided with the rise of young Prime Minister Rajiv Gandhi and Minister of State for Defense Arun Singh, both of whom shared Sunderji's passion for modernizing the armed forces.

No other personality in the Indian Army had as much impact on the security thinking in Pakistan as did General Sunderji. He was feared for his bold and daring decisions and equally admired for his intellect and dedication to military advancement. As part of his military reforms, General Sunderji restructured the Indian infantry into mission-oriented formations. For example, separate units were created for different types of terrain, including the Reinforced Army Plain Infantry Divisions (RAPIDS), which operated in plains and deserts. He also reorganized the Indian Army into seven defensive corps, named the Holding Corps, which were deployed mostly along the Pakistan border. All together, General Sunderji made his own signature air-land mix—a deployment of three strike corps, an armored division at the core, and RAPIDS backed with artillery and air firepower along with helicopter-borne special forces.[65]

Theoretically, under such a formation, India's strike corps would penetrate deep into Pakistan, destroying the Pakistani Army's reserve strike corps and slicing the country into two by severing key lines of communication. In addition, the Indian Air Force would gain air superiority and the Indian Navy would blockade Karachi. Igniting an ethnic insurgency in Pakistan's Sindh would draw Pakistan military forces away from the Indian attack, which would facilitate India's blitzkrieg.

General Sunderji planned to test these operational concepts in 1986 in the four-phased Exercise Brasstacks. The first three phases included the following:

(1) July 21–25, war game for all Indian forces, (2) November 10–14, war game exclusively for India's western command bordering Pakistan, and (3) November–December, amphibious operations with the navy. The fourth and final phase was scheduled for February–March 1987 and involved a full-fledged exercise in Rajasthan. The exercise was to feature two armored divisions and two RAPIDs (with full logistics support and live munitions), all of which were backed by full complements of the air force maneuvering on an east-west axis in the direction of Pakistan's most vulnerable areas. In preparation, India canceled leave for all military personnel, relocated some forces in the Jammu area, and issued operational instructions that were intercepted by Pakistani intelligence.[66]

Upon discovering Exercise Brasstacks, Pakistan rapidly countermobilized and prepared to meet the offensive. As more intelligence intercepts poured in, military maneuvers were hurriedly planned under exercise Saf-e-Shikan and exercise Flying Horse.[67]

Was General Sunderji provoking a war, or was he simply conducting a military exercise? To date no clear conclusion had ever been reached. Several Indian publications revealed the intentions behind the crisis. Ravi Rikhe's book *The War That Never Was*, popularly read in Pakistan at the time, gave stunning revelations that simply reinforced Pakistani belief in India's perpetual intentions to destroy Pakistan. This account revealed a secret plan code-named "Operation Trident" that was embedded in the broader ruse of Exercise Brasstacks.[68] The plan called for provoking Pakistan into a war with a massive deception of force deployment in desert areas of Sindh to the south, drawing away Pakistani forces, and then launching an offensive in the north across the LOC in Kashmir. The ultimate end was the "destruction of Pakistan's enrichment facility at Kahuta."[69]

Some U.S. scholars believe there were plans to conduct a fourth war, which would have been India's one last chance to lead an "attack on Pakistan's nuclear facilities to remove the potential for a Pakistani nuclear riposte."[70] Others thought Sunderji's military action was coercive and designed to send an "unequivocal political and strategic message about India's robust military capability."[71] Some retired Indian military officers serving at the time told me that General Sunderji denied that he had any intention of starting a war with Pakistan.[72]

Pakistani General Khalid Mahmud Arif, Vice Chief of Army Staff, related his version of the story to the author. In late 1986, when Arif learned of preparations for Exercise Brasstacks, he directed the Pakistani defense attache in Delhi to call on the Indian Army chief to seek clarification. Arif contends that if

"Sunderji had informed me that he was going to run an exercise, I would have said fine." But twice the defense attache was rebuffed and was finally told that "India is not obliged to tell you in advance about our exercise or maneuvers." In another instance, an Indian official conveyed to the Pakistani high commissioner in Delhi that "Pakistan is up to some mischief and the Indian Army is on red alert and we will do more unless you withdraw your forces." As tensions mounted, General Arif was fairly certain that action was not imminent. For security purposes, however, "minimum precautionary measures that [were] non-provocative" had to be taken.[73] On the other hand, K. M. Arif's successor, General Mirza Aslam Beg, Vice Chief of Army Staff (March 1987–August 1988), felt that the Indian exercises were obviously innocuous, and thus Pakistan's actions were escalatory and "foolishly deployed."[74]

After having made his assessment, General Arif deployed two strategic reserves in a pincerlike move that would envelop two major Indian cities and cut off its access to Kashmir. In response, the Indian Army redeployed to cover the areas and, further, launched a military thrust to capture critical Sikh territory in Punjab, out of fear that Pakistan might fuel a Sikh insurgency. In India's perception, any Pakistani-captured territory in Indian Punjab would be seen as "liberating the land" for the Sikhs and thus enabling them to declare an independent state (Khalistan).[75] Since then, Pakistan has remained hypersensitive to Indian military mobilizations on its border, and both are wary of intervention in domestic upheavals. South Asia had become a tinderbox once again.

In late January 1987, some bold diplomacy by Islamabad and New Delhi, together with unpublicized U.S. intervention, helped diffuse the crisis. Although war was averted, the Brasstacks crisis left scars. The region was infused with new threat perceptions, which gave rise to innovative military doctrines, as nuclear capabilities were emerging.[76]

Had war broken out and a preventive strike been successfully executed over Kahuta, Pakistan would have certainly been pushed back in its centrifuge program. It would have recovered eventually, but the sure consequences of war with India—once again, as in 1984—would have changed the course of the region's history.

Operation Falcon and Chequerboard

While Brasstacks was unfolding, General Sunderji shifted his gaze toward India's northeast border with China. Operation Chequerboard was underway in Sumdorong Chu Valley, lasting from October 1986 to March 1987.

Prior to this military confrontation, relations between India and China had been steadily improving. However, the amiable relationship came to an abrupt end on December 1986, when India upgraded the disputed territory with China known as the North East Frontier Agency (NEFA) and declared it to be the state of Arunachal Pradesh within India. China was infuriated and, as expected, Beijing lodged a strong protest, charging India with "seriously violating" China's territorial integrity and sovereignty. In response, India accused China of occupying the Sumdurong Chu Valley. By that point, the two countries' militaries were preparing for a standoff.[77]

General Sunderji launched another military operation code-named Falcon. This plan ordered the Indian Air Force to lift the infantry brigade into Zimithang, from where troops took their positions on Hathung La Ridge across Namka Chu River. China became alarmed and responded with a counterforce buildup, sending ominous signals of another war.[78]

In just over a year, the Indian general had brought his country to the brink of war with both China and Pakistan. When the Indian political leadership realized that its army chief had triggered two potential wars, Prime Minister Rajiv Gandhi's office charged General Sunderji with recklessness. The general stood his ground, suggesting that they "make alternate arrangements if they think they were not getting adequate professional advice."[79] Although the two crises were disconnected, their proximity and timing brought three nuclear-armed neighbors to a potentially catastrophic military standoff.

Cricket Diplomacy and the Glib-tongued Scientist

South Asia crises are always accompanied by considerable drama—exaggeration of events or their significance—that often leads to rumors and conspiracy theories. Two events toward the end of the Brasstacks crises have been overdramatized by tales that have left an impact on future perceptions about nuclear capability and intentions.

Despite the high level of military tension, routine diplomatic and sports activities were continuing uninterrupted during the crises (November 1986–February 1987). Pakistani diplomats believed they were managing the crises well, and Prime Minister Muhammad Khan Junejo and his counterpart, Prime Minister Rajiv Gandhi, as well as Indian diplomats believed they were effectively diffusing the crises. Many analysts, however, attribute the crisis de-escalation to President Zia-ul-Haq's famous cricket diplomacy. Zia invited himself to India to watch a cricket match between the two countries, claiming "cricket for peace is my mission." He said that he "wanted to watch good cricket and see how we could solve our problems." By the time Zia visited India, the military crisis was already de-escalating, but his visit did reduce tensions and revive the peace track, which he had initiated with Rajiv Gandhi in a previous visit in December 1985. That visit included a declaration of nonattack on their respective nuclear installations that was eventually formalized in December 1988, after Zia's death.[80]

As mentioned in Chapter 9, in January 1987, during the peak of the military crises and amid tense negotiations among the United States, India, and Pakistan, Khan Research Laboratories (KRL) chief Dr. A. Q. Khan created a controversy with an interview he granted to a Pakistani journalist. On January 28, A. Q. Khan expected at his residence the famous journalist Mushahid Hussain Syed, then working for the *English Daily Muslim*, who requested the visit to personally invite A. Q. Khan and his wife to his wedding. When Mushahid Hussain arrived, however, he was accompanied by a guest journalist from India, Kuldip Nayar. A. Q. Khan claims to have had no prior knowledge of this arrangement, but he extended courtesy and conversed with candor, disregarding security considerations of which a scientist of his caliber and responsibility should be acutely aware. But A. Q. Khan, well known for self-aggrandizing his achievements, needed only a slight boost to his ego to become uninhibited. The two journalists were experienced in the art of extracting information from an egotistic scientist, and Khan went into overdrive, confirming the success of Pakistan's enrichment capability and even boasting of Pakistan's possession of a nuclear bomb.[81] The two journalists were stunned by the confessions of the top Pakistani scientist and national hero. Mushahid Hussain construed Khan's candor to be deliberate nuclear signaling to influence the intense ongoing diplomacy between the two countries to diffuse the Brasstacks military crisis. Kuldip Nayar became the self-appointed messenger to convey the "nuclear threat" to India. He is believed to have reported the matter to the Indian embassy in Islamabad that very evening.

Although conducted in January, the interview was not published until March. As would be expected, it caused an uproar in Islamabad, New Delhi, and Washington. Indian analysts still believe that the January 28 date of the interview was timed to convey a nuclear threat to Delhi.[82] Pakistan, on the other hand, points to the March publication date, believing it was timed to influence the U.S. congressional debate on aid to Islamabad.[83] In reality, the timing of the interview and its publication were simply coincidental. These perceptions exemplify the regional strategic culture, always fraught with drama in an attempt to interpret deeper meanings from disconnected events. Notwithstanding A. Q. Khan's exclamations, the interview had no impact on the positive diplomatic engagement that helped the region escape the quagmire created by the two militaries. India and Pakistan inked an agreement on January 31, 1987, to begin phased withdrawal of the countries' troops. The Brasstacks crises had veritably ended by the time the interview was made public. But the implications of A. Q. Khan's faux pas were severe.

President Zia had three worries to tackle immediately. First was what the ramifications would be of Khan's interview on U.S.-Pakistan relations and the new $4.2 billion economic and military aid package undergoing tough congressional scrutiny in Washington. Zia was sensing emerging shifts in the international system as relations warmed between the Cold War superpowers. Second, at the regional level, Zia worried about India's reactions and the implications of this kind of signaling by a top scientist.[84] Zia had watered down the nuclear rhetoric; he was using all political and diplomatic means to diffuse the "Sunderji-created crises,"[85] and as General K. M. Arif was prepared to vouch, Zia was "not the kind of personality to convey naked threats."[86] Third, and probably of greatest concern to Zia's security managers, was oversight and security of the nuclear program. How could an Indian journalist reach a top Pakistani nuclear scientist entrusted with the most classified program of the country—especially while India and Pakistan were at the brink of war? Pakistani intelligence was focused on security of Kahuta from external spies, not on tracking visitors to A. Q Khan's residence in Islamabad.[87]

A. Q. Khan's freelancing was allowed for a particular purpose: to procure nuclear weapons technology. His indiscretion with a reputed journalist had not just caused a national embarrassment but also had severe consequences for the country and its nuclear program. Avoiding sanctions under the Pressler Amendment to the Non-proliferation Act required the U.S. president to certify to Congress that Pakistan did not have a nuclear device and that its nuclear program was kept in control as agreed between the two states.

Islamabad's reaction to the publication of the interview was swift and severe. A. Q. Khan was first called to explain himself to Senate Chairman Ghulam Ishaq Khan; next he was directed to report to General K. M. Arif, the Vice Chief of Army Staff, who supposedly grilled Khan in his office. A. Q. Khan claimed that "he was tricked (by Mushahid) into meeting the Indian journalist."[88] Finally, he was summoned to the president's house. Lieutenant-General (ret.) Syed Refaqat Ali, who was chief of staff to President Zia-ul-Haq, narrated to the author how the wrath of Zia fell on A. Q. Khan: "Zia-ul-Haq was always [a] warm-hearted man and courteous to all invited guests in his home regardless of rank or status. President Zia himself told me the next morning, 'I have never given any rough treatment to any guest in my house but A. Q Khan is the only one left trembling and perspiring when he left my house last evening.'"[89]

Soon afterward, Zia directed the bomb-designing project to be taken away from A. Q. Khan and returned to the dedicated team in the R block in PAEC, as was discussed in Chapter 9. The newly wed Mushahid Hussain soon lost his job at the Muslim newspaper. The Zia government deprived the newspaper of all government advertisements, isolated it, and economically crippled it, putting it out of business. The damage to the nuclear policy could not be reversed.[90]

In comparing Munir Khan and A. Q. Khan, General K. M. Arif said, "Munir was a sober, quiet and unassuming person dedicated to his work. A. Q. Khan was a glib-tongued flamboyant individual always in search of publicity and glory."[91]

Security Dynamics in Times of Change

As the decade of the 1980s drew to a close, the regional security and political landscape once again began to change. In April 1988, the two superpowers signed the famous Geneva Peace Accord, paving the way for the Soviet withdrawal from Afghanistan, albeit with no clear roadmap for stability in Afghanistan or regionally. The Berlin Wall came down in December of 1989, signaling tectonic shifts in the international system.

In August 1988 President Zia-ul-Haq, along with his top military leadership and the accompanying U.S. ambassador and defense attache to Pakistan, died in a mysterious plane crash. President Zia had worn two hats in office—president and army chief. The presidential hat went to Ghulam Ishaq Khan, who was at the time chairman of the Senate. Vice Chief of Army Staff Mirza Aslam Beg was made the new army chief. Together they decided to hold new elections in the fall of 1988 and hand over power to elected representatives.[92]

The new election returned the Pakistan People's Party (PPP) to power. Under the popular leadership of thirty-six-year-old Benazir Bhutto, PPP had waged an impressive campaign against Zia-ul-Haq for two years. General Beg convinced Benazir to put the past behind her, not to seek revenge against the family of the late president for the execution of her father,[93] and to move to a new era. On behest of President Ghulam Ishaq Khan, Beg brokered a five-point deal with Benazir as quid pro quo for her becoming prime minister: (1) not to be vindictive toward the family of Zia-ul-Haq; (2) not to change defense policies or interfere in the affairs of the armed forces; (3) not to make sweeping bureaucratic/administrative policy changes; (4) not to alter the Afghan policy, and to keep the experienced Sahabzada Yaqub-Khan as foreign minister; and, most important, (5) not to alter nuclear policy, and to let the veteran President Ghulam Ishaq Khan guide and control the secret nuclear program.

Beg convinced Benazir that President Ghulam Ishaq Khan, in various capacities, had remained associated with the nuclear program since her father's time, when he initiated the nuclear weapons program. There was no substitute for his experience, which was critical to the development and secrecy of the nuclear program and was in the supreme national interest.[94]

According to General Beg, prime minister–elect Bhutto amicably agreed, paving the way for the return of full democracy after a hiatus of more than a decade. On nuclear matters in particular, Beg suggested forming a troika comprising the president, prime minister, and Chief of the Army Staff—which he called the national command authority—to decide on all security and nuclear issues. Ostensibly this arrangement was balanced; in reality, it was the president and army chief who were the most powerful decision-makers; Benazir Bhutto was only a co-opted member. General Beg maintains that she was an intrinsic part of all nuclear decisions. Indian Prime Minister Rajiv Gandhi reached out to the new Pakistani prime minister in December 1988 in a bid to revive the spirit of the 1972 Simla Accord, signed by the parents of the two young prime ministers. There was new hope of democratic peace and entente in the region. Unbeknownst to the two leaders, a new crisis was on the horizon, one that has remained the Achilles' heel of India-Pakistan relations—Kashmir.

The Kashmir Uprising and a Third Military Crisis

Since the 1965 war, Kashmir had enjoyed relative peace until the late 1980s, when Kashmiri youths began denouncing the rampant corruption, nepotism, and injustices of the region. India and Pakistan soon lobbed familiar allegations against each other as to who fueled the ensuing conflict. The fall of the Berlin Wall and the prodemocracy demonstrations at Tiananmen Square must have inspired the region's citizens. Kashmiri violence flared in 1989 and only grew more severe until it transformed into a full-fledged insurgency. This event, coupled with a civil war in Afghanistan, left Pakistan in the middle of the arc of violence from Kabul to Srinagar (Kashmir).

That same year, General Aslam Beg conceived a large military exercise, Zarb-i-Momin, believed to be the Pakistani response to India's Exercise Brasstacks. Like Sunderji, Beg wanted to test new military tactics. The exercise was meant to launch a riposte into Indian territory, after having first absorbed an Indian attack at the holding corps, to "stabilize threatened sectors." The counteroffensive force included several infantry divisions to help establish a bridgehead and allow mechanized forces to break out in an offensive maneuver.[95]

As the insurgency in Kashmir continued, Pakistan completed exercise Zarb-i-Momin, but India detected that army units had not returned to their barracks afterward and assessed that they were deployed to support the Kashmir insurgency.[96] Similarly, in February 1990, the Pakistani Army noticed that a number of Indian tank units in the Rajasthan deserts did not return from their annual exercise and assessed that India might be contemplating another Exercise Brasstacks. The two countries were suspicious of each other, and each military movement led to another, creating a spiral of deployment and counterdeployment. By April, both armies were partially mobilized, some units patrolling the border and mechanized forces activated near their operational areas. Pakistan estimated that India had deployed a hundred thousand men and an armored division within fifty miles of the Pakistani border in the Rajasthan deserts.[97] In Kashmir, some two hundred thousand Indian troops were positioned.[98] It is significant, however, that the majority of the offensive forces of both countries remained well away from the border regions.[99]

Throughout 1990, the violence in Kashmir continued to escalate, as did tensions between India and Pakistan. The Indian government responded to Kashmir with a heavy hand, establishing presidential rule and appointing a draconian governor over the state. As predicted by General Beg, by the summer of 1990, the Kashmiris were engaging the Indian military in guerrilla tactics identical to those used against the Soviets in Afghanistan.[100]

Nuclear Signaling

As described above, the pattern of military deployments did not indicate that there was a deliberate plan for war on either side, although the threat of an accidental war was always present. Rather, mere perception of malfeasance and conspiracy fueled India and Pakistan to escalate tensions. Deepening the crisis were the intelligence reports that Pakistan was receiving, indicating that Israel and India were once again planning a nuclear strike against KRL. Was there a nuclear dimension in the 1990 crises? Scholars have debated this issue for almost two decades now without reaching any definite conclusion.

General Beg explained to the author that in deference to U.S. demands, the Pakistani troika of power—the president, prime minister, and army chief—had voluntarily agreed to formulate a doctrine of nuclear restraint (explained in detail in Chapter 13). General Beg recalls that though the leadership agreed to stop enrichment of uranium beyond 5 percent and refrain from conducting hot tests, the research and development on weapons design and delivery would continue. Pakistan would keep a first-strike option open without declaring the nuclear doctrine, and redundancy for a second-strike option would be maintained.[101]

Even when Pakistan halted HEU production, according to General Beg, Islamabad received further "credible information" that there was yet another Indo-Israeli plan for a preventive strike. On January 20, 1990, the Pakistani troika held a meeting, which was also attended by two scientists. The group decided to "deter this impending threat" and sent Foreign Minister Sahabzada Yaqub-Khan to "tell the Indian government that if such a thing happens, whether it comes from Israel or elsewhere, we will hold India responsible and strike back at India." Beg also told the author that he was informed that "Sahabzada Yaqub-Khan did a good job frightening them." In addition, he said that Prime Minister Benazir Bhutto "ordered the army and air force to get ready. A squadron of F-16s was moved to Mauripur [an air force base in Karachi] and we pulled out our devices and all to arm the aircraft, [which carried out] movement from Kahuta, movement from other places, which were picked up by the American satellites." When the author asked about the purpose of these moves, Beg explained that "all movement was made in a way that is visible, because the purpose was not to precipitate a crisis but to deter."[102]

General Beg's rationale was unclear to the author, who asked for clarification: "Were you not precipitating a crisis by openly pulling out devices or carrying out movements to induce U.S. interventions?" Beg reiterated that the crisis was not precipitated by Pakistan, but that India had brutally repressed the Kashmiris and then was mobilizing its conventional forces to threaten Pakistan, now for the third time in six years. He stated unambiguously that "our sources in the Middle East, our sources in India, our sources outside confirmed it [the joint India-Israeli attack] could happen anytime. The information kept coming about the collaboration between India and Israel and that the Americans wanted it so." When asked, "Do you mean the U.S. would support India [in carrying out this attack]?" General Beg replied, "I mean, they [Americans] were in the knowledge of it. It could only happen with American approval. It was therefore necessary to convey deterrence signaling by letting the Americans pick up Pakistani preparations and convey it to both India (and Israel) about the consequences."[103]

The United States, for its part, possibly detected the deliberate movements and certainly reacted. President George Bush sent Deputy National Security Adviser Robert Gates to the region. This was the first time a U.S. president would send an envoy to publicly intervene in a South Asian crisis, a trend repeated in future crises in the region.[104] According to Beg, "[W]hen Robert Gates came to talk to the president of Pakistan, he [President Ghulam Ishaq Khan] told him exactly what he was briefed [by Aslam Beg]: 'Please tell India not to be funny with us [attacking centrifuge facilities at Kahuta or KANUPP] because this [Pakistani preparation for retaliatory attack] was a suicidal [one-way] mission. Our aircraft could go and strike Trombay [India's Pu production reactor and reprocessing facility near Mumbai] and Trimchomalee [an Indian southern city] and all of those places [far to the east and southernmost parts of India] because they [Pakistani aircraft mission] could not return—there were no fueling arrangements.'"[105]

Beg insisted that he was not leading an offensive or attempting to precipitate a nuclear crisis, but instead was demonstrating resolve, which in his opinion was an essential element of a credible nuclear deterrent. As he explained, credibility comes from both the capability and the resolve to use a nuclear weapon.[106] It seems rather ironic that General Beg, who had dubbed the Pakistani military actions during Brasstacks "foolish," was now, in 1990, prepared to send nuclear messages on the basis of "credible" intelligence reports.

However, in an interview with the author, Sahabzada Yaqub-Khan angrily dismissed any role played by him in conveying a nuclear threat. He dismissed Indian allegations that he had threatened India with nuclear action as "mischievous and ad hominem." When the author told him that General Aslam Beg had stated on record that it was a decision of the highest national leadership, Yaqub-Khan dismissed Beg's assertion that the January 20 meeting had tasked him to deliver any threatening messages to India. Sahabzada Yaqub-Khan— widely reputed as aristocratic, polished, and suave—forcefully rejected General Beg's distortions of events and questioned why he, with such an illustrious diplomatic career, would ever agree to convey a naked nuclear threat.[107] Rather, he said, he simply conveyed to India Pakistan's concerns regarding Kashmir.

In his version of the story, Yaqub-Khan visited Delhi around January 21–23 for a tete-a-tete with I. K. Gujral, his Indian counterpart. Yaqub-Khan was at pains to explain that the tone of his conversation with I. K. Gujral was friendly and lyrical in its use of anecdotes in Urdu poetry—far afield from any propaganda or nuclear threat.[108] Yaqub-Khan did, however, warn Gujral that the entire world at the time was "inflamed," and he advocated that the two countries share responsibility to save the subcontinent from crisis. Perhaps Mr. Gujral had misconstrued his words, thinking that the Pakistani foreign minister meant "nuclear flames" and interpreted this reference as a threat. Yaqub-Khan was emotional and at a loss for why a person of Mr. Gujral's stature and intelligence would misunderstand his words and intentions. He believes that rumors of Pakistan's threats to India are an "utterly false allegation" and a "malicious narrative" that has tarnished his distinguished diplomatic record.

Tanvir Ahmad Khan, who was secretary of Information and Broadcasting under Prime Minister Benazir Bhutto, believes that Pakistan intended to send a veiled nuclear threat during the 1990 crisis in three ways: the media, diplomatic channels, and military movements. Because of his government post, Tanvir Khan was privy to the contradictory accounts of Beg and Yaqub-Khan, but believes that the diplomatic assignment given to Yaqub-Khan was meant to convey Pakistan's strength and determination, and that the talk of "fire and flames" was indeed a nuclear threat. He seems to support General Beg's contention that signaling a nuclear threat to India was an approved policy of the government. To further illustrate his point, Tanvir Khan explained that "around March–April, when things were heating up, GHQ asked me to talk to some media outlet." The message that he was to deliver was that "we [Pakistan] are in a position to destroy targets of value. The implication was Bombay. . . . This was part of the psychological battle that was being fought."[109]

The two contradictory accounts from Army Chief Beg and Foreign Minister Yaqub-Khan reflect the institutional disconnect within Pakistan. The distribution of political power between the troika and the lack of a central, unified command authority—characteristic of the Pakistani system in all previous wars—might well have created the need for crisis management in 1990. For the first time since 1948, a democratic government in Pakistan was handling major crises with India with power diffused between the three power centers of the troika. Organizations and individuals likely were receiving contradictory signals from competing authorities.

The burning question is whether Pakistan possessed a real nuclear capability or a usable nuclear device at the time of these veiled threats. From a technical standpoint, as recalled by Dr. Samar Mubarakmand, Pakistan had developed a device based on several cold tests and could theoretically deliver it by aircraft. But in 1990, Pakistan had only telemetry-transmitted data of neutron bursts, and it was still uncertain whether the device "was deliverable with any degree of assurance or performance, which only came about in 1995."[110] One can thus determine that Pakistani nuclear delivery capability at the time was still in its early evolutionary stages. Nonetheless, top political leadership insisted on raising the nuclear ante.

Post-Mortem

An examination of the three crises in the 1980s reveals four distinct features of the conflict between India and Pakistan. First, the origins of the crises can be found in ongoing insurgencies and low-intensity conflicts, with each side accusing the other of complicity and abetment. All three wars in the prenuclear era (1948, 1965, and 1971) included insurgency as a common feature. Second, both the Indian and the Pakistani militaries were undergoing organizational and doctrinal changes as a result of new leadership and strategic environments. Neither military doctrine took the other's nuclear capabilities into account, but rather relied on coercive deployments and dissuasive tactics. Third, Pakistan constantly feared preventive strikes against Kahuta. Revealed plans and intelligence reports did not ease the concern but further contributed to the military tensions. Finally, the United States took varying approaches in its efforts to diffuse each of the crises. These took the form of sending early warnings, dissuading preventive attacks, and dispatching key officials to the region.

In the 1980s, the nuclear capability present in both India and Pakistan was still in its early stages. Rhetoric and veiled messages were the primary tactics, since the capability to deliver a nuclear warhead was limited. Further, neither country had the national technical means to detect the exact progress of the other's nuclear program. The United States possessed the technology but did not know how to mediate a regional conflict occurring on three levels simultaneously: the subconventional, conventional, and nascent nuclear. All three levels were interwoven through intense regional competition. India and Pakistan were engaged in a game of chicken that would lay the foundation for strategic doctrine emerging two decades later.

12   Pakistan's Missile Quest

Although ballistic missiles today are the mainstay of Pakistan's nuclear delivery system, the acquisition, development, flight-testing, and introduction of ballistic missiles into Pakistani strategic arsenals was as arduous a process as was the development of the nuclear program a decade earlier. As in the case of its approach to the nuclear program, Pakistan initially avoided investing in rockets, ballistic missiles, or a space program when there existed an opportunity to acquire technology through cooperation. Then a series of military crises in the mid-1980s and the successful Indian *Prithvi* and *Agni* missile tests spurred the development of a modest Pakistani rocket program. However, it was the summer 1990 military crises and subsequent shock of the U.S. nuclear sanctions in the same year that propelled missile technology acquisition into full speed.

Pakistan's ballistic missile procurement program immediately encountered global barriers—even more so than the Nuclear Suppliers Group (NSG)–created obstacles to its nuclear acquisitions. Industrialized Western nations banded together in 1987 to form yet another supplier control cartel—the Missile Technology Control Regime (MTCR)—which created new requirements for missile technology trade. When Pakistan attempted to respond to India's series of missile-flight tests in 1988 and 1989, the West provided the same advice to Islamabad that it had regarding the nuclear program: India's acquisitions should be ignored and Pakistan should take up the moral high ground and adhere to nonproliferation norms. As before, dependence on economic and military aid made Pakistan more vulnerable to Western coercion. The United States virtually abandoned the region, imposed nuclear sanctions, and refused to supply Pakistan with more F-16s—Pakistan's primary delivery vehicle for nuclear warheads. So the more that the West, specifically the United States, pressured Pakistan to exercise restraint, the more its resolve grew to match India's strategic force. Once again, Islamabad perceived India's treatment as preferential, and Pakistan's as punishment for redressing its security concerns.

Indeed, Pakistan's strategic culture is the best explanation for its near panic to meet the new challenges posed by its chief adversary. As nationalism gripped the isolated country, missile scientists and technicians found a new sense of pride and motivation in their tasks. Finding no prospects for cooperation in Europe in the 1990s, Pakistan again looked to its strategic ally China and willing suppliers in the Far East. Predictably, another familiar pattern would emerge—interlaboratory rivalry between the Pakistan Atomic Energy Commission (PAEC) and Khan Research Laboratories (KRL), this time to master solid fuel and liquid fuel technologies for missiles.

Initial Pakistani Missile Development

In the early 1980s, the arrival of F-16 jet fighter aircraft from the United States provided Pakistan with an operationally reliable method of delivery for its nascent nuclear arsenal. Cold tests that included bomb-delivery simulations relied upon these aircraft and Mirage-V attack aircraft from France. However, because President Bush could not certify to Congress that Pakistan did not possess a nuclear weapon in 1990, a procedure required by the Pressler Law obliged the government to halt F-16 shipments. While the aircraft were collecting dust at the Davis-Monthan Air Force Base in Arizona, the United States also froze nearly $300 million in military supplies to Pakistan.[1] Never before had U.S.-Pakistani relations been so bitter.

Pakistan's long reliance on U.S. assistance forced the leadership to offer a freeze of its nuclear program in return for renewed military cooperation. In response, the United States made new demands: to destroy the existing nuclear cores and to "roll-back its capability to the other side of the line."[2] Clearly, a few F-16s were not worth sacrificing the nuclear program, so, after absorbing the disbelief and shock, Pakistan began to consider an alternative delivery system. The United States had overestimated its leverage and inadvertently fueled the Pakistani missile program. From that point on, missile development joined nuclear weapons at the top rung of Pakistan's national security priorities.

Throughout the 1960s and 1970s both Pakistan and India had developed some basic rocketry and space-launch technologies through their civilian space programs,[3] but it was not until the latter began its Integrated Guided Missile Development Program (IGMDP) in 1983 that the missile race began in earnest.[4] Although India began with a modest technological base, it developed its *Agni* and *Prithvi* missiles by skillfully deriving technologies from its existing space program and combining them with reverse engineering of Russian missile hardware.[5] In contrast, the Pakistani missile program began in the 1980s with no technological base to speak of and nearly no experience. General Mirza Aslam Beg was made the Vice Chief of Army Staff in 1987. Earlier as CGS he had spearheaded military modernizations, and among the many changes he brought was his brainchild of establishing the Combat Development Directorate (CD Directorate), which became functional around 1985. He now tasked CD Directorate to examine emerging missile technologies for induction into the army.[6] The CD Directorate acted as a bridge between operational requirements and available technologies, and it examined the efficacy of ballistic missiles in concert with the Space and Upper Atmosphere Research Commission (SUPARCO).

Established in 1961, SUPARCO was originally in the Space Sciences Research wing of the PAEC before it became a separate organization in 1964. Although it was directly under the president's command, Ayub Khan entrusted Dr. Abdus Salam with supervising the operations. Under Salam's leadership, an aerospace engineering program was initiated in cooperation with the Air Force and SUPARCO. These entities collaborated with the U.S. National Aeronautics and Space Administration (NASA) in June 1962 to launch Pakistani research "sounding rockets" *Rehbar-I* and *Rehbar-II,* which were propelled using a combination of the U.S. Nike and Cajun motors.[7] Between 1962 and 1964, Pakistan launched a number of these sounding rocket tests, but the project was seemingly cost prohibitive and eventually fizzled out within the next decade.

Nevertheless, Pakistan reaped a number of benefits from this cooperative project. Its scientists were trained at Wallop Island and Goddard Space Flight Centers, and it received technologies and ammonium perchlorate, an ingredient of solid rocket fuel, from France and Germany, respectively. According to one report citing a U.S. official, Pakistan's capability to develop a ballistic missile program derived from the knowledge its scientists obtained through its cooperation with NASA on sounding rockets.[8]

Solid-Motor *Hatfs*

Aside from a few inaccurate ballistic missiles and Soviet Scuds that were fired into Pakistani tribal areas from Afghanistan, Pakistan had very little with which to start a missile program.[9] SUPARCO was never adequately funded, and basic knowledge on rocketry and space remained rudimentary at best. Army Chief General Aslam Beg asked SUPARCO to develop a ballistic missile quickly and, with the assistance of KRL, a team hastily combined various available technologies to produce the first surface-to-surface missiles, dubbed *Hatf-I* and *Hatf-II*.[10] The *Hatf-I* is a single-stage, solid-motor, battlefield-range missile capable of delivering a five hundred-kg payload over a maximum range of eighty to one hundred km. *Hatf-II* was a modified version of the *Hatf-I* and is composed of a second stage and a new boost motor added to the first stage—still a short-range missile but with increased reach and payload capabilities.[11]

Western experts have varying opinions about the development of these *Hatfs*. Some believe SUPARCO had obtained technology from the French company Aerospatiale (formerly Sud Aviation) in the early to mid-1980s. These French transfers most likely included propellant ingredients, rocket components, and equipment for solid-fuel casting, curing, and solid-rocket testing facilities. Others believe that the short time frame forced SUPARCO scientists simply to copy the French *Dauphin* and *Eridan* sounding rockets for the *Hatf-I* and *Hatf-II*, respectively.[12]

In response to India's demonstration of the *Prithvi* ballistic missile, in February 1989 Pakistan tested the two *Hatf* missiles and declared the tests a success, prompting Prime Minister Benazir Bhutto to congratulate the nation for "entering the missile age."[13] General Aslam Beg formally announced at the National Defense College, Rawalpindi, that the two "indigenously manufactured surface-to-surface missiles ... with a payload of 500kg and range of 80–300 km" were successfully tested and were "extremely accurate systems." International observers and U.S. experts, however, dismissed the missiles as "inaccurate battlefield rockets," and one U.S. official characterized the *Hatf-II* as simply "'two *Hatf-I*s put together' [that] cannot fly 300 kilometers."[14]

After the initial tests, the *Hatf* series was shelved for more than a decade, until in February 2000, a modified *Hatf-I*, dubbed *Hatf-IA*, was tested and claimed to reach a range of one hundred km with a five-hundred-kg payload. An improved version, the *Hatf-II* (*Abdali*), emerged with the same payload but a longer 180-km range.

In May 2002, at the peak of crises with India, the *Hatf-II/Abdali* was flight-tested along with other categories of missiles and later was finally inducted into the army's strategic force command. Currently, the accuracy of this short-range ballistic missile is improving, and although it is declared capable of carrying a nuclear payload, its limited range suggests it might be carrying only a conventional warhead instead. Pakistan, however, has not declared any of its ballistic missiles as non-nuclear weapon systems, essentially to retain ambiguity.

Strategic Missile Cooperation: China

As mentioned above, Pakistan's missile program faced two major problems from the outset: a limited indigenous technological base and the constraints imposed by the MTCR.

The CD Directorate conducted a comprehensive analysis and recommended that the army chief seek both liquid fuel and solid fuel ballistic missile platforms of varying ranges for its nuclear weapons. A single off-the-shelf purchase could meet immediate needs, but self-sufficiency was the ultimate goal. And so a transfer of technology (TOT) was recommended to redress the country's lack of technical expertise and help develop infrastructure and equipment to produce missiles indigenously in the future.[15] Islamabad's logical option was to turn to its long-time strategic ally, China, for help. Conveniently, China was not a member of the MTCR at the time and was opposed on principle to export control cartels.[16]

Ghaznavi (Hatf-III)

The most cited strategic collaboration between China and Pakistan is related to the sale of M-series technologies, specifically the M-11 or DF-11 (NATO designation CSS-7), developed by China in the 1980s. These short-range, solid propellant, road mobile, single-warhead ballistic missiles were first flight tested in 1990 and deployed into the People's Liberation Army (PLA) in 1992.[17] Some experts say that the M-11 missile is able to carry a payload of 800 kg to a maximum range of 280 km. But by trading off payload for increased range, a five hundred-kg warhead could be delivered to a target three hundred km or more away.[18] The missile is believed to have jet vanes in the exhaust that provide the boost phase.[19] After the warhead assembly separates from the missile frame during flight, the warhead section has four small fins at the rear to provide stability. The separated warhead also has a miniature propulsion system that corrects for the altitude before re-entry and helps adjust the final phase of the trajectory, making this missile very accurate.[20]

U.S. sources believe that initial transfers of some thirty assembled M-11 missiles were made to Pakistan in 1992. These missiles were stored in crates at the

Pakistan Air Force base in Sargodha. This area in Central Punjab became yet another source of Western intelligence curiosity and interest. Western spy satellites captured images that revealed the existence of shelters for missile crates, mobile launchers, and missile maintenance areas, as well as crew quarters.[21] The location having been compromised, the leadership looked for alternative sites from which to disperse missiles.

After the discovery of these transfers, China began supplying the M-11s in unassembled form, which then necessitated the creation of a dedicated missile assembly facility.[22] Chinese experts helped customize designs and also extensively trained Pakistani technicians to become self-reliant for future production.

The exact number of missiles transferred remains classified, but the more important benefit of cooperation with China was the creation of a permanent base for solid fuel technology in Pakistan. Under direction of Chief of the Army Staff (COAS) General Abdul Waheed, the Project Management Organization (PMO) was created in 1994 with Major General Raza Hussain as its head. Along with the National Development Complex (NDC) and Air Weapons Complex (AWC), PMO was the third major organization that would play a primary role in the development of delivery systems. The principal task of the PMO was to create the foundations for a solid fuel missile, absorb the transfer of technology, and learn the art of reverse engineering and assembly techniques for the unassembled M-11 (DF-11) and M-9 (DF-15) ballistic missiles.

In 1995, when NDC and AWC successfully completed the cold tests for aircraft delivery, General Abdul Waheed directed Dr. Samar Mubarakmand to lead the Pakistani missile program.[23] Later, in 2001, the three organizations were merged under the National Engineering and Scientific Commission (NESCOM), which was Pakistan's third major strategic organization after PAEC and KRL.

The Chinese transfer of M-11 technology was only for high-explosive warheads. The designs were significantly changed after years of hard work at NDC and PMO to make them nuclear capable. As Samar Mubarakmand told the author, "Any missile scientist would tell you that even a slight change in the diameter or configuration of the missile warheads would necessitate redesigning it as if starting from the scratch."[24]

Having undergone the design modifications, a new missile named *Ghaznavi* could carry a five-hundred-kg payload, sufficient for a second-generation nuclear warhead, but not suitable for Pakistan's heavier first-generation weapons.[25] The missile has an inertial guidance system and uses jet vanes in the nozzle to make trajectory corrections during the boost phase. The *Ghaznavi* grew accurate after several improvements to the circular error probability (CEP), which settled between two and three hundred meters. CEP, which measures the radius of a circle within which 50 percent of the missiles aimed at the center will strike, is the most common statistical measure of missile accuracy.[26]

The Pakistani Army first conducted a flight test of the *Ghaznavi/ Hatf-III* on May 26, 2002, marking the peak of a military crisis with India and the fourth anniversary of its nuclear tests. After one more flight test, President Pervez Musharraf formally inducted the first batch of missiles into the Pakistani Army's Strategic Forces Command (ASAF) in February 2004.[27]

Over the next three years further technical improvements were made to the heat shielding areas, and after several tests a new batch of *Ghaznavi* missiles were inducted into the Second Missile Group of the Army Strategic Forces Command (ASAF) in April 2007.[28] Finally, February 2008 marked the successful flight test of this missile by the ASAF.[29] As the new *Ghaznavis* were produced and inducted into operational units, they were dispersed to secret locations throughout the country.

Shaheen: Hatf-IV and VI

Early feasibility studies in the CD Directorate recognized that the M-9 fulfilled the technical and strategic requirements. In addition to the M-11, it also recommended a TOT of the M-9 series, believed to have been transferred from China from 1991 onward.[30] Most likely, alongside the PMO facility for the M-11 assembly, China also helped build a turnkey facility for the NDC Fatehjung, near Rawalpindi. The Fatehjung missile facility would build the components and subsystems of the Pakistani solid fuel missiles.

Like the M-11, the M-9 was developed in the mid-1980s and underwent its first flight test around June 1988 in China—the same period in which India was conducting its initial *Prithvi* tests—and was inducted into the PLA around 1990.[31] While the transfer of M-9 technologies gave Pakistani a head start, scientists insist that they worked for several years to design the *Shaheen*. By July 1997 the *Shaheen* engine tests had been conducted at various secret locations, but were erroneously reported as flight tests in Western media.[32] Just as in the case of the M-11, the M-9 was meant to carry a high-explosive conventional warhead and so had to be modified to become nuclear capable.[33] The missile designated as *Shaheen-I (Hatf-IV)* was first publicly displayed at the National Day parade in March 1999 and then underwent several flight tests thereafter.[34]

Like the *Ghaznavi*, the *Shaheen-I* is a single-stage, solid fueled, road-mobile, short-range ballistic missile with a maximum range of seven hundred km and able to deliver a five-hundred-kg payload. The control systems are exercised identically to those of the M-11; the missile has a "strap down inertial guidance system with a digital computer onboard that helps with accuracy." Originally the CEP of the *Shaheen* was a maximum of three hundred meters, but with numerous tests, by the time it was put into operational service the CEP had considerably improved. Testing to improve accuracy continued even after the missile's induction into the army's arsenal, until 2006.[35] In an interview on Geo TV in 2004, Dr. Samar Mubarakmand declared the CEP to be ninety meters at a range of seven hundred km.[36] U.S. missile experts assert that this CEP is possible only if there is a homing system associated with the missile. *Shaheen-I* was formally inducted into the Pakistani Army in March 2003 and was deployed in field exercises.[37] In January 2008, the Strategic Missile Group (SMG) of the ASFC conducted a flight test during the culmination of annual exercises, and currently, the *Shaheen-I* missile is operational.[38]

Shaheen-II/Hatf-VI

Missile experts with U.S. intelligence knowledge suggest that yet another Chinese contribution to Pakistan was the M-18/DF-11, originally a two-stage system with a payload capacity of 500 to 800 kg over a range of a thousand km.[39] Pakistani scientists deny this claim and insist that the improved solid fuel missile *Shaheen-II* (*Hatf-VI*), at a range of two thousand km, was their original work and derived from their base technology transfers. Even today, Pakistani officials and scientists insist that they are self-reliant, but U.S. missile experts continue to believe that *Shaheen-II* remains dependent on Chinese support.[40]

The *Shaheen-II* was first displayed during an October 2003 National Day parade. As with the *Ghaznavi* and *Shaheen-I*, it uses inertial navigation and jet vanes to control the flight, and the warhead separates after the boost phase. Accuracy is limited, with a likely CEP of between two and three hundred meters. The first flight test of the twenty-five-ton *Shaheen-II* occurred in March 2004 at Somiani Flight Test Range on the Arabian Sea and was claimed to have covered 1,880 km.[41] *Shaheen-II* underwent four more tests, in March 2005, April 2006, February 2007, and April 2008. The last test was conducted by ASFC, an indication that it was inducted into the army arsenal.[42]

While these road-mobile missiles greatly enhance the survivability of Pakistan's nuclear force structure, the solid propellants used in the M-series missiles have a finite shelf life. If properly stored, the propellants can be reliable for about a decade to fifteen years.[43] After that time safety and reliability are increasingly compromised. For Pakistan to sustain its nuclear delivery capabilities into the future, it needed to establish the know-how and industrial infrastructure to produce these missiles or equivalent systems. To that end, the Chinese built the turnkey missile factory at Fatehjung, which not only allowed production of the M-series missiles but also provided Pakistan with tremendous know-how and potential means to develop and produce larger, more capable systems in the future. And by constructing such facilities, China spared itself from transferring large, observable missile components such as solid propellant motors. Pakistan now has an infrastructure as well as a training facility to bring a new generation of missile scientists into the art of solid propellant production.

Why Liquid Fuel?

Pakistan developed a strategic connection with the unpopular North Korea regime, which was selling untested and relatively unattractive technologies, in an attempt to acquire a liquid fuel platform. Why would Pakistan want a liquid fueled missile when it had access to solid fuel from China? After all, Islamabad was already under nuclear sanctions, making this acquisition a political risk that could alienate Japan and the United States.

Three rationales might explain why this choice was made. First, the range-payload characteristics of the solid propellant systems from China limited Pakistan's ability to deliver a nuclear weapon to the heart of Indian territory. The North Korean *Nodong* missile has a larger maximum payload capacity (700 to 1,000 kg) and can cover more territory (one thousand to thirteen hundred km). Moreover, the liquid fuel technology from North Korea was offered at inexpensive rates, as both the buyer and seller were poor countries with high-premium national security requirements and economic exigencies. Second, interinstitutional rivalries between the PAEC and KRL prompted the latter to seek an independent channel for missile acquisition. The two institutions had a history of competition throughout the nuclear weapons program, and it seemed only logical that the rivalry would extend to missile delivery systems.[44] Finally, both North Korea and Pakistan were desperate: Pyongyang needed another party willing to test the *Nodong* technology, as North Korean geography did not permit frequent tests, and the Pakistanis knew that their supply routes would be cut off sooner or later. This fear of rejection was not restricted to the West, but extended even to China. Consequently, Pakistan sought to diversify acquisition routes to ensure supplies in the future should international pressures compel China to withdraw its assistance.[45] Establishing a second, independent acquisition channel was also necessary because by the mid-1990s, Pakistan had not yet successfully built an indigenous production line for the solid propellant missiles. Pakistan therefore accepted the risks necessary to meet an urgent national need for an alternative to Chinese-supplied missiles and technologies.[46]

The decision to cooperate with Pyongyang resulted in a competition between China and North Korea, as the former discouraged Pakistan from closely cooperating with Pyongyang. Islamabad's dealings with the pariah state could have had negative consequences that could have dragged China into controversy. More important, Beijing enjoyed the market monopoly it held with regard to missile technology transfers to Pakistan.

North Korea and KRL

KRL technicians and scientists were involved in nearly every security project, especially after the death of President Zia-ul-Haq. The top national leadership of President Ghulam Ishaq Khan and General Mirza Aslam had almost blind faith in A. Q. Khan's messianic ability to trouble-shoot and complete any assigned task regardless of odds. Army Chief Aslam Beg directed A. Q. Khan to work in close coordination with the CD Directorate in General Headquarters (GHQ) on two major conventional weapons projects: *Anza* and *Baktar Shikan*. The former was an antiaircraft missile and the latter an antiarmor rocket. KRL was also directed to work with the Defense and Science and Technology Organization (DESTO), a research organization under the Ministry of Defense Production, and, as needed, with SUPARCO.

As early as June 1992, representatives from KRL and government officials from key agencies visited the Sanum-dong guided missile development center in North Korea to examine the *Nodong*. Sometime in August or September 1992, North Korea's deputy premier and foreign minister, Kim Yong-nam, traveled to Pakistan to discuss possible missile cooperation. In May of the following year it was alleged that Pakistani and Iranian engineers visited North Korea by invitation to witness the first test flight of the *Nodong* missile. Apparently pleased with the results, Prime Minister Benazir Bhutto visited Pyongyang on December 30, 1994, and penned a contract to purchase *Nodong* missiles and the technical design data.

The deal was cemented in late 1995, with North Korea responsible for providing between twelve and twenty-four unassembled missiles and their transporter erector launcher (TEL) vehicles.[47] The missiles were delivered in the fall
of 1997 in several cargo flights from Pyongyang that also included telemetry
crews. These flights were predictably under the watch of Western intelligence
agencies that were monitoring the traffic and increased frequency of visitors
from KRL and Pakistan. Having received the shipments, A. Q. Khan chose the
name *Ghauri* for the liquid missile derivative of the *Nodong*.[48]

The *Nodong* technology is based on a Soviet missile system speculated to be
"an upscale version of the Soviet R-17 missile."[49] The missile's basic airframe is
made from steel, while other sections are made with aluminum. The propulsion system is a liquid-fueled engine that uses a combination of inhibited red
fuming nitric acid and kerosene. During the boost phase, four jet vanes are
used for thrust vector control, and the missile is also believed to use three body-
mounted gyros for altitude and lateral acceleration control. With a payload of
700 to 1,300 kg, the *Nodong* is capable of carrying both high-explosive conventional and nuclear warheads.[50]

Facilities for assembling the *Nodong* missiles were established at KRL. This
missile project, as well as others involving antiaircraft missiles and other conventional weapons, was located in separate areas and distant from the centrifuge plant. The North Korean scientists and technicians were housed separately
with special security arrangements. Just as the Chinese had established a turnkey facility for the M-series solid fuel missile, North Korea undertook a parallel
effort for the liquid fuel missiles.

Ghauri/Hatf-V

The *Ghauri (Hatf-V)* is a single-stage, liquid-propelled missile capable of
delivering a 700 to 1,300 kg payload an estimated eight hundred to fifteen hundred km. It was first tested in Pakistan in April 1998, with North Korean crews
reportedly participating in the launch, but the test was disappointing and the
results were inconclusive. The inertial guidance system, which is likely similar
to that used by Scud missiles, was said to be very poor.[51] Pakistani observers
at the terminal end were divided whether reentry was effectively made. Most
likely the missile burned-up upon reentry, which indicated needed improvements in the heat shielding.

Two additional test flights were conducted, in April 1999 and May 2002, at
which North Korean crews were present for assistance. Since then, Pakistan has

conducted several flight-tests of the *Ghauri-I:* in April 1999, May 2002, May 2004, June 2004, October 2004, and November 2006.[52] Although *Ghauri* was inducted into the military in January 2003, as indicated above, it had to undergo several tests afterward before becoming fully operational.[53] In February 2008, the Strategic Missile Group (SMG) of the ASFC tested *Ghauri* as part of an exercise, indicating operational deployment.

Ghauri II and III

Improvements, reverse engineering, and synergizing expertise from various strategic organizations allowed the *Ghauri* project to continue into *Ghauri II* and *III* missiles, whose ranges were intended to reach more deeply into India. They both boasted a two-stage design that was similar to North Korea's *Taepodong-I* missile, indicating a possible link between the two missile series. Not only were North Korean scientists present in Pakistan, but in August 1998, Pakistani missile scientists and engineers were supposedly present during North Korea's *Taepodong* launch.[54] Both the United States and Japan pressured Islamabad to cut off ties with North Korea; however, A. Q. Khan dragged his feet and did not immediately send the North Korean technicians back to Pyongyang. One reason for KRL's reluctance was possible ongoing training and assistance in engineering the *Taepodong-I.*[55]

The Combat Development Directorate of General Headquarters was consistently pursuing the policy of transfer of technology (TOT) to achieve self-reliance, especially regarding strategic weapons delivery systems. Mounting U.S. pressure to cap and roll back and the nondelivery of F-16 aircraft (a consequence of nuclear sanctions) reinforced the belief that no single source could be entirely dependable. And as in the past, KRL vigorously competed to match any feat that PAEC or its subsidiaries (PMO/NDC) could claim. Because China had transferred the M-series solid fuel production line in the early 1990s, KRL pushed the North Koreans for a similar transfer of an entire production line of liquid fuel technologies (*Nodong* and possibly *Taepodong*). KRL was a late starter and was lagging, an affront to the reputation of A. Q. Khan—the hero for whom nothing was impossible. Western intelligence was much more vigilant in this case, especially because North Korea, unlike China, was a pariah regime.

Under these challenges, the development of longer-range *Ghauri II* and *III* was progressing slowly. There were periodic reports that disclosed testing of more powerful engines, indicating development of longer-range versions. Some

Western sources believe that simple reverse engineering of *Nodong* or transfer of technology would not have been sufficient for the development of longer-range weapons (*Ghauri II* and *III*).[56] To develop the second stage of the rockets, an indigenous Scud production line would have been necessary. But it is unclear if such a capability was fully transferred or such a line exists; therefore this research concludes that Ghauri's maximum demonstrated range is thirteen to fifteen hundred km with a payload capacity of 700 kg (See Table 12.1). Western sources believe it would take a decade for Pakistan to indigenously master production of liquid engines.[57] Pakistani sources, based on background briefings to the author, dismiss Western speculations and claim that they are constantly testing and improving new engines and do not need to import material they needed two decades ago.[58]

Open sources indicate that the *Ghauri* propellant tanks were lengthened by about two meters, which meant that the missile had a longer burn-up time and range.[59] The longer *Ghauri* were flight tested in 2004 after a gap of several years. It took several years for KRL to complete the *Ghauri* production line for a two-stage system. In addition, *Ghauri*'s technology had shortcomings, which created the need for technical upgrades. By 2004, Pakistan had a functioning nuclear command authority secretariat—the Strategic Plans Division (SPD)—under whose direction the efforts of all strategic organizations were synergized, rather than being in competition with each other. KRL was now receiving complementary support from other strategic facilities, from NESCOM, and vice versa. After several tests a "new-look *Ghauri*" has been inducted into Pakistani strategic forces.[60]

Pakistan's long-term plans are classified, but from several briefings and interviews it is evident that ballistic missiles will remain the mainstay of the arsenal and that technicians will focus on improving ranges and accuracy, as well as reentry, telemetries, and guidance systems.

Quid Pro Quo or Money?

One major concern among Western analysts is whether centrifuge technology was traded for liquid fuel missiles. The deal struck with North Korea and the subsequent delivery in 1997 was a state-to-state strategic trade, and although secret, it remained accounted for. The Pakistan government formally paid for twelve to twenty-five *Nodong* missiles, TOT for a facility, and the services rendered by North Korean technicians. North Korea was strapped for cash, and demand from Pakistan was high. Pakistani Prime Minister Benazir Bhutto in

February 2004 publicly admitted that the missile technology from North Korea had been obtained with cash.[61]

Pakistani officials insist that the North Koreans left KRL after the technology transfers and contractual obligations were completed. However, U.S. press reports in 2002 revealed that Pakistani C-130 military transport aircraft were flying between Islamabad and Pyongyang, indicating continued missile and nuclear cooperation between the two countries. Authorities within Pakistan, including President Pervez Musharraf, admitted to the author that C-130s were sent to Pyongyang, but that these flights were meant to transport newly purchased shoulder-fired surface-to-air weapons (RBS-70), leaving Pakistan short of air-defense weapons for all vulnerable areas.[62] Pakistani authorities maintain that the air sorties to and from North Korea had no nuclear connections.[63] Nevertheless, the United States imposed sanctions on KRL and North Korea's Changgwang Sinyong Corporation in March 2003 for engaging in proliferation activities.[64]

Cruise Missiles

Babur/Hatf-VII

Islamabad came under further pressure to respond when India's cooperative program with Russia on the development of the *Brahmos* supersonic cruise missile began. Once again Pakistan was compelled to follow suit and began to secretly develop a land-attack cruise missile to match the *Brahmos* threat. In August 2005, Pakistan conducted the first test of its *Babur (Hatf-VII)* cruise missile. *Babur* is a subsonic missile that can carry both nuclear and conventional payloads and has a range of seven hundred km, although its range after the test was five hundred km. It is a terrain-hugging missile, making detection by ground-based radars difficult.[65] Pakistan's cruise missile tests came as a surprise internationally and demonstrated a technical leap and improved strategic stability. Riding the momentum, Pakistan had development plans covering all possible cruise missile launch platforms—ground, air, and sea.

Pakistan's means of acquiring cruise missile capability is subject to debate and controversy. Like the F-16 sales, cruise missiles are a sore point in U.S.-Pakistan relations. On August 20, 1998, several U.S. *Tomahawk* missiles (TLAMs) were fired from the Arabian Sea to target camps in Afghanistan in response to an attack on U.S. embassies in Africa. Just before the attack, General Ralston, vice chairman of the Joint Chiefs of Staff, was tasked to visit Islamabad and inform the military leadership about the U.S. operation underway over Pakistan's Baluchistan Province into Afghanistan. From the U.S. standpoint, Pakistan was informed at the last minute to maintain the element of surprise and to prevent Pakistan from reacting against India in a misunderstanding. However, Pakistan considered this act a violation of its airspace and many were angry about the intentional subterfuge.

That night, villagers in Baluchistan reported missiles falling from the skies, as several TLAMs malfunctioned and landed unexploded in Pakistani territory. Each TLAM has a self-destruct mechanism to prevent the missile's technology from falling into the wrong hands; however, the self-destruct mechanism had malfunctioned in some of the fallen missiles. Pakistani helicopters carrying a rescue team recovered an unspecified number of TLAMs, although the United States reportedly attempted to retrieve them through the local tribal leaders in Baluchistan but failed. Later the United States pressured Pakistan to return the fallen *Tomahawks*. But Pakistan denied having ever been in possession of these missiles, and by late summer relations between the two countries soured further.[66]

Pakistan maintains that its cruise missile technology was developed indigenously, but U.S. experts suspect that *Babur* was derived from the recovered TLAMs, possibly through reverse engineering. Allegedly some TLAMs were passed on to China. Other experts claim that *Babur* is based on the Chinese DH-10 missile and that most likely, both cruise missiles were derived from reverse engineered *Tomahawks*. In an interview, General Mirza Aslam Beg told the author, "Give credit to our scientists. What happened in the case of cruise missiles? They see it and say we can do it." Beg implied that for quality scientists it was sufficient to simply examine the concept and configuration of the technology and produce the rest.[67]

Ra'ad/ HATF-VIII

In August 2007, Pakistan tested a new air-launched cruise missile, the *Ra'ad* ("Thunder," in Arabic) from a *Mirage III EA* fighter aircraft.[68] This nuclear-capable missile reportedly has a 350-km range along with stealth capabilities. Although Western analysts believed that it would be deployed on the American F-16A and F-16C fighter aircraft, Pakistan instead chose the *Mirage* aircrafts.[69]

Ra'ad is not an offshoot of the land version of *Babur*. Pakistani missile experts told the author that any new missile has to be redesigned, and to develop a land-based version is much different from developing a cruise missile. As with all other Pakistani weapons, Western sources dismiss Pakistani claims of indigenous development and speculate on possible foreign suppliers or collaboration. Chinese collaboration is alleged for the development of the land-based *Babur*, but for the *Ra'ad* air-launched cruise missile (ALCM), Jane's Intelligence report suggests that the design indicates it was derived from South African engineering. These speculations are based on a resemblance to several South African stand-off weapon projects and known defense collaboration with South Africa's Kentron (now Denel), believed to have supplied its Raptor-powered glide bomb (Raptor) to the Pakistan Air Force (PAF).[70]

Battlefield Nuclear Missiles

Nasr/HATF-IX

In April 2011, Pakistan introduced a new weapons system. A short-range surface-to-surface, two-tubed rocket launcher, believed to be an adaptation of a Chinese-design multiple rocket launcher (possibly A-100 type), is mounted on an eight-wheeler transporter erector launcher (TEL) carrying a twenty-foot ballistic missile with a diameter of about 300 mm (11.8 inches). The system is slated to be capable of carrying either conventional or nuclear warheads and is declared to have added "another layer to the deterrence capability" and to close the gap at the tactical or operational level. Several analysts speculate that this system was a response to the new Indian military doctrine of waging a limited war against Pakistan, which will be controlled to remain below the Pakistani nuclear threshold.[71]

The introduction of *Nasr/Hatf-IX* has made a qualitative change in the security landscape and has triggered a debate on the question of deterrence stability. Several questions are raised both in terms of technical efficacy as well as implications for deterrence, war fighting, and command and control. From a technical standpoint, the small warhead with a diameter of less than 12 inches will more likely use a plutonium warhead with an implosion assembly, which is quite challenging. Given the fact that Pakistani tests in 1998 were not plutonium based makes it even more challenging.[72]

The debate rages on at the time of this writing whether such a weapon system will have a deterrence effect in the battlefield or otherwise. One view is that it will have a "deterrent effect at least on unilateral India employment of fast moving integrated battle formations undertaking ground offensive opera-

TABLE 12.1

Missile Inventory

System Name	Range (km)	Fuel	Warhead/ Payload (Kg)	Origin
Hatf-I	80–100	Solid	500	SUPARCO
Hatf-II/Abdali	180–200	Solid	480	SUPARCO/NESCOM
Hatf-III/Ghaznavi	280	Solid	800	PMO/NESCOM
Hatf-IV/Shaheen-1	650–900	Solid	850	NDC/NESCOM
Hatf-IV/Shaheen-1A	1000–1500	Solid	700–1000	NDC/NESCOM
Hatf-V/Ghauri	1300–1500	Liquid	700	KRL/NESCOM[a]
Hatf-VI/Shaheen-II	2000–2500	Solid	1000–1100	NDC/NESCOM
Hatf-VII/Babur	700	Solid	250–300	NDC/NESCOM
Hatf-VIII/Raad[b]	350	Solid	450	NDC/AWC/NESCOM
Hatf- IX/Nasr[c]	60	Solid	Unknown	NESCOM

NOTE: Pakistan has not as of yet tested a naval version of any missile. Presumably Maritime Technology Organization (MTO) is working on a Submarine Launched Cruise Missile (SLCM), which could be a naval version of Babur cruise missile.

[a]KRL and NESCOM have been synergizing their technical efforts for past decade or so.

[b]*Hatf-VIII/Raad* is an Air-Launched Cruise Missile (ALCM).

[c]*Hatf-IX/Nasr* was flight-tested in April 2011. This is slated as battlefield weapon system with a warhead which was declared as capable of carrying a nuclear warhead.

tions."[73] Another view is that the small-yield weapon system will not cause the requisite damage to mechanized forces.[74]

Regardless, the introduction of such a battlefield nuclear weapon system will pose three major challenges affecting stability. First, its short range would warrant its deployment close to Pakistan's own troops, close to the border, which will increase field security issues; second, the command and control of such a system will be very complicated, bringing into question whether to retain central control or delegate it to field formations for greater battle effectiveness; and lastly, such a battle system with its peculiar signals will likely induce preemptive pressures on India or any other adversary to attack with conventional weapons, thus triggering a premature or even unintended war.[75]

Missile Deployments and Strategic Impact

As the first decade of the twenty-first century ends, Pakistan possesses a wide variety of fighter planes, including the French Mirage-V, Chinese JF-17 Thunder, and American F-16 fighter jets. Nevertheless, India fields a quantitatively superior air force. Given the current imbalance, if a war were to take place between the two adversaries, in its initial stages India would attempt to gain air superiority and could indeed dominate the skies even in a prolonged war. Faced with such strategic circumstances, Pakistan relies on its ability to deliver conventional warheads to the battlefield and beyond using its ballistic missiles.

While Pakistan's F-16 aircraft are effective delivery platforms, mobile ballistic missiles offer greater survivability, especially if Pakistan engages in an extended conventional conflict. Furthermore, Pakistan does not have the industrial capacity to build its own fighter, nor can it produce replacement parts indigenously. A healthy ballistic missile arsenal serves as a hedge against possible supplier cutoffs of replacement aircraft, spare parts, or training and maintenance assistance. Finally, medium-range ballistic missiles provide Pakistan with the capacity to threaten targets over all of India's territory, whereas aircraft have a limited radius of combat. To be sure, ballistic missiles are recognized as Pakistan's primary strategic delivery vehicle, and creating the infrastructure to produce them is a military priority second only to the production of nuclear bombs.

While outsiders credit the West or Chinese support for Pakistan's progress in missile development, predictably, Islamabad insists that all credit is due to indigenous efforts. The reality is a mixture of both. It is true that technology transfers from the West helped Pakistan, and equally true that China helped Pakistan jump over key technical hurdles. However, what is also true is the sense of nationalism and pride felt by the Pakistani scientists for their achievements. After all, these technical experts did master an indigenous capability—when their technological capacity base was weak and denial from the West was strong.

Pakistan's missile forces satisfy most of the country's strategic needs, at least those that relate to India. And since Pakistan does not currently have large regional aspirations or other threatening adversaries, developing intercontinental missiles will not be a priority for Islamabad. Rather, increasing its self-sufficiency in the area of short- and medium-range missile development and production will very likely be the focus of Pakistan's future activities.

13   The Grazing Horse in the Meadows

On August 17, 1988, President Zia-ul-Haq, accompanied by top military hierarchy, U.S. ambassador to Islamabad Arnold Raphael, and a U.S. defense attache, boarded a C-130 Hercules aircraft to return to Islamabad after witnessing a tank demonstration near the desert border town of Bahawalpur. Within minutes of takeoff, the presidential plane crashed, exploding on the ground. To date, the cause of the plane crash remains a mystery. The timing of this event—months after the controversial Soviet withdrawal agreement from Afghanistan and the transitory phase of Pakistani domestic politics after Zia-ul-Haq dismissed the Parliament and government of Prime Minister Muhammad Khan Junejo—raised many suspicions. Zia-ul-Haq had stood as a bulwark against the Soviet expansion, but the execution of the global Islamic *jihad* waged from bases in the tribal areas of Pakistan brought a backlash, which Pakistan and the rest of the world continue to suffer from to this day.

As explained in Chapter 11, Zia's sudden death brought Ghulam Ishaq Khan (GIK), then chairman of the senate, to the presidency, and the formation of a troika comprising the president, Prime Minister Benazir Bhutto, and Chief of the Army Staff Mirza Aslam Beg to decide on all security and nuclear issues.

In the closing stages of the Cold War, Prime Minister Bhutto faced new challenges for Pakistan. The United States and Pakistan had maintained a fragile partnership based on four measures: (1) the United States would not pressure Pakistan to become democratic, (2) Pakistan would regain its status from the 1959 bilateral treaty, (3) Pakistan would execute covert operations against Soviet forces in Afghanistan with support from the United States, and (4) nuclear issues would be kept on the back burner.[1] However, these conditions were becoming increasingly irrelevant. With the dramatic end of the Cold War, and specifically the end of the Soviet Union's withdrawal, the United States had little incentive to follow through on any of the four pledges. The 1959 bilateral treaty had made Pakistan significant only because of its geographical location, making it key to the U.S. "containment" policy. By the time the Cold War had ended Pakistan had already returned to a parliamentary democracy, which boosted its image in the U.S. Congress. Further, Pakistan's role on the future of Afghanistan was all but over as far as U.S. objectives in Afghanistan were concerned.

It was the fourth pillar—Pakistan's nuclear ambitions—that the United States could no longer brush aside, especially after its being downplayed in the 1980s and norms against proliferation coming into international focus. After a fifty-year alliance with the United States, Pakistan had difficulty adjusting to the new global order and its diminished significance, as well as renewed U.S. scrutiny, especially of its nuclear program. Furthermore, regional security was deteriorating and domestic politics were in constant flux throughout the decade of the 1990s.

Domestic Tensions and a Policy of Restraint

Thus, Benazir Bhutto inherited the delicate balancing act of appeasing the United States while maintaining the strength of Pakistan's nuclear program. According to her bargain with Army Chief General Mirza Aslam Beg (see Chapter 11), decisions regarding regional security policy and the nuclear program would remain under the supervision of President GIK, and her government would avoid interference in the army's internal affairs, in exchange for a smooth transition to democracy.

Beg believes he advised Ms. Bhutto to the best of his ability and in the interest of the nation. After all, GIK had been involved in the nuclear program's development since the beginning, and his experience was unmatched. In addition, the complex nature of foreign policy (that is, the impending withdrawal of Soviet forces from Afghanistan and rising tensions with India over Kashmir) required the assistance of veteran Foreign Minister Sahabzada Yaqub-Khan. According to General Beg, Benazir agreed to these arrangements, creating a balance of power among the president, prime minister, and the army chief.[2]

But U.S. influence and involvement disrupted this tenuous harmony. Within a month after Benazir Bhutto took the seat as prime minister, during an official visit to Islamabad, a CIA team presented her with a briefing on the status of the Pakistani nuclear program.[3]

In March 1989, Army Chief General Mirza Aslam Beg went to Washington,

DC, where he met with the outgoing national security adviser, General Colin Powell, and his replacement, Brent Scowcroft. Beg was given an opportunity to anticipate the goals of the new Bush administration and the changing geopolitical circumstances.[4] He clearly understood the U.S. position and anticipated that nuclear issues would resurface. Upon his return to Pakistan and in anticipation of Benazir's first official visit to Washington, DC, that summer, there was a meeting of top leaders to deliberate what was to become Pakistan's first nuclear policy.

According to General Beg, this meeting of the "national command authority, jointly chaired by Ghulam Ishaq Khan and Benazir, took a decision to frame a policy of nuclear restraint."[5] This policy included five elements: (1) maintain the minimum force posture necessary for a credible deterrent, (2) refrain from conducting hot tests, (3) freeze fissile stocks at the current level, (4) reduce uranium enrichment to below 5 percent, and (5) affirm that nuclear weapons do not replace conventional force capabilities.[6] Beg did not explain the criterion used to determine the sufficient levels of fissile material necessary for a credible deterrent.[7] When asked if there were a cap on warhead numbers, Beg ambiguously stated that "there was no cap or freezing—at the time we talked, the Indians had 50–70 warheads and what we had was good enough to deter." When asked how it was determined in 1989 that the stockpiles were sufficient, Beg replied, "There was no need to stockpile because it is dangerous. And if you study the intrinsics of weapons of mass destruction, beyond a certain level it loses its value . . . diminishing returns." He went on to explain that the purpose of decreasing enrichment levels to 5 percent was to feed "the nuclear power plants for peaceful purposes that were coming up with the assistance from China (Chashma) and for KANUPP."[8]

To any outside analyst, Pakistan's carefully calibrated policy of nuclear restraint was rational and realistic. It was simply a prudent choice in the face of changing international circumstances. Not only did it clear the way for the upcoming visit of the Pakistani prime minister to the United States, but it also enabled Washington to continue its support of the newly elected democratic government in Pakistan. At the same time, it did not compromise nuclear capability and still allowed Pakistan to maintain both a nascent nuclear deterrent and conventional force balance with India. Benazir Bhutto maintained that a policy of nuclear restraint was developed as an "understanding" with Washington, leading up to her U.S. visit, and that it was favorable to Pakistani national interests; nonetheless, General Beg denied that the United States had any influence on this new nuclear policy and insisted that the national command decision was based solely on Pakistan's national security needs.[9]

In June 1989, Ms. Bhutto completed her Washington trip, in which she pledged to a joint session of the U.S. Congress the peaceful nature of Pakistan's nuclear program.[10] On the sidelines, however, during the visit, CIA Director William Webster exclusively briefed her on U.S. intelligence regarding Pakistan's nuclear program under the pretext that the Pakistani military was withholding information from her.[11] Ariel Levite, however, reports that "the U.S. government may have extracted a 'follow-up agenda for action,'" and that Ms. Bhutto had "conceded to work on any assessment by the CIA of the Pakistani program."[12] Benazir Bhutto's commitment to U.S. officials remains hearsay, but the meeting itself, in which the elected head of Pakistan relied on foreign intelligence briefings about her own country's nuclear program, reveals a level of distrust and secrecy among the highest ranks in Pakistan.[13]

Overall, given the history of U.S.-Pakistan relations on nuclear issues, President GIK and General Beg were unimpressed and even suspicious of the prime minister's fraternizing with U.S. intelligence. However, the briefing laid the foundation of mistrust. While GIK and Beg thought it best to involve her in all decision-making processes, Ms. Bhutto insisted to the West that the Pakistani Army did not keep her in the loop. General Beg argues that "she plays out to the gallery, the truth is what I am telling you .... [S]he was the architect of the nuclear policy of restraint. Can she deny the meeting of nuclear command authority?" As Benazir Bhutto's relationship with the president and the army continued to deteriorate, the classified program became more hidden from any structural oversight other than direct access of the heads of Pakistan Atomic Energy Commission (PAEC) and Khan Research Laboratories (KRL) to the president and army chief.

On August 6, 1990, President GIK dissolved Bhutto's government. At the time, the focus of the world was on Saddam Hussein's invasion of Kuwait, so Pakistani domestic politics drew little attention. Under the constitution an interim government was formed and elections held within ninety days. A new prime minister, Nawaz Sharif, was sworn into office in 1990.

Sharif was the "blue-eyed boy" of the now deceased General Zia-ul-Haq. He was chief minister of the largest province, Punjab, from 1988 to 1990. His party, the Pakistan Muslim League (PML), was the largest political party in a coalition of religious parties known as *Islami Jamhoori Ittehad* (*IJI*), meaning Islamic Democratic Alliance—allegedly brokered by Pakistan intelligence agencies. This alliance was in opposition to Benazir Bhutto's PPP and helped to force her out of office. In the 1990 election, PML won a plurality, and Sharif was sworn in as prime minister.

Sharif was reform minded, but his tenure began under the shadow of two major events. First was the U.S. nuclear sanctions applied in October 1990 when, under the Pressler Amendment to the U.S. nonproliferation law, U.S. President George H. W. Bush declined to certify to the Congress that Pakistan's nuclear program was peaceful and that it did not have a nuclear capability. The application of sanctions implied that the United States was not impressed with the so-called self-imposed nuclear restraint, as General Aslam Beg had claimed. Pakistan had never allowed verification of the restraint. Moreover, as explained in Chapter 11, General Beg's ordering of nuclear posturing to induce U.S. intervention in the summer crisis with India was clearly on the metaphorical radar of the United States. Indeed, General Beg was warned as early as March 1989 by U.S. National Security Adviser Brent Scowcroft that certification of a clean bill for Pakistan's nuclear activities would no longer be business as usual.[14]

Sharif faced a second defining moment when President Bush was building the coalition of military forces to oust Saddam Hussein from Kuwait. Pakistan joined the coalition, sending troops to Saudi Arabia for its defense. But when the operation commenced in January 1991, Army Chief General Beg was not fully behind Pakistan's support of the U.S.-led offensive against Iraq, and he called for "strategic defiance" of the West.

Sharif managed the crisis, but his relations with the army and President GIK soured. In August 1991, when General Beg was due for retirement, friction with the president was exacerbated over the appointment of a new army chief. President GIK appointed General Asif Nawaz Janjua against the wishes of the prime minister. Sharif and the army also disagreed over the military operations being conducted in Karachi and urban Sindh at the time. When General Janjua suddenly passed away as a result of a heart attack in January, the replacement of the army chief again became an issue between the president and the prime minister. Once more, GIK was dismissive of Sharif and appointed General Abdul Waheed as the army chief, surpassing other contenders that the prime minister favored.

For the second time in five years, President GIK faced a prime minister with problems of bad governance—corruption, nepotism, inefficiencies, and friction with the armed forces. President GIK dismissed the Sharif government in April 1993. But Sharif challenged the decision in the Supreme Court and eventually won the case and was restored to power. The tussle between the president and prime minister turned ugly, prompting Army Chief General Abdul Waheed to intervene. He asked both to resign and that an interim government hold elections.

Nonproliferation Challenges in the New World Order

President GIK was by far the greatest silent patron and contributor to the Pakistani nuclear program. As explained in previous chapters, since Zulfiqar Bhutto formed the interministerial coordination committee, GIK had remained involved in the development of the program, and, especially in the Zia era, was the architect of its financial support. In his five years as president (1988–93), he presided over the country's transition from a military dictatorship to a civil democracy amid international upheaval. U.S.-imposed sanctions and increased pressure from Washington on the nuclear issue led GIK to pioneer economic and financial reforms. In 1990, Islamabad embraced economic liberalization, which led to an average growth rate of 5 percent until 1993. However, Pakistan's nuclear program bogged down any further potential economic progress. Former finance minister Sartaj Aziz summed up the true meaning of "eating grass" at that time:

> It is ironic to recall that the much-delayed economic liberalization programme of 1991–1993 coincided with the Pressler sanctions . . . . Pakistan undertook these investments in the expectation that multilateral and bilateral donor agencies . . . would support the required investments. But the stoppage of American assistance reduced the net flow of foreign assistance from \$3.4 billion in 1990 to \$1.9 billion in 1993 . . . . [M]any industrial units closed down and the rate of that brought down the overall GDP growth rate from 6.5% in the 1980s to 4.6% in the 1990s.[15]

Economic woes were compounded by the side effects of the Afghan war as opium poppies and other illegal drugs spilled over Pakistan's borders. The United Nations estimated that by 1993, about 1.7 million Pakistanis (nearly 1.5 percent of Pakistan's population) were drug addicts, mostly in the Pashtun belt of the Pakistan-Afghanistan borderlands. Pakistan was the crossing point for narco-trafficking and small arms smuggling, which fueled violence in the region.[16]

The interim government led by Moeenuddin Ahmad Qureshi, an economist and former vice president of the World Bank, took power from July until October 1993. The outgoing president, GIK, was unwilling to hand over sensitive documentation regarding the nuclear program to a transitory government. Anticipating political uncertainty and having overseen the fragile political leadership for five years, GIK in his wisdom considered it best to hand over the custody of nuclear matters to Army Chief General Abdul Waheed.[17] In General Headquarters (GHQ), the army chief tasked Director General of the Combat Development Directorate (DGCD) Major General Ziauddin, a two-star general, to take charge of the documents and become the point person on all nuclear issues on his behalf. For the first time in the nation's history, the locus of nuclear program decision-making was transferred from the president's office to army headquarters.[18]

President Bill Clinton had taken over the U.S. leadership when the "new world order" began to take shape. By the end of 1993, nonproliferation was the single most popular issue in international relations, one that the Clinton administration embraced with full vigor. Geopolitical considerations were no longer relevant, and regional security was worsening, as Afghanistan was embroiled in a civil war and uprisings in Kashmir had reached unprecedented levels.

Under these circumstances, U.S. Deputy Secretary of the State Strobe Talbott and Deputy Assistant Secretary of State on Nonproliferation Robert J. Einhorn led U.S. efforts to obtain a nonproliferation commitment from Pakistan. They first attempted to press Pakistan to "cap" its nuclear program and roll it back. By April 1994, however, there was realization that rolling back the nuclear program was ambitious. A more realistic option could be to get Pakistan to agree on freezing the nuclear program in return for the embargoed F-16s. An additional caveat was a nonintrusive verification inspection of Kahuta by U.S. inspectors.[19] This proposal got no traction either in Washington or in Islamabad. Opposition within the U.S. Congress, led by Senator Larry Pressler and the Indian lobby in Washington, created uproar over the supply of the F-16s to Pakistan under a quid pro quo. Further, Pakistani Army Chief General Abdul Waheed, on an official tour to the United States, let it be known in no ambiguous terms that any such deal was unacceptable. DGCD Major General Ziauddin was accompanying the army chief to Washington, DC; he was called back to Islamabad for a meeting between a U.S. delegation and Prime Minister Benazir Bhutto, who had been elected to the office for a second time. Unlike in her previous term (1988–90), Ms. Bhutto was in full harmony on nuclear issues with all institutions, especially the army, to which GIK had handed over nuclear responsibility. The prime minister had asked the DGCD Major General Ziauddin to be present for advice on nuclear matters during her meetings, which surprised the visiting U.S. delegation. Analysts surmise that Ziauddin's presence was to ensure that the prime minister did not commit anything to the U.S. delegates that could be rejected by the army chief and to ensure that Pakistan's political leadership and the army were on the same page.[20]

By the mid-1990s, American pressure on the Pakistani nuclear policy had unintended effects. U.S.-Pakistani relations progressively soured over the nuclear question, and as Islamabad felt isolated under sanctions, greater national consensus and harmony within the domestic political leadership emerged over the national commitment to acquire the nuclear deterrent. This sense of national resolve coincided with the intense international focus on the conclusion of the Comprehensive Test Ban Treaty (CTBT). Despite this sense of isolation, it was India's aborted attempt to conduct a nuclear test in 1995 that determined the Pakistani pathway to its own nuclear tests and its position on the CTBT in 1995–96.

The Debate on Nuclear Testing: Cautionists and Enthusiasts Redux

DGCD Major General Ziauddin realized he needed a dedicated staff to handle nuclear diplomacy and to coordinate the various scientific organizations. General Waheed approved the establishment of a "research cell" within the CD Directorate, which was composed of qualified military officers with a strong educational background in strategic studies. In November 1993, on the recommendation of Ziauddin and Lieutenant-General Jehangir Karamat, Army Chief General Abdul Waheed selected this author (then lieutenant colonel) to head this "research cell" in order to examine nuclear arms control and related regional and global developments that could impact Pakistan's strategic policy and nuclear development plans. Some four years later, on July 15, 1997, this cell was officially redesignated as the Directorate of Arms Control and Disarmament Agency (ACDA), headed by the author, now in the rank of brigadier.[21]

The Combat Development (CD) Directorate reported to the Chief of General Staff (CGS), a three-star general officer (lieutenant-general) who is the pivotal principal staff to the army chief at GHQ. Under the CGS were the Director General of Military Operations (DGMO) and the Director General of Military Intelligence (DGMI); each of the three directorates—DGMO, DGMI, and DGCD, headed by a two-star major general—was supposed to synergize its efforts toward the objectives set by the COAS and CGS. Now with the nuclear responsibility, the DGCD gained new importance in his role and influence. Sensitive nuclear developments were reported directly to the army chief, and his decisions were conveyed to the CGS, DGMO, and/or the foreign secretary. All scientific organizations were required to coordinate with DGCD. With this new significance, the CD was often viewed as transgressing into traditional domains of the other directorates within GHQ, all vying to compete for the attention of the army chief on nuclear issues. The expanded role of the CD necessitated expansion and reorganization. By the time nuclear tests were conducted in 1998, the CD had four subdirectorates (divisions), each headed by a brigadier and dealing with acquisition of conventional weapons and strategic weapons development, including missiles and nuclear weapons. The organization of the CD Directorate in 1998 is further discussed in Chapter 17.

Working in close concert with the scientific community, other directorates within GHQ, and the diplomatic core, the director of ACDA advised DGCD on Pakistan's position on arms control issues, especially on the outlines of the CTBT. The ACDA Directorate was soon assisting Pakistan's negotiations in bilateral and multilateral negotiations on nuclear issues and also participating in international conferences and think tanks. Pakistani nuclear diplomacy directly received military inputs and developed a coherent security analysis on nuclear issues, which was further echoed by increasing synergy between the Foreign Office and the CD. Professor Stephen P. Cohen, renowned South Asian scholar, in his book on the Pakistani Army, observed that the "establishment of an arms control cell in GHQ [was] a welcome development," a step that reflected "fresh thinking." It indicated that the army was aware of the need to both participate in and to understand the "nuances of international negotiations."[22]

By 1994, the hot topic of international debate was the CTBT negotiations. DGCD was tasked to assess the need to conduct hot tests within the context of the CTBT. To do this involved a delicate balancing act between technical requirements, military necessity, and diplomatic caution—and the knowledge that maintaining a credible deterrent was key to national security policy. Overall, scientists agreed that cold tests could demonstrate the functionality of nuclear weapons design, but it remained undecided if hot tests were still necessary to provide uncontestable proof.

One side surmised that avoiding hot tests had both strategic and diplomatic advantages. This side argued that, like Israel, Pakistan must maintain a policy of ambiguity. Nuclear ambiguity creates uncertainty in the minds of adversaries, which in turn contributes to strategic deterrence. In addition, the political benefits associated with nuclear restraint were critical for an economically strapped country that could not afford further sanctions. From a technical standpoint, if cold tests sufficiently demonstrated the effectiveness of the weapon designs, they should be just as functional as the Hiroshima bomb, which had been untested until it was actually used. This side argued further that major military crises with India were diffused by Pakistan's nonweaponized deterrent and prevented war. Indeed, this thought process was reminiscent of that of the "nuclear cautionists" during Ayub's era.

The opposing side mirrored the erstwhile "nuclear enthusiasts" camp of the 1960s. Its proponents contended that there was no substitute for a demonstrated nuclear capability. An actual explosion produces a physically measurable yield, and the results are seismically recorded worldwide. From a strategic deterrence standpoint, a proven weapons capability leaves no room for doubt, boosts public morale, and heralds the nation's entry into the nuclear club. Dismissive of the political and economic consequences, proponents of the hot tests argued that Pakistan was no stranger to nuclear sanctions and although suffering, could certainly afford the risk. Most important, if Pakistan signed the CTBT, then it would be severely constrained to respond to future Indian tests.

Throughout most of the 1990s, the more cautious side prevailed as Pakistan was already under economic duress and further international pressure because of its missile technology exchanges with North Korea and China. Upping the nuclear ante would have been counterproductive and would have only increased already existing sanctions. However, a shift occurred between December 1995 and September 1996 as the debate turned to favor the opposing school of thought.

In August 1995, Pakistani Inter Services Intelligence reported unusual activities in Pokhran—the same area where India had conducted the first test in 1974—and concluded possible preparations for another Indian test, later confirmed by the *New York Times*.[23] In October of 1995, the U.S. Senate passed the Brown Amendment to the Nuclear Non-Proliferation Act, which mitigated the impact of the Pressler sanctions.[24] The passage of the Brown Amendment briefly relaxed diplomatic relations between the United States and Pakistan,[25] but even this reprieve was short-lived when the U.S. media—based on a possible tip from U.S. intelligence—made public the Chinese transfer of some five thousand ring magnets to KRL.[26] These ring magnets helped the functioning efficiency of the centrifuges, rotating at great speeds, to enrich U-235.

As activities in Pokhran continued to increase, the Indian position on the CTBT began to harden, and its tone and tenor toward Pakistan and the United States became increasingly acerbic. On June 20, 1996, India's ambassador to Geneva, Arundhati Ghosh, stood at the podium at the plenary session of the Conference on Disarmament on CTBT negotiations and slammed the discriminatory and "flawed nature of the CTBT," asserting that only India's "national security considerations" would determine its decisions.[27]

This turn of events was drastic, as India had worked closely on the treaty text along with the Group of Twenty-one countries (G-21). Perplexed, Pakistan discovered that the Indian delegation was simply implementing directives from Delhi and so summoned Pakistan ambassador Munir Akram to Islamabad for consultations.[28]

The Horse in the Stable

Meanwhile, Pakistan's military leadership was undergoing several changes. General Abdul Waheed retired in January 1996, handing the baton to General Jehangir Karamat, who was CGS at the time. A professional leader with an illustrious career, Karamat's appointment—reflecting the institutional strength and moderate leadership dominant in the military—lasted until October 1998.[29] Ultimately the transition was smooth, but the new army chief inherited several impending issues. In September 1995, Pakistani military intelligence discovered that Major General Zahir-ul-Islam Abbassi and his Islamist followers had been planning a coup d'etat. A speedy court martial and jail sentence eliminated the threat, but the attempt by fundamentalists to forcefully seize power raised concerns just two years after the military was given jurisdiction over the nuclear program.[30] General Karamat was a welcome leadership transition to moderation, which marginalized the more radical factions within the army. Later in 1998, Deputy Secretary of State Strobe Talbott would call him a "cool customer."[31]

Within a week of taking over command, General Jehangir Karamat had held a meeting in GHQ with key diplomats, scientists, and concerned directors of the CD and MO directorates to assess the potential of an Indian nuclear test and the larger CTBT negotiations. The meeting concluded that India was miffed at the passage of the Brown Amendment, which marginally mitigated nuclear sanctions, but was taking advantage of the KRL ring-magnet scandal to divert international focus to Pakistan so that it could conduct a test. If such an Indian test were to reoccur, attendees predicted that U.S. reactions would be similar to those during the 1974 nuclear test. As in the past, there would be an initial uproar, a mild rap on the knuckles, and possible sanctions under the Glenn Amendment that would be quickly lifted. Ultimately, America's efforts would be directed to prevent Pakistan from following suit.

Armed with these findings, General Karamat ordered the immediate preparation of a test site. PAEC Chairman Ishfaq Ahmad and the DGCD supervised the preparations in the Ras Koh Hills, and Brigadier Muhammad Sarfaraz along with Colonel (later Brigadier) Muhammad Anwar reactivated sealed tunnels.[32] Samar Mubarakmand and his team were charged with repairing the shaft, changing its original L-shape to "somewhat like an S-shaped shaft that could withstand the explosion and seal it."[33] By June 1996 the tunnel was ready and Pakistani intelligence was working around the clock to monitor activities at the Pokhran site. It was predicted that India would conduct the tests at the very last minute and then sign the CTBT. Pakistan had to be ready to respond with all options open to the government.[34]

Meanwhile CTBT negotiations continued to advance, and major nuclear weapons states (China and France in particular) began conducting nuclear tests in anticipation. Indian and Pakistani diplomats were in agreement that the objective of the CTBT was to prevent Nuclear Non-Proliferation Treaty (NPT) hold-out states (especially India and Pakistan) from conducting tests. Diplomats at the Conference on Disarmament in Geneva began to coordinate their positions and jointly oppose or support each other on substantive issues.[35] Pakistani negotiators, however, noted a subtle shift in India's position as India became less conciliatory and took more independent positions on the CTBT. Finally, when India threatened to block consensus on the CTBT, it was sent to the United Nations for a vote under an Australian initiative. By September 1996, India was standing alone against the CTBT. The Pakistani government was in a tough spot to decide its course of action.

In Pakistan the government of Ms. Benazir Bhutto came under pressure from President Clinton to sign the treaty. Unlike India, Pakistan did not block the passage of the CTBT to the United Nations. The U.S. administration sought Pakistani signatures when the treaty was opened for signature.

General Karamat had been closely following the CTBT negotiations and presided over a policy meeting on the issue, in which the author presented the substance of the treaty. The meeting deliberated political, strategic, and technical pros and cons for Pakistan. The central question before this meeting was determining the technical requirements of conducting hot tests in a day and age in which other forms of cold testing (such as hydronuclear, hydrodynamics, or computerized simulations) were deemed effective ways of validating the design and reliability of stockpiles. As related above, the opinions of the scientists were divided, though all agreed in principle that cold tests were technically reliable. Some scientists still insisted that there was no substitute for hot testing, which was necessary for safety and reliability; others reinforced the argument that to avoid political costs, Pakistan should rely on its successful cold tests. Yet a point of debate was domestic public opinion. The Pakistani public would certainly question the credibility of a nuclear deterrent if it were not demonstrated. By joining CTBT Pakistan would be foreclosing this option, which would be politically unacceptable.

When it was A. Q. Khan's turn to speak, he addressed General Karamat directly and alluded to India's 1974 nuclear test, saying, "Sir! The Indian horse is grazing in the meadows along with six others; ours is stuck in the stable. Let my horse go into the open and graze in the meadows with the others and then you can sign as many treaties as you like." This powerful statement closed the debate and the conclusions were sent to Prime Minister Benazir Bhutto for the final policy decision.[36]

After weeks of suspense, Ms. Bhutto announced Pakistan's policies on the issue: (1) Pakistan would not sign the CTBT unless India signed it first, (2) Pakistan reserved the right to conduct nuclear tests should its national security demand it, (3) Pakistan would vote in favor of CTBT's passage to the United Nations, (4) despite not signing the treaty, Pakistan would adhere to the letter and spirit of the treaty, and (5) Pakistan would willingly participate in the CTBT monitoring system and allow its seismic station to be part of the CTBT verification network.

Benazir Bhutto's decision reflected a rare institutional consensus within Pakistan. Aware that India could test and then sign the CTBT, Islamabad's new policy would allow it to react in turn. Detractors argued that this position allowed India to make the first move, leaving Pakistan vulnerable. They argued that instead, Pakistan should bite the bullet and test immediately. After all, other countries outside of the NPT had tested—why shouldn't Islamabad release its horse into the meadow? Once the horse is out of the stable, they argued, Pakistan would negotiate with the United States and trade off CTBT signatures for the removal of nuclear sanctions. In the final analysis, as the weaker nation, Pakistan had to withhold signing the CTBT first and simply watch for India's next move.

The Benazir government did not last long after creating this nuclear policy.

The prime minister's younger brother, Mir Murtaza Bhutto, who had long challenged the legitimacy of Benazir Bhutto as heir to Bhutto's party, was gunned down in a police encounter in Karachi on September 20, 1996. On November 5, Benazir's government was dissolved and her husband arrested for alleged involvement in the assassination of Murtaza Bhutto. Allegations of massive corruption forced President Farooq Leghari to dismiss the government for the third time in six years. This move allowed Nawaz Sharif to fill the seat of prime minister, winning by a landslide of 137 parliamentary seats.[37] The CTBT debate receded into the background until Musharraf's government reignited it in 1999.

Since the early 1950s in general but specifically since May 1988, Pakistan had faced continuous political crises in search of an acceptable balance between the powers of the president and the prime minister, and in this context, the position and role of two other national institutions—the military and the Supreme Court. Nawaz Sharif, having won a substantial majority in the Parliament, clipped the powers of the president to dismiss the elected government by passing an amendment to the constitution (the 13th Amendment).[38] Sharif's accumulation of all power into his hands provoked the hapless president to seek support from Supreme Court Chief Justice Syed Sajjad Ali Shah. As nepotism and corruption increased with the augmented power of the prime minister, an intriguing tug-of-war ensued between the president, prime minister, and Supreme Court chief justice, with all three dragging the army to their side.[39] This game eventually came to an end with the resignation of both the president and the chief justice in December 1997, leaving only one institution to be tamed—the army. Nawaz Sharif emerged as an all-powerful prime minister, a position enjoyed by no one other than Zulfiqar Ali Bhutto of the 1970s.

Like Zulfiqar Ali Bhutto, who had selected Zia-ul-Haq, Sharif selected Pervez Musharraf as his chief. Both prime ministers thought their new chiefs lacked institutional support and hence would remain subservient to them. But both overestimated their power and underestimated the institutional strength of the military. The political future of Sharif met the same fate Bhutto's had in 1977. By the autumn of 1999, Nawaz Sharif's confrontations with two successive army chiefs had resulted in a military coup that brought Musharraf into power.

During this drawn-out game of political musical chairs, Pakistan underwent dramatic domestic and economic changes in order to adjust to the new world order.[40] Amid the institutional turmoil during the decade of democracy, from 1989 to 1999, the Pakistani nuclear program was profoundly affected by the fragility of domestic political challenges, which also weakened cumulative national power. The military's strength and combat effectiveness was hurt by U.S.-led nuclear sanctions, but the most deleterious effect was on the economy, which was in dire straits. The United States had veritably abandoned the region after the Cold War. Its relationship with Pakistan was purely utilitarian and issue-based, with Pakistan's nuclear program and its role in global arms control initiatives topping the U.S. agenda. Pakistan was on its own to revive its economy in light of the three dimensions of its national security requirements: stability in Afghanistan, relations with India based on a settlement of unresolved issues (Kashmir in particular), and preservation of its nuclear deterrent.

Pakistan and the Gujral Doctrine

Mr. Inder Kumar Gujral was among the most influential and intellectual politicians of South Asia in modern times. He was prime minister of India for eleven months (from April 21, 1997, to March 19, 1998), and during that time he instituted his famous "Gujral doctrine," which proffered reconciliation and magnanimity toward smaller regional neighbors, with the exception of Pakistan. This doctrine was viewed as a departure from the "Indira Gandhi Doctrine" of the 1980s, which sought a dominant posture and assertive policy.[41]

In Pakistan, Prime Minister Nawaz Sharif was extending an olive branch to his neighbor, which raised hopes for rapprochement between the two countries. On May 12, 1997, a summit for the South Asian Association for Regional Cooperation (SAARC) was hosted in Male, Maldives, where the Indian and Pakistani prime ministers met privately and agreed to form a peace process to encompass all issues affecting relations between the two neighbors. However, the excitement was short-lived, when on June 3, 1997, the U.S. press reported India's deployment of about a dozen *Prithvi* missiles at Jullandhar, a garrison about eighty miles from Lahore.[42]

Pakistan's CD and MO directorates immediately went to work and discovered that India had stored (which is distinct from having deployed) *Prithvi* missiles in its 333 Missile Group garrison in an attempt to provoke Islamabad.[43] The Pakistani leadership decided not to react. Years later, George Perkovich assessed that "hawks in India had welcomed the prospects that deployment of *Prithvi* would compel Pakistan finally to take the M-11 missiles it had obtained from China out of their storage crates. This would then force the United States to apply sanctions against China."[44]

Nevertheless, Indian and Pakistani diplomats were undeterred, and from June 20–July 2, 1997, the foreign secretaries transformed the summit into a concrete bilateral dialogue framework comprising eight working groups, including topics such as Jammu and Kashmir, as well as confidence-building measures (CBMs).[45]

A Request for Strategic Pause

In March 1998, the Hindu right-wing Bhartiya Janata Party (BJP) won elections, returning Atal Bihari Vajpayee to the post of prime minister of India. In addition, the mainstream Hindutva Party came to power and often remembered Pakistan as the destroyer of the Babri Mosque in Ayodhya in 1991, which led to Hindu-Muslim riots. The new Indian coalition promised a hawkish stand on political and security issues and vowed to take back Pakistani-administered Kashmir and to "reevaluate the country's nuclear policy and exercise the option to induct nuclear weapons."[46]

In light of these events, on March 20, 1998, U.S. Secretary of State Madeline Albright wrote a letter to Prime Minister Nawaz Sharif seeking Pakistan's cooperation in what was described as a "strategic pause." The Pakistanis were told that a similar letter was on its way to India. As it was interpreted in Islamabad, the United States was offering to calm down the hawkish proclivities of the new Indian government and was seeking Pakistani cooperation on five major measures: (1) avoid a public display of new weapons, (2) avoid a public announcement heralding the accomplishment of a nuclear/missile program, (3) avoid flight testing ballistic missiles, (4) avoid deploying missiles near a common border, and (5) refrain from declaring nuclear weapons status.

The timing of this proposal was interesting because earlier that month, Pakistan had planned to conduct the first test of the liquid-fueled *Ghauri* missile and then parade it on the country's Republic Day, March 23. Both India and Pakistan had a tradition of military parades held on national holidays in which major weapons were featured. After the request for a "strategic pause," General Karamat, who was on a visit to the United States in the first two weeks of March, advised the government to postpone the *Ghauri* missile test and directed the army not to display the weapon at the national parade. Pakistan had agreed to cooperate even before knowing what the Indian government's response might have been, assuming that a similar request had been made to it.

Testing Ghauri

Predictably, there were parties within Pakistan that were disappointed by the postponement of the *Ghauri* missile test. Why had Pakistan exercised restraint when India did not? How long would Pakistan wait before conducting a missile test? These questions and others reached the ears of Prime Minister Sharif, especially from a very unhappy A. Q. Khan. Swayed by this domestic pressure, the Sharif government gave the green light to conduct the first *Ghauri* test on April 6, 1998.

Upon a directive from the prime minister, the Foreign Office and GHQ were tasked to evaluate the strategic implications of a governmental shift within India, specifically with regard to a possible nuclear test. Two central questions were at the heart of the analysis: (1) What would be the future of Indian-Pakistani relations, specifically the fate of the peace initiatives begun the previous summer? and (2) Should India conduct nuclear tests, what policy options were available to Pakistan?

Assessments within GHQ varied regarding the future of the region's security. One view was that BJP would execute what it had promised in the election campaign and present the fait accompli to the world. The international community would eventually accept India's actions and apply pressure on Pakistan not to follow suit. BJP was a different political animal, and if the election rhetoric were any indication, there was little that would deter its ambitious plans. In terms of a possible Indian nuclear test, ACDA Directorate in CD thought that Vajpayee was a cautious man and would not stray from his predecessors' course. The author argued that when in the hot seat, Vajpayee would know the difference between the real world and election sloganeering. I was simply proved wrong.

14 The Nuclear Test Decision

At 3:45 p.m. on May 11, 1998, India conducted three nuclear tests, claiming the first test to be a two-stage thermonuclear experiment (Shakti-I), the second to be a fission test (Shakti-II), and the third, a subkiloton explosion to "validate new ideas and [the] subsystem" (Shakti-III).[1] The declared yields were 43 kt, 15 kt, and 0.2 kt, respectively.[2] In completing the tests, New Delhi announced its position as a de facto nuclear power, ensuring its national security.[3]

As the Pakistani nation received the news with shock, India celebrated. Indian Home Minister L. K. Advani brushed away his tears of joy long enough to warn Pakistan of the shift in the region's strategic balance and how it may affect the Kashmir conflict. Another leader, Krishan Lal Sharma, asserted that India was "now in a position to take control of *Azad Kashmir*."[4] Some Hindu fundamentalists—clad in saffron robes—went even so far as to attempt to collect radioactive sands as sacred souvenirs from the test site.[5]

Back in Pakistan, General Jehangir Karamat ordered an immediate assessment of the situation, and by 5:00 p.m. all principal staff and key directors in General Headquarters (GHQ) were summoned to their posts. Major General Zulfiqar Ali Khan, who had replaced Ziauddin as Director General of the Combat Development Directorate (DGCD), called Samar Mubarakmand, then Member (Technical) Pakistan Atomic Energy Commission (PAEC), to evaluate the Indian test. Samar Mubarakmand said to the DGCD, "Congratulations!" but Major General Zulfiqar was in no mood for humor and remarked, "You are congratulating us on India's tests?" Samar replied, "Yes, because now we would get a chance to do our own."[6]

He went on to inform the DGCD (in the presence of the author) of the measurements taken at the nearest seismic station to India in Nilore. At first the data seemed to indicate that the tests were fission tests yielding between twelve and fifteen kt. However, as the PAEC further studied the data, it became clearer that India could not claim a thermonuclear test.[7]

Expecting a crisis to arise from this event, GHQ alerted all corps commands and began securing the country's most sensitive areas. Specifically, Headquarters 12 Corps (Quetta) was tasked to secure the Ras Koh (Chagai) test site, and the Pakistan Air Force (PAF) was ordered to fly Combat Air Patrols (CAPs) covering all sensitive strategic locations. Air defense regiments of the army were alerted to monitor the entire air space. Clearly, Pakistan's armed forces were making defensive preparations as if a war were imminent. Based on their long-held threat perceptions, they were bracing for the possibility of preventive strikes.[8]

During this time, Prime Minister Nawaz Sharif was visiting Uzbekistan, and after hearing the news, decided to cut his visit short and return to Pakistan the next day. Chief of the Army Staff (COAS) General Jehangir Karamat advised the prime minister that, upon his return, he should immediately call a meeting of the Defense Committee of the Cabinet (DCC) to examine the full spectrum of implications and bring in all stakeholders for a comprehensive discussion.[9] Sharif returned on May 12 and immediately met General Karamat for a one-on-one meeting. Sharif was briefed on the entire situation and the preparations already underway. The army chief assured the prime minister that the appropriate response to the Indian tests was to be a national decision of historic significance and thus should be officially formalized by taking all the national security institutions on board.[10]

Internal Deliberations

The DCC meeting convened at 10 a.m. on May 13 and was chaired by the prime minister. Among the attendees were the chairman, Joint Chiefs of Staff Committee and the Chief of the Army Staff, General Jehangir Karamat; the Chief of the Air Staff, Air Chief Marshal Perviaz Mehdi Qureshi; the Chief of the Naval Staff, Admiral Fasih Bokhari; the Minister for Finance, Mr. Sartaj Aziz; the Minister for Foreign Affairs, Mr. Gohar Ayub Khan; and the Foreign Secretary, Shamshad Ahmad. In addition, the heads of the PAEC and Khan Research Laboratories (KRL) were invited to present their views, with Dr. Samar Mubarakmand representing the PAEC (Ishfaq Ahmad was traveling in the United States at the time) and A. Q. Khan representing KRL.

The DCC deliberated the full spectrum of the political, security, and economic implications of Pakistan's response to India's nuclear tests. First, the PAEC provided its assessment of the Indian tests and stated that seismic stations recorded only one test on May 11, and not three as India had claimed. The PAEC believed that the thermonuclear test probably failed to ignite its secondary, and the third test probably fizzled out or might have been an experiment.[11] The PAEC concluded that at best, India conducted one successful test with a twelve to fifteen kt yield—an improvement since 1974.

That same day, just as the DCC meeting was coming to a close, India announced having conducted two more subkiloton tests. However, Pakistani seismic stations recorded no activity, and the PAEC surmised that these two tests were experiments or possibly safety tests for a low-yield weapon. Western sources would later validate the conclusions Dr. Mubarakmand had presented before the highest national leadership.[12]

In addition to these assessments, the meeting deliberated possible Indian objectives for conducting the tests and agreed on five points: (1) India had forced itself into the nuclear club simply to be on par with nuclear weapon states of the Nuclear Non-Proliferation Treaty (NPT), (2) without signing the NPT, India had none of the legal obligations to the treaty, (3) the tests were status oriented to claim permanent membership in the UN Security Council, (4) India's policy toward Pakistan would now be aggressive, especially on the issue of Kashmir, and (5) India wanted to push Pakistan to follow suit and be faced with the political and economic consequences of sanctions.[13]

Pakistani decision-makers were caught in a catch-22. If Islamabad responded in kind to the test, it would join India in the proverbial "dog house" and would be the target of sanctions. This would cripple Pakistan's already weak economy, which in turn would further weaken its conventional defenses, leaving it vulnerable to coercion and exploitation. On the other hand, if Pakistan did not respond to the test, the credibility of its nuclear deterrent would be undermined and could encourage India to take aggressive action in Kashmir and Pakistan. Political opponents within Pakistan would demand justification for the inaction, thus risking the regime's political survival. Opposition leader Benazir Bhutto had already begun pressuring Nawaz Sharif for a strong response, and other opposition members had moved resolutions in the Parliament demanding immediate testing; right-wing religious parties were threatening to take to the streets.[14]

As all of these concerns were brought to bear, the economic cost of testing was the fundamental consideration for the DCC. Finance Minister Sartaj Aziz was the only representative on economic issues present at the meeting and saw great economic opportunities in exercising restraint.[15] At the same time, he realized that long-term national interest and public sentiment demanded a different approach. During a conversation with the author, Mr. Sartaj Aziz clarified that he did not oppose the test decision on purely financial grounds. Rather, it was his job to provide the DCC with accurate economic analysis to inform an appropriate strategy. Mr. Aziz believed that although forgoing a nuclear test would result in immediate economic benefits, in the long run such stalling would have placed Pakistan at a permanent strategic disadvantage of living with a noncredible deterrent. In the end, he supported the public demand of a "befitting response."[16]

Samar Mubarakmand assured the DCC that if the decision to test were made, the PAEC would need only ten days to prepare the tests. Concerned that his rival would earn the honor, A. Q. Khan claimed that since KRL had enriched, designed, and cold tested the weapon, it therefore deserved to conduct the hot test.[17] The prime minister was too focused on the decision itself to get into this debate and so left the question of who would test the weapon to the army chief. However, in those days no one had the stomach to handle the competition between the KRL and the PAEC.[18] No final test decision was made in the DCC meeting, but the outcome could be predicted. Pakistan had little choice but to respond.[19]

In anticipation of a decision to test, DGCD coordinated with Samar Mubarakmand and members of the PAEC to prepare for transportation of the nuclear weapons, testing equipment, and personnel to the test site under directive of GHQ (Military Operations [MO] and Combat Development [CD] directorates). Brigadier Muhammad Anwar of Special Development Works (SDW) was ordered to move to the test site and prepare the test tunnel.[20] As arrangements were being made for the impending test, Fakhar Hashmi of KRL visited the PAEC on May 14 and requested that Samar Mubarakmand give two bombs to KRL for testing. He spoke with such authority as to give the impression that the government had chosen KRL to conduct the test.[21] Samar was surprised at the request, but recalled A. Q. Khan's demand at the DCC meeting. This development triggered much anxiety within the PAEC and its members, as many felt that the chance to prove their credentials was being stolen. To add insult to injury, A. Q. Khan purportedly wrote a letter to the prime minister in which he ridiculed the PAEC team, calling them "carpenters and blacksmiths" and requesting that a "joint team" of PAEC and KRL personnel be formed with A. Q. Khan at its head.[22]

Apparently the idea of a joint task appeared sound to the prime minister, but it did not come without technical implications. The PAEC was miffed and made a compelling case that it had been preparing for a nuclear test for more than a decade, and responsibilities could not simply be shifted at the last minute. The design, triggers, diagnostics, tunnel preparations, and every other aspect relating to the test were within the PAEC's control. Eventually the matter was referred to GHQ. Overall, the entire competition seemed petty when taken into the context of the panic and worry surrounding these events. Finally, General Karamat assured the PAEC that no new team would be brought in and that if and when the prime minister made a decision to test, it would occur under Samar Mubarakmand's existing team.[23]

On May 14, Prime Minister Sharif called a full cabinet meeting at his residence, in which three perspectives were represented. The hawks (three members) insisted on conducting the test immediately to resume parity and restore the strategic balance, convinced that no other opportunity would arise. The doves (six members) suggested that Pakistan set its own time to test rather than jump into a trap laid by India. Pakistan had a rare opportunity to isolate India, bolster conventional defense, and reap economic benefits. The third group (six members) advocated a middle position of simply waiting to make a more informed decision—Sartaj Aziz referred to this group as neither hawks nor doves, but "hoves."[24]

At the same time, DGCD Major General Zulfiqar Ali Khan and the Ministry of Foreign Affairs were keeping a close eye on the external situation. As director of the Arms Control and Disarmament Agency (ACDA), CD Directorate, the author worked closely with Mr. Salman Bashir (director general, United Nations) of the Ministry of Foreign Affairs to anticipate and prepare for the reaction from the United States.[25] Later in June 1998, Mr. Riaz Mohammad Khan took office as additional secretary, United Nations and Policy Planning, and his office was the focal point of nuclear diplomacy.[26] President Clinton had already made phone calls to Prime Minister Sharif, and Strobe Talbott, as special envoy for the U.S. president, was on his way to Islamabad. In this vein, the Pakistani foreign office and GHQ mulled over several policy options to deal with the incoming pressure from the United States. Pakistan had an opportunity to make demands of the United States, such as extended deterrence or a nuclear umbrella, mediation in the Kashmir conflict, or a visit by President Clinton that excluded Delhi. Most significant from Pakistan's strategic culture standpoint was a public acknowledgment from the United States that Islamabad faced a genuine security threat from India—something the United States must now admit after forty years of alliance with Pakistan.

Another significant aspect of the internal debate was the potential for failure of the nuclear test. Time was critical; yet moving too quickly could lead to technical failure, leaving Pakistan in the worst possible position. The more Pakistan stalled and took time, the better technical preparations would be made. These factors were all taken into account in several meetings in Islamabad and GHQ involving civil bureaucrats, scientists, and the military as deliberations for a final decision by the prime minister took place.

External Pressures

On May 11, the same day that India conducted its nuclear test, Indian Prime Minister Vajpayee wrote a letter to President Clinton stating that China's threat was the primary reason for India's having broken the international testing moratorium.[27] Brajesh Mishra, national security adviser to the Indian prime minister, later explained that India had "to show a credible deterrent capability not only to the outside world, but to our own people."[28]

The "outside world," however, was deeply disturbed. U.S. Secretary of State Madeleine Albright was appalled that in response to the U.S. "strategic pause" request, the "Indian diplomats had lulled us into thinking that they were not going to undertake any precipitous action in the nuclear area without careful review of the their options."[29] U.S. efforts were now focused on preventing Pakistan from following suit and testing a nuclear device.[30]

President Clinton spoke by phone with Prime Minister Sharif, urging him to take the high moral ground and promising handsome dividends in return. Clinton found Nawaz Sharif's response to be similar to "the guy wringing his hands and sweating."[31] Islamabad knew that the phone calls were just the beginning of American pressure tactics and that they needed to prepare to host a flurry of visitors from Washington.

Soon, Deputy Secretary of State Strobe Talbott and General Anthony Zinni, Commander of U.S. Central Command, were sent to Islamabad.[32] Just as the U.S. team was rehearsing talking points about "restraint and maturity," officials in Islamabad were bracing themselves to counter the U.S. coercion. Talbott and Robert Einhorn were familiar personalities in Islamabad, well remembered for the aborted initiative of "freeze, cap and roll back" during the first term of the Clinton administration. The Pakistani Foreign Office called an interministerial meeting—at which the author represented the DGCD—to formulate a joint strategy and common talking points in anticipation of Talbott's visit.

The result of this meeting was a "Strategic Policy" paper that, in anticipation of the range of carrots and sticks that could be used by the United States, recommended that Pakistan assume a noncommittal position during the negotiations but remain ready to listen. It was also suggested that Pakistani representatives pose hypothetical questions that would compel the U.S. team to place themselves in Pakistan's shoes. Since the government was still discussing options, the best strategy would be to demonstrate unity and resolve at all levels. Above all, the most difficult aspect was to hold in anxieties related to the country's increasing economic and financial burdens, and for this the Finance Ministry was specifically instructed to remain firm. The author recalls that at the end of these sessions, the prime minister approved the positions in the strategic policy paper, and the Foreign Office, the Finance Ministry, and GHQ were all believed to be on the same page in preparation for the U.S. team.

The Talbott Mission

By and large, both the Foreign Office and GHQ stood by the formulated national position during the Talbott mission. Strobe Talbott's written account indicated that the U.S. team left empty-handed and with the impression that despite Pakistan's difficult economic situation, the "Pakistani establishment" was forcing the political leadership to go forward with the nuclear test.[33] The account mentions a one-on-one meeting with the Pakistani prime minister that emphasized the prime minister's fear of political ruin in relation to the nuclear test decision.[34] The author recalls, however, that by the time Talbott had arrived there was little doubt in anyone's mind as to which direction the decision was heading. While Pakistan would assiduously work hard to mitigate the nuclear sanctions under the Pressler Amendment to the U.S. laws, there would be no compromise on the nuclear program. Bhutto's prophetic "eating grass" euphemism had created a national spirit of defiance, despite the fact that it was badly damaging the country's economy.[35]

In anticipation of the U.S. response, Pakistan went to a war footing against a potential preventive strike by India, the United States, Israel, or all three. Also, some Pakistani officials could not believe that the U.S. with all its resources would not have known beforehand that India would test. By implication, they surmised that the United States had granted silent consent to India. In contrast, Washington was applying intense diplomatic pressure on Pakistan in the form of economic sanctions—a devastating prospect in light of the already dire conditions in the country. When faced with such acute threats, U.S. "carrots"—promises of F-16s, aid, or the removal of economic sanctions—meant little. Pakistan would "choke on the carrots" even as they ate grass. These sentiments resulted in a flawed political decision by Sharif to assign the foreign secretary, a civil servant, to lead a team of bureaucrats who, during the diplomatic talks with Talbott, accused the United States of knowing about India's test. In contrast, a top political leader and foreign minister led India's negotiations with the United States.[36]

Islamabad was surprised at the accuracy of its own anticipation of the U.S. reaction and the typical incentives that Talbott and his team would offer to Pakistan. Since early 1994, Islamabad's considered policy had been to refuse to accept any carrots in exchange for a deal that affected the nuclear force goals. Talbott nevertheless tried his best to convince Pakistan not to test a nuclear weapon. The purpose of Talbott's mission was to dissuade Pakistan, rather than to empathize with its security concerns and redress its security dilemma. As usual, the U.S. had no patience for Pakistani strategic anxieties, especially the litany of complaints it had about India. Some senior officials accompanying Talbott were outwardly dismissive of Pakistani threat perceptions, rolling their eyes over any mention of India and its threat, while the Pakistanis strained under the tension and pressure. According to Talbott, at one point a heated exchange in the Pakistani Foreign Ministry escalated to near physical assault by a Pakistani diplomat, "who lunged across the table as though he were going to strangle either Bruce Riedel or me depending on whose neck he could get his fingers around first. He had to be physically restrained."[37] The Pakistani version of the story is somewhat different.[38]

Earlier, during Strobe Talbott's first visit in May immediately after the Indian test, the United States argued that Pakistan would suffer more if it responded to India's nuclear test. When Pakistani Foreign Minister Gohar Ayub Khan asserted that the Pakistani public would protest if Pakistan did nothing in response to India's provocation, Strobe Talbott was poignant in his response: "The Pakistani public would protest if they did not have jobs."[39] The two contrasting positions underscored the wide difference of approach to national security. From the U.S. perspective, Pakistan should take the political high ground and escape from economic sanctions and the cycle of tit for tat with India. From Pakistan's perspective, not responding to India's provocative tests was domestically unpopular and strategically would weaken security from a nuclear deterrence standpoint. For Pakistan to choose between security and economic opportunities was a tough call. It was for this reason that the Pakistanis were "hunkering down, lashing out, or flailing about" during negotiations with Talbott.[40] However, given Pakistan's experience of U.S. abandonment in times of extreme crisis, U.S. offers of aid in exchange for forgoing the opportunity to prove its nuclear capability appeared no more than a hollow promise and ruse to stop Pakistan from doing the obvious.

In hindsight, the author believes that the hawks in Pakistan were proved right. The Pakistani leaders in favor of the "now or never" approach in May 1998 were vindicated eight years later, when in March 2005 the United States offered India an unprecedented nuclear deal that resulted in the famous U.S.-India Peaceful Atomic Energy Cooperation legislation (the Hyde Act of 2006).

It is interesting to note that, despite claims from Western sources that China had conducted a nuclear test for Pakistan in 1990, neither Strobe Talbott nor any other U.S. diplomat ever mentioned the allegation during negotiations. Nor did they use the claim to try to convince the Pakistanis that they already had secretly hot-tested a weapon design and thus did not need another. Some of these allegations had come from a story circulated by Danny Stillman, former director of Los Alamos Laboratory Technical Intelligence Division. A physicist and expert on nuclear diagnostics and tests, Stillman visited China several times between 1990 and 2001. During that time, Stillman "saw clear evidence of Pakistani visitors within the heart of the Chinese nuclear complex" and received many briefings in China. One of these was about "Event no. 35," a nuclear explosion test conducted on May 26, 1990, at the Lop Nur test site in China. The weapon design was described to him as a "CHIC-4 derivative," and so he concluded that it must be a Pakistani design. Stillman speculated further that the "detonation of an imploded, solid-core, enriched, but unboosted uranium bomb matched the performance of a May 1998 test within Pakistan."[41] Both Pakistan and China have dismissed such allegations.

When the author asked Samar Mubarakmand about the Chinese test allegation, he gave a dismissive laugh and said, "[T]hese are figments of imagination—typical of the Western arrogance never to give credit to the Pakistani scientists. We worked on nuclear designs and test preparations for 25 years . . . . The Chinese never help in such an outlandish manner . . . . They only provided subtle help—limited technical help—and only when we asked for it. And we have always been careful not to ask of them [China] anything that would embarrass them. Moreover China would not risk being defamed at our cost, and we would not like that to happen to our best friends, who were always on our side—in times of need, trial and tribulations."[42] Samar further explained that "if we had secretly tested our device in China, our position on nuclear testing and CTBT would have been like the Israelis. And who should know more than you (referring to the author) on our CTBT position . . . . [In] fact we were constantly miniaturizing our designs to make them 'light and deliverable' based on the assumption that the F-16 aircraft may or may not come, so we must have an alternative means (ballistic missiles), so miniaturizing was our compulsion. It was important for us to get an opportunity to test to validate our design and that is why May 1998 was such a great opportunity for which we should thank the Indians."[43]

The Decision to Test

On May 16, 1998, after Strobe Talbott and his team had left, Prime Minister Sharif held another secret DCC meeting and gave the green light to proceed with the nuclear test. Immediately the DGCD gave instructions to Brig Muhammad Anwar, director of SDW, to move back to the tunnel and begin the necessary arrangements. Headquarters 12 Corps, Quetta tasked Brigadier Nadeem Taj, commander of the 61st Infantry Brigade, to move troops in order to secure the test sites in the Ras Koh Hills and Kharan shaft. The 70th Baluch regiment was to secure the first ring of defenses and to assist at the Ras Koh test site. The 8th Sind regiment was to form the outer ring of defenses, and the Frontier Corps paramilitary group was responsible for the third ring. The second shaft in Kharan was secured by the 5th Punjab regiment.[44] In the meantime, the PAF was on alert and was on a constant CAP mission at all sensitive strategic locations. From May 16 until after the tests were conducted, military movements surrounding the Pakistani test resembled wartime operations.

On May 18, Prime Minister Sharif personally summoned PAEC Chairman Dr. Ishfaq Ahmad and said in Urdu, "*Dhamaka kar dein*" ("Carry out the explosion").[45] Ishfaq Ahmad then called a meeting of top PAEC executives, scientists, and engineers. Simultaneously, GHQ and Air Headquarters (AHQ) issued orders to the relevant quarters. Headquarters 12 Corps, Quetta, Army's National Logistics Cell (NLC), the Army Aviation Corps, and No. 6 Air Transport Support (ATS) Squadron were tasked to extend support to the PAEC. The Civil Aviation Authority (CAA) directed the national airline, Pakistan International Airlines (PIA), to make available a Boeing 737 passenger aircraft on short notice for ferrying PAEC officials, scientists, engineers, and technicians to Baluchistan.

Dr. Samar Mubarakmand led the tests. Under his supervision, five horizontal shaft tunnels were made at the Ras Koh Hills, Chagai, and were redesigned in a way so as to collapse in on themselves upon exploding, thus creating a shield. Another vertical L-shaped shaft had been prepared at Kharan, some one hundred km away, for another nuclear explosion.

It was decided that there would be six nuclear tests, each with different bomb designs that had been cold tested earlier. The PAEC could not have afforded to explode six bombs from its inventory, and so only two bombs were selected for tests, one for each site, and the four remaining designs would be tested at Chagai with triggers and natural uranium packed around the weapon.

Beginning on May 19, a massive logistical operation under direction of the Pakistani Army began to transport the men, equipment, and devices to the Chagai test site. Two teams of 140 PAEC scientists, engineers, and technicians arrived, along with teams from the Wah Group, the Theoretical Group, the Directorate of Technical Development (DTD), and the Diagnostics Group.

Needless to say, A. Q. Khan was not happy that the army chose a PAEC team to conduct the nuclear explosion. He complained with such vigor to both the prime minister and the Chief of the Army Staff that a directive resulted, which sent a team from KRL to work with Samar Mubarakmand. On May 21, 1998, a team of four KRL scientists and technicians who had worked on earlier weapons designs arrived at the test site, including Dr. Javed Mirza, Dr. Fakhar Hashmi, Dr. Mansoor, and Dr. Naseem Khan. This team worked amicably with Samar Mubarakmand until May 30, 1998.[46] Javed Mirza told the author, "Our teams (PAEC and KRL) moved together. We were there as observers during [test] preparations, we would discuss together how to put everything together, and we worked together to make sure mistakes didn't happen. Of course the test was done by them (Samar and his team)."[47]

Support facilities were established at both the test sites, including bunkers, observation posts, lodging, communications, and tunnel portals, all of which were camouflaged using canvas and net. To deceive satellite surveillance, all facilities were made of adobe and constructed to resemble a local village—even the tunnel portal itself was located inside an adobe hut. Teams of soldiers were assigned the task of continually erasing vehicle tracks caused by incoming and outgoing trucks and jeeps.

In order to transport the nuclear devices safely, the bomb mechanism, shields, and casing were separated from the fissile material components and flown on a separate flight of PAF C-130 Hercules tactical transport aircraft. These transports from PAF base Chaklala to Dalbandin Airfield were escorted by four PAF F-16s armed with air-to-air missiles. Security was so tight that "the F-16s were ordered to escort the two flights with their radio communications equipment turned off, to ignore any orders during the flight, and, in case of a hijacking, to shoot down the aircraft immediately."[48]

Once the nuclear cargo had arrived at the Dalbandin airfield, the subassembled parts were unloaded separately and taken to the two test sites. In the Ras Koh Hills they were taken into the five "Zero Rooms" located at the end of a kilometer-long horizontal tunnel where Dr. Samar Mubarakmand personally supervised the complete assembly of all the nuclear devices. Later, diagnostic cables were laid from the tunnel to the telemetry and connected to all five nuclear devices, after which a complete simulated test was carried out by telecommand. In total, it took five days to prepare the nuclear devices, lay down the cables, and establish a fully functional command and observation post.

On May 25, 1998, supervised by numerous teams of engineers and technicians, soldiers from the 70th Baluch Regiment helped seal the tunnel. Dr. Samar Mubarakmand himself walked a total of five km checking the devices and the cables. A day later, the tunnels were sealed with a mixture of six thousand bags of cement and twice that amount of sand. By the afternoon of May 27, 1998, the cement had dried and the engineers certified that the concrete had hardened enough and declared the site fit for testing.

The date and time for the test were set for 3:00 p.m. on May 28. Prime Minister Nawaz Sharif called President Clinton and apologized for what was about to happen. He had no choice but to go ahead with the test.[49]

The Chagai Test

At dawn on Thursday, May 28, 1998, an air alert was declared over all military and strategic installations in Pakistan. Based on an intelligence tip-off from Saudi Arabia, PAF F-16A and F-7P air defense fighters were ordered to remain alert in the case of an Israeli attack on the nuclear test sites. Islamabad approached the United States to ascertain the veracity of the tip-off, after which "Washington promptly contacted the chief of Israeli Defense Force and put him into direct contact with the Pakistani ambassador in Washington to lay the fears to rest."[50] Also at the start of the day, the automatic data transmission link from all Pakistani seismic stations to the outside world was switched off. All personnel were evacuated from "ground zero" except for members of the Diagnostics Group and the firing team.[51] At 2:30 p.m., an Mi-17 helicopter arrived at the site carrying the team of observers, including Dr. Ishfaq Ahmed, Dr. A. Q. Khan, and Major General Zulfiqar Ali Khan.

Samar Mubarakmand told the author that A. Q. Khan wanted to push the button for the test, which created a last-minute disagreement. Major General Zulfiqar Ali Khan was told that this was not acceptable to the PAEC team that had done all the hard work, so it was decided that the honor of pushing the button should be given to a junior person who had made the largest contribution in designing the trigger mechanism. At 3:00 p.m., Islamabad awaited the news of the explosion. General Karamat paced in the operations room in MO Directorate (GHQ), but there was no news from the test site for the next fifteen minutes. Apparently, a truck carrying soldiers of the 70 Baluch regiment had become stuck in the sand after sealing the tunnel. In Islamabad each minute seemed like an hour.[52]

The "all clear" signal was given once the site was completely evacuated. Among the twenty men present, Chief Scientific Officer of DTD Muhammad Arshad, the man who had designed the triggering mechanism, was selected to push the button. At exactly 3:16 p.m. Pakistan Standard Time, Arshad prayed "All Praise be to Allah" as he pushed the button.[53]

At that point, the computer took over the control system, which turned on power supplies for each stage and recorded each step. A high-voltage electrical power wave simultaneously reached, with microsecond synchronization, the triggers in all of the five nuclear devices.[54] The earth in and around the Ras Koh Hills trembled as smoke and dust burst out through the five points where the nuclear devices had been buried. From the moment the button was pushed to the detonations, thirty seconds passed. Observers then began to shout, *Allah-o-Akbar* ("God is great"). The mountain shook and changed color, its dark granite rock turning white from deoxidization. Finally, a huge, thick cloud of beige dust enveloped the mountain.[55]

That evening, Pakistan announced the five tests of boosted fission highly enriched uranium (HEU) devices, boasting a total yield of forty kt. The main device produced thirty to thirty-five kt, and the remaining four were designed as low-yield weapons. The international community believes it was a single weapon fission test with a six to twelve kt yield, with the possibility of some other experimental explosions. Although the yield is disputed, the test was clearly a full nuclear explosion heralding the arrival of a seventh nuclear-capable state in the world. After the Chagai tests, the PAEC's DTD formally declared the test a "total success" and "completely safe" from any release of radiation.[56]

Prime Minister Sharif announced that Pakistan had "settled the score," meaning it had met India's mark. Jubilation spread throughout the nation, sweets were distributed, and special prayers were held in Faisal Mosque, Islamabad, to thank the Almighty for the success of the first Muslim country to acquire a nuclear capability. Pakistanis were proud as all Islamic countries sent them their congratulations.

The Kharan Test

Two days later, on Saturday, May 30, 1998, Pakistan conducted its sixth nuclear test, at 1:10 p.m. PST in the Kharan Desert.[57] The day before, on May 29, Dr. Samar Mubarakmand, along with a new testing team, had moved to the test site carrying the subsystem of a "miniaturized device."[58] The Kharan test site had an L-shaped tunnel, so that the nuclear device was assembled in the ground zero room at the end of the horizontal leg of the tunnel.[59]

This particular device, a design created by the Theoretical Group, produced a yield about 60 percent that of the first test—that is, eighteen to twenty kt. An observation post was built fifteen km way, and the men inside did not feel the vibrations or the tremor, but the oscillators did register the data from the test.[60]

The May 30 test was of immense significance because it was the latest and best design that the PAEC had developed, and the test validated the theoretical design parameters. A miniaturized device, it was very small and still powerful in yield. It is this very design that was meant for Pakistan's ballistic missiles and aircraft.[61]

The Finest Hour

Dr. Samar Mubarakmand has claimed that the five devices tested at Chagai and the one at Kharan were all based on PAEC designs.[62] He has also insisted that the nuclear tests at Chagai had been performed entirely by the nuclear test team of PAEC scientists, engineers, and technicians. He told the *Business Recorder,* "It is a wrong impression that these explosions in Chagai were jointly conducted by scientists belonging to various organizations."[63] In a later interview, he credited the success of the tests to the years of practice and training the teams received over years of conducting cold tests. The PAEC was able to accomplish the nuclear tests on such short notice only because it had been preparing for the event for more than two decades.[64] And he said of the Chagai test that it had demonstrated Pakistan's nuclear capability, "which is now with us and it is a tribute to thousands of our scientists, engineers, geologists, metallurgists and theoretical physicists who have really spent more than two decades in this program."[65]

In a speech to the Pakistan Nuclear Society, Dr. Samar praised the PAEC and its excellence. "The PAEC should be very proud of itself. Nobody works in this organization for money or fame. Only a dedication to duty and a high philosophy in life could make us all do this work."[66] He also dismissed speculation that Pakistan's nuclear weapons were based on any foreign design or help. He said, "I can swear to you that nobody in the world, no matter how friendly he is to Pakistan, has ever helped Pakistan. This I can say on oath. This is an indigenous technology and this should be really hammered in because this gives you pride. You have done it. Pakistan has done it. It is not borrowed technology. No one would give us literature, hardware, components, technology. For everything we have [had] to struggle. We had worked under these adverse circumstances and in spite of this adversity, my colleagues took it up as a challenge."[67]

The immense shock wave produced by the Chagai test was detected and monitored by seismic centers in the United States, Russia, Australia, and many other countries. A statement issued by the PAEC Directorate of Technical Development said, "The mission has, on the one hand, boosted the morale of the Pakistani nation by giving it an honorable position in the nuclear world, while on the other hand it validated scientific theory, design and previous results from cold tests. This has more than justified the creation and establishment of DTD more than 20 years back."[68]

The Pakistani Foreign Ministry reportedly described it as "Pakistan's finest hour."[69] Others boasted that Pakistan had become the world's seventh nuclear power and the first nuclear weapons state in the Islamic World.[70] As Pakistanis congratulated themselves and Prime Minister Sharif beamed with pride and enjoyed popularity, the nation prepared to stomach whatever punishment followed.

Part IV: Toward an Operational Deterrent

15   The Dawn of a New Nuclear Power

With the successful tests of Pakistan's nuclear weapon, Nawaz Sharif trium-phantly declared to have "settled the score," and restored strategic balance with India.[1] In Islamabad, a fiberglass model of the Ras Koh Hills was placed at the entrance to the capital, and replicas of *Ghauri* and *Shaheen* were situated on the main rotaries. Billboards of the prime minister, A. Q. Khan, and Samar Mubarkmand were all around the city. The Sharif government's domestic pop-ularity was at its zenith. However, national jubilation over the nuclear tests and congratulatory messages from Muslim countries were short lived.[2] By the end of May, and as the summer began, the true meaning of being an overtly nuclear power finally began to hit.

The national economy was in dire straits and crippled further by multiple sanctions, leading the Sharif government to adopt controversial fiscal policies. Meanwhile, intense diplomatic pressure from the West was aiming to place Paki-stan and India in restraints and to reintegrate the two countries into the interna-tional system. For India, nuclear weapons were the currency of power, a political tool, and the mark of a rising power. For Pakistan, a nuclear capability was the instrument for national survival and a manifestation of the "never again" men-tality that Zulfiqar Ali Bhutto had adopted some twenty-six years before. With no plan in place for the repercussions of conducting the nuclear tests, Pakistan engaged in intense diplomatic negotiations with the United States, leading to doctrinal thinking and the evolution of a command and control system. The circumstances under which decisions were made and international diplomacy conducted eventually shaped the Pakistani operational deterrent.

The Aftermath and Crises

A. Q. Khan's horse was now grazing in the meadows as the Sharif govern-ment braced itself to deal with the political and strategic ramifications of the tests. Almost immediately, multiple crises rose to the surface. A battle in the print media ensued between the Khan Research Laboratories (KRL) and the Pakistan Atomic Energy Commission (PAEC) over credit for the nuclear bomb. It became so vicious that General Karamat directed Director General of the Combat Development Directorate (DGCD) Major General Zulfiqar Ali Khan to intervene and "bring an end to this nonsense."[3] The unenviable responsibility to mediate between the two rival organizations finally fell on the author.[4]

At the same time, economic and financial experts informed the prime minister that remittances from the diaspora were not doubling; rather, foreign exchange in the country was flowing out—and so quickly that if not stopped, the country's reserves would decrease to dangerous levels. Pakistan's foreign debt was a staggering $30 billion, and the foreign exchange reserves were valued at between $600 million and $1.3 billion.[5] In an attempt to solve the problem, a national emergency was proclaimed under Article 232 of the constitution, allowing the government to freeze Pakistani citizens' foreign currency accounts (FCAs), which totaled some $7 billion, and convert them into local currency. Another $4 billion of FCAs belonging to nonresident Pakistanis was brought under severe restrictions.[6] These controversial steps shocked the nation, and rumors quickly spread that the ruling elites had been tipped off and had transferred overnight their wealth and FCAs into foreign accounts. The elites were spared while the rest of the population was made to "eat grass."

Although Pakistan's finance minister presented the fiscal logic behind this economic policy decision to freeze the dollar account, the Pakistani public had limited patience for such a sacrifice, as the government was already marred by myriad corruption scandals and accounts of lavish spending. As a result, Prime Minister Sharif's popularity plummeted, and he never recovered politically. Combined with several other missteps over the following eighteen months, the die was cast: in October 1999, the Sharif regime met its predictable end and the military returned to power.

In the meantime, on the international front, Pakistan was met with hostility. A few days after the nuclear test, President Clinton held a press conference in the Rose Garden and described the situation as a "self-defeating, wasteful, and dangerous" event that would make people "poorer and less secure."[7] Each foreign minister from the five permanent members of the UN Security Council (UNSC) followed suit and made their own denunciations on June 4, 1998, in Geneva. Two days later, Resolution 1172 (1998) was passed condemning both India's and Pakistan's nuclear tests and outlining numerous provisions for the two countries: (1) refrain from any further nuclear testing, (2) cease nuclear weapon development, (3) cease production of fissile material, (4) refrain from making weapons and from deploying them, (5) cease development of ballistic missiles, and (6) prevent the export of equipment, materials, and technology. More important, it urged India and Pakistan to resume dialogue on all outstanding issues, including Kashmir.[8]

The reference to Kashmir in the UNSC resolution hit a sensitive nerve with India, but in Pakistan it was received positively. It was the first time since November 5, 1965, that the Security Council had taken notice of this outstanding dispute as the root cause of problems in the region. In a month's time, however, the United States was trying to find a way to help India and Pakistan out of the impasse. While still trying to retain the spirit of the UNSC resolution, Washington understood that Pakistan faced the prospects of defaulting on debt servicing payments and needed financial help. And so the United States did not oppose Pakistan's seeking assistance from the International Monetary Fund (IMF), and even helped negotiate the IMF agreement.[9]

A Minimum Deterrence Posture for Pakistan

On July 17, 1998, President Clinton wrote a letter to Prime Minister Sharif in which he expressed a desire to move beyond the sanctions quagmire. Derived from UNSC 1172, Clinton set five benchmarks for the region: (1) unconditional adherence to the Comprehensive Test Ban Treaty (CTBT), (2) significant constraints on missiles, including a commitment not to deploy ballistic missiles, (3) termination of unsafeguarded fissile material production and accelerated progress on the negotiation of a Fissile Material Cut-off Treaty (FMCT), (4) adoption of international norms and policy guidelines to control the export of dangerous technology, and (5) resumption of direct political dialogue with India to settle Kashmir and other disputes. This set of benchmarks came to be known as the four legs and trunk of an elephant, or the 4+1. Clinton also indicated that, should Pakistan link the U.S. proposed nuclear restraint measures with a resolution on Kashmir, it would be a "prescription for diplomatic paralysis."[10]

On July 23, Strobe Talbott was sent on another mission to the region with a team of arms control experts led by Robert J. Einhorn. In anticipation of the visit, the author was tasked to prepare a comprehensive brief for Chief of the Army Staff (COAS) General Karamat that included the following aspects:

1. A pattern in the U.S. approach throughout the 1990s was that it sought unilateral self-restraint from Pakistan. The United States was seemingly going out of its way to accommodate India, while Pakistan was buckling under pressure. Pakistan's dilemma lay in its economic vulnerability, which allowed the United States to extract strategic concessions in exchange for providing succor to the ailing economy. How much does Pakistan trade off its vital security interests to keep its economy afloat?

2. The United States had identified two pressure points in Pakistan: economy and conventional force erosion. American clout in the Bretton Woods institutions (World Bank and IMF) enabled it to manipulate Pakistan through U.S. laws (Pressler, Glenn, and so forth), which acted as levers to extract strategic concessions from Pakistan. In contrast, this pressure tool did not apply to India, since India's economy was not as dependent on international financial institutions.

3. Pakistan's objective was to prevent Indian hegemony, retain strategic capability, and overcome economic difficulties. Pakistan's strategy would be to scuttle India's bid to legitimacy as a recognized nuclear weapons state and/or permanent member of the UNSC. Pakistan needed to avoid being entrapped in a debilitating arms race with India, while seeking to balance (not to achieve parity) with a carefully calibrated, finite deterrence policy. A minimum deterrence posture and negotiated agreement with the United States would enable it to do both: retain strategic capability and get on the road to economic recovery and growth.

4. Pakistan needed to approach the United States with a broad response, and identify an arc of interaction whereby it could strengthen converging strategic interests and narrow differences. In this vein, Pakistan needed to insist that Washington distinguish between India's status-oriented objective and Pakistan's security-driven response. The United States wanted to make sure that Pakistan did not damage the nonproliferation regime, while for Pakistan it was important not to buckle under pressure and economic vulnerability.

5. Finally, a separate policy review would need to be conducted in detail, which would consider a broader set of national policies on regional issues (Kashmir, relations with India, Afghanistan); relations with the Great Powers (United States, China, Europe, and Japan); and relations with Islamic countries, all embedded in an economic revival strategy. A nuclear-capable Pakistan would then be able to deter India from attacking Pakistan with its conventional forces. Thus nuclear deterrence would provide the peace dividend

and a window of opportunity through which Pakistan could restore economic order.

The COAS approved the policy review and sent it to the Foreign Office in order to coordinate a solid negotiating position. As previously mentioned, in his account of the negotiations, Strobe Talbott observed that in contrast to India, the "Pakistanis had no game plan. They always seemed to be hunkering down, lashing out, or flailing about."[11] But in reality, there was a flurry of activity in all government departments in preparation for his meeting. It was quite clear that the U.S. negotiating team was dismissing Pakistan's security concerns, while Islamabad was in a handicapped position in comparison to India.

In the last week of July, Robert Einhorn—accompanied by Alan Eastham, Deputy Chief of Mission to Pakistan at the U.S. embassy, Islamabad—visited General Headquarters (GHQ) and held a meeting in the Combat Development Directorate with Major General Zulfiqar Ali Khan and the author. Earlier that morning the U.S. embassy had sent the author an advance copy of a nonpaper titled "Elements of Minimum Deterrence Posture." In it Einhorn explained how assurance on recessed arsenals and several arms control steps would instill regional stability and if Pakistan adopted them might help mitigate U.S. sanctions. In essence the United States was seeking to segregate the conventional delivery systems from the nuclear delivery systems and geographically separate the aircraft/missile frames from the warheads. Einhorn asked Pakistan to take some steps unilaterally that would strengthen the U.S. ability to put pressure on India.

Einhorn explained the three key elements of the "minimum deterrence posture" suggested in the paper: (1) missile elements, (2) nuclear-capable aircraft, and (3) nuclear weapons elements.

Missile Elements

A minimum deterrence posture would require that Pakistan not conduct flight-testing of ballistic missiles or Missile Technology Control Regime (MTCR) Category 1 missiles other than *Ghauri* (liquid propellant) and one type of solid propellant short-range ballistic missile (SRBM), which would be limited to one test each annually. A ballistic missile flight-test notification should be given to the United States and to Pakistan's neighbors fourteen days prior to the intended test date. Pakistan would adhere to specified limits to missile airframes (live and training). Finally, "locational restrictions on missiles and associated equipment" were proposed with a demand that the United States be notified of missile, storage, and testing facility locations. Missiles of different types could not be located in the same place. The United States demanded that the storage of ballistic missiles and launchers be separated by at least one hundred km and also be located at least one hundred km from the border with India.

Nuclear-Capable Aircraft

The United States identified F-16s, Mirages, and A-5s (Fantan) as nuclear-capable aircraft and asked that they be separated from other types of combat aircraft. Explaining the proposal, Einhorn clarified that he realized that all fighter planes are dual-use, but simply requested that Pakistan separate the ones with nuclear missions.

Nuclear Weapons Elements

Pakistan was told it could not possess nuclear weapons in an assembled state, meaning that fissile material components would not be *mated* or armed, and the tritium or firing set not inserted into the system. The United States also demanded that nuclear storage sites maintain the minimum one hundred km distance from the Indian border and the minimum one hundred km between nuclear capable aircraft, missiles launchers, storage sites, and even flight-testing facilities.

Unlike Army Chief General Jehangir Karamat, DGCD Major General Zulfiqar Ali Khan was not known to be a "cool customer."[12] He had a Type A personality: although he was sharp and intelligent, he also was very impatient. Needless to say, when Zulfiqar Ali Khan read the nonpaper, he blew up. His first reaction was to cancel Einhorn's visit just two hours before the meeting. He then calmed down, when I suggested we should meet the team and give a logical professional response to the U.S. proposal. I then provided him with talking points that gave a preliminary response to the U.S. nonpaper and suggested that a detailed response would be given after due deliberations and interagency coordination. Major General Zulfiqar was well prepared before the U.S. team arrived.[13] My talking points included point by point response to U.S. proposals and broad contours:

- Welcoming the effort to help Pakistan think through conceptually what ought to be its "deterrence posture."

- Politely informing the U.S. experts that the presented concepts were relics of the Cold War, and that unlike the Soviet Union, Pakistan required a more nuanced approach.
- Postponing talk of concepts and the role of nuclear weapons in the national security policy. Although the weapon had been tested, it was not operational in any sense.

The meeting with Einhorn and Eastham was cordial and professional. Major General Zulfiqar Ali Khan and the author explained that Pakistan had no desire to up the ante by demonstrating nuclear prowess and challenging international norms against testing, but instead was forced to test because India chose the timing for tests for the second time after 1974, but now the regional security environment has changed. Einhorn was then assured that Pakistan would be forthcoming on all the 4+1 benchmarks, with varying degrees of emphasis, but would also observe New Delhi's position on these benchmarks. Islamabad would abide by its declared moratorium on further testing and would seriously consider CTBT signing proposal, if New Delhi was amenable. In addition it would be willing and open to discuss export control practices and laws, and finally, to commence a bilateral dialogue with India on all issues, especially regarding the core issue of Kashmir.

On the issue of fissile material, we expressed reservations. Pakistan would have been unable to declare a production moratorium, but was still willing to commence FMCT negotiations. Finally, Pakistan addressed missile restraint by assuring the United States that its arsenals were not deployed and that its delivery systems and warheads were already separated. However, Pakistan politely declined the segregation of aircraft proposal as well as refused to disclose the locations of its aircraft or to accept any means of their verification. Zulfiqar asked Einhorn if someone in the United States had cared to research Pakistan's size and physical geography before suggesting a minimum one hundred km barrier between facilities. Einhorn clarified that the U.S. proposals were merely suggestive and not prescriptive.

Overall, we explained that in principle Pakistan was amenable to discussing a range of possibilities that were realistic and that did not compromise Pakistani national security. Einhorn and Eastham appreciated the quick professional response at such short notice. Later, at a U.S. embassy reception, Eastham and other participants thanked me personally and told the author that the "U.S. experts team left positively surprised" at the interim response from GHQ and the

Foreign Ministry. The team is returning with better understanding of Pakistani positions and sensitivities. Islamabad promised a comprehensive response to the U.S. "minimum deterrence posture" nonpaper that would be discussed in a month's time before the UN General Assembly. Meanwhile, the United States mounted intense pressure on India and Pakistan to force the two countries to commit publicly to signing the CTBT within a year.

Amid upheavals, on August 7, 1998, terrorists struck two U.S. embassies, in Nairobi and Darussalam in East Africa, killing more than 250 people.[14] For the first time in public discourse, Osama bin Laden and Al-Qaeda were blamed for the crime, which originated from neighboring Afghanistan. The very next day, the Taliban announced the capture of the city of Mazar Sharif in western Afghanistan as a demonstration that it then held 80 percent of Afghanistan.

On August 21, 1998, General Jehangir Karamat was informed that General Joseph Ralston, Vice Chairman of the U.S. Joint Chiefs of Staff, would be making a stop in Islamabad and requested to meet with him at the airport. The United States had decided to strike back at Osama bin Laden in Afghanistan, and U.S. Navy ships were to fire some sixty Tomahawk cruise missiles over Pakistani territory. General Ralston's job was to convey to the army chief that the missiles flying over Baluchistan's airspace were American and not Indian, lest Pakistan attack India in retaliation. Needless to say, General Karamat felt slighted and did not appreciate the short notice. Even before the meeting was over, Tomahawk missiles were flying over Baluchistan.

The next morning, both the United States and Pakistan faced embarrassment. The Tomahawks were fired at an Afghanistan camp and did not kill Osama bin Laden, but rather, eleven Pakistanis belonging to Harkat Al Ansar who were allegedly training for *jihad* in Kashmir. Further reports arrived that several missiles fell short of the target and into Pakistan. As explained in Chapter 12, the Pakistanis scrambled to get the debris while the United States relied on the self-destruct mechanisms. Pakistan managed to recover some cruise missiles for examination. Brigadier Muhammad Anwar, Special Development Works (SDW) director, later told the author, "Technologies can fall from the skies. God was being kind to Pakistan."[15]

Pressure mounted on the Sharif government to overhaul Pakistan's security policy. Fast-paced nuclear diplomacy and the increasing threat of terrorism forced Pakistan to respond to the emerging challenges. On General Karamat's directive, the author wrote a comprehensive strategic policy review that is outlined here from memory and some personal notes. The fundamental premise of the analysis was that Pakistan had entered a phase of its history in which it must make tough choices. Pakistani behavior as a nuclear power would likely come under severe scrutiny; the long shadow of India would always be politically, diplomatically, and economically challenging; and the increasing unacceptability of the Taliban regime in Afghanistan would become a handicap for Pakistan. The paper included the following major points:

1. Pakistan must make a choice between its Taliban policy and the preservation of a nuclear capability; Pakistan cannot afford to engage on both fronts.

2. Attacks in East Africa have provided Pakistan with an opportunity to reverse the Afghan policy by forcing the Taliban regime to deport the Al Qaeda leadership or else withdraw Pakistani support. The United States would need Pakistan's help in fighting Al Qaeda. As such, Pakistan has a chance to throw off nuclear sanctions, and begin an economic revival.

3. Pakistan must immediately harness all security and strategic organizations under a cohesive and accountable command system. Supporting asymmetric strategies in Afghanistan and Kashmir is likely to come under the radar of the world; hence the policy must now be reviewed or calibrated.

4. Pakistan's nuclear diplomacy must continue to engage constructively with the United States to mitigate sanctions and continue close communications with China.

Unbeknownst to the author, another paper was privately sent to the army chief by former Pakistan ambassador to the United States Maleeha Lodhi. At the time, she was editor of *The NEWS*, a major English daily in Islamabad. In this paper she argued that changed circumstances require immediate re-evaluation of national security policy, that preserving Pakistan's nuclear deterrent was a top national priority, and that Pakistan had to be flexible on other issues, especially review of its Afghanistan policy. General Karamat was in agreement. He endorsed both papers and sent them to the Foreign Office and possibly the Inter-Services Intelligence (ISI) for further inputs and comments. Before sending them to the prime minister, the Foreign Office decided to invite all key ambassadors from major countries to Islamabad for a two-day envoy's conference in order to deliberate the new challenges Pakistan faced.

Meanwhile GHQ was focused on three principal tasks: (1) develop a nuclear doctrine; (2) provide inputs to nuclear diplomacy and the deterrence posture; and (3) plan the command and control organization. Military Operations (MO) Directorate was the veritable secretariat of GHQ, where all inputs were coor-

dinated, and the Arms Control and Disarmament Affairs (ACDA) Directorate in close concert with ministry was already working on nuclear diplomacy.
Another organization, called the Evaluation and Research (E&R) Directorate,
had been functional for some time and analyzed emerging concepts and military doctrines. After the nuclear test, E&R was directed to coordinate with the
MO Directorate, examine the future doctrinal compulsions, and undertake the
planning of command and control organization. By late summer three directorates within GHQ were tasked as "working groups" on doctrine, command
and control, and nuclear diplomacy, what were often referred to as next steps
after becoming an overt nuclear power.

Strategic Restraint Regime

The author prepared a comprehensive response to the U.S. minimum deterrence response nonpaper that was presented in several in-house meetings
in GHQ and the Foreign Office and subjected to intense debate and review.
This proposal was an offshoot of the Strategic Policy Review paper that had
been prepared earlier in June and had become the overall basis of the post-test
negotiations with Strobe Talbott. The Pakistani nonpaper revolved around two
central tenets. The first argument was based on an altruistic notion that arms
control makes better security sense for Pakistan; given its structural weaknesses
and a prostrate economy, strategic competition with India was unwise. Pakistan's focus was regional and its nuclear weapons were specific to deterring India from aggression against it. Pakistan's avowed policy was to maintain deterrence at a sustainable level—that is, minimum credible deterrence and avoiding
a debilitating arms race. Establishing constraints and keeping the force goals at
low levels made sense, but could come about only if India could be netted into
reciprocal constraints that would affect Pakistan security directly. The second
principle was that nuclear restraint could not be an end in itself. It is essentially
tied to conventional force restraint. The purpose of acquiring a nuclear capability was to possess a force multiplier as the ultimate balancer against India, so as
to deny it victory and deter aggression at either level, nuclear or conventional.

With these premises, the Strategic Restraint Regime (SRR) for South Asia
was conceived and consisted of three interlocking elements: (1) agreed reciprocal measures for nuclear and missile restraint to prevent deliberate or accidental use of nuclear weapons; (2) establishment of a conventional restraint

measure; (3) and establishment of a political mechanism for resolving bilateral conflicts, especially the core issue of Jammu and Kashmir.

The SRR concept is a regional restraint arrangement based on the acknowledged importance and tradition of confidence building measures (CBMs) in South Asia. It encompasses reciprocal constraints on nuclear, missile, and conventional force capabilities under a mutually agreed verifiable regime. The India-Pakistan regime ought to be based on five fundamental principles: (1) political climate and culture of conflict resolution conducive to reduction of tension; (2) fair regime that proffers proportionate and balanced obligations on all sides; (3) recognition that nuclear deterrence posture is affected by conventional force imbalance and structural asymmetry; (4) the creation of an institutionalized mechanism to prevent escalation of crisis; and (5) recognition that supreme national security interests might warrant withdrawal from the restraint arrangement. No regime works in a vacuum, and thus an overarching political framework is necessary. A triad of peace, security, and progress would include a process of dialogue to identify issues of peace and security and to find a mechanism for peaceful settlement of all outstanding disputes, including Jammu and Kashmir; an agreement to exercise restraint on military forces; and high-level interaction to promote trade and transit to help development of each other and to create a climate of cooperation and investment.

Based on the above framework, the SRR proposal examined in depth each element of the U.S. minimum deterrence proposal and suggested a regional approach along the following lines.

Nuclear Restraints

In terms of nuclear weapons, ambiguity helps achieve better stability. Operational necessity demands ambiguity on the state of preparation, assembly, location of fissile material components, and location and state of arming, fusing, and firing mechanisms. By ensuring secrecy and perceived retention of retaliatory strike capability (that is, credible deterrence), the Pakistani proposal enhances stability.

On the segregation of nuclear-capable aircraft, Pakistan had a dilemma. Its small inventory of strike-capable aircraft, as in any other tactical air force around the world, was utilized in a variety of roles. Thus the "nuclear-capable" classification could not refer to any particular set of aircraft. This aspect of the proposal was therefore not feasible.

Missile Restraints

A missile stability regime involved three kinds of restraints—deployment, developmental, and locational. Pakistan boldly proposed nondeployment of ballistic missiles, including not mating nuclear-capable missiles with the launching unit/delivery vehicles and not acquiring a ballistic missile system.

Pakistan found rationale in the U.S. proposal of exercising developmental restraint and proposed a mutually acceptable minimum ceiling of missile production and categories of missiles, as well as a range/payload limit for the subcontinent. Both India and Pakistan could restrict missile development to a maximum range of twenty-five hundred km and 1,000 kg payload. In addition, both countries could create a fixed limit for launcher production. However, limits on the number of missiles and warheads produced could not be agreed on for operational reasons.

SRR unambiguously opposed deploying antiballistic missiles (ABMs) and sea-based nuclear weapons such as submarine launched ballistic missiles (SLBMs). The proposal went further to declare South Asia land and sea areas as ABM- and SLBM-free zones (that is, no acquisition, development, or deployment).

Flight-Testing

With regard to restrictions on flight-testing, Pakistan agreed with the U.S. proposal to give prior notification of flight tests. India and Pakistan would mutually negotiate the number of days and location of the flight tests. Pakistan was open to a mutually agreed upon limit for annual flight tests, but cautioned that this requirement would impede design development. In addition, both countries should avoid testing during an escalation of tensions, and in general the tests should be conducted away from shared borders.

Finally, on the question of locational and training restrictions, Pakistan clarified that asymmetries in geographical depth and terrain preclude a symmetrical locational arrangement between India and Pakistan. It was not possible to have a fixed agreement on geographical separation. Instead five steps were proposed: (1) all missiles must be maintained in a 'nonready to launch' state—that is, missile frames and launchers kept separate; (2) peacetime garrisons of all missile units must be kept transparent and, if possible, be included in the verification mechanism; (3) both countries must agree not to use live missiles for training; (4) locations of storage sites for missiles and warheads must be adequately distant from the borders; and finally, for obvious operational reasons, (5) neither India nor Pakistan could agree to a U.S. proposal of sharing the actual location of warhead and missile storage.

Conventional Force Restraints

Conventional force restraint allows a step-by step approach to minimize the risk of war and keep nuclear weapons on a nondeployed status. As long as a safety firewall exists between warheads and the delivery systems, a restraint regime promises nuclear stability. Use of force as an instrument of policy or coercion is unacceptable in the nuclear environment. The only way to prevent nuclear deployment or the possible use of a weapon, whether deliberate or accidental, is to avoid a conventional war and resolve all conflicts by other means—for example, political initiatives and imaginative sustained negotiating (the third component of the SRR).

Given the history of wars and crises in the region, it was surmised that strategic assembly of conventional forces (for example, Brasstacks and the 1990 Kashmir crises) constitute a threat to the neighboring country. Pakistan proposed four steps in the short and long run: (1) both sides identify the offensive strike forces of the other, agree to keep their own immobilized in peacetime locations, and negotiate a process of notification if these forces are to move; (2) both countries may designate low force zones or exclusion zones for a certain weapon system near the border areas; (3) should either country desire to move forces in the designated low force zones, a regime should exist to notify/monitor movement of forces; and (4) in the long run, both sides must have agreed on a proportionate force reduction similar to the pattern of conventional forces in Europe.

In addition, the SRR suggested three unique concepts for the region: red alert notification; a joint verification commission (JVC); and the establishment of a Nuclear Risk Reduction Centre (NRRC). The concept of "red alert notification" was to formally notify the JVC in the event of an emergency. Notification of a red alert implies that any restraint, for example on nonmating, will no longer be valid and consequently the verification commission will no longer be provided access to information that was agreed upon for normal circumstances. Acts by either side that could trigger a red alert would be specified in the regime.

The anticipated JVC was to comprise officials from India, Pakistan, and neutral countries who would function under the aegis of the United Nations. This entity could also be expanded from the existing UN mission known as UN Military Observer Group in India and Pakistan (UNMOGIP), which had lost its significance since it was formed in 1949. JVC would monitor the restraint regimes, agreed upon by both countries, and would receive notification on the red alert status.

Finally, in order to reduce other risks associated with nuclear weapons and their means of delivery, an NRRC was proposed. It would be established in the capital cities of Pakistan and India and follow a Soviet-U.S. precedent. Its 24/7 system would be constantly staffed with professionals who would adhere to procedures in order to avoid misunderstandings. The NRRC would augment the existing hot lines between the two Military Operational Directorates.

As with most international treaties and agreements, a duration and withdrawal clause was also suggested. Should supreme national security considerations necessitate that the agreed arrangement could no longer be implemented, either side could invoke the withdrawal clause. A notification to this effect would be given to the JVC, which would immediately inform the depository (for example, the UN secretary general) and specify the cause for such a move. This notification would be a method of preventing and eliminating a nuclear surprise.

U.S. Response to the Pakistani Initiative

U.S. diplomatic strategy in South Asia was to deal directly with both India and Pakistan separately and at the same time to urge the two countries to talk bilaterally with each other. On September 15 and 16, 1998, just a week before a UN General Assembly session, a team of Pakistani experts led by Ambassador Munir Akram and assisted by Major General Zulfiqar Ali Khan, DGCD, and the author presented the above SRR proposal to a U.S. delegation led by Bob Einhorn. The U.S. delegation was surprised at the deliberation and details, especially given that Pakistan had no prior experience of arms control diplomacy of this kind. After about nine months, Einhorn and his team gave preliminary responses and a comprehensive critique of the Pakistani SRR proposal in an expert-level dialogue held in Geneva on June 30, 1999.

The United States reiterated its position that nuclear tests reduced the security of both countries and that the ongoing competition to develop nuclear forces and ballistic missiles raised the stakes. Both India and Pakistan had declared a desire to avoid an arms race and to establish a "minimum deterrent," but statements had not been supported by actions. The United States viewed Pakistan's perception of threat in a different light, and considered Pakistan's estimates of India's fissile stockpiles to be exaggerated.

It was agreed that the regional environment was very different from the Cold War, and it was acknowledged that Pakistan would not be able to move forward on U.S. proposals of restraint unless India took certain steps. While Pakistan thought that it needed to maintain a balanced force structure, the United States suggested that competition be dampened in the near term and a basis established for elimination of such strategic capabilities. Pakistan could not agree with this latter objective.

Pakistan and the United States generally agreed that missiles should not be mated with the launchers and that separate storage would provide time buffers—necessary in order to reduce the chances of a quick response in a crisis situation. In addition, the United States sensed Pakistan's desire to establish an elaborate command-and-control system promptly. It advised that a robust system required acquisition of an advanced intelligence collection capability, which would require enormous expenditure by both India and Pakistan.

Responding to the concept of "red alert" notification, the United States felt it could be useful only if it served as a means of reducing tensions, but would be counterproductive if used as a tool to "up the ante" in a crisis. From Pakistan's standpoint, Washington was apparently concerned only with containing nuclear/missile development and continued to ignore the conventional imbalance and India's threat to Pakistan.

The Lahore Agreement

Interaction with the United States became an intensive learning experience for Pakistan. Substantive exchange of ideas in meetings and nonpapers with U.S. teams helped both sides understand the obstacles to and prospects for a minimum deterrence posture. However, this process also created suspicions, as India and Pakistan were blind to the discussions held between the United States and the other country. Some quarters of the Pakistani bureaucracy felt suspicious of the growing public friendship between Strobe Talbott and Indian Foreign Minister Jaswant Singh, which lent credence to the theory that the United States was favoring India.[16]

In September 1998, during the UN General Assembly, the prime ministers of India and Pakistan met on the sidelines and decided to resume the composite dialogue that had been stalled since February after the arrival of the new right wing, Hindu government in India and the nuclear tests.

Responding to the concerns of the international community and pressure from the nonproliferation regime, India and Pakistan in their bilateral discussions decided to prioritize two segments of the eight-legged composite dialogue that had been started by the Sharif-Gujral initiative the previous year. The two segments were Jammu and Kashmir; and Peace, Security, and CBMs. An Indian team led by Foreign Secretary K. Ragunath was due in Islamabad on October 15 and 16, 1998. Pakistan decided to offer the SRR to India in the Peace, Security, and CBMs segment of the dialogue.

The dialogue's timing was not entirely favorable for Pakistan. Unexpectedly, General Jehangir Karamat tendered his resignation after a disagreement with the prime minister on October 7, 1998. Two days earlier, General Karamat had publicly emphasized the need for institutionalized decision-making in the country; he preferred the idea of a national security council. The Sharif regime regarded this incident as a rare criticism of his authority and style of governance. Sharif asked Karamat to resign and appointed in his place General Pervez Musharraf, who began making appointments and transfers.[17] DGCD Major General Zulfiqar Ali Khan was promoted to three stars and posted immediately on a civil assignment in Lahore. His replacement was Major General Amjad Ali, who was to report after a few weeks.

With India's delegation arriving in Islamabad for a composite dialogue on Jammu and Kashmir and Peace Security and CBMs next week, the new Chief of Army Staff summoned the Director General Military Operations Major General Tauqeer Zia and the author to brief him on the two segments of the forthcoming dialogue with India. In the meeting I explained the contours of the Strategic Policy Review, which was the master document that outlined the premise of the new security environment and formed the basis of the SRR. It also gave the backdrop of its origin and summary of its outcome with the United States in New York. General Musharraf approved the SRR proposal from GHQ that was passed on to Foreign Secretary Shamshad Ahmad, who was leading negotiations with India. General Musharraf told the author to report back and brief him after the event, not just on the outcome of dialogue with India but also on the entire gambit of nonproliferation and nuclear policy issues. I handed him relevant files on the subject for his study.

Pakistan presented an abridged version of the SRR to India, and the resulting discussion emphasized three interlocking elements: (1) non-use of force, and peaceful settlement of disputes; (2) a Strategic Restraint Regime for South Asia, which included nuclear and conventional force restraint and stabilization measures; and (3) CBMs that included a review of existing measures, prevention and violation of air space and territorial waters, revision of ground-border rules, prior notification of military exercises, upgrading of communication links between DGMOs, activation of new hotlines between the prime ministers, and restraint on propaganda hostile to each other.

This dialogue was the first major discussion between India and Pakistan on security issues that included nuclear and conventional force arms control. However, the Indian delegation had no military officer at the meeting, and the diplomats barely anticipated such an elaborate proposal. The author was representing the GHQ in the delegation, and it became clear that India was prepared only to have generalized discussions on these issues.

India dismissed the notion of conventional force restraint with Pakistan outright, informing the delegation that India faced threats besides Pakistan. However, it was willing to discuss nuclear and missile restraints and nuclear doctrines only. India offered a "no first use" doctrine agreement. Indian diplomats interpreted the link between conventional force restraints and nuclear restraints as containing an implicit threat of upping the nuclear ante.[18] India insisted that the conventional force option was open as long as "proxy wars" continued to be waged against India.[19]

Pakistan responded by dismissing the "proxy" allegation, and insisted that insurgencies are a result of injustices and unresolved disputes. The Pakistanis further argued that tying down the nuclear hand while freeing up the conventional hand was tantamount to legitimizing use of conventional force by India, and delegitimizing the use of nuclear weapons by Pakistan. What, then, was the logic of undergoing the three decades of sanctions and international opprobrium to acquire capability? The dialogue deadlocked on the fundamental concepts. Pakistan could not accept India's "no-first-use" proposal, and India could not accept "no use of conventional force." In fact, Pakistan did not want to bring into the negotiations doctrinal aspects, which it deemed as classified. Rather, Pakistan wanted both nuclear-capable countries to finally agree on the principle of nonaggression and "no use of force" to settle disputes and address the root causes of conflict. India was not interested.

As the dialogue was coming to an end, an Indian delegate admitted to the author that the security and arms control concepts proposed by Pakistan seemed alien to them, a relic of the Cold War not applicable to the current circum-

stances. Indian diplomats advised the Pakistanis not to "speak the Western language," and boasted that "we are the keepers of great civilizations; quite capable
of inventing our own terminologies and developing regional security concepts
rather than borrowing it from the West." India and Pakistan exchanged at least
twenty new proposals for peace and security and several ideas on arms control
issues to review as homework for the next meeting.[20]

For the next three months India and Pakistan deliberated in their respective
capitals over how to bridge the differences for the next round of discussions to
be held in New Delhi on February 15, 1999. Around February 5, it was disclosed
that the expert-level dialogue would be elevated to the executive level, as a dramatic political initiative was being undertaken by the Indian prime minister
to travel to Lahore on the inaugural bus service between the Indian town of
Amritsar and Pakistan's Lahore. The peace and security landscape was about to
change completely, prompting the political leadership from both countries to
pressure the bureaucrats on reaching a draft agreement within ten days, so as to
ensure success at the Lahore summit scheduled for February 20.

On the day of the summit, Prime Minister Vajpayee arrived in Lahore. The
Chinese defense minister was also paying an official visit, which had been scheduled much earlier. This unexpected turn of events created a conflict of interest,
and Pakistan wanted neither side to feel slighted or rebuffed. The Pakistanis
decided to manage both visits with the foreign minister and the three chiefs of
the armed forces remaining in Islamabad in the morning, then flying to Lahore
to meet the Indian prime minister in the afternoon, and then returning back to
Islamabad in the evening to attend a banquet for the Chinese defense minister.
This particular day is recorded as one of the hallmarks of Pakistan's diplomatic
history.

The following day was another monumental event between India and Pakistan. First, Prime Minister Vajpayee visited Minar-e-Pakistan (the national
monument), and recorded in the guestbook that a strong and prosperous Pakistan was in India's interest.[21] The same day, the two prime ministers signed
what was called the Lahore Declaration, in which they shared a vision for peace
and stability with three major commitments: (1) identify efforts to resolve all
issues, including Kashmir; (2) identify a composite and integrated dialogue
process; and (3) take immediate steps for reducing the risks of unauthorized
use of nuclear weapons. Attached to this declaration was a Memorandum of
Understanding (MOU) signed between the two foreign secretaries on nuclear
and security issues. In essence, the Lahore MOU subsumed the peace, security

and CBM dialogue that had transpired since the previous October. For three consecutive days and nights, Indian and Pakistan bureaucrats (including the author) consolidated those multiple security concepts, doctrines, arms control issues, and CBMs into eight concrete agenda items for the future.[22]

In effect, the Lahore MOU created a framework on which to build serious arms control measures and CBMs in South Asia. In many ways, these concepts, though derived from Cold War arms control ideas, were fairly advanced and could have been formulated into a comprehensive treaty that subsumed an arms control regime.

The two sides committed to bilateral consultations on security concepts and nuclear doctrines and to undertake national measures to reduce the risks of accidental or unauthorized use of nuclear weapons. In specific terms, both India and Pakistan agreed to provide advanced notification on ballistic missile flight tests, with a potential to include a bilateral agreement; to prevent incidents at sea; and to maintain their respective moratoria on conducting further tests.

Three additional measures were adopted in the process: to notify each other of any accident or unexplained incident in which there is risk of nuclear fallout or misinterpretation of signals, and to this end identify and establish an appropriate communication mechanism. Next, they agreed to improve and upgrade the existing communication link between respective DGMOs to make it fail-safe and secure. And thirdly, they agreed to set up a mechanism to ensure the effective implementation of the CBMs.

The Lahore MOU promised to let the experts decide on the strategy to reach a bilateral agreement and set a deadline for mid-1999. Unfortunately for the region, by that time both countries were in the midst of a mini war in the frozen heights of a place called Kargil.

16   A Shaky Beginning: Kargil and Its Aftermath

General Pervez Musharraf's tenure as army chief began under tense domestic circumstances and burgeoning regional crises. Pakistan's security policy on Afghanistan had been on the U.S. radar since the Al Qaeda attack on U.S. embassies in East Africa, and tensions with India over Kashmir and the LOC were continuing.[1] The economy faltered under intense pressure from international sanctions, fiscal indiscipline, and Sharif's policies of extravagant spending on mega projects. The army worried that the economic situation would erode the national defense capability.[2]

Within a week of Musharraf's takeover as Chief of Army Staff, two contradictory developments were shaping up. As explained previously, on October 16–18 the foreign secretaries of Pakistan and India were engaged in peace and security dialogues, which also included discussions on Jammu and Kashmir in Islamabad. On the day negotiations commenced, the Indian military reported Pakistani military attacks from across the LOC in the Siachin glacier area, which India supposedly beat back.[3] This seemingly contradictory approach of dueling on the battlefield in Kashmir while discussing peace and security at the diplomatic level was nothing new for Pakistani policy-makers and was considered to be a continuation of a familiar pattern in the region. In the summer of 1997, prime ministers Sharif and Gujral took bold peace initiatives to Maldives, giving birth to the composite dialogues, while the two militaries lobbed artillery shells across the LOC, especially in the Neelum/Kishanganga Valley. These operations would become the tactical cause of the infamous Kargil conflict.

At the outset of his command, and against this backdrop, the new army chief created two avoidable problems. First, he set out to restore confidence between General Headquarters (GHQ) and the civilian government, but instead faced a new source of friction over the role and responsibility of the newly appointed Inter-Services Intelligence Directorate (DGISI). Second, he set the stage for the Kargil conflict by approving a series of bold, controversial moves along the LOC.[4] These two events provoked a series of missteps and decisions that determined the course of history for Pakistan—barely a year after its nuclear tests.

The Kargil episode in particular set Pakistan on a dizzying course of domestic and regional crises that produced further deterioration in the country's civil-military relations, underscoring the incoherence in Pakistani governance and strategic decision-making. This period was indeed a very shaky beginning for Pakistan as a nuclear power. In the end, the United States pressured an isolated Prime Minister Sharif into an unconditional withdrawal from the LOC based on questionable intelligence about a planned nuclear deployment in the conflict. A loss of confidence in Sharif led the military to take power on October 12, 1999, causing another layer of military sanctions overlaid with nuclear sanctions. Millions of Pakistani citizens were in line for eating more grass.

Musharraf in the Line of Fire

One factor that immediately affected Musharraf's leadership was the manner in which his predecessor, General Jehangir, was made to resign. Prime Minister Nawaz Sharif had a reputation for cultivating poor relationships within the government.[5] Sharif's maverick governing style had pitted him against the presidency and the judiciary in his two tenures as prime minister (first from 1990 to 1993, and then from 1997 to 1999) and against four consecutive army chiefs in the same period. He hastened the resignation of two presidents, one chief justice of the Supreme Court, and one army chief.[6] The military felt that these actions were an unnecessarily punitive attempt on the prime minister's part to assert power and undermine not only the role of other state institutions but also the morale of the armed forces.[7]

Musharraf was acutely conscious of the fate of his predecessor. Referring to the Karamat episode when the army chief was suddenly and unceremoniously forced to resign, Musharraf wrote in his memoir, "We would not allow another humiliation to befall us in case the prime minister tried something like this again, but we would only react, never act unilaterally."[8] However, Musharraf also knew that the difficult times required the army's support to the government. With this in mind, in his very first address to officers in GHQ in October 1998, Musharraf promised a new era for civil-military relations in which the military would lend institutional assistance to the civilian government in all areas.

In his first few days as army chief, Musharraf reshuffled commanders and staff and made several key organizational changes. The most significant of these were three appointments: the replacement of the Rawalpindi corps commander with Lieutenant-General Mahmud Ahmed, the promotion and appointment of Lieutenant-General Muhammad Aziz Khan to Chief of General Staff, and the posting of Lieutenant-General Ziauddin as director general of DGISI.[9] These three personalities greatly influenced future organizational and leadership changes, as well as domestic and regional crises that profoundly affected Pakistan for the next decade.

The latter appointment deserves close attention, because it was Prime Minister Sharif who personally demanded Lieutenant-General Ziauddin's appointment as DGISI. That the two were family friends and both ethnically Kashmiri made the military suspicious of favoritism and manipulation of senior military leadership.[10] Like his predecessors, Musharraf was vehemently opposed to civilian interference within the military command, and so he demanded oversight of DGISI's activities, which created tensions between GHQ and ISI.[11]

This development had severe repercussions on the national security apparatus. Within six months of Pakistan's becoming a de facto nuclear power, two premier security institutions—GHQ and ISI—were engaged inwardly in undermining each other rather than synergizing efforts to assess the new security environment. Apparently, Prime Minister Sharif played off the two, hoping to keep the military at bay—further strengthening his grip on power.[12] As decisions were being made on nuclear issues, inputs from the national security bureaucracy and the military were sidelined—this proved to be a dangerous practice.[13]

Meanwhile, international pressure was mounting on Islamabad over its nuclear ambitions. The United States was applying pressure on Pakistan on four issues: signing the Comprehensive Test Ban Treaty (CTBT), commencing negotiations on a Fissile Material Cut-off Treaty (FMCT), enacting export controls laws, and emplacing nuclear and missile restraints on deployments and developments. It was also seeking cooperation from Pakistan on Afghanistan, especially regarding Al Qaeda. However, Islamabad was occupied with the central objective highlighted in the 1998 "Strategic Policy Review": how to mitigate the economic impact of nuclear sanctions without compromising national security objectives, the core of which was to preserve a nuclear capability.[14]

At this juncture, seemingly disconnected and oblivious to the political context outlined above, General Musharraf was presented with the problems at the LOC in the Northern Areas. The new army chief had inquired about the details of an Indian report of a Pakistani attack on some Indian posts in Siachin that India had repulsed. When Musharraf was informed there was no Pakistani attack and this fake report was propagated to coincide with October 16, 1998—the same day that the Indian and Pakistani foreign secretaries were meeting in Islamabad—he suspected something was amiss.[15] So he brought in his close confidante Lieutenant-General Mahmud Ahmad to monitor the region as Commander 10 Corps, Rawalpindi.

Lieutenant-General Mahmud Ahmed, himself newly appointed as pivotal corps commander, was determined to improve security in his command and did not leave anything to chance.[16] In this context, a core group of senior military officers, composed of Lieutenant-General Mahmud Ahmad, Lieutenant-General Muhammad Aziz, and Major General Javed Hassan, who was General Officer Commanding (GOC) Force Command Northern Areas (FCNA), presented a bold plan to Musharraf to strengthen defenses by gaining ground in the watershed on the LOC in Kashmir. The military operation, known as the Kargil plan, was to be conducted in the FCNA region in Kargil by troops under the command of Javed Hassan.[17]

FCNA created a plan to take a forward defensive posture by moving deployed troops to occupy the watersheds on the mountaintops. This move would require expanding the defenses into several new positions into the gaps, as well as establishing new posts on crests and ridgelines. When troops moved in and found vacated areas resulting from the winter retreat of Indian forces, they simply occupied those vacant posts, just as had been done by Indian troops for the past several decades. Not only were the FCNA defenses improved, but also at places they dominated the strategic highway linking Srinagar, capital of Kashmir, with Leh (Ladakh province). A tactical operation thus became one of strategic significance.[18]

For the operation to succeed, utmost secrecy was essential, and so only a few individuals were involved in the planning. The maneuvers required stealth and deception to operate on those treacherous heights where movements are painfully slow and sustaining logistics is a nightmare. Most likely, this plan was originally meant as a war contingency, but under the circumstances it would demonstrate the bold and decisive character of the new military leadership.[19] The plan was possibly first presented to the new army chief in late December 1998 and perhaps a more detailed one later, in mid-January.[20]

Musharraf was consumed with the secrecy and surprise aspect of the plan and made sure that its details were on a need-to-know basis.[21] Prime Minister Sharif visited Skardu in the Northern Areas and held briefings in FCNA on

January 29, 1999, which suggests that he was at least secretly tipped off about the impending operation. Again on February 5, 1999, Sharif visited the Neelum Valley (Kel sector), where Corps Commander Lieutenant-General Mahmud Ahmed personally briefed him.[22] In his address to troops in Skardu, Prime Minister Sharif rewarded the army by raising their pay scale.[23] However, Sharif denies that he was knowledgeable or gave any prior approval of the Kargil operations and was only briefed on the operations after they were well advanced.[24]

By the spring of 1999, Pakistan had embarked on two contradictory tracks with India. As Pakistani soldiers were crossing the LOC and occupying abandoned positions, Sharif was receiving the Indian prime minister in Lahore. The latter led to an upbeat summit culminating in the famous Lahore Agreement that promised peace and security. But after the Lahore process was underway, Sharif did not reverse the daring military operation that continued until late spring.[25]

War on the Roof of the World

On the icy peaks in the Northern Areas along the LOC, Indian troops had vacated posts in October and November 1998, a routine measure both Indian and Pakistani forces undertook during the harsh winter months. The vacating troops retreat to lower heights only to return in the spring or summer of the following year. Some of these posts are at elevations ranging from twelve to seventeen thousand feet above sea level and are strategically located to overlook major valleys and roads. One such road is Highway 1A, which passes through the major town of Kargil. It serves as a link between Srinagar (capital of Indian-administered Kashmir) and Leh (capital of Ladakh Division in Kashmir) and as an artery for supplies to Indian troops deployed on the Siachin glacier, which was occupied in 1984.[26]

A consistent feature of the Pakistani strategic culture since the Siachin episode was to maintain constant vigilance and an aggressive defense posture in the area. Nowhere else in the army did the axiom "Never again" dominate routine activities as much as in the FCNA, which was held responsible for the humiliating loss of Siachin glacier. And so any new commander posted in the Northern Areas was obsessed with never losing an inch of territory under his command.[27] This culture of aggressiveness along the LOC in the northern fringes of LOC had continued, even as India and Pakistan were engaged in several peaceful dialogues throughout the 1990s.[28]

When Indian troops vacated the posts in 1998, Pakistan's brigade-size force of four infantry battalions comprising the Northern Light Infantry (NLI) stealthily occupied the empty positions. NLI soldiers lived in the vicinity, were acclimated to the environment, and belonged to a paramilitary organization, the members of which were routinely integrated with regular army brigades for LOC duties. These soldiers were armed primarily with antipersonnel land mines, man-portable air defense missiles, light artillery pieces, rifles, machine guns, mortars, and other small arms. Speaking their local languages (Balti, Shinai, and Gilgiti dialects) and wearing civilian clothes, the troops deceived Indian intelligence into believing that they were local *mujahideen* (freedom fighters), who were lightly armed or part of the ongoing Kashmir insurgency.[29]

Between December 1998 and April 1999, the NLI was able to establish positions in five distinct areas: Mushkoh, Dras, Kargil, Batalik, and Shyok. From Dras, the Pakistani troops could interdict Highway 1A. According to Pakistani sources, such deep penetration of Indian-held territory had not been planned but was the result of "mission creep."[30] By the beginning of May, Pakistan held approximately 100 to 130 positions within a five-hundred-square-mile area up to five miles deep across the LOC.

The first encounter between NLI soldiers and Indian soldiers occurred on May 2, 1999, when an Indian patrol near the Shyok sector was fired upon. Five days later, on May 7, a second encounter took place, in the Batalik sector, and then a third on May 10 in the Dras sector.[31] Panic and confusion reigned in the Indian camps when the penetration was discovered. India realized that the intruders were not militants but well-trained troops better organized than had originally been assessed. As clashes broke out between India and Pakistan on the LOC, the Indian Army brought forward its 3rd Infantry Division and by mid-May was engaging all of the penetrations. That summer India was lucky. Mountain passes over those heights usually remain blocked for long periods in winter. Two such passes—Zoji La on the Indian side and Burzil on the Pakistani—were important lifelines for the deployed troops. Zoji La pass, which usually does not open up for movement of supplies until late spring or early summer, opened earlier, allowing India to send in troop reinforcements. Burzil pass on Pakistan's side, equally important for supply deliveries, remained closed for much longer.[32]

This situation upset Pakistan's Kargil plan, which was based on consolidating key positions before the Indian passes reopened. The tables began to turn around mid-June, when India was able to bring in reserve forces from far distances, escalating the conflict vertically. The Indian Army launched mass attacks with brigade-size forces as well as its Mirage 2000 aircraft with laser-guided munitions and artillery. The Pakistani troops hunkered down, but the improvised bunkers in their new defense lines across the LOC were not strong or hardened sufficiently to sustain that kind of firepower. Furthermore, troops from Indian Corps 15 and 16 that were deployed on counterinsurgency duties were redeployed because of a potential conventional war.[33] In addition, the 6th Mountain Division deployed on the Chinese border was also moved by the end of May, increasing India's military readiness to expand operations anywhere. Even though this war was being fought on those freezing heights, the Indian Navy also wanted to engage by moving its Eastern Command ships from the Bay of Bengal to Western Command in the Arabian Sea. The forces also included an amphibious brigade from the Andaman and Nicobar islands (Operation Talwar, or "Sword").[34]

Fear of horizontal escalation by India or Pakistan began to mount as the month of June was ending. A massive retaliation from India caught Pakistan by surprise.[35] India realized that many NLI positions were unsustainable and that the troops had overextended themselves without any defensive support or ability to resupply. Consequently, many of the posts were captured or destroyed.[36]

Kargil's planners had calculated that India's war-expanding capacity would be limited. They thought that India's forces were worn thin from the ongoing Kashmiri insurgency and constant tensions.[37] Pakistan also believed that the international community would view the Kargil incursions as a normal pattern of military activity along the LOC, similar to India's occupation of the Siachin glacier fifteen years before.

However, these calculations proved flawed. India's information campaign and tactical successes within the Kargil area began gaining popularity domestically and internationally. The story began to emerge that the conflict was a deliberate escalation by Pakistan less than a year after its nuclear test. Worse still, while Pakistan was embroiled in Kargil, its civil-military relations began to unravel.[38]

The Blair House Meeting and Nuclear Brinkmanship

Because of the ongoing friction between GHQ and ISI, there came a point when Prime Minister Sharif was receiving information from sources other than his own national security institution, such as Indian television propaganda and phone calls from senior U.S. government officials, including President Clinton himself. As a result, the prime minister was unprepared to assess the true gravity of the situation. Panicked and running out of options, he first reached out to India but was rebuffed; efforts to get support from China went nowhere.[39]

Finally Sharif decided to seek U.S. intervention. On July 2, Sharif placed a call to President Clinton, requesting that he intervene. Sharif desired to visit Washington personally. Clinton, after consulting with Indian Prime Minister Vajpayee, told Sharif point-blank that Pakistan must withdraw back to the LOC and that Sharif could come to the United States only if he were ready to accept that agreement. The Pakistani prime minister decided to fly on July 4 to meet with President Clinton.[40]

Sharif brought his family, in addition to a team of close aids, indicating to the Americans that he might have had a one-way ticket or feared a military coup. On the morning of their meeting, President Clinton was briefed that there was "disturbing evidence that the Pakistanis were preparing their nuclear arsenal for possible deployment."[41] One briefer was Bruce Riedel, former CIA official, who recommended to the president that he "use this [information] only when Sharif was without aides."[42] He particularly advised isolating Foreign Secretary Shamshad Ahmad, whom Riedel believed to be "very close to Pakistani military intelligence."[43]

Riedel had been part of Strobe Talbott's negotiating team in the summer 1998 after the nuclear tests. Shamshad was leading the Pakistani negotiations when, as alleged by Talbott (and mentioned in the previous chapter), a Pakistani diplomat nearly physically assaulted them during the negotiations.[44] It was all but clear to the Pakistani bureaucrats that the two senior U.S. democrats had kept a personal grudge since then, and subsequent writings of Bruce Riedel in particular about Pakistan reflected this resentment that reinforced the suspicion.[45]

The agenda at the Blair House summit was dominated by different sets of worries. President Clinton was concerned about escalation of tensions between India and Pakistan and possible use of nuclear weapons, and Prime Minister Sharif worried about the final outcome of the crisis and his own fate as prime minister. Sharif soon found himself trapped when the United States presented him with two options: if he agreed to withdraw completely without any conditions, the United States would assist with mediation; alternatively, the United States would make a public statement blaming Pakistan for the crisis and force it to bear the consequences. Sharif now realized the perils of coming to Washington without having given the strategy deeper thought. The beleaguered prime minister requested a one-on-one meeting with Clinton. The president agreed, but on the condition than an American note-taker, Bruce Riedel, be present. Riedel's is the only existing account of what occurred in that meeting.[46]

Riedel claims that Clinton confronted Sharif directly about whether or not he had ordered a nuclear tipped missile for deployment, and stated that "if the United States appeared to be acting under the gun of a nuclear threat its ability to restrain others from threatening use of their nuclear forces would be forever undermined." Sharif was shocked and confused over the allegations that the Pakistani military would have upped the nuclear ante. Alone, and having neither means to verify the information nor the ability to consult any member of his team, Sharif could only deny the allegation. President Clinton was most likely provided with overstated intelligence in order to pressure Prime Minister Sharif.[47]

After being grilled for an hour, Sharif literally broke down. The United States then wrote a short statement that the prime minister of Pakistan was prepared to take quick and immediate steps toward the restoration of the LOC. To placate Sharif, President Clinton agreed to insert a paragraph that he would take personal interest in Indo-Pakistani efforts to resolve outstanding issues.[48] In the absence of a cease-fire, however, NLI soldiers were forced to disengage from defensive positions and withdraw in broad daylight under relentless Indian fire carried out in anger and revenge. The retreat caused more Pakistani casualties than those incurred during the entire war, and the embarrassment of defeat further undermined Sharif at home and abroad.[49]

Pakistani officials have forcefully denied any nuclear preparations, contending that Pakistan did not at the time possess the capability to make nuclear weapons operational. Further, even if they had wanted to do so, a military skirmish in a remote mountainous corner involving no more than a brigade front on a disputed area was not the dire condition that warranted a nuclear threat. Upon returning from Washington, Prime Minister Sharif never ordered a full investigation of the Kargil operations, which ought to have included information about the alleged nuclear preparations, on which he was so ruthlessly grilled.[50] Instead, Sharif simply dismissed the allegation and no Pakistani ever took it seriously. Within knowledgeable circles in Pakistan, it has been agreed that the United States used the nuclear card simply to shock an already isolated prime minister into an unconditional withdrawal.

Sharif's public silence on the issue, especially given his acrimonious relationship with Army Chief Musharraf, reinforces the fact that no nuclear preparations were made or even considered. In his memoir, Musharraf called any preparation for nuclear strikes in Kargil a "myth" and "preposterous."[51] Lieutenant-General Khalid Ahmad Kidwai, who was the Director General Strategic Plans Division (DGSPD) at the time, dismissed the allegation. In fact, on June 30, 1999, Kidwai and the author met in Geneva with a team of U.S. experts led by Robert Einhorn to discuss the next phase of minimum deterrence posture and the progress on the Pakistani Strategic Restraint Regime proposal. In response to the nuclear preparation allegations, Kidwai remarked, "Would I be sitting in Switzerland if nuclear weapons were being readied for deployments?" (Kidwai recalled this meeting in a June 2006 background briefing to a research team from the U.S. Naval Postgraduate School that included the author. Kidwai believes that the United States probably interpreted large truck activity at the Kirana Ammunition Depot, near Sargodha Air Force Base, to mean nuclear activity, since the Western sources believed the location to house missiles.)[52]

Curiously, in 2000, respected Indian journalist Raj Chengappa, claiming to have inside information, revealed India's preparations of nuclear delivery vehicles during the Kargil conflict.[53] Reportedly, at the peak of crisis, "India then activated all three types of nuclear delivery vehicles to Readiness State 3—meaning some nuclear bombs would be ready to be mated with delivery vehicle[s] at short notice." The report claimed that the "Indian air force kept Mirage fighters on standby," and Indian scientists helped the military to ready "at least four *Prithvi* ballistic missiles for possible nuclear strike . . . and an *Agni* missile capable of launching a nuclear warhead was moved to a western Indian state and kept in a state of readiness."[54]

It is unclear whether U.S. intelligence detected Indian nuclear preparations. If Chengappa's description were true, it would have been nearly impossible for U.S. satellites to miss these signals. What would explain Washington's silence on this question? It can be surmised that either the United States did not consider India's actions as menacing as those of Pakistan, or as a matter of policy it was decided not to make India's preparations public. Alternatively, perhaps President Clinton was not informed of India's nuclear actions, or Raj Chengappa's account is simply not credible.[55]

In the context of the U.S. response to Pakistan's nuclear tests and its subsequent engagements with both India and Pakistan, it became evident to strategic planners in Islamabad that the scope of international reactions would be immeasurable if they ever truly contemplated brandishing nuclear weapons in a war. Feeling falsely accused and misunderstood, Pakistan resolved to ensure that its conventional and nuclear forces would be better prepared for any future crisis.[56] More important, Pakistan became convinced that there was a deep-seated bias against it in the international community and that embarrassing international episodes would be used to label Pakistan as irresponsible.

The Aftermath

The Kargil conflict remains by far the most controversial event in the history of the region. Pakistan's narrative of the rationale behind the operations is contested; the impact on Pakistan's relations with India and the United States remains a subject of intense debate. And the questions surrounding the conduct of a new nuclear power and the role of nuclear weapons in national security policy remain a subject of close scholarly examination.

Versions of the Kargil story vary according to the agenda of any one narrator. Indian scholars view Kargil as the outgrowth of a revisionist Pakistani state seeking to alter the status quo and challenge India's regional dominance.[57] Many Indian commentators and some Pakistani scholars have asserted that Kargil typifies the Pakistani military leadership's attempt to derail the civilian government's peace initiative with India.[58] Western publications and statements by U.S. policy-makers have analyzed the conflict through the exclusive lens of nuclear weapons. Most analysts consider the 1999 events to be a classic case of nuclear deterrence, in which the weapons limited the conflict.[59]

The most acrimonious narrative lies within Pakistan because Kargil revealed the fragility of civil-military relations and the contentious role of the military in the decision-making process. Nawaz Sharif solely blames Musharraf and absolves himself, while Musharraf blames the weak leadership of Sharif. On the other hand, some quasi-official Pakistani accounts present Kargil as the natural outgrowth of historical grievances and a continuation of typical military practices on the LOC.[60]

Hindsight reveals that the planners of the Kargil operation made several serious miscalculations. First, the NLI troops were discovered a month earlier than planned, giving India extra time to organize a response. Second, unseasonable spring weather allowed India to bring heavy weapons, such as the Bofors artillery that proved to be deadly against Pakistani positions in the Kargil-Dras sector, through the Zojila pass. Additionally, Pakistani reinforcements reached the FCNA during June, too late to affect the outcome of the battle. Third, the ruse that the NLI were insurgents instead of Pakistani troops was quickly dispelled, leaving Pakistan in an untenable political position, having publicly stated that the fighting forces were independent *mujahideen*.[61] Fourth, Pakistani planners did not anticipate India's coordinated and relentless counterattack. Musharraf did not expect vertical escalation involving Indian artillery and air force attacks and considered it to be "overreaction" and an "unreasonably escalated Indian response."[62] Fifth, and perhaps most important, the Kargil planners did not realize that such an operation was being carried out in a distinct international environment. The priorities for the primary external actors—the United States and China—had changed over the years. Pakistan's ties with both countries were weak in 1999, while conversely both American and Chinese leaders had sought to improve relations with New Delhi.[63] Pakistan believed that the international community would step in to end the war by enforcing a ceasefire instead of allowing a humiliating withdrawal under continued fighting. However, the international community, especially the United States, had become opposed to the idea of limited conflicts occurring between two nuclear-armed neighbors.[64]

Nuclear Pessimists and Optimists Redux

Contrary to assertions made by some Western authors, the planners of Kargil were not directly emboldened to undertake this operation because of Pakistan's nuclear weapons capability. Instead, it was their limited understanding of the meaning of nuclear revolution that made Kargil planners act as if nothing had changed. They acted as if they lived in a prenuclear, conventional world, mainly concerned with operational imperatives and restoring honor.

Nuclear proliferation pessimists argue Kargil to be a classic case of the stability-instability paradox, a theory developed in the Cold War and attributed to Glenn Snyder. According to this theory, the strategic balance provided by nuclear deterrence prevents a low-level war from escalating to a full conventional or nuclear level. This condition, in turn, paradoxically allows low-level military operations or low-intensity violence to continue under the shadow of nuclear stability. Applied to the Kargil operation, having acquired the ultimate weapon, Pakistan was confident that it could prevent India from waging a conventional war for fear of escalation to the nuclear level; thus, a limited escalation to improve the defensive posture and continuation of support for a low-intensity insurgency to tie down Indian forces was thought feasible at the time.[65]

At first glance, the above theory seems to be palpable. But upon closer examination, there are nuances that cannot be explained by this logic alone. Pakistan was a new nuclear power, still learning and too nascent to know of the stability-instability paradox, much less plan around it. Kargil's military planners were very new to their jobs, involved in secret "need-to-know" planning, and with little to no experience in nuclear theory or joint nuclear and conventional force planning. The same was true for the political leadership and the civil bureaucracy, which were in the process of absorbing the meaning of a nuclear Pakistan.[66] Additionally, the operation was planned impulsively and was based on tactical rationales. Overall, the planners assumed that it was the conventional force balance, operational challenges of retaking lost grounds on such difficult terrain and India's military force commitments elsewhere, not nuclear weapons, that would prevent escalation.[67]

What the Kargil operation did reveal were the gaps between Pakistan's competing bureaucratic and political entities. As Maleeha Lodhi, a highly respected scholar noted, "The Kargil affair has exposed systematic flaws in a decision-making process that is impulsive, chaotic, erratic, and overly secretive. The elimination of internal checks and balances . . . yielded a personalized system of governance which delivers hasty decisions, whose consequences are not thought through, and which are predicated on lack of consultation and scrutiny even within the establishment, much less based on public consent."[68] India's coordinated military, political, and diplomatic responses stood in sharp contrast to a confused and disarrayed Pakistan. Pakistan's Foreign Office had been left out of Kargil's planning and was unprepared to rebut India's diplomatic maneuvers. As the Sharif government attempted to disassociate itself from the Kargil operation, and the military seethed over a Washington-brokered withdrawal, the civil-military divide widened, eventually laying the groundwork for the October 1999 coup.

Military Coup

Beginning late August 1999, tensions between the government and Musharraf were visible as rumors began to circulate about the removal of the army chief or a possible military coup.[69] Sharif had probably made up his mind to remove Musharraf as early as mid-June, at the peak of the Kargil crisis.[70] Indeed, there were those who "stood to gain" from Musharraf's removal. The potential aspirants to the appointment of army chief were Lieutenant-General Ziauddin

(DGISI) and Lieutenant-General Tariq Pervez (Corps Commander Quetta and brother-in-law of Federal Minister Raja Nadir Pervez).[71]

In the midst of such intrigue, Prime Minister Sharif decided to send his brother, Chief Minister of Punjab Province Shahbaz Sharif, to Washington, DC. The visit, in the third week of September, was coordinated to coincide with DGISI Lieutenant-General Ziauddin's official visit to the U.S. capital.[72] Shahbaz Sharif was ostensibly visiting as the "Prime Minister's special envoy" for a "confidential talk on Kashmir."[73] But in reality, the brother came to express concern about a military coup, prompting the U.S. Department of State to issue a warning. Unintentionally, this public warning became the tipping point that unraveled civil-military relations in Pakistan.

The following month, in October 1999, Shahbaz Sharif met with the army chief to remove any misunderstandings and clarify his visit to Washington, DC. Musharraf told him point blank that he would not accept being "kicked up" to become the ceremonial Chairman Joint Chief of Staff Committee (CJCSC). The army chief recommended immediate retirement of Lieutenant-General Tariq Pervez. To Musharraf's surprise, the prime minister accepted both demands. In fact, Sharif appointed General Musharraf with dual hats: CJCSC as well as Chief of the Army Staff (COAS).[74] The prime minister thought that this would lull Musharraf into complacency so he could devise a plan to remove him during an official visit to Sri Lanka.

On October 12, just as Musharraf flew from Colombo, Sri Lanka, on Pakistan International Airlines (PIA), the prime minister issued orders to retire General Pervez Musharraf and replace him with Lieutenant-General Ziauddin as the new COAS. Pakistani national television showed Sharif personally placing new ranks on the promoted chief. This was the second time in a year that Sharif had dismissed the army chief without warning. In the words of one of Sharif's colleagues, Sartaj Aziz, "He had overplayed his hand and effectively derailed the democratic process for nine long years."

The prime minister instructed the PIA plane carrying Musharraf to divert its course to anywhere outside the country. Newly appointed Army Chief Ziauddin, while still in the prime minister's house, attempted to issue his first instructions to GHQ. Lieutenant-General Muhammad Aziz, Chief of General Staff, informed him that the army recognized him only as DGISI and that GHQ awaited the return of General Pervez Musharraf, from Sri Lanka, whom they recognized as the rightful army chief. GHQ told Ziauddin that it could not act on the basis of TV clippings, but would wait for the formal retirement orders and the official appointment of the new chief by the Ministry of Defense.

The prime minister's office then directed authorities in Karachi to physically block the PIA plane's landing at Karachi Airport. Meanwhile, Ziauddin made telephone calls to two serving lieutenant-generals. Lieutenant-General Saleem Haider, who was playing golf at the time, was instantly appointed the Commander 10 Corps and was summoned to the prime minister's house for briefing and instructions. Ziauddin also made Lieutenant-General Muhammad Akram the new Chief of General Staff (CGS) to replace Aziz Khan and directed him to go to GHQ. However, by the time the two acted, it was too late.[75]

While Prime Minister Sharif was busy diverting or delaying the PIA flight, GHQ issued instructions to all corps commands of the army to take over administrative responsibilities in each province by removing the civilian government and taking key leaders into custody. Troops moved in to take over Islamabad and elsewhere. The PIA plane carrying Musharraf eventually landed in Karachi after the military took over the airport. Musharraf fulfilled what he had promised—that he would not allow another "humiliation" of an army chief.[76]

So began the fourth military takeover in the country's history. As many times before, the people expressed new hopes for the destiny of the nation—the Pakistani public was celebrating the change. In May 1998, sweets were distributed to herald the arrival of Pakistan's status as a nuclear power. Now the same public distributed sweets to celebrate the departure of its incumbent regime. This military coup stood out in comparison to the previous three. Pakistan had become a de facto nuclear power, and nuclear powers have norms and constitutional practices to effect political transitions.

On the evening of October 14, 1999, I was summoned by the COAS to his official residence. The COAS asked me to assist him in preparing his first speech to the nation. With the help of close family members, the speech writing took three nights before it was delivered. On October 17, 1999, the author accompanied General Pervez Musharraf to Pakistan Television (PTV) headquarters for his first public appearance. The world waited anxiously to hear what the new military leader had in store for a new nuclear power. That speech was remembered for its famous "seven point agenda" and a roadmap for Pakistan at the turn of the millennium.[77]

17 Establishment of Robust Command and Control

As Musharraf prepared to address his nation, across the border in India, Prime Minister Atal Bihari Vajpayee was sworn in on October 14, 1999. To international observers, the contrast between the two countries was striking. Just as democracy strengthened in India, the military seized power in Pakistan for the fourth time.

The author prepared Musharraf for his speech. He politely reminded the army chief to congratulate Indian Prime Minister Vajpayee on his resumption of office. By doing this, Musharraf could take the initiative to mitigate the tensions that arose from the Kargil episode and emerge as a moderate leader. Musharraf graciously accepted the advice and offered an olive branch to India by declaring a unilateral removal of additional forces deployed during the summer conflict. Encouraged, the author suggested further that the "international community [was] anxious to hear the perspective of the new leader of a new nuclear power." Musharraf smiled and exclaimed, "Oh! I almost forgot—you are the nuclear guy."

Initially Musharraf wanted to include specific nuclear policies in his speech, such as offering nonaggression pacts to India or announcing elements of a nuclear doctrine. But after discussion with the author, he agreed that broad contours of the nuclear policy would be more appropriate in his first speech. So he stressed "restraint and responsibility" as the twin pillars of Pakistan's national nuclear policy, in addition to the strengthening of nonproliferation measures.

In his October 17 speech, Musharraf delivered a subtle message regarding Indo-Pakistani relations and security, with President Clinton in mind, saying this:

> Pakistan has always been alive to international non-proliferation concerns. Last year, we were compelled to respond to India's nuclear tests in order to restore strategic balance in the interest of our national security and regional peace and stabili-

ty. In the new nuclear environment in South Asia, we believe that both Pakistan and India have to exercise utmost restraint and responsibility. We owe it to the world. I wish to reassure the world community that while preserving its vital security interests, Pakistan will continue to pursue a policy of nuclear and missile restraint and sensitivity to global non-proliferation and disarmament objectives.[1]

Musharraf then congratulated the Indian prime minister and said:

At the turn of the century, South Asia stands at a crucial juncture of history. The twentieth century saw our transition to independence but the region has unfortunately remained mired in conflicts and economic deprivation. Together we can change the scenario .... [B]oth must sincerely work towards resolving their problems, especially the core issue of Jammu and Kashmir .... Pakistan would welcome unconditional, equitable and results-oriented dialogue with India .... [It] is our desire that the situation on our borders and the Line of Control should remain calm and peaceful. I take this opportunity to announce unilateral de-escalation on our international borders with India and initiate the return of all our forces moved to the borders in the recent past.

Musharraf's policy speech raised hopes both domestically and abroad. The seven-point agenda was ambitious and provided national direction and hope for a coherent national policy. The new military leader closely monitored national economic conditions and was well aware that further international sanctions resulting from the military coup were approaching. With barely $600 million in the foreign exchange reserve, Pakistan stood at the brink of default.[2] By emphasizing military restraint and nonproliferation, Musharraf attempted to mitigate the international sanctions by opening up dialogue and reducing Pakistan's isolation, all with the goal of mitigating economic pressure.

Just a few months later Musharraf delivered on his promise by opening a debate on the implications of signing the Comprehensive Test Ban Treaty (CTBT).[3] Hopes that the United States might show some interest in this dialogue were dashed, however, when the U.S. Senate rejected the CTBT, and the Clinton administration was not forthcoming toward Pakistan. Musharraf dropped the idea, especially after President Clinton's five-hour visit to Islamabad stood in stark contrast to his five-day visit to India.[4] Even so, Musharraf wanted to smooth relations with India and overcome the bitterness of Kargil to steer the relationship onto a positive track.

One year ago, upon assuming his Chief of the Army Staff (COAS) position in October 1998, General Musharraf was keen on examining the study on the implications of Pakistan's overt nuclear status. As mentioned earlier, that summer his predecessor, General Jehangir Karamat, had directed the study, focusing on three areas: (1) nuclear diplomacy, (2) nuclear doctrine, and (3) nuclear command and control. Specifically, in the wake of Strobe Talbott diplomacy, General Karamat sought answers to the following questions, which ACDA was tasked to examine: What changes are necessary for a coherent national strategy after Pakistan declared itself a new nuclear power? What is the best course for nuclear diplomacy that would mitigate economic sanctions and preserve nuclear deterrence? What nuclear doctrines ought to be adopted? How can nuclear conventional force planning be integrated into a new strategic doctrine? What should be the new nuclear command-and-control arrangements? What organizational changes are necessary to create a coherent decision-making body and how can it best function?

Musharraf was faced with the choice of declaring either a nuclear command authority or a nuclear-use doctrine to the world. Eventually, he approved the former in an effort to reflect Pakistan's assumption of responsibility as a nuclear power, but the path to that decision was long and arduous.

Oversight of the Nuclear Program: Redux

As we have learned from previous chapters, from the inception of Pakistan's nuclear program, only a small group of individuals was privy to the bomb mission. The military was not aware of the program until 1977, although it had begun providing technical and logistical support a year earlier to Khan Research Laboratories (KRL).[5] A decade of military rule had forged a nexus between the military and scientific communities, which has continued to date. However, even with the change of regime and power, from 1972 to 1993, only one office— the president's or the prime minister's—and the same personalities directed the course of Pakistan's nuclear program.

The year 1993 was significant in Pakistan's nuclear history and was yet another tumultuous one in its political history. In January, following the sudden death of COAS General Asif Nawaz Janjua, President GIK had appointed General Abdul Waheed to replace him. The new COAS hit the ground running. By spring of that year, the relationship between President Ghulam Ishaq Khan (GIK) and Prime Minister Nawaz Sharif had begun to sour.[6] On April 17, 1993, Prime Minister Sharif in a public television address lashed out at the president. The following day, President Ghulam Ishaq Khan dismissed the government and Parliament and installed a caretaker government led by a new interim prime minister, Balk Sher Mazari. Sharif challenged the decision in the Supreme Court, won the case, and was restored on May 26, 1993. For the next three months, a bitter power struggle between the president and prime minister met an impasse, making a laughing stock of Pakistan both domestically and abroad. Finally, COAS General Abdul Waheed intervened by shuttling between the president and prime minister, conveying to both that they must resign and allow elections to bring in a fresh leadership.[7] With both the president and the prime minister out, a new interim government was installed led by Moeenuddin Qureshi, a senior official of the World Bank, until elections were held on October 24 and 27. Predictably, the elections brought Benazir Bhutto back to office for the second time. Nawaz Sharif met the same fate, as did Benazir Bhutto in 1990, turning the national politics half a circle after five years of democratic return.

Little was it realized to what extent control over the nuclear program would be compromised with President GIK out of the scene. GIK was truly a veteran and the only person who had been consistently overseeing the program from its very beginning—possibly since 1972. As discussed in Chapter 8, it was GIK's ingenious methods that financed the program and kept procurement strategies afloat even when the country's economy was failing.[8]

GIK was a serious-minded bureaucrat—quiet and reputed for his integrity and honesty. A no-nonsense person who would not trust the nuclear secrets of the state to any interim government, on his final day in public office GIK reluctantly handed over all nuclear-related documents, including details on decisions and projected force goals, to General Abdul Waheed.[9] GIK never appeared in public after that day. Contrary to common belief, this was the first time the army had inherited the responsibility for the nuclear program—the result of a power breakdown at the center between the president and the prime minister. Until that point, the role of General Headquarters (GHQ) in nuclear decision-making had never been formal.

The nuclear decision-making and command-and-control apparatus of Pakistan was completely revamped between 1999 and 2001. As the first army chief to assume power after Pakistan had become an overt nuclear weapons state, Musharraf had both the motivation and the means to put Pakistan's nuclear house in order. One of his first acts was to order a reorganization of the military bureaucracy within the GHQ. Specifically, he ordered the creation of a Strategic Plans Division (SPD), which began operations in December 1998. The Sharif government had previously tasked the army to prepare a new command-and-control arrangement but did not approve it.

After President GIK resigned and handed over nuclear responsibility to GHQ, nuclear issues in the period between July 1993 and December 1998 were handled at the Combat Development Directorate, which supervised Pakistan's transition to being a declared nuclear power.

The Rise and Fall of the Combat Development Directorate

The Combat Development Directorate (CD Directorate), the brainchild of General Mirza Aslam Beg, was formed in 1985 and was composed of technically qualified officers who could scientifically study and analyze the optimal technology modernization strategy for the armed forces.[10] It acted as the bridge between the General Staff (GS) requirements laid down by the Chief of General Staff and the Weapons and Equipment Directorate (W&E), which procured the approved system and sent final recommendations to the Ministry of Defense. The CD Directorate primarily worked on evaluation, analysis, and concepts of conventional weapons use and related doctrines. After General Beg was appointed Vice Chief of the Army Staff (VCOAS) in March 1987, he infused new energy in the CD to secretly analyze India's ballistic missile development and coordinate a response by working closely with Space and Upper Atmosphere Research Commission (SUPARCO), as discussed in Chapter 14. The CD played a major role in the conduct trials of the *Hatf* series in 1989 and later was the focal point of ballistic missile acquisition—the only contribution of the Combat Directorate toward the nuclear program before 1993.

In July 1993, when President GIK and Nawaz Sharif resigned, all nuclear documents went to Army Chief General Abdul Waheed. Soon afterward, General Waheed appointed Major General Ziauddin as Director General of the Combat Development Directorate (DGCD) and entrusted him with the responsibility of coordinating nuclear issues on his behalf. Faced with this new responsibility, Ziauddin began reorganizing the CD in GHQ; before long, Ziauddin was the face of all things nuclear, and from 1993 to 1998 the CD was the center of the nuclear program.

Within a few years, the CD had been reorganized into four divisions, each headed by a brigadier. "A Division" evaluated conventional weapons and doctrines. "B Division" was responsible for artillery, air defense, and ballistic missiles, and was especially significant in missile acquisitions and technology transfers. The author worked in "C Division" (later renamed Arms Control and Disarmament Affairs), which analyzed nuclear, chemical, and biological issues, along with regional security developments. The C Division worked closely with the Ministry of Foreign Affairs and its role in multilateral and bilateral negotiations, which has been discussed in previous chapters.[11]

The "D Division" had two subgroups: Decision Support System (DESTEM), which dealt with operational research methodologies, and another that coordinated all strategic organizations in the country. The entire division would later be known as Directorate of Strategic Weapons Development (SWD), headed by then-Brigadier Ahmad Bilal.[12]

From 1993 until 1998, the CD Directorate became the central office of coordinating nuclear-related policy on behalf of the COAS. Ziauddin was promoted to three-star and left to command a corps; he was replaced by Major General Zulfiqar Ali Khan, another officer from the army's corps of engineers, as DGCD. In the five years after President Ghulam Ishaq Khan departed, two army chiefs, General Abdul Waheed and General Jehangir Karamat, ensured that the nuclear weapons mission came to fruition. At the same time, the military's combat potential was eroding under seven years of U.S. nonproliferation sanctions, commonly referred to as the Pressler sanctions (after the Pressler Amendments to the nonproliferation laws), and decreasing defense expenditures under the economic crunch. With the lack of supplies and funding and deficiencies in spare parts, equipment, and replacement weapons, Pakistan's conventional force balance with India, which had marginally improved in the 1980s, began to plummet, forcing it to seek more reliance on nuclear force goals.

Under these conditions, the principal task of the CD Directorate to develop combat capabilities through modernization became very challenging, especially because Western sources were becoming increasingly reluctant suppliers. The buzzwords in the CD Directorate were *self-reliance* and *transfer of technology* (TOT). The military ensured that it would take the hit and not allow erosion of the nuclear force goals. As Dr. Ishfaq Ahmad told the author, "We were never short of budget from all governments."[13] One of the crowning achievements of the CD Directorate was to create a military-scientific camaraderie in national security objectives. To mitigate military deficiencies, Pakistan Atomic Energy Commission (PAEC), KRL, and other scientific organizations also expanded conventional weapons programs to build new systems indigenously, such as short-range rockets, antitank weapons systems, and antiaircraft missile systems for the army.

The combined pressure of conventional force erosion and diplomatic pres-

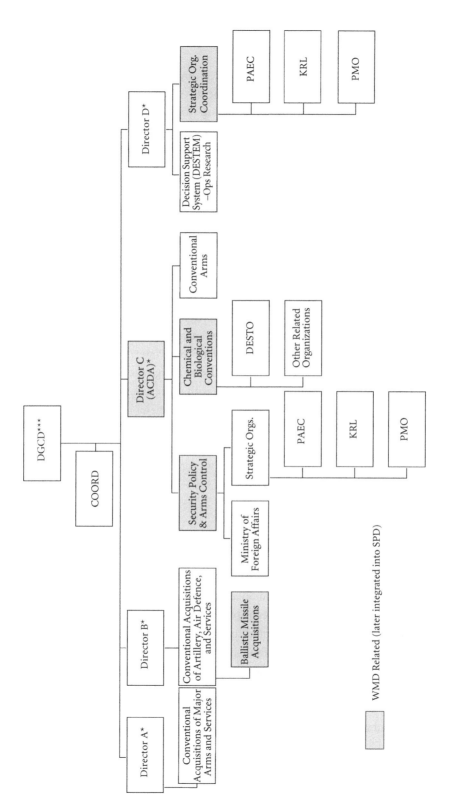

Figure 17.1. Organizational Chart: Combat Development Directorate (CD Directorate, 1985–1998)

sure from the United States to cap the nuclear program further pushed Pakistan to seek alternative sources both for fissile stocks and for means of delivery. By that time the missile program was making strides, especially with turnkey technologies transferred from China and North Korea (see Chapter 12). In 1997, however, CD came under additional pressure when competition between PAEC and KRL was becoming problematic, involving the media to glorify one camp and demonize the other. The DGCD became more assertive in attempting to control the ugly rivalry, especially reports in the local press. On CD recommendation COAS General Karamat suggested to Prime Minister Sharif that he audit KRL, which had been exempt from oversight for more than two decades. The role of the CD Directorate had qualitatively changed—its nuclear responsibilities now included complementing nuclear diplomacy at the Foreign Office.

The expanded responsibilities of the CD Directorate somewhat overshadowed the role of other directorates in GHQ. Consequently, within a week of taking power, General Musharraf posted Lieutenant-General Zulfiqar Ali Khan on a civil assignment as chairman of the Water and Power Development Authority (WAPDA). The new army chief decided to reorganize GHQ—he closed the CD Directorate and merged its divisions with other directorates in GHQ.[14] In particular, Musharraf was focused on establishing a new organization, which would exclusively oversee the nuclear program. In the meantime, the C and D Divisions of CD Directorate were to report directly to the CGS or COAS on all nuclear issues until a new organization was created with which these two nuclear-related divisions would be merged.

The Birth of the Strategic Plans Division

The Military Operations Directorate (MO) is the hub and veritable secretariat of the GHQ. It is the central clearinghouse of all military orders and instructions; its responsibilities span from operational planning to procurements. By the mid-1990s the spectrum of security issues expanded and required additional directorates in GHQ that could complement the MO responsibilities. In 1996 one such organization, the Evaluation and Research (E&R) Directorate was created with an ambiguous mandate to conduct research on doctrines or any other subject directed by the COAS.[15] Kidwai, a brilliant professional from the artillery corps, became the new director general of E&R around late June 1998 and had very little exposure to nuclear issues. Two months after being appointed to E&R, the division was directed to conduct research on command

and control models that were to be presented to the civilian government. As with most large organizations, many factors make interagency coordination difficult.

The 1998 nuclear tests suddenly made nuclear issues much more attractive, and soon afterward, all three GHQ directorates (MO, CD, and now E&R) were working simultaneously on overlapping issues, often in secrecy and with intense competition.[16] By early October 1998, E&R and MO had created the main outlines of the command and control system, which comprised a National Command Authority (NCA) headed by political and military leaders, a supporting secretariat to that NCA, and specialized strategic forces. This plan was then approved within the military.

In December 1998, Major General Kidwai was tasked to take over the nuclear portfolio as potential head of the new organization. From then on nuclear issues came under the jurisdiction of E&R Directorate until SPD was formed, of which Kidwai became the head. Zulfiqar Ali Khan, the outgoing DGCD before leaving for his new assignment, handed Kidwai three briefcases filled with documents and no accompanying guidance. The documents made little sense to Kidwai, who then visited various strategic organizations and listened to detailed briefings. Regardless of his limited experienced, he had under his command two directors—Brigadier Ahmad Bilal and the author, both from the erstwhile CD Directorate heading D and C divisions, respectively, who had considerable experience and institutional memory to help the new E&R Directorate convert into a new nuclear organization. Bilal would later be promoted to major general and head the newly created Security Division and at the time of this writing is Chairman SUPARCO.[17]

In February 1999, then-Army Chief General Musharraf submitted the military-approved NCA plan, which included proposal of a secretariat that would take charge of operations, finances, and security of all strategic organizations on behalf of the NCA. In April 1999, the army made a formal presentation to Prime Minister Sharif and his team, including Foreign Minister Sartaj Aziz and Finance Minister Ishaq Dar. Although Sharif appreciated the presentation, he did not formally approve the plan. Instead, he tasked the foreign minister to conduct a further evaluation. There were two possible reasons for Sharif's reluctance. First, the NCA model presented resembled the National Security Council (NSC), which carried heavy political baggage. Second, Foreign Minister Aziz desired a more influential role than that of other military officials. However, just a month later, the Kargil crisis would explode, and all NCA plans

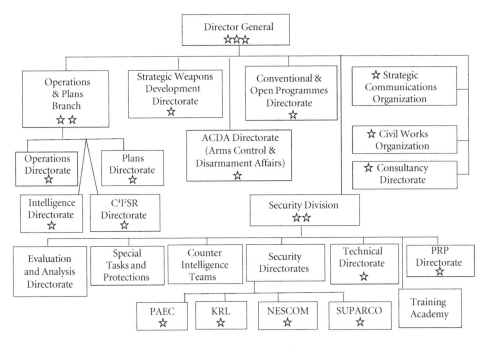

Figure 17.2. Organization of Strategic Plans Division (SPD)

would be put on hold. Despite the political impasse, the military would proceed to merge the CD and E&R to form its new secretariat, the SPD.[18]

The first goal of the SPD was to establish an operational nuclear deterrent, for which the organization followed the standard military method—that is, a basic policy framework followed by a nuclear doctrine. The ten-point nuclear doctrine emphasized a minimum deterrent. The next stage was to translate minimum deterrence into a development strategy, the first step of which was to define the quality and quantity of nuclear weapons necessary to match India's threat. This strategy was later refined to include land-based and air-based delivery systems. The next step was to develop a third-tier strategic force command. SPD would lead the field forces, and since the strategic forces were both land- and air-based, SPD had to be moved to the Joint Services Headquarters (JSHQ). At the time, however, GHQ had no budget for SPD. In March 1999, when General Musharraf was appointed as acting Chairman Joint Chiefs of Staff Committee (CJCSC) in addition to his appointment as COAS, he requested the secretary of defense to grant special funding for SPD. With 5 million rupees (approximately U.S. $0.8 million), SPD was able to move to its new location at the Joint Services Staff College (JSSC), adjacent to JSHQ, and it remains there to this day.[19]

Kidwai, now the head of SPD, was tasked with structuring and shaping the Strategic Force Command (SFC), but this too came with its hurdles. The first was to create the organizational structure, which was eventually modeled after the conventional Corps Headquarters of the army. The second issue was determining the strength level of the SFC in terms of force size, quantity, targeting requirements, and geography. After all, it was not easy for strategic forces to cover the entire Indian landmass, although this was Pakistan's goal.[20] In addition, although some officers who had taken courses at U.S. military institutions had marginal experience of fire planning with nuclear weapons, Pakistan lacked experience in nuclear force training, delivery systems, and authority. The only knowledge the military had was based on theoretical exercises and U.S. field manuals. This experience was insufficient to create the entirety of Pakistan's nuclear forces.

Within a year of its formation, the SPD had evolved into a true nuclear enclave; currently, with a decade of experience, it is the key to Pakistan's nuclear management. The growth of SPD led to systematic control over strategic organizations and provided direction for the nuclear program. In the past, Pakistan lacked oversight over its covert nuclear program, leading to the A. Q. Khan network and other mishaps. But today SPD has a firm hold of Pakistan's nuclear organization and policy.

Nevertheless, the exact nature of launch authorization procedures is ambiguous.[21] Several sources refer to a system of two separate codes—one civilian and the other military—amounting to a "dual-key" system.[22] However, several authoritative accounts mention a three-man rule. In particular, the code to arm a weapon can only be inserted in the presence of three persons. It is possible that a two-man rule is adopted for movement of warheads and a three-man rule is adopted for employment authorization. According to Pakistani planners, the number of persons involved varies "for technical reasons"—three at some points in the chain of command, two at other points.

Pakistan is not explicit about its arrangements for weapons security, but it has developed physical safety mechanisms and firewalls both in the weapon systems themselves, as well as in the chain of command. No single individual can operate a weapon system, nor can one individual issue the command for nuclear weapons use. The NCA command and control system ensures that weapons can be operationally ready on short notice, yet unauthorized arming and/or use never takes place.

Pakistan does not keep its nuclear weapons on hair-trigger alert. The nuclear weapons are few in number and probably kept in disassembled form; their components are reportedly stored separately, at dispersed sites. Keeping the weapons in a disassembled form, along with the use of authorization codes, reduces the risk of capture or unauthorized use. Naturally, there is considerable uncertainty about the location of Pakistani nuclear weapons and about procedures for actual use. After September 11, Pakistan ordered a redeployment of the country's nuclear arsenal to at least six secret new locations, according to one account.[23] Fissile materials are obviously stored in secret locations; probably in initial stages they are near installations such as Kahuta or Khushab, or close to Rawalpindi. Additionally, from a security standpoint sensitive material sites are carefully chosen, in safe areas and within quick reach of designated rapid reaction forces, which are specially trained and operate under command of the security division of SPD. Although Pakistan's system is not as sophisticated as the U.S. permissive action links (PALs), it is deemed reliable enough to preclude unauthorized arming or launching of its nuclear weapons.

Dummy locations are also reportedly employed to minimize the risks of destruction or capture.[24] SPD Head Lieutenant-General Khalid Kidwai, in a lecture at the U.S. Naval Postgraduate School in October 2006, clarified that "no delegation of authority concerning nuclear weapons is planned."[25] The conclusion, therefore, is that centralized control is retained by the NCA at the Joint Services Headquarters. Beyond this clarification, operational control plans cannot be made public by any nuclear state and thus remain a national security secret, as was the case with the United States and other nuclear powers during the Cold War.

As of 2012, SPD comprises 150 officers, with Kidwai at its head after he retired from active duty in October 2007. The organization now functions under the CJCSC and reports directly to the prime minister. It also functions as the secretariat to the National Command Authority, which is responsible for formulating nuclear policy, force postures, development plans, arms control, finances, and nuclear security.

National Security Council

As the new military regime took national responsibility, Musharraf quickly realized the growing need for an established national body to make key security decisions. The army had been a proponent of creating a body like the

National Security Council (NSC) as the best remedy for strained civil-military relations. The NSC would bring together the top civil and military leadership that together would forge a coherent national policy and consensus on strategic affairs. However, the logic of this proposal was mired in controversy.

President Zia-ul-Haq had introduced the idea of the NSC in 1985. His vision was seen as an effort to entrust the army with the constitutional role of supervising the government.[26] Since then, the political leadership in Pakistan, Nawaz Sharif in particular, loathed the concept of the NSC or any arrangement that included the military. Some politicians feared that such an action would legitimize the political role of the military and give it undue influence in decision-making.[27] The military took this mindset to be unwarranted paranoia. In its point of view, the complex nature of the changing security environment warranted an "institutional system of checks and balances."[28] In typical military parlance, the NSC would bring "all stake-holders on board," implying consensus on national security affairs.[29] An existing forum that bore close resemblance to the NSC was the Defense Committee of the Cabinet (DCC). But it had not been effective in decision-making or managing crises. The DCC did not have a functioning secretariat that could monitor or analyze the complex nature of defense and security affairs; in fact, it served as more of a conference room where members assembled on short notice.[30]

Notwithstanding the potential political backlash, after Musharraf seized chief executive power, he created the NSC, which remained in service until 2002. The NSC was convened and chaired by the president and was composed of a total of thirteen civilian and military leaders.[31] Musharraf's NSC included the "Leader of the Opposition" in the National Assembly and the elected chief ministers of all four provinces. As such, the forum could not discuss particularly sensitive strategic issues and so was not involved in nuclear decision-making, although it did formalize the role of the military in Pakistan's policy-making machinery. The NSC remained controversial throughout Musharraf's tenure. It was never clear if it was an advisory or a decision-making body, whose deliberations were legally binding the national policy or otherwise.[32]

National Command Authority

Musharraf directed SPD to make a formal presentation to the NSC for approval of the NCA.[33] He strongly believed that the formation of the NCA was critical, especially at a time when the CTBT was on the agenda, when the United

States was keeping a watchful eye on Pakistan, and when India had announced its own nuclear doctrine. All of these events made it clear to Musharraf that the NCA was needed to create an informed forum for debate and to demonstrate to the international community that Pakistan was becoming a responsible nuclear nation.

The NSC was called to a formal meeting on February 1, 2000, under the chairmanship of Chief Executive Musharraf to discuss the NCA in the current political context. It was a marathon session that examined all the implications of India's nuclear doctrine, the contours of Pakistan's own doctrines, and nuclear diplomacy. From the outset, Musharraf was determined to keep nuclear weapons issues within the jurisdiction of the highest-level civilian and military decision-makers, all of whom would be represented on the NCA. Nuclear force planning would be integrated with conventional war plans at the joint planning level within SPD, but the president, prime minister, cabinet ministers, and the four service chiefs would decide on actual nuclear weapons use. After considerable debate, Pakistan decided to announce its national command and control system.

On February 2, 2000, Musharraf announced Pakistan's NCA, which was under the direction of the SPD. To this day, the nuclear command-and-control setup is an overlay of the existing national command structure and has two segments. The NCA is made up of top civilian and military officials and is the center of all decisions related to nuclear policy, procurement, planning, and use. Until 2010, the president chaired the NCA with the prime minister acting as vice chairman.[34] Following the 18th amendment to the Constitution, the president handed over the responsibility to the prime minister. The NCA now consists of the Employment Control Committee (ECC) and the Development Control Committee (DCC), both chaired by the prime minister. The foreign minister is deputy chairman of the ECC, the body that defines nuclear strategy, including the deployment and employment of strategic forces, and decides on nuclear use. The committee includes the main cabinet ministers as well as the military chiefs. The ECC reviews presentations on strategic threat perceptions, monitors the progress of weapons development, and decides on responses to emerging threats. It also establishes guidelines for effective command-and-control practices to safeguard against the accidental or unauthorized use of nuclear weapons.

The chairman of the Joint Chiefs of Staff is deputy chairman of the DCC, the body responsible for weapons development and oversight. It includes the nation's military and scientific leadership, but no political leadership except the prime minister. The DCC body exercises technical, financial, and administrative control over all strategic organizations, including national laboratories and research and development organizations associated with the development and modernization of nuclear weapons and their means of delivery.

With ECC and DCC as the first tier of the NCA, the second tier is the SPD, which assists both committees and oversees the systematic progress of weapons systems. At the third tier, separate strategic force commands had been created within each of the services: the Army Strategic Force Command (ASFC), the Air Force Strategic Command (AFSC), and the Naval Strategic Force Command (NSFC). These three services retain training, technical, and administrative control over their respective forces; however, operational control is under the jurisdiction of the NCA, which provides military direction through the Chairman Joint Chiefs of Staff Committee (CJCSC), housed in the National Military Command Centre (NMCC). The NCA is the final authority over launching a nuclear strike; such a decision is based on consensus within the NCA, with the chairman casting the final vote.[35]

With the formal announcement of the NCA, for the first time all national laboratories were brought under de jure control of the SPD, which rapidly established a military-style control and sought full accountability of the laboratories, which PAEC and KRL had never been subjected to before. By November 2000, all organizations participating in the nuclear and missile programs had been put under the tight control of the NCA.

In January 2001, the National Engineering and Scientific Commission (NESCOM), under the leadership of Samar Mubarakmand, separated the nuclear and conventional programs.[36] In NESCOM, a new division of labor was instituted: PAEC became solely responsible for mining and reprocessing, KRL for enrichment, and NDC for all weaponization issues.[37] The new organization became fully operational in 2001.

These sweeping structural changes brought with them numerous challenges; the largest of these was A. Q. Khan and his influential political standing. Khan was accustomed to dealing directly with previous presidents, prime ministers, and army chiefs. For any officer lower than these ranks to challenge him would have been seen as unpatriotic and dangerous. Therefore the SPD instituted standard operating procedures for all the strategic organizations. For example, contacts between media and scientific organizations were monitored, requiring approval from SPD before the release of any publications. In addition, clear-

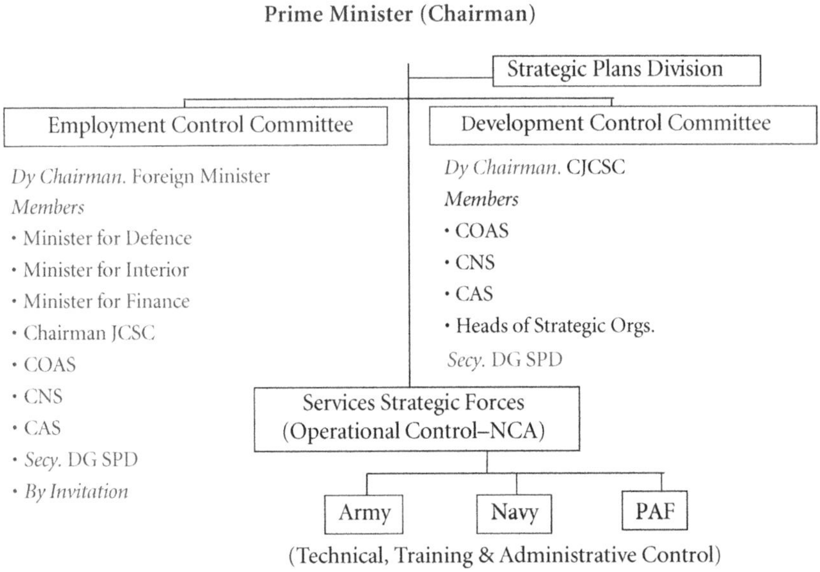

Prime Minister (Chairman)

Strategic Plans Division

Employment Control Committee

Development Control Committee

Dy Chairman. Foreign Minister

Members

• Minister for Defence

• Minister for Interior

• Minister for Finance

• Chairman JCSC

• COAS

• CNS

• CAS

• *Secy.* DG SPD

• *By Invitation*

Dy Chairman. CJCSC

Members

• COAS

• CNS

• CAS

• Heads of Strategic Orgs.

Secy. DG SPD

Services Strategic Forces
(Operational Control–NCA)

Army   Navy   PAF

(Technical, Training & Administrative Control)

Figure 17.3. Organization of National Command Authority (NCA)

ances were required for all travel abroad by members of the scientific organizations. Finally, reporting on all financial expenditures was required. These three requirements placed pressure on A. Q. Khan, who constantly clashed with SPD while attempting to sell unauthorized conventional military equipment to foreign governments.

Within a year of NCA's formal announcement, A. Q. Khan, in March of 2001, had been removed from Khan Research Laboratory and appointed scientific advisor to the government. He was fired from that position as well, after the exposure of his illegal nuclear supply network in 2004. Khan's network came to light following a full disclosure to the International Atomic Energy Agency by Libya about the source of its nuclear program. Pakistan enacted export control legislation in 2004 and established the Pakistan Nuclear Regulatory Authority. Indeed, as will be explained in Chapter 19, it was the evolving command and control that contributed to unraveling A. Q. Khan's network, as the NCA rapidly upgraded security, oversight, and export control legislation.

Pakistan, still on the nuclear learning curve, would have its newly acquired deterrent tested in 2001–2. The Kargil crisis of 1999 and the post-9/11 war in Afghanistan had already created a tense regional environment for a nascent nuclear power and had forced resetting of security priorities in the light of new realities. Institutional control of the nuclear weapons program was under way when two back-to-back crises occurred. First was a terrorist attack on India's Parliament in New Delhi on December 13, 2001. This event led to India's military mobilization and Pakistan's countermobilization, resulting in a ten-month-long military standoff. The India-Pakistan crises would barely be diffused when the discovery of A. Q. Khan's nuclear proliferation network shook the world, and all fingers pointed toward the beleaguered newly nuclear nation. These testing times nevertheless enabled Pakistan to establish an operational nuclear deterrent and improve the robustness of its nuclear command and control.

18   Testing the Deterrent

Since the end of the Cold War, Pakistan's external environment had challenged its strategic significance in the region. The emergence of the United States as a hegemonic power created tensions with China, which in turn brought together Washington and New Delhi. This alliance had serious long-term repercussions for Pakistan. As India inched closer to the United States, it continued its military relationship with Russia, and ostensibly maintained normalcy with China. New Delhi's consistent policy was to isolate Pakistan by running propaganda portraying it as a failed state and emphasizing its alliance with communist China. The military coup provided India with even more fodder for its campaign to delegitimize Pakistan. Musharraf had inherited a sanctioned country that became overtly nuclear during times of domestic turmoil and international opprobrium. Musharraf's seven-point agenda promised to the world in his first address seemed like milestones on a very steep hill.

As Robert Jervis has noted, realizing the true meaning of nuclear revolution is a slow process.[1] In the case of Pakistan, it was bound to be even slower. International circumstances and regional crises, however, accelerated the pace of the nuclear learning curve. It was the post-9/11 international environment and a ten-month military standoff with India that would shape Pakistan's nascent nuclear doctrine and command-and-control system. Acquiring a nuclear capability is one thing; turning it into a viable nuclear force and the state into a nuclear power is another matter. Significant above all were two lessons: (1) nuclear and conventional weapons could be integrated to create a combined deterrent, and (2) deterrence is not automatic: effective deterrence requires will and credible force structures configured to convey resolve. The pathway to acquiring an operational nuclear deterrent required a close examination of national security policy, embedded in which would be the nuclear doctrine and an organizational structure that could implement the decisions.

Security Policy under Musharraf

Musharraf's seven-point agenda would never reach fruition unless he pulled Pakistan out of the sanctions that had crippled the economy. He faced the dilemma of determining what policy concessions could be negotiated in order to lift economic sanctions and relieve Pakistan from international isolation. He sought the right balance of economic exigencies and national security interests as the best strategy to "help the United States help Pakistan."[2] The typical even-handedness of the United States in its policy toward the region, however, began tilting toward India. By the time Musharraf took power, the tilt had become outright discrimination. Nevertheless, Musharraf remained pragmatic and patient. In his first address as army chief to officers in GHQ, he answered a barrage of questions on Pakistan's relationship with the United States: "I am aware of the history . . . . But let me tell you clearly, that you have a choice: you may love America, you may hate America; but you cannot ignore America. Such is the reality of our times and we must live with it."[3]

On October 12, 2000, the same day Musharraf was commemorating the first anniversary of the military coup, Al Qaeda struck at the United States in the Middle East. As the U.S. warship USS *Cole* refueled in Aden Harbor in Yemen, two suicide bombers detonated their explosives-packed boat next to the warship, killing seventeen U.S. sailors and wounding thirty-nine.[4] The Clinton administration, which had largely ignored substantive contacts with the Pakistani military regime, now began to realize the need for cooperation with Islamabad to deal with Al-Qaeda in Afghanistan. From Islamabad's perspective, U.S. officials were less focused on the developments in Afghanistan, but rather were obsessed with nuclear issues.[5] Regardless, it was rather unrealistic for an outgoing administration to expect unsolicited support from a sanctioned ally and a military regime that had been largely cold-shouldered. These disconnects in U.S.-Pakistan relations on nuclear and security issues continued for the next decade, well after the USS *Cole* incident and partnership after 9/11.[6] By the turn of the century, Islamabad's strategic community strongly believed that the United States was a fickle ally that had only a utilitarian view of Pakistan. Far from expecting favors from Washington, Pakistan stayed the course to preserve its nuclear capability and security interests.

Seeking Strategic Relevancy

Like the Carter administration two decades earlier, the Clinton administration faced a dilemma of choosing between nonproliferation and national security. Both Democratic regimes applied nuclear sanctions, but soon realized that the exigencies of national security required Pakistan's partnership and strategic cooperation. Pakistanis characterize their value in this relationship as the "most allied ally" in the 1960s, the "most sanctioned ally" in the 1990s, and the "most bullied ally" in the 2000s.[7]

For Islamabad to preserve its strategic relations with the United States, it had to remain important to U.S. security interests and do all it could to avoid ideologically clashing with it. Pakistan's relevancy rested on an honest net reappraisal of its national assets and liabilities. The new military regime was aware that its geographical location, basic resources, people talent, and relative military strength were tangible assets. But it was lacking in a high-tech industrial base, national coherence, domestic stability, and international prestige.[8]

On balance, Pakistan's cumulative national power was enough to withstand shocks, but not enough to compete with India. Seeking parity with India or engaging in competition would be unwise. Yet throwing in the towel and capitulating under pressure would be equally dangerous. In this catch-22, Pakistan could neither compete nor give up. The middle path was the only realizable course—to follow a policy of finite deterrence. This policy had three main components: (1) seek strategic balance without entering a debilitating arms race, (2) stymie India's machinations of isolating Pakistan through adroit diplomacy and strategic alliances, and (3) maintain an adequate nuclear and conventional force posture that would make any Indian attack prohibitively costly.[9]

Musharraf's quest to seek a solution soon ran into an impasse. Finding consensus among competing stakeholders within the bureaucracy, branches of the military, and policy-makers was difficult.[10] The interagency process, in which the author was involved, underwent prolonged and meaningless deliberations. On the hawkish side were suggestions that Pakistan should demand that the United States accept the country as a nuclear weapons state in the Nuclear Non-Proliferation Treaty (NPT), provide dozens of F-16s in return for a Comprehensive Test Ban Treaty (CTBT) signature, allot $100 billion in economic aid, and relieve Pakistan's foreign debt (approximately $38 billion at the time). At the dovish end of the spectrum were suggestions that Pakistan concede fundamental national security objectives on India, Afghanistan, and Kashmir, and even freeze the nuclear program in exchange for economic gain. Many Pakistani officials were either lacking in sufficient acumen to comprehend the gravity of its national situation or had no clue about the basics of international relations. Overall, the officials were too rigid and in some cases even disingenuous to allow any initiative to come to fruition.[11]

By the end of the year, national security compulsions were forcing the Clinton administration to reengage with Pakistan. However, the decision to open channels of communication came a bit late. Pakistan needed time to reflect on its own security policies and waited for the new administration to take office before starting negotiations. Islamabad's policy response was no different than in 1980, when changing regional dynamics in a U.S. election year compelled the United States to deal with a military regime under sanctions and for Pakistan to wait for the election outcome in the United States.[12]

Change of the Guard in Washington

With George W. Bush's Republican government in the White House, hope was rekindled in Islamabad. Colin Powell's appointment as secretary of state was a welcome change because he was highly respected in Pakistan and was a former general, making diplomacy with another military leader in Pakistan more fitting. But more significantly, he had been national security advisor under President Reagan, when U.S.-Pakistani relations had seen sunnier days. By the summer of 2001, Pakistani-U.S. relations had begun to thaw, since President Bush was not an enthusiast of arms control issues. There was anticipation in Pakistan that the nuclear issue would not be the centerpiece of their strategic affairs. Under these changing circumstances, Musharraf's security policy evolved in about a year's time.[13]

As briefly explained in Chapter 17, Musharraf's security policy was based on four pillars. First, economic revival and national prosperity would be at the core of national policy.[14] The revival of the economy would require support from international finance institutions and major Western countries. To gain Western support, however, Pakistan needed to address issues such as terrorism, peace with India, and democratic reform. And to better manage its finances, the budget deficit had to be reduced, defense expenditures monitored, and fiscal discipline enforced. All of these steps would enhance credibility for a positive investment climate.

The second pillar was the preservation of a nuclear and conventional force deterrent as a cornerstone of national defense policy. Pakistan required a balanced force posture to deter India and at the same time placate nonproliferation enthusiasts. Pakistan would consider signing the CTBT, negotiating the Fissile Material Cut-off Treaty (FMCT), and strengthening export control measures. Third, detente and rapprochement with India had to complement deterrence and would be a necessary component of Pakistan's security policy. It needed to revive a dialogue with India and move past the bitterness of Kargil toward finding peaceful conflict resolution.

The fourth and final pillar of its security policy was to ensure stability in Afghanistan. A friendly and stable Afghanistan was a must for Pakistani national security. Islamabad was convinced that political stability in Afghanistan was guaranteed only under the authority of an ethnically balanced and legitimate, tribally supported regime. Pakistan had supported the Taliban in the past because they brought a semblance of stability to Afghanistan; however, the Taliban regime was anything but Islamabad's puppet and had in fact become a liability for Pakistan. Several Pakistani envoys from abroad suggested to Musharraf that he find a resolution to the Osama bin Laden problem. For example, the Taliban regime could evict the Al Qaeda leadership from Afghan territory and hand over bin Laden to the Saudi Arabian authorities. Afghan policy would simply be to ensure the stability and balanced settlement of all stakeholders in Kabul.[15]

Prelude to 9/11

Prior to 9/11, three events in Pakistan reshaped its image internationally. First, on April 1, 2001, Musharraf removed A. Q. Khan from the Khan Research Laboratories (KRL) and retired Ishfaq Ahmad, who had completed ten years as Chairman PAEC. He appointed both of them as advisors to the government. This was the first sign that the military regime was tightening its control and that Khan could no longer freely conduct his activities. Second, on June 18, 2001, Pakistani Foreign Minister Abdul Sattar gave a keynote speech at the Carnegie Endowment's Nonproliferation Conference in which he announced Pakistan's nuclear policies. He explicitly stated that his country's doctrine rested on the premise of no use of force—conventional or nuclear.[16] Third, in July 2001, India's prime minister, Atal Bihari Vajpayee, invited Musharraf to pay an official visit and Musharraf accepted. As he boarded the plane for New Delhi, he was an all-powerful man wearing four hats simultaneously: president, chief executive, Chairman Joint Chief of Staff Committee (CJCSC), and Chief of the Army Staff (COAS).[17]

Taken together, the three events in 2001 painted Pakistan in a positive light and generated considerable interest in the United States and abroad. Islamabad was publicly assuming the responsibilities as a new nuclear power, easing regional tensions, and improving proliferation controls. Furthermore, Musharraf's image had begun to shift from that of a maverick to one of a capable leader, whose liberal outlook and willingness to rein in extremist groups had raised hopes for better international cooperation on both nuclear and terrorism issues.[18]

The 9/11 Attacks

The evening of September 11, 2001, was probably one of the tensest moments in Pakistan's history. As news of the terrorist attack on U.S. soil shocked the world, Pakistan was sucked into a vortex of international calamity. No other event in recent history had sparked an overnight change in the international system. Suddenly, the world began to depend on Pakistan's cooperation in the aftermath of the tragedy. Musharraf aptly notes in his memoir that it was "one day that changed the world . . . . September 11 marked an irrevocable turn from past into an unknown future. The world would never be the same."[19]

The very next morning Secretary of State Colin Powell called President Musharraf to ask simply, "Are you with us or against us?" Director general of the Inter-Services Intelligence (ISI), Lieutenant General Mahmud Ahmad, was on an official visit in Washington, DC, and was asked the identical question by his CIA counterpart. In a later meeting with Deputy Secretary of the State Richard Armitage, he was allegedly warned that should Pakistan decide to oppose the United States it "should be prepared to be bombed back to the Stone Age."[20]

Pakistani authorities were nonplussed by the undiplomatic manner with which Washington requested their cooperation. Even before Powell had called Musharraf, the latter had already publicly condemned the attack and offered assistance.[21] Whether or not outright threat was conveyed, Musharraf had no doubt that the United States would react "like a wounded bear."[22]

Dispersal and Survivability

At the first sign of a veiled U.S. threat, Islamabad went into action.[23] Powell's phone call coupled with Armitage's statement (irrespective of whether Mahmud exaggerated the threat) rattled Pakistan; both were perceived as an attempt to disarm the nascent nuclear country.[24] As Washington planned an urgent strike against Afghanistan, Islamabad's decades-long fear of preventive strikes sent it into high alert.

In the week of September 11–19, Pakistan's armed forces were ordered to be on enhanced readiness. Musharraf considered the demands placed before him by U.S. Ambassador Wendy Chamberlain. These demands included: sharing intelligence, deconflicting Pakistani airspace for use by the U.S. Air Force, and providing logistical bases for operations in Afghanistan. Historically, these requests were not inconsistent with the nature of cooperation expected between the allies and so raised only one concern—the safety of Pakistan's strategically sensitive sites.[25] Conceding to the U.S. demands, especially on providing air space, compromised strategic assets. Musharraf deliberated on how to respond.[26]

Before he could make a decision, however, President Musharraf directed Strategic Plans Division (SPD) to secure all strategic weapons without delay. It was here that the true value of SPD was realized. In the previous two plus years, SPD had prepared hardened silos at secret locations for storage of nuclear warheads and their means of delivery.[27] A "Consultancy Directorate" had been created in SPD whose exclusive task was to study and design the silos to withstand external attacks (for the organizational structure of SPD, see Figure 2 in Chapter 17).[28] Like all other nuclear projects, this one was yet another on-the-job learning experience. No blueprint or template for such silos existed, so experts had to rely on open sources and their own ingenuity. There were constant studies and in-house deliberations between scientists, engineers, and security experts about the best means of ensuring secrecy, dispersal, and survivability of Pakistan's strategic weapons. The exact number, location, and quality of sites are classified, as would be any nation's most treasured secret.

Planning and coordination of this mission was done under the supervision and control of the National Military Command Centre (NMCC) at Joint Services Headquarters (JSHQ).[29] The Pakistan Air Force (PAF) and Army Aviation moved nuclear weapons to several secret sites, during which time airports in Islamabad and elsewhere shut down all commercial flights.[30] Once President Musharraf was given assurances that all strategic assets had been secured, he was prepared to respond to the United States.

In the end, Musharraf reversed policy on Afghanistan and abandoned the Taliban. He later wrote in his memoir that this decision was made in part to preserve Pakistan's nuclear capability. He observed, "The security of our strategic assets would be jeopardized. We did not want to lose or damage the military parity that we had achieved with India by becoming a nuclear weapon state. It is no secret that the United States has never been comfortable with a Muslim country acquiring nuclear weapons, and the Americans undoubtedly would have taken the opportunity of an invasion to destroy such weapons. And India, needless to say, would have loved to assist the United States to the hilt."[31]

The Hammer and the Anvil

On October 7, 2001, the United States attacked Afghanistan in "Operation Enduring Freedom." For three weeks before the U.S. attack, Pakistan tried in vain to convince Mullah Omar and the Taliban regime to expel or hand over the perpetrators of 9/11 to avoid a U.S. attack on the territory. The effort was futile.

When the operation started, nearly two-thirds of Pakistani airspace was de-conflicted for use by U.S. forces, and several bases were provided for logistical support. While air, naval, and amphibious landings as well as the delivery of almost 75 percent of supplies were conducted from south to north using Pakistani territory and cooperation, the ground operations were conducted from north to south using Northern Alliance (predominantly non-Pashtun) forces. This strategy forced the Taliban to melt into the Pashtun tribal belts in eastern and southern Afghanistan and across the porous border into Pakistani tribal areas, or Federally Administered Tribal Areas (FATA). The swift and kinetic U.S.-led operation resulted in the sudden collapse of the Taliban regime and capture of Kabul.

Two major operations followed, in December 2001 and March/April 2002, Operation Tora Bora and Anaconda, respectively. Both were conducted close to the mountainous region of the Pakistan-Afghanistan border and involved a dual strategy: hammer (U.S.-led offensive) and anvil (Pakistani forces defending the border). Both operations failed to decisively decimate the senior Al-Qaeda leadership, which allowed Taliban fighters to escape across into FATA.

The hammer-and-anvil strategy had several planning and execution flaws. First, the military operations using Northern Alliance partners pushed the Taliban toward familiar areas in which the militants had waged war against the Soviets and further alienated the Pashtun community at large. The location of U.S. offensives was not coordinated with Islamabad, making it impossible to create an anvil.[32] The Pakistani Army was led into the porous border, an area with which they were very unfamiliar and which was essentially a "no-go" zone per a previous agreement with the tribes. Despite little or no coordination on operations near its western borders, efforts were underway to "peacefully penetrate" tribal areas.[33] By the middle of December, some 100,000 Pakistani forces involving almost the entire 11 Corps in Peshawar, the North West Frontier Province (NWFP), or Khyber Pakhtun Khwa (new name) and 12 Corps in Quetta, Baluchistan, were deployed to seal the Afghan border as U.S. forces struck the "hammer" in nearby Afghanistan. It was then that reports of full-scale mobilization of the Indian Army began to emerge. By early January, across its eastern border, a million-strong Indian army was deployed. The Pakistani Army knew that India could not stomach the fact that Pakistan had become a "key frontline state," and the predominant view in the U.S. embassy in Islamabad was that India was an irritant in the execution of Operation Enduring Freedom and that India's mobilization interfered with the primary objective of the United States to ensure Pakistani military focus on the ongoing operations in Afghanistan.[34] Never before in Pakistan's history had it faced two fronts as it did in the period from December 2001 to October 2002.[35] The time for Pakistan to test its deterrent capability was approaching. Finally, at the end of 2002–early 2003, the United States shifted its focus from Afghanistan to Iraq.

Military Stand-off with India

Almost two years before, on the eve of India's Republic Day, January 25, 2000, India's defense minister, George Fernandez, formally announced a new doctrine of "limited war under the nuclear umbrella." Buoyed by the success of Kargil and unprecedented U.S. support, Indian Army Chief General Ved Prakash Malik had often surmised that conventional wars and victory were achievable goals, a view now endorsed by Defense Minister Fernandez. They argued that there exists space between low-intensity wars and nuclear war, in which India's conventional force advantage can prevail over the weaker Pakistan. This limited war would hypothetically terminate without triggering a nuclear attack and would be put to the test in the 2001–2 military standoff.

Musharraf had barely begun to enjoy Pakistan's new, positive image when five suicide militants attacked the Indian Parliament with guns and hand grenades on December 13, 2001. Nine people were killed in a shootout that lasted for ninety minutes.[36] Two months earlier, a nearly identical terrorist attack on the State Assembly in Indian administered Kashmir had been reported.

The very next day India blamed Lashkar-e-Tayyaba (LET), a Pakistani-based organization that was waging *jihad* in support of Kashmiri freedom. U.S. ambassador to India Robert Blackwill explicitly characterized the attack on India as "no different in its objective from terror attacks in the United States on September 11."[37] By drawing the analogy with 9/11, the U.S. envoy was inciting India to up the ante and take advantage of the post-9/11 environment. But the Indian army hardly needed that; it was raring to go.[38]

The First Phase of Crisis: December 13–May 2002

On December 15, 2001, India's Cabinet Committee on Security (CCS) decided to mobilize for war. Three weeks later, on January 3, 2002, the army was ready for offensive actions dubbed Operation Parakaram.[39] Not since the 1971 war had India mobilized 500,000 troops, including its three strike corps.[40] Pakistan then began to countermobilize. For the fifth time since the occupation of Siachin in 1984, India and Pakistan were again on the brink of outright war, though this time the scale of mobilization on Pakistan's borders was full and unprecedented since the 1971 war.

In a strategic choreography, India then progressively upped the diplomatic and political ante. New Delhi recalled its high commissioner in Islamabad, Vijay K. Nambiar, on December 21, 2001.[41] On December 25, the press reported that Indian *Prithvi* ballistic missiles had been deployed.[42] Just a day later, Indian newspapers reported that the Army Day parade was to be canceled under the pretext that the troops were needed on the borders.[43] On December 27, India barred Pakistani National Airlines from flying over its airspace and ordered 50 percent of its diplomats to return to New Delhi within forty-eight hours.[44] Indian Foreign Minister Jaswant Singh publicly denounced Pakistan for not taking India's concerns seriously and declared that India's prime minister would not meet President Musharraf at the upcoming South Asian Association for Regional Cooperation (SAARC) summit.[45] Shortly thereafter, India announced its "biggest military exercise in 15 years" to be conducted in the Rajasthan desert and the plains of Punjab. Finally, on December 31, 2001, India submitted a list of twenty alleged terrorists, demanding their extradition.[46]

Reactions in Pakistan matched India's escalation. Musharraf sent his condolences and condemned the terrorist attacks on Indian soil. However, as soon as India began to mobilize, Pakistan put its troops on alert and warned on December 14 that "India will pay heavily if they engage in any misadventure."[47] But in two acts of good faith, Pakistan offered a joint investigation of the attacks, which India then rejected, and kept its high commissioner in New Delhi, stating that cutting off communications during a crisis is not a good precedent.[48]

Furthermore on January 12, 2002, Musharraf addressed the nation, stating that Pakistan would not tolerate groups that "carry out terrorism under the pretext of the Kashmir issue."[49] This announcement was followed by widespread arrests of leaders from the organizations that India accused and the banning of several other organizations. Over the next few days 1,430 people were arrested and more than four hundred militant group headquarters were sealed.[50]

As India's force mobilization was completed, the Pakistan military had already taken up its defensive position. On January 10, 2002, Pakistan notified the United States in advance that it might need to retake some of its airbases, specifically Jacobabad, which had been dedicated to U.S. operations in Afghanistan. Some of Pakistan's troops that were designated to deploy on the western borders were stalled in preparation for a move to the Indian border. Meanwhile, the United States declared that it was shifting its operational bases to Central Asia.

On January 25, India conducted a flight test of its new solid-fuel, single-stage *Agni I* missile, which had a range of seven hundred to nine hundred km and a payload of 1,000 kg. The next day it was paraded in New Delhi, advertised as a "Pakistan-specific missile."[51] The test, coupled with the parade, indicated that India did not take Musharraf's speech seriously.[52] Meanwhile, one of India's offensive strike corps, commanded by Lieutenant-General Kapil Vij, made threatening moves close to Pakistan's border that were picked up by U.S. satellites. The United States provided this information to Indian authorities, and General Vij was quickly removed from command.[53]

Although traditionally Pakistan might have responded in kind to India's actions, especially the missile flight-tests, this time it held back.

The Second Phase of Crisis: May 14, 2002–June 17, 2002

Amid a flurry of international diplomatic activity in the region in January, Prime Minister Vajpayee's political leadership overruled the war-hungry bureaucrats in New Delhi. Behind this decision was the quick mobilization of Pakistan's troops into a counterstrike position, leaving India with no advantage.[54] The first surge of crisis was diffused by January; however, troops remained deployed along the border, which was becoming a costly affair for India, both in economic terms as well as soldier and civilian casualties in deployed areas.[55] As winter turned to spring, another tension brewed when a violent Hindu-Muslim clash began in the Indian state of Gujarat in late February/March 2002. By the first week of March hundreds of Muslims had been killed or left homeless in refugee camps. This situation created yet another tense environment with frustrated troops deployed on either side of the border.[56]

Meanwhile, on Pakistan's western borderlands, U.S. forces began Operation Anaconda. Pakistan's forces were distracted on two borders and were obviously less effective in those areas as force deployment deepened with India on Pakistan's eastern border. The foundation was laid for potential mistrust between the United States and Pakistan. The U.S. accused Pakistan of not doing enough to prevent Al Qaeda from crossing the border, and Pakistan alleged that the United States never coordinated effectively with Pakistan. One senior officer told the author, "[F]ar from being sympathetic to the Pakistani two-front dilemma, the United States brushed it aside and India could not digest the fact that Pakistan was a front-line state, once again."[57]

By May 2002 things had seemingly calmed down. At the same time, the "largest ever" India-U.S. military exercise was to take place for two weeks in Agra, demonstrating the "growing strategic cooperation between the two countries."[58] The Indian defense minister stated that India had no plans to launch a military attack over the next few months.[59]

War Closes In

It seems as if the defense minister spoke too soon. Around the same time, another terrorist attack occurred at an Indian military camp in Kashmir, killing thirty-one people.[60] The next day India blamed Pakistan and threatened retaliation. Indian Army Chief General S. Padmanabhan stated that "the time for action has come."[61] Pakistan dismissed the allegations and was convinced that New Delhi was attempting to divert attention away from the Muslim genocide in Gujarat.[62]

On May 18, 2002, New Delhi demanded that Pakistan High Commissioner to India Ashraf Jahangir Kazi leave India, and Islamabad recalled him. Meanwhile, heavy shelling began on the Line of Control (LOC) and other border regions. Four days later, moderate Kashmiri leader Abdul Ghani Lone was assassinated in the Kashmir Valley, just when Indian Prime Minister Vajpayee was visiting the area and had announced India to be ready for "the decisive fight."[63] Kashmir was in an uproar as the Indian Army moved more troops to the border and the Indian Navy moved five Eastern Fleet warships into the Arabian Sea toward Pakistan.[64] The following day India threatened to scrap the forty-two-year-old

Indus Water Treaty, and Minister of Water Resources Bijoya Chakraborty said, "[If] we decide to scrap the Indus Water Treaty, then there will be drought in Pakistan and people of that country [will] have to beg for every drop of water."[65] Pakistan was quick to call these actions "economic strangulation" and a part of India's strategy to stifle Pakistan with a combination of shutting off river flows from dams in Indian-administered Kashmir and blockading Karachi, the sole port of Pakistan.[66]

President Musharraf declared that the two countries "were closer to war than at any time since the Dec. 13th attack on the Indian Parliament." India's heightened aggressive rhetoric could no longer be ignored.[67] Pakistan began shifting troops from Afghanistan, and the PAF was placed on full alert as Pakistan braced for an attack.

Deterrence Signaling

It was during this time that Pakistan conducted three back-to-back missile flight tests of *Ghauri* and *Hatfs* (*Ghaznavi* and *Abdali*) (see Chapter 12).[68] The flight tests occurred at the height of tensions and were the country's most explicit warning to India.[69] Addressing Pakistani scientists on June 17, 2002, President Musharraf said,

> We were compelled to show then, in May 1998 that we were not bluffing and in May 2002, we were compelled to show that we do not bluff . . . . By testing with outstanding success the delivery systems of our strategic capability, these men validated the reliability, accuracy, and the deterrence value of Pakistan's premier surface-to-surface ballistic missile systems of the *Hatf* series, namely—*Ghauri, Ghaznavi, and Abdali* . . . . [We] need to ensure that the three basic ingredients of deterrence—capability, credibility, and resolve—never got compromised.[70]

A new norm of signaling deterrence emerged in South Asia, in which missile flight tests at the peak of crises were used as messages to adversaries and other audiences. The continued military standoff allowed Pakistan to develop a subtle politico-military response by integrating three elements: conventional force deployment and rapid countermobilizations; missile testing; and diplomatic offensive.[71] On May 29, Islamabad sent five special envoys to the United States, Europe, and Islamic countries to explain and defend Pakistani positions.[72]

By May 31, the two sides had come very close to war. President Musharraf told the author that on one night we had authenticated intelligence that India would attack the next morning. He said, "[We] ordered the armed forces to be ready and the PAF was ordered to attack back immediately. We would have not waited but our retaliation plans were ready." He did not elaborate what the "retaliation plans" were, but clearly stated there was no plan to employ nuclear weapons.[73]

In the midst of the conflict, a flurry of international diplomatic activity began. U.S. Defense Secretary Donald Rumsfeld traveled to the region to calm tensions.[74] On June 7, U.S. Deputy Secretary of the State Richard Armitage arrived to speak with both countries. Three days later, the first signs of thaw emerged when India lifted its ban on Pakistani fly-overs and sent its naval warships in the Arabian Sea back to their original bases.[75] By the middle of the month the crisis had subsided. On June 20, the Indian defense minister confirmed that cross-border infiltration had nearly ended.

From Pakistan's standpoint, India's force mobilization in 2001–2 was yet another example of how New Delhi uses its superior military might to force Pakistan into submission. The terrorist attack on the Indian Parliament could not have come at worse moment for Pakistan.[76] India was frustrated at the renewed importance of Pakistan as a critical ally of the United States and found the attack to be a timely excuse to test its limited war doctrine.[77]

Nuclear Dimensions

Significant in the crisis was the reduced rhetoric about nuclear weapons. By and large, the Pakistani leadership downplayed the role of nuclear weapons.[78] Despite speculation to the contrary, to this author's knowledge, nuclear weapons were not readied during the 2001–2 crisis. However, several Western and Indian sources claim that there were indeed veiled nuclear threats made by Musharraf.[79] These allegations cite two interviews as evidence: (1) Lieutenant-General Khalid Kidwai's interview with Italian physicists in January 2002, and (2) a *Der Spiegel* interview with Musharraf on April 6, 2002. This first interview had no connection with the evolving military crisis, but rather was a discussion on the policy of nuclear use in his office. "Pakistani nuclear weapons would be used only if the very existence of Pakistan as a state is at stake. . . . Nuclear weapons are aimed solely at India." Kidwai explained that in case that deterrence fails, they will be used if:

A. India attacks Pakistan and conquers a large part of its territory (space threshold)

B. India destroys a large part either of Pakistani land or air forces (military thresholds)

C. India engages in economic strangling of Pakistan (economic strangling)

D. India pushes Pakistan into political destabilization or creates a large-scale internal subversion in Pakistan (domestic destabilization).[80]

The above criterion on employment of nuclear weapons was deliberately imprecise. These are the factors that will govern the decision-making of the National Command Authority (NCA). However, it clarifies Pakistan's approach to deter India's conventional and nuclear threat, and to dissuade India from making nonmilitary threats to Pakistan's territorial integrity.

In the second aforementioned interview, President Musharraf responded to a question by stating, "Nuclear weapons are the last resort. I am optimistic and confident that we can defend ourselves with conventional means, even though the Indians are buying up the most modern weapons in a frenzy. Nuclear weapons could be used if Pakistan is threatened with extinction, then the pressure of our countrymen would be so big that this option too, would have to be considered. In a crisis, nuclear weapons also have to be part of the calculation"[81]

Neither of these two statements was meant as a naked threat of nuclear weapon use, but it was ambiguous enough not to rule it out. Statements from Pakistani officials as well as strategic scholars are unambiguous in that any military attack on Pakistan will be met with equal response. Pakistan would not clarify the red-line risks beyond the four criteria expressed above.

Meanwhile, statements from India were mixed regarding nuclear issues. One day India would threaten that nuclear war was near; then foreigners would evacuate, so the next day it would downplay the threat of war. The same day that Musharraf dismissed the "absolutely baseless" charges that Pakistan had moved missiles to the border, India's defense secretary, Yogendra Narain, stated, "Pakistan is not a democratic country and we do not know their nuclear threshold. We will retaliate and must be prepared for mutual destruction on both sides."[82]

In contrast to his subordinate, Indian Defense Minister Fernandez repeatedly dismissed fears of nuclear war. On June 3, 2002, he stated, "I don't agree with the idea that India and Pakistan are so imprudent and excitable that they will forget what nuclear weapons can do."[83]

With the unlikelihood of Pakistan's accepting a no-first-use policy, the doctrinal puzzle of the Pakistani nuclear program is put to rest.[84] The objectives of its program are twofold. The first objective is to prevent India from destroying or overwhelming Pakistan. Nuclear weapons thus not only ensure physical defense of the nation but also maintain its national sovereignty. The second objective is to deter an Indian conventional attack. For a credible deterrence, it was clearly communicated that nuclear weapons and a robust conventional force were ready to meet limited war threats as a necessary measure for national security.[85]

Pakistan Nuclear Force Postures: The Impact of Military Standoff

The ten-month military standoff only reinforced India's perpetual existential threat to Pakistan. Pakistan would lack the resources to begin major mobilizations whenever terrorists attacked India and instead would be forced to rely even more on nuclear deterrence. In this vein, the 2002 crises guided Pakistan's nuclear force posture, which is now directly related to India's conventional force postures, military doctrines, and periodic force mobilization.

Nuclear weapons ensured Pakistan's national sovereignty, prevented bullying by India, and deterred a physical invasion. However, India is unlikely to be deterred from using its conventional superiority in military scenarios. For Pakistan, any conventional military attack from India would constitute a deterrence failure. As India escapes from deterrence and Pakistan relies on it, the notion of deterrence stability in the region is dubious at best.

By the time of the second peak of the crisis, in May 2002, the Pakistan military had finalized plans for integrating its conventional and nuclear forces. The crisis actually provided Pakistani officials a real-time environment in which they could hypothesize and create scenarios from which to design conventional and nuclear responses. The crisis accelerated the pace of force planning and integration.

However, a number of internal problems and resource limitations would also affect Pakistan's nuclear force posture. Pakistani planners in SPD were cognizant of the constrained economy and understood matching Indian advances exactly would be unwise. By adopting a policy of secrecy and ambiguity, Pakistan avoided the need to match India and also hid deficiencies that could otherwise be exploited.

Pakistan had maintained that a state of nondeployment is an effective means of maintaining centralized control of its assets. The NCA under President

Musharraf recognized that imminent war scenarios would require that key decisions be made before the fighting began, some of which might involve the assembly of nuclear forces. The dilemma lay in how to ready dispersed weapons and at what stage in the conflict strategic forces should shift from an unassembled state to "ready to launch."[86] Fortunately, none of these preparations were necessary during the 2001–2 crisis. In an interview on June 4, 2002, Musharraf said, "The possession of nuclear weapons by any state obviously implies that they will be used under some circumstances. However, our larger policy is de-nuclearization of South Asia. Never in the history of Pakistan has a nuclear arsenal ever been deployed, never even the missiles . . . deployed."[87] By far this statement was the most categorical on nondeployment of nuclear weapons, especially given that the crisis was at its peak and all foreigners were evacuating the area. Several Indian analysts also acknowledged that India and Pakistan adhered to nuclear discipline in all military crises. Former Lieutenant-General V. R. Raghavan, a respected Indian scholar on strategic affairs wrote, "Though numerous concerns have been expressed through the word of the Western media, the security and safety standards in India and Pakistan have remained relatively high. In South Asia, nuclear weapons have never been put into formal deployments or put into alert status, despite a series of crises."[88]

For nearly four years, SPD functioned to achieve five major NCA directives to guide nuclear force planning. First, minimum credible deterrence would be the guiding principle of strategic planning. Immediate strategic force goals would be based on a threat hypothesis, but periodic review would revise force goals when required. Second, force goal planning would always be considered within the constraints of technical and financial resources. Third, plans would integrate conventional and nuclear forces into operationally effective deterrent forces at the joint services level—with control firmly within the NCA. Fourth, conventional war plans would be independent of nuclear forces. Finally, nuclear weapons and related activities would be under centralized control to ensure safety, security, survivability, and readiness.

Pakistan's Strategic Force Command (SFC) took its final shape during the period of the conflict. By 2002, Pakistan had established its air and land nuclear forces and created ballistic missile units. The PAF air squadrons under the Strategic Air Commands operated under a coherent command, control, communication, and intelligence (C3I) system that was linked with Pakistan's national military operation centers at the JSHQ.

By October 2002 the crisis had ended and Pakistan had a newly elected Parliament. By this time the nation had established a fully operationalized nuclear capability. For ten months there was never a need to put its nuclear forces on alert.[89] The crisis, however, gave Pakistan confidence in its nuclear deterrent and provided important lessons for nuclear planners who continued to develop concepts and procedures to ensure the security and readiness of the nuclear forces. From then on, every crisis involving India and Pakistan would have a nuclear backdrop.

Pakistani confidence in its national security was aptly summarized in Musharraf's memoir. "We went through a period of extreme tension throughout 2002, when Indian troops amassed in an eyeball-to-eyeball confrontation. We responded by moving all our forces forward. The standoff lasted 10 months. Then the Indians blinked and quite ignominiously agreed to a mutual withdrawal of forces."[90]

Part V: Meeting New Challenges

19   The Unraveling of the Khan Network

Sultan Bashiruddin Mahmood and A. Q. Khan were the two stalwarts of the nuclear program in the 1970s; both contributed immensely, yet both acted in controversial ways that nearly brought the program to its knees. The Khan nuclear proliferation network and a meeting between Mahmood and Osama bin Laden in summer of 2001 left their marks on the history of the program and continue to haunt Pakistan even today.

During an interview at his residence on June 18, 2006, President Pervez Musharraf was asked by the author, "In your seven years in power, there were four major crises that you faced: namely, the 1999 coup, 9/11, the 2001–2002 standoff with India, and finally, the exposure of the A. Q. Khan network in 2004. In your opinion, which was the most worrying or dangerous?" Before the author had even finished his question, President Musharraf answered unequivocally: "The A. Q. Khan crisis." He elaborated that in all the other crises he had had an intuitive sense of how to lead and confidence in finding a solution. However, the A. Q. Khan episode was "like a fast train coming head on . . . . [It] was a puzzle whose pieces were unknown . . . . [N]ot knowing the depth of a situation [was] the most difficult thing to deal with." Musharraf explained further, "[T]he public image of A. Q. Khan was that of a legend and father of the bomb. He certainly was a hero for his role and contribution to the nuclear program, but at the same time no other person brought so much harm to the nuclear program than him."[1]

A. Q. Khan had been granted autonomy to procure a nuclear capability for Pakistan and he delivered. The nation honored him with the highest awards and respect, and he was granted the utmost freedom, more than any other individual or organization. Yet he behaved as if he were larger than life and answerable to no authority, and he indulged in activities dangerous to Pakistan's national interests. It is a matter of personal judgment whether he was a hero or villain, but in either case, the A. Q. Khan crisis was undoubtedly the darkest chapter in the country's nuclear history.

A Nuclear Program Stigmatized

Early Suspicions and Removal of A. Q. Khan from KRL

In February 2000, after the National Command Authority (NCA) was officially created, the Strategic Plans Division (SPD) began to execute institutional oversight and control over all strategic organizations. Clearance was now required for all travel, media appearances, interviews, and official visits or transactions with any foreign government or entities. SPD also began to work closely with the Ministry of Foreign Affairs and Ministry of Defense to tighten measures and streamline procedures for clearance and control processes, which were hitherto loose and lacking accountability. No other strategic organization had difficulties with these new measures except for the Khan Research Laboratories (KRL). A. Q. Khan resisted, and soon his activities came into question—especially his suspicious travels abroad. President Musharraf directed intelligence agencies and SPD to monitor Khan. Close surveillance revealed three incidents that caused A. Q. Khan's removal from KRL.

The first was when A. Q. Khan requested a chartered flight from Turkey and was unable to explain why the flight was to be refueled at Zahidan, Iran. In a second instance, North Korean nuclear scientists visited KRL, possibly in disguise, and unbeknownst to the president. Khan flatly denied that there were any scientists involved.[2] Finally, there were allegations that a chartered flight to North Korea, typical for carrying conventional munitions, was carrying unauthorized cargo—possibly centrifuges. The plane was raided by Inter-Services Intelligence (ISI) but failed to yield any evidence, indicating that A. Q. Khan had most likely been tipped off.[3] Khan could not reconcile himself to the fact that he could be questioned, much less have his plane raided. Continued tension between A. Q. Khan and state authorities eventually resulted in his removal as KRL's chairman in March 2001.

Retired Scientists Meet Osama bin Laden

As mentioned in the previous chapter, the relationship between the United States and Pakistan took on a new dimension after September 11, 2001. In addition to enlisting Pakistan's cooperation in counterterrorism efforts, the United

States became especially concerned with the security of Pakistan's nuclear arsenal. These concerns were triggered when the U.S. discovered in early October 2001 that two retired Pakistani nuclear scientists, Chaudhry Abdul Majid and Sultan Bashiruddin Mahmood, had met with Al Qaeda leaders in Afghanistan in August of that year. Chaudhry Abdul Majid had been a nuclear fuel expert at the Pakistan Institute of Nuclear Science and Technology (PINSTECH), from where he had retired in 2000. Sultan Bashiruddin Mahmood, the chief designer and director of Pakistan's Khushab Plutonium Production Reactor, retired in 1999 after bitterly opposing the government's stance on the Comprehensive Test Ban Treaty (CTBT) and Pakistan Atomic Energy Commission (PAEC) policies.[4] It may be recalled that Mahmood's aggressive management style created a rift between him and A. Q. Khan, and was only exacerbated when the former was removed from Pakistan's uranium enrichment program, which was then handed over to Khan.[5]

Mahmood founded the *Ummah Tameer-e-Nau* (UTN), loosely translated Reconstruction of Islamic Community, a charity relief agency that included a number of retired engineers, physicists, chemists, and former military officers. Regarding Mahmood's and Majid's meeting with Osama bin Laden and other Al Qaeda members, Mahmood explained in an interview with the author that UTN was working toward economic reconstruction and had nothing to do with bombs or nuclear technology. He claimed, "The allegation that we were selling nuclear expertise is all drama and lies," and he complained bitterly that UTN was unfairly disbanded and its accounts were frozen, taking away the livelihood of many honest workers. According to Mahmood, "UTN was not working clandestinely or engaged in any terror activities and our dealings were transparent and above board. We met Mullah Omar several times and Osama only once."[6] In the several meetings with Mullah Omar and Afghan ministers, he said that he was promoting the idea of economic integration, and in 2000 proposed a five-year plan for development of Afghanistan that would target the country's vast mineral ores. He also suggested that Pakistan's industrial and technical sector could be employed to help further explore and extract the natural resources. He explained to Taliban authorities that industrial progress could not occur unless they developed a skilled labor force, and for that purpose Mahmood proposed the establishment of a Polytechnic Institute in Kabul. Mullah Omar directed the Taliban authorities to arrange a meeting between Mahmood and Sheikh Osama bin Laden, who had the money. In August 2001, a UTN team that included both Majid and

Mahmood met Osama bin Laden solely to request funding for the proposed institute.

Mahmood claimed that Osama bin Laden and his Al Qaeda colleagues listened but refused to provide any financial assistance. Impressed by the scientific background of the two visitors, Osama was more interested in knowing how Pakistan had achieved a nuclear capability. In Mahmood's own words, "Osama brought up the nuclear subject in a very general sense and I explained the benefits of nuclear energy and emphasized the difficulties and challenges in building and maintaining nuclear weapons." According to Mahmood, he dissuaded the Al Qaeda leader from pursuing a nuclear program. He said, "If at all they were thinking [about a nuclear capability], after this meeting they [must have realized] this was all very challenging."[7]

Once U.S. intelligence sources informed Pakistani authorities of this meeting, Mahmood and Majid were arrested on October 23, 2001, and several other UTN members were called in for questioning. Sultan Bashiruddin Mahmood told the author that the Central Intelligence Agency (CIA) and other U.S. experts interrogated him and Majid, as well as two UTN members, Yousef Beg and Arshad Ali Chaudhry. Mahmood said to the author, "[We] gave the CIA officials the entire detail of our meeting with Osama. Majid [who had passed away in 2006] and I told them everything truthfully that was discussed in our meeting with Osama bin Laden. But the Americans never believed it." The author asked Mahmood whether he was questioned under duress, to which Mahmood replied, "I was never physically tortured by anyone, neither by the ISI nor the CIA or the Americans . . . and I had no reason to lie . . . . My family and friends were worried of course we may be transferred somewhere else like Guantanamo or somewhere but by the Mercy of Almighty, we were safe. We told the truth, but the Americans did not believe it."[8]

The scientists were released from detention in late January 2002 without trial. The United States did not insist, for fear of embarrassing both governments and of disclosing nuclear secrets.[9] Mahmood insisted that there was no wrongdoing, but U.S. doubts that UTN was involved in solely benign activities were further exacerbated by the fact that Mahmood and Majid failed several polygraph tests. Mahmood told the author that he had declined to take any polygraph tests but was forced to do so, and that he had informed the authorities that he considered them "unreliable and inaccurate." In addition, Libya's Head of Intelligence Musa Kousa claimed that the UTN had approached his country to offer assistance with building a nuclear bomb. Mahmood dismissed this allegation, insisting that his nongovernmental organization (NGO) had nothing to do with Libya.

In any case, Mahmood and Majid were not experts in nuclear bombs. Speculations that the two scientists might have discussed radioactive or dirty bombs with Al Qaeda were vehemently denied. In another published account, it is alleged that in response to Mahmood's admonition to bin Laden about the difficulty of setting up a uranium enrichment plant, Osama bin Laden asked, "What if you already have the enriched uranium?"[10] Sultan Bashiruddin Mahmood, however, denies that Osama asked him such a question, or ever reporting this story to his CIA or ISI interrogators.

The Beginning of the End

With the removal of A. Q. Khan from KRL in March 2001, Musharraf thought that illicit proliferation activities were over. But A. Q. Khan kept an office at the KRL, as well as one in the prime minister's secretariat. His successor, Dr. Javed Mirza, was not pleased that Khan still had influence over his subordinates.[11] In an interview with the author, he said, "I initially had no objection. Dr. Khan was my boss and mentor and we all respected him. But then he would sit for hours with KRL employees conducting business." Khan's routine presence and fraternizations with the KRL staff was undermining Mirza's authority.[12] Mirza clarified that A. Q. Khan never visited the centrifuge plant at Kahuta after he left office, but he was very active and close with the director of procurement, Muhammad Farooq. Mirza reported his concerns to his superiors, leading the SPD to prohibit Khan's visits to KRL.[13]

Closing in on A. Q. Khan

In early 2003, the International Atomic Energy Agency (IAEA) confirmed Iran's construction of a pilot centrifuge facility in Natanz and revealed evidence that Pakistan had a role in this event. Blame was being placed on A. Q. Khan, and SPD was immediately alerted. Officials questioned Khan about his involvement with Iran's centrifuges and he flatly denied any role.

According to President Pervez Musharraf's memoir, his most embarrassing moment came when CIA Director George Tenet presented evidence in September 2003 that A. Q. Khan was peddling nuclear technology. "The ugly episode leaked out and blew straight into Pakistan's face."[14] Later that year, the German-owned ship *BBC China* was seized in the Mediterranean and found to be carrying nuclear equipment from Malaysia to Libya. The shipment on the boat and its route were similar to those of other Khan network cargoes. The equipment had originated in Malaysia, where Urs Tinner oversaw the production of specialized centrifuge parts at the Scomi Precision Engineering Factory. Five large cargo containers full of these specialized parts were initially sent from Malaysia to Dubai, where they were relabeled as "used machinery" and transferred to the *BBC China*.[15] This tactic of disguising the end-user by relabeling and changing shipping routes was nothing new, but on this particular occasion spy satellites had tracked the shipment.

The Sri Lankan Connection: Letters on Extortions and Bribes

By February 2004 the U.S. media announced the discovery of the proliferation network with A. Q. Khan at its head. One revelation was how A. Q. Khan was abusing his position of special adviser to the prime minister to conduct his illicit business. He even wrote several letters on the official letterhead and signed them as "Federal Minister." Some of these letters to Sri Lanka with Khan's signature were intercepted by authorities in Islamabad as well as abroad, underscoring the extravagant nature of Khan's audacity and the utter disregard for the consequences of his actions apparent in the conduct of his business.[16]

The letters offer a window through which to analyze why A. Q. Khan had been removed from KRL in April 2001. By that time, Khan had already moved most of his operations to his Dubai office, SMB Computers. From Dubai, the network's proliferation activities in Middle Eastern countries were coordinated, most notably in Iran and Libya. B. S. A. Tahir, a Sri Lankan national and nephew of Mohammad Farooq, was running the office.[17] Farooq and A. Q. Khan sometime before had had a falling out, and Farooq conspired with a Sri Lankan middleman by the name of Harry Jayewardene to extract money from B. S. A. Tahir by threatening to expose him to U.S. authorities. In late February to March 2003, A. Q. Khan became aware of the extortion plot and, in an effort to preemptively prevent exposure of the network, appealed to President Chandrika Bandaranaike Kumaratunga of Sri Lanka, and eventually General Gerry de Silva of the Sri Lankan military, to help him find Jayewardene and recover the funds.

On April 28, 2003, A. Q. Khan wrote a letter on Pakistani government letterhead to General DeSilva (evidently as a follow-up to a phone call referred to in the letter) to explain how Mr. Jayewardene had blackmailed B. S. A. Tahir. The letter ends with:

Dear General, I am sending all the papers [*sic*] please see if you can use your connections to get this money back. If any lawyer can arrange it we can pay him $300 000/–$200 000/– to you for your help and assistance. If we are unable to get back this money easily I will get in touch with Mr. Prabhakaran or Balasinghe to get this blackmailer and extortionist.

I shall be extremely grateful if you can help in this matter.

With my most profound personal regards.

Yours sincerely,
Dr. A. Q. Khan
Federal Minister

Prabhakaran and Balasinghe are names of leaders of the rebel Liberation Tigers of Tamil Eelam (LTTE), an indication of the lengths to which A. Q. Khan was willing to go to recover what must have been a much larger sum of money than indicated in the letter, as well as to perpetuate and protect his proliferation network.[18]

The second intercepted letter, dated May 5, was sent as official communication from the prime minister's office to President Kumaratunga, asking her to intervene in the blackmail case.[19] On November 8, 2003, Khan wrote yet another letter to General DeSilva, well after the *BBC China* was seized, emphasizing further that Khan was oblivious of the consequences of his actions while his network was being publicly exposed.[20]

Internal Investigation

As early as November 2003, Pakistani authorities had begun investigating the Khan network. Lieutenant-General Ehsan-ul Haq, Director General Inter-Services Intelligence Directorate (DGISI), and Lieutenant-General Khalid Kidwai, Director General Strategic Plans Division (DGSPD), and the SPD head of security, Major General Ahmad Bilal, conducted the investigation. President Musharraf shared the findings with U.S. authorities, several allies, and the IAEA. The Pakistani investigators were shocked to discover the extent and reach of the Khan network. In a background briefing to the author, the conclusions were startling.[21]

The network had been very innovative by exploiting globalization for the growth of its business. While successful for many years, however, the proliferation network could not sustain itself in the long term because it was flawed by design. The demise of the A. Q. Khan network was caused by three distinct yet interrelated factors: (1) the network's transition from procurement to proliferation—the clients Khan targeted in his export business were all pariah states, which drew attention to their activities; (2) the network's failure to adapt to increased national and international suspicion—Khan continued business as usual even while numerous countries were beginning investigations; and (3) the tremendous greed, hubris, and sheer audacity of A. Q. Khan and his associates.

From State Procurement to Private Sector Proliferation

After decades of procuring critical components for Pakistan's nuclear program, the network had taken on a life of its own. A. Q. Khan had built a business that had little regard for who or what was at the receiving end of its product. The network operated more like a corporation than an arm of the state. While the PAEC procurement strategy in the 1970s was designed to jump over bureaucratic hurdles, KRL identified loopholes in the system and exploited them.

Khan's exporting business was conducted from his Dubai office because of its convenient location in the Jebel Ali Free Trade Zone. A. Q. Khan functioned as the chief executive officer and relied heavily on his inner circle of trusted contacts to act as the board of directors. They included: Hank Slebos, Gotthard Lerch, Heinz Mebus, Gerhard Wisser, Daniel Geiges, Abdus Salam, Peter Griffin, Ernest Piffl, Günes Cire, and Friedrich Tinner and his sons Urs and Marcos. These contacts, made during Khan's time in Europe, had helped him to establish a uranium enrichment program in Pakistan.[22] For several decades, the combined expertise and resources of the members of this board made the procurement and proliferation network possible. All nearing the age of retirement, they were in favor of turning a quick profit and were unfazed by the consequences of their activities. What distinguished A. Q. Khan in the network was that he acted as the chief executive of the board and none of the associates of the centrifuge business network was head of a nuclear weapons program in his country.[23]

Khan was innovative in his transition from procurement to proliferation. Not only did Khan maintain a Rolodex of contacts, but he also had close relationships with companies from which he and his associates procured parts.[24] Increasingly, trade in nuclear materials and technologies was not in the form of a turnkey product, but rather in the form of individual components such as ring magnets, aluminum and maraging steel, flow-forming and balancing equipment, vacuum pumps, noncorrosive pipes and valves, and end-caps and baffles. The network conducted extensive business with Scomi Precision Engineering (Malaysia), ETI Electroteknik (Turkey), EKA (Turkey), Trade Fin (South Africa), Kirsch Engineering (South Africa), Bikar Mettale Asia (Singapore), and Habando Balance, Inc. (South Korea), among others.

The network stayed a step ahead of regulations and export controls. Khan and his associates bought into established manufacturing companies, developed relationships with middlemen and front companies, and recruited technical experts through bribery or deception. In addition, the Dubai office established offshore agents and purchasing companies through which parts and capital were funneled, often paying about a 15 to 25 percent markup and above-market prices along with lucrative kickbacks. Clandestine funding methods were utilized to make payments using credit and bank transfers and launder money, all through unscrupulous financial institutions such as the Bank of Credit and Commerce International (BCCI). In some cases, he was able to order more than what was necessary of a particular item for Pakistan's program and then sell off the additional parts. For example, when Pakistan updated its technology from the P-1 centrifuge to the P-2, Khan sold the older, used technology for a profit to Iran.

The Iran Connection

Khan began his dealings with Iran as early as 1987, which lasted into two phases. Reportedly, three Iranian officials met with Heinz Mebus, Mohammed Farooq, and B. S. A. Tahir in Dubai, where they offered the following items: a disassembled sample machine (including specifications, drawings, and descriptions); specifications, drawings, and calculations for a complete plant of two thousand machines; auxiliary vacuum and electric equipment; and uranium reconversion and casting capabilities.[25] Phase I lasted from 1987 to 1992, during which time Khan network approached Iran with a so-called shopping list for P-1 centrifuge designs. Iran used Khan's shopping list as a buyer's guide to procure on its own.[26] Iran probably did not completely trust A. Q. Khan and had complained that the old P-1 centrifuges were, in many cases, faulty and damaged.

The P-1 centrifuges handed over to Iran were the ones that had been used at the pilot project at Sihala in the early years of the highly enriched uranium (HEU) experiments, when KRL was still under construction, as mentioned in Chapter 7. After Pakistan began HEU enrichment with advanced P-I and P-2 centrifuges, the P-1 centrifuges were redundant and not in use. A. Q. Khan secretly traded some of these to Iran. Later, when the IAEA found that the centrifuges had traces of distinct HEU particles, Iran admitted to the IAEA that the used centrifuges had come from an outside source. Later, on request from the IAEA, Pakistan provided samples of its centrifuge to help the IAEA match the isotopes of the traces and bring an end to its investigation. With cooperation from Pakistan, it was proved that Iran at the time had not produced those centrifuges domestically.[27]

Phase II of the Iran deal lasted from 1994 to 1999 and involved duplicate P-1 centrifuge designs, components for 500 P-1 centrifuges, P-2 centrifuge designs, and technical consulting. Iran has admitted to meeting with network intermediaries thirteen times between 1994 and 1999.[28] The P-2 samples and accompanying detailed specifications and drawings allowed Iran to skip ahead in its research and make thousands of centrifuges on its own, ordering parts individually from the Khan network as well as from other sources in Europe and elsewhere.[29]

North Korean Connection

Although North Korea was already on the plutonium route, it was interested in centrifuge technology as a backup for a possible HEU route in future. Khan was able to provide it with approximately twelve old centrifuges, drawings, sketches, technical data, depleted uranium hexafluoride, and a shopping list of what could be bought. It was much easier for Khan to ship nuclear components to North Korea than to Iran because trade in sensitive military equipment with Pyongyang had already been authorized. As explained in Chapter 12, North Korea and Pakistan have had state-to-state dealings on missiles and conventional munitions since the 1970s, but there was no quid pro quo for ballistic missiles in exchange for nuclear technology; cash payments of $210 million were made to North Korea for the ballistic missiles package, which included the transfer of technology.[30] Unlike Libya, North Korea had seemingly no connection with the other members of the network. It is not known if there were any financial transactions between North Korea and the Dubai office. Apparently Khan provided a dozen centrifuges to North Korea in the mid-1990s to speed up deliveries of *Nodong* missiles as well as technical assistance to transfer the technology. At the time, PAEC projects, especially the solid-fuel-missile transfer of technology from China at the Project Management Organization (PMO), were proceeding well ahead of schedule.

A. Q. Khan's key incentive was to beat rival PAEC in the race by demonstrating the liquid-fuel prowess first. It may be recalled that PAEC had conducted a cold test of a nuclear weapon in 1983, one year ahead of KRL. Khan wanted to beat PAEC this time. He bribed North Korea with the lure of centrifuges to spur more deliveries and technical assistance.[31] As described in Chapter 12, the flight test of the *Nodong* (dubbed *Ghauri* in Pakistan) failed to meet the technical parameters and would take some years to improve; Khan's ego was nevertheless satisfied at the time, since this flight test was a full one year before PAEC could demonstrate the solid-fueled *Shaheen*.[32]

The Libya Connection

Taking place between 1997 and 2003, the Libya deal was by far the most important, riskiest venture of Khan's career and involved close collaboration with individuals and companies all around the world. It differed from the Iran and North Korea deals in three main ways: (1) the bulk of the execution took place after A. Q. Khan was removed from KRL; (2) it was the first time the network managed to produce outside any single country the entire array of materials, tools, and technologies required to fabricate gas centrifuges for uranium enrichment; and (3) the scale was much larger because Libya was starting from scratch with no infrastructure on the ground.[33]

Libya contracted with A. Q. Khan to manufacture centrifuge components and assemble them offsite, after which they were installed and operated at a location outside of Tripoli. A. Q. Khan suggested that the Libyans build sheds to camouflage the centrifuges that would look like goat or camel farms. The offsite construction maximized profits for Khan and his associates and kept the Libyan program dependent on them for advice.[34] The Libyan deal involved the following: twenty complete L-1 centrifuges and components for an additional two hundred; two sample L-2 centrifuges; uranium hexafluoride (which is speculated to have come from the Democratic People's Republic of Korea [DPRK]); a machine shop to produce and repair centrifuges and to train Libyan technicians; and nuclear bomb designs and instructions. The Dubai office placed the orders for dual-use machinery, which Scomi Precision Engineering (SCOPE) constructed. SCOPE then shipped the relabeled equipment via various ships and ports, from which they were transshipped and bound for Libya.

Libya ultimately ordered components for ten thousand L-2 centrifuges and a uranium hexafluoride piping system that was manufactured but not delivered. The centrifuge equipment included ring magnets, aluminum and maraging steel, flow forming and balancing equipment, vacuum pumps, noncorrosive pipes and valves, end caps and baffles, and power supply inverters. As Victoria Burnett and Stephen Fidler explained in their *Financial Times* article in 2004, supplying ten thousand centrifuges, each of which had ninety-six parts, meant that the supplier would have had to procure or manufacture more than a million components and ship them all to Libya—an enormous and dangerous task.[35] To meet this challenge, Khan increased the capacity of existing front companies and established factories in nontraditional supplier companies to procure, assemble, and manufacture the components.[36]

Ultimately, Khan's proliferation network fed a growing demand within key countries that were willing to procure nuclear materials and technologies at any cost. Unfortunately for Khan, these clients also happened to be pariah states that by their very nature attracted international interest and scrutiny.

The Libyan connection was probably the lead thread that contributed to the unraveling of the network. Unbeknownst to the Khan network in Dubai, as early as March 2003, Libya was secretly negotiating with the United Kingdom and United States to lift sanctions in connection with the infamous Lockerbie bombings. Gaddafi's son Saif was negotiating the deal for normalization of relations, which included the dismantling of Libya's strategic program.[37] Libya decided to provide evidence of its dealing with the network and eventually all the technologies and documentation.[38] The Khan network had apparently been tracked since then, and to the network's ill luck, the lure of profit was too intoxicating for it to keep up with changing times.

Failure to Adapt to Changing National and International Dynamics

Before the network began to come undone, A. Q. Khan had free rein to do what he liked in Pakistan. As Javed Mizra told the author, KRL never existed on paper as a legitimate government entity, and KRL was essentially unaccountable. Once KRL became an independent commission, A. Q. Khan had even more independent authority.[39] With tacit protection from the government, KRL was able to operate with near impunity and without informing authorities of its activities. A. Q. Khan's program was secret, and he was no longer accountable to anyone for his outside activities.

The Pakistani government overlooked Khan's activities because it believed the benefit he provided outweighed the cost of corruption. A. Q. Khan was a go-getter, a people-pleaser, and a hero. He was a master at kickbacks and bribes, which kept scrutiny away from his activities—at least temporarily. Also, many of those who observed his bureaucratic malpractices were themselves beneficiaries of the system.

For example, the Pakistani Army was a big beneficiary of the KRL. In the 1980s under Army Chief General Aslam Beg's modernization program, KRL manufactured conventional weapons for the army, for which the defense budget was used. A. Q. Khan had successfully argued with Beg at the time that he should be allowed to generate his own funds, which would free up national resources and make KRL self-sufficient.[40] General Beg was willing to allow this, which fed speculation that he was prepared to condone the corrupt practices of A. Q. Khan,[41] which he in effect did in an interview with Douglas Frantz:

> If a scientist is given 10 million dollars to get the equipment how would he do it? He will not carry the money in his bag. He will put the money in a foreign bank account in someone's name. The money lies in the account for some time, and the mark-up that fetches may probably have gone into his account. It is a fringe benefit. It is very logical that somebody contacts a scientist telling him that ARY Gold determines gold [prices] in the region, so why not invest a million dollars or have it invested on his behalf? This may have happened. Is it a crime? No.[42]

In general, if objections were raised they were quickly silenced for reasons of national security. Indeed security reigned so supreme that the government was willing to overlook corruption on its behalf. As President Musharraf put it on February 5, 2004: "Security was under the organization [KRL] itself. No one was monitoring them . . . . [T]here was no external audit . . . . And this was the correct approach I tell you. Otherwise, we would have been unable to move ahead."[43] It was generally accepted that the ends justified the means.

Further, in a culture in which corruption is the norm, especially where those with power and influence are hardly questioned, A. Q. Khan did little wrong. In popular perception in Pakistan, he is a hero; at least he delivered to Pakistan what the state had expected of him and indeed tasked him with in his twenty-five-year career in KRL.[44]

By early 2000, the collaboration between Western intelligence and Khan network insiders was a major turning point for the unraveling. Insider information, specifically from the Tinners, helped U.S. officials obtain information about specific activities. Former Director of the CIA George Tenet boasted, "We pieced together subsidiaries, his clients, his front companies, his finances, and manufacturing plants. We were inside his residence, inside his facilities, inside his rooms. We were everywhere these people were."[45] Gary Samore, former head of the National Security Council Nonproliferation Office, commented that the relationship with the Tinners "was very significant." In his words, "That's where we got the first indications that Iran had acquired centrifuges."[46] A former CIA official told journalists Douglas Frantz and Catherine Collins that "[Urs] Tinner gave us the final ability to know what the network was doing."[47] The Tinners' cooperation is widely credited as the important link that led to an American operation to funnel sabotaged nuclear equipment to Libya and Iran.[48]

Khan and his associates were similarly unfazed by major exogenous shocks to the international system—such as the attacks on September 11, 2001—that led to further scrutiny of their program. Feeling invincible, they continued business as usual, with little disruption to their day-to-day practices. After September 11, Western intelligence tightened, making the Tinners all the more crucial. In August of 2002, Iran's Natanz nuclear site was exposed, but Khan's Dubai business still continued to do business with Iran in spite of these revelations.

Just like Khan and the rest of his "board of directors," the Tinners were motivated by greed and were lured into providing information to the CIA and MI6 with hefty sums of money. They are believed to have received as much as $10 million over the course of four years—much of it in cash—for their information.[49]

Audacity and Greed

The simple reason behind the A. Q. Khan network's transition from a state procurement network to a virtual private sector export network was the greed of Khan and the business people in his inner circle. In many cases, Khan's hubris went so far as to admit publicly the tactics that allowed him to be successful over the years. He boasted of his contacts from his time in Europe, and of his manipulation of the grey market in dual-use commodities. Of the nearly one hundred Dutch companies that supplied centrifuge parts and materials to Pakistan's procurement program, Khan said, "They literally begged us to buy their equipment." At the twenty-fifth anniversary of KRL in 2001, he admitted, "My long stay in Europe and intimate knowledge of various countries and their manufacturing firms was an asset."[50] He explained that the equipment he ordered was known as "conventional technology" that had "1,001 uses in other disciplines."[51] According to a *New York Times* article that broke the story in February 2004, Khan was "eager to defy the West and pierce 'clouds of the so-called secrecy,' as he once put it."[52] He boasted, "Notwithstanding the fact that we were handicapped by not being able to hold open discussions with foreign experts or organizations, we attacked all the problems successfully."[53]

Even though the Dutch government was suspicious of Hank Slebos's activities in behalf of Pakistan's nuclear program, Slebos was able to avoid conviction and, miraculously, continue supplying the Khan network. Beginning in 1996, Dutch export control authorities tried to undermine Slebos's export business with a so-called catch-all clause that allowed them to impose ad hoc export licenses on unregulated dual-use commodities that were suspected of being destined for WMD-related programs.[54] In the absence of clear regulations on dual-use items, the catch-all clause enabled the Dutch government to legally prevent Slebos from exporting anything that had a potential military purpose. Of the catch-alls invoked by the Dutch government between 1996 and 2004, approximately two-thirds can be attributed to Slebos.[55] Always the crafty businessman, Slebos got around the catch-all clause by creating new business channels abroad, which made Dutch intervention difficult.[56]

Hank Slebos was not the only network member to narrowly escape prosecution for export control violations. In 1996, Friedrich Tinner was questioned by Swiss authorities about a shipment of specialized valves the IAEA had discovered in Jordan on its way to Iraq before the Gulf War.[57] Tinner claimed to have no idea how the valves arrived in Jordan. He said that they had been shipped legally to Singapore, and it was not his responsibility where they had gone after that.[58] The Swiss statute of limitations on export violations had at that point expired, so authorities did not press the matter with Tinner.[59]

What did Pakistan gain in the end? From its nuclear procurement, Pakistan gained a nuclear deterrent and suffered the collateral damage associated with it. It gained nothing, however, from Khan's proliferation to Iran, North Korea, and Libya. To date, none of these countries have even acknowledged or given credit to Pakistan or any related entity. The Iranians have been openly cynical about the technology A. Q. Khan provided them. Khan gave them a head start by sending samples that allowed them to move forward with their program, even if he did not supervise their activities as intricately as he did with Libya. The Libyans never acknowledged the role of the state of Pakistan in their nuclear acquisitions when they gave up their nuclear program in 2003. Likewise, the North Koreans do not acknowledge that they received anything of significance for their nuclear program.

SPD Reforms

Despite the setback, the undoing of the A. Q. Khan network brought the United States and Pakistan closer together via close cooperation and information exchange. In a background briefing, the author was informed that the

United States never officially demanded any access to A. Q. Khan and that U.S. officials had been very careful in offering assistance that Pakistan would accept. There was renewed emphasis on strengthening command and control, and the SPD began reforming its own system through the help of the United States.

One of the greatest flaws in Pakistan's nuclear security system was the lack of any formal oversight of the strategic organizations. The security arrangement since the beginning of the nuclear program was designed to protect it from outside interference, spying, and physical threats. But there was no formal reporting channel within the security apparatus to account for imports and exports, personal travel, and other details that may have revealed suspicious activity.

A Personnel Reliability Program (PRP) was created, and several technical persons were trained in advanced material protection, control, and accounting procedures at various U.S. labs.[60] Although there were limits to this cooperation, SPD developed good contacts and received education and cooperation in developing its own PRP procedures with U.S. systems, but it kept its standards classified. As the author was told in a background briefing, "[We] seek cooperation in a non-intrusive manner, and education is always useful, and there are no limits to improving standards of nuclear management."[61]

Each person dealing with strategic forces or programs undergoes reliability tests—either the PRP for civilian scientists, engineers, and others, or the Human Reliability Program (HRP) for military personnel. All strategic organizations and programs were put under one of three categories: the classified nuclear weapons program, which requires the highest level of clearance; a sensitive but not classified category—that is, power reactors and nuclear energy–related facilities; and an open program that involves agriculture, medicine, conventional weapons, and so forth. The PRP criteria vary with each category. The background check involved a cumulative assessment of factors such as psychological, medical health, political affiliation, and financial background. These criteria were established after a series of security checks and certification that are conducted and renewed annually or biannually, depending on the sensitivity of the position or program involved.[62]

The foremost reform was the creation of the Security Division within SPD that now has three levels of physical security: (1) the laboratories' own set of procedures, (2) an eight to ten thousand–person security force, and (3) ISI intelligence. In addition, SPD includes a technical directorate that conducts technical upgrades including, inter alia, infrared and motion sensors, locks, video cameras, and communication devices.[63]

The SPD force is endowed with its own intelligence unit with up to ten thousand employees led by a two-star general. The entire SPD nuclear security department is in charge of all nuclear installations, using its own paramilitary force and multilayered perimeter security. This organization coordinates with all intelligence agencies about any external military or espionage threat to Pakistan's nuclear infrastructure. (See SPD organization chart in Chapter 17.)

The ISI operates in conjunction with the nuclear security division but does not have a formal role. Even now, the director general of the ISI is invited only to meetings and is not a full member of the Pakistani National Command Authority. The security operations of all major organizations are coordinated by four separate security directorates that report directly to the director general of the Security Division, who in turn reports to the head of SPD, and finally to the chairman of the Joint Chiefs of Staff Committee. The latter is the highest level of military integration, which also houses the National Military Command Centre (NMCC) and is the focal point of intelligence and the nuclear command authority.

SPD took lessons from the Mahmood-Majid episode, and since then has focused on securing sensitive material and know-how, including retired persons with relevant knowledge.[64] This approach gave birth to a policy that required all scientists and officials with sensitive knowledge and expertise to be re-employed within the strategic organizations, even after their retirement. In short, no scientists would retire until their death.

Over the past eight years, the SPD has reportedly screened all relevant personnel, granted varying levels of security clearances, and determined the requisite degree of access for those handling sensitive nuclear materials. According to a report by Italian experts, "[K]ey people are screened and controlled by four agencies [ISI, Military Intelligence, Intelligence Bureau, and SPD]. Every aspect of each person's life is reported, including his or her families and relatives. Such screenings are repeated every two years."[65]

Pakistan has faced two fundamental challenges in establishing its personnel reliability requirements. First, religious extremism is increasing in Pakistani society as a whole. Therefore, the reliability program must distinguish between those who are merely pious and those with tendencies toward religious extremism. Second, because Pakistan does not have sophisticated technological controls over personnel, it has to rely on the rationality and loyalty of individuals who are thoroughly screened to handle sensitive nuclear responsibilities.[66] Generally, reliance on personnel and on technology is balanced and exercises assertive control over strategic assets.

Negative Consequences

Musharraf's best strategy for dealing with the A. Q. Khan dilemma was explained in his memoirs: "I had to act fast to satisfy international concerns, and yet, also avoid inflaming the masses of Pakistan in support of their hero."[67] On the one hand, the political fallout from Khan's public trial was untenable, especially for the newly formed civil government, and the information revealed could have compromised the nuclear program's security.[68] On the other hand, Pakistan could not simply ignore it. Eventually it was decided that A. Q. Khan would confess his crime and seek apology from the Pakistani public, and Musharraf would pardon him in return. His legal council was S. M. Zafar—the same lawyer who had defended Khan in his Netherlands trial. A. Q. Khan was, however, kept "under protection," a euphemism for house arrest without indictment.

Eight years later, the repercussions of the Khan network are still reverberating both in Pakistan and internationally. A. Q. Khan continues to cause national embarrassment with routine diatribes in the media, especially against former president Musharraf, and by fighting battles in Pakistani courts. In addition, Pakistan's image has suffered an irreparable loss, and now the country is considered to be grossly irresponsible. After signing a lucrative nuclear deal with India, President Bush visited Pakistan in March 2006 and said in reply to the possibility of a similar deal with Islamabad, "India and Pakistan have different histories." His remarks not only rubbed salt to Pakistani wounds but also crystallized the real consequences of the A. Q. Khan network.

20   Nuclear Pakistan and the World

Pakistan has suffered multiple shocks in the eight years since the A. Q. Khan network exposure. The strategic landscape has drastically changed, and the domestic situation is especially worrisome. Terrorists and violent extremism threaten to impose their will by continuous challenge to state authority. After ten years of fighting in Afghanistan, the prospects for stability and peace appear dim. The United States has increased counterterror strikes against suspected militant strongholds in the tribal borderlands, and Pakistan's armed forces are spread thin assisting these missions. Meanwhile, hundreds of suicide attacks have targeted Pakistani hotels, marketplaces, Sufi shrines, government offices, and military headquarters. As political forces struggle for power and influence, sectarian and ethnic conflicts span the whole country—most notably in Karachi and Baluchistan. The ensuing political instability and the plummeting economy are eating the state from within, even while the country steadily progresses toward its strategic weapons force goals.

Having survived forty years of trials and tribulations, the nuclear program has been fueled by a strategic culture filled with historic grievances, military defeats, and paranoia. Pakistan has procured, built, secured, and managed one of the most advanced technologies in the world and has good reason to be proud of its capability. There is almost no other comparable achievement in the country's history. Today the armed forces and the civilian bureaucracy, from religious right to liberal left, all support Pakistan's continued nuclear weapons capability. The nuclear factor is so deeply embedded in national security thinking that any step toward disarmament would be met with stiff resistance. Moreover, there is a strong consensus that Pakistan's nuclear weapons are under a constant threat from hostile countries, which include the United States, Israel, and India. Pakistanis believe that their nuclear arsenal remains vulnerable to preventive or preemptive attacks, and thus even a rumor of attack prompts the armed forces to take precautionary measures.[1] Undoubtedly, the people of Pakistan have paid a heavy price, and many of their economic woes are the consequence of national security decisions taken since 1972. Indeed, preserving the nuclear capability has been the cornerstone of many leaders' decision-making processes. To attain the nuclear capability was an end in itself and any means were justified, including forcing a people to eat grass in sacrifice. So how will Pakistan's nuclear arsenal impact the country's future trajectory?

Proliferation pessimists worry that a nuclear Pakistan will encourage other states to follow suit and increases the likelihood of nuclear weapons use in South Asia. Still others believe that nuclear weapons have actually exacerbated regional security problems and caused crises, and still others worry about terrorists acquiring the weapons or materials.[2] Optimists credit the absence of wars and contained military crises to a nuclear weapons arsenal.[3] These same positive-minded individuals point out that there has been no major breach either of safety or of nuclear security in the country.[4] After all, Pakistan cooperated with the international community to shut down the A. Q. Khan network and to improve its command and control over weapons and materials.[5]

Nevertheless, Pakistan's biggest challenge to its deterrent has nothing to do with fissile material stocks, delivery means, or an ambiguous nuclear doctrine, but rather rests on future internal threats. In an exclusive background briefing for this book at the Strategic Plans Division (SPD) it was emphasized that "Pakistan has no external threat it cannot meet. It is the ability of internal cohesion and control over sectarian divide that will remain the biggest challenge." For Pakistan to maintain a strategic balance and avoid increased conflict with India, it must uphold social cohesion, government stability, and sustained economic growth.[6]

The Fall of Musharraf

The 9/11 catastrophe not only allowed Musharraf to change Pakistan's strategic orientation but also provided an opportunity to jumpstart the economy with new aid and cash flows. In a few years the economy had turned around and boasted about 8 percent annual GDP growth in 2006.[7] Musharraf overturned the policy of confrontation with India in an effort to resolve Kashmir and began supporting President Hamid Karzai and the Bonn Process. His back-channel diplomacy with India had progressed very well, but he could not develop a rapport with Afghanistan, where relations got worse after an initial positive start.[8] By and large Musharraf handled the delicate security situations reasonably well, and until Spring 2007 he was popular, boasting over 60 percent approval ratings.[9]

In March 2007, President Musharraf tried to remove the chief justice of the Supreme Court, which triggered a civil society movement led by lawyers. In the summer, after months of dialogue had failed to disarm the militant *Lal Masjid* (Red Mosque) in the heart of Islamabad, which for years had been a source of violent religious extremism, he ordered an ideological cleansing operation of the mosque.[10] The two seemingly disconnected events created domestic chaos, prompting hundreds of suicide attacks and demonstrations. Sensing a weakened military regime, the two former prime ministers, Benazir Bhutto and Nawaz Sharif, returned from exile and politically challenged Musharraf.[11]

Even in this hostile environment, Musharraf ran in the presidential elections as a military general and was reelected in October 2007. The election itself was controversial, and the results were challenged in the Supreme Court on the grounds that a military leader cannot run for president. Sensing that he might lose the court case, General Musharraf declared a national state of emergency on November 3, 2007, replaced judges who declined to take a new oath, and banned electronic media.[12] By the end of 2008, Musharraf's popularity had plummeted and his grip on the country was lost.

After her return from exile, Benazir Bhutto began campaigning and was assassinated on December 27, 2007, just ten days before the parliamentary elections. In February 2008, Benazir's husband, Asif Ali Zardari, quickly seized power. In six months he exiled Musharraf and became the president of Pakistan. With Benazir and Musharraf gone, the political landscape completely changed and became marred by weak leadership, inefficiency, and corruption. Eventually, right-wing political parties and ethnic groups began to call the shots.

Two significant events in November 2008 had a dramatic impact on Pakistan. A terrorist attack on Mumbai, India, killed more than 160 people and wounded nearly twice that number.[13] In the ensuing sixty-hour gun battle between Indian security forces and the terrorists, all but one assailant was killed. The surviving terrorist turned out to be a Pakistani national.[14] India and Pakistan were in conflict once again, bringing the four previous years of peace talks and back door diplomacy to an end.[15]

Analysts in Pakistan grew increasingly aware that the arc of terrorism had now expanded to the entire subcontinent. There was no greater opportunity for cooperation among regional states. But that was not to be. Instead India blamed the entire terrorist threat on Pakistan, and adversarial policies continued to dominate on both sides.

By this time Asif Ali Zardari's coalition had grown weak.[16] In early 2009 the lawyer's movement picked up momentum and tried once again to restore the judges, who were removed in November 2007. Joined by the opposition, including Nawaz Sharif, a long march toward Islamabad finally convinced the ruling party to restore all the judges. The Supreme Court judges made a jubilant return to their offices as civil society celebrated its victory. There were hopes for rule of law and justice, but as of 2012 the prospects look dim, especially as the democratically elected government is seemingly in a clash with the judiciary. In an open clash with the Supreme Court, the prime minister is defiantly refusing to step down after being indicted in a case of contempt of court. As this book goes to print, the son of Chief Justice Iftikhar Chaudhry—the same who Musharraf had fired in March 2007—is facing court investigation for alleged bribes. This is a defining moment for the Pakistani political and justice system to prove itself.

Despite these domestic upheavals, the nuclear program has continued unabated. But the departure of a strong leader and the death of a popular leader, Benazir, created a void that fueled instability and put into question the role of nuclear weapons in a state that seems to be unraveling at the seams.

The Role of Nuclear Weapons

The Pakistanis see no role for nuclear weapons other than to deter India from waging a conventional war. This was the original purpose for the program, and it stands to this day—notwithstanding the fact that Pakistan is vulnerable to an Indian attack because it is internally weak and divided. This situation poses a paradox because nuclear deterrence can work effectively only if other vulnerabilities and weaknesses do not exist. Vulnerabilities are tempting and challenge the credibility of deterrence. In fact, India's basic premise to wage a limited war against Pakistan is to punish the country in response to what it calls state-sponsored terrorism or threats that are hatched and waged from the Pakistani soil with or without the connivance of the state or its entities (implying Pakistani intelligence services). The Pakistanis dismiss this rationale and argue that Pakistan has suffered more from violent extremists and spillover of Afghan instability, and that India is simply using the post 9/11 environment to wage a war against its long-term adversary. Should India wage a limited war and succeed in terminating it on its terms, deterrence will have failed. From the Pakistani perspective, to enhance its credibility, it is forced to risk the use of nuclear weapons simply to stop India in its tracks. However, the bottom line is that nuclear weapons alone cannot constitute an effective national security if other elements of national power remain dangerously weak.

The Cold Start Doctrine

In the mid-eighties, India's military doctrine toward Pakistan was based on deep strikes with major mechanized strike corps formations. The advent of nuclear weapons, however, made this doctrine unfeasible, and India has been contemplating a limited conventional war doctrine since the 1999 Kargil conflict. In the 2002 military standoff, India failed to commence a war, which led to new thinking within the military.[17]

The Indian military has been embroiled in counterinsurgency in Kashmir for two decades. It has two options: (1) strike deep without the fear of escalation, assuming that Pakistan would be deterred against a nuclear response; or (2) strike hard but shallow, based on destruction-oriented operations on a broad front, assuming that the operations would not cross Pakistan's nuclear red lines—the so-called Cold Start Doctrine.

India would lose the element of surprise with the assembly and mobilization of large strike formations, which would prompt Pakistan to mobilize defenses quickly. India's dilemma is to find a way to undercut Pakistan's countermobilization strategy and retain surprise. The Cold Start Doctrine requires proactive capability with defensive formations by breaking larger formations into division-size integrated battle groups (IBGs), backed by air and firepower. Cold Start is also based on the assumption that rapid military action would trump India's domestic political leadership and outside intervention, and that a fait accompli would resolve the conflict politically and diplomatically.

Pakistan's response to Cold Start has been relatively muted because of domestic political compulsions. From the findings of several conferences and background briefings, it is evident that the Pakistani strategic community challenges the assumptions on which Cold Start is based and is confident that Pakistan is prepared to match India's preparation as it manifests.

However, this doctrine has complicated Pakistan's security requirements, forcing the country to be torn in multiple directions and dimensions. Islamabad must balance the Cold Start threat from India against rising counterinsurgency, counterterrorism, and counterextremism. Should a Cold Start threat manifest from India, two consequences can be predicted. First, Pakistani forces would likely abandon every other security requirement to meet this threat as primary. Second, Islamabad would be under intense pressure to deploy nuclear weapons against Indian conventional forces.[18]

It cannot be decisively concluded whether this doctrine is a theoretical proposition or whether there is serious understanding and sponsorship within the Indian government. Regardless, the Indian Army continues to undertake military exercises for implementing this doctrine each year. Given Pakistani strategic culture and the crisis-ridden history with India, Pakistan cannot lower its guard even in the face of rumored threats.

Geo-Politicking

For Pakistan it is the paradox of geography that determines both its strategic relevance and the instabilities of surrounding areas. For decades its geopolitical location, professional armed forces, and external alliances have allowed it to be, as President Obama put it, "a strategically important country whose stability and prosperity would greatly benefit India."[19] Pakistan is conscious of its significance, and the last thing it would want is to be pushed to the geopolitical margins. As it seeks to remain an active player in the geopolitical game, strategic relevancy remains a cornerstone of its maneuvering.

But from Pakistan's perspective, India's diplomatic maneuvers encircle it with hostile and nonfriendly neighbors, making Islamabad's partnership with China more costly and with the United States so complicated that Washington might consider it counterproductive. To Pakistan's west, in Afghanistan and Iran, India makes effective inroads ostensibly for economic and infrastructure development. The Indian military base at Ayni in Tajikistan and its infrastructural development in Kabul make Pakistan wary. India is also actively engaged with Iran by building strategic roads from its port city Chahbahar to Afghanistan. These projects seem to be a rebuttal to China's construction of the Pakistani port of Gwadar. India perceives China's building of a series of harbors and ports for outlets to the Indian Ocean as stifling, whereas Pakistan considers Indian activities on its western borders as geopolitical outmaneuvering. These little games of perceived encirclements and alliances add new roles for nuclear deterrence and added pressures on strategic stability in the region. In terms of the Asian power balance in the twenty-first century, China is the only major power that sees the utility of a nuclear Pakistan as a balance against India and in the long run, as a hedge against the growing Indian-U.S. strategic relationship.

There are fears in Western countries that other Muslim nations could be influenced by Pakistan's nuclear program. In the late 1970s, Zulfiqar Ali Bhutto introduced the notion of an "Islamic bomb," which made observers suspicious of technology-sharing with other Muslim countries. Pakistan and Saudi Arabia have extremely close military ties and several formal defense agreements. Saudi Arabia provided generous financial support to Pakistan that enabled the nuclear program to continue, especially when the country was under sanctions. To the author's best knowledge, there is no concrete evidence of any nuclear-related agreement between Pakistan and Saudi Arabia.[20] However, among Pakistan's political parties, some on the religious right are in favor of providing extended deterrence to Muslim countries. Jamaat-i-Islami's Senator Khurshid Ahmad has said, "Pakistan as an Islamic state has a responsibility to the broader Umma . . . . Pakistan's nuclear weapons will inevitably be seen as a threat by Israel, and therefore Pakistan must include Israel in its defense planning . . . . Under the circumstances, the future of the Muslim world depends on Pakistan."[21] To the author's knowledge, there has been no plan to provide extended deterrence to any other country or to sell nuclear technology.[22] The Pakistanis do, however, proudly stick to the rhetoric of being the first Muslim country to acquire nuclear weapons. And this still remains a popular theme in the country's political culture.

Emerging Force Goals

Even though the purpose of nuclear weapons is clear, Pakistan is still in the early stages of nuclear learning. The Kargil episode demonstrated that Pakistani strategic thinking was dominated by conventional military logic. In the 2002 crisis, the ambiguity of its nuclear-use doctrine was scrutinized, and its nuclear deterrent was tested. As head of state, Musharraf demonstrated his statesman-like qualities by adopting a pragmatic response to international scrutiny and to military crisis with India. And when the A. Q. Khan crisis struck, he carefully balanced domestic and international concerns.

For Pakistan, these experiences were its first steps along a steep learning curve in an increasingly complex world.[23] Decades of experience in nuclear diplomacy are useful but not sufficient for the self-declared nuclear power to tackle the nuances of international relations.

The purpose of possessing nuclear weapons for deterrence against a conventional attack was established, but what constitutes deterrence success or failure was not easy to determine. The knowledge that a bomb exists in the basement was not sufficient for India to give up plans for fighting and winning a conventional war. Even when Pakistan's nuclear capability was demonstrated, the threat of conventional war did not disappear. It became clear that deterrence requires a mixture of credible force, demonstrative capability, and a manner to convey a country's will to its opponents. Furthermore, Pakistanis recognize that deterrence works primarily in the eye of the beholder, and as a political weapon, nuclear weapons can be credible only once they are perceived as militarily usable. For over a decade now, after three major crises, Pakistan's National Command Authority has matured in formulating strategic doctrines, thresholds, targeting, and survivability plans.

In the decade of President Pervez Musharraf's rule, nuclear weapons played a prominent but a silent role in his policy focus and strategic orientation. Like Zia, he downplayed the nuclear-use aspect and relied primarily on conventional capabilities. Musharraf depended on a nuclear capability as a buffer in time and space to focus on strengthening the other elements of national power and to avoid a debilitating arms race.

Based upon historical pattern, Pakistan would most likely monitor developments and advances in India and determine its own force postures, while bearing in mind the stark reality of resource constraints. Matching all Indian advances is not necessary to maintain a strategic balance. And periodic review by the NCA for a qualitative match and force goal ceilings as well as oversight of safety, security, and survivability will remain a regular feature in Pakistan's nuclear future.[24]

As mentioned earlier, Pakistan's arsenals are maintained in nondeployed form. The NCA maintains centralized control of the assets, and an elaborate system of security and the Security Division have installed safety measures that ensure the physical security of storage and transport. Security is tough, with strict access control within each organization and a personnel reliability program similar to that of Western countries.

The system, however, must learn to respond to the rapidly changing strategic environment. A Mumbai-type attack can speedily deteriorate a normal situation in the region. Therefore, in an unfolding crisis and conventional force assembly, nuclear weapons could well be brought closer to battle readiness, just in case. It is therefore the duty of NCA to ensure readiness in the event of a sudden strike or conventional war. For effective deterrence, nuclear forces are integrated into conventional war planning. And under circumstances in which the security situation rapidly shifts from peace to crisis to war, the alert postures of nuclear weapons would most likely shift rapidly from a low state to a high state of alert. If the security situation continues to remain tense, at some point nuclear weapons would be mated with delivery systems in peacetime, much as in the early periods of the Cold War in Europe.[25]

Pakistan's delivery means were expanded and diversified, including in the arena of cruise missiles, which have recently been tested. The auxiliary assertions about the role of nuclear weapons, however, are still in flux. Until the end of the first decade after the nuclear tests, there has been little focus on influential factors such as the political status of becoming a nuclear power, especially in terms of regional and international affairs. That might change in the coming decade, especially after India is conferred with special status in the nuclear world order and Pakistan is made an outlier.

Future Trajectories

Pakistan's efforts toward nuclear pragmatism were dashed when its initiatives to develop a strategic restraint regime failed to gain traction. The new nuclear partnership between the United States and India has sparked nuclear nationalism and strategic anxiety in Pakistan (and possibly China), and now has the potential to destabilize the strategic balance in South Asia.

Under the emerging Indo-U.S. nuclear partnership, India is allowed to keep eight heavy-water power reactors, its fast breeder reactor (FBR) program, its heavy water and tritium production, and uranium enrichment and fuel reprocessing facilities outside International Atomic Energy Agency (IAEA) safeguards. India is rapidly expanding its uranium enrichment program and may add another three thousand gas centrifuges for producing more highly enriched uranium (HEU) for its nuclear submarine program.[26]

From Pakistan's point of view, the Indo-U.S. Civil Nuclear Cooperation enables India to increase its fissile material stocks substantially and complete its triad-based nuclear arsenal. India will be able to add several hundred kilograms of weapons-grade and unsafeguarded reactor-grade plutonium and HEU to its nuclear stockpiles each year. Until now, India has used only two production reactors, CIRUS (shut down in December 2010) and Dhruva, for the production of fissile material, which may have given India 500 kg of weapons-grade plutonium, sufficient for some seventy to ninety weapons. Now under the deal, eight of its unsafeguarded heavy-water reactors—if operated on low burn-up—can produce another 1,250 kg of plutonium-laden spent fuel per year. In addition, one Indian 500-MW FBR can potentially produce 130 kg of weapons-grade plutonium each year. India has plans for four more breeder reactors by 2020, which in theory could produce more than 500 kg a year of weapons-grade plutonium. Western observers, especially the supporters of the nuclear deal with India, might disagree with the above, but others share these same concerns.

Islamabad's Response

Several nonproliferation experts have testified to the U.S. Congress, warning of the implications of the exceptional deal to India, claiming that it would weaken the nonproliferation regime and complicate future arms control negotiations, creating conditions for a regional arms race in South Asia and affecting India's relationship with Pakistan. All of these warnings have manifested just as the United States has cemented its nuclear relationship with India. Pakistani reactions to the Indo-U.S. deal were as predicted.

Pakistan is single-handedly blocking the commencement of the Fissile Material Cutoff Treaty (FMCT) at the Conference of Disarmament in Geneva. The Pakistanis have argued that a fissile material agreement in its existing form would place Pakistan at a perpetual disadvantage and disturb strategic stability in the region. Further, Pakistan has stated that in order to maintain its minimum credible deterrent, it cannot be expected to accept any cap in fissile material production while the FMCT legitimizes India's vast fissile material stocks.

India's material advantage has presumably led Pakistan to accelerate its plutonium program in order to develop advanced, miniaturized warheads that will enable it to maintain minimum credible deterrence and strategic balance with India. Further, the recent controversy in India over the success or failure of its thermonuclear test in 1998 has raised the prospect of a resumption of nuclear testing in the region, although this debate seems to have been triggered by the Indians themselves to pave the way for future testing. The Pakistani assessment is that such an event might take place, given the Indian reluctance to give categorical assurances of no future tests during negotiations of the Indo-U.S. deal. Should an Indian test occur, Pakistan would again be forced to respond and carry out tests of its own. Some in Pakistan, especially the scientific community, may be encouraged to suggest that the opportunity to test a new generation of fission weapons and plutonium-based weapons should not be lost.

Future Fissile Stocks: Capacities and Constraints

Khan Research Laboratories (KRL) continues to produce HEU for weapons at a rate of at least one hundred kilograms per year and is expanding its existing capacity by introducing and installing a new generation of P-3 and P-4 gas centrifuges, having much higher separative work unit (SWU),[27] which will exponentially increase the plant's enrichment capacity.[28] This projected increase in uranium enrichment capacity is also being backed by parallel expansion of the Chemical Plants Complex (CPC) which provides feedstock for the centrifuges.[29]

Meanwhile, plutonium-based warheads are also on the production lines. The 50-MWt Khushab-I plutonium and tritium production reactor has been operating since 1998. The Pakistan Atomic Energy Commission (PAEC) is constructing three additional heavy-water reactors of the same size at the same site, which would considerably expand Pakistan's plutonium production capacity in the next decade.[30] The New Labs reprocessing plant at Pakistan Institute of Nuclear Science and Technology (PINSTECH) is also being expanded to double its existing capacity.[31] In addition, Pakistan is nearing completion of a much larger commercial-scale reprocessing facility located at Chashma, which was abandoned by the French in 1978.[32] With the addition of three more Khushab reactors, Pakistan will also be able to replenish its stocks of tritium, which may have outlived their half-life.[33] This move would signal a shift in emphasis from HEU-based fissile material stocks to plutonium-based stocks.

In addition to the above military program, the civilian fuel cycle program is being set up in parallel by PAEC to meet future nuclear fuel requirements of a nuclear power program. These requirements include the construction of another nuclear fuel fabrication plant and a commercial-scale centrifuge enrichment plant at Chak Jhumra, with an estimated production capacity of 150,000 to 600,000 SWU of low-enriched uranium (LEU) for light-water reactors. This project, along with associated civil fuel cycle infrastructure, would be completed within the next few years and would be placed under IAEA safeguards. At this time, however, there is no report of any work commencing on this project.[34]

Delivery Means: Future Trends

Until the 1990s, aircraft were the only means of nuclear delivery for Pakistan. However, once solid- and liquid-fueled ballistic missile technologies were transferred to Pakistan from North Korea and China, respectively, ballistic missiles became the mainstay for delivery. Nevertheless, Pakistan's ensured delivery capabilities have been continuously challenged because of India's possible acquisition of ballistic missile defense systems with the assistance of the United States and Israel. As India bids for the Arrow antiballistic missile (ABM) systems and Patriot PAC-3 system to back up its S-300 aircraft systems, Pakistan's ability to deliver its warheads through ballistic missiles and aircraft becomes adversely affected.

These developments have triggered the impulse to introduce cruise missile technology in the form of the *Babur* cruise missile. In the future, Pakistan's means of ensured destruction would comprise *Hatf-III* (*Ghaznavi*) and *Hatf-IV*(*Shaheen-I*) for short ranges from 290 to 650 kilometers, respectively, and short-range ballistic missiles (SRBMs) and *Hatf-V* (*Ghauri*) and *Hatf-VI* (*Shaheen-II*) for medium-range ballistic missiles with the purpose of covering the entirety of India to the east and south, with ranges up to 1,250 and 2,200 kilometers, respectively. In addition, cruise missiles based on land, air, and sea platforms would be ideal for penetrating Indian air defense and ballistic missile defense (BMD) systems.[35] India's acquisition of force multipliers and ABM systems are the ingredients for destroying the regional strategic balance seemingly in place.

In April 2011, Pakistan tested the *Hatf-XI/Nasr* missile system, which was introduced as adding "another layer of deterrence" to its arsenals. As of this writing the weapon system is not a deployment decision, but the two-tube missile system adapted from a multiple rocket launcher with a range of sixty km is slated to be tipped with a nuclear warhead. The implication of this system is that Pakistan has acquired the capability to build a miniaturized nuclear warhead. Given the size of the warhead, it will be a plutonium-based system that requires an implosion device with a diameter of less than twelve inches—quite a technological achievement.[36] The introduction of a strategic weapon (any weapon with a nuclear warhead is strategic) for battlefield use has several implications for the future. Clearly, the battlefield situation would become more complex, raising questions about preemption, command and control, and field security.[37] Yet if Pakistan achieves mastery in making small warheads, then the future warheads on the *Babur* and *Ra'ad* cruise missiles will almost be a certainty.[38]

Delivery Means Constraints

Pakistan still faces difficulties in purchasing Western technologies freely. Except for the F-16 C/D Block-52, which it recently acquired in small numbers, state-of-the-art modern aircraft are outside the reach of Pakistan, because of both financial constraints and the reluctance of suppliers as a result of regional instability and in deference to India's objections. These limitations force Pakistan to rely on China for aircraft deliveries, such as *JF-17 Thunder* multirole aircraft. Given the nature of Sino-Pak relations, Pakistan would also be confident of receiving Chinese technologies, including new fighter aircraft.

Pakistan's current fleet of solid-fueled SRBMs has numerous deployment limitations. In order to maximize their range into India, they would need to be deployed closer to the Indo-Pakistani border, which would make them vulnerable to pre-emptive strikes. The medium-range *Shaheen* and *Ghauri* systems can overcome these drawbacks. As indicated in Chapter 12, KRL received about two-dozen North Korean *No-Dong* missiles in the mid-1990s. Over a period of time, transfers of missile technology from North Korea and the synergy between various strategic organizations such as the National Development Complex (NDC) and KRL have enabled Pakistan to indigenously improve and produce the *Ghauri* system.[39]

A Nuclear Pakistan: Tale of Two Futures

What role nuclear weapons will likely play in Pakistani policies and in its regional and international engagements will depend primarily on four developments: (1) how the war on terrorism proceeds and what role Pakistan will play in it; (2) how regional dynamics affect conflict resolution and regional power balance between India and Pakistan; (3) how the United States acts in Asia (particularly with respect to China and India) and toward the Islamic world (particularly with respect to Iran); and (4) how Pakistan's own domestic politics progress under, or after, military rule. Depending on these developments, Pakistan's nuclear policy is likely to evolve into one of two futures.

The first future is moderate and pragmatic and would occur if Pakistan has a moderate government that ensures balanced civil-military relations. This course would perpetuate the national security establishment's perception of nuclear force as purely a national security instrument. Even with the changing regional dynamics, it will likely follow the predictable pattern that has been seen in the past. Pakistan would continue to rely on a combination of internal and external balancing techniques to meet emerging threats. Pakistani nuclear and conventional forces would grow in tandem with India's force modernization. Its external balancing would likely rely on China, Muslim countries, and the United States. If Pakistan's economy grows and if relations with India improve, the probability of Cold War–style nuclear learning, to include arms control and confidence-building measures with India, should not be ruled out.

The other nuclear future is a radical shift away from Pakistan's traditional approach to international relations. Such an outcome is more likely if a radical right-wing government assumes power. A domestic change of this nature could shift the emphasis of nuclear weapons from a purely national security tool to a more ideologically based power instrument. This would result in confrontation, most likely with Pakistan's non-Muslim neighbors and the West, and perhaps extended deterrence to the Muslim world. This scenario is plausible, since right-wing political parties have hinted to this effect. However, this future would complicate Pakistan's relationship with the world and could put the country's nuclear program into jeopardy.

In sum, Pakistan's decades-old struggle to improve its precarious security predicament has provided security from its principal adversary—India. However, as Pakistan becomes an advanced nuclear state, it faces asymmetric threats to its security that require different instruments of conventional force backed up with political, diplomatic, and economic efforts.

No other nuclear power acquired a nuclear capability under such obstacles and in the face of efforts to derail the program; no other power without experience and support turned its rudimentary nuclear capability into operational deterrent forces; and no other power created a robust command-and-control system and constructed a nuclear security regime under immense pressure from Western cynicism and internal security threats.

At the time of this writing, Pakistan has shown tendencies that reveal potential to move toward either future described above. At the beginning of 2012 Pakistan was seen in the throes of an identity crisis that has been simmering for several decades and was catalyzed in 2011 by the assassinations of the governor of Punjab province and the minister of minority affairs, both of whom were outspoken defenders of minority rights. The country stands divided between moderates, with a liberal outlook of a modern state, and conservatives who have a vision of a theocratic state.[40] This division has brought the nature of Pakistan into question, pointing to the potential for the second future of radical tendencies, raising concerns in the international community. By the end of 2011, however, Pakistan has shown maturity in its policies. Civil-military relations are better, and relations with India have begun to improve, promising the restoration of ties that were severed as a result of the terror attack in Mumbai in November 2008. Should this trend gain momentum, the Pakistani trajectory could well be toward the first future.

As a young nation-state, Pakistan's identity is still in flux. For the international community, Pakistan presents the first encounter with a modern nuclear-armed nation state whose destiny is uncertain. The kind of Pakistan that emerges out of this traumatic period will determine its nuclear future.

In the summer of 2010, the Pakistani nation was devastated by one of the worst recorded floods in history. Nearly one-third of the country was submerged under raging waters, and nearly two-thirds of its prime crops and livestock were destroyed, displacing nearly 25 million people (almost the population of California). Meanwhile, double-digit inflation, poor growth, unemployment, and massive corruption have brought the country into a state of "stagflation." As the military balances multiple contingencies and its nuclear arsenal continues to grow and mature into a robust deterrent force, the Pakistani masses seem destined to "eat grass . . . even go hungry." Perhaps it never crossed Zulfiqar Ali Bhutto's mind that his words would become a self-fulfilling prophecy.

Epilogue

Pakistan possesses close to one hundred nuclear weapons, while its search for security continues. In 2011, several major events rocked the state of Pakistan, raising a litany of concerns: a crisis of national identity between moderates and conservatives; the fate of its fledgling democracy; and the future of U.S.-Pakistan relations. Indeed, Pakistan sits on a tinderbox as the narrative of this book comes to a close.

The internal and external struggles continue to mount. The year 2011 began with the brutal assassinations of Punjab's liberal governor Salman Taseer, on January 4, 2011, and a few months later of Christian minority minister Shahbaz in Islamabad, incited by Islamic fundamentalism that saw that state under the fear of reprisals. As a result, these incidents sparked an internal debate about the fate of the country.[1] That same month, CIA contractor Raymond Davis killed two Pakistani citizens in Lahore, triggering unprecedented anger among the Pakistanis. This issue was eventually resolved after blood money was paid to the family of the victims, but it triggered a level of distrust among allies in the war against terrorism.

On May 2, 2011, in a spectacular raid deep inside Pakistan in the city of Abottabad (some sixty miles north of Islamabad), U.S. Navy SEALs killed Osama Bin laden. No incident in recent history was as sensational and shocking. The Abottabad operation created intense controversy in the country, since it was viewed as a breach of Pakistan's sovereignty.[2] This was followed by official statements by U.S. government officials alleging either complacency or complicity of the Pakistani security forces.[3] Then came the November 26, 2011, attack led by U.S. forces on the Pakistani Army check-post at Salala on the border with Afghanistan, which killed twenty-seven soldiers and officers; it proved to be the proverbial "straw that broke the camel's back" and brought U.S.-Pak relations to an all-time low. Professor Anatol Lieven of King's College, London, described the relationship with the United States in this way: "[There] is a thin veneer of friendship over a morass of mutual distrust and even hatred."[4] Such remarks are a true reflection of the challenges that both the United States and Pakistan face to balance two realities in the relationship: one of friendship, and one of raised skepticism and contempt.

These military operations punctured the balloon of uncertainty and mistrust that had progressively matured over the decade since Pakistan joined the war against terrorism in the aftermath of September, 11, 2001. The combination of these factors has served to aggravate the anti-American sentiment within the country, which is enhanced by conspiracy theorists and right-wingers on both sides.

Notwithstanding this deteriorating situation, there have been some positive developments in the region. The Pakistani military has shown remarkable restraint from intervening in the political process despite increasing political instability and worsening economic crisis in the country. Additionally, relations with India have gradually improved with regard to trade and commercial concessions by granting India the Most Favored Nation (MFN) status. The commencement of a dialogue process with India is encouraging, but not promising enough to become a sustained process that could lead to a genuine era of peace and detente. This brings us full-circle to the question of strategic stability in South Asia.

Generally speaking, effective nuclear deterrence between nuclear-armed neighbours relies on a shared conception of risk and reality. Without this, the robustness of nuclear deterrence is questionable. India and Pakistan have yet to find the common denominator on security doctrines that does not challenge deterrence stability. Pakistan has taken India's military doctrine of punitive operations against a perceived terror attack (Cold Start Doctrine/Proactive Operations) as literal and real. Of particular note is India's expansion of its air-land capabilities, which have been perfected in a series of regular exercises and technological innovations. At this stage, Pakistani conventional forces are deployed on both its eastern and western borders in order to balance military contingencies simultaneously—one being the traditional defense against India, and the other counterinsurgency and stability operations on the western border. Under these operational conditions Pakistan has no choice but to rely upon nuclear weapons and modern conventional capabilities. The policy is designed to make India's conventional force adventure against weakened Pakistani defenses as costly as possible. The introduction of short-range, nuclear-capable weapons systems (*Hatf-XI/Nasr*) in 2001 as "another layer of deterrence" is aimed at obtaining such an objective.[5]

Given such an environment, there are four primary technological innovations and force modernizations that will most likely change the strategic landscape of the region in the next decade: cruise missiles, battlefield nuclear weapons or tactical nuclear weapons (TNW), sea-based deterrence, and ballistic missile defense (BMD). Parallel improvements in intelligence, surveillance, and reconnaissance (especially space-based communication satellites) in the region are gradually shifting employment doctrines from pure countervalue targeting to counterforce targeting.

Also, India is reportedly expanding its uranium enrichment capabilities for its nuclear submarine program and completing new reprocessing plants and production and breeder reactors. The combination of the Indo-U.S. nuclear deal and India's Cold Start Doctrine forced Pakistan to further expand its plutonium production capabilities by beginning work on three additional reactors, bringing the total to four. In February 2011, the Pakistani prime minister visited the Khushab Nuclear Complex, signaling the completion of the second production reactor at Khushab. At the same time a third facility is nearing completion, with plans in motion to initiate a fourth project, which could be operational by 2014–15.

The planned fourth reactors appear to be slightly bigger than the first reactor, with an estimated maximum capacity of 50–100 MWt. The commercial-scale reprocessing plant at *Chashma* is also nearing completion. This is the same reprocessing project that France had abandoned in 1978 that since then had been lying dormant for twenty-five years. Following the commissioning of the Khushab-1 reactor in 1998 spent fuel became available for reprocessing, and President Pervez Musharraf made the decision to begin reprocessing plutonium production in 2002.

Along with expanded New Labs, the new Chashma processing plant (nearly 100-ton capacity) will enable Pakistan to reprocess significant quantities of weapons-grade plutonium from the fuel produced at the Khushab Complex. Assuming that the facility operates at 70 percent capacity, each of these would be able to produce an estimate of 12 kg of weapons-grade plutonium annually, resulting in an estimated yearly production of roughly 46–50 kg, enough to manufacture six to seven plutonium-based bombs.

As I was finishing this book manuscript, I received a final "background briefing" in Islamabad on the latest strategic developments. The gist was that

Pakistan has no plans to move toward battlefield weapons. The introduction of *Nasr* is a purely defensive measure meant to bolster conventional deterrence by creating strong barriers that will deter assaulting forces at the tactical level. The Pakistani strategic command authorities do not think that *Nasr* is a tactical nuclear weapon in the classic sense. Any system, in their belief, that is capable of carrying a nuclear warhead cannot be dubbed tactical. Should a nuclear warhead system be used in a tactical role, it will still have strategic impact; regardless of terminology it crosses the threshold from the conventional to the nuclear realm. This warrants the highest level of command and control and use authorization from the National Command Authority (NCA).

In the Pakistani strategic belief, as of 2001 and 2002 the country had restored the strategic balance in the region; it was disturbed by India's military doctrine of limited war under the nuclear overhang and nuanced through the Cold Start Doctrine. *Nasr*, therefore, re-restores "the strategic balance by closing in the gap at the operational and the tactical level." Pakistan's security managers surmise that in India's calculations, Pakistan would not have used the "big strategic weapons if the attacks were shallow and occurring in the vicinity of the battlefield close to the border." So in their assessment, "*Nasr* pours cold water to Cold Start … thus this is a weapon of peace. It restores the balance; it should convince India to think long before deciding to attack."

In terms of the cruise missile systems that have been added to the inventory, specifically the air-launched cruise missile (*Hatf-VIII/Raad*) has a stand-off capability to target anything within the range of 450 km, including Delhi. *Raad* solves the PAF problem of penetrating Indian air defenses and air force disparity. For PAF, penetrating Indian air defenses would require a major operations fleet of fighter aircraft to escort, fight, and to deliver a bomb. And compared with India, Pakistani resources, especially in air force and naval assets, are far smaller. Hence Pakistan's air-launched cruise missile capability to offset this imbalance. This capability is now all the more important since India displays intentions of acquiring 126 state-of-the-art Medium Multi-Role Combat Aircraft (MMRCA) and 42 *Sukhoi* SU-30 MKI aircraft, in addition to its existing inventory of fighter aircraft.

Finally, both India and Pakistan are actively pursuing a sea-based deterrent. On the Pakistani side, such a capability would most likely be based on a naval version of the cruise missile. The Maritime Technology Organization (MTO) is nearing completion of the project, which, once tested or inaugurated, will be commissioned under the Naval Strategic Force Command (NSFC), completing the third leg of the triad. Both countries are also developing assured second-strike capabilities, with aggressive navies in South Asia in the northern Arabian Sea.

Pakistan's National Engineering and Scientific Commission (NESCOM) has also developed the *Burraq* Unmanned Aerial Vehicle (UAV), which in the future could be armed like Predator with increased range, giving it the capabilities of an unmanned combat aerial vehicle or a cruise missile. Its current range stands at 1,250 km, which can provide enhanced coast-to-coast capability one way.

In South Asia there are clear trajectories in nuclear trend-lines indicating new security doctrines, force modernizations, and technological innovations that are leading the region into a nuclear arms race. An end to the rivalry with India, stabilization of Afghanistan, and resolving the variety of domestic issues would be an ultimate gain for the whole region, especially if it opens up the trade and energy corridors between Central Asia and South Asia.

Specifically, in the case of Pakistan, achieving balance in conventional force numbers and modernization, in tandem with progress in bilateral relations with India, is the key to lowering numbers of nuclear weapons. Pakistan's political stability is still uncertain, and the future of strategic stability in the light of these developments and modernizations is still not assured. Undoubtedly, the coming decade will be one of continued strain and skepticism. A continued dialogue and understanding of the nuclear environment and security doctrines in the region are necessary to keep any conflict at bay.

Notes

Preface

1.   "Background briefing" implies official briefs that can be used for substance and clarification but not attributed, because of the rules of engagement for the research.

Chapter 1

1.   For identical questions posed in their study, see John Wilson Lewis and Xue Litai, *China Builds the Bomb* (Stanford University Press, 1988).

2.   The studies that have influenced this endeavor the most include Richard Rhodes, *The Making of the Atomic Bomb* (New York: Simon and Schuster); David Holloway, *Stalin and the Bomb: The Soviet Union and Atomic Energy, 1939–1956* (New Haven: Yale University Press, 1994); Lewis and Xue, *China Builds the Bomb*; George Perkovich, *India's Nuclear Bomb: The Impact on Proliferation* (Berkeley: University of California Press, 1999); and Avner Cohen, *Israel and the Bomb* (New York: Columbia University Press, 1998).

3.   Early and incomplete accounts of the Pakistani program include Ashok Kapur, *Pakistan's Nuclear Development* (New York: Croom Helm, 1987); Ziba Moshaver, *Nuclear Weapons Proliferation in the Indian Subcontinent* (New York: St. Martin's, 1991); and Shahid-ur-Rehman, *Long Road to Chagai* (Islamabad: Print Wise Publications, 1999). A more recent account is Bhumitra Chakma, *Pakistan's Nuclear Weapons* (New York: Routledge, 2009). A recent Pakistani contribution, though one focused only in part on Pakistan's nuclear history, is Naeem Salik, *The Genesis of South Asian Nuclear Deterrence* (New York: Oxford University Press 2009). Extensive journalistic accounts on the A. Q. Khan nuclear supplier network include Douglas Frantz and Catherine Collins, *The Nuclear Jihadist: The True Story of the Man Who Sold the World's Most Dangerous Secrets—And How We Could Have Stopped Him* (New York: Twelve, 2007); Gordon Corera, *Shopping for Bombs: Nuclear Proliferation, Global Insecurity, and the Rise and Fall of the A. Q. Khan Network* (New York: Oxford University Press, 2006); and William Langewiesche, *The Atomic Bazaar: The Rise of the Nuclear Poor* (New York: Farrar, Straus and Giroux, 2007).

4. For the concept of orphan states, see Michael Mandelbaum, "Lessons of the Next Nuclear War," *Foreign Affairs* 74, 2 (March/April 1995), 22–35.

5. Bernard Brodie, ed., *The Absolute Weapon: Atomic Power and World Order* (Harcourt Brace Jovanovich, 1972).

6. See John J. Mearsheimer, *The Tragedy of Great Power Politics* (New York: W. W. Norton, 2001), 156–57.

7. Kenneth N. Waltz, *The Theory of International Politics* (New York: Random House, 1979), 128; and Stephen M. Walt, *The Origins of Alliances* (Ithaca, NY: Cornell University Press, 1987), 21–26, 263–66.

8. Ibid. For an analysis of external and internal balancing, see Scott D. Sagan, "The Origins of Military Doctrine" in Peter R. Lavoy, Scott D. Sagan, and James Wirtz, eds., *Planning the Unthinkable: How New Nuclear Powers Will Use Nuclear, Biological and Chemical Weapons* (Ithaca, NY: Cornell University Press, 2000), 23. See also Scott D. Sagan, "Why Do States Build Nuclear Weapons?: Three Models in Search of a Bomb," *International Security* 21, 3 (Winter 1996), 73–85.

9. Waltz, *The Theory of International Politics*, 168; and Walt, *The Origins of Alliances*, 21–26, 263–66.

10. Peter R. Lavoy, "Nuclear Proliferation over the Next Decade: Causes, Warning Signs, and Policy Responses" in Peter R. Lavoy, ed., *Nuclear Proliferation in the Next Decade* (New York: Routledge Taylor and Francis Group, 2008), 2.

11. Ibid., 2–3. For detailed application of this point, see Jacques Hymans, *The Psychology of Nuclear Proliferation: Identity, Emotions, and Foreign Policy* (Cambridge: Cambridge University Press, 2006).

12. Hasan Askari Rizvi, "Pakistan's Strategic Culture," in Michael Chambers, ed., *South Asia in 2020: Future Strategic Balances and Alliances* (Carlisle Barracks, PA: Strategic Studies Institute, U.S. Army War College, 2002), 307. Rizvi draws from Alistair Iain Johnston's work on strategic culture. See Iain Johnston, "Thinking about Strategic Culture," *International Security* 19, 4 (Spring 1995), 46, and Iain Johnston, *Cultural Realism: Strategic Culture and Grand Strategy in Chinese History* (Princeton: Princeton University Press, 1995), ch. 1. See also Feroz Hassan Khan, "Comparative Strategic Culture: The Case of Pakistan," *Strategic Insights* 4, 10 (October 2005).

13. Michael C. Desch, "Culture Clash: Assessing the Importance of Ideas in Security Studies," *International Security* 23, 1 (Summer 1998), 141–70.

14. Rizvi, "Pakistan's Strategic Culture," 306–8.

15. See Peter R. Lavoy, "Nuclear Myths and the Causes of Nuclear Proliferation," *Security Studies* 2, 3/4 (Spring/Summer 1993), 192–212. See also Lavoy, "Nuclear Proliferation over the Next Decade," 4–8.

16. Lavoy, "Nuclear Proliferation over the Next Decade," 3.

17. The author is indebted to Peter R. Lavoy for sharing the above thoughts. This book's research originated in coauthorship with him. See Lavoy, "Nuclear Myths and the

Causes of Nuclear Proliferation," 192–212. See also Lavoy, "Nuclear Proliferation over the Next Decade," 4–8.

18. The delay between the shock and the Indian test is explicable, largely inasmuch as the principal proponents of nuclearization, Nehru and Bhabha, died in 1964 and 1966, respectively.

19. Cited in Kausar Niazi, *Zulfiqar Ali Bhutto of Pakistan: The Last Days* (New Delhi: Vikas, 1992), 99.

20. See Holloway, *Stalin and the Bomb,* 154.

21. See Lewis and Xue, *China Builds the Bomb,* 4, 36.

22. See Perkovich, *India's Nuclear Bomb,* 13–25, 46–47.

23. See Avner Cohen, "Israel: A *Sui Generis* Proliferator," in Muthiah Alagappa, ed., *The Long Shadow: Nuclear Weapons and Security in 21st Century Asia* (Stanford: Stanford University Press, 2008), 242–44.

24. George Perkovich, *India's Nuclear Bomb,* 67.

25. Lewis and Xue, *China Builds the Bomb,* 36.

26. N. M. Butt, "Nuclear Developments in Pakistan," in Pervaiz Iqbal Cheema and Imtiaz H. Bokhari, eds., *Arms Race and Nuclear Developments in South Asia* (Islamabad: Islamabad Policy Research Institute, 2004), 44.

27. Peter Edidin, "Pakistan's Hero: Dr. Khan Got What He Wanted, and He Explains How," *New York Times*, February 15, 2004.

Chapter 2

1. See Eisenhower archives, at http://www.eisenhower.archives.gov/all_about_ike/Speeches/Chance_for_Peace.pdf.

2. Cited in Dennis Kux, *The United States and Pakistan 1947–2000: Disenchanted Allies* (Washington, DC: Woodrow Wilson Center Press, 2001), 52.

3. Ibid.

4. Centre for Global Security Research, *Atoms for Peace after 50 Years: The New Challenges and Opportunities* (Livermore, CA: Lawrence Livermore National Laboratory, December 2003).

5. Ashok Kapur also begins his history of the Pakistan nuclear program in 1953. Ashok Kapur, *Pakistan's Nuclear Development* (New York: Croom Helm, 1987).

6. Lawrence Ziring, *Pakistan: At the Crosscurrents of History* (Oxford: Oneworld Publications, 2003), 45.

7. See Stanley Wolpert, *Shameful Flight: The Last Years of the British Empire in India* (New York: Oxford University Press, 2006).

8. Ziring, *Pakistan*, 45.

9. Wolpert, *Shameful Flight*, 1.

10. In 1956, Pakistan's eastern wing, East Bengal, was legally redesignated East Pakistan. It is now the independent state of Bangladesh. Ziring, *Pakistan*, 64.

11. On February 21, 1952, the Bengali language movement began after protesting students were killed outside Dhaka University. A monument to their memory became a symbol of secession from Pakistan. Ibid., 57.

12. The Ahmediyya sect belonged to the followers of Ghulam Ahmed, a nineteenth-century preacher who claimed revelation from God. Devout Muslims considered his followers apostates. Ibid., 58–59.

13. Husain Haqqani, *Pakistan: Between Mosque and Military* (Washington, DC: Carnegie Endowment for International Peace, 2005), 20–21.

14. Altaf Gauhar, *Ayub Khan: Pakistan's First Military Ruler* (Lahore: Sang-e-Meel Publications, 1994), 103.

15. Selig S. Harrison, "Ethnic Conflict and the Future of Pakistan," in Wilson John, ed., *Pakistan: The Struggle Within* (New Delhi: Pearson Longman, 2009), 20–24.

16. Sindh had long campaigned to separate from the Bombay presidency and succeeded in separating in 1936. This gave Karachi, the capital, to the Sindhis. With Karachi becoming a federal district, city jobs were taken by Urdu-speaking Muhajirs, causing deprivation among the local Sindhis. Harrison, "Ethnic Conflict and the Future of Pakistan," 24–26.

17. Ziring, *Pakistan*, 46–61. See also Harrison, "Ethnic Conflict and the Future of Pakistan," 29–31.

18. Feroz Hassan Khan, "Rough Neighbors: Afghanistan and Pakistan," *Strategic Insights* 2, 1 (January 2003), http://www.ccc.nps.navy.mil/si/jan03/southAsia.asp.

19. Kux, *The United States and Pakistan*, 52–55.

20. Shuja Nawaz, *Crossed Swords: Pakistan, Its Army and the Wars Within* (New York: Oxford University Press, 2008), 111; see also Kux, *The United States and Pakistan*, 54–64.

21. Kux, *The United States and Pakistan*, 60.

22. Ibid., 61. Cited in Nawaz, *Crossed Swords*, 106.

23. Memoranda of discussions at National Security Council (NSC), December 16 and 23, 1953, and Richard Nixon, *RN: Memoirs of Richard Nixon* (New York: Simon and Schuster, 1978). Cited in Nawaz, *Crossed Swords*, 111.

24. Pakistan became a member of SEATO in 1954 and CENTO a year later. In 1959 Pakistan and the United States signed a bilateral treaty.

25. Kux, *The United States and Pakistan*, 72.

26. Nawaz, *Crossed Swords*, 112.

27. Kux, *The United States and Pakistan*, 63.

28. Ibid.

29. In the early 1950s, Major General N. M. Raza—twice Pakistan's ambassador to China after 1950—was a critical link in paving and bridging relations. Ambassador Maqbool Bhatti, interview by author, Islamabad, June 2004. Anwar Hussain Syed, *China and Pakistan: Diplomacy of an Entente Cordiale* (Amherst: University of Massachusetts, 1974), xii.

30. Abdul Sattar, *Pakistan's Foreign Policy 1947–2005: A Concise History* (Islamabad: Oxford University Press, 2007), 51; Abdul Sattar, interview by author, Islamabad, June 20, 2006.

31. See Yair Evron, *Israel's Nuclear Dilemma* (Ithaca, NY: Cornell University Press, 1994), 3.

32. Feroz Hassan Khan, "Pakistan's Evolving Strategic Doctrine," in John, ed., *Pakistan: The Struggle Within*, 118–44.

33. Feroz Hassan Khan, "Toward Cooperative Security: Prospects for Nonproliferation and Arms Control," in Joseph F. Pilat, ed., *Atoms for Peace: A Future after Fifty Years?* (Washington, DC: Woodrow Wilson Center Press, 2007), 99. For the entire speech, see Appendix 1, 239–46.

34. Pilat, *Atoms for Peace*, Appendix 1, 239–46.

35. Leonard Weiss, "Atoms for Peace," *Bulletin of Atomic Scientists* (November–December 2003), 34–44.

36. Peter Lavoy, "The Enduring Effects of Atoms for Peace," *Arms Control Today* 33, 10 (December 2003).

37. Weiss, "Atoms for Peace," 34–44.

38. Ibid.

39. Bhumitra Chakma, "Road to Chaghi: Pakistan's Nuclear Program, Its Sources and Motivations," *Modern Asian Studies* 36, 4 (2002), 874, fn. 3.

40. Lavoy, "The Enduring Effects of Atoms for Peace."

41. Ishfaque Ahmed, interview by author, Islamabad, December 2005.

42. See Peter R. Lavoy, "Learning to Live with the Bomb? India and Nuclear Weapons, 1947–1974," Ph.D. diss., Berkeley, University of California, 1997.

43. Chakma, "Road to Chaghi," 874.

44. Salimuzzaman Siddiqui, "The Pakistan Council of Scientific and Industrial Research: A review of Its activities," *Pakistan Quarterly* 7, 4 (Winter 1957), 42–45.

45. S. Z. H. Siddiqui, "Scientific Research in Pakistan," *Pakistan Quarterly* 15, 1–2 (Winter 1957), 26.

46. Kapur, *Pakistan's Nuclear Development*, 36; see also Government College, Lahore, "Center for the Advanced Studies in Physics," http://www.gcu.edu.pk/CASP.htm (accessed January 25, 2010).

47. N. M. Butt, "Development of Solid-State Physics in Pakistan," in Hameed A. Khan et al., eds., *Physics in Developing Countries: Past, Present and Future* (Islamabad: Commission on Science and Technology for Sustainable Development in the South, April 2006), 37. N. M. Butt was a student of Chaudhry's at Government College, Lahore.

48. N. M. Butt, "Nuclear Radiation Education and Nuclear Science and Technology in Pakistan," paper presented to the 2nd International Congress on Radiation Education, Debrecen, Hungary (August 20–25, 2002), available at http://www.pakdef.info/pak-

military/army/nuclear/radiation.html (accessed January 25, 2010). See also "Nucleus of Nuclear Power," *Daily Times*, January 12, 2004, http://www.dailytimes.com.pk/default. asp?page=story_12–1-2004_pg7_27.

49. Butt, "Nuclear Radiation Education."

50. In interviews, several PAEC scientists who had studied under Chaudhry used this phrase.

51. The irony is that Prof. Abdus Salam is internationally recognized as the first Muslim Nobel laureate in physics, while at home, as an Ahmadi, he is legally a non-Muslim.

52. There is some confusion as to where Ahmed undertook his graduate education. In Butt, "Nuclear Radiation Education," Butt states that Ahmed "apparently" pursued higher studies at the University of Manchester under Lord Rutherford. Given the timing of Ahmed's Ph.D. (1925), however, Rutherford would already have transferred from the University of Manchester to Cambridge. Further, British physicist Leslie Fleetwood Bates, as an aside in his account of the life of another British physicist, Edmund Clifton Stoner, recounts that Stoner discussed Ahmed quite favorably in his recollection of his time at the Cavendish Laboratory in the 1920s. See L. F. Bates, "Edmund Clifton Stoner, 1899–1968," *Biographical Memoirs of Fellows of the Royal Society* 15 (April 1969), 211–13.

53. The above account somewhat simplifies a more complex governance structure. A twelve-member Atomic Energy Committee created an Atomic Energy Council (AEC) and an Atomic Energy Commission in March 1956. The Council, as delimited in a February 1956 resolution, included five persons: the chairman of the Atomic Energy Committee, the finance minister, the industries minister, the finance secretary, and the industries secretary. (In Pakistan, a minister is politically appointed, while a secretary is the senior-most civil servant in the ministry.) The Commission, reporting to the Council, was composed of the chair and six other scientists. See Kapur, *Pakistan's Nuclear Development,* 35. See also I. H. Qureshi, "Recollections from the Early Days of the PAEC," *The Nucleus* 42, 1–2 (Islamabad: Quarterly Scientific Journal of Pakistan Atomic Energy Commission, 2005), 7–11.

54. Nazir Ahmad, "The Atomic Energy Commission," *Pakistan Quarterly* 7, 3 (Autumn 1957), 14.

55. Argonne National Laboratory: History, http://www.anl.gov/Science_and_Technology/History/Anniversary_Frontiers/eduhist.html.

56. Ibid.

57. Shirin Tahir-Kheli, *The United States and Pakistan: The Evolution of an Influence Relationship* (New York: Praeger, 1982), 116.

58. Shahid-ur-Rehman, *Long Road to Chagai,* 22.

59. Ibid.

60. Ibid., 23. See also S. N. Burney, "Development of Atomic Energy in Pakistan," vol. 1, cited in ibid.

61. Shahid-ur-Rehman, *Long Road to Chagai*, 23.

62. Ibid., 24.

63. Ibid.

64. Ibid., 23.

65. Kapur, *Pakistan's Nuclear Development*, 38–39, 42.

66. Lieutenant-General (ret.) Syed Refaqaut Ali, interview by author, December 2005, Islamabad.

Chapter 3

1. The president had the authority to appoint the prime minister and provincial governors; was supreme commander of the armed forces, with authority to appoint the commander-in-chief of the three services; and was the ultimate authority on the civil services of Pakistan. Shuja Nawaz, *Crossed Swords: Pakistan, Its Army, and the Wars Within* (New York: Oxford University Press, 2008), 128–29.

2. Husain Haqqani, *Pakistan: Between Mosque and Military* (Washington, DC: Carnegie Endowment for International Peace, 2005), 15–25.

3. Ahmad Faruqui, "Pakistan's Security Environment in the Year 2015: Scenarios, Disruptive Events, and U.S. Policy Options," paper presented at a workshop held under the aegis of the Strategic Studies Institute, U.S. Army War College, Washington, DC, June 27, 2001.

4. Lieutenant-General Majeed, interview by author, October 11, 2009, Islamabad. When Ayub Khan was appointed defense minister, in addition to his responsibilities as commander-in-chief, he began to think more in terms of "running the country," rather than running the army.

5. Altaf Gauhar, *Ayub Khan: Pakistan's First Military Ruler* (Lahore: Sang-e-Meel Publications, 1994), 39–41; see also Hasan Zaheer, *The Times and Trial of the Rawalpindi Conspiracy 1951: The First Coup Attempt in Pakistan* (New York: Oxford University Press, 1998).

6. Gauhar, *Ayub Khan*, 120.

7. One issue was to persuade the Americans to agree with Pakistan Air force chief Asghar Khan's desire to get B-66 aircraft, whereas the U.S. was prepared to give twenty B-57 aircraft.

8. Gauhar, *Ayub Khan*, 131.

9. Lieutenant-General Malik Abdul Majeed, interview by author, October 11, 2009, Islamabad. Malik Abdul Majeed was a young staff officer in GHQ when martial law was declared in 1958. Recalling the earlier martial law of 1953, Majeed commented that the military was unfamiliar with this term "martial law." By 1958, he believed there were five major actors within the military who were active in bringing about martial law, overthrowing President Mirza. These five generals were: Muhammad Ayub, Yahya Khan, Abdul Hamid Khan, Atiq-ur Rehman, and S. G. M. Pirzada. He recalls that for

young officers in the 1950s, the frequent changes of the political leadership were disturbing.

10. *Dawn,* editorial, October 10, 1958, cited in Gauhar, *Ayub Khan,* 159.

11. Samuel Huntington, *Political Order in Changing Societies* (New Haven: Yale University Press, 1968), 251.

12. Mohammad Ayub Khan, *Friends Not Masters: A Political Autobiography* (Karachi: Oxford University Press, 1967), 30, cited in Gauhar, *Ayub Khan,* 157.

13. Gauhar, *Ayub Khan,* 161.

14. Ayub Khan, *Friends Not Masters,* 19.

15. Ibid.

16. Nawaz, *Crossed Swords,* 192.

17. Richard Sisson and Leo E. Rose, *War and Secession: Pakistan, India, and the Creation of Bangladesh* (New York: Oxford University Press, 1992), 17.

18. Stanley Wolpert, *Zulfi Bhutto of Pakistan: His Life and Times* (New York: Oxford University Press, 1983), 46–54.

19. Pakistan's new constitution would come into affect in 1962.

20. Gauhar, *Ayub Khan,* 191.

21. Nawaz, *Crossed Swords,* 183–85; see also discussion in Pervaiz Iqbal Cheema, *Pakistan's Defence Policy, 1947–58* (New York: St. Martin's, 1990).

22. Nawaz, *Crossed Swords,* 185–86.

23. Dennis Kux, *The United States and Pakistan 1947–2000: Disenchanted Allies* (Washington, DC: Woodrow Wilson Center Press, 2001), 112–13.

24. Gauhar, *Ayub Khan,* 198–200.

25. Wolpert, *Zulfi Bhutto of Pakistan,* 60.

26. Ibid. Later, Bhutto denounced "Basic Democracies," which he had done so much to implement, as "Basic Fascism."

27. Bhutto's style was seen as too ambitious, and he was crossing swords with his senior colleagues. Bhutto was selected by the president to represent Pakistan in the UN General Assembly. He made the most of his journey to and from New York, with stopovers in Turkey, France, the United Kingdom, Canada, Japan, and the Philippines. Ibid., 61–62.

28. Ibid., 64–65.

29. Ibid., 65.

30. Ibid., 66.

31. Zulfikar Ali Bhutto, "Impressions of the United Nations," address to the Pakistan UN Association, May 22, 1961, quoted in ibid.

32. Wolpert, *Zulfi Bhutto of Pakistan,* 67.

33. Kux, *The United States and Pakistan,* 130–32.

34. Ibid.

35. Lieutenant-General (ret.) Abdul Majeed Malik, interview by author, Islamabad, October 11, 2009.

36. Kux, *The United States and Pakistan*, 135.

37. Ayub Khan, *Friends Not Masters*, 170.

38. Wolpert, *Zulfi Bhutto of Pakistan*, 73–74; see also Abdul Sattar, *Pakistan's Foreign Policy 1947–2005: A Concise History* (New York: Oxford University Press, 2007), 70–71.

39. Wolpert, *Zulfi Bhutto of Pakistan*, 73–74.

40. Ibid., 75.

41. Ibid.

42. Ibid., 80.

43. Gauhar, *Ayub Khan*, 268.

44. As a goodwill gesture, Chou En-Lai made a gift of some grazing areas for Pakistan. Ibid., 290.

45. Ibid., 291–95.

46. Ibid.

47. Ibid., 301.

48. Nawaz, *Crossed Swords*, 202–3; and Gauhar, *Ayub Khan*, 308–9.

49. Nawaz, *Crossed Swords*, 202–3.

50. Gauhar, *Ayub Khan*, 310.

51. Ibid., 309.

52. B. C. Chakravorty, *History of the Indo-Pak War, 1965* (New Delhi: History Division, Ministry of Defense, 1992), 39, cited in Nawaz, *Crossed Swords*, 205.

53. Gul Hassan Khan, *Memoirs* (New York: Oxford University Press, 1993), 178. General Gul Hassan Khan was Director Military Operations (DMO) at General Headquarters at the time.

54. Gauhar, *Ayub Khan*, 322.

55. Ibid.

56. Ibid., 323.

57. Ibid., 322.

58. Nawaz, *Crossed Swords*, 219–47.

59. Ibid.

60. For a detailed military history of the 1965 war, see Lieutenant-General Mahmud Ahmed, *Illusion of Victory: A Military History of the Indo-Pak War 1965* (Karachi: Lexicon Publishers, 2002).

61. Lieutenant-General Majeed, interview by author, Islamabad, October 11, 2009. See also Feroz Hassan Khan, Christopher Clary, and Peter Lavoy, "Pakistan's Motivations and Calculations for the Kargil Conflict," in Peter R. Lavoy, ed., *Asymmetric Warfare in South Asia: The Causes and Consequences of the Kargil Conflict* (New York: Cambridge University Press, 2009), 68–74.

62. Kux, *The United States and Pakistan*, 161–62.

63. Ibid.

64. Gauhar, *Ayub Khan*, 348.

65. Ibid.

66. Ibid., 352.

67. Ibid., 353.

68. Kux, *The United States and Pakistan*, 169.

69. Lieutenant-General Majeed, interview by author, Islamabad, October 11, 2009.

70. Kux, *The United States and Pakistan*, 165.

71. Ibid., 169.

72. Ibid., 172.

73. Zia Mian, "How to Build the Bomb," in Mian, ed., *Pakistan's Atomic Bomb and Search for Security* (Lahore: Gautam Publishers, 1995), 135–36.

74. Bhutto, *If I Am Assassinated* (New Delhi: Vikas, 1979), 137.

75. Abdus Salam, Z. Hassan, and C. H. Lai, *Ideals and Realities: Selected Essays of Abdus Salam* (Singapore: World Scientific, 1984), 156.

76. S. A. Hasnain, "Dr. I. H. Usmani and the Early Days of the PAEC," *The Nucleus* 42, 1–2 (Islamabad: Quarterly Scientific Journal of Pakistan Atomic Energy Commission, 2005), 13.

77. Dr. Ishfaq Ahmad, interview by author, Islamabad, December 2005.

78. Hasnain, "Dr. I. H. Usmani and the Early Days of the PAEC," 15.

79. Dr. Ishfaq Ahmad, interview by author, Islamabad, December 2005.

80. Ibid., 14.

81. A. M. Faruqui, "A Pakistani Who Made Dreams Come True," *Pakistan Link,* editorial, November 21, 2003. Quoted in Hasnain, "Dr. I. H. Usmani and the Early Days of the PAEC," 17.

82. The name *The Nucleus* for the Quarterly Journal of the PAEC was suggested by Dr. Anwar Hossain, director of the Atomic Energy Center in Dacca.

83. Zulfiqar Ali Bhutto remained responsible for atomic energy affairs after Ayub Khan appointed him as a federal minister in 1959. As minister of Fuel, Power and Natural Resources, his ministry was also responsible for the PAEC. When Bhutto became the foreign minister in 1963, the PAEC was directed to report to the Foreign Ministry. Until Bhutto was sacked in 1966, he was a veritable political father of atomic energy affairs. When Bhutto became the president and later prime minister, the PAEC and all organizations dealing with atomic matters reported to the head of the government (president/ prime minister) directly, and not to any ministry of the government.

84. Riazuddin, "Contribution of Professor Abdus Salam as Member of PAEC," *The Nucleus* 42, 1–2 (2005), 31–34.

85. Hasnain, "Dr. I. H. Usmani and the Early Days of the PAEC," 18.

86. Ibid.

87. Ibid.

88. Ibid., 14; and S. A. Hasnain, interview by author, Islamabad, June 2006.

89. Hasnain, "Dr. I. H. Usmani and the Early Days of the PAEC," 18.

90. Ibid. In total, the PAEC sent ten engineers to ORSORT, mostly in the operations

option. Of the ten, only one, Saeed Zahid, opted to do the hazards evaluation special-ization, but he did not remain long in the PAEC. That is one reason that safety analysis remained rather weak in the PAEC in those days.

91. Ibid.

92. Bhumitra Chakma, *Pakistan's Nuclear Weapons* (New York: Routledge, 2009), citing Shirin Tahir-Kheli, "Pakistan's Nucleus Option and U.S. Policy," *Orbis* 22, 2 (Summer 1978), 358.

93. Chakma, *Pakistan's Nuclear Weapons*, 12.

94. Ziba Moshaver, *Nuclear Weapons Proliferation in the Indian Subcontinent* (London: Macmillan, 1991), 100.

95. S. B. Guha, "Pakistan's Atomic Energy Programme," *Institute for Defence Studies and Analysis Journal* (New Delhi) 3, 1 (July 1970), 120.

96. Ibid.

97. Ibid.

98. M. Nasim and S. D. Orfi, "Evolution and Development of Nuclear Safety Regime in Pakistan," *The Nucleus* 42, 67–72.

99. Shahid-ur-Rehman, *Long Road to Chagai* (Islamabad: Print Wise Publications, 1999), 24. The turnkey contract had a fixed cost of $60 million, carrying a 4 percent interest rate and a supplier credit of $24 million.

100. The negotiations over CIRUS for India ran into objections by the Canadian bureaucracy over the question of imposing strict safeguards. Indian prime minister Nehru was able to convince Canadian prime minister Lester Pearson, who overruled the bureaucratic objections. It appears that the Canadian bureaucracy regained control on this issue when the turn for Pakistan came. George Perkovich's account indicates that the Canadian bureaucracy obtained a commitment from India in a secret annex to the treaty that the reactor and the resulting fissile material would be used only for peaceful purposes. Also, while India agreed to pay for the reactor, it did so in rupees, not having to use foreign exchange. See George Perkovich, *India's Nuclear Bomb: The Impact on Global Proliferation* (New York: Oxford University Press, 2000), 27.

101. Agha Shahi, interview by author, Islamabad, June 19, 2005.

102. Rehman, *Long Road to Chagai*, 25.

103. Ibid. Shahid-ur-Rehman contends that the PAEC submitted proposals for fuel fabrication, a heavy water plant, and a reprocessing plant, but the "relevant department shot them down." This claim has not been verified by any other source. Ibid., 25–26.

104. I. H. Qureshi, "Recollections from the Early Days of the PAEC," 10–11.

105. Ibid., 7–11, 9.

106. Hasnain, "Dr. I. H. Usmani and the Early Days of the PAEC," 70.

107. Ibid., 16.

108. Ibid.

109. Qureshi, "Recollections from the Early Days of the PAEC," 9.

110. Ibid.

111. Kux, *The United States and Pakistan*, 165–71.

112. Qureshi, "Recollections from the Early Days of the PAEC," 41–47, 42.

113. Pakistan Institute of Engineering and Applied Sciences, http://www.pieas.edu.pk/about/genesis.php (accessed August 10, 2009); Qureshi, "Recollections from the Early Days of the PAEC," 41–47; and B. A. Hasan, "Human Resource Development at PIEAS—A Brief Historical Account," *The Nucleus* 42, 1–2 (2005), 113–22.

114. In 1966, PINSTECH was composed of the following divisions: Nuclear Physics Division, Radio Isotope Production Division, Reactor Operation Division, Health Physics Division, and Reactor Design Group and Reactor School. However, by 1992, the expanded PINSTECH was made up of the following divisions, including R&D support divisions and special lab centers: Nuclear Physics, Nuclear Materials, Nuclear Chemistry, Nuclear Engineering, Health Physics, Radioisotope Applications, Applied Physics, Applied Chemistry, Radiation Physics, R&D Support Divisions (Electronics, Computer, General Services, Scientific Information, Special Labs/Centers, Center for Nuclear Studies, Micro-seismic Studies, Optics/Laser Laboratories).

115. N. M. Butt, M. A. Shaikh, and I. E. Qureshi, "Development of Physical Sciences at PINSTECH," *The Nucleus* 29, 1–4 (1992), 2.

116. Munir Ahmad Khan, "Medal Award Ceremony," speech at the Pakistan Nuclear Society, PINSTECH Auditorium, Islamabad, March 20, 1999.

117. Lieutenant-General Syed Refaqat, interview by author, Islamabad, June 19, 2005.

118. Perkovich, *India's Nuclear Bomb*, 66.

119. Ibid., 67.

120. Ibid.

121. Ibid., 68–69.

122. Ibid.

123. Ibid., 84.

124. Faruqi, "Pakistan's Security Environment in the Year 2015." Cited in Feroz Hassan Khan, "Pakistan's Nuclear Future," in Michael R. Chambers, ed., *South Asia in 2020: Future Strategic Balances and Alliances* (Carlisle Barracks, PA: Strategic Studies Institute, 2002), 157.

125. Chakma, *Pakistan's Nuclear Weapons*, 16.

126. Steve Weissman and Herbert Krosney, *The Islamic Bomb* (New York: Times Books, 1981).

127. See Anwar Hussain Syed, *China and Pakistan: Diplomacy of an Entente Cordiale* (Amherst: University of Massachusetts Press, 1974), 10–11.

128. Henry D. Sokolski, "The Nuclear Nonproliferation Treaty," in *Best of Intentions: America's Campaign against Strategic Weapons Proliferation* (Westport, CT: Praeger, 2001), 40–46; and Joseph Cirincione with Jon B. Wolfsthal and Miriam Rajkumar, eds.,

Deadly Arsenals: Tracking Weapons of Mass Destruction (Washington, DC: Carnegie Endowment of International Peace, 2002), 25.

129. Agha Shahi, interview by author, Islamabad, June 19, 2005.

130. Ibid.

131. B. Sinha and R. R. Subramanyam, *Nuclear Pakistan: Atomic Threat to South Asia* (New Delhi: Vision Books, 1980), 30–32.

132. Kux, *The United States and Pakistan,* 165–68.

133. Munir Ahmad Khan, "Medal Award Ceremony."

134. Farhatullah Babar, "Bhutto's Footprints on Nuclear Pakistan," *The News,* April, 4, 2006, 3.

135. S. K. Pasha, "Solar Energy and the Guests at KANUPP Opening," *Morning News* (Karachi), November 29, 1972, 20.

136. Ayub Khan, *Friends Not Masters,* 206.

137. Agha Shahi, interview by author, Islamabad, June 19, 2005.

138. Rehman, *Long Road to Chagai,* 25.

139. Agha Shahi, interview by author, Islamabad, June 19, 2005.

140. Craig Baxter, ed., *Diaries of Field Marshal Mohammad Ayub Khan 1966–1972* (New York: Oxford University Press, 2007), 55.

141. Ibid.

142. Lieutenant-General Syed Refaqat, interview by author, Islamabad, December 19, 2005. The Dacca quotation was specifically provided by Refaqat during the interview.

143. Wolpert, *Zulfi Bhutto of Pakistan,* 111–12. Wolpert cites Bhutto's speech to the All-Pakistan Students Federation, London, August 13, 1966, in Hamid Jalal and Khalid Hasan, eds., *Politics of the People,* vol. 2, *Awakening the People* (Rawalpindi: Pakistan Publications, n.d.), 4–15.

Chapter 4

1. Stanley Wolpert, *Zulfi Bhutto of Pakistan: His Life and Times* (New York: Oxford University Press, 1983), 110.

2. Ibid., 112.

3. Ibid., 112–13.

4. Ibid., 113.

5. Ibid., emphasis added.

6. Feroz Hassan Khan, "Nuclear Proliferation Motivations: Lessons from Pakistan," in Peter R. Lavoy, ed., *Nuclear Weapons Proliferation in the Next Decade* (New York: Routledge, 2007), 70.

7. Michael Mandelbaum, "Lessons for the Next War," *Foreign Affairs* 74 (March/April 1995), 28–30.

8. Stephen P. Cohen, *India: Emerging Power* (Washington, DC: Brookings Institution Press, 2001), 204.

9. John Lewis and Xue Litai, *China Builds the Bomb* (Palo Alto: Stanford University Press, 1988), 4.

10. John H. Gill, "India and Pakistan: A Shift in the Military Calculus," in Ashley J. Tellis and Michael Wills, eds., *Military Modernizations in an Era of Uncertainty, Strategic Asia, 2005–06* (Washington, DC: National Bureau of Asian Research, 2005), 239–40. See also Ashley J. Tellis, *India's Emerging Nuclear Posture: Between Recessed Deterrent and Ready Arsenal* (Santa Monica, CA: RAND Publications, 2001), 58–75.

11. Lewis and Xue, *China Builds the Bomb*, 62–70.

12. This conspiracy refers to alleged meetings in the Indian town of Argatala, Tripura, between Mujibur Rehman; the first secretary of the Indian embassy, N. Ojha; and Indian Army officers Lieutenant-Colonel Misra and Major Menon. Several other contacts were also reported between the Indian embassy in Dhaka and the Awami League. Mujibur's six-point plan was thought by some to have grown out of these meetings. Twenty-eight East Pakistanis were arrested on January 6, 1968. See Wolpert, *Zulfi Bhutto of Pakistan*, 115.

13. Altaf Gauhar, *Ayub Khan: Pakistan's First Military Ruler* (Lahore: Sang-e-Meel Publications, 1994), 408–9.

14. See Wolpert, *Zulfi Bhutto of Pakistan*, 115.

15. Ibid., 117.

16. The author, then a student, and along with other student leaders, personally met Zulfiqar Ali Bhutto in Flashmen's Hotel, Rawalpindi, in December 1968. He later participated in some of the student demonstrations against the Ayub regime.

17. Dennis Kux, *The United States and Pakistan 1947–2000: Disenchanted Allies* (Washington, DC: Woodrow Wilson Center Press, 2001), 179.

18. For Johnson's remarks to Ayub, see ibid., 167. For Kosygin's reply to Yahya Khan, see ibid., 181.

19. Richard Sisson and Leo E. Rose, *War and Secession: Pakistan, India, and the Creation of Bangladesh* (Berkeley: University of California Press, 1991), 160. Abdul Sattar, interview by author, Islamabad, June 20, 2006. See also Abdul Sattar, *Pakistan's Foreign Policy 1947–2005: A Concise History* (New York: Oxford University Press, 2007), 113–15.

20. Sahabzada Yaqub-Khan, interview by author, June 19, 2006. See also Anwar Dil, ed., *Strategy, Diplomacy, Humanity: Life and Work of Sahabzada Yaqub-Khan* (San Diego, CA: Intercultural Forum, 2005), 280–81.

21. Shuja Nawaz, *Crossed Swords: Pakistan, Its Army and the Wars Within* (New York: Oxford University Press, 2008), 267.

22. Sisson and Rose, *War and Secession*, 160.

23. Ibid., 173–74.

24. Ibid., 166–72.

25. In the middle of 1969, President Nixon sought help from President Yahya Khan to secretly open up relations with China. The Soviets would learn of the covert arrange-

ments. In return the Soviets signed a twenty-year Treaty of Friendship with India. See Kux, *The United States and Pakistan,* 181–83.

26. The Pakistani riposte was never launched with full ground forces in this war. The author was then serving in a unit that was part of the strike corps in southern Punjab, which was to launch an offensive across Rajistan and Punjab in India on December 5–6. The order to attack never came, and the war on the western front ended in a stalemate.

27. Nawaz, *Crossed Swords,* 282.

28. Ibid., 310.

29. Kux, *The United States and Pakistan,* 206.

30. Henry Kissinger, *The White House Years* (New York: Little Brown, 1979), 856. Cited by Sattar, *Pakistan's Foreign Policy 1947–2005,* 115.

31. Sisson and Rose, *War and Secession,* 207–8.

32. CIA Memorandum "Implications of an Indian Victory over Pakistan," December 9, 1971. Declassified PA/HO, Department of State. E. O. 12958, as amended June 9, 2005. Assembled by Centre for Indian Military History. Cited by Nawaz, *Crossed Swords,* 308.

33. The mission of the *USS Enterprise* was ostensibly to be available for the evacuation of U.S. personnel from East Pakistan. However, Henry Kissinger declared that he intended to give emphasis to U.S. warnings against an attack on West Pakistan. Kux, *The United States and Pakistan,* 201.

34. V. Langer, *The Defence and Foreign Policy of India* (New Delhi: Sterling Publishers, 1998), 205. Cited in Sattar, *Pakistan's Foreign Policy 1947–2005,* 119.

35. Nawaz, *Crossed Swords,* 322.

36. Wolpert, *Zulfi Bhutto of Pakistan,* 170.

37. Lieutenant-General Syed Refaqat, interview by author, Islamabad, June 19, 2005.

38. Ibid.

39. Lieutenant-General (retired) Majeed Malik, interview by author, Islamabad, October 9, 2009.

40. Lieutenant-General Syed Refaqat, interview by author, Islamabad, June 19, 2005.

41. Ibid.

42. Ibid.

43. Sultan Bashiruddin, interview by author, Islamabad, December 14, 2006.

44. Ibid.

45. Ibid.

46. Ibid.

47. Sultan Bashiruddin Mahmood volunteered to join the army and leave PAEC, to "go and fight *jihad.*" By the time he was ready for training the war was already over. Sultan Bashiruddin Mahmood, interview by author, Islamabad, December 14, 2006.

48. Ibid.

49. Ibid.

50. Ibid.

51. Wolpert, *Zulfi Bhutto of Pakistan*, 172–73.

52. Ibid.

53. Ibid., 176.

54. Ibid.

55. Sultan Bashiruddin Mahmood, interview by author, Islamabad, December 14, 2006.

56. Ibid.

57. Ibid.

58. Shahid-ur-Rehman, *Long Road to Chaghi* (Islamabad: Print Wise Publications, 1999), 16–18; and Sultan Bashiruddin Mahmood, interview by author, Islamabad, December 14, 2006.

59. Sultan Bashiruddin Mahmood, interview by author, Islamabad, December 14, 2006.

60. Ibid.

61. Ibid.

62. Ibid.

63. Ibid.

64. Ibid.

65. Ibid.

66. Steve Weissman and Herbert Krosney, *The Islamic Bomb* (New York: Times Books, 1981), 45–46; Zulfikar Ali Bhutto, *Awakening the People: Speeches of Zulfikar Ali Bhutto, 1966–1969,* comp. Hamid Jalal and Khalid Hasan (Rawalpindi: Pakistan Publications, 1970), 21.

67. Ishfaq Ahmad, interview by author, Islamabad, December 20, 2005.

68. Munir Ahmad Khan, quoted in Shahid-ur-Rehman, *Long Road to Chaghi*, 27. "Homi Bhabha had struck a synthesis with the political leadership soon after independence in 1947 and secured political commitment for his country's nuclear program. Munir Khan achieved this synthesis with the political leadership [Bhutto] in 1972. Since then, the country's nuclear program has enjoyed bipartisan political support." Farhatullah Babar, "Founder of Nuclear Program," *The News*, April 23, 1999.

69. Munir Ahmad Khan was Professional Grade-P5 till 1972, beginning as first officer in the Reactor Division in 1958, followed by senior officer in 1961, and then serving as section chief of the Nuclear Power Reactor Technology and Application from 1964 to 1968. He then served as head of the Nuclear Fuel Cycle and Reactor Engineering Section in the same division, from 1968 to 1972. While he was there, his responsibilities included developing major international programs relating to nuclear power, including thermal and fast breeder reactors; heavy water and gas-cooled reactors; research reactor utilization in developing countries; review of design, construction, and operation of demonstration power reactors in the United States and Canada; coordination of programs

for research contracts for theoretical estimation of uranium depletion and plutonium buildup in nuclear power reactors in developed countries; nuclear desalination; and small and medium power reactors and market surveys for nuclear power plants. S. A. Hasnain, "Dr. I. H. Usmani and the Early Days of the PAEC," *The Nucleus* 42, 1–2 (2005), 13–20, 19. See also Bio-data of Munir Ahmad Khan, Chairman, PAEC, 1972–91 and 20 Years (1979–99), *ECHO: Journal of the IAEA Staff* 202 (1999), 24–25.

70. Munir Ahmad Khan also organized more than twenty technical conferences on these subjects and served as a scientific secretary to the Third and Fourth UN Geneva Conferences on the Peaceful Uses of Atomic Energy, held in 1964 and 1971, respectively. As chairman of the PAEC, he was elected a member of the IAEA Board of Governors for twelve years and was the leader of Pakistan's delegation to nineteen IAEA general conferences. He also served as chairman of the IAEA Board of Governors from 1986 to 1987. He was the second Pakistani to serve as chairman of the IAEA Board after Dr. I. H. Usmani. *IAEA Bulletin,* 41, 2 (1999).

71. Ibid.

72. Munir Ahmad Khan. "Medal Award Ceremony," speech to the Pakistan Nuclear Society, PINSTECH Auditorium, Islamabad, March 20, 1999.

73. Bio-data of Munir Ahmad Khan.

74. Ibid., and I. H. Qureshi, "Recollections from the Early Days of the PAEC," *The Nucleus* 42, 1–2 (2005), 7–11, 11.

75. Ashok Kapur, *Pakistan's Nuclear Development* (London: Croom Helm, 1987), 54–55.

76. This practice is also called radionuclide monitoring, which is now part of the Comprehensive Test Ban Treaty. There are peculiar isotopes in the air after any nuclear test that, if present, can be obtained through air sampling.

77. S. N. Burney, "Death of a Visionary and a Man of Substance," *The News,* June 23, 1992.

78. Weissman and Krosney, *The Islamic Bomb*, 46.

79. Neil Joeck, *Maintaining Nuclear Stability in South Asia*, Adelphi Paper 312 (London: International Institute of Strategic Studies, 1997), 38.

80. Several definitions have been used by various studies and organizations in the U.S. government to describe nuclear capacities or nuclear thresholds. The CIA defines "standby capacities" as possession of all facilities needed to produce nuclear weapons. See Ariel Levite, "Never Say Never Again: Nuclear Reversal Revisited," *International Security* 27 (Winter 2002/2003), 66.

81. Ariel Levite defines "nuclear hedging" in its advanced form as developing the capacity "to produce fissionable materials as well as scientific and engineering expertise to package final product into nuclear explosive charge" at a short notice. Ibid., 69. See Also Feroz Hassan Khan, "Nuclear Proliferation Motivations," 71.

82. Stephen Meyer, *The Dynamics of Nuclear Proliferation* (Chicago: University of

Chicago Press, 1984), 1–3. See also Feroz Hassan Khan, "Nuclear Proliferation Motivations," 70–71.

83. Ishfaq Ahmad, interview by author, Islamabad, December 20, 2005.

84. Ibid.

85. Ibid.

86. Feroz Hassan Khan, "Nuclear Proliferation Motivations," 69.

Chapter 5

1. Z. A. Bhutto became the prime minister after the 1973 Constitution was promulgated on August 14, after which he abolished martial law and established a parliamentary form of government. Bhutto was deposed in a military coup in 1977, which then returned the office of the president.

2. General (ret.) Khalid Mahmud Arif, interview by author, Rawalpindi, June 20, 2005.

3. John Lewis and Xue Litai, *China Builds the Bomb* (Palo Alto: Stanford University Press, 1988), 35.

4. Dennis Kux, *The United States and Pakistan 1947–2000: Disenchanted Allies* (Washington, DC: Woodrow Wilson Center Press, 2001), 208.

5. After the Simla Accord, India perceived Kashmir to be a bilateral issue. Pakistan's interpretation is that the Simla Accord in no way inhibits Pakistan from raising the issue on the international stage.

6. Stanley Wolpert, *Zulfi Bhutto of Pakistan: His Life and Times* (New York: Oxford University Press, 1983), 213.

7. Dr. Mubashir Hasan, interview by the author, Lahore, June 20, 2007.

8. After partition, Jinnah had worn *Sherwani* (tunic) and *Karakuli* cap. Zulfiqar Ali Bhutto for his public addresses always wore what he called Awami dress.

9. Tanvir Ahmad Khan, interview by author, Islamabad, June 19, 2006. See also Kux, *The United States and Pakistan 1947–2000*, 211.

10. Kux, *The United States and Pakistan 1947–2000*, 207.

11. Ibid., 208.

12. In one such incident artillery guns and infantry were ordered to quash a police mutiny in Peshawar. In another incident the air force was asked to conduct "dummy runs" by fighter planes over Faisalabad. Such practices were deemed illegal and unacceptable by the military. See Gul Hassan Khan, *Memoirs of Lt. Gen. Gul Hassan Khan* (New York: Oxford University Press, 1993), 361–68.

13. Shuja Nawaz, *Crossed Swords: Pakistan, Its Army and the Wars Within* (New York: Oxford University Press, 2008), 325.

14. The dismissals were controversial. Both the army and the air chief were removed on March 2–3, 1972, after allegedly refusing to accept illegal orders about the use of force within the country. Following their resignations, Bhutto's ministers Mustafa Khar,

Mumtaz Bhutto, and Mustafa Jatoi forced the chiefs into a car at gunpoint and drove them to Lahore. See Gul Hassan Khan, *Memoirs of Lt. Gen. Gul Hassan Khan*, 367–69. See also Nawaz, *Crossed Swords*, 324–26.

15. Nawaz, *Crossed Swords*, 324.

16. Wolpert, *Zulfi Bhutto of Pakistan*, 217.

17. J. A. Rahim was later exiled to Europe. See ibid., 239–40.

18. Dr. Riazuddin, interview by author, June 18, 2006; and Sultan Bashiruddin Mahmood, interview by author, Islamabad, December 14, 2006.

19. Sultan Bashir Mahmood, interview by author, Islamabad, December 14, 2006.

20. Ishfaq Khan, interview by author, Islamabad, December 2005; and Sultan Bashir Mahmood, interview by author, Islamabad, December 14, 2006.

21. The Zangger Committee, also known as the Nuclear Exporters Committee, sprang from Article III.2 of the Treaty on the Non-Proliferation of Nuclear Weapons (NPT), which entered into force on March 5, 1970. "The Committee was formed in 1971, under the chairmanship of Claude Zangger (Switzerland), to draft a 'trigger list' of (a) source or special fissionable materials, and (b) equipment or materials especially designed or prepared for the processing, use, or production of special fissionable materials. Under Art. III.2 of the Nuclear Non-Proliferation Treaty (NPT), these items should be subject to International Atomic Energy Agency (IAEA) safeguards if supplied by NPT parties to any non-nuclear weapon States (NNWS). In 1974, the Zangger Committee published a Trigger List, a list of items that would 'trigger' a requirement for safeguards and guidelines ('common understandings') governing the export of those items to NNWS not party to the NPT. These guidelines establish three conditions of supply: a nonexplosive use assurance, an IAEA safeguards requirement, and a re-transfer provision that requires the receiving state to apply the same conditions when re-exporting these items. The Trigger List was first published in September 1974 as IAEA document INFCIRC/209 and has been amended several times since then." For details see http://www.nti.org/e_research/official_docs/inventory/pdfs/zang.pdf.

22. Shahid-ur-Rehman, *Long Road to Chaghi* (Islamabad: Print Wise Publications, 1999), 29; Munir Ahmad Khan, "Medal Award Ceremony," speech to the Pakistan Nuclear Society, PINSTECH Auditorium, Islamabad, March 20, 1999.

23. Other fissile materials exist, such as californium and neptunium, but are harder to produce, making their use impractical.

24. Joseph Cirincione, Jon B. Wolfsthal, and Miriam Rajkumar, *Deadly Arsenals: Nuclear, Biological and Chemical Threats* (Washington, DC: Carnegie Endowment for International Peace, 2002), 35–42.

25. U-233 also has a significant quantity of 8 kg, but this isotope is difficult to find. It is important to note that nuclear weapons can be made, depending on their design, using lesser quantities of fissile materials.

26. This same weapons-grade uranium can be used for propulsion of nuclear submarines and, in rare cases, as feedstock to another power reactor.

27. Natural uranium reactors can come in four types: heavy water reactor, graphite reactor with light water, graphite reactor that is gas cooled, and a research reactor. Each produces spent fuel, with varying degrees of impurities. It is usually the spent fuel from the heavy water reactor that is a special target for plutonium extraction, and is burned at low level for a short duration so as to prevent impurities from entering the spent fuel. If the power production is at high-level burn up, the resulting spent fuel has significant amounts of impurities, such as Pu-241, Pu-242, and Pu-243. These impurities make it extremely difficult to extract Pu-239.

28. "The Nuclear Fuel Cycle," World Nuclear Association, http://www.world-nuclear.org/education/nfc.htm (accessed September 13, 2009).

29. Munir Ahmad Khan, "Medal Award Ceremony."

30. Ibid.

31. Shahid-ur-Rehman, *Long Road to Chaghi*, 29.

32. Ibid.

33. Cirincione, Wolfsthal, and Rajkumar, *Deadly Arsenals*, 35–50.

34. Munir Ahmad Khan, "Medal Award Ceremony."

35. Maulana Kauser Niazi, *Aur Line Cut Gai* ["And the Line Was Cut Off"] (Lahore: Jang Publishers, 1987), 77. Niazi dedicated the chapter "The Truth behind the Veil of the Reprocessing Plant" to this issue.

36. Dr. Mubashar Hassan, interview by author, Lahore, June 16, 2007.

37. In the 1960s, Usmani selected some 600 students for higher studies. By this time, in the early 1970s, 106 of them would return with doctorate degrees. See Nawaz, *Crossed Swords*, 340. Nawaz cites Carey Sublette, "Pakistan's Nuclear Weapons Program—The Beginning," Nuclear Weapon Archive, http://www.nuclearweaponarchive.org/Pakistan/PakOrigin.html (accessed January 2, 2002).

38. George Perkovich, "Could Anything Be Done to Stop Them?: Lessons from Pakistan's Proliferation Past," in Henry Sokolski, ed., *Pakistan's Nuclear Future: Worries beyond War* (Carlisle Barracks, PA: Strategic Studies Institute, Army War College, 2008), 64. Almost all former PAEC scientists interviewed by the author emphatically stated that there was never any plan to deceive foreign partners or to abuse the nuclear trust regarding foreign assistance, but that it is the sovereign right of the state to determine how it uses its gained expertise for national security purposes.

39. George Perkovich, *India's Nuclear Bomb: The Impact on Proliferation* (New York: Oxford University Press, 2000), 86–105.

40. Pakistani scientists insist that, unlike some countries that joined the NPT to get cooperation and then used the knowledge, Pakistan never signed the deal. And also unlike India, it did not abuse the technology given to Pakistan under Atoms for Peace. Again, they believe they did nothing illegal or immoral, and it is within the right of a

sovereign state to use the know-how of its citizens for any role deemed necessary for its national security.

41. Munir Ahmad Khan, "Development and Significance of Pakistan's Nuclear Capability," in Hafeez Malik, ed., *Pakistan: Founders' Aspirations and Today's Realities* (Karachi: Oxford University Press, 2001), 153.

42. Munir Ahmad Khan, "How Pakistan Made Nuclear Fuel," *The Nation*, February 7, 1998.

43. Munir Ahmad Khan, "Bhutto and the Nuclear Programme of Pakistan," *The Muslim*, April 4, 1995.

44. Ishfaq Khan, interview by author, Islamabad, December 2005.

45. Munir Ahmad Khan, "Significance of Chashma Plant," *Dawn*, August 8, 1993.

46. Sultan Bashiruddin Mahmood, interview by author, Islamabad, December 14, 2006. See also Naeem Salik, *The Genesis of South Asian Nuclear Deterrence: Pakistan's Perspective* (New York: Oxford University Press, 2009), 78.

47. M. A. Chaudhri, "Pakistan's Nuclear History: Separating Myth from Reality," *Defence Journal* 9, 10 (May 2006).

48. "History," Pakistan Atomic Energy Commission, http://www.paec.gov.pk/pinstech/history.htm (accessed August 10, 2009); and I. H. Qureshi, "Development of Physical Sciences Program at PINSTECH," *The Nucleus* 42, 1–2 (2005), 41–47, 42.

49. "History," Pakistan Atomic Energy Commission.

50. Chaudhri, "Pakistan's Nuclear History"; N. M. Butt, "Nuclear Radiation Education and Nuclear Science and Technology in Pakistan," paper presented at the 2nd International Congress on Radiation Education, Debrecen, Hungary (August 20–25, 2002), http://www.paec.gov.pk.

51. Munir Ahmad Khan, "How Pakistan Made Nuclear Fuel."

52. Ibid.

53. PINSTECH at this time already had a functioning 5-MW Pakistan Atomic Research Reactor (PARR-1). In addition, in 1967 an Electronics and Operation Division was added to this reactor, which enhanced its technical capabilities. As part of Bhutto's plan, the capacity of PARR-1 was doubled, and the PAEC acquired a Chinese 27-KW Miniature Neutron Source Reactor (MNSR, or PARR-2), which reached criticality on November 2, 1989.

54. Munir Ahmad Khan, "Nuclearization of South Asia and Its Regional and Global Implications," *Regional Studies* (Islamabad) 26, 4 (Autumn 1998).

55. Sultan Bashiruddin Mahmood, interview by author, Islamabad, December 14, 2006.

56. Ishfaq Ahmad, interview by author, Islamabad, December 2005; and Sultan Bashiruddin Mahmood, interview by author, Islamabad, December 14, 2006.

57. Sultan Bashiruddin Mahmood, interview by author, Islamabad, December 14, 2006.

58. Pakistan Atomic Energy Commission, http://www.paec.gov.pk/kanupp (accessed November 20, 2009).

59. PAEC Supplement Publication on KANUPP's Inauguration, 1972.

60. Ibid.

61. Ibid., emphasis added on the words of President Eisenhower's speech in December 1953.

62. Mahmood claims that he invented a kind of troubleshooting probe to find and prevent leaks from the heavy water reactor. Sultan Bashiruddin Mahmood, interview by author, Islamabad, December 14, 2006.

63. Ishfaq Khan, interview by author, Islamabad, December 2005; and Sultan Bashir Mahmood, interview by author, December 14, 2006.

64. Lieutenant-General (ret.) Syed Refaqat Ali, interview by author, December 19, 2005; and Pervez Butt, interview by author, December 15, 2006.

65. Sultan Bashiruddin Mahmood, interview by author, Islamabad, December 14, 2006.

66. Ibid. and Dr. Pervez Butt, interview by author, December 15, 2006.

67. Pervez Butt, interview by author, Islamabad, December 15, 2006.

68. KANUPP is heavy water cooled and heavy water moderated. CIRUS was light water cooled and heavy water moderated. Sultan Bashiruddin Mahmood, interview by author, Islamabad, December 14, 2006.

69. Ibid. In separate interviews, Ishfaq Ahmad and Dr. Pervez Butt, successive PAEC chairmen, both took the same position.

70. This was an off-the-record remark in Urdu by a PAEC scientist who did not want attribution during the interview in June 2006. Author's written notes, paraphrased and translated by author.

71. Steve Weissman and Herbert Krosney, *The Islamic Bomb* (New York: Times Books, 1981), 53.

72. Ibid.

73. Ibid., 54.

74. Ibid., 60.

75. Ibid., 61.

76. Wyn Q. Bowen, *Libya and Nuclear Proliferation: Stepping Back from the Brink,* Adelphi Paper #380 (London: International Institute for Strategic Studies, 2006), 30–31.

77. Weissman and Krosney, *The Islamic Bomb,* 72–73.

78. Ibid., 63.

79. Bowen, *Libya and Nuclear Proliferation,* 29–31.

80. Ibid., 62.

81. IAEA director-general Eklund coined the term "Moslem Oil Money" in 1979

in discussion with U.S. officials about the efficacy of economic sanctions on Pakistan. Cited in Salik, *The Genesis of South Asian Nuclear Deterrence*, 91.

82. Weissman and Krosney, *The Islamic Bomb*, 162.

83. Dr. Ishfaq Ahmad (chairman PAEC, 1991–2001), quoted in Shahid-ur-Rehman, *Long Road to Chaghi,* 50.

84. Munir Ahmad Khan, "Medal Award Ceremony."

85. Munir Ahmad Khan, "How Pakistan Made Nuclear Fuel."

86. Ibid.

87. Shahid-ur-Rehman, *Long Road to Chaghi,* 69. The first national award for uranium exploration was given to the geologist Mr. Khalid Aslam.

88. Ibid., 69–70. See also Ishfaq Ahmad, interview by author, Islamabad, December 2005.

89. "NTI: Pakistan Nuclear Chronology," Nuclear Threat Initiative, http://www.nti.org/e_research/profiles/Pakistan/Nuclear/5593_5596.html (accessed November 19, 2009).

90. Ibid.

91. Ibid.

92. Ishfaq Ahmad Khan, interview by author, December 20, 2005. See also Shahid-ur-Rehman, *Long Road to Chaghi*, 50.

93. Shahid-ur-Rehman, *Long Road to Chaghi*, 50. See also Weissman and Krosney, *The Islamic Bomb*, 210; and Jeffrey T. Richelson, *Spying on the Bomb* (New York: W. W. Norton and Company, 2006), 338.

94. Bowen, *Libya and Nuclear Proliferation.*

95. Weissman and Krosney, *The Islamic Bomb*, 212.

96. Chaudri, "Pakistan's Nuclear History."

97. Shahid-ur-Rehman, *Long Road to Chaghi*, 70.

98. Ibid., 71.

99. Sultan Bashiruddin Mahmood, interview by author, Islamabad, December 14, 2006.

100. "NTI: Pakistan Nuclear Chronology."

101. Munir Ahmad Khan, "Development and Significance of Pakistan's Nuclear Capability," 155–56.

102. Munir Ahmad Khan, "How Pakistan Made Nuclear Fuel."

103. Shahid-ur-Rehman, *Long Road to Chaghi*, 97.

104. "Karachi Nuclear Power Plant (KANUPP): Milestones & Achievements," Pakistan Atomic Energy Commission, http://www.paec.gov.pk/kanupp/ma.htm (accessed November 20, 2009).

105. Ibid.

106. Samar Mubarakmand, "A Science Odyssey: Pakistan's Nuclear Emergence,"

speech to the Khwarzimic Science Society, Centre of Excellence in Solid State Physics, Punjab University, Lahore, November 30, 1998. "The most difficult part of the whole process is the production of highly volatile, dangerously toxic and extremely corrosive fluorine gas that requires special electrodes and the production of hydrofluoric acid. PAEC scientists and engineers had to acquire complete mastery over vacuum and welding technology for precluding any possibility of a potential leak that could be fatal for any human coming into contact with hydrofluoric acids and fluorides. Those working at CPC also had to acquire complete mastery over uranium and nuclear chemistry, especially fluorine chemistry. The fact that fluorine is the most reactive of all elements in the periodic table made it a formidable challenge for them. After initial refining at the uranium refining plant, uranium ore concentrate or yellow cake is converted into uranium dioxide. The uranium dioxide then undergoes a further reaction with hydrogen fluoride, which involves the production of hydrofluoric acid and fluorine gas, to form uranium tetra-fluoride or UF4. Production of UF4 was a major accomplishment, for which Dr. Aminuddin Ahmed of PAEC was awarded the first-ever Tamgha-I-Imtiaz in 1981. The UF4 obtained undergoes a further reaction with fluorine gas to produce uranium hexafluoride gas or UF6." See also Kamal Matinuddin, *Nuclearization of South Asia* (Karachi: Oxford University Press, 2002), 101.

107. Weissman and Krosney, *The Islamic Bomb*, 218.

108. Shahid-ur-Rehman, *Long Road to Chaghi*, 67.

109. The CPC comprises seven independent chemical plants where UF6 is produced: a uranium mill that extracts uranium in the form of yellow cake, a plant to refine yellow cake to produce ammonium diuranate (ADU), a plant to convert ADU to uranium dioxide (UO2), a plant to produce hydrofluoric acid, a plant to produce fluorine gas, a plant to convert UO2 to uranium tetrafluoride (UF4), and a plant for the conversion of UF4 to uranium hexafluoride (UF6). Mubarakmand, "A Science Odyssey."

110. Weissman and Krosney, *The Islamic Bomb*, 211, 218–20.

111. Munir Ahmad Khan, "Medal Award Ceremony."

112. Shahid-ur-Rehman, *Long Road to Chaghi*, 68. High-ranking officials within Pakistan, including Lieutenant-General (ret.) Ghulam Jilani Khan, the governor of Punjab, and Nawaz Sharif, who was then chief minister, were kept in the dark about the nature of work at CPC.

113. "NTI: Pakistan Nuclear Chronology."

114. Butt, "Nuclear Radiation Education."

115. Richelson, *Spying on the Bomb,* 232.

116. Ibid.

117. Ibid., 233–34.

118. Farhatullah Babar, "Munir Ahmad Khan—A Splendid Contribution," *The Nation* (Islamabad), April 24, 1999.

119. *The Pakistan Times*, article on Zulfiqar Ali Bhutto's press conference of May 19, 1974, Lahore, May 20, 1974.

120. Perkovich, *India's Bomb*, 185.

121. "The Prime Minister of Pakistan, Z. A. Bhutto's reply," June 5, 1974, printed in *Pakistan Horizon* 27, 3 (Third Quarter 1974), 198–200, quoted in Bhumitra Chakman, "Road to Chaghi: Pakistan's Nuclear Program, Its Sources and Motivations," *Modern Asian Studies* 36, 4 (2002), 871–912.

122. Central Intelligence Agency (CIA), "Bhutto Seeks Nuclear Policy Assurances," *National Intelligence Daily*, May 24, 1974.

123. Daniel Moynihan, personal discussion with author, April 2002. See also Daniel Moynihan, quoted by N. Ram, "From Nuclear Adventurism to Appeasement," *Frontline*, Chennai, June 19, 1998, quoted in Munir Ahmad Khan, "Nuclearization of South Asia and Its Regional and Global Implications."

124. Syed Refaqat, interview by author, December 19, 2005.

125. Munir Ahmad Khan, "Nuclearization of South Asia and Its Regional and Global Implications."

126. Weissman and Krosney, *The Islamic Bomb*, 134.

127. CIA, "Bhutto Seeks Nuclear Policy Assurances."

128. Ibid.

129. Munir Ahmad Khan, "Development and Significance of Pakistan's Nuclear Capability," 155.

130. Ibid.

131. Munir Ahmad Khan, "Nuclearization of South Asia and Its Regional and Global Implications."

132. Ibid.

133. Cirincione, Wolfsthal, and Rajkumar, *Deadly Arsenals*.

134. Shahid-ur-Rehman, *Long Road to Chaghi*, 44–45.

135. Feroz Hassan Khan, "Nuclear Proliferation Motivations: Lessons from Pakistan," in Peter R. Lavoy, ed., *Nuclear Weapons Proliferation in the Next Decade* (New York: Routledge, 2007), 71.

136. Dr. Riazuddin, interview by author, Islamabad, June 18, 2006.

Chapter 6

1. Among those superseded was Lieutenant-General Majeed Malik. Nearing ninety years of age in October 2009, he was interviewed by the author. Majeed Malik was probably the most qualified to become Chief of the Army Staff, as he had an impressive career and commendable performance on duty. Majeed Malik had commanded the 11th and 12th Infantry Divisions in 1971 and 1972, respectively, and had gained fame as a bold military commander. In the spring of 1972, he conducted a tactical military opera-

tion in Lipa Valley that restored the Line of Control (LOC) in Kashmir and successfully pushed back Indian army incursions beyond the LOC. His career record included the prestigious appointment as Director of Military Operations and Chief of General Staff in GHQ before becoming corps commander, 11th Corps, in Peshawar.

2. This information is derived from the author's personal recollection of General Zia-ul-Haq's military records. The author was posted in the Military Secretary's branch in General Headquarters between 1986 and 1988, in a section (MS-4) that managed the military careers and postings of senior officers; the author had access to this record.

3. After his return to Pakistan, Zia-ul-Haq appealed against the negative report. He contended that he had had no intention of bypassing embassy channels, had instead been penalized for petty personal reasons, and that King Hussein had personally commended him for his advisory role. Zia's plea was accepted, and the unfavorable remarks were officially expunged from his official military record. The record of the entire proceedings, however, is kept in the confidential dossier. Author's personal recollection.

4. Author's personal recollection.

5. Shuja Nawaz, *Crossed Swords: Pakistan, Its Army and the Wars Within* (New York: Oxford University Press, 2008), 343–44. Zia-ul-Haq offered and Zulfiqar Ali Bhutto accepted an honorary appointment of colonel-in-chief of the Pakistan Armored Corps. British military tradition had reserved such an honorary position for retired senior military leaders. Under the constitution, the prime minister was already the civilian supreme commander of the armed forces, but Bhutto loved the open affection of the military.

6. In general, both the United States and Pakistan refrained from public recriminations against each other on proliferation issues from the 1970s to the 1990s.

7. Dr. Ishfaq Ahmad, interview by author, Islamabad, December 2005. Dr. Pervez Butt also reiterated the same view in interview by the author, Islamabad, December 15, 2006.

8. Dr. Pervez Butt, interview by author, Islamabad, December 15, 2006.

9. Sultan Bashiruddin Mahmood, interview by author, Islamabad, December 14, 2006; and Muhammad Afzal, interview by author; and S. A. Hasnain, interview by author, June 2006. See also Munir Ahmad Khan, "Development and Significance of Pakistan's Nuclear Capability," in Hafeez Malik, ed., *Pakistan: Founders' Aspirations and Today's Realities* (Karachi: Oxford University Press, 2001), 155–56.

10. John Lewis and Xue Litai, *China Builds the Bomb* (Palo Alto: Stanford University Press, 1988), 60–72.

11. As mentioned in Chapter 3, after the 1965 war the United States placed an arms embargo on Pakistan (and India). Since the mid-1960s, the Pakistani military's inventory had included Russian and Chinese weapons and equipment, including tanks, artillery, and even small arms. After the 1971 war, and Bhutto's reign, it was only natural to continue relations with China and North Korea, primarily for acquiring ammunition

and spare parts. The interactions between the major defense industries of the countries became ongoing.

12. The Warsaw Pact and communist countries were subject to technological denials throughout the Cold War under the Coordinating Committee for Multilateral Export Controls (COCOM). Today similar controls are maintained in the Wassenaar Arrangement, which in essence also selectively denies defense and Western technologies to countries of concern.

13. Munir Ahmad Khan, "Nuclearization of South Asia and Its Regional and Global Implications," *Regional Studies* (Islamabad) 26, 4 (Autumn 1998).

14. Dennis Kux, *The United States and Pakistan 1947–2000: Disenchanted Allies* (Washington, DC: Woodrow Wilson Center Press, 2001), 238–39.

15. In reality the timing of the announcement was coincidental, because deliberations over applying sanctions had been in the works for quite some time. The U.S. government was probably forced to announce as a result of a media leak. Ibid.

16. Munir Ahmad Khan, "Franco-Pak Nuclear Relations," *The News,* October 31, 1994.

17. Steve Weissman and Herbert Krosney, *The Islamic Bomb* (New York: Times Books, 1981), 70–72.

18. Ibid., 147.

19. George Perkovich, "Could Anything Be Done to Stop Them?: Lessons from Pakistan," Nonproliferation Policy Education Center, July 26, 2006, http://www.npec-web.org/Essays/20060726-Perkovich-CouldAnythingBeDone.pdf.

20. Weissman and Krosney, *The Islamic Bomb,* 74.

21. Dr. Mohammad Afzal, interview by author, Islamabad, December 20, 2005. During the interview Dr. Afzal explained that the high-temperature, gas-cooled pebble bed reactor design differed in concept from reactors in the United Kingdom. The Australian design used fuel in the form of small, one-centimeter spheres coated with beryllium, with which he gained experience while working at the Australian Atomic Energy Commission at Lupasite. This technique did not involve classic reprocessing, but handling the "messy" beryllium was "almost as complex as plutonium."

22. Shahid-ur-Rehman, *Long Road to Chaghi* (Islamabad: Print Wise Publications, 1999), 31. See also author's interview with Ishfaq Ahmad, June 17, 2006.

23. Shahid-ur-Rehman, *Long Road to Chaghi,* 31.

24. Dr. Muhammad Afzal, interview by author, December 20, 2005.

25. Weissman and Krosney, *The Islamic Bomb,* 75.

26. Charles K. Ebinger, *Pakistan Energy Planning in a Strategic Vortex* (Bloomington: Indiana University Press, 1981), 84. See also debate in Naeem Salik, *The Genesis of South Asian Nuclear Deterrence: Pakistan's Perspectives* (New York: Oxford University Press, 2009), 79.

27. Bashiruddin and others denied that Pakistan had any plans to use the spent fuel

from KANUPP for extracting weapons-grade plutonium. He gave technical reasons to explain that KANUPP fuel was unsuitable for this purpose. PAEC scientists and officials such as Ishfaq Ahmad, Pervez Butt, Sultan Bashir, Muhammad Afzal, S. A. Hasnain, N. M. Butt, and others have denied any plans to divert fuel from KANUPP.

28. Weissman and Krosney, *The Islamic Bomb*, 76.

29. Ibid., 76–78.

30. Dr. Muhammad Afzal, interview by author, December 20, 2005. See also Weissman and Krosney, *The Islamic Bomb*, 78–79.

31. Weissman and Krosney, *The Islamic Bomb*, 79–80.

32. Agha Shahi, interview by author, June 19, 2005.

33. Ibid.

34. Maulana Kauser Niazi, *Aur Line Cut Gai* ["And the Line Was Cut Off"] (Lahore: Jang Publishers, 1987). See also Weissman and Krosney, *The Islamic Bomb*, 167–71.

35. Weissman and Krosney, *The Islamic Bomb*, 167. In the author's interview with several PAEC scientists, who asked to remain anonymous for this claim, this assertion of SGN is validated; however, they question the 95 percent transfer claim in the Weissman and Krosney account.

36. Agha Shahi, interview by author, June 19, 2005.

37. Ibid. See also Sahabzada Yaqub-Khan, interview by author, June 20, 2005. For Ambassador Iqbal Akhund's account, see Iqbal Akhund, *Memoirs of a Bystander: A Life in Diplomacy* (New York: Oxford University Press, 1997), 256–93.

38. Weissman and Krosney, *The Islamic Bomb*, 67. See also Jeffrey T. Richelson, *Spying on the Bomb* (New York: W. W. Norton and Company, 2006), 339.

39. Sultan Bashiruddin Mahmood, interview by author, Islamabad, December 14, 2006.

40. Salik, *The Genesis of South Asian Nuclear Deterrence*, 81–83.

41. Richelson, *Spying on the Bomb*, 341.

42. Perkovich, "Could Anything Be Done to Stop Them?"

43. Shahid-ur-Rehman, *Long Road to Chaghi*, 37. See also M. A. Chaudhri, "Pakistan's Nuclear History: Separating Myth from Reality," *Defence Journal* 9, 10 (May 2006).

44. Dr. Muhammad Afzal, interview by author, December 20, 2005.

45. Shahid-ur-Rehman, *Long Road to Chaghi*, 36–37.

46. Sultan Bashiruddin Mahmood, interview by author, Islamabad, December 14, 2006.

47. Kux, *The United States and Pakistan 1947–2000*, 214.

48. Ibid., 215.

49. Ibid., 216.

50. Ibid., 218.

51. Ibid.

52. Ibid., 219.

53. Ibid.

54. Ibid., 221.

55. Ibid. Kux cites an interview with Brent Scowcroft, Washington, DC, May 4, 1999.

56. Ibid., 222.

57. Ibid.

58. Ibid., 223.

59. Ibid., 224.

60. Ibid., 231.

61. Ibid., 233.

62. Ibid., 235.

Chapter 7

1. Javed Arshad Mirza is one of the only KRL officers with insider knowledge on the centrifuge program. He remained closely associated with the enrichment program and worked specifically on initial centrifuge experiments. Mirza holds a Ph.D. in electronics from Glasgow University, UK, and as postdoctorate fellow he spent time at the Technical University in Munich, Germany, working on neutron capture gamma ray spectroscopy. He also has work experience with the UK Atomic Energy Research Establishment in Orwell.

2. A. Q. Khan was born on April 27, 1936, but his education certificate shows April 1, 1936. This change of date and registration was done to allow him to seem sixteen years old for a school examination, which is held in the first week of April. See Zahid Malik, *Dr. A. Q. Khan and the Islamic Bomb* (Islamabad: Hurmat Publications, 1992), 36.

3. Douglas Frantz and Catherine Collins, *The Nuclear Jihadist* (New York: Hachette Book Group, 2007).

4. Malik, *Dr. A. Q. Khan*, 53.

5. Ibid.

6. Douglas Frantz and Catherine Collins, *The Man from Pakistan: True Story of the World's Most Dangerous Nuclear Smuggler* (New York: Hachette Book Group, 2008), 17.

7. International Institute for Strategic Studies (IISS), *Nuclear Black Markets: Pakistan, A. Q. Khan and the Rise of Proliferation Networks, a Net Assessment,* IISS strategic dossier (London: International Institute for Strategic Studies, 2007), 17.

8. Bhutto's press secretary, Khalid Hassan, quoted in Frantz and Collins, *The Nuclear Jihadist,* 19–21.

9. Ibid.

10. In his letter to President Roosevelt, Albert Einstein explained how the atomic experiment could be made into a bomb, which would not only revolutionize warfare but also change the fate of mankind. For the Einstein letter see: U.S. Department of Energy,

Argonne National Laboratory, "Research," http://www.anl.gov/Science_and_Technology/History/Anniversary_Frontiers/aetofdr.html.

11. Translated excerpts from "Islamabad Tonight" discussion program hosted by Nadeem Malik, "Dr. Abdul Qadeer Khan Discusses Nuclear Program," *Aaj News Television* in Urdu, Karachi, August 31, 2009.

12. IISS, *Nuclear Black Markets*, 17.

13. Ishfaq Ahmad, interview by author, Islamabad, December 20, 2005.

14. Ibid.

15. In the words of Sultan Bashiruddin Mahmood, "Soon after submission of this report [on enrichment feasibility], the PAEC Chairman called me in the evening at 7 p.m. to his office. . . . Munir Ahmad Khan got up from his seat, and sat on the sofa, next to me, and put on his transistor radio (to muffle his voice) and said slowly, 'Today I am going to share a secret with you. I had given you a job and it had a purpose. I have studied the reports that you have prepared, and heard you also, and we have taken a decision that I want to share with you. This is extremely confidential and it is so confidential that you cannot even share it with your wife. We have decided to start the enrichment program and I have decided that you will head that program. So you should prepare yourself and I will again say that it is a most secret project.'" Sultan Bashiruddin Mahmood, interview by author, Islamabad, December 14, 2006.

16. Sultan Bashiruddin claims that he was able to prepare a report on centrifuges based on the experience and knowledge derived from the 1967 centrifuge study group and from his discussions with South Africans at the Rizley center for the United Kingdom Atomic Energy Authority (UKAEA). Sultan Bashiruddin Mahmood was a research fellow at Rizley in 1969, and he held detailed discussions with South African engineers who were then working on the Becker-nozzle and centrifuge methods for enrichment. Bashiruddin and many other PAEC scientists asserted that PINSTECH made use of much open-source literature on centrifuges available at the time.

17. Dr. Riazuddin, director general, National Centre for Physics, former Member Technical, PAEC, interview by Mansoor Ahmed, Islamabad, February 15, 2007. The author is grateful to Mansoor Ahmad, who also provided useful research for this book, for sharing this additional information with the author.

18. For an explanation of the basic principles of enrichment, see Allan S. Krass, Peter Boskma, Boelie Elzen, and Wim A. Smit, *Uranium Enrichment and Nuclear Weapon Proliferation*, Stockholm International Peace Research Institute (New York: Taylor and Francis, 1983), 9–11.

19. U.S. Congress, Office of Technological Assessment, *Proliferation of Weapons of Mass Destruction: Assessing the Risks*, OTA-ISC-559 (Washington, DC: Government Printing Office, August 1993).

20. Ibid.

21. "Maraging steel is a high-strength iron alloy used for the G2 [and P2] rotors; the term derives from 'martensite age hardening.'" IISS, *Nuclear Black Markets*, 19.

22. Ibid.

23. The names Project 706 and 786 were used interchangeably for local communication inside the PAEC. Project 786 was a reference to the sacred and quantitative expression of the Arabic saying *Bismillaah,* "in the name of God." Sultan Bashiruddin Mahmood, interview by author, Islamabad, December 14, 2006.

24. Sultan Bashiruddin Mahmood, interview by author, Islamabad, December 14, 2006.

25. Dr. Riazuddin, director general, National Centre for Physics, former Member Technical, PAEC, interview by author and research assistant, Islamabad, February 15, 2007; See also Bashiruddin Mahmood, interview by author, Islamabad, December 14, 2006.

26. Agha Shahi, interview by author, June 19, 2005.

27. Sultan Bashiruddin Mahmood, interview by author, Islamabad, December 14, 2006; Farhatullah Babar, "Apportioning Credit for the Bomb," *The News,* June 21, 1998; and Shahid-ur-Rehman, *Long Road to Chaghi* (Islamabad: Print Wise Publications, 1999), 50.

28. Sultan Bashiruddin Mahmood, interview by author, Islamabad, December 14, 2006.

29. The defense secretary tasked superintendent-engineer of the Civil Aviation Authority, Abdul Karim, to help renovate and remodel these barracks for the "secret project."

30. Javed Arshad Mirza, interview by author, Islamabad, June 14, 2007.

31. Sultan Bashiruddin Mahmood, interview by author, Islamabad, December 14, 2006.

32. Javed Arshad Mirza, interview by author, Islamabad, June 2007; Sultan Bashiruddin Mahmood, interview by author, Islamabad, December 14, 2006. See also Shahid-ur-Rehman, *Long Road to Chaghi*, 57.

33. Sultan Bashiruddin Mahmood, interview by author, Islamabad, December 14, 2006.

34. Ibid.

35. A. Q. Khan asserts, "We searched a location for the program and sketched out a detailed map of the construction site. We purchased land from the local people." Translated excerpts from "Islamabad Tonight."

36. There are competing versions of the story as to who selected the site of Kahuta. A. Q. Khan and his supporters claim that he selected the site a year later when he joined the centrifuge plant in 1976.

37. Sultan Bashir Mahmood, interview by author, Islamabad, December 14, 2006.

38. Sajawal Khan Malik was posted to Project 706 in 1976 and remained in the program until 2001. He was originally posted to assist A. Q. Khan in the CWO, but would remain in charge of security and would later move departmental positions. He was arrested along with A. Q. Khan in 2004. Sultan Bashir Mahmood, interview by author, Islamabad, December 14, 2006; Javed Arshad Mirza, interview by author, Islamabad, June 14, 2007.

39. Sultan Bashiruddin Mahmood, interview by author, Islamabad, December 14, 2006.

40. Ibid.

41. Ibid.

42. Ibid.

43. Ibid.

44. Given A. Q. Khan's knowledge of German, Dutch, and English, his job as a translator exposed him to very interesting information. Ibid.

45. Ibid.

46. Ibid.

47. Javed Arshad Mirza, interview by author, Islamabad, June 14, 2007.

48. Ibid.

49. Ibid.

50. Ibid.

51. Ibid.

52. Sultan Bashir Mahmood, interview by author, Islamabad, December 14, 2006. See also Shahid-ur-Rehman, *Long Road to Chaghi*, 59.

53. Sultan Bashir Mahmood, interview by author, December 14, 2006.

54. Shahid-ur-Rehman, *Long Road to Chaghi*, 53.

55. Ibid.

56. Javed Mirza, interview by author, Islamabad, June 14, 2007.

57. A. Q. Khan's wife, Henny, was quoted explaining her husband's frustration: "My husband realized he was not getting anywhere [with the centrifuge program]. Only two options were available—either call it a day or take the government into confidence." Quoted in Adrian Levy and Catherine Scott-Clark, *Deception: Pakistan, the United States, and the Secret Trade in Nuclear Weapons* (New York: Walker Publishing Company, 2007), 34–35ff.

58. Javed Arshad Mirza, interview by author, Islamabad, June 14, 2007.

59. Sultan Bashiruddin Mahmood, interview by author, Islamabad, December 14, 2006. Shahid-ur-Rehman, *Long Road to Chaghi*, 53.

60. Javed Arshad Mirza, interview by author, Islamabad, June 14, 2007.

61. Ibid.

62. Sultan Bashiruddin Mahmood, interview by author, Islamabad, December 14, 2006.

63. Javed Arshad Mirza, interview by author, Islamabad, June 14, 2007.

64. Shahid-ur-Rehman, *Long Road to Chaghi*, 59.

65. Lieutenant-General Syed Refaqat Ali, chief of staff to President Muhammad Zia-ul-Haq, interview by author, December 19, 2005. See also IISS, *Nuclear Black Markets*, 19.

66. Javed Arshad Mirza, interview by author, Islamabad, June 14, 2007.

67. General (ret.) Khalid Mahmud Arif, interview by author, Rawalpindi, June 19, 2005; and Lieutenant-General Syed Refaqat Ali, interview by author, Islamabad, December 19, 2005.

68. Javed Arshad Mirza, interview by author, Islamabad, June 14, 2007.

69. Shahid-ur-Rehman, *Long Road to Chaghi*, 72–74.

70. Jeffrey Smith and Joby Warrick, "A Nuclear Power's Act of Proliferation: Accounts by Controversial Scientist Assert China Gave Pakistan Enough Enriched Uranium in '82 to Make 2 Bombs," *Washington Post*, November 13, 2009, http://www.washingtonpost.com/wpdyn/content/article/2009/11/12/AR2009111211060.html (accessed March 18, 2010).

71. Shahid-ur-Rehman, *Long Road to Chaghi*, 73.

72. Ibid. See also Dr. Ishfaq Ahmad, interview by author, December 20, 2005.

73. Sultan Bashiruddin Mahmood, interview by author, Islamabad, December 14, 2006.

74. Ibid.

75. Javed Arshad Mirza, interview by author, Islamabad, June 14, 2007.

76. Ibid.

77. Ibid.

78. Ibid.

79. Ibid.

80. G. D. Alam was a British-educated computer programmer and mathematician. Fakhar Hashmi also received a British education in metallurgy from South Hampton University and was deputy director under Alam. Finally, Anwar Ali was a physicist and would later become PAEC chairman.

81. G. D. Alam, "Dr. Qadeer Was Ready to Secretly Sell Nuclear Technology to an Arab Country: Dr. G. D. Alam," interview in *Assas-o-Lashkar* (Urdu), June 12, 1998.

82. Ibid. See also Shahid-ur-Rehman, *Long Road to Chaghi*, 59.

83. Translated excerpts from "Islamabad Tonight."

84. Munir Ahmad Khan, interview by Hamid Mir and Saeed Qazi in *Daily Ausaf* (Urdu), June 18, 1998.

85. Shahid-ur-Rehman, *Long Road to Chaghi*, 59.

86. Levy and Scott-Clark, *Deception,* 50–52.

87. Ibid., 53.

88. Ibid., 71n.

89. Ibid., 56.

90. Ibid.

91. Ibid.

92. Frantz and Collins, *The Man From Pakistan*, 95.

93. Ibid., 79.

94. Ibid.

95. Dr. A. Q. Khan, "Pakistan's Nuclear Programme: Capabilities and Potentials of the Kahuta Project," speech to the Pakistan Institute of National Affairs, Islamabad, September 10, 1990; and Dr. A. Q. Khan, "Capabilities and Potentials of the Kahuta Project," *Frontier Post*, September 10, 1990.

96. Ibid.

97. Ibid.

98. Ibid.

99. U.S. Department of State, "The Pakistani Nuclear Program," secret memorandum, declassified June 23, 1983, cited in Andrew Winner and Toshi Yoshihara, *Nuclear Stability in South Asia* (Medford, MA: Institute for Foreign Policy Analysis, 2002), 22, http://www.gwu.edu/~narchive/NSAEEBB/NSAEBB6/ipin22_1.htm (accessed July 19, 2005).

100. Levy and Scott-Clark, *Deception*, 440. This information is not verified from a background briefing given to the author June 14, 2006, at Strategic Plans Division (SPD), Joint Services Headquarters (hereafter referred to as "background briefing") and interviews with former officials. Contrary to A. Q. Khan's written assertions, his successor, Javed Mirza, in interview by author, downplayed the impact of earthquakes on the centrifuges. He clarified to the author that centrifuges break mostly because of wear and tear and other technical reasons, especially the delicate balancing; after all, they are rotating at extremely high speeds.

101. The maraging steel is produced in People's Steel Mill in Karachi. Author's discussions with President Pervez Musharraf, Islamabad, June 18, 2006, and background briefing at SPD, June 14, 2006.

102. A. Q. Khan, interview by Tariq Warsi in *Nawa-i-Waqt*, February 9, 1984; A. Q. Khan, interview in *Jang*, February 10, 1984; quoted in Levy and Scott-Clark, *Deception*, 101–2. See also Dennis Kux, *The United States and Pakistan 1947–2000: Disenchanted Allies* (Washington, DC: Woodrow Wilson Center Press, 2001), 275.

103. IISS, *Nuclear Black Markets*, 20.

Chapter 8

1. Four major publications in the West with identical themes were: Gordon Corera, *Shopping for Bombs: Nuclear Proliferation, Global Insecurity, and the Rise and Fall of A. Q. Khan Network* (New York: Oxford University Press, 2006); Douglas Frantz and Cath-

erine Collins, *The Nuclear Jihadist* (New York: Hachette Book Group, 2007); Adrian Levy and Catherine Scott-Clark, *Deception: Pakistan, the United States, and the Secret Trade in Nuclear Weapons* (New York: Walker Publications Company, 2007); and David Albright, *Peddling Peril: How the Secret Nuclear Trade Arms America's Enemies* (New York: Simon and Schuster, 2010). In addition to these the author made key contributions to the research project organized and published under the aegis of the International Institute of Strategic Studies, London. See International Institute for Strategic Studies (IISS), *Nuclear Black Markets: Pakistan, A. Q. Khan and the Rise of Proliferation Networks, A Net Assessment,* IISS strategic dossier (London: International Institute for Strategic Studies, 2007).

2. Steve Weissman and Herbert Krosney, *The Islamic Bomb* (New York: Times Books, 1981) 182.

3. Ibid.

4. Translated excerpts from "Islamabad Tonight" discussion program hosted by Nadeem Malik, "Dr. Abdul Qadeer Khan Discusses Nuclear Program," *Aaj News Television* in Urdu, Karachi, August 31, 2009.

5. The term was coined by IAEA director General Mohamed ElBaradei, quoted in Wyn Q. Bowen, *Libya and Nuclear Proliferation: Stepping Back from the Brink*, Adelphi Paper 380 (London: Routledge for Institute for Strategic Studies, 2006), 37.

6. For example, A. Q. Khan's closest partner, Hank Slebos, stated unambiguously that "Pakistan was within its right to build nuclear weapons to maintain the balance of power against India." Quoted in Frantz and Collins, *The Nuclear Jihadist,* 77.

7. Ibid.

8. Weissman and Krosney, *The Islamic Bomb,* 182, 185.

9. Frantz and Collins, *The Nuclear Jihadist,* 43.

10. IISS, *Nuclear Black Markets,* 24–25.

11. Sultan Bashiruddin Mahmood, interview by author, Islamabad, December 14, 2006.

12. Ibid.

13. Sultan Mahmood told the author that after acquiring the aluminum rotor machine for ADW, they looked for more advanced German G-S designs for maraging steel rotors. Mahmood claims to have gone back to Dusseldorf to the same person who also sold him one G-S machine, which arrived around June 1976 in Wah. Ibid.

14. Ibid. See also M. A. Chaudhri, "Pakistan's Nuclear History: Separating Myth from Reality," *Defence Journal* 10 (May 2006).

15. M. A. Chaudhri, "Pakistan's Nuclear History: Separating Myth from Reality," *Defence Journal* 10 (May 2006).

16. Ibid.; see also Shahid-ur-Rehman, *Long Road to Chaghi* (Islamabad: Print Wise Publications, 1999).

17. Shahid-ur-Rehman, *Long Road to Chaghi,* 62.

18. Corera, *Shopping for Bombs*, 23. See also Dr. G. D. Alam, quoted in Shahid-ur-Rehman, *Long Road to Chaghi*, 61; and Sultan Bashiruddin Mahmood, interview by author, Islamabad, December 2006.

19. IISS, *Nuclear Black Markets*, 29.

20. Ibid., 24.

21. Ibid.

22. Corera, *Shopping for Bombs*, 23.

23. Ibid.; Weissman and Krosney, *The Islamic Bomb.*

24. Friedrich Tinner would later become a CIA informer on the network and played a key role in supplying the Iranian nuclear program. He and his son, Urs Tinner, would be part of the Libyan nuclear program network. Corera, *Shopping for Bombs*, 78, 161, 246–47, 249.

25. Ibid., 58, 184.

26. Ibid.; Shahid-ur-Rehman, *Long Road to Chaghi,* 57–58.

27. Levy and Scott-Clark, *Deception,* 467; Frantz and Collins, *The Nuclear Jihadist,* 74.

28. Shahid-ur-Rehman, *Long Road to Chaghi,* 58.

29. Frantz and Collins, *The Nuclear Jihadist,* 74.

30. A. Q. Khan was tried in absentia, indicted, and convicted for espionage. To date, A. Q. Khan insists that he did not seek any classified information. He wrote in his regular column: "A case was initiated against me in Holland for writing two letters from Pakistan to two of my former colleagues. The letters were said to be an attempt to obtain information, which the Public Prosecutor interpreted as being classified. I was prosecuted without my knowledge and in my absence. The information I had asked for was ordinary technical information available in published literature for many decades. I submitted certificates from six world-renowned professors from Holland, Belgium, England and Germany stating that the information requested by me was public knowledge and was not classified. I filed an appeal against this unjust case and the High Court of Amsterdam quashed the verdict of the lower court. On 16th June, 1985, the Dutch government finally dropped all charges." See A. Q. Khan, "Kahuta—A History," *News International*, http://www.thenews.com.pk/editorial_detail.asp?id=191448 (accessed April 21, 2010).

31. Weissman and Krosney, *The Islamic Bomb,* 184; Frantz and Collins, *The Nuclear Jihadist,* 77.

32. Frantz and Collins, *The Nuclear Jihadist,* 76–77. The friendship between A. Q. Khan and Slebos spanned almost forty years, and Slebos considers himself to be A. Q. Khan's best friend and key partner. Cited in Frank Slijper, "Project Butter Factory: Henk Slebos and the A. Q. Khan Nuclear Network," briefing paper (The Netherlands: Transnational Institute/Campagne tegen Wapenhandel), September 2007, http://www.tni.org/detail_pub.phtml?know_id=200 (accessed November 20, 2008).

33. Weissman and Krosney, *The Islamic Bomb,* 185.

34. Frantz and Collins, *The Nuclear Jihadist,* 186.

35. Ibid., 186–87; Shahid-ur-Rehman, *Long Road to Chaghi,* 62. Ernst Piffl also supplied inverters to the centrifuge plant of the United Kingdom Atomic Energy Authority (UKAEA) at Capenhurst, operated by British Nuclear Fuels Ltd. See IISS, *Nuclear Black Markets,* 24.

36. Levy and Scott-Clark, *Deception,* 54–55.

37. Weissman and Krosney, *The Islamic Bomb,* 87.

38. Shahid-ur-Rehman, *Long Road to Chaghi,* 62.

39. Ibid.

40. Levy and Scott-Clark, *Deception,* 55.

41. Dr. G. D. Alam, interview in *Assas-o-Lashkar,* June 12, 1998.

42. Weissman and Krosney, *The Islamic Bomb,* 187.

43. Mossad targeted Heinz Mebus's home with a letter bomb that killed his dog. CORA managing director Eduard German was threatened with bombings in Bern, Switzerland, February 20, 1979. See Levy and Scott-Clark, *Deception,* 87.

44. Ibid., 88.

45. Frantz and Collins, *The Nuclear Jihadist,* 93.

46. Shahid-ur-Rehman, *Long Road to Chaghi,* 63.

47. Weissman and Krosney, *The Islamic Bomb,* 216–17. The Dubai-based company was run by the Indian national Abdus Salam and involved A. Q. Khan's friend in Canada, Abdul Aziz Khan.

48. Frantz and Collins, *The Nuclear Jihadist,* 93.

49. A. Q. Khan, "Uranium Enrichment at Kahuta," in Zahid Malik, *Dr. A. Q. Khan and the Islamic Bomb* (Islamabad: Hurmat Publications, 1992), 96.

50. IISS, *Nuclear Black Markets,* 24–26.

51. Ghulam Ishaq Khan (G. I. Khan) was the key initiator of this idea. He was always privy to the nuclear program, until he became president himself after Zia-ul-Haq died in a plane crash in 1988. G. I. K. remained president until July 1993.

52. IISS, *Nuclear Black Markets,* 26–27.

Chapter 9

1. President Zia-ul-Haq was livid when he learned of A. Q. Khan's interview with Indian journalist Kuldeep Nayyar, which was arranged through Pakistani journalist Syed Mushahid Hussain and published in London on March 1, 1987. In his interview A. Q. Khan, ranting indiscreetly, boasted of his achievement in enriching uranium and made a veiled threat to India by exaggerating Pakistani bomb capability. Khan's indiscretion caused tremendous trepidation in President Zia, who had pledged to the world to keep the Pakistani nuclear program peaceful and especially "never to embarrass his friend, President Ronald Reagan." Syed Refaqat Ali, interview by author, Islamabad, June 19, 2006.

2. As will be shown in Chapter 10, Zia approved the plutonium program, which was the first sign of his changed opinion about the PAEC and Munir Ahmad Khan, whom he had earlier suspected of being a "Bhutto loyalist." Ibid.

3. Riazuddin and Samar Mubarakmand were the two leading scientists involved in the bomb design and later with the 1998 nuclear test.

4. The U Equation of State and/or HE Equation of State would eventually help in designing the triggering of the device.

5. Another method to produce tritium is irradiating lithium-6 targets in a nuclear reactor. Tritium also serves as a neutron initiator.

6. Dr. Samar Mubarakmand, interview by author, Islamabad, June 14, 2010.

7. Dr. Riazuddin, interview by author, Islamabad, June 18, 2006.

8. Dr. Ishfaq Ahmad, Riazuddin, and Samar Mubarakmand, interviews by the author, Islamabad, December 19, 2005, December 14, 2005, and June 14, 2009, respectively.

9. M. A. Chaudhri, "Pakistan's Nuclear History: Separating Myth from Reality," *Defence Journal* 9, 10 (May 2006); and *The News*, special ed. (Nuclear), May 31, 1998.

10. In an effort to instill a sense of pride, Salam noted that the heads of the Manhattan Project were also theoretical scientists, and informed the Pakistani scientists that a similar theoretical physics group was being established within the PAEC.

11. Shahid-ur-Rehman, *Long Road to Chaghi* (Islamabad: Print Wise Publications, 1999), 38.

12. Dr. Riazuddin, interview by author, Islamabad, June 18, 2006.

13. Shahid-ur-Rehman, *Long Road to Chaghi,* 75.

14. Ibid., 39.

15. Beryllium is one material used as a damper because it is a good neutron reflector, which helps initiate the chain reaction. But beryllium reflectors are difficult to manufacture and handle, given their brittle and toxic nature. Therefore, the first design that was prepared by the Theoretical Group used U-238 as a reflector. Pakistan may have also used polonium-210 mixed with beryllium as the neutron source for its first-generation weapons. Subsequent weapons may have used tritium as a neutron source.

16. Dr. Riazuddin, interview by Mansoor Ahmed, Islamabad, February 15, 2007. The author is grateful to Mansoor for sharing his interview findings.

17. Samar Mubarakmand, "A Science Odyssey: Pakistan's Nuclear Emergence," speech to the Khwarzimic Science Society, Centre of Excellence in Solid State Physics, Punjab University, Lahore, November 30, 1998.

18. Shahid-ur-Rehman, *Long Road to Chaghi,* 74.

19. Ibid., 41.

20. Ibid., 5.

21. Ibid., 41.

22. Sultan Bashiruddin Mahmood, "Obituary: A Great Scientist Passes Away," *The Post,* August 15, 2007.

23. Mansoor Jafar, "Nation Loses an Unsung Hero," *The News,* August 16, 2007.

24. POF at Wah included a facility to produce RDX, a powerful explosive. But the PAEC required something far more powerful, known as Her Majesty's Explosive (HMX).

25. Shahid-ur-Rehman, *Long Road to Chaghi,* 40.

26. Mubarakmand, "A Science Odyssey."

27. Pervez Butt, former chairman PAEC, interview by author, Islamabad, December 15, 2006.

28. Shahid-ur-Rehman, *Long Road to Chaghi,* 75–76.

29. Dr. Samar Mubarakmand, interview by author, Islamabad, June 14, 2010.

30. *The Proceedings of the Pakistan Academy of Sciences: Citation of New Fellows* 41, 1 (June 2004), http://www.paspk.org/41–1.htm (accessed June 16, 2007).

31. Pakistan tested simple fission designs in May 1998; PAEC, however, had a facility for tritium purification and recovery. Tritium has a half-life of twelve years only.

32. Mubarakmand, "A Science Odyssey."

33. Pakistani scientists were able to develop solid state krytons for triggering the implosion devices. Shahid-ur-Rehman, *Long Road to Chaghi,* 76. During the early 1980s, it was reported that Pakistan had also tried to procure krytons from the United States.

34. Dr. Samar clarified to the author that KRL developed a parallel UML-like facility from 1987 onward, in which the enriched gas was converted into metal and bomb cores. Javed Mirza, interview by author, Islamabad, June 14, 2007; Samar Mubarakmand, background briefing to author and interview by author, Islamabad, June 14, 2010.

35. Mubarakmand, "A Science Odyssey."

36. Ibid.

37. Central Intelligence Agency, "Pakistan's Nuclear Program: Personnel and Organization," CIA Electronic Reading Room, November 1985, 24–25, http://www.foia.cia.gov (accessed June 29, 2010).

38. Shahid-ur-Rehman, *Long Road to Chaghi,* 75–76.

39. Mubarakmand, "A Science Odyssey."

40. Ibid.

41. Ibid.

42. Ibid.

43. Ibid. Samar Mubarakmand, interview by author, Islamabad, June 14, 2010.

44. Ishfaq Ahmad, interview by author, Islamabad, December 19, 2005; see also Mubarakmand, "A Science Odyssey."

45. Ishfaq Ahmad, interview by author, Islamabad, December 20, 2005, and June 17, 2006.

46. Ibid. See also Rai Muhammad Saleh Azam, "When Mountains Move: The Story of Chagai," *Defence Journal* (June 2000), http://www.defencejournal.com/2000/june/chagai.htm (accessed June 16, 2007).

47. Ishfaq Ahmad, interview by author, Islamabad, December 20, 2005, and June 17, 2006; Samar Mubarakmand, interview by author, Islamabad, June 14, 2010.

48. Brigadier Mohammad Sarfaraz was chief of staff of a corps in 1976, who was assisting with logistics for Dr. Ishfaq and his team.

49. SDW reported directly to the Chief of the Army Staff and partnered with the Ministry of Defense, the Ministry of Foreign Affairs and Finance, the Frontier Works Organization (FWO), and intelligence agencies.

50. Shahid-ur-Rehman, *Long Road to Chaghi,* 79.

51. Ishfaq Ahmad, interview by author, Islamabad, December 20, 2005. See also Brigadier (ret.) Sarfaraz Ahmad, quoted in Shahid-ur-Rehman, *Long Road to Chaghi,* 77–78.

52. Shahid-ur-Rehman, *Long Road to Chaghi,* 78.

53. Mubarakmand, "A Science Odyssey."

54. Ibid.

55. Samar Mubarakmand, interview by author, Islamabad, June 14, 2010.

56. Mubarakmand, "A Science Odyssey."

57. Brigadier (ret.) Mohammad Sarfaraz, quoted in Shahid-ur-Rehman, *Long Road to Chaghi,* 77–78.

58. Samar Mubarakmand, interview by author, Islamabad, June 14, 2010. See also Shahid-ur-Rehman, *Long Road to Chaghi,* 77–78.

59. Samar Mubarakmand, interview by author, Islamabad, June 14, 2010.

60. Shahid-ur-Rehman, *Long Road to Chaghi,* 82–83.

61. Munir Ahmad Khan, "Medal Award Ceremony," speech to the Pakistan Nuclear Society, PINSTECH Auditorium, Islamabad, March 20, 1999.

62. Samar Mubarakmand, interview by author, Islamabad, June 14, 2010. See also Brigadier (ret.) Sarfaraz Ahmad, quoted in Shahid-ur-Rehman, *Long Road to Chaghi,* 77–78.

63. Samar Mubarakmand, interview by author, Islamabad, June 14, 2010.

64. Brigadier (ret.) Sarfaraz Ahmad, quoted in Shahid-ur-Rehman, *Long Road to Chaghi,* 77–78.

65. Mubarakmand, "A Science Odyssey."

66. Ibid.

67. Mubarakmand interview, June 14, 2010.

68. Shahid-ur-Rehman, *Long Road to Chaghi,* 82–83. Ishfaq Ahmad and Samar Mubarakmand also endorsed this report in separate interviews with the author.

69. Mubarakmand, interview, June 14, 2010. See also Shahid-ur-Rehman, *Long Road to Chaghi,* 82–83.

70. Mubarakmand, interview, June 14, 2010.

71. Shahid-ur-Rehman, *Long Road to Chaghi,* 81–84.

72. Mubarakmand, interview, June 14, 2010.

73. Adrian Levy and Catherine Scott-Clark, *Deception: Pakistan, the United States, and the Secret Trade in Nuclear Weapons* (New York: Walker Publishing Company, 2007), 85. The author cannot conclusively confirm the exact date when Zia-ul Haq directed A. Q. Khan to commence work on the bomb design. According to some interviews, in the early 1980s, Zia-ul Haq directed Lieutenant-General Syed Zamin Naqvi, then in charge of security and coordination, to provide a copy of the PAEC design work to both KRL and PAEC and generate a competition between the two. Zia-ul-Haq at the time did not trust Munir Ahmad but was much impressed with A. Q. Khan's achievement and had full faith in him.

74. Dr. Riazuddin, interview by author, Islamabad, June 18, 2006. Riazuddin recalled to the author that after the briefing on the weapons designs, Zia-ul Haq asked only one question: "How many Ahmadis/Qadianis were in the nuclear program?" Earlier, Z. A. Bhutto had ordered an investigation of all Ahmadis in the nuclear program. All appointees or students of Dr. Abdus Salam were viewed with suspicion, including Munir Khan, Sultan Bashiruddin Mahmood, and Riazuddin.

75. PAEC official, interview by author on nonattributable basis, Islamabad, June 14, 2006. The story within PAEC was that A. Q. Khan had spread a rumor to discredit PAEC and thus have the entire classified program moved to KRL. The author could not verify this claim.

76. In the words of Syed Refaqat, "Zia was feeding A. Q. Khan's ego knowing he was a man who wanted to be crowned everyday if possible, an ambitious man—Julius Caesar." Syed Refaqat Ali, interview by author, Islamabad, June 19, 2006.

77. This information was based on a letter that A. Q. Khan had purportedly written to his wife, which was leaked to a journalist friend in the UK, Simon Henderson. It may have been a way of blackmailing the military government against legal action. Khan threatened to reveal state secrets through Simon Henderson, who claims to be a close personal friend. See *Washington Post,* November 13, 2009. See also Dennis Kux, *The United States and Pakistan 1947–2000: Disenchanted Allies* (Washington, DC: Woodrow Wilson Center Press, 2001), 345.

78. After the Israeli attack on Osirak, the Pakistani leadership began to get nervous. Earlier reports indicate that Israel attempted to convince the United States to attack Kahuta or KANUPP.

79. *Washington Post*, December 13, 2009. See also Andrew Koch, *Jane's Intelligence Review*, cited in International Institute for Strategic Studies (IISS), *Nuclear Black Markets: Pakistan, A. Q. Khan and the Rise of Proliferation Networks, a Net Assessment,* IISS strategic dossier (London: International Institute for Strategic Studies, 2007), 32. The KRL design would eventually be copied and sent to Libya, where it was discovered in 2004. That warhead design was later handed over to U.S. authorities and was reported to be less than 1 meter in diameter and weighing exactly 453 kilograms.

80. Anwar Iqbal, "Pakistan Assails US Report about Chinese Help for N-plan,"

Dawn, November 14, 2009. A. Q. Khan has denied the assertion that he wrote any such letter, and Pakistan officially rejects the report.

81. Ibid.

82. Samar Mubarakmand, interview by author, Islamabad, June 14, 2010.

83. Shahid-ur-Rehman, *Long Road to Chaghi,* 104–5.

84. IISS, *Nuclear Black Markets,* 32.

85. Background briefing at Strategic Plans Division (SPD) to the author on A. Q. Khan network, Rawalpindi, June 2007.

86. *Washington Post,* December 13, 2009. With attribution to A. Q. Khan, Pakistan had obtained a CHIC-4 implosion bomb design, along with fifty kilograms of HEU in 1981. A. Q. Khan has denied having written the purported letter.

87. Shahid-ur-Rehman, *Long Road to Chaghi,* 83.

88. Samar Mubarakmand, interview by author, Islamabad, June 14, 2010. See also General K. M. Arif, interview by author, Islamabad, June 19, 2005; General Mirza Aslam Beg, interview by author, Islamabad, September 1, 2005; and Lieutenant-General Syed Refaqat Ali, interview by author, Islamabad, June 19, 2006.

Chapter 10

1. Munir Ahmad Khan, interview by *Urdu Digest,* October 1981, Lahore.

2. Muhammad Afzal, interview by author, Islamabad, December 30, 2005.

3. Sultan Bashiruddin Mahmood and Pervez Butt, interview by author, Islamabad, December 14, 2006. See also Central Intelligence Agency, "Pakistan Nuclear Weapons Program: Personnel and Organizations," research paper, Directorate of Intelligence, November 1, 1985, CIA Electronic Reading Room, October 20, 2010, http://www.foia.cia.gov/search.asp.

4. Ishfaq Ahmad, interview by author, Islamabad, December 20, 2005.

5. All reactors have their power outputs measured in thermal energy (t); output of reactors dedicated to power or electricity production is measured in electric energy (e). Plutonium production reactors such as Khushab or research reactors such as PARR-1 are labeled 50 MWt or 10 MWt, respectively. In the case of India's Dhruva power reactor, for example, output is 100 MWt. Typically, a 300-MWe power reactor will produce at least three times the thermal power or energy (or 900 MWt). Capacity for those dedicated for power production is written as MWe.

6. Munir Ahmad Khan, "How Pakistan Made Nuclear Fuel," *The Nation,* February 7, 1998.

7. Jeffrey T. Richelson, *Spying on the Bomb* (New York: W. W. Norton and Company, 2006), 339.

8. Henry D. Sokolski, ed., *Pakistan's Nuclear Future: Worries beyond War* (Carlisle Barracks, PA: Strategic Studies Institute, U.S. Army War College, 2008).

9. International Institute for Strategic Studies (IISS), *Nuclear Black Markets: Paki-*

stan, A. Q. Khan and the Rise of Proliferation Networks, a Net Assessment, IISS strategic dossier (London: International Institute for Strategic Studies, 2007), 24–25.

10. Pervez Butt, interview by author, Islamabad, December 15, 2006; Sultan Bashiruddin Mahmood, interview by author, Islamabad, December 14, 2006; Ishfaq Ahmad, interview by author, Islamabad, December 20, 2005; Muhammad Afzal, interview by author, Islamabad, December 2005.

11. Agha Shahi, interview by author, Islamabad, June 19, 2005.

12. George Perkovich, "Could Anything Be Done to Stop Them?: Lessons from Pakistan," Nonproliferation Policy Education Center, July 26, 2006, http://www.npec-web. org/Essays/20060726-Perkovich-CouldAnythingBeDone.pdf.

13. Steve Weissman and Herbert Krosney, *The Islamic Bomb* (New York: Times Books, 1981), 67.

14. Pervez Butt, interview by author, Islamabad, December 15, 2006; Sultan Bashiruddin Mahmood, interview by author, Islamabad, December 14, 2006.

15. CIA, *Pakistan Nuclear Study,* April 26, 1978, 23–24, CIA Electronic Reading Room, accessed October 20, 2010, http://www.faqs.org/cia/docs/44/0000252641/PAKI-STAN-NUCLEAR-STUDY.html.

16. David Fischer, *History of the International Atomic Energy Agency: The First Forty Years* (Vienna: IAEA, 1997), http://www-pub.iaea.org/MTCD/publications/PDF/Pub1032_web.pdf (accessed October 20, 2011).

17. Munir Ahmad Khan, "Significance of Chashma Plant," *Dawn,* August 8, 1993.

18. In 1985, Zia-ul-Haq had held non–party based national elections and a hybrid civil-military government had emerged with Prime Minister Mohammad Khan Junejo, an assertive civilian prime minister, in office, who often challenged Zia-ul-Haq and the military.

19. Shahid-ur-Rehman Khan, "Zia Orders Pakistan AEC to Design Indigenous Nuclear Reactor," *Nucleonics Week,* November 13, 1986, 3–4; Sultan Bashiruddin Mahmood, interview by author, Islamabad, December 14, 2006; Pervez Butt, interview by author, Islamabad, December 15, 2006.

20. Chashma reactors would run at 30,000 MWd/t (megawatt day per ton) burn-up or higher, while KANUPP runs at 7,000 MWd/t burn-up.

21. Ishfaq Ahmad, interview by author, Islamabad, December 20, 2005; Pervez Butt, interview by author, Islamabad, December 15, 2006; Sultan Bashiruddin Mahmood, interview by author, Islamabad, December 14, 2006; and Muhammad Afzal, interview by author, Islamabad, December 2005.

22. Pervez Butt, interview by author, Islamabad, December 15, 2006; Sultan Bashiruddin Mahmood, interview by author, Islamabad, December 14, 2006.

23. As explained in Chapter 7, earthquakes in the lower Himalaya region were common, and had destroyed four thousand centrifuges operating at Kahuta centrifuge plant in 1981.

24. Shahid-ur-Rehman, *Long Road to Chaghi* (Islamabad: Print Wise Publications, 1999), 96.

25. "Pakistan Needs Help to Make Plutonium and Tritium," *The Risk Report* 1, 5 (June 1995), 9, Wisconsin Project on Nuclear Arms Control, http://www.wisconsinproject.org/countries/pakistan/pak-help-pu-tritium.html (accessed October 20, 2010).

26. Sultan Bashiruddin Mahmood, interview by author, Islamabad, December 14, 2006.

27. Ibid.

28. "Pakistan Needs Help to Make Plutonium and Tritium," 9.

29. Shahid-ur-Rehman, "Zia Orders PAEC to Design Indigenous Nuclear Reactor," *Nucleonics Week,* November 13, 1986, 3–4, quoted in Andrew Koch and Jennifer Topping, "Pakistan's Nuclear Related Facilities," Center for Nonproliferation Studies Data Abstracts, Monterey Institute of International Studies, 1997, cns.miis.edu/pubs/reports/pdfs/9707paki.pdf, www.paec.gov.pk/ncndt/about.htm (accessed October 20, 2010); "Nuclear Official Claims Reactors Being Produced," *AMN* (Karachi), January 17, 1991, 6; "Pakistan Nuclear Developments," NTI Nuclear and Missile Database, April 23, 1991, Nuclear Threat Initiative, http://www.nti.org/e_research/profiles/Pakistan/Nuclear/5593_6323.html (accessed October 20, 2010).

30. Mark Hibbs, "German Firm's Exports Raise Concern about Pakistan's Nuclear Capabilities," *Nuclear Fuel*, March 6, 1989, 13–14.

31. The Heavy Mechanical Complex is run under the Pakistan Defense Ministry and headed by a three-star general. It produces tanks, guns, armored personnel carriers, and other heavy machinery, including tractors. HMC-1 and HMC-II are dedicated to such projects.

32. Sultan Bashiruddin Mahmood, interview by Mansoor Ahmed, written notes, Islamabad, August 3, 2007.

33. Weissman and Krosney, *The Islamic Bomb*, 83.

34. Central Intelligence Agency, *Pakistan Nuclear Study*, 24–25.

35. Ibid.

36. Weissman and Krosney, *The Islamic Bomb*, 298.

37. Ibid., 82–83.

38. Central Intelligence Agency, "Pakistan Nuclear Weapons Program."

39. Samar Mubarakmand, interview by author, Islamabad, June 14, 2010.

40. PUREX, or plutonium uranium extraction, is a method for chemical separation of plutonium and unspent uranium from other fission by-products in spent nuclear fuel. Also known as the solvent extraction method for fuel reprocessing, it was first invented during the Manhattan Project and is a well-known method for reprocessing around the world.

41. Jack Boureston, "Pakistan's Past, Current and Future Reprocessing Facilities,"

profile, Firstwatch International, October 1, 2006, http://www.firstwatchint.org/docs/pakistan_reprocessing.pdf (accessed October 10, 2010).

42. Weissman and Krosney, *The Islamic Bomb*, 222.

43. "Hot Laboratories," *Der Spiegel*, February 27, 1989, 113, in JPRS-TND-89–006 (March 28, 1989), 33–34.

44. This was confirmed to the author by a PAEC scientist involved in reprocessing.

45. Mark Hibbs, "Pakistan Separation Plant Now Producing 8–10 Kg of Plutonium/Yr," *Nuclear Fuel*, June 12, 2000.

46. "Minister Wants to Stiffen Export Controls," *Der Spiegel*, June 26, 1989, 87–89, quoted in Koch and Topping, "Pakistan's Nuclear Related Facilities."

47. "Nuclear Contacts with Pakistan," *Der Spiegel*, February 27, 1989, 113, quoted in Koch and Topping, "Pakistan's Nuclear Related Facilities."

48. Background briefings with former PAEC officials, Islamabad, June 2007.

49. "Nuclear Contacts with Pakistan," 113.

50. "Nuclear Weapons Technology," Section V, Federation of American Scientists, www.fas.org/irp/threat/mctl98–2/p2sec05.pdf (accessed December 20, 2010).

51. Munir Ahmad Khan, "Nuclearization of South Asia and Its Regional and Global Implications," *Regional Studies* 26, 4 (Autumn 1998).

52. IISS, *Nuclear Black Markets,* 24–25.

53. Sultan Bashiruddin Mahmood, interview by Mansoor Ahmed, written notes, Islamabad, August 3, 2007.

54. Usman Shabbir, "Remembering Unsung Heroes: Munir Ahmad Khan," *Defence Journal,* May 2004.

55. Shahid-ur-Rehman, *Long Road to Chaghi,* 65–66.

56. Ibid., 65–66.

57. "Nuclear Weapons Technology."

58. Ibid.

59. Hibbs, "German Firm's Exports Raise Concern about Pakistan's Nuclear Capabilities," 12.

60. Ibid.

61. Ibid.; see also Samar Mubarakmand, interview by author, Islamabad, June 14, 2010.

62. Ibid.

63. Hibbs, "German Firm's Exports Raise Concern about Pakistan's Nuclear Capabilities," 13–14.

64. "Tritium Transfer to Nuclear Weapons Program Detailed," *Nuclear Developments,* July 18, 1990, 26–30, quoted in Koch and Topping, "Pakistan's Nuclear Related Facilities."

65. "Nuclear Exports to Pakistan Reported," *Der Spiegel,* February 20, 1989, quoted in Koch and Topping, "Pakistan's Nuclear Related Facilities."

Chapter 11

1. See Husain Haqqani, *Pakistan: Between Military and the Mosque* (Washington, DC: Carnegie Endowment for Peace, 2005); Hassan Abbas, *Pakistan's Drift into Extremism* (New York: ME Sharpe, 2005). For Pakistani security policy under Zia, refer to Robert G. Wirsing, *Pakistan's Security under Zia, 1977–1988: The Policy Imperatives of a Peripheral Asian* State (London: Macmillan Academic and Professional, 1991).

2. For China, the acceptance of "One China" and its permanent membership in the UN Security Council heralded China's rise as a major power. Post-Mao China needed the space for modernization. Among the several bilateral agreements signed with the United States, the most significant was the Agreement on Cooperation in Science and Technology, which was to become the largest bilateral program. Zbigniew Brzezinski, *Power and Principles: Memoirs of the National Security Advisor 1977–1981* (New York: Basic Books, 1983), 240–45; and Brzezinski, *Grand Chessboard: American Primacy and Its Geostrategic Imperatives* (New York: Basic Books, 1997).

3. Pakistan had played a secret facilitating role in 1971, which was now bearing fruit with the exchange of visits of Vice Premier Deng Xiaoping to Washington, DC, in January and later Vice President Mondale to Beijing in August. On March 1, 1979, the United States and China formally established embassies in Beijing and Washington. See Dennis Kux, *The United States and Pakistan, 1947–2000: Disenchanted Allies* (Washington, DC: Woodrow Wilson Center Press, 2001).

4. Syed Refaqat Ali, interview by author, Islamabad, June 19, 2006; India voted against a resolution in the UN General Assembly that condemned the Soviet occupation of Afghanistan. India also stood firm when the international community boycotted the Moscow Olympics.

5. Thomas Perry Thornton, "India and Afghanistan," in Theodore L. Eliot, Jr., and Robert L. Pfaltzgraff, Jr., eds., *The Red Army on Pakistan's Border: Policy Implications for the United States* (Washington, DC: Pergamon-Brassey's International Defense Publishers, 1986), 46–47. See also Wirsing, *Pakistan's Security under Zia*, 10.

6. Wirsing, *Pakistan's Security under Zia*, 10. Wirsing cites the *New York Times*, May 29, 1980, A16, and May 30, 1980.

7. President Jimmy Carter had visited India on January 1, 1978. Unlike previous high-level visits, this one did not include a visit to Pakistan, which reflected U.S. acceptance of India's rise as a regional hegemon and worsening relations with Pakistan. See Kux, *The United States and Pakistan*, 235.

8. Under the Glenn and Symington amendments to the Foreign Assistance Act, U.S. aid to countries that were nonsignatory to the Nuclear Non-Proliferation Treaty and who either conducted nuclear tests or imported fuel would be cut off. See ibid., 235.

9. Ibid.

10. Wirsing, *Pakistan's Security under Zia*, 10.

11. Ibid., 235–41.

12. Ibid., 240.

13. Pakistan had formally withdrawn from CENTO in 1979 and joined the Non-Aligned Movement.

14. In the summer of 1979, the Carter administration approved less than a million dollars in funding for covert support of the Islamic resistance against the communists. In the Bhutto era the covert operations were the responsibility of Inspector General Frontier Corps (Peshawar), but as new sources for covert operations were funded, Zia shifted responsibility to his trusted confidant Lieutenant-General Akhtar Abdur Rehman, who was director general of Inter-Services Intelligence (DGISI). Since then, ISI has been responsible for the resistance movement in Afghanistan in close cooperation with the CIA. See Kux, *The United States and Pakistan,* 242.

15. For a debate on the determinants of Pakistan's security policy in the 1980s, see Wirsing, *Pakistan's Security under Zia,* 16–21.

16. See Zulfikar Ali Bhutto, *If I Am Assassinated* (New Delhi: Vikas, 1979), 136–37.

17. Gordon Corera, *Shopping for Bombs* (New York: Oxford University Press, 2006), 29.

18. Adrian Levy and Catherine Scott-Clark, *Deception: Pakistan, the United States, and the Secret Trade in Nuclear Weapons* (New York: Walker Publishing Company, 2007), 92–93.

19. In another story, a student traveling on the back of a truck fell off, striking his head against a mysterious rock that was found to be an electronic device with all sorts of "whirring and blinking bits." This "rock" was later kept in a Pakistan "museum for trainee spies." Cited in ibid., 93.

20. Kux, *The United States and Pakistan,* 240.

21. Unclassified Document of Department of State, General Advisory Committee on Arms Control and Disarmament, Friday Morning Session, September 14, 1979, 309–477. See also Naeem Salik, *The Genesis of South Asian Deterrence: Pakistan's Perspective* (New York: Oxford University Press, 2009), 93–96.

22. Ibid.

23. Agha Shahi, interview by author, Islamabad, June 19, 2005. Also quoted verbatim in Kux, *The United States and Pakistan,* 241.

24. Ibid.

25. Levy and Scott-Clark, *Deception,* 87–88.

26. George Perkovich, *India's Nuclear Bomb: The Impact on Global Proliferation* (Berkley: University of California Press, 1999), 240.

27. Levy and Scott-Clark, *Deception,* 104.

28. Bharat Karnad, *Nuclear Weapons and Indian Security: The Realist Foundations of Strategy* (New Delhi: Macmillan, 2002), 349–50. See also Levy and Scott-Clark, *Deception,* 110–12.

29. Javed Mirza, interview by author, Islamabad, June 13, 2007. See also General (ret.) Mirza Aslam Beg, interview by author, Rawalpindi, September 1, 2005. General Beg at the time was Chief of General Staff at the General Headquarters, which was responsible for defense of the country.

30. See Feroz Hassan Khan, "Nuclear Security in Pakistan: Separating Myth from Reality," *Arms Control Today* 39, 5 (July/August 2009), 16–17.

31. Kux, *The United States and Pakistan*, 256.

32. Ibid., 257–59.

33. Ibid.

34. Agha Shahi, interview by author, Islamabad, June 19, 2005; and General (ret.) K. M. Arif, interview by author, Islamabad, Rawalpindi, June 19, 2005.

35. Syed Refaqat Ali, interview by author, June 19, 2006.

36. Feroz Hassan Khan, "Security Impediments to Regionalism in South Asia," in Rafiq Dossani, Daniel C. Sneider, and Vikram Sood, eds., *Does South Asia Exist?: Prospects of Regional Integration* (Washington, DC: Brookings Institution, 2010), 235–36.

37. "Leaders Pay Tribute to Doyen of India's Strategic Community," special correspondence, *The Hindu,* February 3, 2011, http://www.thehindu.com/news/national/article1150646.ece (accessed October 10, 2011).

38. K. Subramanyam's realpolitik nature was recognized in Pakistan when he famously said, in April 1971, after the Pakistani Army cracked down in Dhaka, that this was "an opportunity the like of which will never come again." See Kux, *The United States and Pakistan*, 206.

39. Wirsing, *Pakistan's Security under Zia,* 86–87.

40. The Pakistani security establishment is convinced that India's aggressive security policies are driven by the Kautliyan principle, which is India's Machiavellian influence. See, for example, General K. M. Arif, *Estranged Neighbors: India-Pakistan 1947–2010* (Islamabad: Dost Publications, 2010), 281–82.

41. The U.S. embargo enforced in 1965 was lifted in 1976, but Pakistan was again embargoed under the Carter administration. It was meaningfully opened up by the Reagan administration.

42. See Feroz Hassan Khan, "Security Impediments to Regionalism in South Asia," in Dossani, Sneider, and Sood, eds., *Does South Asia Exist?,* 227–50.

43. From the author's personal recollection of the exercise, when he was posted on operational staff assignment and participated in the exercise planning and conduct. President Zia and top civil and military leadership of the country attended the exercise, including some future army leaders and army chiefs.

44. Sumit Ganguly and Devin T. Hagerty, *Fearful Symmetry: India—Pakistan Crises in the Shadow of Nuclear Weapons* (New Delhi: Oxford University Press, 2005), 49.

45. For details, see Feroz Hassan Khan, Christopher Clary, and Peter Lavoy, "Pakistan Motivations and Calculations in Kargil," in Peter Lavoy, ed., *Asymmetric War in*

South Asia: The Causes and Consequences of the Kargil Conflict (New York: Cambridge University Press, 2009), 74–80.

46. Lieutenant-General V. R. Raghavan, *Siachin: Conflict without End* (New Delhi: Penguin Books, 2002), 51–52.

47. India had been probing the Siachin Glacier areas since 1979, but more aggressive patrolling began in 1983. The Pakistani Army dispatched a team of the Special Services Group (SSG) to confirm intrusion, after which both sides accused the other of preparing to occupy the glacier. See Khan, Clary, and Lavoy, "Pakistan Motivations and Calculations in Kargil," 74–80. Siachin continues to bleed both militaries twenty-five years later. See Nora Boustani, "From Pakistani War Front to Strategic Ivory Tower," *Washington Post*, April 12, 2002.

48. For an Indian account, see Raghavan, *Siachin*, 58–85. For the Pakistani narrative referred to here, see Pervez Musharraf, *In the Line of Fire: A Memoir* (New York: Simon and Schuster, 2006), 68–69.

49. See Zafar Iqbal Cheema, "The Strategic Context of the Kargil Conflict: A Pakistani Perspective," in Lavoy, ed., *Asymmetric War in South Asia*, 47–55.

50. Musharraf, *In the Line of Fire*, 87.

51. India by this time was facing multiple insurgencies and crises elsewhere within the country, most notably in the eastern states where there were leftist movements such as Naxalite movements in Andhra, Jharkand, and the Nagaland militancy. In northeast India, yet another autonomous movement, United Liberation Front for Assam (ULFA), was shaping up for liberation in Assam.

52. For details, see Jugdeep S. Cima, *The Sikh Separatist Insurgency in India: Political Leadership and Ethno-nationalist Movements* (New York: Sage Publications, 2010).

53. Ramachandra Guha, *India after Gandhi: The History of the World's Largest Democracy* (New York: Harper Perennial, 2007), 562–65.

54. Scott D. Sagan and Kenneth Waltz, *Spread of Nuclear Weapons: A Debate Renewed* (New York: W. W. Norton and Company, 2002), 91. Western intelligence concluded that India might move to "smother Pakistan's nuclear baby in its crib." Cited by Ganguly and Hagerty, *Fearful Symmetry*, 57.

55. The Indian authorities later claimed that the squadron had been hidden in the woods in an adjacent airfield as part of a passive air defense drill. See Ganguly and Hagerty, *Fearful Symmetry*, 58.

56. Levy and Scott-Clark, *Deception*, 110–11. See also Ganguly and Hagerty, *Fearful Symmetry*, 57–58.

57. Perkovich, *India's Nuclear Bomb*, 258. See also Ganguly and Hagerty, *Fearful Symmetry*, 57.

58. K. M. Arif, cited in Levy and Scott-Clark, *Deception*, 111.

59. Mirza Aslam Beg, interview by author, Rawalpindi, September 1, 2005.

60. As quoted in Levy and Scott-Clark, *Deception*, 104.

61. Ganguly and Hagerty, *Fearful Symmetry,* 58.

62. This was a classic situation in which the difference between preventive attack and preemptive attack becomes clear. Preventive attack is a deliberate plan to destroy the emerging capability of an adversary before it matures into a full capability and to nullify the existing military advantage (which India was contemplating in this case). Preemptive attack means seizing the initiative from the adversary through a first blow when an attack is imminent (which in this case India feared Pakistan might do either in panic or in the knowledge that the missing Jaguars signified an impending assault on Kahuta.)

63. Mrs. Gandhi had been warned by intelligence agencies about threats to her life in the aftermath of Operation Blue Star, especially about her Sikh bodyguards. She dismissed the concerns. Guha, *India after Gandhi,* 565.

64. According to Stephen Cohen, General Sunderji's scholarly achievements far exceeded his legacy as a military commander. Stephen Cohen, discussions with the author, Brookings Institution, Washington, DC, 2002.

65. Walter C. Ladwig III, "A Cold Start for Hot Wars? The Indian Army's New Limited War Doctrine," *International Security* 32, 3 (Winter 2007/8), 158–90.

66. Shuja Nawaz, *Crossed Swords: Pakistan, Its Army, and the Wars Within* (New York: Oxford University Press, 2008), 393; and Ganguly and Hagerty, *Fearful Symmetry,* 73–75. The author, then in the rank of major and posted in General Headquarters, remembers how a directive of imminence of war had put the entire Pakistani Army on alert and that mobilizations for war had commenced.

67. Exercise Saf-e-Shikan south of Sutlej placed Army Reserve South (ARS) in locations and Exercise Flying horse in the Jhelum-Chenab corridor region. Meanwhile, the PAF conducted exercise Highmark. Ganguly and Hagerty, *Fearful Symmetry,* 74.

68. Ravi Rikeye, *The War That Never Was: The Story of India's Strategic Failures* (New Delhi: Chanakya, 1982), 2.

69. Wirsing, *Pakistan's Security under Zia,* 178.

70. See Sagan and Waltz, *Spread of Nuclear Weapons,* 95.

71. See Ganguly and Hagerty, *Fearful Symmetry,* 72.

72. Ibid. General Sunderji, after his retirement, participated in several Track-II initiatives with retired Pakistani officials and always maintained this position. Brigadier (ret.) Gurmeet Kanwal reiterated the same view to the author in private discussions, in Sofia, Bulgaria, July 28, 2011.

73. General K. M. Arif, interview by author, Rawalpindi, June 20, 2005.

74. General (ret.) Mirza Aslam Beg, interview by author, Rawalpindi, September 1, 2005. In General Beg's view, "[We] foolishly deployed. And this is where the reaction started . . . . India halted its exercise to cover the Ravi-Chenab and Ravi-Beas areas and then continued with the exercise." General Beg, however, maintains that during the same crisis period, a joint India-Israel preventive strike threat existed.

75. Ganguly and Hagerty, *Fearful Symmetry,* 74.

76. There are many claimants for the cause of de-escalation. Some attribute it to President Zia's cricket diplomacy in March; others attribute it to the two prime ministers' meeting in Bangalore for the South Asian Association for Regional Cooperation (SAARC) summit that had already diffused the crisis. The Indian and Pakistani army chiefs do not think there were any plans to carry out maneuvers, and there is no way to verify if there were. Some attribute the de-escalation to the nascent nuclear capability. Whatever the case, Brasstacks left perceptions of threat in its wake.

77. Manoj Joshi, "Warrior as Scholar," *India Today*, February 22, 1999. General Sunderji passed away on February 8, 1999, after a prolonged illness of over a year.

78. Ibid.

79. Ibid.

80. Ron Tempest, "War Talk Evaporates on First Pitch: Zia's Cricket Diplomacy Gets High Score in India," *Los Angles Times,* February 23, 1987, http://articles.latimes.com/print/1987–02–23/news/mn-3286_1_cricket-fans (accessed October 13, 2011).

In November 1986, when the crises began, India was hosting a summit of the South Asian Association for Regional Cooperation (SAARC) at Bangalore. The Indian and Pakistani prime ministers met on the sidelines, and the latter received assurances that the military exercise would be scaled down to alleviate Pakistani concerns. When that did not happen, Pakistan countermobilized in December 1986, which led to the crises. In January, as result of telephone exchanges, diplomacy between the two foreign secretaries was opened to deactivate the crises, taking place between January 31 and February 4, 1987, after which the troops began to withdraw. Abdul Sattar, *Pakistan's Foreign Policy 1947–2005: A Concise History* (New York: Oxford University Press, 2007), 194–95.

81. Senior Pakistani officials at the time were unanimous in describing A. Q. Khan as egotistic, and no amount of glory was sufficient for him. Ambassador Sahabzada Yaqub-Khan, interview by author, Islamabad, June 18, 2005; General K. M. Arif, interview by author, Rawalpindi, June 20, 2005; and Syed Refaqat Ali, interview by author, Islamabad, June 19, 2006. See also Arif, *Estranged Neighbors.*

82. Many Western authors assert that the A. Q. Khan interview was deliberate nuclear signaling. See Ganguly and Hagerty, *Fearful Symmetry*, 76–77.

83. The timing of the interview in relation to the India-Pak Crises and its publication a month later led to many speculations. The Indian lobby claims the interview was officially designed to convey nuclear threat to Indian authorities, knowing well that Kuldip Nayyar would do so. There is evidence that Mr. Nayar conveyed the message that same evening at a dinner at the residence of the Indian high commissioner, Mr. S. K. Singh. The interview was actually published on March 1, 1987, in the United Kingdom. By that time the military crises had all but subsided, and troop withdrawal began within the next month. The timing of the publication led Pakistani nationalists to believe this to be another conspiracy to derail U.S. military and economic aid to Pakistan. The pub-

lication was timed to coincide with the U.S. congressional hearing that was to deliberate the $4.2 billion aid package to Pakistan.

84. At the time of the interview (January 28), it made no sense whatsoever to give a nuclear signal to India. On January 27, Prime Minister Rajiv Gandhi and Junejo had discussed ways to defuse the crisis, and the Pakistani foreign secretary had arrived on January 31, which led to five days of successful talks with an agreement on February 4, 1987. Beginning on February 11, troops began a phased withdrawal. Mr. Abdul Sattar, interview by author, Islamabad, June 20, 2006. See also Sattar, *Pakistan's Foreign Policy 1947–2005*, 194–95; Ganguly and Hagerty, *Fearful Symmetry*, 75–76.

85. Ambassador Sahabzada Yaqub-Khan, interview by author, Islamabad, June 18, 2006; General K. M. Arif, interview by author, Rawalpindi, June 20, 2005; and Syed Refaqat Ali, interview by author, Islamabad, June 19, 2006.

86. General (ret.) K. M. Arif, interview by author, Rawalpindi, June 20, 2005; Lieutenant-General (ret.) Syed Refaqat Ali, interview by author, June 19, 2006. Both were former chiefs of staff with President Zia-ul Haq in the 1980s.

87. Ambassador Sahabzada Yaqub-Khan, interview by author, Islamabad, June 18, 2006; General K. M. Arif, interview by author, Rawalpindi, June 20, 2005; and Syed Refaqat Ali, interview by author, Islamabad, June 19, 2006.

88. Arif, *Estranged Neighbors*, 289.

89. Syed Refaqat Ali, interview by author, December 19, 2005. As General K. M. Arif put it, "Zia had a firm talk with A. Q. Khan," Arif, *Estranged Neighbors*, 289.

90. Syed Refaqat Ali, interview by author, Islamabad, June 19, 2006.

91. Arif, *Estranged Neighbors*, 289.

92. In May 1988, Zia-ul-Haq had dismissed the civil government of Prime Minister Muhammad Khan Junejo, as well as the Parliament. New elections were scheduled for November. Prime Minister Junejo had challenged his dismissal in the Supreme Court. Although Junejo won the case after Zia's death, the Supreme Court, on the advice of Army Chief Mirza Aslam Beg, decided not to restore the government back to power and instead held new elections in November.

93. General Mirza Aslam Beg, interview by author, Islamabad, September 1, 2005; Syed Refaqat, interview by author, Islamabad, June 19, 2005.

94. Author's interviews with Sahabzada Yaqub-Khan, Syed Refaqat Ali, Tanvir Ahmad Khan, and Mirza Aslam Beg.

95. Nawaz, *Crossed Swords*, 418–29. Beg was conscious not to repeat the misunderstanding of Brasstacks, so he moved the axis of the exercise to the south and away from the Indian border.

96. Ganguly and Hagerty, *Fearful Symmetry*, 88–89.

97. Ibid., 93.

98. Ibid., 94–95.

99. Michael Krepon and Mishi Faruqee, eds., *Conflict Prevention and Confidence*

Building Measures in South Asia: The 1990 Crisis, occasional paper 17, Henry Stimson Center, Washington, DC, 1994, 5.

100. In an open letter to former Prime Minister Rajiv Gandhi, Governor Jagmohan cited sixteen hundred violent incidents, including 351 bomb blasts in eleven months in 1989. In his words, "[T]hen between January 1 and January 19, 1990, there were as many as 319 violent acts—21 armed attacks, 114 bomb blasts, 112 arsons, and 72 incidents of mob violence." For the open letter, see http://www.kashmir-information.com/jagmohan/jagmohan2rajiv.html.

101. General Mirza Aslam Beg, interview by author, Rawalpindi, September 1, 2005.

102. Ibid.

103. Ibid.

104. Feroz Hassan Khan, "The Independence-Dependence Paradox: Stability Dilemmas in South Asia," *Arms Control Today* 33, 8 (October 2003), 15–19.

105. General Mirza Aslam Beg, interview by author, Rawalpindi, September 1, 2005.

106. Ibid.

107. Sahabzada Yaqub-Khan, interview by author, Islamabad, June 20, 2006.

108. Sahabzada Yaqub-Khan shared with the author a copy of the poetry that Yaqub-Khan had recited in his exchange of poetic anecdotes with his Indian counterpart, Mr. I. K. Gujral. Khan read verses from an Urdu translation of a Persian poem from *Payam-i-Mashriq* (*Message from the East*) written by the famous poet Dr. Mohammad Iqbal. Another great poet of the subcontinent, Faiz Ahmad Faiz, translated the famous poem. The use of the poetry was intended to send a message that neither side wanted conflict; in competition both are "picking-up sea shells, but neither finds the beautiful pearl." Neither desires the "distress of the hot-blood," yet "we fail to kindle the small candles to light the common heritage and hope for our people."

109. Tanvir Khan, interview by author, Islamabad, June 19, 2006.

110. Samar Mubarakmand, interview by author, Islamabad, June 14, 2010.

Chapter 12

1. Dennis Kux, *The United States and Pakistan, 1947–2000: Disenchanted Allies* (Washington, DC: Woodrow Wilson Center Press, 2001), 309–10.

2. Ibid.

3. "Rocket" is a common term in modern military terminology that refers to an unguided weapon, which is a self-propelled cylinder using liquid or solid fuel. A missile, in the military context, is an unmanned rocket with a guidance system that adjusts its flight path to the target after launch. Military missiles fall into two major categories: ballistic and cruise. The main difference between the two is that ballistic missiles leave the earth's atmosphere during flight, while cruise missiles do not. Ballistic missiles have an initial powered boost phase followed by supersonic free flight along a high, arching trajectory that terminates at the objective. Guidance occurs during the boost phase and,

in more advanced systems, during the re-entry and terminal phases. Cruise missiles are automatically guided, self-propelled, air-breathing vehicles that sustain flight through the use of aerodynamic lift. Missiles can also be categorized by virtue of their points of launch and impact, type of propulsive system, and guidance system. For definitions, see Brigadier Feroz Hassan Khan with Gaurav Rajan and Michael Vannoni, *A Missile Stability Regime for South Asia*, Cooperative Monitoring Center, occasional paper 35 (Albuquerque, NM: Sandia National Laboratories, 2004).

4. The missile program was launched by India's Defence Research and Development Organisation (DRDO), which was composed of a basket of five missiles: *Prithvi* and *Agni* were strategic delivery systems; *Trishul* (short range) and *Akash* (medium range) were air defense surface-to-air missiles (SAMs); and finally *Nag,* which was an antitank guided missile (ATGM). See also Gurmeet Kanwal, "Bridging the Gap," *Geopolitics* 1, 11 (June 11, 2010), http://www.ezinemart.com/Geopolitics/01062010/Home.aspx (accessed July 1, 2010).

5. Some U.S. experts in discussion with the author shared their belief that reverse engineering is a fallacy and that one cannot make an exact replica. For the Indian missile program and Soviet assistance, see Rodney Jones, Mark McDonough, Toby Dalton, and Gregory Koblentz, *Tracking Nuclear Proliferation: A Guide in Maps and Charts* (Washington, DC: Carnegie Endowment for Peace, 1998), 127–29.

6. General Aslam Beg was widely respected for his role as Chief of General Staff in modernizing the army in the 1980s. Like General Sunderji in India, Beg was amenable to new organizational and operational changes that met the demands of the times. In August 1988, after Zia's death, he became the army chief, which gave him full authority to execute his vision of modernizing the army.

7. Wisconsin Project on Nuclear Arms Control, "Pakistan Derives Its First *Hatf* Missiles from Foreign Space Rockets," *Risk Report* 1, 8 (October 1995), 4, http://www.wisconsinproject.org/countries/pakistan/hatf.html (accessed October 23, 2011).

8. Ibid.

9. Naeem Salik, "Missile Issues in South Asia," *Nonproliferation Review* 19, 2 (Summer 2002), 50–51.

10. The Arabic name *Hatf* means "lance" or "spear." The entire missile series is named *Hatf,* but each category of missile had individual nicknames. Most of these are named after major Muslim kings who defeated Hindu armies at various points in history and established dynasties in India. *Shaheen* means "eagle," a poetic symbol of the great philosopher Muhammad Iqbal, who founded the ideology of Pakistan.

11. Nuclear Threat Initiative (NTI), Country Profiles, Pakistan Profile, Missile Overview, http://www.nti.org/e_research/profiles/Pakistan/Missile/index.html (accessed October 23, 2011).

12. Khan, Rajan, and Vannoni, *A Missile Stability Regime for South Asia*, 17.

13. Wisconsin Project, "Pakistan Derives Its First Hatf Missiles," 5.

14. Ibid.

15. Author's personal knowledge and recollection. The author served in CD Directorate, GHQ, from November 1993 until December 1998; the organization has since merged into the newly formed Strategic Plans Division (SPD).

16. The Coordinating Committee for Multilateral Export Controls (COCOM) was created in 1949 for the purpose of preventing Western companies and countries from selling strategic goods and services to the Eastern bloc countries, which included China. After the Cold War, COCOM's relevancy diminished as it removed restrictions for Eastern Europe and morphed into another export control cartel named "The Wassenaar Arrangement on Export Controls for Conventional Arms and Dual-Use Goods and Technologies," established in 1995. See Robert Rudney and T. J. Anthony, "Beyond COCOM: A Comparative Study of Five National Export Control Systems and Their Implications for a Multilateral Nonproliferation Regime," *Comparative Strategy* 15 (January/March 1996), 41–57. See also Lynn E. Davis, *The Wassenaar Arrangement* (Washington, DC: U.S. State Department, 1996), www.acda.gov/wmeat95/davis95.htm (accessed October 23, 2011); and Richard T. Cupitt and Suzette R. Grillot, "COCOM Is Dead, Long Live CO-COM: Persistence and Change in Multilateral Security Institutions," *British Journal of Political Science* 27 (July 1997), 361–89.

17. R. Jeffrey Smith, "China Said to Sell Arms to Pakistan; M-11 Missile Shipment May Break Vow to U.S.," *Washington Post*, December 4, 1992, A10; Jim Mann, "China Said to Sell Pakistan Dangerous New Missiles," *Los Angeles Times*, December 4, 1992, 1.

18. Any missile with this range/payload tradeoff is held as a Category I system under the MTCR.

19. Duncan Lennox, ed., "CSS-7 (DF-11/M-11)—People's Republic of China: Offensive Weapons," *Jane's Strategic Weapon Systems* 25 (Coulsdon: September 1997), 25. See also http://www.fas.org/nuke/guide/china/theater/df-11.htm.

20. Ibid.

21. R. Jeffrey Smith and David B. Ottaway, "Spy Photos Suggest China Missile Trade; Pressure for Sanctions Builds over Evidence That Pakistan Has M-11s," *Washington Post*, July 3, 1995, A01 (in Lexis-Nexis Academic Universe, www.lexis-nexis.com).

22. According to the NTI, Chinese technology transfers might have included solid-fuel propellants, manufacture of airframes, re-entry thermal protection materials, post-boost vehicles, guidance and control, missile computers, integration of warheads, and the manufacture of transporter-erector launchers (TELs) for the missiles. See NTI, "Pakistan Profile, Missile Overview, Nuclear Threat Initiative," http://www.nti.org/e_research/profiles/Pakistan/Missile/index.html (accessed July 1, 2010).

23. Samar Mubarakmand, interview by author, Islamabad, June 14, 2010.

24. Ibid.

25. *Ghaznavi* is named after Mahmoud Ghaznavi, the Afghan ruler who invaded India in the tenth century and is famous for the destruction of the Hindu temple of Somnath.

26. It may be possible to achieve Circular Error Probability (CEP) of two to three hundred meters, but that would require terminal guidance and control systems for the re-entry vehicle (RV). A ninety-meter CEP is possible only if one uses a homing system on the missile's RV. Typical missiles in regional countries have CEPs of between three hundred and a thousand meters. Advances in guidance technology, including global positioning systems (GPS), and advances in guidance technology will significantly increase accuracy. See Khan, Rajan, and Vannoni, *A Missile Stability Regime,* 29.

27. "President Says Pakistan Nuclear Programme 'Here to Stay,'" BBC Monitoring International Reports, February 21, 2004, Lexis-Nexis Academic Universe, www.lexis-nexis.com; and B. Muralidhar Reddy, "We Will Never Roll Back N-Programme: Musharraf," *The Hindu*, February 22, 2004, Lexis-Nexis Academic Universe, www.lexis-nexis.com.

28. "Pakistan Test-Fires New Version of Nuclear Capable Missile," BBC Monitoring South Asia, December 9, 2006, and "Army Gets Ghaznavi Missiles," *The Nation*, April 26, 2007, http://nation.com.pk.

29. "Pakistan PM, Army Chief Witness 290-km Range Ballistic Missile Launch," BBC Monitoring South Asia, February 13, 2008.

30. Bill Gertz, "China Can't Say No to Arms Buyers," *Washington Times*, May 28, 1991, A1, Lexis-Nexis Academic Universe, www.lexis-nexis.com.

31. The DF-15/M-9 (NATO designation CSS-6).

32. "Government Confirms Test-Firing of New Missile," *Agence France Presse,* July 3, 1997, in FBIS Document FTS19970703000413.

33. Joseph Cirincione, Jon B. Wofsthal, and Miriam Rajkumar, *Deadly Arsenals* (Washington, DC: Carnegie Endowment for International Peace, 2005), 214.

34. Western experts surmise from the photographs of the missile displayed during the national parade, flight tests, and disclosed range/payload data that it closely matches the parameters of the Chinese M9. See NTI, Pakistan Profile, Missile Overview, Nuclear Threat Initiative, http://www.nti.org/e_research/profiles/Pakistan/Missile/index.html (accessed July 1, 2010).

35. "After Ghauri, Shaheen Shines in Pakistan," *The Statesman*, November 3, 2006.

36. Samar Mubarakmand, interview with Hamid Mir, Geo TV, March 2004.

37. "Strategic Force Gets Shaheen-1 Missile," *Japan Economic Newswire*, March 6, 2003, International News, Lexis-Nexis Academic Universe, www.lexis-nexis.com.

38. "More on Pakistan Test-Fires Nuclear-Capable Missile," BBC Monitoring South Asia, January 25, 2008.

39. "Shaheen-II/Hatf-6/Ghaznavi: Pakistan Missile Special Weapons Delivery Systems," Federation of American Scientists, December 2003, www.fas.org.

40. David E. Sanger and Eric Schmitt, "Reports Say China Is Aiding Pakistan on Missile Project," *New York Times,* July 2, 2000; "Unclassified Report to Congress on the Acquisition of Technology Relating to Weapons of Mass Destruction and Advanced Conventional Munitions," Central Intelligence Agency, January 1–June 30, 2001, www. cia.gov.

41. "Pakistan Scientist Says Missile Test Reassures Nation over Nuclear Programme," BBC Monitoring International Reports, March 10, 2004.

42. NTI, Pakistan Missile Overview.

43. The author is grateful to U.S. missile scientist Michael Elleman for this insight. (Personal discussion in Washington, DC, October 2010.)

44. NTI, Pakistan Missile Overview.

45. In the early 1990s the United States applied intense pressure on China over its missile supplies to developing countries in the Middle East and South Asia. And China was negotiating with the U.S. to join supplier cartels such as Nuclear Suppliers Group (NSG) and MTCR.

46. This story is largely one of hedging. Khan began procuring parts for the *Ghauri* in the early 1990s, just as the production lines for the *Ghaznavi* and *Shaheen* missiles were being established at PMO. It follows that Pakistani authorities must have encouraged Kahn to acquire the *Ghauri* as a hedge against disappointment. Besides, *Ghauri*'s procurement represented a long-range capability in a shorter time frame and with fewer technical risks. Given the test dates, it is obvious that the technical procurement of *Ghauri* was faster than the production line setup, which took longer. This explains why *Shaheen* was tested six years later than *Ghauri*.

47. The *Nodong* deal was likely finalized during the visit of the former vice chairman of the National Defense Commission, Marshal Ch'oe Gwang, to Islamabad in December 1995. See NTI, Pakistan Missile Overview.

48. Ghauri was an Afghan king who ousted the Ghaznavi Empire in India in the twelfth century.

49. NTI, Pakistan Missile Overview.

50. Ibid.

51. U.S. missile expert, personal communication with author, 2006.

52. NTI, Pakistan Missile Overview.

53. Ibid.

54. The author was personally told by U.S. and Japanese officials about the presence and ongoing cooperation during several arms control bilateral negotiations. Japan in particular was concerned about the implications of a Pakistani role in *Taepodong* tests. This will be analyzed in subsequent chapters.

55. Retired officials and missile experts, personal discussions with author, Pakistan and United States.

56. "Ghauri-III Engine Said Successfully Tested," *Ausaf* (Islamabad), June 24, 1999,

in FBIS Document FTS19990624000013, June 24, 1999; and "Pakistan Reportedly Begins Preparations for Testing Ghauri-3 Missile," BBC Monitoring International Reports, April 21, 2002, in Lexis-Nexis Academic Universe, April 21, 2002, www.lexis-nexis.com.

57. NTI, Pakistan Missile Overview. Author's personal discussions with U.S. missile experts.

58. Background briefing to the author, Islamabad, June 14, 2007.

59. *Nodong* was also transferred to Iran, where it was modified as *Shahab*. The two-meter extension is similar to what Iran did when it modified the *Shahab* nose cone and reduced the warhead mass. For a photograph of the *Ghauri II*, see http://www.b14643.de/Spacerockets_1/Diverse/Nodong/Dong.htm (accessed June 2010).

60. Background briefing to the author, Islamabad, June 14, 2007.

61. "Bhutto Says Pak Paid N Korea for Missile Tech," *Economic Times*, February 11, 2004. See also NTI, Pakistan Missile Overview.

62. President Pervez Musharraf, personal communication with author, June 18, 2006; and background briefings, Rawalpindi, June 14, 2007.

63. Background briefings with author, December 15, 2007.

64. It is unclear if the sanctions were based on past transactions. A U.S. State Department spokesperson explained that missile proliferation sanctions were imposed on North Korea for "its involvement in the transfer of Missile Technology Control Regime Category 1 items" to a "Category 1 missile program in a non–Missile Technology Control Regime country." See "State Department Regular Briefing," *Federal News Service*, March 31, 2003, Lexis-Nexis Academic Universe, www.lexis-nexis.com. See also NTI, Pakistan Missile Overview.

65. Neelam Mathews, "Pakistan Tests Nuclear-Capable Subsonic Cruise Missile," *Aerospace Daily and Defense Report*, July 27, 2007.

66. The author was Director Arms Control and Disarmament Affairs in Combat Development Directorate, General Headquarters, at the time and has personal knowledge and recollection of these events.

67. General (ret.) Mirza Aslam Beg, interview by author, Rawalpindi, September 1, 2005.

68. S. M. Hali, "Ra'ad Roars," *The Nation*, August 29, 2007. See also Doug Richardson, "Pakistan Tests Hatf 8 Air-Launched Cruise Missile," *Jane's Missiles & Rockets*, September 1, 2007, and "Pakistan Military Test-Fires Nuclear Capable Cruise Missile," *International Herald Tribune*, August 25, 2007, http://www.iht.com/articles/ap/2007/08/25/asia/AS-GEN-Pakistan-Missile-Test.php.

69. Richardson, "Pakistan Tests Hatf 8 Air-Launched Cruise Missile."

70. "Ra'ad (Hatf-8) (Pakistan), Air-to-surface missiles—Stand-off and cruise," Jane's Air-Launched Weapons, Air-to-surface missiles—Stand-off and cruise, August 12, 2011, http://articles.janes.com/articles/Janes-Air-Launched-Weapons/Ra-ad-Hatf-8-Pakistan.html (accessed October 25, 2011).

71. Rodney Jones, "Pakistan's Nuclear Poker Bet," *Foreign Policy* 27 (May, 2011).

72. See Rodney Jones, "Pakistan's Answer to Cold Start?" *Friday Times* (Lahore), May 13–19, 2011, 7–8.

73. Ibid., 8.

74. Presentation made on tactical nuclear weapons in a conference on Strategic Stability in Phuket, Thailand, September 20, 2011. Author's name and title withheld due to nonattribution.

75. Feroz Hassan Khan, "Minimum Deterrence: Pakistan's Dilemma," in *RUSI Journal* 156, 5 (October/November 2011), 48.

Chapter 13

1. Dennis Kux, *The United States and Pakistan, 1947–2000: Disenchanted Allies* (Washington, DC: Woodrow Wilson Center Press, 2001), 257–59; Abdul Sattar, *Pakistan's Foreign Policy 1947–2005: A Concise History* (New York: Oxford University Press, 2007), 14–10.

2. Sahabzada Yaqub-Khan, interview by author, Islamabad, June 2005. See also Kux, *The United States and Pakistan*, 257–59.

3. Kux, *The United States and Pakistan*, 299.

4. Ibid.

5. General Mirza Aslam Beg, interview by author, Islamabad, September 1, 2005. Beg described this so-called national command authority as comprising five people: President Ghulam Ishaq Khan, Prime Minister Benazir Bhutto, Chief of the Army Staff General Mirza Aslam Beg, PAEC Chairman Munir Ahmad Khan, and director of the KRL Abdul Qadeer Khan.

6. General Mirza Aslam Beg, interview by author, Islamabad, September 1, 2005.

7. Ibid. When the author pressed General Beg to explain the logic by which the NCA determined the "sufficiency of fissile stocks" in 1989, he insisted, "Stockpiling is dangerous and the study of the intrinsics of WMD show, there comes a point of diminishing returns." He did not elaborate whether he thought that the "point of diminishing return" was already reached in 1989. For a critique of General Aslam Beg's assertion, see Naeem Salik, *The Genesis of South Asian Nuclear Deterrence: Pakistan's Perspectives* (Oxford: Oxford University Press, 2009), 126.

8. Aslam Beg, interview by author, Islamabad, September 1, 2005. Beg refused to admit that nuclear restraint had anything to do with his visit to the United States in the spring of 1989 or the impending visit of Prime Minister Bhutto in the summer of 1989. In fact, General Beg denies that there was any "understanding" with the United States on nuclear issues, something Benazir Bhutto admitted to Dennis Kux in her interview with him. See Kux, *The United States and Pakistan*, 299–300.

9. Kux, *The United States and Pakistan*, 300.

10. Ibid., 299–300.

11.   Feroz Hassan Khan, "Nuclear Proliferation Motivations: Lessons from Pakistan," in Peter R. Lavoy, ed., *Nuclear Weapons Proliferation in the Next Decade* (New York: Routledge, 2007), 77.

12.   Cited in Ariel Levite, "Never Say Never Again: Nuclear Reversal Revisited," *International Security* 27 (2003), 81.

13.   The author has been unable to confirm from any other sources whether or not Ms. Bhutto made any commitment to the CIA or to U.S. officials to this effect. See also Khan, "Nuclear Proliferation Motivations," 84.

14.   Dennis Kux, *The United States and Pakistan.*

15.   Sartaj Aziz, *Between Dreams and Realities: Some Milestones in Pakistan's History* (New York: Oxford University Press, 2009), 126–27.

16.   Kux, *The United States and Pakistan,* 325.

17.   Ishfaq Ahmad, interview by author, Islamabad, December 19, 2005.

18.   Since the day he left office in July 1993, President GIK never spoke a word or came back to public life. He declined the author's request for an interview in 2005, citing heath reasons. He passed away in 2006. His family had no documents.

19.   Kux, *The United States and Pakistan,* 327.

20.   Author's personal recollection; Shuja Nawaz, *Crossed Swords: Pakistan, Its Army and the Wars Within* (New York: Oxford University Press, 2008), 476.

21.   The author was posted to the CD Directorate in November 1993 and assigned the responsibility to coordinate nuclear matters and to head the "research cell," also referred to as the "think tank," a cover name established in the library of the CD Directorate. The author worked closely with the Military Operations Directorate and the Foreign Office, diplomats in Geneva and scientific organizations including PAEC and KRL.

22.   Stephen P. Cohen, *The Pakistan Army* (Oxford: Oxford University Press, 1998), 175.

23.   George Perkovich, *India's Nuclear Bomb: The Impact on Global Proliferation* (New Delhi: Oxford University Press, 2002), 365–66.

24.   In September 1995, Pakistan was able to negotiate successfully with the U.S. Senate a proposed bill called the Brown Amendment, which allowed the release of military equipment to Pakistan.

25.   The Brown Amendment to the Nuclear Non-Proliferation Act was passed after a successful visit of Prime Minister Benazir Bhutto to Washington, DC. Approximately $368 million worth of spare parts and military supplies were finally released that had been withheld under the Pressler sanctions, eroding Pakistan's conventional military capability. See Nawaz, *Crossed Swords,* 478.

26.   International Institute for Strategic Studies (IISS), *Nuclear Black Markets: Pakistan, A. Q. Khan and the Rise of Proliferation Networks, a Net Assessment,* IISS strategic dossier (London: International Institute for Strategic Studies, 2007), 26–27.

27. Ibid., 379–80.

28. The author was present part-time in Geneva to assist Ambassador Munir Akram on several disarmament issues. During the most critical aspects of the CTBT negotiations, Muhammad Afzal, PAEC, and Malik Azhar Ellahi, Foreign Service, assisted Ambassador Akram. The CTBT rolling text was regularly examined in the Foreign Office and GHQ, where critical decisions were made in consultation with the PAEC and KRL. ACDA was the central directorate coordinating CTBT analysis.

29. General Jehangir Karamat was the natural successor to become army chief when General Abdul Waheed declined Bhutto's offer of extension. Karamat was the most qualified and experienced, but in Pakistan there is always a drama associated with a change of command. See Nawaz, *Crossed Swords*, 81–82.

30. Ibid., 477–78.

31. Strobe Talbott, *Engaging India: Diplomacy, Democracy, and the Bomb* (Washington, DC: Brookings Institution Press, 2004), 63. See also Aziz, *Between Dreams and Realities*, 194.

32. Ishfaq Ahmad, interview by author, Islamabad, December 20, 2005; and Brigadier Muhammad Anwar, interview by author, Rawalpindi, April 1, 2009.

33. Samar Mubarakmand, interview by author, Islamabad, June 14, 2010. Mubarakmand explained to the author that reshaping was necessary in order to ensure that each curve of the S collapsed and sealed the explosion.

34. Pakistan's ambassador to the conference in Geneva, Munir Akram, was directly in touch with the army chief, DGCD, and the foreign secretary on this matter. Director of the ACDA (the author), along with the director general of disarmament in the Foreign Office, was present in Geneva during this development.

35. At the Conference of Disarmament in Geneva, although the CTBT was the main event, negotiations on other treaties were ongoing. Significant deliberations took place on the Fissile Material Cutoff Treaty, Convention on Certain Conventional Weapons (Protocol IV on Restrictions on Landmines), and Prevention of Arms Race in Outer Space (PAROS).

36. Nausheen Wasti, "A Chronological Survey of the CTBT: 1996–2000," in Moonis Ahmar, ed., *The CTBT Controversy: Different Perceptions in South Asia* (Karachi: Department of International Relations, University of Karachi, 2000), 140.

37. Nawaz, *Crossed Swords*, 486.

38. Presidential powers to sack the political government were obtained by General Zia-ul-Haq in 1985 under the 8th Amendment to the 1973 Constitution. Nawaz Sharif made the office of the president merely a ceremonial one, much as in India.

39. The political gamesmanship between the president, prime minister, and chief justice of the Supreme Court came to a head in the autumn of 1997. In a series of bizarre political intrigues in late 1997, a politically inspired move by the president and the Supreme Court to oust the prime minister through contempt of court was countered by

an internal judicial revolt—allegedly on the bidding of the prime minister—against the legitimacy of the Supreme Court chief justice. The controversy turned ugly when political supporters of the prime minister interrupted the court hearing with hooliganism, forcing the judges to seek protection in their chambers. The chief justice asked the army to provide protection to the chief justice. This could have been construed as a positive signal for the army to move and remove the prime minister, which would have obviously received support of the Supreme Court.

40. The first manifestation of the new world order was visible in the 1991 Gulf War, in which Pakistani Army brigades were part of the coalition forces.

41. The Gujral doctrine was announced in a speech at Chatham House, London, in September 1996 and again in mid-January in Colombo, Sri Lanka. Perkovich, *India's Nuclear Bomb*, 390–91. See also Feroz Hassan Khan, "Security Impediments to Regionalism in South Asia," in Rafiq Dossani, Daniel C. Sneider, and Virkam Sood, eds., *Does South Asia Exist?: Prospects of Regional Integration* (Washington, DC: Brookings Institution, 2010), 228.

42. R. Jeffery Smith, "India Moves Missiles near Pakistani Border," *Washington Post*, June 3, 1997, A15, http://www.washingtonpost.com/wp-srv/inatl/longterm/southasia/stories/missile060397.htm (accessed October 30, 2011).

43. The author recalls that the analysis in ACDA Directorate, GHQ on *Prithvi* development recommended that Pakistan take reciprocal actions. The idea was to trigger a type of Cuban Missile Crisis in the region.

44. Perkovich, *India's Nuclear Bomb*, 396–97.

45. As of June 1997, the Director ACDA, CD Directorate, GHQ, became an integral part of the bilateral peace, security, and CBM dialogue with the Ministry of Foreign Affairs. This working group would eventually draft the Lahore Memorandum of Understanding in February 1999.

46. Perkovich, *India's Nuclear Bomb*, 406–7.

Chapter 14

1. Thomas Reed and Danny Stillman, *The Nuclear Express: A Political History of the Bomb and Its Proliferation* (Minneapolis, MN: Zenith Press, 2009), 241.

2. George Perkovich, *India's Nuclear Bomb* (Berkeley: University of California Press, 1999), 416; and Reed and Stillman, *The Nuclear Express*, 241–43. Assessments of Indian claims concerning thermonuclear tests were disputed by outside sources.

3. Perkovich, *India's Nuclear Bomb*, 417.

4. Pakistani-administered Kashmir is referred to as *Azad Kashmir*, meaning "Independent Kashmir." See Sartaj Aziz, *Between Dreams and Realities: Some Milestones in Pakistan's History* (New York: Oxford University Press, 2009), 193–94.

5. Sunil Khilnani, *The Idea of India* (London: Farrar, Straus and Giroux, 1999), 1. In

private conversations with the author, Indian scholars clarified that the Hindu devotees were eventually stopped from collecting radioactive sands.

6. Samar Mubarakmand, "A Science Odyssey: Pakistan's Nuclear Emergence," speech to the Khwarzimic Science Society, Centre of Excellence in Solid State Physics, Punjab University, Lahore, November 30, 1998.

7. The author was present in the DGCD's office when Samar Mubarakmand gave his assessment over the telephone to Major General Zulfiqar Khan, which was promptly passed to Army Chief General Karamat. The international assessments that came later were close to Pakistan's initial assessments.

8. Author's personal recollections of the events. Director of Military Operations at the time, Lieutenant-General (ret.) Shahid Aziz, was present during the author's interview with Brigadier Muhammad Anwar, director of the SDW, who said that precautionary steps were taken in the fear that the test preparations would be detected. George Perkovich confirms that U.S. intelligence had more inside information on Pakistan's nuclear program than on India's. See Perkovich, *India's Nuclear Bomb,* 418.

9. General Jahangir Karamat, interview by author, Washington, DC, September 1, 2010. Foreign Secretary Shamshad Ahmad was excited and eager to discuss the issue over the phone from Central Asia, making several references to a "green signal." General Karamat urged caution not to mention sensitive subjects over the phone. The army chief told the foreign secretary to convey to the prime minister that everything was under control and that he would provide a comprehensive brief upon the return home of the prime minister.

10. General Jehangir Karamat, interview by author, Washington, DC, September 1, 2010. This was yet another example of Prime Minister Sharif's decision-making style. His "kitchen cabinet" decisions would come under much criticism in years to come.

11. In a thermonuclear test the fission itself is the primary, which triggers the secondary to cause the explosion.

12. The author visited the Comprehensive Test Ban Treaty Organization (CTBTO) in Vienna a year later, and the data recorded there were not much different. See also Reed and Stillman, *The Nuclear Express,* 242.

13. Indeed, within a decade of the tests, history proved that India had achieved all four of the objectives that the Pakistani DCC meeting had hypothesized. The United States not only accepted India as a de facto nuclear power but, in addition, India was favored with an exceptional nuclear deal in 2005; during his visit to India in November 2010, President Barak Obama offered U.S. support to India's bid for permanent membership in the UN Security Council (UNSC). The Pakistanis note that in deference to India's political status, the international community has consistently turned a blind eye to India's aggressive posturing on Kashmir and human rights violations.

14. The PPP, led by Benazir, introduced a resolution in the Senate and publicly de-

manded a response. Eleven political parties demanded immediate testing. See Aziz, *Between Dreams and Realities*, 193.

15. General Karamat told the author he was surprised that Finance Secretary Chaudhry Moin Afzal was not invited for the DCC meeting, while Foreign Secretary Shamshad Ahmad was. The author recalls that from the moment India conducted its test, GHQ was constantly in touch with the Finance, Defense, and Foreign ministries to assess the complete picture of the military, diplomatic, and financial position of the country. General Jehangir Karamat was personally talking to all stakeholders to keep them informed.

16. Sartaj Aziz, discussions with the author, Dubai, December 11, 2009. See also Aziz, *Between Dreams and Realities*, 192. There are other publications based on accounts of other attendees at the DCC meetings who alleged that the finance minister opposed the test by presenting a very grim economic picture and consequences. See, for example, Naeem Salik, *The Genesis of South Asian Deterrence* (New York: Oxford University Press, 2009), 141; and Rai Muhammad Saleh Azam, "When Mountains Move: The Story of Chagai," *Defence Journal* (June 2000), http://www.defencejournal.com/2000/june/chagai.htm (accessed December 24, 2010).

17. Sartaj Aziz, interview by author, Dubai, December 11, 2009.

18. The PAEC had been responsible for conducting the test since the mid-1980s because it had been designing, cold testing, and preparing the tunnels and trigger mechanism.

19. Samar Mubarakmand, interview by author, Islamabad, June 14, 2010; and General Jehangir Karamat, interview by author, September 1, 2010. The PAEC concluded that these were probably experiments resembling cold tests or safety tests.

20. Brigadier (ret.) Muhammad Anwar, interview by author, Islamabad, April 14, 2009. The tunnels at both testing sites (Chagai and Kharan) were ready by May 6, 1998, just days before India conducted its nuclear tests.

21. Samar Mubarakmand, interview by author, Islamabad, June 14, 2010. Dr. Fakhar Hashmi declined several requests for an interview.

22. A. Q. Khan's letter was sent to GHQ. DGCD Major General Zulfiqar Ali Khan was furious. The CD Directorate had to dampen the interlaboratory rivalry and keep up the morale of the scientists, a distraction that was unwarranted and counterproductive.

23. Author's recollection of the events. Also recalled in author's interview with Samar Mubarakmand, Islamabad, June 14, 2007.

24. Aziz, *Between Dreams and Realities*, 193.

25. Salman Bashir is the foreign secretary in Pakistan at the time of this writing and was the key official with whom the author worked closely in numerous negotiations with the United States and India. He and the author worked closely in drafting the Lahore Memorandum of Understanding signed between India and Pakistan in February 1999.

26. Riaz Mohammad Khan later became the foreign secretary from 2005 till 2008. He is the author of the book *Afghanistan and Pakistan: Conflict, Extremism and Resistance to Modernity* (Washington, DC: Woodrow Wilson Center Press, 2011).

27. Perkovich, *India's Nuclear Bomb*, 417; and Aziz, *Between Dreams and Realities*, 191.

28. Perkovich, *India's Nuclear Bomb*, 417.

29. Ibid., 418.

30. Ibid.

31. President Clinton's remarks cited in Strobe Talbott, *Engaging India: Diplomacy, Democracy, and the Bomb* (Washington, DC: Brookings Institution, 2004), 57.

32. Ibid., 58–59; Perkovich, *India's Nuclear Bomb,* 417; and Aziz, *Between Dreams and Realities,* 194.

33. The term "Pakistani establishment" is a euphemism for military, intelligence, bureaucrats, and right-wing journalists with strong nationalist and often hawkish views on national security. These views are often seen as traditionalist, rejecting any opinions different from "established norms"—especially liberal Western views.

34. For details, see Talbott, *Engaging India*, 52–67.

35. See details in memoirs written by Sartaj Aziz, *Between Dreams and Realities,* 91–93.

36. Talbott, *Engaging India*, 105.

37. Ibid.

38. The author was actively involved in many of the meetings with technical and arms control experts in the Foreign Office throughout the summer. Officials told the author that the attitude of U.S. officials was dismissive and at times mocking of Pakistani anxieties concerning security threats from India, especially when there were disagreements over what the United States thought was in Pakistan's best interest. The Pakistani version of the story is that one U.S. official in the negotiations was using dismissive gestures, including rolling eyes and shrugs of the shoulders, which annoyed a Pakistani diplomat, who lost his cool and got up angrily to leave in protest. Several participants intervened and persuaded him to calm down and remain seated. Such gestures were diplomatically unwise and culturally impolite, given Pakistan's traditional hospitality and courtesy to visiting guests. For the Talbott version, see ibid.

39. Strobe Talbott recalled the carrot analogy when a visiting Pakistani army chief, General Abdul Waheed, had declined to accept lifting of economic sanctions and delivery of F-16s in exchange for rolling back the nuclear program by symbolically gesturing the choking of throats with carrots. Ibid., 61.

40. Ibid., 106.

41. Reed and Stillman, *The Nuclear Express,* 252–53.

42. Samar Mubarakmand, interview by author, Islamabad, June 14, 2010.

43. Ibid. Samar Mubarakmand maintained that the CHIC-4 design was not deliverable.

44. Brigadier Muhammad Anwar, interview by author, Islamabad, April 14, 2009. Brigadier Anwar passed away a few months after the interview, which was probably the last time he spoke on the subject.

45. Azam, "When Mountains Move."

46. Javed Mirza, interview by author, Islamabad, June 13, 2006; Brigadier Muhammad Anwar, interview by author, Islamabad, April 14, 2009.

47. Ibid.

48. Ibid.

49. Talbott, *Engaging India*, 70; Aziz, *Between Dreams and Realities*, 194.

50. Saudi intelligence reportedly provided the intelligence tip-off during Israeli Prime Minister Benjamin Netanyahu's official visit to China. His plane, escorted by Israeli fighters, flew over Saudi territory and Central Asia on May 24, 1998, arriving in China on May 25. The radar signature prompted some Saudi intelligence to warn the Pakistani air attache in Riyadh. This began a cascade of alerts along Pakistan's chain of command. The author recalls that the threat was taken very seriously. Lieutenant-General (ret.) Shahid Aziz told the author, "[We] had no choice but to prepare for any eventuality on the principle of 'better safe than sorry.'" Brigadier Muhammad Anwar, interview by author, Islamabad, April 14, 2009. The issue was settled when the U.S. government confirmed with Israel that no such action was underway. Talbott, *Engaging India*, 70–71. See also Sumit Ganguly and Devin Hagerty, *Fearful Symmetry* (New Delhi: Oxford University Press, 2005), 131; and Adrian Levy and Catherine Scott-Clark, *Deception: Pakistan, the United States, and the Secret Trade in Nuclear Weapons* (New York: Walking Publishing Company, 2007), 273.

51. Talbott, *Engaging India*, 70; and Aziz, *Between Dreams and Realities*, 194.

52. Brigadier Muhammad Anwar, interview by author, Islamabad, April 14, 2010.

53. Ibid.

54. Ibid.

55. Talbott, *Engaging India*, 71.

56. Ibid.

57. Mubarakmand, "A Science Odyssey."

58. Shahid-ur-Rehman, *Long Road to Chaghi* (Islamabad: Print Wise Publications, 1999), 14.

59. Ibid., 15.

60. Samar Mubarakmand, interview with Hamid Mir, *Capital Talk*, Geo Television, March 5, 2004.

61. Shahid-ur-Rehman, *Long Road to Chaghi*, 11.

62. Samar Mubarakmand, "Samar Insists PAEC Staff Conducted Blasts," *Business Recorder*, June 3, 1998.

63. Samar Mubarakmand, interview with Hamid Mir, *Capital Talk*, Geo Television, March 5, 2004.

64. Mubarakmand, "A Science Odyssey."

65. Samar Mubarakmand, "Medal Award Ceremony," speech to the Pakistan Nuclear Society, PINSTECH Auditorium, Islamabad, March 20, 1999.

66. Ibid.

67. Ibid.; see also M. A. Chaudhri, "Pakistan's Nuclear History: Separating Myth from Reality," *Defence Journal* 10 (May 2006).

68. Shahid-ur-Rehman, *Long Road to Chaghi*, 14.

69. Azam, "When Mountains Move."

70. Levy and Scott-Clark, *Deception*, 273.

Chapter 15

1. Strobe Talbott, *Engaging India: Diplomacy, Democracy, and the Bomb* (Washington, DC: Brookings Institution, 2004), 71; Adrian Levy and Catherine Scott-Clark, *Deception: Pakistan, the United States, and the Secret Trade in Nuclear Weapons* (New York: Walker Publishing Company, 2007), 275.

2. Some of these symbols were removed only in January 2004, in observance of a visit by Indian Prime Minister Atal Bihari Vajpayee.

3. The author recalls COAS General Karamat's written directive to DGCD in response to a slurring campaign in the media between the PAEC and the KRL in the month following the nuclear tests.

4. Major General Zulfiqar Ali Khan, DGCD, personally conveyed the message to both chairmen and asked them to stop giving statements to the media. The author followed up with the two organizations at all levels and ensured that such leaks stopped.

5. See Dennis Kux, *The United States and Pakistan, 1947–2000: Disenchanted Allies* (Baltimore: Johns Hopkins University Press, 2001), 347; Sartaj Aziz, *Between Dreams and Realities: Some Milestones in Pakistan's History* (New York: Oxford University Press, 2009), 197.

6. For a detailed explanation, see Aziz, *Between Dreams and Realities,* 196–99; 361–63. The FCA scheme was introduced by the Sharif regime in February 1991 to liberalize capital accounts in the hope of raising the level of savings. This scheme yielded the intended results. The FCA increased from $2.1 billion in February 1991 to $11.1 billion by April 1998. However, successive governments spent the money to finance the current account deficit rather than keep it as reserves; as a result the country's foreign exchange reserves were a meager $1.3 billion at the time of the nuclear test.

7. Levy and Scott-Clark, *Deception,* 275.

8. UN Security Council Resolution (S/RES/1172), United Nations, June 1998.

9. Kux, *The United States and Pakistan,* 347.

10. Author's memory, from the contents of President Clinton's letter to Prime Minister Nawaz Sharif, July 17, 1998.

11. Talbott, *Engaging India*, 106.

12. Strobe Talbott accurately described General Jehangir Karamat as a "cool customer" who would politely listen to his interlocutors and respond with gentle firmness in his conversation. Ibid.

13. The author was in close contact with Foreign Secretary Shamshad Ahmad and Director General Salman Bashir in the Pakistan Foreign Office. The interim responses to U.S. minimum deterrence posture were faxed to the Foreign Office and the Ministry of Defense so that all officials were on the same page.

14. Aziz, *Between Dreams and Realities*, 207.

15. Brigadier Muhammad Anwar, interview by author, Islamabad, April 14, 2009.

16. Talbott, *Engaging India*, 85. See also Feroz Hassan Khan, "Reducing the Risk of Nuclear War in South Asia," in Henry Sokolski, ed., *Pakistan's Nuclear Future: Reining in the Risk* (Carlisle Barracks, PA: U.S. Army War College, Strategic Studies Institute, December 2009), 72.

17. Pervez Musharraf, *In the Line of Fire: A Memoir* (New York: Simon and Schuster, 2006), 81.

18. Ibid., 71.

19. India never used the word "terrorism" on the issue of Kashmir in the negotiations. Since September 2001, the Kashmir struggle has been conflated with terrorism.

20. Author's discussion with Mr. Rakesh Sood and Jassal Singh, Indian diplomats accompanying the Indian delegations, during the foreign secretary's bilateral talks on peace, security, and CBMs in Islamabad on October 16, 1998.

21. Aziz, *Between Dreams and Realities*, 223–24.

22. Ibid., 364–67 (Appendix II).

Chapter 16

1. See Feroz Hassan Khan, Christopher Clary, and Peter Lavoy, "Pakistan Motivations and Calculations in Kargil," in Peter Lavoy, ed., *Asymmetric War in South Asia: The Causes and Consequences of the Kargil Conflict* (New York: Cambridge University Press, 2009), 80–81.

2. General Jehangir Karamat, interview by author, Washington, DC, September 1, 2010; and Dennis Kux, *The United States and Pakistan, 1947–2000: Disenchanted Allies* (Baltimore: Johns Hopkins University Press, 2001), 347. In his memoirs, Sartaj Aziz, who was then the foreign minister, described Pakistan as the "melting pot of global fault-lines." Sartaj Aziz, *Between Dreams and Realities: Some Milestones in Pakistan's History* (New York: Oxford University Press, 2009), 203–48.

3. Pervez Musharraf, *In the Line of Fire* (New York: Simon and Schuster, 2006), 85–86.

4. Ibid.

5. Nawaz Sharif took issue with General Mirza Aslam Beg (served 1988–91) during the 1991 Persian Gulf War, especially over General Beg's assertion on the concept of strategic defiance, which implied appreciating Saddam Hussein's aggression in Kuwait. Next, General Asif Nawaz (1991–93) died in office, amid allegations of foul play. His successor, General Abdul Waheed (1993–96), was a no-nonsense army chief who intervened to break the deadlock forcing both the president, GIK, and the prime minister, Sharif, to pack and leave home. General Waheed's successor, General Karamat, was the fourth army chief forced to resign. Musharraf was the fifth army chief in a row, whose attempted sacking brought in the inevitable military takeover.

6. Prime Minister Sharif had clashed with both President Ghulam Ishaq Khan and Farooq Leghari, who had resigned, in 1993 and 1997, respectively. Chief Justice Sajjad Ali Shah was next to resign, after a bitter confrontation with the Sharif government. In the preceding years, in widely known secret deals, the Sharif government had bribed the bureaucracy, judiciary, and other state institutions, which led to the demise of President Farooq Leghari and Chief Justice Sajjad Ali Shah of the Supreme Court. Finally, General Karamat was due to retire in January 1999 but was forced to retire in October 1998.

7. Sharif's close and trusted associate Sartaj Aziz described the removal of General Jehangir Karamat a "blunder." Aziz, *Between Dreams and Realities,* 202.

8. Musharraf made these remarks in his first address to officers in the GHQ auditorium after taking over as COAS. He urged officers to get on with their jobs, as a new era had commenced and clearly emphasized that his leadership would be bold and pragmatic and different from the previous one. The author was present when these remarks were made. See also Musharraf, *In the Line of Fire,* 86.

9. When Musharraf was promoted, his army course-mate (29th Pakistan Military Academy (PMA long course) and aspirant for the appointment of COAS, Lieutenant-General Ali Kuli Khattak, Chief of General Staff, resigned and never returned to office. (See ibid., 85.) Sharif also ignored Sartaj Aziz's suggestion to compensate Lieutenant-General Ali Kuli Khattak by appointing him chairman, Joint Chiefs of Staff. Sharif was led to believe that Ali Kuli had supported a military takeover during the judiciary crises. Aziz, *Between Dreams and Realities,* 201.

10. General Jahangir Karamat told the author that he had observed Lieutenant-General Ziauddin, then adjutant general of the Pakistani Army, often visiting the Sharif family in Lahore. On one occasion Karamat politely inquired of Ziauddin the purpose of visits and fraternization with the family. Since the author had served under Lieutenant-General Ziauddin as DGCD, General Karamat asked the author, "Did Ziauddin not know that movements of senior military leadership were closely monitored? Was he not intelligent enough not to get the message what it means when the COAS inquires into such a thing personally?" Seemingly Lieutenant-General Ziauddin did not understand the message and continued fraternizing with Sharif's father. General Jehangir Karamat, interview by author, Washington, DC, September 1, 2010.

11. After being appointed DG-ISI, Ziauddin had direct access to the prime minister, which Musharraf found uncomfortable and made his concerns known. In another incident, in the summer of 1999, the Quetta Corps Commander Lieutenant-General Tariq Pervaiz was found privately meeting with the prime minister (in Rawalpindi) and other civilian leaders without clearance from the army chief. Tariq Pervaiz's first cousin was Raja Nadir Pervaiz, who was then a federal minister in the Nawaz Sharif cabinet. Musharraf retired the corps commander immediately. The purpose of this action was to serve as a deterrent to other senior military leaders and to protect the army's institutional discipline.

12. Nawaz Sharif's tactics were similar to those of Z. A. Bhutto in the 1970s. Bhutto played off General Muhammad Sharif and General Zia-ul Haq by appointing one as chairman, Joint Chiefs and the other as COAS, knowing fully of their personality clash in Multan earlier. Nawaz Sharif seemingly borrowed a page from Bhutto's Machiavellian mindset. Both Bhutto and Sharif enjoyed unchallenged power as prime ministers, yet both wanted complete dominance as all-powerful personalities.

13. Musharraf, *In the Line of Fire*, 85.

14. "Strategic Policy Review of Summer 1998" was among the few papers the new army chief was given to read in October 1998.

15. Musharraf, *In the Line of Fire,* 87.

16. Lieutenant-General Mahmud Ahmed, interview by Peter R. Lavoy, Lahore, January 13, 2004. See Lavoy, *Asymmetric War in South Asia*, 85.

17. John H. Gill, "Military Operations in the Kargil Conflict," in Lavoy, *Asymmetric War in South Asia*, 96. See also Shaukat Qadir, "An Analysis of the Kargil Conflict 1999," *Journal of the Royal United Services Institution* (April 2002), 24–30.

18. Khan, Clary, and Lavoy, "Pakistan Motivations and Calculations in Kargil," 80.

19. Ibid., 19.

20. See Musharraf, *In the Line of Fire*, 88. However, Peter Lavoy records Lieutenant-General Mahmud giving a full briefing to the army chief in mid-January. Lavoy, *Asymmetric War in South Asia,* 85.

21. Ibid., 97.

22. Ibid., 85.

23. Lavoy, *Asymmetric War in South Asia,* 85; Musharraf, *In the Line of Fire*, 96. See also Shirin Mazari, *The Kargil Conflict 1999: Separating Myth from Reality* (Islamabad: Feroz and Sons, 2003), 28–32. In both publications, photographs of Sharif's visit to Skardu and Kel are shown to prove that he was briefed on those dates about the impending and ongoing operations. Sharif continues to deny he was briefed about the operations.

24. Aziz, *Between Dreams and Realities,* 258–59, 284.

25. "Lahore Declaration," India and Pakistan, February 21, 2009, Inventory of International Nonproliferation Organizations and Regimes, James Martin Center for Nonproliferation Studies, Monterey Institute of International Studies.

26. Lavoy, *Asymmetric War in South Asia*, 64.

27. This knowledge is based on the author's personal experience commanding an infantry battalion in 1991–92 in the FCNA. See also ibid., 64–91.

28. In the summer of 1997, when India and Pakistan began the eight-point composite dialogue as a result of the Gujral-Sharif meeting, heavy fighting continued along the LOC, especially in a valley called Kishanganga (on Indian maps) and Neelum Valley (on Pakistani maps). See Feroz Hassan Khan, "Security Impediments to Regionalism in South Asia," in Rafiq Dossani, Daniel Sneider, Vikram Sood, and Walter H. Shorenstein, eds., *Does South Asia Exist?: Prospects for Regional Integration* (Stanford, CA: Walter H. Shorenstein Asia–Pacific Research Center, 2010), 236–39.

29. Gill, "Military Operations in the Kargil Conflict," 96; and Christine Fair, "Militants in Kargil Conflict," in Lavoy, *Asymmetric War in South Asia*, 232–33.

30. Musharraf, *In the Line of Fire*, 90–91.

31. Ibid. See also official briefing given to Peter Lavoy at FCNA by Major General Nadeem Ahmad in January 2003. Lavoy, *Asymmetric War in South Asia,* xiv.

32. Zojila pass on the Indian side and Burzil pass on the Pakistani were critical to maintaining logistical supplies to both military forces. Typically, these passes close during early winter and open for traffic during the summer months. In the opening phases, troops dump supplies and food, water, and munitions for the winter deployments. The opening and closing of the passes was an important factor in the planning of the tactical operation.

33. Gill, "Military Operations in the Kargil Conflict," 107.

34. Ibid., 110. The Indian Navy had planned an exercise code-named "Summerex" on the east coast near the Bay of Bengal. However, it shifted this exercise to the west coast to demonstrate naval deterrence.

35. Musharraf, *In the Line of Fire,* 91. He [Musharraf] also believed that India had "unreasonably escalated" its response. He does not clarify why he believes India's escalation was unreasonable.

36. Author's personal discussions with many officers and soldiers of 5 NLI battalion who participated in the battle. The author had commanded the 5 NLI battalion from 1991 to 1993. I paid a visit to the unit as the colonel of the battalion (an honorary position of old British tradition) after the Kargil conflict was over. Also at the U.S. Naval Postgraduate School, Monterey, California, the Kargil conflict was analyzed for several years. A study in Pakistan's Command and Staff College, Quetta, revealed that the posts established were far too deep to be logistically sustainable and were not hardened or mutually supporting to provide any coherent defensive lines. They were incapable of withstanding sustained military attacks that very summer.

37. Musharraf, *In the Line of Fire*, 96–97. Musharraf personally briefed the defense committee of the cabinet on July 2, 1999, explaining to them that India was in no position to launch an offensive. Indian troop induction in Kashmir would create a strategic

imbalance in the Indian system and, despite India's strength, it would be unable to dislodge the NLI positions from those heights.

38. The prime minister began to be skeptical of the briefings of GHQ on Kargil. The source of his doubts were primarily counterbriefings of Lieutenant-General Ziauddin, DGISI, that countermanded the position taken by the Corps Headquarters and the army chief. In addition, the prime minister was influenced by Indian and Western television, as well as relentless pressure from the U.S. president during the operation.

39. Aziz, *Between Dreams and Realities*, 268–76.

40. Musharraf gave Nawaz Sharif an "optimistic military situation" in his briefing. Aziz, *Between Dreams and Realities*, 28. Musharraf believed that the "political decisions had to be his own." He did not clarify why he believes "political decisions" and "military decisions" should be separate realms when indeed they should be in sync with each other. On the prime minister's decision to go to Washington for a July 4 meeting with President Clinton, in Musharraf's own words: "[It] remains a mystery to me why he was in such a hurry." Musharraf, *In the Line of Fire*, 97

41. See Bruce Riedel, "The 1999 Blair House Summit," in Lavoy, *Asymmetric War in South Asia*, 136–37.

42. Ibid.

43. Ibid.

44. Strobe Talbott alleged that during the meeting in Islamabad one diplomat aggressively "rose out of his chair and lunged across the table as though he were going to strangle either Bruce Riedel or me, depending on whose neck he could get his fingers around first. He had to be physically restrained." Strobe Talbott, *Engaging India: Diplomacy, Democracy, and the Bomb* (Washington, DC: Brookings Institution, 2004), 105. Pakistan's Foreign Ministry officials called the incident—as reported in Talbott's book— grossly exaggerated and smacking of preconceived bias against Pakistan for the failure of Talbott's diplomacy to dissuade Pakistan from a nuclear test response. Background briefings to the author in June 2007, April 2009, and March 2011; and the author's personal discussions at the time of the incident in 1998, as well as recollections with former Foreign Secretary Shamshad Ahmad in Palo Alto, July 2011.

45. Background briefings in June 2007, April 2009, and March 2011. Author's personal conversations with several officials who wish not to be quoted by name but remain convinced that Bruce Riedel, in particular, and some others were the drivers of an anti-Pakistan agenda since the so-called physical assault incident of 1998. The pro-India tilt was plain and visible to the Pakistanis since the negotiations began after the nuclear tests.

46. The exclusive inclusion of Bruce Riedel as notetaker in a one-on-one meeting between President Clinton and Prime Minister Sharif was objected to by the Pakistani delegation, which insisted on the inclusion of Shamshad Ahmad, Pakistan's foreign secretary, as well; the U.S. declined, and Prime Minister Sharif did not insist upon inclusion of a Pakistani notetaker.

47. Avner Cohen, "The Last Nuclear Moment," *New York Times*, October 6, 2003, http://www.nytimes.com/2003/10/06/opinion/the-last-nuclear-moment.html.

48. Aziz, *Between Dreams and Realities*, 279.

49. Khan, Clary, and Lavoy, "Pakistan Motivations and Calculations in Kargil."

50. Although it has been over a decade, Sharif has spoken several times on his position on Kargil but he has never mentioned being confronted on the nuclear question.

51. Musharraf, *In the Line of Fire*, 97–98.

52. Background briefing by Lieutenant-General Khalid Kidwai, June 14, 2006, in Strategic Plans Division, Joint Services Headquarters.

53. Raj Chengappa, *Weapons for Peace: The Secret Quest of India's Quest to Be a Nuclear Power* (New Delhi: Harper Collins Publishers, 2009), 437.

54. Ibid.

55. In discussions with Indian retired military officers and former officials, the author was told that the Chengappa account is a journalist's view. Indian academics and nuclear experts do not mention India's preparations.

56. The author was on active duty in SPD at the time. Armed with this personal knowledge, the author does not believe that nuclear weapons were mated or played any significant role in the Kargil crisis. Aziz Haniffa, interview by author, Washington, DC, June 14, 2002.

57. See Jasit Singh, ed., *Kargil 1999: Pakistan's Fourth War for Kashmir* (New Delhi: Knowledge World, 1999).

58. Ibid.; Gurmeet Kanwal, "Nawaz Sharif's Damning Disclosures," *The Pioneer*, August 16, 2000. For Pakistani critics of the military, see Babar Sattar, "Pakistan: Return to Praetorianism," in Muthiah Alagappa, ed., *Coercion and Governance: The Declining Role of the Military in Asia* (Stanford: Stanford University Press, 2001), 385–412. Samina Ahmed, "Pakistan: Professionalism of an Interventionist Military," in Muthiah Alagappa, ed., *Military Professionalism in Asia* (Honolulu: East-West Center, 2001), 151–61. Both Babar Sattar and Samina Ahmed have argued that the military had justified its unique role in the state by pointing toward the Indian threat. By implication, the disappearance of that Indian threat would also mean the diminishing of the military role in security policy and politics. This perspective complements several Indian analytical perspectives of Pakistani military behavior. See, for example, Aswini Ray, *Domestic Compulsions and Foreign Policy* (New Delhi: Manas Publications, 1975).

59. Strobe Talbott compares Kargil to the Cuban missile crisis and quotes President Clinton referring to Pakistani action as "nuclear blackmail." Talbott, *Engaging India*, 161, 165, 167. Bruce Reidel also discusses Clinton's worry that "if the United States appeared to be acting under the gun of a nuclear threat its ability to restrain others from threatening use of their nuclear forces would be forever undermined." See Reidel, "American Diplomacy and the 1999 Kargil Summit at Blair House," Policy Paper Series (Philadelphia: University of Pennsylvania, Center for the Advanced Study of India, 2002),

http://www.sas.upenn.edu/casi/reports/RiedelPaper051302.htm (accessed December 23, 2010). Sumit Ganguly's invocation of the "stability-instability" paradox is typical of academic analysts in the United States. See Sumit Ganguly, *Conflict Unending: India-Pakistan Tensions since 1947* (Washington, DC: Woodrow Wilson Center Press, 2001), 122, 127. See also Sumit Ganguly and Devin Hagerty, *Fearful Symmetry: India-Pakistan Crises in the Shadow of Nuclear Weapons* (New Delhi: Oxford University Press, 2005), 143–66.

60. Shirin Mazari, *The Kargil Conflict 1999*.

61. Based on interviews with senior Pakistani officials, it appears that the Foreign Office, which was not involved in the initial planning of the incursion, lobbied to keep the *mujahideen* story alive, arguing that international legal problems would arise if the government of Pakistan admitted that the army was complicit in the infiltration.

62. Musharraf, *In the Line of Fire*, 91, 97.

63. For background, see Feroz Hassan Khan and Christopher Clary, "Dissuasion and Regional Allies: The Case of Pakistan," *Strategic Insights* 13, 10 (October 2004).

64. Talbott, *Engaging India*, 165; and Reidel, "American Diplomacy and the 1999 Kargil Summit at Blair House."

65. See Scott D. Sagan and Kenneth Waltz, *Spread of Nuclear Weapons: A Debate Renewed* (New York: W. W. Norton and Company, 2002), 97; Michael Krepon, "The Stability-Instability Paradox, Misperception, and Escalation Control in South Asia," in Rodney W. Jones, Michael Krepon, and Ziad Haider, eds., *Escalation Control and the Nuclear Option in South Asia* (Washington, DC: Henry L. Stimson Center, 2004), 2–24.

66. Lavoy, *Asymmetric War in South Asia*, 90.

67. Ibid., 32–33. See also S. Paul Kapur, "India and Pakistan's Unstable Peace: Why Nuclear South Asia Is Not Like Cold War Europe," *International Security* 30, 2 (Fall 2005), 127–52.

68. Maleeha Lodhi, "The Kargil Crisis: Anatomy of a Debacle," *Newsline*, July 1999.

69. Aziz, *Between Dreams and Realities*, 280–90.

70. Ibid., 287.

71. Ibid. Musharraf was aware of the hushed campaign against him involving several actors with their own agendas. Admiral Fasih Bokhari, Chief of Naval Staff, was an aspirant for the post of Chairman Joint Chief of Staff Committee (CJCSC), as he was nearing completion of his tenure as naval chief. Air Chief Marshal Pervez Mehdi, chief of Air Staff, was unhappy for not being brought into the loop when Kargil was planned. The PAF found itself caught unawares when the Indian Air Force escalated the conflict in Kargil. Unprepared, the PAF could only helplessly watch IAF bombarding its own troops, in no position to respond. See also Aziz, *Between Dreams and Realities*, 288–89.

72. DGISI Lieutenant-General Ziauddin was believed to be visiting the United States to discuss secret operations against Al Qaeda in Afghanistan.

73. Kux, *The United States and Pakistan*, 353–54.

74. General Musharraf was appointed to both assignments until October 16, 2001. See Aziz, *Between Dreams and Realities*, 289.

75. Both Lieutenant Generals Saleem and Akram found the gates at the prime minister's house, GHQ, and HQ 10 Corps sealed by troops.

76. Musharraf, *In the Line of Fire*, 85.

77. For three days inputs poured in from the various government departments, personalities, and intellectuals, making it very complicated for the author to put together a coherent policy speech. Meanwhile General Musharraf was making up his mind, taking major decisions, and mulling over the next steps. After considerable deliberation, General Musharraf set a seven-point agenda: (1) revive national confidence and morale; (2) strengthen the federation, remove interprovincial disharmony, and restore national cohesion; (3) revive the economy and restore investors' confidence; (4) ensure law and order and dispense speedy justice; (5) depoliticize state institutions; (6) devolve power down to the grassroots; and (7) ensure swift accountability across the board. See Ibid., 149–50.

Chapter 17

1. The author took one full day to draft the two pages, which included portions covering support of global nonproliferation and improving relations with India. For a detailed analysis, see Feroz Hassan Khan, "Pakistan's Perspectives on Global Elimination of Nuclear Weapons," in Barry M. Blechman and Alexander K. Bollfrass, eds., *National Perspectives on Nuclear Disarmament: Unblocking the Road to Zero* (Washington, DC: Henry L. Stimson Center, 2010), 211–41.

2. For detailed analyses, see Shahid Javed Burki, *Changing Perceptions, Altered Reality: Pakistan's Economy under Musharraf, 1999–2006* (New York: Oxford University Press, 2007), 13–14.

3. Moonis Ahmar, *CTBT Controversy: Different Perceptions in South Asia* (Karachi: Department of International Relations, 2000), 43. Musharraf's foreign minister, Abdul Sattar, took the lead in the debate on the CTBT. See "CTBT Not against National Interest," *Dawn*, February 26, 2000. His inclination to support the treaty prompted the right-wing political party Jamaat Islami (JI) to declare a virtual *jihad* against the CTBT. Abdul Sattar's address at the Institute of Policy Studies, a JI-funded think tank in Islamabad, was marred by hostile polemics and interruptions during his speech. For Abdul Sattar's comments, see Sattar, *Pakistan's Foreign Policy 1947–2005: A Concise History* (New York: Oxford University Press, 2007). See also Sattar, interview by author, Islamabad, June 20, 2006.

4. President Clinton's visit to Pakistan included a video address to Pakistan. He declined a photo-op handshake with Chief Executive Pervez Musharraf.

5. Ishfaq Ahmad, interview by author, Islamabad, December 20, 2005 and June 20, 2006. See also Zafar Iqbal Cheema, "Pakistan's Nuclear Use Doctrine and Command

and Control," in Peter R. Lavoy, Scott D. Sagan, and James Wirtz, eds., *Planning the Unthinkable: How New Nuclear Powers Will Use Nuclear, Biological and Chemical Weapons* (Ithaca, NY: Cornell University Press, 2000), 171–75.

6. Among hosts of issues, one was the choice of appointing General Abdul Waheed. Sharif privately raised concerns over GIK's selecting a fellow Pashtun as COAS. See Shuja Nawaz, *Crossed Swords: Pakistan, Its Army, and the Wars Within* (New York: Oxford University Press, 2008), 470–71.

7. Ibid. Nawaz states that Sharif talked to DGISI Lieutenant-General Javed Ashraf Qazi in Punjabi and said, "Make sure you don't forget to take care of us! These two Pathans [Ishaq and Waheed] may gang up against us."

8. See International Institute for Strategic Studies (IISS), *Nuclear Black Markets: Pakistan, A. Q. Khan and the Rise of Proliferation Networks, a Net Assessment*, IISS strategic dossier (London: International Institute for Strategic Studies, 2007), 27–30; and Gordon Corera, *Shopping for Bombs: Nuclear Proliferation, Global Insecurity, and the Rise and Fall of the A. Q. Khan Network* (New York: Oxford University Press, 2006), 13.

9. Dr. Ishfaq Ahmad, interview by author, Islamabad, December 20, 2005.

10. General Beg had initiated a program to send military officers to Western civil universities for advanced degrees. By the early 1990s several military officers had postgraduate degrees from top Western universities in operational and technical fields. The author was one of the beneficiaries of this initiative, bringing him to the Paul Nitze School of Advanced International Studies (SAIS) of Johns Hopkins University, Washington, DC, from 1989 to 1991. The author was posted to the CD from 1993 to 1998, after which the CD was merged with the Strategic Plans Division (SPD), where I served until my retirement.

11. In the summer of 1994, under the directive of General Abdul Waheed, nuclear-related documents were transferred to DGCD. In a joint meeting presided over by CGS, Lieutenant-General Jehangir Karamat, some specific nuclear-related documents were formally transferred from MO Directorate to CD Directorate, and handed over to the author. Thereafter DGMO and DGCD continued coordination on a regular basis under directive of CGS and COAS.

12. Later promoted to Major General, Ahmad Bilal has remained part of the nuclear establishment. Bilal was later entrusted with the responsibility of becoming head of the newly created security division.

13. Ishfaq Ahmad, interview by author, Islamabad, December 20, 2005.

14. DGCD was replaced with Major General Syed Amjad, who stayed for less than six months. Amjad did not take over the nuclear responsibility; in fact, he only oversaw the dismemberment of the CD Directorate and ensured smooth transfers of its subordinate directorates (C and D Divisions) to SPD and other branches in GHQ by December 1998. The CD Directorate officially ceased to exist by the end of March 1999.

15. Naeem Salik, *The Genesis of South Asian Nuclear Deterrence* (New York: Oxford University Press, 2009), 234–35.

16. The sudden significance of nuclear matters after the 1998 tests made each branch within GHQ compete. Discussions on nuclear issues became a hot topic in GHQ.

17. At the time of this writing Major General Ahmad Bilal is Chairman SUPARCO, where he has served since August 2010.

18. Pervez Musharraf, *In the Line of Fire* (New York: Simon and Schuster, 2006), 288–89.

19. In April 1999, the COAS also was appointed as acting CJCSC. Arguably, this move enabled GHQ to allow SPD to move to JSHQ.

20. Author's personal knowledge and background briefing at SPD in June 2007.

21. Paolo Cotta-Ramusino and Maurizio Martellini, "Nuclear Safety, Nuclear Stability and Nuclear Strategy in Pakistan: A Concise Report of a Visit by Landau Network—Centro Volta," Como, Italy, January 21, 2002, 4, http://www.mi.infn.it/~landnet (accessed June 10, 2012).

22. Bennett Jones, "Will Pakistan Fall Apart?" *Prospect* 46 (November 1999), 209.

23. Molly Moore and Kamran Khan, "Pakistan Moves Nuclear Arsenal and Tightens Control over Arms," *International Herald Tribune*, November 12, 2001.

24. Seymour M. Hersh, "Watching the Warheads," *New Yorker*, November 5, 2001.

25. Lieutenant-General Khalid Kidwai, lecture to the Naval Postgraduate School, Monterey, CA, October 27, 2006. See also Cotta-Ramusino and Martellini, "Nuclear Safety, Nuclear Stability and Nuclear Strategy in Pakistan," 4.

26. Sartaj Aziz, *Between Dreams and Realities: Some Milestones in Pakistan's History* (New York: Oxford University Press, 2009), 238.

27. For example, see ibid., 238–40.

28. Musharraf, *In the Line of Fire,* 171.

29. Within military circles, some believe that the proper functioning of NSC would eliminate the maverick decision-making conducted both by politicians and military leaders and prevent military takeover in the future. Others believe that the real reason politicians are opposed to NSC is that it will give military and state bureaucracy oversight over their corruption and moneymaking agendas. The tragedy of weak political structures and failed democracy in Pakistan is the result of the unending cycle of frequent military takeovers and corrupt and inefficient civil governance. See ibid., 171–72.

30. Aziz, *Between Dreams and Realities,* 241.

31. Legal Framework Order 2002 (Chief Executive's Order no. 24 of 2002). In December 2003, as a concession to the Islamist opposition, Musharraf agreed to drop his demand that the NSC be recognized by the constitution.

32. In all NSC deliberations, however, the opposition leader Maulana Fazl-ur Rehman never attended the meetings, saying he never agreed to the concept. Musharraf thinks

that he backed out to "sabotage my political reforms so that they can return to their bad old ways of bad old days." Musharraf, *In the Line of Fire*, 172.

33. In the first few months of his reign, Musharraf was focused on consolidating power and creating an image of himself as a liberal leader. In this vein, Musharraf established the NSC to advise on policy for the military government. From there, two policy issues emerged that were believed to have an impact on Pakistan's overall image. The first issue was the Blasphemy Law, which was often abused and targeted minorities, and the second was the debate surrounding the CTBT. Right-wing political parties were against Musharraf's proposed changes on both counts and took to the streets in protest. Although key changes could have been made, Musharraf backed away from both issues, indicating that he did not want to alienate the public on issues of minor significance early in his regime. Observers were eerily reminded of Z. A. Bhutto's appeasement of religious parties and how that placed him on a slippery slope. Musharraf, who had spent his childhood in Turkey and speaks Turkish fluently, was rumored to follow in the footsteps of Mustafa Kemal Atatürk, who was the founder of modern and secular Turkey. However, in truth Musharraf was not going to follow in those steps. In an informal dinner discussion he explained the mistake of Atatürk and the shah of Iran in trying to wipe out religion, which, he believed, only came back to haunt them. He was, however, never clear enough, nor had enough support from liberal civil society, to implement liberal ideas, as civil society saw him as a usurper and dictator. Hence, Musharraf soft-peddled religious groups. One such move was his withdrawal of administrative steps on the Blasphemy Law in January 2000.

34. When first established, those positions were not filled, and the NCA was chaired by Musharraf in his role as chief executive.

35. Mahmood Durrani, *Pakistan's Strategic Thinking and the Role of Nuclear Weapons,* CMC occasional paper (Albuquerque, NM: Sandia National Laboratories, July 2004), 31.

36. Andrew Koch and Christopher F. Foss, "Pakistan Strengthens Nuclear Security," *Jane's Defence Weekly*, October 9, 2002, 25.

37. Paul Guinessey, "Pakistan Reshuffles Weapons Programme," *Physics Today* (May 2001); Peter R. Lavoy, "Islamabad's Nuclear Posture," in Henry D. Sokolski, ed., *Pakistan's Nuclear Future: Worries beyond War* (Carlisle Barracks, PA: Strategic Studies Institute, January 2008), 149–53.

Chapter 18

1. Robert Jervis, *The Meaning of the Nuclear Revolution: Statecraft and the Prospect of Armageddon* (Ithaca, NY: Cornell University Press, 1989).

2. U.S. officials often used the phrase "help us help you," which was another way of conveying that if Pakistan were ready to concede on some issues, the United States would be willing to find compromise.

3. The author was present at the new COAS address to GHQ officers in GHQ auditorium in October 1998.

4. George Tenet with Bill Harlow, *At the Center of the Storm: My Years at the CIA* (New York: Harper Collins, 2007), 128. See also U.S. Department of Defense, "USS Cole Commission Report," http://www.fas.org/irp/threat/cole.pdf (accessed December 20, 2010).

5. See, for example, Strobe Talbott, *Engaging India: Diplomacy, Democracy, and the Bomb* (Washington, DC: Brookings Institution, 2004). Pakistani officials thought that if CTBT signatures were that important to the United States, then Washington should have applied pressure on India, whose adherence to the CTBT would have automatically led Pakistan to follow suit. Instead U.S. diplomats were openly courting India and pressuring Pakistan.

6. Jeffery Souter, "Is Pakistan an Ally?" *Kansas City Star*, December 26, 2010, http://www.kansascity.com/2010/12/26/2543471/is-pakistan-an-ally-in-the-war.html.

7. Cyril Almeida, "Pakistan, the Most Bullied Ally," *Dawn*, November 30, 2010, http://www.dawn.com/2010/11/30/pakistan-the-'most-bullied-us-ally'.html.

8. These are drawn from a modified version of the list originally coined by Harvard professor Joseph Nye, Jr. The author is grateful to Dr. Syed Riffaat Husain, chairman of the Department of Defense and Strategic Studies, Quaid-e Azam University, Islamabad, for this reference and for presenting a modified version in a detailed presentation on the subject of Asian power balance, held in Singapore, October 8–9, 2010. For the original version, see Joseph Nye, Jr., *Bound to Lead: The Changing Nature of American Power* (Boston: Harvard University Press, 1990).

9. The three points were the author's original recommendations in the post–nuclear test "Strategic Policy Review." In a background briefing in Islamabad, June 2006, provided to the author and team from the Center for Contemporary Conflict at the U.S. Naval Postgraduate School, it was reemphasized that Pakistan remained a strategically relevant actor in the region. As long as the Pakistani armed forces remained a viable force and the nation retained its geographical significance, Pakistan would never be marginalized.

10. Abdul Sattar, *Pakistan's Foreign Policy 1947–2005: A Concise History* (New York: Oxford University Press, 2007), 138.

11. The author recalls that the range of ideas demonstrated a lack of basic understanding of diplomacy and national security. See ibid.

12. The author recalls that in Clinton's last year, he wanted extensive discussions on three main issues: (1) nuclear issues, including Pakistani options on the CTBT, (2) counterterrorism cooperation in Afghanistan, and (3) the fate of deposed Prime Minister Nawaz Sharif. On December 10, 2000, Sharif signed a deal with Musharraf to go into exile, which was brokered by the Saudi monarch with Clinton's personal intervention and approval.

13. Deliberations in the National Security Council (NSC), National Command Au-

thority (NCA), and the Strategic Plans Division (SPD), a comprehensive strategic policy review.

14. President Pervez Musharraf, "Pakistan: A Vision for the Future," address at the Woodrow Wilson International Center for Scholars, Washington, DC, February 12, 2002.

15. Abdul Sattar, interview by author, Islamabad, June 20, 2006. Sattar explained that Mullah Omar refused to listen when Pakistan, under international pressure, attempted to persuade him not to destroy the Buddha statues in Bamyan, Afghanistan. Mullah Omar argued that he was answerable only to God's commands.

16. The author and Major General Khalid Kidwai were present during the foreign minister's speech. Several U.S. arms control experts and scholars engaged with the author to interpret and elaborate on Pakistan's nuclear policies and what Pakistan desired to learn from the United States. Earlier, on January 25, 2001, Pakistan's foreign secretary, Inam-ul Haq, addressed the plenary session of the Conference on Disarmament and offered "a strategic restraint regime for the region" that included a proposal for the nondeployment of ballistic missiles, no operational weaponization of nuclear capable missiles, and formalization of the notification of ballistic missile flight tests. See Naeem Salik, *The Genesis of South Asian Nuclear Deterrence* (New York: Oxford University Press, 2009), 232–33.

17. In October 2001, Musharraf would appoint a new Chairman Joint Chief of Staff Committee and Vice Chief of the Army Staff. A year later, after the October 2002 parliamentary elections, he would hand over powers as chief executive to the prime minister. Despite this shift, Musharraf retained power as the president because of the 17th Amendment to the constitution. See Pervez Musharraf, *In the Line of Fire* (New York: Simon and Schuster, 2006), 177–78.

18. U.S. government officials were divided on their approach to dealing with the increasing terrorism threat from Al Qaeda. One group, led by Cofer Black, director of CIA Counterterrorism Center (CTC), sought to bolster the Northern Alliance against the Taliban. See Tenet and Harlow, *At the Center of the Storm*, 141. Others sought cooperation with Pakistani intelligence, including training commandoes to capture bin Laden. See Bob Woodward, *Bush at War* (New York: Simon and Schuster, 2002), 5.

19. Woodward, *Bush at War*, 200.

20. The Pakistani narrative continues to mention that a threat to its nuclear program was made, and U.S. officials deny it. For the Pakistani version, see Musharraf, *In the Line of Fire*, 200–201. For the U.S. perspective, see Tenet and Harlow, *At the Center of the Storm*, 180–81.

21. Musharraf, *In the Line of Fire*, 200–202.

22. Ibid.

23. Ibid.

24. Richard Armitage has denied that he conveyed any threat. See Melissa Block, "Ar-

mitage Denies Making 'Stone Age' Threat," National Public Radio, September 22, 2006, http://www.npr.org/templates/story/story.php?storyId=6126088. Ambassador Maleeha Lodhi, then Pakistan's ambassador to the United States, was present at the meeting and told the author that she did not believe a naked threat of the kind had been made.

25. Peter R. Lavoy, "Islamabad's Nuclear Posture: Its Premises and Implementation," in Henry D. Sokolski, ed., *Pakistan's Nuclear Future: Worries beyond War* (Carlisle, PA: Strategic Studies Institute, 2008), 143–47.

26. Background briefing to the author and off-the-record interviews.

27. In hindsight one of the benefits of establishing SPD and moving it to JSHQ was that Pakistan had created a dedicated, hardened, and secure storage.

28. Brigadier Pervez Niazi was a qualified engineer and a graduate from George Washington University. He had served with the author in the Combat Development Directorate as his deputy director ACDA (C Division) in 1996 and 1997.

29. The dispersal of nuclear assets was coordinated efficiently between JSHQ, DGMO in GHQ, and SPD. The DGMO at the time was Major General Ashfaq Pervez Kayani, now COAS since November 2007.

30. Background briefing in Islamabad. Pakistan embassy sources, on conditions of anonymity, told the author about the closure of the Islamabad Airport during the second week of September. See also "Pakistan's Special Weapons Facilities, Weapons of Mass Destruction, Global Security," http://www.globalsecurity.org/wmd/world/pakistan/facility.htm (accessed January 3, 2011).

31. Musharraf, *In the Line of Fire,* 202.

32. Lieutenant-General Shahid Aziz, discussions with author, Islamabad, April 14, 2009. Shahid Aziz was Chief of General Staff at General Headquarters at the time. He told the author that GHQ formally complained to General Tommy Franks about this lack of information and coordination.

33. Background briefing provided by Major General Shaukat Sultan, director general of Inter-Service Public Relations, to the author and research team from the U.S. Naval Postgraduate School in June 2006. Presentation by Commandant Pakistan's National Defense College, Lieutenant-General Tariq Waseem Ghazi, at the U.S. Naval Postgraduate School, September 16, 2004. Lieutenant-General Shahid Aziz, discussions with author, Islamabad, April 14, 2009.

34. Colonel (ret.) David Smith, "The 2001–2002 Standoff: The Real-time View from Islamabad," in Zachary Davis, ed., *The India-Pakistan Military Standoff: Crisis and Escalation in South Asia* (New York: Palgrave Macmillan, 2011), 191–92.

35. Riaz Mohammad Khan, *Afghanistan and Pakistan: Conflict, Extremism, and Resistance to Modernity* (Washington, DC: Woodrow Wilson Center Press, 2011) 121–22. See also Smith, "The 2001–2002 Standoff," 195.

36. Rama Lakshmi, "Gunmen with Explosives Attack Indian Parliament," *Washington Post,* December 14, 2001; Rasul Bailey and Joanna Slater, "Terror Strike in India Fuels

Old Tensions—Crises with Pakistan May Ensue if Culprits Prove to Be Kashmiri," *Wall Street Journal*, December 14, 2001.

37. Celia W. Dugger, "Group in Pakistan Is Blamed by India for Suicide Raid," *New York Times*, December 15, 2001; Rama Laskshmi, "Indians Blame Attacks on Pakistan-based Group: Fears of Renewed Tension Increase," *Washington Post*, December 17, 2001.

38. Background briefing at Joint Services Headquarters to the author in July 2005.

39. Gurmeet Kanwal, "Lost Opportunities," *Tribune India*, December 13, 2010, http://www.tribuneindia.com/2010/20101213/edit.htm#6.

40. Ibid.

41. "India Calls Back Envoy to Pakistan," *Hindustan Times*, December 21, 2001.

42. Vishal Thapar, "Prithvi Missiles Move Near Border in Punjab," *Hindustan Times*, December 24, 2001; Rajiv Chandrasekaran, "India Missiles Put in Position: Tensions Rise on Pakistani Border," *Washington Post*, December 27, 2001.

43. "No Army Day Parade, Troops Needed," *Hindustan Times*, December 26, 2001. The army parade was later held on January 15, 2002. The author is grateful to Brigadier (ret.) Gurmeet Kanwal, director, Center for Land Warfare Studies, for clarifying the event.

44. Joanna Slater and Daniel Pearl, "India-Pakistan Ties Take Another Dip—New Delhi Bans Flights from Rivals, Curtails Diplomatic Missions," *Wall Street Journal*, December 28, 2001.

45. During the SAARC summit, however, President Musharraf in full media glare walked up to Indian Prime Minister Vajpayee and greeted him; the Indian prime minister gracefully accepted by standing up to shake his hand. South Asian crises are often sprinkled with dramatic moments such as these.

46. "India's Most Wanted List of Terrorists, Criminals Handed over to Pakistan," *Hindustan Times*, December 31, 2001.

47. "Pakistan Puts Troops on High Alert along LoC: Report," *Hindustan Times*, December 14, 2001.

48. Celia W. Dugger, "India Rebuffs Pakistanis over Inquiry Into Attack," *New York Times*, December 18, 2001; "Pakistan Won't Withdraw its Envoy in India," *Hindustan Times*, December 21, 2001.

49. Erik Eckholm, "Pakistan Pledges to Bar Any Groups in Reply to Indian Appeal," *New York Times*, January 13, 2002.

50. Eric Eckholm with Celia Dugger, "Pakistan Has Rounded Up 1430 as Part of Plan to Curb Militants," *New York Times*, January 16, 2002.

51. "Future—Fire—The Shorter Smarter Agni Heralds a New Genre of Missiles Directed towards Pakistan," *India Today*, January 29, 2002.

52. Feroz Hassan Khan, "Nuclear Signaling, Missiles and Escalation Control in South Asia," in Michael Krepon, Rodney Jones, and Ziad Haider, eds., *Escalation Control and the Nuclear Option in South Asia* (Washington, DC: Henry L. Stimson Center, 2004), 88.

53. Celia W. Duggar, "India Tests Missile, Stirring a Region Already on Edge," *New York Times*, January 26, 2002.

54. Lavoy, "Islamabad's Nuclear Posture, 132.

55. One Indian study estimates that 70 million rupees (USD $1.7 million) per day were spent during that time. This affected agriculture in the borderlands. Gurmeet Kan wal, "Lost Opportunities," *Tribune India*, December 13, 2010, http://www.Tribuneindia.com/2010/20101213/edit.htm#6.

56. Ainsle Embree, "Who Speaks for India? The Role of Civil Society," in Rafiq Dossani and Henry S. Rowen, eds., *Prospects for Peace in South Asia*, Studies of the Asia-Pacific Research Center (Stanford: Stanford University Press, 2005), 180.

57. Lieutenant-General Shahid Aziz, discussions with author, Islamabad, April 14, 2009. Gen Aziz was the Chief of General Staff (CGS) at GHQ at the time and current Army Chief General Ashfaq Pervez Kayani was the Director General Military Operations (DGMO).

58. "Indo-US Military Exercise Has Long Term Objectives," *Dawn*, May 15, 2002.

59. Masood Haider, "No Intention to Attack Pakistan: Fernandez," *Dawn*, May 15, 2002.

60. Feroz Hassan Khan, "Reducing the Risk of Nuclear War in South Asia," in Henry Sokolski, ed., *Pakistan's Nuclear Future: Reining in the Risk* (Carlisle Barracks, PA: Strategic Studies Institute, December 2009), 74.

61. "New Delhi Threatens Retaliation for Jammu Killings," *Dawn*, May 17, 2002.

62. "Pakistan Rejects Indian Charge," *Dawn*, May 17, 2002.

63. Aamer Ahmad Khan, "Pakistan, India Close to War, Says Musharraf," *Dawn*, May 23, 2002. See also "Warships Move as Vajpayee Warns of Decisive Fight," *Dawn*, May 23, 2002.

64. "Warships Move as Vajpayee Warns of Decisive Fight," *Dawn*, May 23, 2002.

65. "India Threatens to Scrap Indus Water Treaty," *Dawn*, May 24, 2002.

66. See Paolo Cotta-Ramusino and Maurizio Martellini, "Nuclear Safety, Nuclear Stability and Nuclear Strategy in Pakistan: A Concise Report of a Visit by Landau Network—Centro Volta," January, 21, 2002, lxmi.mi.infn.it/~landnet. Lieutenant-General Khalid Kidwai, director general, Strategic Plans Division, reiterated this point in an address on October 27, 2006, to the Center for Contemporary Conflict at the U.S. Naval Postgraduate School, Monterey, CA. For a summary of Kidwai's talk, see www.ccc.nps.navy.mil/news/kidwaiNov06.asp.

67. Aamer Ahmed Khan, "Pakistan, India Close to War, Says Musharraf," *Dawn*, May 23, 2002.

68. Indian Foreign Ministry Spokeswoman Nirupama Rao stated, "India is not impressed with missile antics by Pakistan," May 26, 2002. See Feroz Hassan Khan, "Nuclear Signaling, Missiles and Escalation Control in South Asia," 74.

69. Ibid., 88.

70. Ibid. The author is grateful to Lieutenant-General Khalid Kidwai for sharing this quotation from President Musharraf's speech to Pakistani scientists and missile engineers on June 17, 2002, Islamabad. See also Smith, "The 2001–2002 Standoff," 201.

71. Feroz Hassan Khan, "Nuclear Signaling, Missiles and Escalation Control in South Asia," 88–99.

72. "Emissaries Set to Visit U.S.; Europe" *Dawn,* May 30, 2002.

73. President Pervez Musharraf, discussions with author, Islamabad, June 18, 2006.

74. On June 4, 2002, at a regional summit in Central Asia, Musharraf offered to have unconditional talks with India, which India rejected. When Musharraf walked up to Vajpayee to shake his hand, the latter did not reciprocate.

75. "Jawed Naqvi India Lifts Ban on Overflights: Rumsfield May Propose LoC Monitoring Today," *Dawn,* June 12, 2002.

76. India's grievance regarding the attack on its Parliament was a serious matter. An attack on an Indian democratic institution is unacceptable under any circumstances anywhere in the world. However, India's assumption of Pakistani culpability and rapid mobilization created more complications than it solved. India had many options for seeking Pakistani cooperation in handling the crisis. An earlier effort at the Agra Summit in July 2001 could not form an agreement. In this regard India sought military coercion as opposed to diplomacy.

77. Author's discussions with Pakistani military and civilian officials during a workshop, "The India-Pakistan Military Standoff 2001–2002," sponsored by the U.S. Naval Postgraduate School and the Institute of Policy Research, Islamabad, held in August 2005.

78. In a CNN interview on June 1, 2002, Musharraf said, "Nuclear war is unthinkable for South Asia. I don't think either side is that irresponsible to go to that limit." Transcript of CNN interview with Musharraf, http://articles.cnn.com/2002–06–01/world/musharraf.transcript_1_general-musharraf-prime-minister-vajpayee-nuclear-weapons?_s=PM:asiapcf (accessed November 26, 2011). See also "Musharraf Rules Out Possibility of Nuclear War," *The Hindu,* June 2, 2002.

79. On May 12, 2002, Bruce Riedel, former national security staffer, broke the story that the Pakistan military had prepared nuclear weapons in Kargil. The timing of the publication insinuated that Pakistan was eager to use its nuclear arsenal at the first opportunity.

80. Cited in Lavoy, "Islamabad's Nuclear Posture," 135–36.

81. Ibid. See also Roger Boyes, "Musharraf Warns India He May Use Nuclear Weapons," *London Times*, April 8, 2002.

82. "India Will Use Nuclear Weapons, If Pakistan Does: Defence Official," *Hindustan Times,* June 3, 2002.

83. "Fernandez Dismisses Nuclear Fears," *Times of India,* June 3, 2002.

84. Munir Akram, Pakistan's ambassador to the United Nations, defended Pakistan's

nuclear policy, saying, "We have the means, and we will not neutralize it by any doctrine of no-first-use." Masood Haider, "Islamabad Refuses to Accept 'No First Strike Doctrine,'" *Dawn*, May 31, 2002.

85. Ibid., 138–39.

86. Once the nuclear warheads are mated and ready to launch, the NCA would then be prepared to contend with three possible launch conditions: launch on warning, launch under attack, or launch on orders.

87. "Vajpayaee Rejects Talk Offer," *Dawn*, June 5, 2002. See also "N-Arms Possession Implies Usage: Musharraf," *The Hindu*, June 5, 2002.

88. V. R. Raghavan, "Limited War and Nuclear Escalation in South Asia," *Nonproliferation Review* 8 (Fall–Winter, 2001), 84.

89. There is no public information as to whether anyone in the Bush administration found evidence that Pakistan mated nuclear weapons. If it were to happen, the most probable circumstances would have been those between mid-May to mid-June 2002. But if we are to believe the statements of the leaders, nuclear weapons were never brandished in either of the two crises after the nuclear tests.

90. Musharraf, *In the Line of Fire,* 301.

Chapter 19

1. Pervez Musharraf, discussions with author, Rawalpindi, Pakistan, June 18, 2006.

2. See also Pervez Musharraf, *In the Line of Fire* (New York: Simon and Schuster, 2006), 286–87. On several occasions U.S. and Japanese officials had conveyed their suspicions to this author about the nature of cooperation and possible presence of North Korean nuclear scientists in KRL. A. Q. Khan constantly denied the presence of any nuclear scientists, claiming that missile experts from Korea were training Pakistani engineers to be self-sufficient. On one such report Musharraf confronted A. Q. Khan directly, but again Khan flatly denied everything.

3. Background briefing to the author on June 14, 2007. The three incidents led to the removal of A. Q. Khan as chairman of KRL. See also Musharraf, *In the Line of Fire,* 287–88.

4. Sultan Bashiruddin Mahmood, interview by author, Islamabad, December 14, 2006.

5. Ibid. See also Ishfaq Ahmad, interview by author, Islamabad, December 19, 2005; Javed Mirza, interview by author, Islamabad, June 13, 2006; and Agha Shahi, interview by author, Islamabad, June 19, 2005.

6. Sultan Bashiruddin Mahmood, interview by author, Islamabad, December 14, 2006.

7. Ibid.

8. Ibid.

9. Ron Suskind, *The Way of the World: A Story of Truth and Hope in an Age of Ex-*

tremism (New York: HarperCollins, 2008), 27, 47–49; David Albright and Holly Higgins, "Pakistani Nuclear Scientists: How Much Nuclear Assistance to Al Qaeda?" Institute for Science and International Security, August 30, 2002.

10. Suskind, *The Way of the World,* 70.

11. Musharraf, *In the Line of Fire,* 289.

12. Javed Mirza, interview by author, Islamabad, June 13, 2007.

13. Ibid. Also background briefing to the author, June 14, 2007.

14. Musharraf, *In the Line of Fire,* 291.

15. William J. Broad, David E. Sanger, and Raymond Bonner, "A Tale of Nuclear Proliferation: How Pakistani Built His Network," *New York Times*, February 12, 2004.

16. A. Q. Khan's handwritten letters addressed to General Gerry DeSilva, no. SA/PM/04/03, dated April 28, 2003, and SA/PM/11/03, dated November 11, 2003, on the letterhead of Government of Pakistan, Prime Minister's Secretariat. A. Q. Khan's typed letter addressed to Her Excellency Chandrika Bandaranaike Kumaratunga, President of the Democratic Socialist Republic of Sri Lanka, no. SAPM/05/2003, dated May 5, 2003, on the letterhead of Government of Pakistan, Prime Minister's Secretariat. (Copies of A. Q. Khan letters to Sri Lanka were obtained from open sources during extensive research on the A. Q. Khan Proliferation Network at the Center on Contemporary Conflict at Naval Postgraduate School during a period from 2004 to 2007.)

17. Ibid. President George W. Bush referred to B. S. A. Tahir in a speech to National Defense University about the A. Q. Khan network, February 11, 2004. See also David Albright, *Peddling Peril: How the Secret Nuclear Trade Arms America's Enemies* (New York: Simon and Schuster, 2010), 45.

18. A. Q. Khan's handwritten letter addressed to General Gerry DeSilva, no. SA/PM/04/03, dated April 28, 2003, on the letterhead of Government of Pakistan, Prime Minister's Secretariat.

19. A. Q. Khan's typed letter addressed to Her Excellency Chandrika Bandaranaike Kumaratunga, President of the Democratic Socialist Republic of Sri Lanka, no. SAPM/05/2003. dated May 5, 2003, on the letterhead of Government of Pakistan, Prime Minister's Secretariat.

20. In the same letter to the president, the name of G. Lerch appears. A third intercepted letter, dated November 8, 2003, which was sent well after the *BBC China* incident, was again addressed to General DeSilva, in which A. Q. Khan again complains of not having received the money despite all of his efforts. He further explains that many of his friends are continuing to put pressure on "Harry" to return the extorted money. In the letter he writes that "Harry is the real crook, he has everyone in his pocket [in Sri Lanka]."

21. SPD's background briefing to the author, June 14, 2007.

22. The Tinners are widely credited with helping Western intelligence agencies to bring down the Khan network. Though there has yet to be official confirmation, they allegedly turned spies for the CIA/MI6. See Albright, *Peddling Peril,* 208.

23. The author is indebted to Selina Adam, research associate at the Institute of Strategic Studies, Islamabad, for pointing out this fact during a seminar on Strategic Stability in South Asia in March 2010.

24. In many cases, Khan did business with these companies because he knew an individual in them, or had a personal friend doing business with that company.

25. Gordon Corera, *Shopping for Bombs: Nuclear Proliferation, Global Insecurity, and the Rise and Fall of the A. Q. Khan Network* (Oxford: Oxford University Press, 2006), 60.

26. Dafna Linzer, "Iran Was Offered Nuclear Parts," *Washington Post*, February 27, 2005.

27. International Institute for Strategic Studies (IISS), *Nuclear Black Markets: Pakistan, A. Q. Khan and the Rise of Proliferation Networks, a Net Assessment,* IISS strategic dossier (London: International Institute for Strategic Studies, 2007), 69–70.

28. International Atomic Energy Agency, "Implementation of the NPT Safeguards Agreement in the Islamic Republic of Iran," Report by the Director General, GOV/2004/83, November 15, 2004, 8.

29. Ibid. See also IISS, *Nuclear Black Markets,* 71.

30. IISS, *Nuclear Black Markets,* 75.

31. The author recalls A. Q. Khan pressing DGCD Major General Zulfiqar Ali Khan in early 1998 to allow the *Ghauri* flight-test. There were several considerations at the time not to up the ante. Eventually Prime Minister Sharif and General Karamat agreed to the flight-test on April 6, 1998, when A. Q. Khan convinced them he was ready. The test, however, did not succeed at that time.

32. IISS, *Nuclear Black Markets,* 76.

33. Ibid., 76–77.

34. Musharraf, *In the Line of Fire,* 295–96.

35. Victoria Burnett and Stephen Fidler, "Animal Lover, Egoist, and National Hero," *Financial Times,* April 7, 2004.

36. Christopher Clary, "The A. Q. Khan Network: Causes and Implications," master's thesis, National Security Affairs, Naval Postgraduate School, Monterey, CA, 2006, 77.

37. It is unclear whether the U.S. attack on Iraq in March 2003 induced fear of a similar fate in Gaddafi or whether its desire to get Libya back into the international system caused Gaddafi's change of mind. Regardless, the 2011 fate of Gaddafi after the NATO role in his demise might lead many countries to draw their own lessons.

38. IISS, *Nuclear Black Markets,* 76.

39. The chairman of the PAEC, Ishfaq Ahmad, informed the GHQ authorities in 1997 about the fact that KRL was not accountable and that the PAEC was responsible. The army chief decided to refer the matter to the government, which led to KRL's becoming an independent commission. Ishfaq Ahmad, interview by author, Islamabad, December 19, 2005.

40. General Mirza Aslam Beg, interview by author, Rawalpindi, September 1, 2005.

41. Many believe that A. Q. Khan conducted the Iran deal with a wink from General Beg, both of whom received kickbacks from the transaction.

42. Quoted in Douglas Frantz, "From Patriot to Proliferator," *Los Angeles Times*, September 23, 2005.

43. Ibid. See also Musharraf, *In the Line of Fire*, 295–96.

44. In almost all interviews in Pakistan, and in the author's interactions with academics, scholars, policy-makers, and students, the theme arose that corrupt elites had looted the country but failed to meet its needs. Why must A. Q. Khan be made an exception when he gave to the nation what may possibly be the tools of ultimate national survival?

45. Douglas Frantz and Catherine Collins, *The Man from Pakistan: The True Story of the World's Most Dangerous Nuclear Smuggler* (New York: Twelve, 2007), 250.

46. William J. Broad and David E. Sanger, "In Nuclear Net's Undoing, a Web of Shadowy Deals," *New York Times*, August 25, 2008.

47. Frantz and Collins, *The Man from Pakistan*, 248.

48. Broad and Sanger, "In Nuclear Net's Undoing, a Web of Shadowy Deals."

49. Ibid.

50. *Dr. A. Q. Khan Research Laboratories 1976–2001: 25 Years of Excellence and National Service*, Khan Research Laboratory, Islamabad, July 31, 2001.

51. Ibid.

52. Broad, Sanger, and Bonner, "A Tale of Nuclear Proliferation."

53. Dr. A. Q. Khan, "Pakistan's Nuclear Programme: Capabilities and Potentials of the Kahuta Project," speech to the Pakistan Institute of National Affairs, September 10, 1990. See also Dr. A. Q. Khan, "Capabilities and Potentials of the Kahuta Project," *Frontier Post*, September 10, 1990.

54. Frank Slijper, "Project Butter Factory: Hank Slebos and the A. Q. Khan Nuclear Network," briefing 2007/01, Transnational Institute in association with Campagne tegen Wapenhandel, 24.

55. See full list of catch-alls at Campagne tegen Wapenhandel, http://stopwapenhandel.org/projecten/Khan/kamer/Karimi080404.html.

56. Frank Slijper, "Project Butter Factory," 24.

57. A. Q. Khan's business association with Tinners goes back to 1979. He explains how sensitive equipment purchases were diverted to third locations—even when authorities in the original purchasing country had been alerted and had stopped shipment. See A. Q. Khan, "Hidden Truth," *The Nation*, June 8–14, 2012, http://thenation.org.uk/140612/page28k.htm, and http://thenation.org.uk/140612/page25k.htm (accessed June 8, 2012).

58. Frantz and Collins, *The Man from Pakistan*, 248.

59. Ibid.

60. Background briefings to the author, June 14, 2007.

61. Ibid.

62. Background briefing, June 14, 2007. See also Feroz Hassan Khan, "Nuclear Security in Pakistan: Separating Myth from Reality," *Arms Control Today* 39, 5 (July/August 2009).

63. For details of security and physical protection, see Major General Mahmood Ali Durrani, *Pakistan's Strategic Thinking and the Role of Nuclear Weapons*, occasional paper 37, Cooperative Monitoring Center, Sandia National Laboratories, July 2004, 53.

64. Corera, *Shopping for Bombs*, 162.

65. Paolo Cotta-Ramusino and Maurizio Martellini, "Nuclear Safety, Nuclear Stability and Nuclear Strategy in Pakistan: A Concise Report of a Visit by Landau Network—Centro Volta," Como, Italy, January 21, 2002.

66. Feroz Hassan Khan, "Challenges to Nuclear Stability in South Asia," *Nonproliferation Review* 10, 1 (Spring 2003), 69.

67. Musharraf, *In the Line of Fire*, 292.

68. Background briefing to the author, June 2007. Prime Minister Zafarullah Jamali, vice chairman of the NCA, was not willing to hold a public trial of A. Q. Khan. He advised the president against such a step.

Chapter 20

1. This vulnerability has existed since the mid-1980s when reports about a joint Indo-Israeli attack against Kahuta circulated inside Pakistan, only later to be confirmed when it became evident (at least to Pakistani defense planners) that India seriously contemplated such a plan.

2. Most arguments are drawn from Scott D. Sagan's arguments in Scott D. Sagan and Kenneth Waltz, *Spread of Nuclear Weapons: A Debate Renewed* (New York: W. W. Norton and Company, 2002).

3. Ibid.

4. Almost all Pakistani scientists interviewed have testified to their record of safety and certification by the IAEA.

5. President Barack Obama, 100th-Day Press Briefing transcript, April 29, 2009, http://www.nytimes.com/2009/04/29/us/politics/29text-obama.html?_r=1&pagewanted=print. See also Paul K. Kerr and Mary Beth Nikitin, "Pakistan's Nuclear Weapons: Proliferation and Security Issues," Congressional Research Service, Report RL 43248, July 20, 2001, 1–2.

6. Background briefing in SPD on June 14, 2007.

7. For several months Pakistan has appeared as an emerging market. See, "Emerging-market Indicators," *Economist,* March 11–17, 2006, 89.

8. "A meeting of Afghan political leaders was organized by the UN in Bonn in late November 2001, culminating on 5 December in the signing of an agreement that set out the step-by-step transition towards increasingly legitimate power structures, culminating in the establishment of a fully representative and freely elected government. The UN Security Council endorsed the outcome the following day in Resolution 1383

(2001). Under the Bonn Agreement, the parties agreed to establish an Interim Authority comprising three main bodies: a 30-member Interim Administration headed by Chairman Hamid Karzai, a moderate Pashtun, which took power on 22 December; an independent Supreme Court; and a Special Independent Commission for the Convening of the Emergency Loya Jirga (a traditional meeting of Afghan tribal, political and religious leaders)." Tim Youngs, "Afghanistan: The Culmination of the Bonn Process," research paper 05/72, House of Commons Library, October 26, 2005, 12.

9. Musharraf explained to the author his negotiating formula to put the positions of all stakeholders (India, Pakistan, and Kashmiris) on the table, eliminate such positions that were not acceptable to the other parties, and carve a common denominator for settlement. Musharraf and Karzai had a falling out in later years as each accused the other of bluffing. Pakistan was disconcerted that Karzai allowed ingresses by India into Kabul with the purpose of destabilizing Pakistan. Afghanistan blamed Pakistan for facilitating hostile activities of the Taliban/Pashtuns.

10. The military operations against *Lal Masjid* (Red Mosque) in Islamabad were ordered after repeated dialogue attempts had failed to disarm the militant mosque in the heart of Islamabad, and its vigilantes harassed ordinary citizens in Taliban style. The operation was conducted when some Chinese women were kidnapped from a beauty parlor in Islamabad. The operation lasted from July 3 to July 10, in which ninety-three militants and women were killed in a gun battle (official figures). This operation came in the midst of judiciary crises.

11. U.S. and UK officials had brokered an agreement between Benazir Bhutto and Pervez Musharraf. At the same time Benazir Bhutto had worked on a "charter of democracy" with her political opponent Nawaz Sharif.

12. The national emergency was lifted on December 15, 2007.

13. Ian Black, "Attacks Draw Worldwide Condemnations," *The Guardian*, November 28, 2008.

14. Eric Schmitt, Somini Sengupta, and Jane Perlez, "U.S. and India See Link to Militants in Pakistan," *New York Times*, December 3, 2008.

15. Musharraf's departure had stalled back door diplomacy on a settlement of Kashmir and other issues. On the day of the Mumbai attack, Pakistan's foreign minister was in New Delhi for peace dialogues.

16. The ruling Pakistan's People's Party and Pakistan Muslim League (Nawaz Sharif) had joined hands with other political forces with a single agenda to oust President Musharraf from office. Ironically, he was the glue to the coalition, which fell apart within months.

17. Walter Ladwig III, "A Cold Start for Hot Wars? The Indian Army's New Limited War Doctrine," *International Security* 32, 3 (Winter 2007/8), 158–90. For another view on the concept of limited war, see S. Paul Kapur, "India and Pakistan's Unstable Peace: Why Nuclear South Asia Is Not Like Cold War Europe," *International Security* 30, 2 (Fall 2005), 127–52.

18. On April 19, 2011, Pakistan tested a *Nasr/Hatf-IX* missile announced to be capable of carrying a nuclear warhead. Rodney W. Jones, "Pakistan's Nuclear Poker Bet," *Foreign Policy*, May 27, 2011.

19. President Barack Obama, answering a question in Mumbai during his state visit to India in November 2010. See "Remarks by U.S. President Barack Obama and First Lady Michelle Obama with Students at St. Xavier's College, Mumbai," *The Hindu*, November 8, 2010, http://www.thehindu.com/news/resources/article874180.ece (accessed November 28, 2011).

20. International Institute for Strategic Studies (IISS), *Nuclear Black Markets: Pakistan, A. Q. Khan and the Rise of Proliferation Networks, a Net Assessment,* IISS strategic dossier (London: International Institute for Strategic Studies, 2007), 83. Saudi Defense Minister Sultan bin Abdulaziz reportedly visited KRL in May 1999 and again in August 2002. Most likely he is the only foreign official to have visited a strategic facility in Pakistan. Such visits are opportunities for Pakistan to boast of technical capabilities and do not constitute Saudi Arabian interest in acquiring nuclear technology from Pakistan.

21. Khurshid Ahmad, "Nuclear Deterrence, CTBT, IMF Bail-outs and Debt Dependence," *Tarjuman al-Qur'an*, December 1998, cited in Sohail H. Hashmi, "Islamic Ethics: An Argument for Nonproliferation," in Sohail H. Hashmi and Steven P. Lee, eds., *Ethics and Weapons of Mass Destruction: Religious and Secular Perspectives* (New York: Cambridge University Press, 2004), 341.

22. The NCA statement of December 14, 2010, however, indicates Pakistan's right under IAEA safeguards to provide nuclear power expertise and infrastructure for peaceful purposes to friendly countries in this new era of nuclear renaissance. See also "Head of Pakistan's Nuclear Program: Pakistan Has the Right to Use Nuclear Weapons Should the Need Arise," interview of Lieutenant-General Khalid Kidwai by Sameh 'Abdallah of the Egyptian government daily *Al-Ahram,* http://www.memri.org/report/en/0/0/0/0/0/0/4714.htm#_edn1 (accessed January 22, 2011).

23. In their own way, these events in South Asia were the Bay of Pigs and Cuban Missile Crisis of the region.

24. Pakistan's NCA (through its Employment Control Committee) periodically monitors the strategic development in the region and determines the force goals that are followed up by the Development Control Committee of the NCA.

25. For detailed examination of such trends, See Feroz Hassan Khan, "Challenges to Nuclear Stability in South Asia," *Nonproliferation Review* 10, 1 (Spring 2003), 59–74, http://cns.miis.edu/npr/pdfs/101khan.pdf (accessed November 28, 2011).

26. Zia Mian, A. H. Nayyar, R. Rajaraman, and M. V. Ramana, "Fissile Materials in South Asia: The Implications of the U.S.-India Nuclear Deal," International Panel on Fissile Materials, September 2006.

27. SWU is the measure of unit of productive capacity of each centrifuge for enriching uranium. Typically, SWU represents the cumulative productive output of an

entire centrifuge. With the installation of advanced centrifuge designs (P-3, P-4), the KRL's output is expected to increase from the current 15–20,000 SWU to 45–60,000 SWU.

28. Mian et al., "Fissile Materials in South Asia"; and David Albright, "Securing Pakistan's Nuclear Infrastructure," in Lee Feinstein, James Clad, Lewis Dunn, and David Albright, *A New Equation: U.S. Policy toward India and Pakistan after September 11* (Washington, DC: Carnegie Endowment for International Peace), May 2002.

29. David Albright, Paul Brennan, and Robert Kelly, "Pakistan Expanding Dera Ghazi Khan Nuclear Site: Time for U.S. to Call for Limits," May 19, 2009, http://isis-online.org/uploads/isis-reports/documents/PakistanExpandingCPC_19May2009.pdf (accessed November 28, 2011).

30. David Albright and Paul Brannan, "Update on Khushab Plutonium Production Reactor Construction Projects in Pakistan," Institute for Science and International Security, April 23, 2009; Mark Hibbs and Shahid-ur-Rehman, "Pakistan Civilian Fuel Cycle Plan Linked to NSG Trade Exception," *Nuclear Fuels* 27 (August 2007).

31. According to a 1983 State Department document, the New Laboratories facility was "capable of extracting small quantities of plutonium," but large enough to "allow for expansion of reprocessing capacity." U.S. State Department, "The Pakistani Nuclear Program," declassified report, http://www.gwu.edu/~nsarchiv/NSAEBB/NSAEBB114/chipak-11.pdf (accessed November 27, 2011).

32. David Albright and Paul Brannan, "Chashma Nuclear Site in Pakistan with Possible Reprocessing Plant," Institute for Science and International Security, January 18, 2007.

33. The typical half-life of tritium is twelve years.

34. Sajid Chaudhry, "CDWP Okays Rs 13.7bn N-fuel Enrichment Plant," *Daily Times*, July 27, 2007.

35. John H. Gill, "India and Pakistan: A Shift in the Military Crisis?" in Ashley J. Tellis and Michael Willis, eds., *Military Modernization in an Era of Uncertainty* (Seattle, WA: National Bureau of Asian Research, 2005), 257.

36. Paul K. Kerr and Mary Beth Nikitin, "Pakistan's Nuclear Weapons"; Rodney W. Jones, "Pakistan's Answer to Cold Start?" *Friday Times* (Lahore), May 13–19, 2011, 7–8.

37. Feroz Hassan Khan, "Minimum Deterrence: Pakistan's Dilemma," *RUSI Journal* 156, 5 (October/November 2011), 48.

38. Mansoor Ahmed, "Why Pakistan Needs Tactical Weapons," *Weekly Pulse*, May 6, 2001, Islamabad.

39. Background briefing at SPD, June 14, 2007, Rawalpindi.

40. Carlotta Gall, "Pakistan Faces a Divide of Age on Muslim Law," *New York Times*, January 11, 2011.

Epilogue

1. Governor Salman Taseer stood up to provide justice for a poor Christian woman against the abuse of an existing blasphemy law that warrants the death sentence. His bodyguard murdered him on January 4, 2011, after several extremist groups issued a *Fatwa* (decree) and reward for his head. The assassin admitted that he killed because the governor had opposed the blasphemy law and was in favor of abrogating it. For detailed comments, see Najam Sethi, "The Price of Passion," editorial, *Friday Times* (Lahore), January 7–13, 2001, 1.

2. The breach of Pakistan's sovereignty went both ways. Al Qaeda's penetration within the Pakistani state, as well as the state's inability to prevent an external intervention, has cumulatively created a state of helplessness as far as Pakistan's security is concerned. Both circumstances have resulted in public ire against Pakistani intelligence and armed forces alike.

3. In his parting testimony to the Congress, Admiral Michael Mullen, former chairman of the Joint Chiefs of Staff, alleged the operation of the Haqqani Terrorist Network as the veritable arm of the Inter-Services Intelligence (ISI). This statement initiated exchanges of rhetoric between both countries questioning the vitality of the relationship.

4. Anatol Lieven, "With a Friend like This," *New York Times*, op-ed, November 1, 2011.

5. See Rodney W. Jones, "Pakistan's Nuclear Poker Bet," *Foreign Policy*, May 27, 2011.

Index

CD Directorate, 325; as DGISI, 308, 318–320, 468n11, 470n38; Musharraf coup and, 319–320; nuclear program and, 325; Sharif family and, 467n10; U.S. visit, 319, 472n72

Zia-ul-Haq, Mohammad: as army chief, 124, 125; Bhutto and, 124, 125; civilian government and, 441n18, 450n92; coup, 137, 160; cricket diplomacy, 224–225, 449n76; death, 227, 252; Islamic extremists and, 124; A. Q. Khan and, 181, 188, 189–190, 226–227, 435n1, 439n76; military record, 124–125, 424n3; National Security Council proposal, 333; as president, 459n38;

relations with United States, 208–210; security policies, 226

Zia-ul-Haq, Mohammad, nuclear program and: bomb design work and, 174, 187–188, 189–190, 439n73; nuclear reactor construction, 195; PAEC and, 152, 174; plutonium production, 196; scientists and, 27, 150–151, 152, 188; secret directives after agreement with Reagan, 214–215; support, 210; tests, 185, 189; uranium enrichment, 156, 157, 161; uranium mining, 113

Zifferero, Maurizio, 145

Zinni, Anthony, 274